An Introduction to Parapsychology

FIFTH EDITION

An Introduction to Parapsychology

FIFTH EDITION

Harvey J. Irwin and
Caroline A. Watt

McFarland & Company, Inc., Publishers
Jefferson, North Carolina, and London

LIBRARY OF CONGRESS CATALOGUING-IN-PUBLICATION DATA

Irwin, H. J. (Harvey J.)
An introduction to parapsychology / Harvey J. Irwin and Caroline A. Watt — 5th ed.
p.   cm.
Includes bibliographical references and indexes.

ISBN-13: 978-0-7864-3059-8
(softcover : 50# alkaline paper) ∞

1. Parapsychology — Textbooks.   I. Watt, Caroline A.   II. Title.
BF1031.I79   2007   133.8 — dc22   2006039579

British Library cataloguing data are available

Cover image ©2007 PhotoDisc; background images ©2007 clipart.com

Manufactured in the United States of America

*McFarland & Company, Inc., Publishers
Box 611, Jefferson, North Carolina 28640
www.mcfarlandpub.com*

ACKNOWLEDGMENTS

This book has grown out of my experiences in teaching parapsychology at the University of New England over a period of 25 years. In this context I benefited by the efforts of my students, who provided feedback on my teaching programs and who worked hard to educate me. Reliance upon earlier course notes as a framework for my book was enabled by the university's agreement to release copyright.

The content of the book has been influenced by numerous researchers whose parapsychological work I have found to be a source of inspiration. I have endeavored to acknowledge these contributions through appropriate citations in the text, but I would like especially to record my intellectual indebtedness to the work of John Beloff, Susan Blackmore, John Palmer, Louisa E. Rhine, and Rex Stanford.

Thanks are due to the following people who graciously read and offered constructive comment upon various sections of the manuscript of the first edition: Carlos Alvarado, Alan Gauld, Ray Hyman, Jürgen Keil, Gertrude Schmeidler, Sybo Schouten, Michael Thalbourne, and Debra Weiner. Additionally, I acknowledge with gratitude the suggestions of teachers and researchers for revision of the text, some of which have been incorporated in subsequent editions: Richard Broughton, Frank Dilley, Joop Houtkooper, Stanley Krippner, Karlis Osis, Philip Stander, Rex Stanford, Jessica Utts, and Nancy Zingrone offered thoughtful advice in this regard.

In preparing this fifth edition of the book I had to face the dilemma that since my formal retirement from academia my access to the current literature in parapsychology had become more limited. The obvious solution was to solicit the assistance of a younger parapsychological researcher who is both active and eminent in the field. My first choice as co-author was Dr. Caroline A. Watt of Edinburgh University, and I was highly delighted when she accepted my invitation to revise the book. Almost all of the updated material has been contributed by Caroline, and her insightful input has served to strengthen substantially the quality of this introduction to parapsychology. It is with unqualified gratitude that I thank Caroline for her expertise, diligence, tenacity and unwavering good humor in completing the new edition.

Cases of out-of-body experience from my book *Flight of Mind* are quoted in Chapter 12 by permission of the publisher, Scarecrow Press. The quotation in Chapter 16 from an article in the *Applied Psi Newsletter* by Mishlove and Kautz (1982) is made by courtesy of the authors and the publisher, the Center for Applied Intuition.

Eric Eisenbud (on behalf of the late Jule Eisenbud), Stanley Krippner, William Roll, Helmut Schmidt, Ian Stevenson, and Charles Tart provided photographs for reproduction in the book: their generosity here is greatly appreciated. Other figures were supplied by the Rhine Research Center (RRC) and by the Mary Evans Picture Library (MEPL). The source of each figure is given in the text. The technical expertise of the University of New England's Media Resources Unit in various photographic tasks and of Ivan Thornton in preparing the line drawings is acknowledged with thanks.

— H. J. Irwin
University of New England
Armidale, Australia
September 2006

Harvey Irwin generously invited me to join him as co-author in preparing this updated edition of *An Introduction to Parapsychology*. Throughout our collaboration, Harvey has been unfailingly rapid in response, gracious in accepting my revisions, and kind and constructive in his feedback. Harvey, it has been a joy working with you. Throughout the process I enjoyed the support of my partner and colleague, Professor Richard Wiseman, who has the rare ability to both make me laugh and think. Thank you, Richard.

Finally, I would like to acknowledge my sorely-missed colleague and mentor, Professor Robert Morris. Bob was Koestler Professor of Parapsychology at the University of Edinburgh from 1985 until his sudden death in 2004, and was responsible for my entering parapsychology twenty years ago. If even a little of his wisdom has rubbed off on me, how fortunate I am, and it is to him that I dedicate my efforts toward this book.

— C. A. Watt
University of Edinburgh
Edinburgh, Scotland
September 2006

CONTENTS

LIST OF FIGURES

1

INTRODUCTION

Parapsychology is the scientific study of experiences which, if they are as they seem to be, are in principle outside the realm of human capabilities as presently conceived by conventional scientists. Thus parapsychological phenomena ostensibly indicate the operation of factors currently unknown to or unrecognized by orthodox science, popularly referred to as *paranormal* factors. More formally, parapsychology has been defined by its proponents as the study of "apparent anomalies of behavior and experience that exist apart from currently known explanatory mechanisms that account for organism-environment and organism-organism information and influence flow" (Parapsychological Association, 1989, pp. 394–395). Familiar examples of such anomalous phenomena are experiences that seemingly involve extrasensory perception (ESP) and apparitions (e.g., ghosts). The objective of this book is to provide an introductory survey of parapsychologists' efforts to explore the authenticity and bases of these anomalous, apparently paranormal phenomena.

As a general delineation of the scope of parapsychological research the above paragraph has several features warranting consideration. Most important is the point that in no way is there any presumption here of the existence of "the paranormal," contrary to the approach of many contemporary parapsy-chologists who actually regard parapsychology as the study of the paranormal. Certainly people report having experiences in which it seemed to them there was, for example, some information acquired without the involvement of the recognized human senses. But when such an "extrasensory" experience is termed *parapsychological* no conclusion has necessarily been reached that there exists a paranormal process by which information can be mediated outside the individual's sensory capacities.

As far as the definition of parapsychological experiences is concerned it is purely a matter of appearances, of how an experience *seems* to be. A fundamental task of researchers then is to investigate the actual bases of these experiences, determining the extent to which the phenomena are explicable within the framework of accepted principles of mainstream science and if appropriate, defining the respects in which that framework should be extended in order to accommodate empirical findings on the phenomena.

Although parapsychological experiences appear to be paranormal they therefore are not defined to be so; rather, the question of their paranormality is a matter for investigation. It is important to appreciate the distinction between *parapsychological experiences* that unequivocally do occur and underlying *paranormal processes* that are mere hypotheses

1

for scientific investigation. All ESP experiences thus are parapsychological, but we require proof that any of them could be paranormal.

The foregoing representation of parapsychology also highlights the discipline's paradoxical relationship with science. Despite the fact that parapsychological phenomena ostensibly are contrary to conventional scientific wisdom it is through the methods of science that the phenomena are studied. Sociologically speaking, parapsychology is undertaken as a scientific endeavor regardless of its subject matter, flaws in any of its research procedures, and the skeptical rhetoric of its critics. More specifically, the perspective adopted in this book is that parapsychology is very much allied to psychology, the science of behavior. In other words, parapsychological research rightly is conducted predominantly within the broader context of the scientific investigation of behavior and its phenomena are best understood in the light of an appreciation of the principles of psychology. Thus a feature of modern parapsychology is that investigation of its phenomena is staged in the controlled environment of the psychological laboratory whenever possible. Scientific methodology is emphasized also in field studies of the sort that predominated in the days when such interests were known as *psychical research*, the study of phenomena apparently mediated directly by the mind or "soul."

In part the scientific orientation in parapsychology demands that the design and the conduct of an investigation be as impervious as possible to the beliefs of the research personnel (except of course where such beliefs are the focus of the study.) It is as well to note at the outset that a similar approach ideally should be adopted by you as a student of parapsychology. This is no simple achievement, in essence because the subject matter of parapsychology tends to evoke extreme reactions in people, either of uncritical, soft-minded gullibility in the paranormal or of unyielding, closed-minded skepticism. To

get the most from your study of parapsychology it will be necessary to set aside such narrow preconceptions of the subject and consciously to strive for a more objective, evenhanded style of weighing up arguments and data on both sides of an issue.

As it is depicted in this text parapsychology additionally is centered on experiences of *people*. This is not to claim that infrahuman animals are devoid of so-called psychic abilities. Indeed there has been some investigation, both in the laboratory and in the field, of parapsychological phenomena associated with animals. But like their counterparts in psychology these studies derive their pertinence largely from their role as simplified and highly controlled models of human behavior and from the comparative or evolutionary perspective they bring to the human context. The quantitative and qualitative data on people's parapsychological experiences also are manifoldly more extensive, detailed and diverse than that for animals; the human focus in parapsychology thereby is apt in relation to its empirical footing and its capacity for theoretical productivity. At the same time, when behavioral scientists seek to address the experiences of people rather than the behavior of animals they appreciate the difficulty of the task. Human cognitive, social, cultural, emotional, motivational, perceptual, neuropsychological, psychodynamic, and other psychological factors are so complex and variable that no individual experience can possibly be understood completely in terms of one basic dimension or process. Although parapsychology's emphasis upon people as the object of its study may make the discipline more personally meaningful you therefore should not have unduly high expectations of finding simple, comprehensive, scientifically sound answers to your queries about the nature of parapsychological experiences.

The scope of the field of parapsychology has drawn comment from both conceptual and pragmatic perspectives. In conceptual terms there has been some unease that parapsychology in essence is defined negatively, that is, a phenomenon is held to lie within the field's boundaries for no other reason than that it is defined not to lie outside them. This is a feature of the widely endorsed alternative notion of parapsychology as the study of the paranormal or of processes as yet undiscovered and unrecognized by science. That approach is founded upon a negative definition because parapsychologists are unable to specify what it is (as opposed to what it is not) that indicates an experience's involvement of the paranormal. It is thought insufficient to define extrasensory perception (ESP), for example, as direct apprehension of information by the mind, for the reason that "direct apprehension" is specifiable not in any affirmative way but only as something that is *not* via the usual sensory channels and is *not* derived inferentially from previous knowledge. A problem with this negative definition is that it is a difficult task to rule out all possible normal explanations: we might be unaware of some possible normal explanations, other individuals might deliberately deceive us, or we might unconsciously deceive ourselves (Alcock, 2003). Presumably what would be required here is a means of nominating what this paranormal transfer of information actually is, enabling its discrimination from other, superficially similar experiences that are based on mere delusion and hallucination.

The common notion of parapsychology as the study of the paranormal is not embraced in this book. Rather, parapsychology here is defined as the study of experiences having the appearance of being in principle outside the realm of human capabilities as conceived by conventional scientists. Within the theoretical framework of modern behavioral science an extrasensory experience, for example, simply could not have occurred as it is reported to have done. But now the task of the parapsychologist is not the study of negatively defined underlying paranormal

factors; rather, it is deemed to entail a systematic exploration of various possible bases and characteristics of experiential reports. Certainly this work will include investigation of the occurrence of extrasensory experience when sensory and inferential sources of information have procedurally been eliminated, but this is quite distinct from a pursuit of the paranormal. By defining parapsychology in terms of *appearances* the discontent over negative definition should lose some of its potency. It is unnecessary, for example, to define extrasensory experience in a way that will distinguish it from delusory or hallucinatory experience, because conceivably "ESP" might one day be shown to be just that. Admittedly, if paranormality is negatively defined then ultimately so too must the "appearance of being paranormal," but at least the latter is not predicated simply upon the exclusion of any list of scientifically accepted processes.

This raises the possibility that the terms of our adopted definition are temporally relative, that is, a given phenomenon might not be classified as parapsychological forever. Suppose that ESP were shown conclusively to be due to some presently recognized psychological processes and was relabeled with some name less provocative of the paranormal. In time people then might come to view such an experience no longer as incompatible with scientific principles nor as suggestive of a paranormal event, in which case the phenomenon rightly would shift from the parapsychological domain to some other area of psychology. But in that event the phenomenon should at least remain a legitimate issue for psychological research. If on the other hand extrasensory experience was defined explicitly as a *paranormal* phenomenon, a demonstration that this was not so more likely would prompt psychologists to believe the phenomenon had been eliminated as a matter of research. Temporal relativity therefore does not loom as an unacceptable limitation of our definition of parapsychology.

Cultural relativity could be another

type of conceptual limitation. Certainly if parapsychology is depicted as the study of the paranormal there is the problem that what people classify as paranormal will vary from one culture to another. In some societies, for example, ESP is regarded as a human skill that falls entirely within the natural order, yet in our society it generally is thought of as paranormal. On the other hand by defining parapsychology in terms of its phenomena's apparent relation to conventional scientific principles, the issue of cultural relativity becomes somewhat less contentious because science is an international and comparatively cross-cultural activity. A phenomenon's status in the framework of conventional science therefore is accorded greater significance than its interpretation by members of individual societies. The definition of parapsychology may still be culturally bound to the extent of its scientific perspective, but in any event that is quite consistent with the view that parapsychology has a claim to being part of the world of science.

The demarcation of parapsychological phenomena in terms of appearances nevertheless encounters a few practical problems. One is that some instances of stage magic, especially mentalism, might be held to have the superficial form of the paranormal and hence have grounds for being classified as parapsychological. Although most researchers properly would reject this categorization it could have merit in some respects. A parapsychologist's knowledge of legerdemain certainly can be advantageous as a guard against fraudulent psychics (Hansen, 1985; Truzzi, 1997), and magical tricks can be used in a laboratory setting as a context for exploring the foundations of people's interpretation of events as paranormal (e.g., see Benassi, Singer & Reynolds, 1980). But while the superficial form of stage magic may be that of the paranormal these performances typically are not *perceived* by the audience as actually being paranormal.

By presenting himself or herself as a magician instead of as a medium or psychic the performer communicates the illusory character of the act and hence people do not see it as involving processes currently unrecognized by conventional science. For that reason a piece of stage magic generally would not be regarded as a parapsychological experience. If magicians do depict themselves as psychic, however, their performance may well be accepted by the audience as paranormal. In that case magic falls in much the same class as fraud. The stance taken here is that if the public is deceived into construing a phenomenon as paranormal then their experience should nonetheless be deemed parapsychological and be the subject of study by parapsychologists. The result of such research of course may be that people become aware of the deception, the phenomenon becomes decreasingly viewed as paranormal, and its study shifts from the predominantly parapsychological domain to that of social psychologists and sociologists.

Again, there may be other phenomena interpreted as paranormal by the general public and yet excluded from study by parapsychologists. The considerable majority of scientific parapsychologists would not concede as legitimate issues in their field such things as witchcraft, popular astrology, fairies, the Bermuda Triangle, numerology, and Tarot readings, despite the common image of these matters as paranormal in the mind of the public and indeed for many skeptics (e.g., see Frazier, 1981). I suspect that parapsychologists' rejection of these topics springs in part from political motives; to give serious consideration to the above phenomena would severely prejudice parapsychology's already tenuous status as a science in the eyes of the rest of the scientific community. In any event, parapsychologists effectively have restricted the scope of their study to phenomena that are ostensibly paranormal in relatively specific respects. These respects may be depicted in the following terms. First, the focal phenomena may present as a paranormal form of communication; cases of apparent ESP are an instance of this type. Second, other phenomena accepted for investigation by parapsychologists seem to imply a metaphysical facet of human existence; for example, a reported sighting of a ghost might be taken as putatively paranormal under this perspective. Additionally, a phenomenon such as a spiritualist medium's apparent communication with the spirit of a deceased person may be of interest to parapsychologists on both of the above counts. Regardless of the rationale for such demarcation of parapsychological endeavor, the fact remains that the average citizen's notion of paranormal phenomena is evidently far broader than that of the academic parapsychologist.

Although the exclusion of some particular phenomena from the field may be disputatious there is broad consensus in the view that traditionally there have been three basic domains of parapsychological research, namely extrasensory perception, psychokinesis, and the survival hypothesis. The nature of each of these will be addressed in turn.

An *extrasensory experience* is one in which it appears that the experient's mind has acquired information directly, that is, seemingly without either the mediation of the recognized human senses or the processes of logical inference. By way of illustration, on a few occasions I have been thinking about some friend and have had my thoughts interrupted by a phone call from that very person. Now, with sufficient knowledge of the context of this type of occurrence it could be possible to explain, or explain away, the experience in "rational" terms that do not appeal to the existence of any paranormal process called ESP. To this extent it is presumptuous to label the experience "extrasensory." But as with other parapsychological phenomena, we are concerned just with appearances, and from that perspective the above example superficially suggests the operation of

some paranormal link between my thoughts and those of my friend. The example, no doubt a familiar encounter for many readers, represents a particular type of extrasensory experience that ostensibly entails direct mind-to-mind communication, so-called *telepathy*. In some instances the extrasensory experience relates to information not in another mind but in part of the objective environment. Thus a person's awareness of sensorially inaccessible visual events is termed *clairvoyance*, and ESP of auditory events, *clairaudience*; again, "clairvoyance" commonly is used in a generic fashion to designate extrasensory apprehension of any class of objective events. Sometimes too, ESP apparently is displaced in time. Extrasensory awareness of a future event is known as *precognition*, and that of a past event, *retrocognition*.

Often it can be difficult to determine how a given extrasensory experience should best be classified. Consider an example. From time to time I find myself thinking I have not heard from one of my professional colleagues for a while, and later the same day I receive a letter from that person. Perhaps this may be deemed to entail ostensible extrasensory awareness of the letter itself, in which case my experience would be considered clairvoyant. Or the experience might be construed as apparent awareness of the perceptions of the mail sorter, that is, an instance of telepathic experience. Or again it could be represented as a precognitive experience of the subsequent mail delivery or of my opening the letter, or perhaps even a retrocognitive experience of my correspondent writing the letter some weeks earlier. In practice therefore, the utility of the proposed categories of ESP may be doubtful. Much the same could be said of their application to the description of laboratory data. Thus it was felt necessary to devise the expression *general extrasensory perception* (GESP) to refer to data that could have reflected unknown components of clairvoyance or telepathy or both

(Rhine, 1948, p. 44). In the laboratory context the various terms nevertheless may usefully be employed in conveying the type of experimental procedure followed in an investigation.

In this book one convenient terminological convention is observed as far as possible. The terms extrasensory perception, telepathy, clairvoyance, precognition and the like usually are intended to refer to a hypothetical paranormal process, one that conceivably could account for a given parapsychological phenomenon; of course, the process might or might not actually exist. On the other hand such expressions as extrasensory experience, telepathic experience, clairvoyant experience, and precognitive experience designate events that do occur, experiences that people do have and which on the surface suggest the operation of a paranormal process. It could be said, for example, that a parapsychologist investigates the nature of extrasensory experience and in the course of doing so, gathers evidence on the existence or otherwise of extrasensory perception. The "extrasensory" in *extrasensory experience* therefore pertains to appearances and not necessarily to reality, whereas the "extrasensory" in *extrasensory perception* refers to the nature of a hypothesized paranormal reality. Occasionally this convention is overlooked, usually in order to avoid the tedium of frequent repetition of a given expression, but the sense should nonetheless be evident; for example, reference may be made to ESP when clearly we are speaking of extrasensory experience.

Extrasensory experience and ESP constitute one of the three basic domains of parapsychological research. A second domain is that of *psychokinesis* (PK), a word that translates literally as "movement by the mind." A PK experience entails an apparent mind-over-matter effect, that is, a case where an individual's thoughts or preferences appear to have had a direct influence upon the structure of the physical environment. The influence seemingly occurs without the mediation of recognized physical energies or mechanisms, particularly those comprising the human motor system. In the popular view PK probably would once have been most strongly exemplified by the spoon-bending performances of the Israeli psychic Uri Geller or by the apparently paranormal displacement of objects by the Russian psychic Nina Kulagina. Nowadays there are few, if any, highly publicized individuals claiming PK ability. Psychokinetic experiences, however, need not involve observable movement; the stopping of a clock at the time of a loved one's death, for example, commonly is construed as an event of the mind-over-matter variety.

The labels *extrasensory perception* and *psychokinesis* were devised originally to convey the ostensible nature of the respective phenomena in a vividly descriptive fashion. Today, however, they are rather unsatisfactory as technical terms because they are so presumptive of the paranormal processes that hypothetically could underlie the experiences. Even if ESP exists it might well operate by way of some (as yet undiscovered) sort of sensory modality, a "sixth sense," and hence not be "extrasensory." Again, if ESP is truly extrasensory then it might be more akin to ideation than to "perception." Similar objections can be leveled at the term psychokinesis.

Although it is convenient to have graphically descriptive nomenclature for a phenomenon it should also be atheoretical, and unfortunately neither of the two above terms meets this criterion. For that reason the British parapsychologist B. P. Wiesner introduced *psi phenomena* as a generic term encompassing both ESP and PK (Thouless, 1942; Thouless & Wiesner, 1948). The Greek letter *psi* here is used to denote the unknown paranormal element in these experiences in much the same way as the letter *x* represents the unknown in an algebraic equation until its identity is determined. In effect, however, psi constitutes more than a blanket term;

there has developed a (sometimes tacit) assumption that the paranormal element in ESP is the same as the one in PK, that these two parapsychological domains share a common underlying process or mechanism (see also Storm & Thalbourne, 2000). Thouless proposed further that the so-called extrasensory facets be known as *psi gamma* and the psychokinetic facets, *psi kappa*. These two terms, unlike that of *psi*, have never attracted broad endorsement, and ESP and PK now are so entrenched in the parapsychological and indeed the popular vocabulary that is unlikely they will be replaced at least until their actual bases become established by researchers and accepted by the public.

Supplementary to the study of psi phenomena a traditional domain of parapsychological research concerns the *survival hypothesis*, the notion that there is some element of human existence that survives death. As we shall see in the next chapter much of the original interest of psychical researchers in the survival hypothesis focused on claims of communication between deceased spirits and mediums during spiritualist seances. Other phenomena also were pursued in this context; thus, evidence for life-after-death was sought in experiences of apparitions, poltergeists, reincarnation, and of one's self being outside the physical body (the out-of-body experience), among others. Modern parapsychologists continue to study these sorts of experience, although more as phenomena in their own right than as avenues for validating the survival hypothesis. Nevertheless these experiences collectively form an important sector of parapsychology; as they usually are differentiated experientially from the fundamental psi phenomena of ESP and PK they have come to be regarded as the third domain of the discipline. Even if the survival hypothesis proves not to provide a legitimate basis for their conceptual integration, each of these experiences *appears* to entail the existence of a nonphysical or spiritual self, and thereby this research domain has coherence beyond that of merely comprising parapsychological phenomena other than the basic psi experiences.

Within each of the domains of parapsychological investigation three central issues arise. These relate respectively to authenticity, underlying processes, and phenomenology. The scope of these three issues now will be considered.

In the opinion of many parapsychologists the principal objective of their research is to determine whether or not the evident paranormal quality of a given class of parapsychological experience is *authentic* or ontologically real. That is, allowing for the instances that can be accommodated by conventional psychological processes, are some parapsychological experiences due to the operation of paranormal factors? Because parapsychology is a scientific discipline there presently is a consensus that this issue properly can be resolved only in the scientific laboratory. Admittedly such an attitude took time to evolve, and in Chapter 2 we shall see the founders of the discipline sought to authenticate the existence of the paranormal in other ways.

The issue of authenticity nevertheless has always been close to the heart of parapsychological research. In the extrasensory experience, for example, the issue is if it is really possible for a person to acquire information when all opportunity for rational inference and input from recognized sensory sources have been ruled out. Similarly, in relation to the notion of PK, can a person's thoughts and preferences affect the state of a physical system when all recognized physical energies and mechanisms are excluded as mediators? And is there a nonphysical element of human existence that can separate from the physical body, can survive organic death, can retain its organization as an integral personality after death, can appear before and haunt the living, can be born again in another body, and so on? All of these inquiries entail the issue of authenticity.

Authenticity relates to the question of "whether"; the issue of *underlying processes* concerns the question of "how." So-called *process-oriented* research is designed to ascertain the processes by which parapsychological experiences are enacted. It is one thing to demonstrate, for example, that a paranormal phenomenon called ESP does exist; it is quite another thing to establish the ways in which it works. Note, however, that process-oriented research is not predicated upon the authenticity issue. In the first place it is both feasible and valid to conduct investigations of the operating characteristics of a parapsychological phenomenon before that phenomenon is shown to be paranormal. Secondly, it is legitimate, and just as instructive, to undertake such investigations even if the phenomenon eventually proves not to be paranormal; like other behavioral scientists parapsychologists seek to understand the bases of human experience, and even if those bases are found to be entirely compatible with accepted psychological knowledge, that knowledge nonetheless is enriched by the demonstration of its capacity to account for parapsychological as well as other psychological phenomena. Process-oriented research therefore is justified irrespective of the issue of authenticity.

The third major issue in parapsychological research is important but currently rather underrated. It focuses on the description of parapsychological phenomena from the *experient*'s point of view; that is, investigators seek to establish the characteristics of the phenomena as actually experienced and the impact such experiences have upon the individual. This approach is known as *phenomenological* research (Irwin, 1994b). It too is independent of the authenticity issue; the phenomenology of people's parapsychological experiences can be documented whether or not those experiences have a paranormal basis. On the other hand, the phenomenological issue can be linked with process-oriented research. Although it certainly is possible to study phenomenological charac-

teristics of the experiences without the slightest concern for underlying processes, such study often does suggest ideas about the nature of underlying processes. In other words phenomenological research is useful in generating hypotheses for investigation in process-oriented research.

More generally, the issue of phenomenology is to do with the question of "what," or to be less elliptical, the discernment of what it is that parapsychology has to explain. There is some tendency among parapsychologists either to be smug over this matter or to ignore it altogether. That is, it commonly is assumed that we know what an extrasensory experience is, what a psychokinetic experience is, what an out-of-body experience is, and so forth, and that the empirical objective is to investigate their paranormality and underlying processes. But there is more to an experience than its definition. Human experience has a range of different dimensions, and specifically, there are facets of parapsychological experience other than its ostensible paranormality. For example, investigation of the hypothetical paranormal process ESP might well help us understand the informational origins of extrasensory experience, but there remain to be addressed the bases of the form taken by the experience, its thematic content, its temporal course, its emotional tenor, its social context, and its impact upon the individual, among other things. The purpose of phenomenological research is to establish all such experiential features of parapsychological phenomena.

In many respects therefore, phenomenological research should set the research agenda in parapsychology, because it has the function of specifying the essential characteristics of the phenomena to be explained. The latter role of course is not exclusive to the phenomenological approach. Process-oriented research also throws up empirical relationships requiring further investigation; these would include observed correlations between the occurrence of parapsychological phenomena and features of the experient's personality and beliefs, for example. And the authenticity issue constantly provides items for the research program.

At the same time phenomenology could rightly be deemed the primary issue of parapsychological research in that it has some degree of logical precedence over the other two major issues; as apparent paranormality is itself a phenomenological feature of parapsychological experiences, the phenomenology issue effectively anticipates that of authenticity, and as noted above, the impetus for process-oriented research sometimes comes from phenomenological data. Many para-

psychologists probably would feel this to be flagrantly overstating the case, but our central argument remains that phenomenological research is too neglected and depreciated at this still early phase of the development of parapsychological science. For that reason the text gives due attention to the issue of phenomenology as well as to those of authenticity and underlying processes.

Before proceeding to consider research on particular parapsychological phenomena, it is appropriate to examine the historical origins of the field. That is the topic of the next chapter.

Key Terms and Concepts

parapsychology
paranormal
psychical research
parapsychological experiences
experient
extrasensory perception (ESP)
extrasensory experience
telepathy
clairvoyance
precognition

retrocognition
general extrasensory perception (GESP)
psychokinesis (PK)
psi
psi phenomena
the survival hypothesis
authenticity
process-oriented research
phenomenology

Study Questions

1. Parapsychology commonly is defined as the science of the paranormal. What are the advantages and the disadvantages of that approach?

2. Honorton (1993, p. 210) argued that the term "paranormal" is an anachronism: if psi is ontologically real it must necessarily be a natural phenomenon. In Honorton's view, the term "paranormal" therefore should be abandoned. If this suggestion was generally accepted how would it change our conceptualization of the discipline of parapsychology?

3. Explain why a phenomenon need not be paranormal in order to be parapsychological. Why then are parapsychologists intent upon investigating the paranormality of such experiences?

4. List some of the phenomena regarded as paranormal by the general public but which you suspect to be disregarded in a science of parapsychology. What are your feelings about the omission of these topics from study?

5. Explore the various facets of the conceptual relationship between parapsychology and science.

6. Many people believe their pets to have psychic abilities. In your view, to what extent should this issue occupy a prominent position in parapsychological research? What might be learned from such research?

7. The subject matter of parapsychology tends to evoke rather extreme reactions in people. Conduct a simple survey of some friends and acquaintances on the issue. What range of reactions is evident? What motives might underlie these reactions?

8. What is the difference between extrasensory perception and extrasensory experience, and what is the significance of the distinction?

9. Recall one of your own extrasensory experiences and try to classify it as telepathic or clairvoyant and as precognitive or contemporaneous or retrocognitive. In light of that exercise what is your impression of the utility of the various categories of extrasensory experience?

10. How apt are the terms extrasensory perception and psychokinesis?

11. Examine a few of your own parapsychological experiences. What interesting hypotheses do these experiences suggest for the respective research issues of authenticity, underlying processes, and phenomenology?

12. To what extent are the three major research issues of authenticity, underlying processes, and phenomenology independent of each other?

13. As objectively as you can, look closely at your own attitudes and beliefs and then specify your preconceptions and prejudices about parapsychological phenomena.

14. Some phenomena other than parapsychological ones are defined negatively. The sudden infant death syndrome (SIDS) or "crib death" for example, is diagnosed by exclusion. That is, a given case is classified as SIDS only when other (positively defined) causes systematically are ruled out. The negative definition of SIDS evidently has acted as a stimulus for researchers to identify the bases of the condition. Why then are parapsychologists taken to task for defining their phenomena in a negative fashion?

2

ORIGINS OF PARAPSYCHOLOGICAL RESEARCH

In the reckoning of most writers the discipline of parapsychology is little more than a hundred years old. The commencement of parapsychology, or psychical research as it then was called, generally is put at February 20, 1882, when the Society for Psychical Research (SPR) was officially constituted in England. The SPR was founded principally on the initiative of some academics at Cambridge University and several other people, all of whom believed that various claims for the existence of paranormal phenomena warranted scientific scrutiny. It may be noted that a number of SPR members in these early days were skeptics; others were philosophers concerned fundamentally with the metaphysical implications of parapsychological experiences if these should prove to be genuinely paranormal. Nevertheless the founders of the SPR were united in their conviction that the objective investigation of parapsychological phenomena was called for, despite the prevailing disinterest in such research among the established divisions of science.

Recorded instances of parapsychological experiences of course may be found among all cultures and in all historic periods. Indeed some cases were documented in much detail: the church's hagiographic records of the lives of the saints provide many such examples.

On the other hand the notion of testing the accuracy and authenticity of reported parapsychological experiences emerged very slowly (Inglis, 1977). In the seventeenth century writers such as Henry More and Joseph Glanvill showed themselves alert to the possibility of fraud, delusion, and unreliable observation in such cases. But concern of this sort was sporadic and had little claim to representing the basis of an academic discipline. The essential perspective of More and Glanvill, for example, was religious rather than scientific; they were endeavoring to ascertain the earthly presence of the devil and diabolical forces. A call by Francis Bacon for objective scrutiny of parapsychological experiences was rather more scientifically motivated, but at the time society was not receptive to such a view and Bacon's arguments went unheeded (Bell, 1956). Some two and a half centuries were to pass before parapsychological phenomena were accorded a degree of serious and sustained academic attention.

Two main factors can be seen to have led to the foundation of parapsychology in 1882 (Beloff, 1993; Inglis, 1977). These were the movements known respectively as Mesmerism and Spiritualism, and we will consider them in turn.

11

Mesmerism

Franz Anton Mesmer was born in Switzerland in 1733 and later studied medicine at the University of Vienna. Mesmer was particularly interested in the influence which physicians can exert over their patients. At the folk level there was a tradition that certain divinely inspired individuals had the power to cure the sick by touch, the so-called "laying on of hands," and some of these healers used magnets to strengthen the healing force that purportedly emanated from them. Mesmer believed that a similar sort of energy was involved in the ability of physicians to promote their patients' return to health. Through experimentation he found, for example, that he could influence the rate of blood flow by movements of a magnet. He subsequently discovered a magnet was not necessary: the same effect could be achieved with any object over which he had passed his hands. Mesmer concluded there exists a healing force or "fluid" known as *animal magnetism* (so named to distinguish it from ordinary mineral magnetism).

Mesmer moved to Paris in 1778 and his method of treatment became highly fashionable, much to the annoyance of the medical fraternity; not surprisingly, he frequently was accused of being a charlatan. Of most interest in the present context are some of the by-products of Mesmer's technique. As Mesmer made magnetic "passes" over his patients they would fall into a deep sleep-like state or trance, although their eyes could be open or closed. In this state the "magnetized" individuals would be remarkably compliant with Mesmer's suggestions, reporting, for example, complete freedom from pain. Today we would designate this state of consciousness a hypnotic trance; there are some differences in the behavior of Mesmer's patients and that of contemporary subjects under hypnosis, but largely these seem to reflect changes in people's expectations of what should happen in such a state.

Other reported by-products of magnetic induction were so-called "higher phenomena" such as the subject's ability to "see" events that were sensorially inaccessible: thus gestures made by the magnetizer in another room might be described accurately. Following these initial observations disciples of Mesmer endeavored to use the magnetic trance as a means of evoking telepathy, clairvoyance, traveling clairvoyance (the impression of transporting clairvoyant awareness to a distant location), and other parapsychological experiences (see Dingwall, 1967–1968).

Broadly speaking, the parapsychological facet of the mesmeric movement either was ignored by the scientific establishment or was used as evidence of the bogus character of animal magnetism (Leahey & Leahey, 1983, Ch. 5). Further, the movement had no direct effect on the foundation of the SPR; that is to say, when the SPR began its investigations of parapsychological phenomena it looked to hypnotism only as an ancillary research technique. Nevertheless mesmerism can be regarded as a factor in the origins of parapsychological research in two important respects. First, the activities of Mesmer's followers raised the possibility that through careful manipulation of test conditions a researcher might be able to ascertain the authenticity of parapsychological phenomena. Thus an individual might be found to exhibit certain behavior which by virtue of the investigator's control over the situation could be due only to paranormal factors. In this sense mesmerism can be regarded as the "forerunner" of parapsychology (Beloff, 1993). Second, mesmerism implied that parapsychological phenomena could be examined outside occultist and quasi-religious contexts. This was of special significance in light of the fact that the major catalyst for the SPR's establishment was indeed a religious movement, that of Spiritualism.

Spiritualism

Parapsychological research as a coherent discipline was precipitated by the Spiritualist movement which began in America in the middle of the nineteenth century. Although one can point to many philosophical antecedents (see Anderson, 1987; Leahey & Leahey, 1983, pp. 162–164), in 1848 Spiritualism was both given an impetus and brought to popular awareness by events in the household of a family named Fox (E. Isaacs, 1983; Weisberg, 2004).

In December 1847 a blacksmith John Fox, his wife, and two of their children, 14-year-old Maggie and 12-year-old Kate, moved into a rented wooden cottage in Hydesville (near Rochester), New York State. The house is said to have had a reputation for being associated with uncanny events, and in the latter half of March 1848 the family began to hear a variety of strange sounds: rappings, bangs and scrapings as if furniture was being shifted. This outbreak of percussive activity became more insistent until March 31 when the inexplicable noises were particularly intense. John Fox decided to check if the window sashes were being rattled by the wind and gave the window frames a strong shake. Young Kate commented that each time her father shook the windows the noises were heard as if in reply. It occurred to her to snap her fingers to see if that would elicit a similar response. The "ghost," as it was taken to be, responded to this challenge with raps in the pattern of Kate's snapping fingers. Maggie also joined in the game. Mrs. Fox then decided to use the "ghost's" percussive responses to questions as a means of communication. She asked if the noises were being produced by a spirit: "If it is, make two raps." Immediately two raps sounded. In this fashion it is said the Foxes ascertained the communicating spirit to be that of a man who at the age of 31 had been murdered and his body buried in the cellar of the Foxes' house.

Several neighbors were called in and they too witnessed the spirit communications. One neighbor had the idea of facilitating communication by calling the letters of the alphabet, the spirit being asked to rap when appropriate and thereby spell out whole sentences. By this means further gruesome details of the murder were conveyed. The deceased man allegedly was Charles Rosma, a traveling salesman who had been robbed and murdered by a former occupant of the house about five years earlier. The latter denied this claim and the occurrence of the murder never was verified. An effort to locate the corpse was thwarted by the fact that the ground under the cellar was waterlogged. Many years later a newspaper reported the finding of a skeleton in the cellar when an old wall collapsed, but corroboration of the report is lacking (Prince, 1930, pp. 155–156).

More and more people flocked to the house to witness the communications. Leah, an older married daughter of the Foxes, realized that her sisters could be exploited as a commercial proposition. Soon the girls were traveling about the country giving demonstrations of their contact with the spirit world. In a rented hall typically a lecture would be given on spiritualism and then questions put to the spirits on behalf of members of the paying audience. The activities of the Fox sisters received much attention in the press. Public interest increased further as new phenomena were reported: people at the Foxes' seances felt themselves touched by an invisible hand; objects moved unaccountably; and musical instruments played without human intervention.

Needless to say there were charges that the percussive noises and other effects were produced by fraudulent means. It was suggested that the raps could have been effected by snapping toe joints. In later years Kate and Maggie used this explanation when they offered confessions of their fraudulent practices (Neher, 1980, pp. 213–214; "Spiritualism exposed," 1888/1985). Some commentators point out that at the time of the confessions the Fox sisters were destitute and hence their statements may have been designed to gain financial advantage and perhaps also to discredit their elder sister Leah with whom they had fallen out. In any event the confessions subsequently were retracted.

For present purposes the authenticity of the Foxes' spirit communications is of peripheral concern. The fact remains that the idea of communicating with deceased persons captured the imagination of the American public. Mediums sprang up in other parts of New York State, and by the early 1850s followers of spiritualism in New York city alone numbered in the tens of thousands (Weisberg, 2004). Within a few years the message of spiritualism had spread throughout America and to Europe. Its growth was soon to accelerate dramatically as people found wanting alternative worldviews based solely on an agnostic science or on a Christianity under siege from Darwin's theory of evolution. Spiritualism offered an appealing compromise, for here was a religious movement that claimed to put religion on a empirical footing, most particularly by seeking direct "scientific proof" of its central tenets through communication with the spirit world.

Although many mediums were caught out in deception reports persisted that there were some trustworthy mediums who were able to produce ostensibly paranormal phenomena under circumstances thought to preclude trickery. Such assertions were all but ignored by the scientific establishment: under the contemporary scientific view of the world paranormal events could not happen and hence were bound to be bogus, undeserving of academic attention. Dissension from these assumptions by a few Cambridge intellectuals and others in Britain led to the formation of the SPR in 1882 (Oppenheim, 1985). They felt the implications of parapsychological phenomena were so great that science could not afford to ignore the phenomena or to re-

ject them out of hand. If investigation should indicate that the prevailing scientific worldview was incomplete, that surely would be worth knowing, they maintained.

Although most mediums incorporated elements of their own style in their seances the basic features of spiritualist seances were surprisingly uniform. The following outline of the phenomenology of trance mediumship draws on the account by Broad (1962, Ch. 10). For convenience of exposition it is assumed that the medium was a woman, as the considerable majority of spiritualist mediums indeed were; this is not to imply of course, that male mediums did not achieve eminence too.

The medium sat quietly in her chair either in the dark or in very subdued lighting and she closed her eyes. Soon she began to breathe deeply and to be rather restless for a few minutes. On becoming calmer she started to whisper to herself, then to talk audibly in a voice and manner unlike her usual self. It was as if another personality had gained control of the medium's vocal cords. This trance personality usually was the same in each seance conducted by the medium and was known as the *spirit guide* or *control*; it was depicted as the medium's "contact" in the spirit world.

The trance-personality or control would converse with the *sitters*, the people attending the seance, for perhaps an hour or more. Often it would present itself as a child and speak in a childish fashion; other controls would claim to be Red Indian, Hindu or Chinese and talk in a false stereotypic style of broken English. The control's narrative typically was entertaining and sometimes it would make remarks derogatory or embarrassing to the medium. It also would refer to its past life on earth and to the nature of postmortem existence. After a period of general conversation the control would claim to be in communication with the spirit of a deceased relative or friend of one of the sitters. Messages to the sitter and references to the spirit's earthly life would be conveyed through the control as an intermediary. With some mediums the voice of the control would actually be replaced by another voice purporting to be that of the spirit or *communicator* itself; this was called "direct voice" communication.

Usually contact would be made with several communicators during a seance, particularly if more than one sitter was present. In some instances the spirit communication would be a discourse in the form of spiritual teachings or literature; this now has come to be termed *channeling* (Alcock, 1996; Hastings, 1987). At the end of the seance the medium again would show a certain amount of restlessness, groaning and whispering, then resume her normal voice and manner. Having come out of the trance state she generally was ignorant of what had happened during the seance.

What were the phenomena of the seance room that moved people in Britain (and later those in other countries) to call for objective investigation in accordance with the fundamental tenets of science? A useful way to address this issue is to examine the careers of some of the more notable mediums. As well as illustrating the reported phenomena the review provides a context for exemplifying the development of investigative techniques.

Four Spiritualist Mediums: Their Careers and Their Investigation

Daniel Dunglas Home (1833–1886). Broadly speaking there are two types of mediums. *Mental mediums* provide information to which they evidently do not have access by normal means. For example they may foretell the future, describe distant events of interest to the sitter, nominate the location of the sitter's lost possessions, give a history of the owner of a particular object presented

to them, and communicate with deceased personalities. *Physical mediums* generally have these abilities of mental mediums but additionally appear to have the power to influence the physical state of objects. The seance table may rise from the floor, "spirit" raps may be heard, furniture in the seance room may be displaced, objects and people may be levitated, and so on. At the spirits' behest these physical effects usually occur under conditions of darkness or of subdued lighting.

Daniel Home (pronounced "Hume") was an exponent of physical mediumship and by some accounts one of the best. Home was born in 1833 near Edinburgh, Scotland, and was raised by an aunt, although he remained emotionally close to his mother. At the age of 9 he and his aunt emigrated to Connecticut; his parents also moved to America but Daniel continued to live with his aunt. Home's mother died when he was 17, much to his distress. Shortly afterwards inexplicable noises and movement of furniture began to plague the house. The young Home was familiar with the recent events in the Fox household and he too tried to communicate with the source of the spirit raps. Using an alphabet technique he eventually obtained a message, ostensibly from his deceased mother, reassuring him and declaring that he had a "glorious mission" in life to cure the sick and to convert people to a belief in spiritualism.

Home began to hold seances for the neighbors in his aunt's parlor. Sitters were told where to find long-lost relatives and the location of misplaced possessions. The participants in these early seances were greatly impressed, but Home's aunt was convinced the whole affair was the work of the devil and after just one week she threw him out of the house. Home moved in with friends and became a full-time medium. His talents were reported in the press and his fame spread.

It would appear that Home never accepted money for his seances, a fact which many spiritualists have taken as proof of his honesty. Nevertheless he lived very well for

Figure 1. Daniel Dunglas Home (photograph: MEPL).

the rest of his life as a houseguest. His personal magnetism, empathy and readiness to display his "gift" made him most welcome in the best of homes.

Some of his mental feats took the form of spirit possession, as in the following instance (Home, 1864/c.1973, pp. 26–27). One day in 1852 the Elmers, a Massachusetts family with whom Home was staying, were visited by a Reverend Brittan. In the middle of a conversation with the visitor Home suddenly fell into a trance. He groaned, then declared "Hannah Brittan is here!" The medium paced the floor, moaning, striking his head and crying "Save them from the pit!" and "There's no light! Where am I?" The Elmer family was mystified but the Reverend Brittan was quite shaken: as far as he was aware no one in Massachusetts knew the story of Hannah Brittan. It emerged that many years earlier a relation named Hannah became insane with worry about hell and eternal torment.

Home suffered from tuberculosis or what the Victorians called consumption, and in the hope of improving his health he sailed for England in the spring of 1855. It is a testimony to his talents and character that having arrived in England virtually penniless and with few contacts Home established himself within a month as a favorite of London's most eminent hostesses.

One of Home's physical phenomena was the appearance of "spirit hands" during his seances. Spiritualists believed that discarnate spirits could become visible to sitters by drawing on *ectoplasm*, a substance allegedly issued from the body of the medium. Sometimes these *materializations* (as they are termed) comprised only parts of a bodily form, and the phenomenon of luminous spirit hands was one relatively common such instance. A spirit hand was observed in an 1855 sitting with the English poets Elizabeth Barrett Browning and Robert Browning. The latter reportedly found spiritualism distasteful and took part in the seance with great reluctance (although that view may in fact have been formulated by Robert after the event; see Jenkins, 1982, pp. 44–45). His wife Elizabeth on the other hand was mystically inclined and as the evening progressed it became clear that she found Home quite captivating. During the seance a large luminous white hand appeared and at Home's command it made the suitably poetic gesture of crowning Elizabeth with a wreath of clematis that had been decorating the table at which they sat. This infuriated Robert Browning and although he had no proof he charged that the spirit hand was actually Home's foot or some device manipulated by the medium's foot.

This incident was the inspiration for Browning's poem "Mr. Sludge the Medium." This vengeful work recounted the fraudulent activities and weak character of a supposedly fictitious spiritualist medium; the latter, however, was a thinly disguised caricature of Home. Although Robert decided not to publish "Mr. Sludge" until after Elizabeth's death his intense animosity toward Home was no secret.

Home responded by publishing a vitriolic attack on Browning in a spiritualist magazine. Now, normally this would have been an unforgivable indiscretion, as the Brownings were the darlings of the English social set. Yet far from becoming a social outcast Home found his reputation if anything enhanced by the affair, so strong was his own position becoming in the higher social circles. In any event Home's fame spread to the Continent and for the remainder of his life he toured Europe as an honored guest of the rich and the privileged.

One of Home's most famous feats occurred in December 1868 at the London apartment of Lord Adare. Home traveled and lived with Adare for over a year. During this period Adare recorded all of the physical manifestations he witnessed, privately publishing his notes in 1869. On the night in question Home conducted a seance in the darkened dining room after dinner. Two sitters other than Adare were present, Lord Lindsay and Adare's cousin Captain Wynne. While in trance Home announced that the spirits would whisk him out of the fourth floor window of an adjacent room and in through the window of the dining room. According to reports from each of the witnesses Home was heard to enter the next room and shortly afterwards appear outside the window of the seance room, floating in mid-air. Home is said to have glided in through the window and sat down at the table.

Many writers have sought to explain how this instance of apparent *levitation* could have been performed by normal means. One of the SPR founders, Frank Podmore (1902), later argued that Home merely crept back past the three sitters in the dark and hopped up on a window sill, making it appear under the poor conditions for observation that he was floating outside the window. It does seem unlikely that none of the seance participants detected Home's passage through the dining

room to the window sill, although it should be said that the three sitters firmly believed in Home's powers and thus may have perceived only what they dearly needed to (Lamont, 2005). On similar grounds Wyndham (1937, p. 199) argues the sitters may simply have hallucinated the experience. Others, including the master magician Houdini, have declared that because there was a small balcony outside each window, it was quite possible for Home to have leapt from one to the other if he was reasonably fit and had no fear of heights (Hall, 1984, p. 120). According to Lambert (1976, pp. 311–312) Home could easily have used rope to swing from one window to the next and into the seance room. There also have been suggestions that the three witnesses were obliged to give testimony in support of Home's levitation because of his homosexual relationship with one or more of them (Hall, 1984). It may be noted there are some discrepancies among the accounts of the three witnesses.

Many people had attended Home's seances in the hope of catching the medium in some fraudulent act but Home's performance never was exposed conclusively as sham. There was one instance of a sitter who claimed to have seen Home's shoulder or body rising and falling in synchrony with the movements of a spirit hand (Jenkins, 1982, pp. 47–48), and of course there were many people like Robert Browning who declared Home a fake on no hard evidence at all. On a few occasions Home did offer himself for testing by skeptical investigators (e.g., Zorab, 1970) and while he came through these tests with his reputation essentially intact it must be said that many of the investigators were ill-qualified for the task they undertook (Lamont, 1999). Indeed techniques for testing mediums were poorly developed at this time. Often the investigator simply observed what the medium did. Even when some simple controls over the medium's movements were imposed they were ones which readily could be circumvented by a skilled conjurer.

One comparatively extensive investigation of Home's seance phenomena was undertaken by the chemist and physicist (later Sir) William Crookes, an eminent figure of the scientific establishment. In the *Quarterly Journal of Science* for July 1870 Crookes announced his intention to determine whether the reported phenomena of spiritualist seances were authentic or bogus. To the extent that other scientists were at all interested in this objective they generally felt assured that the authority of Crookes would do much to dispel the "superstitious attitudes" encouraged among members of the public by the spiritualist movement.

Crookes's work with Home began in 1871. To the astonishment of the scientific community Crookes reported that all of the phenomena associated with Home were genuine! Most of Crookes's conclusions were based on his and his collaborators' passive observation of the phenomena under conditions which he felt were adequate for the purpose of valid investigation. Thus he noted the occurrence of spirit raps governed by some form of intelligence; the movement of furniture and other objects either in contact with Home or at some distance from the medium; levitation of furniture and of Home himself; *materialization* of spirit hands, faces, and "phantasmic forms" or apparitions; *automatic writing* through the medium's hand or with a planchette; and *apports*, the paranormal transference of objects into the seance room from other locations. Crookes also designed a couple of specific tests of the medium's powers. He set up weights in a chemical balance and asked the medium (or the spirits working through the agency of the medium, as Home would have it) to influence the mass of an item to upset the equilibrium of the balance. He also enclosed one end of a small accordion in a cage of copper wire and asked that the instrument be played. According to Crookes Home passed each of these tests.

Not unexpectedly the report by Crookes on Home's performance evoked vehement criticism by other scientists, much of it emotionally rather than rationally based and some involving outright misrepresentation. Because seance phenomena were incompatible with accepted scientific principles the former must be shown to be bogus. Hence, it was argued that Crookes's procedures were not sufficiently tight to preclude trickery. Without any supportive evidence it was charged that Home had attached to the accordion a wire or some such device by which he was able to extract a few notes from the instrument, or that he had smuggled into the room another accordion that was used to produce some music (Wyndham, 1937, p. 231).

Whether or not these criticisms were fair, it must be said that the value of Crookes's investigation of Home is questioned by some recent allegations. It seems possible that Crookes's report on another medium, Florence Cook, was spurious, in part intended to conceal an affair between Crookes and Cook (Hall, 1962). The purported evidence for this scenario certainly has been criticized by Medhurst and Goldney (1964), and in addition, there is no direct indication of any similar collusion between Crookes and Home. Nevertheless, the allegations about the Florence Cook affair, if confirmed, necessarily would undermine the integrity of Crookes and thereby raise doubts about the validity of all of his psychical research including that involving Home.

While it may be true that Home never was detected in fraudulent practices it could be argued that at the time techniques for investigating mediums were poorly developed and that Home was subjected to very few tests by independent, suitably trained researchers of unimpeachable character. In later years as the sophistication of investigative procedures increased the number of physical mediums fell. Indeed after the 1940s the physical medium almost became an extinct species, with the physical phenomena of the spiritualist era having no major parallels until the Uri Geller episode of the mid–1970s.

Leonora Piper (1859–1950). We now turn to a medium who operated at a time when psychical research was better established. Arguably the best known American mental medium, Leonora Piper has a special place in the history of parapsychological research. She was the most extensively studied of all mental mediums, participating in formal investigations over more than thirty years and generating material for numerous reports and other commentaries in the pages of the psychical research journals. Indeed, Mrs. Piper (as she was known throughout her career) is described by one modern biographer as the first mental medium "to provide substantial evidence for the possession of some paranormal faculty" (Gauld, 1982, p. 32). On the other hand, another more skeptical commentator has dismissed her simply as a "clever charlatan" (Gardner, 1992, p. 246).

Mrs. Piper generally was described as an attractive, good-natured but rather unintelligent woman. She reportedly had a few parapsychological experiences as a child (Piper, 1929), but her mediumship usually is said to have begun after her marriage at the age of 22 to William Piper of Boston. In 1884 Mrs. Piper had several consultations about her health with a blind medical (healing) medium. During her second visit she fell into a trance and received a communication that appeared to be from the spirit of the late son of a fellow sitter. In subsequent seances held in her own home, contact was made with various spirit controls including Longfellow, Bach, Commodore Vanderbilt, an actor Sarah Siddons, and an Indian girl with the unlikely name of Chlorine. Spoken communications from the spirit world seemingly were channeled through Mrs. Piper from these controls. Shortly afterwards an eighteenth-century French physician calling himself Phinuit took over as Mrs. Piper's spirit control. It was in this phase of her mediumship that she came to the attention of the eminent Harvard psychologist William James.

Figure 2. Leonora Piper (photograph: MEPL).

In time it became apparent that Phinuit's account of his supposed earthly existence was dubious. No trace of Phinuit's name could be found in official records. During seances this spirit control showed a meager knowledge of medicine and little ability either to speak or to understand French, his alleged native tongue. Thus, even a sympathetic biographer has conceded that the character of Phinuit was "quite certainly fictitious" (Gauld, 1982, p. 114). Moreover, during some sessions Phinuit was inclined to "fish" for information from the sitters, presumably as a basis for generating his supposed communications from the spirit world. Hansel (1980, p. 66) and Gardner (1992, p. 223) dismiss the Piper mediumship in part on this ground.

On other occasions, however, the spirit control Phinuit provided sitters with substantial quantities of detailed, veridical information that often struck those present as impossible for Mrs. Piper to have acquired by normal means. William James therefore was moved to undertake a series of tests with

Mrs. Piper commencing in 1885. He introduced 25 sitters to Mrs. Piper's circle under pseudonyms and found that 15 received impressive factual information, even at their first seance (James, 1886). James concluded that Mrs. Piper had some paranormal ability, but unfortunately he did not have the time to continue his investigations.

James's (1886) report nevertheless impressed the American Society for Psychical Research (ASPR), and the society therefore resolved to pursue the study of Mrs. Piper's mediumship. The opportunity to implement this resolution came in the following year with the appointment of the Australian-born psychical researcher Richard Hodgson as the secretary of the ASPR. Hodgson was a skeptic who had earned an outstanding reputation for his research on behalf of the SPR in England. He had caught several physical mediums, including the Italian woman Eusapia Palladino, in the act of cheating. Further, he had looked into anomalous phenomena said to be associated with the theosophist Madame Blavatsky and the SPR's scathing report of his investigations damned her for fraud and for forgery. Hodgson thus was an experienced investigator to be feared by dishonest mediums. Possibly because of his skeptical attitude Hodgson tended to be rather brusque with Mrs. Piper, and despite their working together for 18 years the two were never close (Piper, 1929). On the other hand, Hodgson's unsociable facade also ensured that during their casual conversations Mrs. Piper had scant opportunity to elicit any data about Hodgson's past life. In sittings he attended anonymously on arrival in Boston in 1887, Hodgson must therefore have been taken aback when he received through the medium some relatively intimate facts about Australian friends and relatives.

As a means of assessing Mrs. Piper's performance, however, Hodgson preferred to rely on mediumistic communications to sitters other than himself. In some seances arranged by Hodgson, sitters were masked,

introduced pseudonymously, instructed to remain silent, and seated behind the medium. These procedures were designed to minimize Mrs. Piper's potential reliance on cues in the sitters' manner about their likely character and background, and to inhibit her use of sitters' involuntary bodily and facial reactions as feedback on the accuracy of the material she was communicating to them; these tricks of stage telepathy were familiar to Hodgson and are known to magicians as "cold reading" techniques (Hyman, 1977). Hodgson even went so far as to employ detectives for some weeks to keep Mrs. Piper and her husband under surveillance. Despite all these precautions Mrs. Piper continued to give impressive readings.

The eminent skeptic Martin Gardner (1992, p. 223) nevertheless insists that Mrs. Piper's performances were achieved largely by means of cold reading in conjunction with a willingness of gullible sitters to overlook all the inaccurate material in the medium's communications. It might also be objected that many sitters at Mrs. Piper's seances came from the area in which the medium lived. That is, Mrs. Piper may have been in a position to speak about her sitters' affairs on the basis of material she had gleaned from the social grapevine or even from agents' surreptitious enquiries. Gardner (1992, p. 245) believes the medium's husband was employed to research the lives of prospective sitters on her behalf. It is usual, too, for sitters to want to contribute information as a part of the social interaction with the medium during the seance (Wooffitt, 2000). Although some of Hodgson's methods of selecting and introducing sitters were designed to circumvent these possibilities, he realized the value of tests that could be conducted in a location completely unfamiliar to the medium. To this end arrangements were made in 1889 to have Mrs. Piper travel to England for investigation by members of the SPR.

Throughout the English visit precautions again were taken to prevent Mrs. Piper from gathering information about the investigators and potential sitters. For example, family records of her hosts were locked away, new servants unfamiliar with the host family were employed, Mrs. Piper's luggage and mail were examined, and she was given an escort wherever she went, even on shopping excursions. The SPR's representatives reported Mrs. Piper's behavior to be fully cooperative and to give no cause for the slightest suspicion. In nearly 90 sittings convened in England the control Phinuit was often noted to make erroneous claims or to make statements that would be true of almost any sitter, and sometimes he would flagrantly fish for information from sitters. But also forthcoming were large amounts of factual material about deceased acquaintances of anonymous sitters. The comprehensive report on Mrs. Piper's performances in England argued strongly for the paranormality of her trance phenomena (Myers, Lodge, Leaf & James, 1890).

On her return to America in February 1890 Mrs. Piper contracted to work with the ASPR. Over the next 15 years detailed records of Mrs. Piper's seances were maintained by Hodgson. In large part because of Phinuit's unconvincing character Hodgson's (1892) first report on the Piper mediumship suggested that she was not in fact communicating with deceased individuals but, rather, she gathered relevant data by some "supernormal" or extrasensory means and dramatized these in the form of a spirit address. Eventually, however, even the skeptical Hodgson (1898) was persuaded to the spirit hypothesis. This change of attitude seems to have been prompted principally by the appearance of a new control, George Pellew or "G.P." A young writer, Pellew had been known to Hodgson and had recently been killed in a riding accident. As a communicator G.P. proved to be a much more credible personation than Phinuit, and gradually G.P. took over as Mrs. Piper's primary control. During the period of G.P.'s control automatic writing became increasingly more frequent as the

mode of spirit communication. Hodgson evidently was impressed by the knowledge of Pellew's life conveyed through the medium. Most impressive was the fact that of 150 sitters introduced to G.P., the 30 who had been known by Pellew in life were recognized as such.

Over the ensuing years of Mrs. Piper's active mediumship several other controls emerged, but most (including a group called the Imperators) seemed superficial characterizations just as Phinuit had been. Due to the persistent efforts of Hodgson and his successor at the ASPR James Hyslop, evidential material gathered in these sittings nevertheless continued to accumulate and reached copious proportions. Mrs. Piper also was involved in a tantalizing mediumship episode known as the cross-correspondences (see Chapter 9). Most notable perhaps is that at no stage during Mrs. Piper's very long career were investigators able to establish any positive evidence of fraudulent activity by her. Critics such as Hansel (1980, p. 66) have rejected this perception with the retort that the investigators were people who were easily deceived; although it might seem inappropriate to thus dismiss Hodgson, a man who was intent on uncovering fraud and who had been successful in exposing many dishonest mediums, in retrospect it could be argued that Hodgson was naive in some respects (Munves, 1997). Certainly there were investigators who remarked on Mrs. Piper's cold reading techniques, occasions on which apparent contact was made with the spirit of a completely fictitious person, and the lack of any evidential material in their particular sittings with the medium (e.g., Tanner, 1910), yet Mrs. Piper was never caught in the act of soliciting information about sitters outside the seance room. Much has been made of Mrs. Piper's so-called "confession," a 1901 newspaper report in which the medium was said to have conceded she herself was uncertain that her controls were genuine spirit entities (e.g., Neher, 1980, p. 218). At the time of the seances there was considerable speculation about the need to appeal to the existence of spirits in order to explain Mrs. Piper's trance phenomena, but many of those who rejected this need still seemed forced to conclude the operation of some paranormal process such as telepathy or clairvoyance.

On balance, may the record of Mrs. Piper's mediumship reasonably be held to document the existence of any paranormal phenomenon? To some extent the answer to this question clearly rests on an assessment of the effectiveness with which psychical researchers ruled out all normal sources of the information communicated by Mrs. Piper. Although such an assessment must inevitably be subjective, it seems fair to say that control over all relevant factors in the highly complex physical and psychological context of a seance must be extraordinarily difficult to achieve. If nothing else, the diverse investigatory procedures implemented by Hodgson and by the SPR committee attest to the substantial logistical problems involved in any attempt to exclude orthodox explanations of mental mediumship.

Hélène Smith (1861–1929). Hélène Smith was the pseudonym of Catherine Elise Muller, a nonprofessional medium in Geneva from the early 1890s. Her career is outlined by Flournoy (1900), from whom the following account is drawn. Smith was the daughter of a Hungarian merchant who had settled in Geneva after traveling extensively and acquiring several languages in the process; the father's facility for languages may have some bearing on the nature of Smith's mediumship, as we shall see.

Hélène Smith first heard of spiritualism at the age of 30 when an acquaintance lent her a book on the subject. Her curiosity roused, she joined a spiritualist circle. At the second of the seances she attended (April 1892) there was received a spirit communication announcing that the spirit of Victor Hugo would be her protector and spirit guide or control. In subsequent seances Smith began

to experience visual and auditory images said to be evoked by her spirit guide, and to develop the ability of automatic writing. While in the dissociated state of a mediumistic trance she would seemingly become possessed by a discarnate spirit who would force her hand to write messages for the sitters attending the seance.

Smith soon became a strong medium and was very well known among spiritualists. During her seances she is said to have moved objects at a distance, apported flowers and Chinese coins, helped sitters to locate misplaced possessions, predicted future events, seen spirit visitors, clairaudiently heard spirits talking, and elicited spirit raps. "Victor Hugo" remained her spirit guide for approximately six months, when there emerged another control identifying itself as "Leopold" and which eventually supplanted the original guide. After a period "Leopold" claimed to be the deceased spirit of Cagliostro, an Italian-born mystic who frequented the French court during the reign of Louis XVI and Marie Antoinette.

In 1894 Professor Theodore Flournoy, a professor of psychology at the University of Geneva, accepted a colleague's invitation to attend some of Smith's seances. To Flournoy's astonishment she was able to give him accurate information about events which had occurred in his family before he was born. Thus motivated Flournoy determined to investigate Smith's psychic talents. One of his first tasks was to undertake a character analysis of the spirit guide Leopold/Cagliostro. He judged Leopold's personality to be quite a contrast to that of Smith. Further, when Leopold wrote through the hand of Smith the handwriting differed from Smith's usual script, showing the style of the previous century. When Leopold spoke through Smith (so-called direct voice communication) the voice was a deep bass with a strong easily recognizable Italian accent.

On the other hand there were other facets of Leopold that did not ring true. His handwriting was strikingly dissimilar to that used in some of Cagliostro's letters preserved in French archives. During the seances Leopold evidently did not understand Italian and would ignore anyone who addressed him in that language. Worse still the spirit guide was very vague or evasive about questions concerning his terrestrial existence and did not furnish a single name, date, or precise fact which could be investigated for its authenticity.

At one seance the spirits revealed that Smith was the reincarnation of Marie Antoinette. Later Smith would go into trance and "become" Marie Antoinette, a character which she carried quite naturally. Nevertheless there again were marked discrepancies between the spirit's handwriting through the hand of Smith and that of the real Marie Antoinette, and Flournoy was able to trap the "Queen" in various malapropisms. Flournoy constructed a psychodynamic interpretation of this phase of Smith's mediumship, arguing that "Leopold" and "Marie Antoinette" were secondary personalities of the medium, reflecting certain unconscious desires and anxieties.

Although Flournoy rejected the notion that Smith literally was in contact with a spirit world he was prepared to countenance the possibility that she had paranormal access to information. For example, in October 1894 there began another cycle of Smith's mediumship in which she took on the role of an Indian princess of the fifteenth century. In these seances the entranced Smith exhibited a good deal of knowledge about Indian historical events, costumes, and language. Flournoy investigated the accuracy of this material and its accessibility in Geneva. He was forced to conclude that the source of Smith's knowledge of these matters was a "psychological enigma." He did not, however, rule out the possibility of *cryptomnesia*, that is, subconscious memory of material read many years previously.

One of the most fascinating phases of

Smith's mediumship began in November 1894 when Smith's own spirit reportedly was transported to the planet Mars in a number of seances. While in trance she would describe the human, animal and floral life of Mars and would also speak and write in the "language" of that planet. Since her spirit guide gave purported translations of the written communications Flournoy was able to examine the Martian language for its structure. He found that the Martian scripts were not random scribblings but indeed exhibited an alphabet which was used consistently across the series of seances. Nevertheless it was clear that the vowels and consonants of Smith's Martian language were those of French (her native tongue) and that the grammar, inflections and construction also were modeled on French. On this basis Flournoy concluded that the Martian language was an extraordinary elaboration by Smith's unconscious mind. As an intellectual endeavor Smith's Martian communications certainly did not impress him, but as a feat of memory and subconscious creativity the effort was remarkable. Smith also provided purported descriptions and sketches of the Martian landscape. Of course Flournoy was unaware of the discrepancies between these accounts and details of Martian topography revealed by recent space probes, but he did comment to Smith on the extraordinarily human-like character of her descriptions of life on Mars. Apparently stung by Flournoy's comments Smith later reported spirit excursions to another planet which had grotesque inhabitants and a language evidently unlike any earthly one.

Whether or not you are persuaded by Flournoy's (1900) analysis it does present an exciting method for investigating mental mediums, and it is unfortunate that similar studies are lacking in the literature. The analysis of the Martian cycle also raises important questions about the creative capacity of the unconscious and serves to caution us that even in those cases of spontaneous

Figure 3. Charles Bailey (photograph: *Harbinger of Light*).

parapsychological experiences where fraud and willful deception confidently may be ruled out there still is a possibility that subconscious fantasy may have played a substantial role.

Charles Bailey (c. 1870–1947). The last of our quartet of mediums, Charles Bailey, is of special interest to the first author (HJI) because he too was an Australian. Bailey merits consideration here because he did generate much interest on the international parapsychological scene and also because investigation of his talents illustrates the role of physical constraints in testing physical mediums. His career is documented by Irwin (1987a).

Charles Bailey reportedly was born in Richmond, Victoria, Australia, in about 1870. He had little education, even being described by one biographer as illiterate. Usually he was employed in poorly paid positions, at one time being a boot operative, and possibly for this reason he expected payment by his sitters. His professional mediumship began in 1889 and eventually he gained the

patronage of an American-born Melbourne millionaire, T. W. Stanford.

Now, Stanford was ardently devoted to spiritualism and psychical research for much of his life (Dommeyer, 1975). He was the brother of the founder of Stanford University in California and he made substantial donations to that university for the purpose of encouraging psychical research. Stanford began his studies of seance phenomena in America and continued this work after migrating to Australia, doing much to stimulate psychical research in that country. Although Stanford arranged private sittings with many mediums his work with Charles Bailey over 12 years represents one of the most detailed and sustained records of mediumship in the history of parapsychology. Between 1902 and 1913 thorough accounts were maintained of each sitting of Bailey's circle in Melbourne and subsequently these were presented as ten bound volumes to Stanford University. In 1903 Stanford published the results of his early observations in a small booklet, and monthly reports of Bailey's seances were printed in an Australian spiritualist magazine, the *Harbinger of Light*.

Bailey's particular specialty was *apportation* of a wide range of objects. While seated in darkness or subdued light, sitters would hear various objects fall on to the seance table. According to spirit communications these apports were conveyed by the spirits with whom Bailey was in contact. Among the apports recorded by Stanford in his 1903 booklet were several live specimens of exotic birds, birds' nests (many containing eggs), live fish, large quantities of seaweed and sand replete with aquatic fauna, a fishing net, a live turtle, exotic plants, ivory, beads and precious stones, a human skull, a leopard skin, and a sizable piece of tapestry. Most sensational, however, were apported clay tablets and cylinders said to bear ancient Babylonian inscriptions, some of which were translated by Bailey's spirit controls. Communications from ancient Aztec personages also occurred apparently through the discarnate personality of an American scholar, Professor Edward Robinson; the biographical details of Robinson are reported to have largely been authentic.

Stanford's work with Bailey was purely documentary. No attempt was made to impose constraints upon the medium's activities, although Stanford reassured his readers that he had not observed anything suggestive of deception. Tests of an apparently more stringent character were conducted in Sydney by Dr. Charles MacCarthy, a physician of some note. In the first series of the MacCarthy sittings the membership of the circle was chosen by MacCarthy. Bailey was not permitted to enter the seance room before the session and he was searched by a number of the sitters (although rarely was he stripped completely), then enclosed in a double-sewn canvas bag with only his arms and head free. The seance room was searched and after Bailey entered the room it was locked for the duration of the sitting. Generally all lights were extinguished before any apports were produced. In seven sessions under these conditions the medium apported 54 objects including some inscribed cylinders and clay tablets, foreign coins, semiprecious stones, an Arabic newspaper, a hot semibaked "Chupatti" cake, live birds, and various marine creatures including a crab and a small barely alive shark. For the second series of seances Bailey was stripped to his underwear and searched, then placed in a "cage" of mosquito netting. On occasions sitters were searched and Bailey was required to wear boxing gloves, to change into a new suit, or to be placed in the canvas bag as well as in the cage as precautions against conjuring. The usual diversity of tablets and cylinders and other apports again were produced.

After consideration of several rival hypotheses MacCarthy felt that the paranormality of Bailey's phenomena was an inescapable conclusion. He did note that the inscriptions and figures on the apported

tablets and cylinders looked remarkably sharp and fresh but he was not perturbed by this, believing the impressions to be too difficult to simulate. When photographs of the tablets were submitted to the British Museum by the SPR's Sir Oliver Lodge, however, the supposed antiquities were declared to be forgeries. A tablet obtained by Sir Arthur Conan Doyle (an ardent spiritualist) in a 1920 sitting with Bailey also was referred to the British Museum and found to be an imitation. Conan Doyle nevertheless did not hold this against the medium, arguing that it may have been easier for the discarnate "transporting agency" to locate and handle one of these forgeries than an authentic tablet buried deep in some archaeological site.

Another Australian researcher, A. W. Dobbie, also reported the communications of Bailey's Hindu control to be nonsensical scribblings and a peepul tree ostensibly apported from India to be a cutting from an olive tree. Be that as it may, it was Bailey's actual production of objects in MacCarthy's extended test series that stood as the medium's principal achievement. MacCarthy's investigations attracted international attention and arrangements were made for the medium to be tested overseas. In 1904 Bailey went to Italy to be scrutinized by a committee of the Milan Society for Psychical Studies. The committee's report was inclined to favor Bailey's apports as being genuinely paranormal phenomena, although it would appear that Bailey was rather more resistant to the researchers' imposition of controls than he is depicted to have been in Australian investigations.

In 1910 Bailey traveled to France to be studied in Grenoble by a group led by the eminent French parapsychologist Colonel Albert de Rochas. Although no sleight of hand was detected, evidence was brought forward that Bailey was recognized as a man who two days earlier had purchased some birds similar to those produced during the test. The spirit control had declared the birds to have been apported from India. Bailey denied purchasing the birds and refused to conduct further sittings for the Grenoble committee. Investigations in London during the following year also found Bailey to be uncooperative in certain respects. In one of these sessions Bailey was unable to produce apports when unexpectedly being required to be enclosed in a satinette bag tied at the neck. Two birds were apported under similar test conditions in the following session, but subsequent inspection revealed a hole had been made in one corner of the bag. As a consequence an adverse report was issued.

Bailey's international reputation rapidly deteriorated. His career as a medium suffered further in 1914 when a "spirit" he materialized was seized by a sitter who in turn had the drapery wrenched from his grasp. The seance, held in Sydney, ended in chaos. Bailey did continue to conduct seances in Sydney and overseas for another thirty years until shortly before his death in 1947, but he was no longer of interest to parapsychologists. Bailey's friends and the faithful members of his circle nevertheless continued to defend his reputation and to reject the reports of the "pseudoscientists."

That sense of mutual antipathy between spiritualists and parapsychologists has persisted to this day. In the main, spiritualists reject the reductionist approach of scientists and now look to personal revelation and faith rather than experimental scrutiny for substantiation of their convictions. Parapsychologists, on the other hand, are determined to emphasize the scientific character of their discipline and therefore they are intent on dissociating parapsychology from anything to do with occultism. They are a little embarrassed by the fact that parapsychology had its roots in spiritualism, or, to be more precise, was inspired by some of the implications of the reported activities of spiritualist mediums. Despite occasional efforts to encourage communication between parapsychologists and spiritualists the gulf between them looms ever large. As we shall see in the section on the

survival hypothesis some parapsychological research does relate to metaphysical matters and in this regard it would be of interest to spiritualists and other religious folk. Nonetheless, perhaps parapsychologists can be more objective in such research if they themselves avoid too close an identification with religious movements.

Conclusions

We now have looked at the careers of four mediums, namely Daniel Home, Leonora Piper, Hélène Smith, and Charles Bailey. Of course there are many other mediums that could have been discussed, but these suffice for present purposes. First, they instance the variety of phenomena that are reported to occur in the seance room and that elicited the interest of the founders of the SPR. Second, they illustrate three broad types of mediumistic performance. Some seance phenomena, like those associated with Bailey, undoubtedly are produced by fraudulent means, even if sitters themselves aver their paranormality (Besterman, 1932; Davey & Hodgson, 1887; Mulholland, 1938/1979; Polidoro, 2003); indeed, the physical and psychological setting of many mediums' seances seems to have been highly conducive to the misdirection of sitters' attention and to the suspension of their capacity for reality testing (Owen, 1990; Wiseman, Greening & Smith, 2003). Seance phenomena produced by other mediums, while not intentionally deceitful, appear to be rooted in subconscious fantasy: Smith's psychic excursions to Mars evidently were of this sort, and at least some of Mrs. Piper's spirit controls appear to have been dramatic productions of the medium's subconscious mind. And in yet other cases there seems to be something going on that we cannot immediately explain, something that warrants further investigation; for example, a few of Home's feats, some of the more evidential material gathered in Mrs.

Piper's seances, and perhaps also the Indian phase of Smith's mediumship remind us that it is appropriate to keep an open mind about parapsychological phenomena and indeed to explore their authenticity under more scientific conditions. It is as well to remain alert to each of these three possibilities when you ponder the performance of contemporary psychics.

What are the lessons to be learned from past investigations of mediums? One is that if parapsychologists are to investigate the talents of mediums the researcher must be in total control of the situation and be alert to the stratagems of fraudulent mediums (Wiseman & Morris, 1994, 1995). The researcher, rather than the medium, must define the circumstances and objectives of the test. On the other hand it must be acknowledged that while spiritualism precipitated psychical research and posed many questions for researchers to pursue, investigation of mediums has failed to authenticate any parapsychological phenomenon.

In the view of the majority of contemporary parapsychologists, before the alleged events of the seance room can be assessed it is necessary to undertake laboratory studies of experimental analogs of such events. For example, if it is asserted that mediums can predict the future by paranormal means the parapsychologist must design an "event prediction" task that can be performed in a laboratory setting where potentially confounding variables can be controlled. Questions other than authenticity might similarly be scrutinized. According to some spiritualists the presence of skeptics at a seance can inhibit the occurrence of the phenomena. That suggestion is one that can be examined through appropriate exercises in the laboratory. (The types of tasks used by modern parapsychologists in their investigations will be described in subsequent chapters.)

Again, if the work of Flournoy is any guide, the study of spiritualist mediums may offer a novel avenue of inquiry into the capacities of the subconscious mind. Certainly

our present understanding of such capacities is meager and any unexploited research technique such as this does warrant attention (see also Braude, 2003). The less than convincing personations represented by some of Mrs. Piper's spirit controls similarly suggest the operation of distinct subconscious "personalities," a notion that has given rise to some discussion of mediumistic performance in relation to the clinical concepts of dissociation and multiple personality or dissociative identity disorder (Kenny, 1986; Negro, Palladino-Negro & Louza, 2002; Reed, 1989; Richeport, 1992; Ross, 1989).

But such advanced questions were far from the minds of the British group that set about the establishment of the SPR in 1882. Their perspective was much simpler, namely that the phenomena of the seance room did deserve some manner of intellectual scrutiny. On the other hand, the scientific community of the time was inclined simply to ignore these phenomena completely. Certainly a few scientists suggested the need for empirical investigation but only with the objective of exposing the reported effects as sham and humbug. The distinguished physicist Michael Faraday (1853), for example, conducted simulated seances with a table fitted with a loose top and showed that when sitters laid their hands on the tabletop they unwittingly exerted lateral pressure on it and made it turn. On this basis he asserted the table-tipping phenomena of seances had a natural explanation. As Inglis (1977, p. 217) notes, however, Faraday's demonstration in no way accommodated the reports of tables moving around the seance room or even rising above the floor. Even more regrettably, Faraday refused to meet with Daniel Home and thus subject his account of the psychic's performance to a direct assessment (Lamont, 2005). Other intellectuals sought simply to ridicule or "debunk" spiritualist phenomena. Thus the Orientalist Richard Burton commented, "In case I ever become a spirit, I trust I shall not be summoned into anybody's drawing-room and there made to play the banjo and rap people's heads, in return for a fee of a guinea" (Wyndham, 1937, p. 135). But in the main, intellectuals believed that the cause of scientific rationalism was best served by ignoring the claims of spiritualism. Psychical research was then very much a protest against the scope of the prevailing scientific zeitgeist, even if the psychical researchers themselves maintained a fervent identification with the fundamental methodological framework of science.

The movements of spiritualism and mesmerism therefore had a significant place in the *origins* of parapsychology. Their influence on the subsequent development of the discipline, however, was rather less substantial.

KEY TERMS AND CONCEPTS

mesmerism
mesmeric trance
animal magnetism
spiritualism
materialization
seance
sitter
reading
ectoplasm
possession
levitation
laying on of hands
table tipping
medium
physical medium/phenomena

mental medium/phenomena
psychometry
spirit hands
Society for Psychical Research (SPR)
Daniel Home
Leonora Piper
Hélène Smith
Charles Bailey
automatism (sensory or motor)
automatic writing
planchette
control, spirit guide
apports
cryptomnesia

STUDY QUESTIONS

1. Interest in paranormal phenomena is as old as history itself. Why then do most commentators maintain that parapsychology has existed for barely more than a century?

2. In the view of almost all nineteenth-century intellectuals the notion of animal magnetism was sheer quackery, yet mesmerism evidently contributed in some way to the foundation of the SPR. How do you account for this?

3. Parapsychologists today would tend to classify the events in the Fox household as an apparent poltergeist outbreak. Similar cases have been documented in many cultures and in many eras. What factors were peculiar to the Hydesville case that led to its inspiration of a religious movement?

4. How can the spiritualist movement be said to have precipitated parapsychology as a discipline?

5. What are the principal differences in the careers of the four spiritualist mediums Home, Piper, Smith and Bailey, and what is the significance of these differences?

6. What purported phenomena were associated with spiritualist mediums and how were these investigated?

7. From the parapsychologist's viewpoint is there anything to be learned from the activities of mediums?

3

THE PHENOMENOLOGY OF EXTRASENSORY PERCEPTION

A phenomenological approach to extrasensory experience, the study of ESP as actually experienced, emerged very gradually from a tradition of gathering case reports primarily for other purposes. Before reviewing the phenomenological characteristics of ESP the conceptual background of case collection will be outlined.

Approaches to Case Collection in Parapsychology

One of the initial tasks undertaken by the Society for Psychical Research (SPR) was the development of precise criteria for the collection of reports on spontaneous parapsychological experiences. The SPR's focal objective here was to educe the existence of paranormal phenomena from case reports and hence it was thought necessary to ensure that each accepted report be strongly indicative of the occurrence of something paranormal.

The most basic of the SPR criteria was that the experience must be on record, preferably in writing but at the very least as an oral communication to another person, *before* the content of the experience was substantiated.

Suppose, for example, a woman dreamt of her son's death. If she happened to have written an account of her dream in her diary or had described it to her husband before news of the son's death was received, this could qualify as an acceptable case of a parapsychological experience. Investigation of the case then would be undertaken by SPR members. The first piece of evidence that would be called for here would be the original diary entry or a statement from the husband on his recollection of events. Additionally, corroborative material would be sought from diverse sources. If possible, investigators would question other witnesses such as people who had been told of the experience and others who had been present at the son's death. A copy of the death certificate and character references for the principals of the case would be obtained. Ideally statements should be procured and interviews conducted as soon after the incident as possible. In this fashion it was hoped to guarantee the case subject's veracity and to eliminate errors of recall, both deliberate and unintentional. If some authentic examples of paranormal phenomena were excluded by application of these criteria then that was deemed a necessary cost of ensuring that the selected cases were evidentially reliable.

29

By this means case collections of parapsychological experiences were compiled by the SPR and by the societies for psychical research that soon were founded in many other countries. The major surveys conducted along these lines include a collection of over 700 cases of telepathic experience by Gurney, Myers and Podmore (1886); Henry Sidgwick's study of telepathic phenomena in the form of an apparition of a person on the verge of death (Sidgwick, Johnson, Myers, Podmore & Sidgwick, 1894); Eleanor Sidgwick's (1888–1889) and Saltmarsh's (1934) collections of precognitive experiences; Eleanor Sidgwick's (1891) study of clairvoyant experiences; Tyrrell's (1942/1963) analysis of apparitional experiences drawn from the SPR files; and Stevenson's (1970) survey of imageless or "intuitive" telepathic impressions, and his series of reports on apparent reincarnation memories (e.g., Stevenson, 1966).

It is clear from the survey reports that the early SPR investigators looked to spontaneous cases very largely as a means of ascertaining the authenticity of parapsychological phenomena, that is, a means of providing evidence that these phenomena stem from the operation of paranormal factors. That orientation is instanced in a most extreme form by a later investigation undertaken by the American psychical researcher Walter Franklin Prince (1928). His study cites parapsychological experiences of scientists, lawyers, clergymen, literary figures and others considered to qualify as unimpeachable witnesses. Like the founders of the SPR, Prince believed that adequately documented case reports from reliable experients could provide sound testimony to the existence of paranormal processes, a view still endorsed by some parapsychologists today (e.g., see Stevenson, 1971, 1987b).

Additionally, some of the SPR investigators began to examine spontaneous case collections for indications of the nature or characteristics of parapsychological experiences. That is, through content analysis of cases researchers hoped to define, for example, the circumstances under which each different type of parapsychological experience occurred and thereby to gain some insight into the ways in which the supposed paranormal processes could operate. While it must be acknowledged that these early studies primarily were concerned with the issue of authenticity they therefore exhibited a measure of appreciation for process-oriented research and even a glimmering awareness of the issue of phenomenology.

Subsequently it was realized by the American parapsychologist Louisa Rhine that for *purposes other than authentication*, cases could be collected under criteria far less stringent than those proposed by the SPR, and thus in the 1950s she undertook analyses of all spontaneous cases which seemed both to have been reported in good faith and to be instances of parapsychological experiences (Rhine, 1951, pp. 165–166). Her argument was that since a given case report will be at least partially reliable, in a sizable collection of uninvestigated cases (such as her own Duke University collection) the elements of unreliability would be random "noise" against which would stand out the reliable and consistent data on the characteristics and occurrence of parapsychological experiences. While validation of individual reports might be thought necessary for the authentication of the phenomena it therefore was not essential to the pursuit of other issues, she maintained. Specifically, uninvestigated case reports could indicate the nature of the processes underlying parapsychological experiences.

From the outset Louisa Rhine (1951) believed that these indications should be scrutinized further by means of controlled experimental research, although as she pursued her work with case analysis she seems to have become increasingly more confident in the evidential value of this material (Stevenson, 1987c, p. 104).

Louisa Rhine's new technique for case surveys certainly facilitated research on spontaneous cases and as we shall see, much interesting material emerged through investigations of this type. Admittedly, the new approach did provide an opportunity for critics to declare (in apparent ignorance of Louisa Rhine's argument) that parapsychologists would accept as "evidence for the paranormal" anyone's delusion or fantasy if only the individual would state that it was a parapsychological experience; if you have grasped the rationale and methodology of Louisa Rhine's technique you should have little difficulty in establishing the fallacy of that criticism. At the same time a few parapsychologists, while acknowledging the value of case analyses, do caution that collections of uninvestigated reports possibly could yield data statistically unrepresentative of carefully investigated cases (Dingwall, 1961; Stevenson, 1987c; White, 1964b). Statistical analyses by Schouten (1983) nevertheless have failed to establish any major differences between investigated and uninvestigated case collections.

In this chapter we will consider the application of case study analyses to a major parapsychological phenomenon, the extrasensory experience, and examine in more depth the strengths and weaknesses of this approach.

Surveys of ESP Experiences

The simplest form of survey is the opinion poll. The great strength of the poll is that if properly carried out it can capture a snapshot of the opinions, beliefs and experiences of a large and demographically representative sample of the general population. On the other hand, polls tend not to ask in-depth questions about particular topics. Although somewhat superficial, then, polls can present useful information about the *frequency* of beliefs and experiences in the general population. There are several polls about ESP beliefs (see Chapter 15), but fewer on the question of

ESP experiences. US sociologist Andrew Greeley and colleagues at the University of Chicago have conducted two National Opinion Research Center polls on spiritual and paranormal beliefs and experiences. In the 1973 poll of 1,467 US adults, 58 percent indicated having had an ESP experience. Over ten years later, the proportion reporting an ESP experience had increased to 67 per cent (Greeley, 1987). Polls such as these suggest that ESP experiences are far from uncommon.

One way in which spontaneous case material can be utilized in greater depth entails a survey technique where people are simply asked if they have had a given parapsychological experience, together with questions on potential psychological correlates of that experience. The objective here is to find the sorts of people who have (or at least who report) the parapsychological experience. Thus the incidence of these experiences can be related to various demographic and other personalistic variables. In the specific context of ESP experiences one such survey in the form of a postal questionnaire was conducted in 1974 by an American parapsychologist, John Palmer (1979). His data indicated that 51 percent of Charlottesville residents and 55 percent of University of Virginia students had had some form of extrasensory experience. Some of Palmer's other findings on waking ESP (as distinct from ESP during dreams) may be summarized by way of illustration of the survey approach. About 38 percent of the sample reported having had an extrasensory experience while awake. People who acknowledged such experiences generally tended to recall their dreams, to analyze their dreams, to have lucid dreams, to have had a moving spiritual or transcendental experience, to have consulted a psychic, to have a positive attitude toward parapsychological research, to place some credence in astrology, to believe in reincarnation, to be divorced or separated, and to have a lower level of education. No trends, however, were found in relation to the variables of gender, age, birth order, political convictions, religiosity, religious denomination, occupation, income, practice of meditation, use of "mind expanding" drugs, or vividness of dreams.

Some of the more recent surveys of ESP experiences have tended to focus specifically on psychological characteristics of the experient. A review of these findings is deferred to the following chapter, where data on ESP experients can be integrated with data on the types of people who perform well in experimental ESP tasks. It might also be mentioned that although research on ESP experients is still relatively meager the psychological profile of the experient seems to be highly similar to that of the *believer* in psi phenomena; correlates of paranormal belief have been much more extensively researched and are addressed in detail in Chapter 15.

In any event the above review of Palmer's (1979) findings suffices to indicate that the survey technique is most pertinent to the issue of underlying processes, that is, in generating ideas about the ways in which extrasensory experiences come about. Those issues also will be taken up in the next chapter. If the survey questionnaire includes items about the experience itself it may well be useful also in studying the phenomenology of extrasensory experience. But the latter sort of information has come predominantly from a rather different perspective on the study of case material.

The Phenomenology of ESP Experiences

Another approach to spontaneous cases, that exploited most notably by Louisa Rhine, is to analyze the content of case reports and locate trends in the characteristics of the various categories of parapsychological experience. It is this method that has provided the most direct access to the phenomenology of a parapsychological experience, that is, the features of the phenomenon as it is experienced by the individual.

Louisa Rhine's data on the phenomenology of extrasensory experiences confirmed some of the categories defined in Chapter 1. In particular she noted the occurrence of precognitive, contemporaneous, and retrocognitive experiences. Because the issue of the temporal displacement of ESP has major theoretical implications Rhine's data in this regard are given separate coverage in Chapter 5. The most basic of her phenomenological results, however, relate to the *form* of the extrasensory experience. Rhine (1953a) observed that broadly speaking, each of the case reports could be categorized as an intuitive impression, a hallucination, a realistic dream, or an unrealistic dream. Each of these forms of spontaneous ESP experience now will be described.

Intuitive impressions. These extrasensory experiences consist of a simple unreasoned impression or hunch. There is no imagery accompanying the experience, nor any conscious process of linear rational thought leading to the impression. The individual reports suddenly "just knowing" something that upon subsequent investigation was borne out. In occasional instances the informational element is minimal and the experience comprises little else than a strong, unexpected emotion; usually, however, the experient has some appreciation of the identity of the person to whom, or the situation to which, the felt emotion relates.

An example of an intuitive impression is given by the following experience of the first author (HJI). The day before he and his family were to leave on a holiday he had a nagging impression that something was wrong with one of the car wheels. He had no logical grounds for this notion but it was sufficiently intense and compelling for him to make a superficial examination of the wheels and he also noted carefully the handling of the car when he went out that evening. During the trip on the following day one of the tires blew out. According to the garage attendant who fixed the tire at our destination the blow-out was due to a small stone lodged between the tire and the inner tube. In time the pebble had abraded the inner tube to the point of disintegration. Note that the content of the original impression ("something is wrong with one of the wheels") is limited and unelaborated: there was no associated imagery nor any conscious ideation converging toward the idea. (HJI cites this personal experience purely for illustrative purposes. In itself it does not convince him of the authenticity of ESP, and nor should it convince you.)

Hallucinations. In a hallucinatory ESP experience the "message" is conveyed in the form of a sensory hallucination. For example, at the time of the unexpected death of a loved one in some distant place, many people report seeing an apparition of the individual or hearing his or her voice calling them. The second author (CW) experienced an apparent case of hallucinatory ESP. For many years she lived close to a busy train track and commuted to work by train. At home one evening, while vacuuming the house, CW heard the screeching of train brakes and a terrible crashing noise. Expecting to see some kind of accident on the nearby track, she rushed outside but was surprised to find that there was no sign of any catastrophe. The next day was a Saturday so CW didn't take the train to work. However, later in the day a train was indeed derailed on that line. It was a minor incident and there were no casualties. Subsequent investigations found a fault with the track. Again, we present this case for illustrative rather than evidential purposes. Certainly ESP is not the only explanation. Perhaps in the preceding days the gradually worsening fault had changed the sound and feel of that section of track and CW had subconsciously become aware of this on her daily commute. This sensing of a change in track conditions, combined with a natural proclivity to worry, could have triggered CW's auditory hallucination.

The information in hallucinatory experiences often is incomplete. In cases where the experient's name is heard being called she or he may speculate about the safety of the person identified with the hallucinated voice but have no precise knowledge of that person's situation at the time of the experience.

Realistic dreams. In some extrasensory experiences information seemingly is acquired by way of a clear, realistic mental image. By far the most common form of this type is a dream which later is confirmed. It is on this basis that Louisa Rhine designated experiences of this sort "realistic dreams." The term, however, is not entirely appropriate because the category also is intended to accommodate waking imagery (e.g., a "vision") which is not projected on to the environment (as is the case with a hallucinatory experience).

The following example of ESP in a realistic dream was sent to HJI some years ago by a young Australian man aged 17. "On a Wednesday night (mid–1977) I had an extremely vivid dream that I was watching an operation which I felt was for cancer. I did not know immediately who the person was who was undergoing the operation, but recognition came slowly. Gradually I sensed that the surgery was taking place in America and I associated it consciously with my sister. [The fellow wrote regularly to his elder sister in America but had had no indication that his sister may have been ill.]... Upon waking I described the dream to my mother. The next night the same dream was experienced except this time ... I became far more agitated.... A certain urgency was felt. As the dream ended this urgency gave way to peace. Once again I told my mother about it. About one week later a letter arrived [in Australia] from America telling my family that my sister had undergone two operations for cancer [each on the night, or day as it was in the U.S., on which the young man had had his dreams]. The operation was a success."

Note that "realistic" in this context does

not necessarily mean completely literal. If the above correspondent's sister had actually had only one operation or if the operation was for something other than cancer the dreams still would be regarded as realistic in the sense that the information they conveyed was not in a disguised form. By their nature realistic cases generally are more detailed in content than those of the two preceding categories, although much of the detail here may well be unconscious elaboration of a single basic item of information.

Unrealistic dreams. These are similar to realistic dream experiences but here the imagery is of a fanciful unreal sort. Although these cases do include a few waking experiences the category is predominated by dreams.

Sometimes the information conveyed by the extrasensory experience is dramatized as a fantasy. By way of illustration Louisa Rhine (1953a, p. 97) cited a case in which an elderly lady dreamt her daughter was pregnant and that she was teasing her daughter about it. Nothing like this interaction between mother and daughter ever took place but it subsequently emerged that the latter indeed was pregnant at the time. In other instances the information may be disguised, as in symbolic form. You may recall the biblical story of the pharaoh who dreamt of seven fat kine (cattle) and seven lean kine, a dream which was interpreted as a precognition of seven years of plenty to be followed by seven years of drought and famine.

As with any taxonomic scheme there are occasional instances of spontaneous extrasensory experience that do not fit conveniently into any single component of Rhine's quadripartite system. A few extrasensory dreams, for example, contain both realistic and unrealistic elements. With continued application of this taxonomy over another two decades of research Louisa Rhine nevertheless was satisfied with its efficacy and saw no substantial reason to revise it. That view generally has been endorsed by other case analysts

who utilized schemes similar to Rhine's (e.g., Green, 1960; Hagio, 1994; Irwin, 1989a; Prasad & Stevenson, 1968; Sannwald, 1963; Schouten, 1981; Virtanen, 1977/1990).

Before surveying more of Louisa Rhine's phenomenological findings it again should be emphasized that none of Rhine's cases is presented as evidence of the authenticity of ESP. The examples cited above serve only to illustrate a taxonomic scheme; any one of them could be "explained away" as a chance event or otherwise attributed to normal rather than paranormal factors.

Over an extended series of analyses beginning in 1951 Louisa Rhine noted several more trends in the phenomenological characteristics of extrasensory experience. The principal findings are summarized below (except that data relating to precognition and retrocognition are deferred for consideration in Chapter 5).

Distribution. The relative incidence of the different forms of ESP experience in Rhine's collection was approximately as follows: intuitive 26 percent, hallucinatory 9 percent, realistic dreams 44 percent, unrealistic dreams 21 percent (e.g., Rhine, 1962a, p. 93.) This pattern generally is confirmed by other surveys: that by Sannwald (1963) in Western Europe put the relative frequencies at 27, 10, 48 and 15 percent respectively. A few studies nevertheless have yielded somewhat different results (Schouten, 1982). It must be said that the incidence of a particular type of case in a collection can be affected by various factors. If in a radio interview the researcher cites as an example a case of realistic dream ESP many listeners who have had this type of experience will write to the researcher with details of their case. If these reports are included in the parapsychologist's case collection, the occurrence of realistic dream ESP then could be exaggerated. The experient's reticence is another pertinent factor. People may be relatively reluctant to report hallucinatory cases, fearing that hallucinations might be taken as indicative of mental disorder. Dreams on the other hand may be acknowledged more readily, even if they seem bizarre, because "after all, they are only fantasy."

Taken simply at face value these data nevertheless generate interesting questions for research into processes underlying the extrasensory experience. That a half or more of the experiences occur in the form of a dream might be taken to suggest these processes operate best when the experient's intellectual defenses are down or when the experient is engrossed in the contents of mentation and largely dissociated from sensory inputs from the environment. The ESP experience's association with dreams and intuition also prompts the notion that the content of the experience has its origins deep in subconscious levels of the human mind. Each of these themes will be addressed again in the context of process-oriented research (see Chapter 4).

Completeness of content. Extrasensory experiences typically incorporate information on only some aspects of the environmental event to which they ostensibly relate. Louisa Rhine (1962a,b) examined the four forms of ESP experience for their completeness of content, the latter being defined operationally in the fairly gross terms of whether or not the experience conveyed the general meaning of *what* occurred and to *whom* (Weiner & Haight, 1986, p. 18). This analysis showed realistic dreams to exhibit the highest level (91 percent) of completeness of content, followed in order by unrealistic dreams (72 percent), intuitive impressions (55 percent), and hallucinatory experiences (32 percent). Similar findings are reported by Virtanen (1977/1990).

The skeptic probably would be inclined to argue that because the content of dreams is so much more complex than that of intuitions and hallucinatory experiences, one would expect purely on the basis of chance that dreams will show the greatest number of points corresponding to reality. On the other hand, if the informational origins of extrasensory experience lie deep below the level of consciousness one might expect dreams also to be relatively efficient vehicles for processing or "working up" the information to the point where it is comparatively available for access to consciousness. In any event the evidently differential completeness of the content of the various forms of ESP experience is a phenomenological feature that warrants appropriate empirical investigation and explanation.

Personal significance of content. In those cases in which the extrasensory experience related to another person, commonly it was someone emotionally close to the experient, according to Louisa Rhine (1956). That general trend has been confirmed in analyses of several other case collections from various countries (Green, 1960; Irwin, 1989a; Prasad & Stevenson, 1968; Sannwald, 1963; Schouten, 1981; Stevenson, 1970). This may indicate that an emotional bond between people is conducive to extrasensory "communication." Again it is possible that there is greater opportunity for the content of the experience to be confirmed by a close individual than by a stranger, so that the impression about the friend is relatively likely to be categorized by the experient as being extrasensory instead of being dismissed as baseless fantasy. In statistical tests of this possibility, however, Schouten (1983) found no evidence in its support. In any event, examination of ESP cases as a whole does suggest that their content has some significance for the experient, that is, the experiences seem to be *purposive*. In this respect the spontaneous extrasensory experience is seen to have a "slice of life" quality, a feature that is central to the phenomenological analysis of any experience.

The theme of personal significance is borne out too by Louisa Rhine's analysis of the events depicted in extrasensory experiences. The vast majority of cases in her collection concerned deaths, personal crises (illnesses, accidents, births, marriages) and other

Figure 4. Louisa Rhine and her file of case reports (photograph: RRC).

events of general importance to the experient. Similar findings are reported for other case collections of extrasensory experience (Prasad & Stevenson, 1968; Schouten, 1981; Stevenson, 1970; Virtanen, 1977/1990), but evidently not for instances of ESP in childhood (Drewes, 2002). Perhaps experiences concerned with personally significant events are intrinsically easy to recall and hence they readily are reported to the collector of case reports, although the trend in the data is so consistent that it seems unlikely to be a mere report artifact. Louisa Rhine (1961) herself attributed this trend to the notion that ESP communicates "news" and these types of events are especially "newsworthy." On the other hand, while extrasensory experiences about other people often concern tragic events, those about oneself may more commonly depict relatively trivial matters (Drewes, 2002; Weiner & Haight, 1986).

While extrasensory experiences generally may relate to personally significant events the various forms of the experience may be differentially associated with particular kinds of events. Schouten (1981), for example, suggests that the death of the referent person is relatively more likely to be depicted in waking imagery than in an imageless intuition.

Conviction. When describing an extrasensory experience people often give particular emphasis to their impression that the experience was highly compelling and meaningful. As we shall see in the following chapter this contrasts markedly with the behavior of subjects in ESP experiments: typically they simply do not know if their impressions of a sensorially concealed target is correct. The sense of conviction in spontaneous extrasensory experience therefore is a matter warranting some study.

Louisa Rhine began her investigation of the issue in 1951. In her most detailed report (Rhine, 1962a) she noted the sense of conviction in the experience's content to vary substantially with the form of the experience, being highest in intuitive impressions (84 percent) and lowest in realistic (23 percent) and unrealistic (19 percent) dreams. This tendency was confirmed by Green (1960) and by Schouten (1981, 1982) for other case collections. Perhaps this is due to the fact that the individual has learned that (normal) dreams usually are based in fantasy and thus not to be accorded much credence. Louisa Rhine (1951) on the other hand suggested that conviction is emotional rather than an objective item of information and hence cannot readily be represented as a mental image. She contrasts the situation for imaginal experiences with that of intuitive ESP in which no imagery and little objective information emerges in consciousness, yet conviction often is high.

Telepathic experiences. In her study of telepathic experiences Louisa Rhine (1953b) focused on an instructive form of the hallucinatory ESP experience known as "call cases." These are ones in which the individual heard a loved one calling and learned later that the "caller" was in distress some distance away. It was noted that in few of these cases did the caller or *agent* actually call to the experient or indeed even think of the latter person. Louisa Rhine speculated that in ESP the notion of an agent sending a message to the experient might be invalid. Rather, the experient may be the "active" member of the association, in some way seeking out information on people emotionally close to him or her. Support for this idea emerged in a later study (Rhine, 1956) in which it was found that although experients in telepathic cases did need to know about the agent, in about a sixth of cases there seemed to be no conceivable reason for the agent to communicate to the experient. Louisa Rhine's suggestion certainly raises questions about the popular view of extrasensory "perception" as a perceptual-like process, a "sixth sense" in which some unidentified sort of environmental "stimulus" is mediated to a percipient.

Louisa Rhine's investigation of the phenomenology of extrasensory experience is a most valuable pioneering effort, but regrettably it has inspired few parapsychologists to continue and to extend her research. As far as its implications for process-oriented research is concerned, arguably the most interesting ideas thrown up by Louisa Rhine's analyses of spontaneous case reports is that ESP seems purposive in its orientation and that it may well be instigated by the experient rather than being received passively by him or her.

Other phenomenological features. The meager information available on other aspects of ESP phenomenology falls into two main classes, that relating to the situation in which the experience occurred and that to do with the experience's impact upon the individual.

The social context of extrasensory experiences was surveyed in a sample of 124 Australian university students (a report on the focal objective of the survey is provided by Irwin, 1989a). Approximately two-thirds of the group reported being alone at the time of the experience. Given that the substantial majority of the sample had had their most recent extrasensory experience before the age of 18 and that a sizable proportion of such experiences arise during sleep, perhaps it is not surprising that most of these respondents claimed to have been without company. Certainly the result should not necessarily be taken as applicable to the general population of extrasensory experients. The social context of an ESP experience might additionally affect its form. In one case collection Schouten (1981) found intuitive impressions to occur more often when the experient was with other people than when alone, while in another sample (Schouten, 1982) other types of waking ESP experiences tended to arise when the experient was alone.

Also surveyed in the Australian study was the experient's level of physical activity at the time. Ninety percent of the sample reported being engaged in minimal activity such as sleeping, sitting, or standing. The activity level was moderate (as in walking or playing a piano) in 7 percent and substantial (as in jogging or playing tennis) in only 3 percent. This tendency for a very low level of physical activity at the onset of the extrasensory experience is found in association also with some other parapsychological phenomena (e.g., Irwin, 1985a, pp. 151–152) and is consistent with the idea that these experiences are facilitated by an unforced engrossment in one's mentation or in a repetitive, highly practiced motor act (Honorton, 1977; Irwin, 1985b).

The latter notion also sits reasonably well with data on the individual's state of mind at the experience's onset. The strong association between extrasensory experience and dreaming already has been noted. In the first author's (HJI) Australian student survey very few people felt they had been concentrating strongly when their experience took place; most were either engaged in minimally demanding mental activity (28 percent) or not really thinking about anything in particular (50 percent).

Apart from Louisa Rhine's attention to the experient's conviction in their extrasensory experience the experience's *impact* upon the individual has received surprisingly little attention from researchers. Stevenson (1970, pp. 23–26) sought to operationalize the issue of conviction by examining whether or not the experient took any action after an intuitive telepathic experience. Action reportedly was taken in about half of the cases, most particularly when the "agent" in the experience was identified and when that person's thoughts were said to have been focused on the experient at the time.

The experience's emotional impact is an important but neglected aspect of ESP phenomenology. Sannwald (1963, p. 282) noted that about 85 percent of cases in his collection referred to unpleasant or sad events, but he did not ascertain how experients actually felt about their extrasensory impression of these events. It is feasible, for example, that if conviction in the experience is low the experient will be relatively unmoved by its negatively toned content. Stevenson's (1970, pp. 26–27) analysis of intuitive telepathic impressions examined original case reports for evidence of the emotions felt by the experient. Although many of the reports made no reference to the matter the dominant emotions educed in the remainder were anxiety (61 percent), depression (36 percent), and joy (3 percent). In the Australian student sample an attempt was made to survey the individual's feelings immediately after their extrasensory experience. Here 18 percent were happy or joyful, 25 percent anxious, and 5 percent depressed. The other 52 percent indicated they had felt "otherwise"; in a written elaboration of this response option many said their reaction was one of surprise/curiosity/intrigue, a few noted they were confused or displeased, and several claimed to have been quite indifferent to the content of their experience. A small survey in Britain by Milton (1992) yielded broadly similar results. Finally, in an Argentinean survey by Montanelli and Parra (2004) 15 percent of people who had had an extrasensory dream and 6 percent of those who had experienced telepathy reported that their experience had been conflictive or traumatic in some respect. Notwithstanding the above findings there clearly is scope for further research into the emotional impact of extrasensory experiences.

Another facet of the experience's impact is whether or not the experient tells anyone about it. This undoubtedly is linked to the experient's level of conviction and the nature of the event depicted in the experience, among other things. Respondents in the Australian survey were asked if they had told someone of their experience before they learned by conventional means of the depicted event's actual occurrence. Thirty percent had done so; of the remainder, 53 percent had not because of no inclination to do so, and 17 percent had not told anyone because of the lack of an opportunity.

This completes the review of ESP phenomenology. It may seem surprising that we know comparatively little about an experience acknowledged to have been had by approximately half the population. But despite the substantial efforts of Louisa Rhine phenomenological research on extrasensory experience is still in its formative stage.

The Value of Spontaneous Case Material

Spontaneous cases may be of use to parapsychologists in several ways. First, it must be said that these "real life" experiences are what we are endeavoring to explain. It is all very well to take ESP into the laboratory for controlled investigation and precise statistical evaluation, but once this is done our hope surely is that we will be in a position to explain how and why people have these parapsychological experiences in the course of everyday life. Collections of spontaneous cases at least should serve to remind experimental parapsychologists of the ultimate goal of their research.

A second function of case material is to indicate the different ways in which ESP (if there is such a thing) may be expressed. For example, ESP experiences in everyday life seem to relate to past, present, and future events, and may take the form of an intuition, a hallucination, or a mental image (e.g., dream). The researcher should be alert to these ecological vehicles of expression and consider the extent to which specific laboratory findings may be generalized to the various forms.

Perhaps a primary role of spontaneous cases is to suggest hypotheses for experimental investigation. Content analyses of case collections provide a valuable source of inspiration on the nature of extrasensory processes. For example, if spontaneous ESP experiences tend to occur when the percipient is in a mentally relaxed state the parapsychologist can examine the effect of relaxation on experimental ESP scoring, then if appropriate go on to explore precisely what specific aspects of relaxation are involved in this relationship and the bases of it. All too often experimental parapsychologists have given insufficient cognizance to the indications of case material for process-oriented research. Given that the subject matter of spontaneous cases seems to be something of particular significance to the experient, why have parapsychologists conducted so much ESP testing with geometric shapes and alphanumeric characters that have little personal meaning for experimental participants?

Finally, as we have seen from Louisa Rhine's work, spontaneous cases can be examined from a phenomenological viewpoint. Quite apart from the matter of the bases of parapsychological phenomena it is legitimate to inquire into the character of the experiences from the percipient's point of view (Giorgi, 1997; Richardson, 1999). Whether or not the phenomena are paranormal, people do have these experiences and we as students of behavior should be interested to ascertain what is distinctive about the content and personal interpretation of these experiences (White, 1990, 1992). Phenomenological data may advantageously be utilized, for example, in testing hypotheses about the psychological or evolutionary functions of extrasensory and other parapsychological experiences (e.g., see McClenon, 2002). Similarly, only by knowing what happens from the experient's viewpoint will we be able to decide, for example, whether the experience of a person we see in the psychological clinic is parapsychological or psychopathological. If experiences of these two types can be distinguished phenomenologically perhaps we can avoid classifying people as schizophrenic when all they require is some counseling to come to terms with their personal parapsychological encounter.

In these respects, therefore, collections and surveys of spontaneous parapsychological experiences can make a substantial contribution to research. At the same time there are certain limitations in such data of which we must take account.

The Limitations of Spontaneous Case Material

The evidential limitations of spontaneous cases essentially spring from the possible incidence of self-deception, deception and fraud on the part of the people reporting the experience. Some of the limitations will be discussed in relation to the issues of au-thenticity and the nature of parapsychological experience.

Case Material and Authenticity

Despite the hopes of the founders of the SPR the general feeling among modern parapsychologists is that no spontaneous experience, no matter how carefully investigated, can be considered to provide unequivocal evidence of the authenticity of parapsychological phenomena (Hövelmann & Krippner, 1986; West, 1982). Any such experience might have been due to the unknown operation of one or more of the following factors.

Inaccuracies of recall. Cognitive psychologists have demonstrated that people's recall of everyday events can be highly inaccurate. Human memory is not a device permitting literal replay of previously experienced incidents. Once a particular interpretation is placed on an event, features of the experience consistent with that interpretation might be recalled but inconsistent features will tend to be forgotten. If, for example, you witness an altercation between Smith and Jones and attribute the blame to Jones you later may tend to recall Jones's provocative actions but not those of Smith. A similar type of distortion may occur in some reports of parapsychological experiences. By way of illustration, we may dream that Uncle John and Aunt Mary have food poisoning and both die. A few weeks later we learn that Aunt Mary has died of cancer. We then may declare that we had a precognitive dream to this effect, quite oblivious to the fact that we conveniently have forgotten that the dream related also to Uncle John and to food poisoning. As time passes the depicted consistency between the event and our precognition of it will tend to increase. Having placed an interpretation on an experience its recall may be embellished to reinforce that interpretation (Wiseman, 1996). If Jones is seen to have provoked the argument with Smith you involuntarily may elaborate on the nature of Jones's provocation.

Similarly, in the retelling of our precognitive dream of Aunt Mary's death we unwittingly may incorporate details about her anger over the doctor's inability to effect a cure. Thus, French (2003) has suggested that reports of parapsychological experiences may be rooted in a human capacity to create false or spurious memories.

Misperception of ambiguous situations. Perceptual psychologists point out that human perception of the world is not veridical but rather is a construction based on sensory inputs, past experience, and expectations. Particularly in perceptually ambiguous situations past experience and expectations play a substantial role in determining what we consciously "perceive."

One way in which past experience influences our perception of an incident as paranormal is in regard to causality. In childhood people have learned that events occurring in quick succession are causally linked, that is, one event is seen to cause the other or both events are seen to be caused by a common factor. This conception has been borne out on so many occasions that it often is taken for granted. Even where two events are causally independent their temporal contiguity is a compelling suggestion of a meaningful connection between them. Someone who happens to be pulling the handle of a poker machine in a distinctive way when the jackpot drops is inclined to believe that this technique of pulling is a cause of poker machine payouts. In a parapsychological context, if we are thinking of a long-lost friend at the very moment that person phones us it is natural to assume a causal connection between these events, yet they may well have arisen coincidentally.

Past experience also governs our assessment of the probability of an incident, and incidents with a low probability are intrinsically more likely to be construed as paranormal. Nevertheless our estimates of probability may be very inaccurate. For example, you may think it extraordinary for two people in a small group to have the same birthday, but for a group of 23 people the odds are better than 50/50 that at least two of them share a birthdate. Often our estimates of probability are distorted by the forgetting of things which at the time were inconsequential. Try to recall how many times you have read your horoscope in a magazine and subsequently found the predictions to be fulfilled. Most likely you will recall having looked at horoscopes but can not really say whether or not they were realized. Yet if you read in tomorrow's horoscope that you were about to make a financial gain and in the afternoon were told that you had won the lottery you probably would be inclined to conclude that horoscopes should be given some credence. Many would proclaim, "The probability of winning the lottery is so small that the horoscope could not have been correct just by chance!" Nevertheless the horoscope predicted not a lottery win but a more probable event, a financial gain; and on closer examination our impression of the probability of a horoscope's fulfillment is based on a very vague memory of the record of past predictions.

Perception also is influenced by expectations and beliefs, particularly in ambiguous situations. Often expectations make perception or cognitive processing more efficient. Having read "They bought some chocolates at the...," we expect to encounter "shop" in the next few words. When "shop" does appear it therefore requires little processing for its recognition and our reading thereby becomes more proficient. On the other hand, expectations can lead to misperceptions. If in the above example a typographical error resulted in "shep" being printed instead of "shop" many readers would not even notice the misprint, that is, their perception would not be veridical. Magicians rely heavily on creating inappropriate perceptual expectations. By various maneuvers they effect the impression that an object is located under a black cloth, and when the cloth is removed to reveal the absence of the object the audience "perceives" the object's dematerialization. In a more parapsychological context the nervous person spending a night in an unfamiliar old house may be prone to perceive naturally occurring noises as the footsteps of a ghost: there is an expectation (even subconscious) that such houses could be haunted.

Beliefs also serve to influence the search for alternative explanations of the perceived event (Jones & Russell, 1980). An individual who is extremely skeptical about the paranormal will look for natural causes of the event and if this should prove unproductive will dismiss the experience as a coincidence or mental aberration and quickly forget it. In contrast a person who is overly gullible about the paranormal will accept any unusual event as such without giving due consideration to other possibilities. A report of a spontaneous experience thus might spring largely from motivated misperception.

Subconscious perceptions. In the literature of cognitive psychology there is evidence that some sensory stimuli may be registered by the individual's processing system without evoking a conscious sensation (an instance of this was formerly termed subliminal perception, but recent researchers now subsume this and allied phenomena under the more neutral label "perception without awareness," e.g. Merikle, Smilek & Eastwood, 2001). This subconscious information later may break through into consciousness in the form of a dream or in thought associations. For example, you may be concentrating on some activity when an old friend happens to speak in your vicinity. Shortly afterwards you may start daydreaming about your old friend; at that moment the latter taps you on the shoulder and you cry in amazement, "Why, I was just thinking about you!" It is conceivable that some reports of ESP are based on such subconscious perception. Consider another example. Some very subtle changes in behavior may signify that a friend is very ill but is hiding the fact from you. If these cues are not perceived consciously they may be registered subconsciously and emerge subsequently as the basis of a "precognitive" dream of your friend's death. Some instances of apparent telepathy between close friends might reflect similar factors. One individual will make a comment and the other will remark that such a thought had just passed through his or her mind too. Rather than attributing this to ESP each person might review their recent mentation to find what prompted that particular thought. It may turn out to be an association to a fleeting image or remark on television which by virtue of the pair's common history and empathy (Donovan, 1998) evoked the same train of thought.

Deception and fraud. The preceding sources of inaccuracy in spontaneous case reports basically are unintentional: the experient has no deliberate objective of deceiving the case collector. Other respondents however, may well engage in premeditated deception and fraud. Their motives may be diverse. Some may have an infantile sense of mischief, others may get a feeling of superiority from misleading a "know-all academic." People aspiring to be professional psychics also may be seeking a university department's "stamp of approval" to enhance their credibility among members of the public.

There is nothing especially difficult in concocting a tale of a fictional parapsychological experience and passing the fabrication on to a collector of case reports, although it seems relatively few reports have been exposed as fraudulent (Stevenson, 1987b, p. 4). Perhaps of more interest are some of the techniques used by professional psychics or stage mentalists to demonstrate they have "extrasensory" abilities (for a broader review see Abbott, 1909; Wiseman, 2001; Wiseman & Morris, 1994). Although these sorts of performance can hardly be deemed "spontaneous" some of the underlying techniques might well be used in instances presented to the parapsychologist as reports of spontaneous ESP.

One technique is called billet reading and is useful for performance before a large group. Members of the audience are each invited to write on a card the name of a loved one and a short description of some distinctive characteristic of that person. Each card is sealed in an envelope and passed to the "psychic" who then selects envelopes at random to read by ESP. After attempting to read a card clairvoyantly the envelope is opened, the card read to the audience to establish the accuracy of the ESP attempt, and the person who wrote that card is asked to acknowledge its authenticity. The mentalist proceeds through several cards in this fashion with great success and the audience's donations are gratefully received to support the good work. How is this performance achieved by sleight of hand?

The trick in billet reading is fiendishly simple. The reading of the first card is sham. There are (at least) two options here. One is to report that little information can be obtained from the card ("because the writer is a skeptic"), make an ostensibly weak stab at the envelope's contents, open the envelope, pretend to read out something which is quite discrepant from the attempted ESP reading, and finally retain the sympathy of the audience by not asking the "obviously embarrassed" skeptical writer of the card to acknowledge it. Alternatively, a reading may be given and a stooge in the audience deceitfully acknowledges its complete accuracy. Under either of these arrangements for the reading of the first card the contents of this envelope in reality are not divulged to the audience and thus can be used as the message that the psychic pretends to obtain from the second envelope. Ostensibly to provide authentication of the second reading this envelope is opened and its contents become the message to be reported for the third reading. This procedure can be repeated indefinitely, although the performer would stop after five or six readings to ensure that cynics will not

have sufficient time to discern the technique being employed. A feature of billet reading is that authentication of readings is given by several members of the audience known to other people there not to be a stooge of the performer.

Let us now consider a method more applicable to the circumstance where there is only one sitter. This is the classical situation of the fortune-teller or consultant medium. Where the sitter is a regular patron the fortune-teller has tremendous scope for obtaining information about the client and presenting it as inspiration from the spirits. Rather extreme measures include engaging a private detective to gather suitable data or recruiting a housebreaker to search the individual's home for information (and also to steal one or two small items of sentimental value which can be "apported" in a sitting some months later). According to one reformed (or retired) medium there is a network of mediums in America within which dossiers of major (wealthy) clients are circulated (Keene, 1976). A rather less extreme but equally effective tactic is to get the client talking during each session and to report some of this information in a reading at a later date; certainly sitters usually disclose information as part of the processes of social interaction that occur during a psychic reading (Wooffitt, 2000). Since sitters are more interested in what the psychic says to them than in what they say to the psychic they often are convinced that the subsequent reading derived from paranormal sources.

Where the fortune-teller has not met the client before some rather different measures must be employed. One possibility with a female sitter is to invite her to leave her coat and handbag in the waiting room where they are searched by an accomplice for any useful data. More subtle avenues however, may be utilized; these are known as "cold reading" techniques (Hyman, 1977). The sitter may unwittingly reveal a good deal of personal information in response to casual questions by the psychic (although not all such questions necessarily serve this purpose; Wooffitt, 2000, 2003). Further, the sitter can be sized up on the basis of grooming, clothing, jewelry, mannerisms and speech, and this information can provide a basis for the initial stages of the reading. The impact of these statements can be noted, even in minor changes of facial expression, and the comment quickly may be hedged and if necessary completely reversed. If data on the individual's background can be extracted a medium familiar with the latest opinion polls and surveys can predict with high probability the client's beliefs on a range of issues. All of this information can be interwoven with statements the client would like to hear: "You have several abilities which you have not been given an opportunity to demonstrate," "You have a tendency to underestimate your achievements," and so forth. Even if the factual material is mistaken the client will remember the reading in glowing terms if it contained a good measure of carefully presented flattery.

Apart from the informational facet of the performance there are points of showmanship involved in a successful reading. The medium will be confident and act as if she or he believed in the performance, at the same time remaining modest and making no excessive claims. The cooperation of the sitter will be sought; then if the reading is a failure it is the sitter's fault. Cooperation is said to be needed particularly because of the "vagaries of language": as it might not be possible for the medium to convey adequately the intended meaning, the sitter is called upon to clarify the message by restating it in their own words or in relation to their own life. This of course, gives the fortune-teller additional information and clues as to the direction the reading should take. Various dramatic devices such as a crystal ball or palm reading will provide an air of mysticism and also an excuse for stalling: while the medium formulates the next part of the reading the medium can be seen to be following the lines of the client's hand or to be peering through the mists in the crystal ball. Stock phrases will be used to fill out the reading and to provide further time in which to organize thoughts. Statements will be given in an uncertain tone or posed as a question, then modified in accordance with the client's reaction so as to leave the sitter with the impression of having received a positive statement. In short, the skills of a fake medium are very much those of an adept used car salesman.

Chance. Perhaps the major argument against the use of spontaneous case material for the purpose of authenticating parapsychological phenomena is that the role of chance in such cases is unknown. You may intuit the unlikelihood of a given case being due purely to coincidence but the fact remains that almost invariably the investigator is not able to specify the statistical probability of the event's occurrence by chance.

Consider for example, the second author's (CW) experience of an auditory hallucination that seemed to predict a train derailment. Our anecdotal description noted that CW has a tendency to worry. Therefore there may be several occasions every day when she thinks of possible accidents, and countless occasions throughout a year. It would be quite likely — inevitable even — that purely by chance there would at some point be a coincidence between one of her cognitions and a later accident. Statisticians Persi Diaconis and Frederick Mosteller call this the Law of Truly Large Numbers: "with a large enough sample, any outrageous thing is likely to happen" (Diaconis & Mosteller, 1989, p. 859). Although official records can quantify the number of train accidents, it is virtually impossible for us to discover the number of times people think or dream of a train accident. So the likelihood of such a coincidence cannot be calculated. Unless the level of statistical significance of a spontaneous experience can be determined parapsychologists cannot justifiably be confident that the event was unlikely to have been a coincidence.

The move toward testing the authenticity of parapsychological phenomena in the laboratory reflected the realization that the level of statistical significance must be ascertained and there must be control exercised over such potentially confounding factors as those cited above, namely, inaccuracies of memory, misperception, subliminal cues, and deliberate deception. This is not to say that parapsychological case collections necessarily are riddled with instances of these artifacts. Indeed, according to Schouten (1983) the coherence of observed patterns in the case collections lessens the likelihood that such sources of error are in any respect substantial. But in the absence of a precise assessment of the extent to which artifacts are influential in any given collection, it is widely conceded that laboratory investigation is the most appropriate means by which to address the authenticity question.

Case Material and the Nature of Parapsychological Phenomena

As you will recall Louisa Rhine argued that collections of spontaneous case material could be used to gather data on the nature of parapsychological phenomena. If such trends are used as hypotheses for experimental investigation there is much merit in Louisa Rhine's position. On the other hand, where the data are to be used for other purposes one must be cognizant of certain limitations in collections of case material. The limitations here generally relate to sampling, that is, the extent to which the collection can be regarded as representative of spontaneous experiences as a whole.

Investigators are one potential source of bias in this respect since they decide which reports will be included in the collection and which will not. Such decisions are by their nature subjective. To reject some reports as not pertaining to a parapsychological phenomenon may in the eyes of other researchers be construed as imposing upon the data one particular interpretation of what should constitute a parapsychological phenomenon. To reject other reports on the grounds that they are too poorly written for use in the analysis might be seen as biasing the sample towards people who are more verbally fluent and perhaps thereby prone to embellishment. To accept all reports would leave the researcher open to the charge that the collection contains identifiable instances of psychotic hallucination, hoaxes, and other non-parapsychological material.

The case collection also may be biased by the manner in which contributions are solicited. If examples of particular parapsychological experiences are given to potential respondents they tend to elicit very similar experiences rather than the full range of forms which the phenomena can take. If researchers make an appeal for cases in the media they may be sampling a population of uncertain, and thus possibly atypical, characteristics. It is not simply a matter of the listeners to a particular radio program being unrepresentative of the general population but also that the researcher has little idea of what sort of people actually listen to the program.

Additionally the composition of case collections may be atypical because of the differing preparedness of people to respond to the researcher's plea for case reports. People who believe in parapsychological phenomena may well be much more inclined to participate in a survey of spontaneous ESP experiences than folk who do not. Individuals sympathetic to the objectives of science and general academic research may be relatively common among the respondents. It is also the case that females tend to be more willing than males to write out an account of their experiences and send it to an investigator. Even if an individual is prepared to take part in the project she or he may tend to report experiences of a certain type, such as the more credible instances or ones less suggestive of maladjustment.

There are procedures for minimizing the effects of these various potential sources of bias but in general it is advisable to seek replication of case study data in other samples and with other research techniques. At the same time it must be said that in spite of the potential for sampling bias, many phenomenological trends do seem remarkably consistent across different case collections.

In this section a number of limitations of spontaneous case material have been highlighted. By means of these arguments it is possible to "explain away" virtually any spontaneous parapsychological experience, and on such grounds many critics maintain that parapsychological research is futile. While acknowledging that case collections cannot be used as conclusive evidence of the authenticity or ontological reality of parapsychological phenomena the position taken here is that this does not warrant the abandonment of research into these experiences.

First, the fact that cases may plausibly have been due to the operation of any number of normal factors does not demonstrate that any given case was indeed due to such factors. The case still could be authentic (paranormal). As Watt (1990–1991) notes, psychological research on human attributional and information-processing errors might equally be used to argue that some people could have been mistaken in construing their anomalous experiences *not* to have involved paranormal processes. The only fair way of assessing the authenticity of a parapsychological phenomenon is to employ a research technique suited to that task, that is, to resort to a carefully designed experimental procedure.

Second, even if the phenomena prove not to be paranormal, people do report them and hence we as behavioral scientists should endeavor to understand why they are reported. Far from prompting an end to research the points raised in this section indicate the necessity of further, if different, research. There are many diverse methods of scientific research, and surveys, case collection, and experiments are just some of the available options (White, 1992). Each research method has its value and the use of multiple methods allows researchers to converge on a multifaceted solution to a given issue (Alvarado, 1996; Watt, 1994a). A convergent strategy in scientific investigation is especially pertinent to the study of the complexities of human experience.

KEY TERMS AND CONCEPTS

intuitive impressions
hallucinations
realistic dreams
unrealistic dreams
Louisa Rhine

telepathic agent
completeness of content
conviction
call cases
billet reading

STUDY QUESTIONS

1. Recall one of your own extrasensory experiences. To what extent does it meet the SPR criteria for the acceptability of a case report? What additional evidence would have been demanded of your case by the founders of the SPR, and why would they think this evidence was necessary?

2. Were the SPR criteria needlessly severe? Or were they appropriate for their intended purpose?

3. Distinguish between a case collection and a case survey. Methodologically speaking, might there be some overlap between the two approaches?

4. How did Louisa Rhine's technique for analysis of case collections differ from that of earlier studies?

5. Try to locate among your own extrasensory experiences instances of intuitive impressions, hallucinations, realistic dreams, and unrealistic dreams. Do any of your experiences not fit neatly into Louisa Rhine's proposed taxonomy?

6. What were the principal results of Louisa Rhine's analyses of spontaneous cases of ESP?

7. Of what use to parapsychologists are spontaneous case reports?

8. What are the evidential limitations of spontaneous case material? In view of these limitations might it be advisable for parapsychologists not to use case collection and surveys as research techniques?

9. Recall one of your own extrasensory experiences and explore ways in which an independent critic might seek to explain your experience in terms of recognized psychological processes. To what extent do you feel your experience demonstrates the existence of the paranormal process ESP?

10. On what sort of evidence should parapsychologists seek to assess the authenticity of ESP?

11. Critically consider the proposition that the laboratory experiment is the only rigorous research method in a scientific parapsychology.

4

EXPERIMENTAL RESEARCH ON EXTRASENSORY PERCEPTION

The Authenticity of ESP

A central issue in ESP research is that of authenticity, that is, whether (some) extrasensory experiences are due to the operation of a process presently not acknowledged to exist by conventional scientists. Parapsychologists' interest in this issue often is represented as a pursuit of the paranormal and thus in a sense a crusade against science itself, but in essence the research on the authenticity of ESP has been a pursuit of the normal, a use of the methods of science in an attempt to establish the bases of ESP and to "normalize" them, either by demonstrating their compatibility with accepted scientific principles or by establishing sufficient reason for that framework to be expanded in order to accommodate the occurrence of extrasensory experiences. In addition to its significance for parapsychology's legitimization as an academic discipline the investigation of ESP's authenticity is a fascinating study in the sociology of science.

The Move to Experimental Inquiry

Following the establishment of the SPR, and particularly in the first quarter of the twentieth century, there was a growing realization that the authenticity of ESP could be investigated only through a controlled test in a laboratory situation. That appreciation evolved naturally from researchers' experience in investigating mediums, although it was to be some time before there developed a standard experimental paradigm for ESP research. The first step toward operationalizing the ESP hypothesis entailed an emphasis upon controlled observation whereby the investigator should select some target material, ensure it was sensorially inaccessible to the subject of the study, and then invite the individual to identify the material by psychic means. Some of the SPR's early investigations of mental mediums or "sensitives" comprised controlled tasks of this sort. Thus, Guthrie's study in 1883 required subjects to telepathically identify sensations concurrently being experienced by agents in visual, gustatory, olfactory and tactile modalities (Guthrie & Birchall, 1883; Gurney et al., 1886, Vol. 1, pp. 36–58).

Controlled tests in which the range of extrasensory targets is unknown (and hence conceptually unlimited) to the subject are known as *free-response* experiments. These investigations were to make a major contribution to our understanding of processes underlying extrasensory experience, particularly through the work of Sinclair (1930/1962) and Warcollier (1938/1975). But in the early period of experimentation their value to the issue of ESP's authenticity was limited because the evaluation of their data necessarily was qualitative. In Guthrie's study with drawings for example, the evidence for the occurrence of telepathy relied upon the apparent similarity between the pictures viewed by the agents and the subjects' sketched impressions of those targets. Whatever their value for process-oriented research such studies did not attest to the reality of ESP because it was not (then) possible to be sure that correspondences between targets and responses were anything more than lucky guesses.

The next step in the development of a paradigmatic ESP experiment therefore was marked by an emerging awareness of the need for quantification of the observed correspondence between targets and responses. This entails both the representation of the subject's performance as a numerical score and the probabilistic assessment of this performance being due simply to guessing or "chance." A few of the earliest SPR investigations instance a glimmering appreciation of this requirement. Beginning in the year before the SPR's statutory foundation ESP tests were conducted by Barrett, Gurney and Myers with the five young daughters of an English clergyman, the Rev. Creery; here an agent (or *sender*) concentrated on the thought of various types of targets including a randomly selected playing card and a two-digit number, and the subject (the *receiver*) sought to determine each target telepathically (Gurney et al., 1886, Vol. 1, pp. 20–31). In the case of these targets the investigators evaluated the girls' performance on the assumption that the probability of correctly guessing the identity of a playing card on the basis of chance alone was 1 in 52, and that of guessing a two-digit number, 1 in 90. The probability of the observed results being due to random guesses thus was determined to be typically very low

(Gurney et al., 1886, Vol. 1, p. 25). (It should be noted in passing that evidence of the girls' cheating was reported a few years later.)

The notions of quantification and probabilistic assessment of ESP data, and the associated need for a large number of "guesses" or trials, were enunciated formally in 1884 by Charles Richet, an eminent physiologist and later Nobel Prize laureate at the University of Paris (Gurney et al., 1886, Vol. 1, p. 31; Richet, 1923, p. 85). Richet suggested that if psychic ability were weakly present in the general population, then if a number of people were tested with long sequences of randomly drawn playing cards, a greater than expected number of successful guesses would be indicative of psychic ability. Richet's thesis was indeed a crucial insight in the history of experimental parapsychology, principally for two reasons. First, although critics of ESP research had ample scope to quibble about the claimed extent of target-response correspondence in free-response studies like that by Guthrie, this became a much more difficult proposition when the data were quantified and objectively evaluated in these *restricted-choice* experiments. Second, quantification permitted the detection of very weak or intermittent extrasensory effects, eventually opening the way for research into the authenticity question with so-called *unselected* subjects instead of people with supposedly high and controllable skills in ESP. Typical of his era however, Richet himself still preferred to have data that encouraged conviction qualitatively as well as quantitatively; in tests to identify extrasensorially the suit of 2927 playing cards Richet recorded 789 correct responses compared to an expected 732, but despite the statistical improbability of achieving this result by chance he could not regard it as conclusive.

Richet's development of probabilistic assessment of card-guessing studies was of great significance not only to experimental parapsychology. Historians such as Ian Hacking and Ted Kaptchuk have argued that the origins of the use of randomization in experimental design can be traced back to the early card-guessing experiments of the SPR (Hacking, 1988; Kaptchuk, 1998). Probability modeling was used in psychophysics at that time, but not for the purposes of drawing inferences. Richet's work was a pioneering application of randomization and is a good example of how the methodological and conceptual challenges facing parapsychologists can lead to developments with mainstream applicability and relevance (Watt, in press; see also Alvarado, 2005; Kelly, 2001; Kelly & Alvarado, 2005).

Although there were relatively few experimentally inclined psychical researchers active during the 50 years immediately following the foundation of the SPR a surprising number of simple card-guessing tests of ESP were undertaken; Pratt, Rhine, Smith, Stuart and Greenwood (1940, Table 29) catalog about 80 such experiments. While many of these had experimental personnel of unknown standing, a small number of trials, an inadequately controlled experimental setting, other methodological flaws, and/or poorly reported procedure, some of the studies do seem procedurally adequate.

A Harvard University researcher George Estabrooks (1927/1961), for example, conducted four series of tests with individual unselected students as subjects in one room and himself as the telepathic agent in another room. Each of the 83 participants completed 20 trials with playing cards as targets. The identification of target color and of target suit were substantially better than expected on the basis of chance.

A few skeptics also undertook card-guessing experiments. One of these was the often-cited study by Coover (1917/1975) at Stanford University in 1915. Individual subjects sat in one room while a telepathic agent sat with Coover in an adjacent room. The targets were a shuffled 40-card deck of playing cards. On the roll of a die each trial was performed under one of two conditions. In the "telepathy" condition the telepathic agent looked at the card while the subject sought to identify it. The other type of trial was designed as a control or "non-telepathic" condition; here the telepathic agent did not view the card when the subject attempted to guess its identity. After some 10,000 trials Coover found no substantial difference between scores under the two conditions and he concluded there was no support for the telepathy hypothesis.

Critics of Coover's study later pointed out that although the control condition may have been "non-telepathic" it was hardly a "non-ESP" procedure; on the contrary, it admitted the operation of clairvoyance, a possibility Coover simply could not take seriously. Comparison of the scores to that expected purely on the basis of random guessing showed performance under both conditions to be above chance, significantly so when data for the two conditions were (rather inappropriately) combined. Coover himself was inclined to attribute the scores' elevation over chance to the possibility of involuntary auditory cues passing from the agent's room to the adjoining subject's room (Kennedy, 1939, p. 63).

But despite all this activity, before 1930 research on the authenticity of ESP had a negligible impact upon the scientific community. In part this was due to the fact that only a small proportion of the work was conducted in a university setting and was published in sources where it might come to the notice of other scientists. A more fundamental factor however, was that the research effort was sporadic and uncoordinated. Although some qualified researchers, such as Troland (1917/1976) and Coover (1917/1975), did perform ESP tests they typically completed just a single study and then made no further empirical contribution to the field. No coherent, sustained program of research had been instigated by this work and no dominant standardized experimental paradigm had evolved. The scientific researchers' sense of frustration was reflected in increasing disunity within the SPR and the American Society for Psychical Research (ASPR), with major rifts arising between the ardent experimentalists and other, more spiritualistically oriented members (Mauskopf & McVaugh, 1980; Tietze, 1985).

The program of ESP experimentation that was to confront the academic world with the authenticity issue began in 1927 at Duke University in North Carolina when J. B. Rhine (husband of Louisa Rhine) developed the classical ESP cards and techniques for their use. This style of research became so fundamental to the discipline that J. B. Rhine generally is regarded as the father of modern experimental parapsychology, although like any intellectual pioneer he had his conceptual predecessors, as we have seen.

Joseph Banks Rhine (1895–1980) studied botany and plant physiology at the University of Chicago, where both he and Louisa obtained their Ph.D. This may seem an odd background for a person who taught psychology and engaged in parapsychological research, but two factors conspired to help Rhine along his chosen path. First, in the 1920s botanists were in the forefront of work in statistical theory and Rhine's knowledge in this area served him well in his later efforts to devise laboratory tests of ESP. Second, Rhine's interest in parapsychological research endeared him to William McDougall, the newly appointed head of the Psychology Department at Duke University. Rhine thus became an instructor in psychology in 1928 and an assistant professor in 1929.

J. B. Rhine's first topic for study was clairvoyance. Although earlier psychical researchers generally felt telepathy had been adequately attested many of them were dubious about the existence of clairvoyance; as was the case with Coover, some even dismissed the notion out of hand, in spite of the formal experiments on clairvoyance by Richet (1888) many years before. Between 1924 and 1928 however, Ina Jephson of the SPR per-

Figure 5. J. B. Rhine (photograph: RRC).

formed a sizable card-guessing investigation the results of which she claimed to support the hypothesis of clairvoyance. She then proceeded to argue that because former experimental studies of apparent telepathy also admitted the possibility of clairvoyance of the cards being viewed by the agent, the concept of telepathy was in fact redundant (Jephson, 1928). The occurrence of ESP without the mediation of an agent or "sender" therefore became a salient issue.

Now, Rhine was aware that previous ESP studies had relied on packs of ordinary playing cards as target material, but there were objections to the use of these cards. The probability of correctly guessing the identity of a playing card theoretically was 1 in 52, but it was clear that subjects had preferences for certain cards (e.g., aces) that might make a random-guessing model of performance invalid regardless of the existence or otherwise of clairvoyance.

Additionally, there was the problem that the identity of playing cards is determined by two bits of information, the suit (hearts, diamonds, clubs, spades) and the face value (ace, two, three, etc.). This made for some inconvenience in scoring. If a guess had to be precisely correct to be credited then a person who, for example, often guessed the suit but rarely the value would unjustly be rated as a poor performer.

The elasticity of scoring criteria also allowed critics to level the charge of "hypothesis saving": if the parapsychologist failed to find significant results when scoring the responses holistically, the data could be reprocessed for correctness of the suit, and then for correctness of the face value, and then for correctness of the suit color, all in the hope of eventually locating a statistically significant effect.

To avoid these various difficulties Rhine sought some simple stimulus cards to which a statistical random-guessing model would be applicable. He initially used digits and letters as targets for the participant to identify by clairvoyant means, but again subjects exhibited marked preferences for some digits/letters over others. An experimental psychologist at Duke University, Karl Zener, suggested some elementary geometrical symbols and thus the now famous ESP symbols (formerly known as Zener symbols) came into being. There are five different symbols: a square (formerly a rectangle), a circle, a cross (or plus sign), a star, and wavy lines. The

standard ESP pack comprises 25 cards, five of each symbol. The essential task of an experimental participant is to guess, perhaps with the assistance of some form of ESP, the identity of each card in a shuffled deck. An unusually high and sustained level of correct responses on the part of an individual was proposed as a demonstration of the authenticity of ESP.

Some basic terminology of card-guessing tests may be collated at this point. The subject's guess is termed a *call*. Correct guesses are *hits*, incorrect calls are *misses*. A set of 25 guesses (for a full pack) is a *run*; often a test session would comprise a number of runs. The symbol on a given trial is known as the *target* for that trial.

Several different experimental techniques were devised by the Rhines. Two are methods for testing clairvoyance. In the "down through" (DT) technique the subject has to guess the order of symbols in a shuffled downward-facing deck, starting from the top and working down. After the 25 guesses are recorded each card is turned over and checked against the subject's corresponding call. In an alternative technique the experimenter takes one card at a time from the shuffled pack, places it face down, records the subject's call, and then repeats the process until all 25 cards have been used. The calls

Figure 6. The ESP symbols (© RRC).

and targets finally are checked for correspondence.

Each of these techniques was held by Rhine to be a test of clairvoyance because at the time of the subject's guesses the experimenter was unaware of the order of the cards and thus telepathy was excluded. Another procedure tapped general ESP (GESP), that is, clairvoyance and/or telepathy. Here the experimenter (or an agent) takes one card from the pack, looks at it, records the subject's call, and continues in this fashion through the whole deck. Since the subject theoretically may rely on extrasensory information either from the card itself (clairvoyance) or from the mind of the experimenter (telepathy) this technique was proposed as a measure of GESP (rather than of telepathy as had been assumed in many earlier studies).

Rhine then formulated the statistical means of evaluating data yielded by these procedures. As the probability of guessing the identity of an ESP card is ⅕ one would expect the subject to produce on average ⅕ of 25, or 5, correct calls purely by random guessing. That is to say, the *mean chance expectation* (MCE) is 5 per run. By conducting the subject through an extended series of runs the actual performance could be compared to MCE. The statistic used for this comparison is a form of a standard or Z score known as a *critical ratio* (CR). For example, if a participant completed 30 runs (750 trials) and had 175 hits, Z would equal 2.28. If you look in a table of areas under the normal curve the two-tailed probability (p) of obtaining $Z = 2.28$ or larger is 0.02. This (hypothetical) subject therefore has exhibited a level of success that statistically is unlikely to have been due simply to chance (p<.05). See Burdick and Kelly (1977) and Edge, Morris, Palmer and Rush (1986, Ch. 6), for more details on how to calculate CR.

After devising an experimental paradigm and suitable statistical procedures Rhine set about finding some people who were "sensitive," that is, who could perform consistently well in his tests. His first significant result was obtained in a series of tests conducted in 1931 to 1932. Using a clairvoyance procedure 24 student subjects gave a total 207 hits in 800 trials (as against a MCE of 160), for which the value of p is less than one in a million (Mauskopf & McVaugh, 1980, p. 90).

Rhine also worked toward tightening his experimental procedure, particularly in regard to the elimination of sensory cues. For example, some of the earlier packs of ESP cards had very slight differences in the pattern on the back of each card and it was realized that if subjects could see the backs of the cards they might learn (either deliberately or subconsciously) to distinguish certain cards by the pattern on the obverse face. Similarly, subjects who could see or hear the experimenter could be aware of subtle changes in the experimenter's facial expression or tone of voice when a correct call was made. With a closed deck, knowing that a square (for example) had been drawn from the deck the subject would have a slightly increased chance of correctly guessing cards bearing other symbols.

When Rhine published his book *Extra-Sensory Perception* in 1934 he described his gradual improvements in technique (although critics were quick to seize upon earlier experiments and criticize them for poor control). Nevertheless, the main function of Rhine's book was to show how the ESP hypothesis could be approached in a rigorously scientific fashion, encouraging other psychologists to undertake similar research. The success of some of his own studies were cited not so much to establish the authenticity of ESP but to indicate that there were individuals who may be able to perform consistently better than chance level and thereby an experimental research program on ESP might well be viable. For example, one of Rhine's outstanding subjects was a Methodist theological student Hubert Pearce who averaged about 8 hits per run (compared to a MCE of

5) over 690 runs (17,250 trials). Rhine's *Extra-Sensory Perception* also reviewed the history of experimental parapsychological research in an attempt to demonstrate that such work could be divorced from occultism and to support some of the trends he had found in the analyses of his own data.

The book initially was received with cautious interest among the American psychological community. The book then caught the public eye and not only became a best seller but also elicited much comment in the popular press and instigated a fad for ESP cards. Reaction among psychologists soon was strongly antipathetic; it is uncertain if this was due to the publicity given to the Duke University research, to the exaggerated claims made in the media, or to a resurgence of awareness that ESP was incompatible with accepted principles of behavioral science. In any event, between 1934 and 1940 ESP raged as a major psychological controversy, with Rhine's work subjected to vehement criticism. Much of the comment was purely rhetorical: for example, the Duke research was ridiculed as being rooted in superstition and mysticism and as such it was held to be putting the science of psychology in disrepute. Some of the more rational arguments of the critics included: invalid statistical analyses, uncontrolled sensory cues, recording errors, inadequate shuffling, optional stopping, suppression of null results, and fraud. Rhine recognized and dealt with many of these criticisms in his later research (Pratt et al., 1940).

For many years the techniques developed by Rhine effectively controlled the agenda for ESP research. Later parapsychologists devised rather more adventurous experimental procedures, in part as a response to the sheer tedium of long series of card-guessing trials. For example, in place of the standard ESP symbols Fisk and Mitchell (1953) used drawings of a clock face with the hour hand pointing to one of the hour positions from 1 to 12; unfortunately these targets proved unsatisfactory because partici-

pants had preferences for certain times and these response biases contaminated the data (Chauvin, 1985, p. 26).

Modern electronic developments also contributed to the design of novel restricted-choice targets. In the late 1960s Schmidt (1969, 1970a) constructed devices by which a sequence of ESP targets was determined in part by the random emission of particles from either a radioactive or an electronic source. These so-called *random event generators* (REGs) can be connected to a panel of target lights as in Tart's (1976) "ten-choice trainer," or to a display of target events on a video screen. Not only are ESP test machines of this sort more entertaining for participants than are card-guessing tests but data can be collected efficiently and processed automatically without the risk of human error.

The popularity of free-response techniques also has revived in the last few decades, particularly in the context of research on extrasensory experiences during various altered states of consciousness. In fact free-response procedures now form the dominant paradigm in this area so it is appropriate to say more about free-response methodology. Target material in free-response studies is unrestricted, for example geographical sites, art prints, and more recently film, video, or digitized clips can be used. Typically free-response targets are more colorful and complex than the simple symbols used in restricted-choice studies. Prior to a study, the experimenters prepare a large number of target possibilities, known as the *target pool,* and they sub-divide the target pool into smaller sets typically of four different targets. So for instance a pool of 120 art print postcards would each be concealed in labeled envelopes and would be subdivided into 30 sets of four. For any one trial, one set is randomly chosen and then one target is randomly chosen from that set to be the designated ESP target for the trial. The other three targets in the set play an important role as *decoy targets.* As we shall see, the target and decoys are needed for the *judging period.*

Once the trial is underway, the sender (if there is one) views the chosen target, while the target's identity is concealed from everyone else involved in the trial. Unlike restricted-choice studies where the receiver makes a single call or guess as to the target identity, in free-response studies the receiver has no idea what target will be chosen for any particular trial. Therefore the receiver can give a number of different impressions about the target identity, and these impressions can be in any form, for example a report of a dream, a series of sketches, or an ongoing verbal report of thoughts and feelings known as a *mentation*. The receiver's impressions may be recorded or transcribed. In restricted-choice studies the occurrence of a hit is unambiguous. For instance with Zener cards if the receiver calls a "star" and the target is a star then the trial is counted as a hit. In contrast, the unrestricted nature of free-response targets and target responses means that a judgment has to be made as to whether or not the receiver has obtained information about the target. In free-response studies, then, the judging period is a key stage. Once the receiver has given his or her impressions of the target, either the receiver or an independent person is given the set containing target and decoys in order to judge the degree of similarity between the receiver's impressions and the four target possibilities. Each of the four target possibilities is given a score or is ranked in order of similarity to the receiver's impressions and a hit is scored if the target that is judged to be most similar to the receiver's impressions was the actual target that had previously been randomly chosen and viewed by the sender. At this point in free-response studies the statistical evaluation becomes similar to that for forced-choice studies. We know the likelihood of obtaining a hit by chance alone (25 percent if there is one target and three decoys), and over a number of trials we compare the chance hit-rate with the actual hit-rate to obtain a probability value. So the rather more complex procedure

in free-response studies in the end boils down to a fairly simple statistical evaluation. Let us now turn to some examples of free-response studies.

At the Maimonides Medical Center in Brooklyn, New York, Ullman, Krippner, and Honorton conducted some fascinating studies on ESP during dreams (Child, 1985; Ullman & Krippner, 1970; Ullman & Krippner, with Vaughan, 1989). These investigators report the content of experimental participants' dreams could relate thematically to sensorially inaccessible pictorial targets, namely, prints of famous works of art. Similar findings were subsequently reported by other research teams (for a review see Sherwood & Roe, 2003). The Maimonides team also compiled a set of 1,024 photographic slides representing all combinations of the presence and absence of ten specific dimensions of pictorial content (Honorton, 1975). A target slide and an experimental subject's imagery during an altered state of consciousness then could independently be coded on these ten dimensions and the correspondence between them assessed in a purely quantitative fashion. This and similar target material made a significant contribution to some major series of free-response studies, most notably those concerned with ESP during sensory restriction or ganzfeld conditions, of which more is said later in this chapter.

An experimental procedure that gained considerable public attention was designed by Targ and Puthoff (1978) at the Stanford Research Institute in California. Dubbed *remote viewing* its experimental subjects are asked to describe a randomly selected outdoor location at which a co-experimenter currently is situated. Judges blind to the identity of the target rate the subjects' imagery protocols for their correspondence to each location in the pool of potential targets. Targ and Puthoff report extra-chance correspondence between subjects' imagery and the actual target under the remote viewing procedure, although there has been some dispute

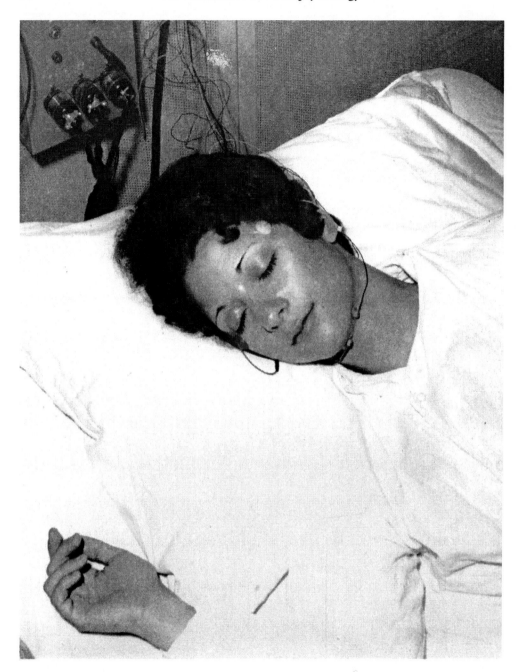

Figure 7. A participant in a Maimonides study of ESP in dreams (photograph: Stanley Krippner).

as to whether their judges in fact were fully blind to the identity of targets (Alcock, 1990; Marks & Kammann, 1980; Tart, Puthoff & Targ, 1980). The procedure has been utilized by other researchers (e.g., Dunne, Jahn & Nelson, 1983), but again there are suggestions of statistical and methodological flaws in some of this work (Hansen, Utts & Markwick, 1992; *cf.* Dobyns, Dunne, Jahn & Nelson, 1992; Targ, 1994). After due consideration of these criticisms Schmeidler (1994a) nevertheless concludes that the evidence supports the hypothesis that the remote viewing procedure is psi conducive, and one of the few more recent studies (Storm, 2003) also showed some evidence of above-chance performance.

Despite this recent flurry of innovative ESP research, for most contemporary psychologists the atmosphere of the 1934–1940 controversy prevails. For example, the arguments presented in Day's (1969) and Marks' (1986) critiques of ESP research essentially are the same as those dating from the 1930s. Recently some attempt has been made to list the claimed methodological flaws and to examine statistically their possible influence on the reported data. A technique known as *meta-analysis* enables the aggregation of results across all known experiments on a given phenomenon (Green & Hall, 1984; Krippner et al., 1993; Steinkamp, 1998). By coding each experiment for apparent or potential methodological flaws the bearing of each flaw on the data then might be assessed. For example, the size of the experimental ESP effect found in studies where motivated recording errors theoretically were feasible can be compared to the effect-size for experiments in which such errors could not have occurred. If the extra-chance scores in ESP tests were due to the flaws alleged by critics meta-analysis should bear this out. Meta-analyses of various specific classes of ESP experiment have been undertaken (e.g., Bösch, 2004; Child, 1985; Crandall, 1991; Haraldsson & Houtkooper, 1995; Haraldsson, Houtkooper & Hoeltje, 1987; Honorton, 1985; Honorton & Ferrari, 1989; Honorton, Ferrari & Bem, 1998; Hyman, 1985; Lawrence, 1993; Milton, 1997; Milton & Wiseman, 1999a,b; Schechter, 1984; Sherwood & Roe, 2003; Stanford & Stein, 1994; Steinkamp, Milton & Morris, 1998; Watt, 1994b). We discuss some of the limitations of meta-analysis in a later section on the cumulative record of ESP research. But on the basis of meta-analyses of one set of ESP studies a critic and a parapsychologist have agreed that at least the experimental effect cannot

reasonably be attributed either to suppression of null results or to invalid statistical procedures (Hyman & Honorton, 1986). It should be added that meta-analysis itself still is regarded as a relatively controversial statistical technique.

In any event the prevailing impression among psychologists today is that so much heat was generated during the original ESP controversy there just has to be something unscientific about parapsychological research into ESP. Although skeptics' rhetoric certainly has served to sustain this attitude the present position has been compounded by the failure of parapsychologists to devise techniques for controlling this hypothesized ability of ESP. If the very best subjects can sustain an average of only 8 hits per run and the now typically short studies of groups of unselected subjects yield means of about 5.2 hits (as against MCE of 5), then *regardless* of the level of statistical significance the data are hardly very persuasive that people in some paranormal fashion can direct their awareness to things inaccessible to the recognized senses. Undoubtedly some scientists would require consistent one hundred percent accuracy (25 hits per run) before they would sit up and take notice. Thus, Gendin (1998, p. 439) muses, "We may well want to know why, if we postulate psi power, the person made any wrong calls at all." Although this extreme requirement is unreasonable the onus now is squarely on the parapsychologist to gain sufficient understanding of the nature of ESP as to permit substantial control over the phenomenon, thereby convincing other scientists not merely in statistical terms but at an *emotional* level as well.

But what is the objective status of the available experimental evidence? Does it establish the authenticity of ESP in the eyes of the fair-minded observer? Three approaches to this issue must be explored. The first concerns the existence of a definitive experiment; the second seeks authenticity in the weight of the cumulative record of ESP experimentation; and the third entails the logical evaluation of what an ESP experiment can achieve. These three approaches are addressed in order.

The Existence of the Definitive Experiment

One means of judging if ESP is genuine is to locate an ESP experiment which is definitive as far as the issue of authenticity is concerned. In particular, can we be persuaded of the paranormality of ESP experience by the results of some study which parapsychologists themselves regard as among the most carefully conducted?

The demand for a definitive ESP experiment has been made by several critics (e.g., Price, 1955, 1956), and parapsychologists intermittently have responded by nominating past studies believed to provide the best evidence for authenticity (e.g., Beloff, 1980; Rao, 1984). The selection of a definitive experiment clearly is a subjective and to some extent arbitrary process. Beloff (1980) suggested the following criteria. First, the experimenter had to be a competent person of good standing and well known to the parapsychological community. Second, the report of the experiment had to be published in a reputable scientific journal that routinely subjects its papers to editorial scrutiny and refereeing by qualified peers. Third, the overall experimental ESP scores had to be so highly significant that selective reporting, optional stopping, or any procedural artifact such as nonrandom target selection could be discounted. Fourth, the experiment had to be deemed by eminent parapsychologists as one of the best available.

Several experiments deemed to meet Beloff's criteria have been nominated (e.g., Beloff, 1980; Rao, 1984). Be that as it may,

Figure 8. Hubert Pearce (left) being tested for ESP by Rhine (photograph: RRC).

there remains a fundamental difficulty in the notion of a definitive experiment. Irrespective of the professional eminence of the investigator and the reported attention to precision in the execution of the study, and regardless too of the standing and the number of scientists who endorse the study's findings, there always is the possibility, no matter how remote we judge it to be, that experimental personnel colluded to manipulate or invent the data. Such an argument was put forward by British psychologist and critic Hansel (1966, 1980) for one experiment that meets Beloff's criteria: Rhine's Pearce-Pratt study (Rhine, 1936; Rhine & Pratt, 1954). Although Hansel's use of that argument may be politically motivated to the extent that he did not seek to apply it to any other phenomenon investigated by psychologists, its validity stands inviolate. In short, there is and can be no definitive experiment on the authenticity of ESP.

The Cumulative Record

Given that some fault can be found with any single experiment perhaps the best evidence for ESP's authenticity may be provided by the trend in the cumulative record of ESP research. Some experiments in the literature may well be based on bogus data; indeed there are a few cases of fraudulent experimenters in parapsychology, just as there are some in psychology and in other sciences. Other experiments may have yielded significant results through shoddy experimental procedures, as in failure to eliminate sensory cues. Still other reports of significant data might be attributable to those uncommon occasions on which significance is achieved purely by chance. Be this as it may, if the substantial proportion of experimental reports cite significant data surely it is unreasonable to maintain that *all* of them were due to these sorts of artifacts. That is, surely we may rely upon at least one of the significant studies in

the cumulative record being indicative of a genuine effect. If one accepts this argument the relative frequency of experiments yielding statistically significant results is such as to indicate there is something here that warrants explaining rather than explaining away.

An assessment of the cumulative record of ESP research recently has been facilitated by the statistical technique of meta-analysis. As mentioned earlier, meta-analysis permits the aggregation of results across all known experiments on a given phenomenon. Additionally, it is possible under this technique to allow for the existence of unknown and unreported experiments that yielded only chance results. In a comprehensive survey of meta-analyses of ESP studies Utts (1991) concluded there was strong evidence for a small but positive effect, particularly in free-response investigations of ESP, that cannot reasonably be attributed to the existence of unreported null findings. On these grounds some parapsychologists have concluded that ESP must now be regarded as a demonstrated phenomenon. It is in this sense that Broughton (1991, p. 279), for example, has provocatively dubbed the meta-analysis of ESP research "the controversy killer."

On the other hand, there are reasons to believe that meta-analysis as currently practiced in parapsychology is not a panacea for our ills (Watt, in press). For example, debate continues about how to interpret meta-analyses of studies of ESP under ganzfeld conditions (e.g., Milton & Wiseman, 1999a, 2001; Storm & Ertel, 2001, 2002). Broughton's depiction of meta-analysis as the controversy killer therefore may have been over-optimistic. Although meta-analysis is regarded as a quantitative form of literature review, in practice some subjectivity remains in how meta-analyses are conducted. Drawing on their experience, parapsychologists can thus point to ways in which meta-analysis can be improved, for instance by using multiple independent and blind coders (Steinkamp, 1998).

An additional problem for a small field like parapsychology is that it is not possible to set the criteria for study inclusion and the coding criteria for meta-analysis blind to the outcome of studies. The criteria for inclusion and for coding need to be set *in advance* of the studies actually being done (Akers, 1985; Kennedy, 2004; Milton, 1999; Scargle, 2000) rather than as happens at present, with the benefit of hindsight. Kennedy's "Proposal and challenge for proponents and skeptics of psi" perhaps goes furthest to recognize this problem and to suggest a solution (Kennedy, 2004). Drawing on his experiences in pharmaceutical research, Kennedy recommends that proposed pivotal studies are identified and planned in advance. A committee of experienced parapsychologists, moderate skeptics and a statistician could review and comment on the proposed protocols so that methodological issues are dealt with before the data are collected. Exploratory studies would continue of course, but would be so designated in advance of the results being known, and excluded in advance from future proof-oriented meta-analyses. So, although a single definitive experiment is not possible, perhaps we may argue that a prospective proof-oriented meta-analysis, consisting of studies done by many different investigators in many different labs, is the closest parapsychology — or any behavioral science for that matter — can come to a definitive conclusion on the authenticity of an experimental effect.

Where does this leave you, the novitiate who is forced to wander between the neighboring camps of psychology and parapsychology? As there are arguments favoring each side you must choose the interpretation that strikes you as logically most satisfactory, or else be forced to accept that the issue of authenticity is unresolved or inherently irresolvable. In our view it is fair to say that the experimental evidence for ESP meets the criteria generally demanded for other psychological phenomena. To be sure, ESP experiments are not replicable in the sense that

anyone could guarantee to obtain a significant ESP score with the first person they happen to meet after ten o'clock next Tuesday morning. But in our experience of undergraduate laboratory exercises psychologists generally delude themselves of the level and quality of replicability entailed in many of their accepted phenomena.

In any event we remain to be convinced that authenticity demands replicability of this sort; an intrinsically weak and unstable phenomenon could be resistant to attempts to elicit it experimentally, yet still be "real" (Beloff, 1985). Again, with any conventional (intuitively acceptable) psychological phenomenon no one would dream of demanding an experiment in which fraud was utterly inconceivable. If a large number of independent investigators had obtained significant data on such a phenomenon, the existence of some null results notwithstanding, psychologists unhesitatingly would conclude that the phenomenon was not an artifact of fraud, poor experimental procedure, or the like. Unless there are to be one set of rules for intuitively acceptable data and another set for parapsychological and other "radical" data, we find ourselves persuaded that the ESP studies are indicative of a genuine phenomenon. That this phenomenon is ESP is equivocal however, as we endeavor to show in the next section.

Logical Scrutiny of the ESP Data

Even if it is conceded that there does exist a definitive experiment or that the cumulative experimental record constitutes an adequate substitute for this requirement it remains to be shown that the statistically significant data are conclusive on the matter of ESP's authenticity.

In essence ESP tests show nothing else than that some subjects, or groups of subjects, are able to guess the identity of sensorially inaccessible targets at a level beyond that expected by chance. This is consistent with the existence of a paranormal means of acquiring information but it does not prove its existence, for the following reason. Parapsychologists have not demonstrated that there was an actual passage of information from the targets to the percipient's mind. The channel for ESP, if it is appropriate to think in those terms, has not been determined and until it is, other explanations of the extra-chance or *anomalous* data are possible. For example, perhaps there is some force in nature that effects a measure of extra-chance convergence or isomorphism between two series of comparable objects (such as a series of targets and a series of calls) without any actual flow of information between the series. Perhaps our current notion of how "chance" processes should operate is invalid. The merits of such hypotheses do not warrant examination at this juncture (see Chapter 8), but the possibility of formulating a range of optional hypotheses illustrates that although the data of ESP experiments may testify to a genuine phenomenon these data might be attributable to factors other than ESP. In short, to promote ESP from a data consistent hypothesis to an authentic phenomenon, parapsychologists must also ascertain there are objective processes which mediate ESP in the ESP test situation.

This is not to say that ESP must be shown to rely on some detectable signal as its vehicle and to be registered by a specifiable organ of the body. Perhaps ESP does not work that way. Whatever its underlying processes they nevertheless must be shown to be open to measurement independently of the extra-chance performance that they enable. In this respect the authenticity of ESP must be resolved in light of some appreciation of the nature of ESP. That is, the significance of proof-oriented research depends upon results from process-oriented research. In addition to determining whether the underlying process is ESP or something more familiar to main-stream psychologists, process-oriented research could yield coherent functional relationships the pattern of which might indicate if the anomalous card-guessing data are likely to reflect ESP or instead some procedural artifact. The focus of experimental research into ESP thus shifts to process-oriented study.

Before we move on to consider ESP research findings in more detail, it is appropriate at this juncture to consider some of the methodological precautions that ought to be implemented by anyone attempting to conduct ESP research.

Methodological Precautions in ESP Research

Let us begin with a cautionary tale. The second author (CW) recently conducted a study looking into the possibility of whether one person (the *helper*) could help another distant and sensorially isolated person (the *helpee*) improve their performance at a focusing of attention task. The study had a simple design: the helper followed a randomized and counter-balanced schedule of "help" and "control" periods. During help periods, the helper thought of the helpee and tried to assist them to focus. The helpee, who was located in a sound-attenuated room, knew nothing of the schedule that the helper was following, and simply had to press a button whenever their attention wandered from the object of focus. The button-press was the dependent variable in the study. All else being equal, there should be no difference in the number of button-presses during help periods compared to control periods. If remote helping was taking place, then it was predicted there would be fewer distractions during help periods compared to control periods. During the study, the helpee was seated in the experimental room and was asked to begin the focusing task. A minute or so later, the experimenter instructed the computer to begin displaying the influence schedule to the helper. The study had 60 participants, each of whom took part in one testing session, and of course the experimenter was blind as to the influence schedule during each session. Careful pilot testing verified that the computer was correctly recording button presses along with its record of the influence schedule. A strong remote helping effect seemed to occur in this study, with participants having dramatically fewer distractions during the help periods compared to control periods. Both intrigued and somewhat concerned at the strength of this effect (the effect was not at all comparable with that obtained in other similar studies), CW designed and conducted a replication study. To cut a long story short, she found that a computer programming error had led to an artifactual excess of "control" button-presses. During the short period before the influence schedule began to be displayed to the helper, any button presses that the helpee made were labeled by the computer as "control" presses (Watt & Brady, 2002).

Why did the pilot testing fail to uncover the programming error? The pilot testing did not exactly duplicate a formal session — lab staff acted as participants in the pilot runs. They knew the design of the study, and didn't press the button during the period prior to data collection. This tale shows us that even though extensive precautions were taken — including sound proofing, double-blind design, randomized and counterbalanced influence schedule, and automated data recording — an artifact still crept in. If CW hadn't been concerned at the size of the effect in her original study, she would not have been motivated to conduct a replication and the flaw might have remained undetected.

Though we have already pointed out that there is no such thing as a definitive study, clearly in order to claim that a study provides evidence in support of the ESP hypothesis it is important to minimize possible alternative hypotheses such as sensory leakage, inadequate randomization, and errors in data recording and analysis. There is a veritable minefield of pitfalls awaiting the inexperienced or careless investigator. Any one of these could introduce into a study an effect that looks like ESP, but is not. It is beyond our scope to provide an exhaustive list of methodological precautions. The interested reader is referred to the following useful texts: *Foundations of Parapsychology* (Edge, Morris, Palmer & Rush, 1986, Chapters 4 and 5), and Milton and Wiseman's (1997) book *Guidelines for ESP Research*. Drawing largely on the latter, the following principal precautions are highlighted.

Pre-specification. Experimental details and statistical tests should be stated in advance. This is to prevent the experimenter from later ignoring data that does not support their hypothesis. Details that should be pre-specified include sample size (the number of trials in the study), which trials are pilot and which are formal, and which statistical tests will be used and whether they will be one-tailed or two-tailed.

Randomization. Statistical tests require that the targets in ESP tests are randomly selected. Different methods of randomization exist, and these differ in their adequacy. In card-guessing, for example, hand shuffling does not adequately randomize target order. Electronic random number generators (RNGS) produce a random output, but the output can be affected by external influences such as power spikes and temperature changes. Pseudo-RNG s (that use an algorithm to produce a random sequence) are deterministic and therefore not susceptible to environmental influence, but the adequacy of their randomness is not always clearly documented. Random number tables avoid many of these problems, particularly the Rand corporation tables (Rand Corporation, 1955). If these are used, it is recommended that researchers report the exact method of determining an entry point (Hyman & Honorton, 1986). The experimental write-up should include a description of who did the randomization. For instance, if the experimenter performed the target randomization then he or she might not be truly blind to the target identity during a session. Finally, tests of the random source used should be conducted and reported.

Participant selection. If selected or special subjects are used, the participant will undergo repeated testing. This might enable the participant to discover ways to circumvent experimental safeguards. Special subjects (e.g., self-professed psychics) may also have a personal investment in obtaining positive evidence of their capabilities, and therefore may have more motivation to attempt to cheat. Using large numbers of unselected subjects reduces the likelihood of participant fraud, but possibly at the cost of having weaker psi effects.

Target selection. If targets are selected prior to a study, their identity should be protected — for instance, stored in a locked filing cabinet or in a password-protected computer. Otherwise, it may be possible to ascertain the identity of a target prior to the session in which it is used.

Sensory shielding. A flaw of the early Rhine card-guessing studies was to have the sender and the receiver in the same room. Although the receiver could not see the face of the target card, it is possible that changes in the sender's posture or breathing could reveal information about the target. Ideally, the sender and receiver should be located in separate, non-adjacent and sound-insulated rooms that do not share a floor or other connection such as a ventilation system. It is vital to protect against any sensory leakage that might convey target information — before, during, and after a session. For instance, if video targets are used during a session, it is important that the sound track is not audible in the receiver's room. If static targets are used, such as art prints, they should be concealed in opaque envelopes prior to the trial. This shielding should extend to other indi-

viduals involved in the study. For example, if there are other laboratory staff who know the target identity, they should have no contact with the receiver.

Target judging. As we have seen, in free-response studies a judge is needed to identify which of the target and decoy possibilities was the actual target. The judge could be the receiver, or an independent judge who considers a number of session transcripts after the study has concluded. The judge needs to be shielded from any knowledge about the actual target identity. Here, it is important that the judge is not looking at any targets that may have been held by the sender because the sender may leave physical traces on a target they have held — such as greasy fingerprints, perfume, or creasing — that would provide a sensory cue as to the target identity. In order to protect against this possibility, it is recommended that there are two identical target sets — one for sending, and one for judging. In addition, if the receiver's impressions need to be transcribed for later judging, it is vital that the person doing the transcription is blind as to the target identity.

A general recommendation also is that someone with expertise in deliberate deception — for example, a magician — is consulted at the design stage of a study (Hansen, 1990). Magicians are not infallible, but they may be able to spot opportunities that other investigators have missed for circumventing the experimental safeguards. Many of these guidelines — particularly adequate randomization, the use of blind methods, and pre-specification of study design, hypotheses and analyses — are not only important in parapsychology but should also be implemented in other disciplines such as medical research, experimental psychology, and physics (Watt & Nagtegaal, 2004). We feel that the methodological challenges facing parapsychologists, and the scrutiny to which their research has been subjected, means that parapsychologists tend to apply higher methodological standards to their research than is the case for many mainstream researchers. This is not to say that parapsychologists' methods are particularly stringent, just that they are often more stringent than other mainstream researchers. As we shall see in the next section, careful scrutiny shows that many parapsychological studies are far from perfect and there are no grounds for complacency in this regard.

Process-Oriented Research on ESP

The remainder of this chapter is devoted to a review of experimental work designed to reveal the characteristics of processes underlying the hypothetical phenomenon of ESP. As noted in Chapter 1 this so-called process-oriented research does not assume the authenticity of ESP per se. If ESP were shown not to exist the results of process-oriented research would still apply to the nature of the anomaly in card-guessing performances whatever its identity.

The authenticity issue nevertheless has had an apparent effect upon the conduct of process-oriented research. Akers (1984) undertook a methodological analysis of experiments concerned with correlates of ESP performance in the domains of personality, attitudes, and states of consciousness. In the considerable majority of these he identified at least the opportunity for such methodological flaws as non-randomness of target sequences, sensory leakage, subject cheating, recording errors, scoring errors, statistical violations (e.g., optional stopping), and experimenter fraud.

Parapsychologists undertaking process-oriented research evidently have tended to assume the authenticity of ESP has been established at a sufficient level of certainty that precision in procedural control no longer is necessary in the investigation of the characteristics of ESP. That assumption of course, is grossly inappropriate. If we cannot be confident that a process-oriented study in fact is tapping ESP or the card-guessing anomaly, then we also cannot be confident that the data of the study reveal anything about the characteristics of that anomaly. Of course, Akers typically could not show that the potential flaws were realized and had an identifiable role in generating the statistically significant results, but his analysis does serve as a caution not to put too much faith in the findings of any single study, but rather to take greater cognizance of process-oriented data that have been replicated by various researchers.

The lower level of procedural control in process-oriented ESP research nevertheless needs to be redressed. According to Milton (1996) some experimental parapsychologists might simply be unaware of the methodological safeguards they should implement, or they may be unaware of the importance of these safeguards in the eyes of critics.

Process-Oriented Research and the Parapsychological Experimenter Effect

Before reviewing research into the nature of ESP one further methodological issue must be raised. It is known as the *parapsychological experimenter effect* and it raises the problem that if ESP and other parapsychological phenomena are authentic and can operate outside the individual's conscious control, parapsychologists may have no reliable avenue for determining the nature of ESP. That is, process-oriented research might well be futile.

As in other types of psychological research the performance of subjects in ESP experiments can be influenced by the behavior of the experimenter (e.g., see White, 1977). The experimenter's level of motivation and handling of the participants can influence the subjects' motivation and expectations which in turn may have an effect on the level of their scores. Similarly, if any of the experimenter's actions suggest to the subjects the precise nature of the experimental hypothesis they may strive to perform in a way that otherwise they would not. These sorts of biases in the procedure of human experiments are familiar to psychologists and deliberate steps can be taken to minimize their operation and influence. Methodological problems arising from the influence of the experimenter on the data generically are termed *experimenter effects*.

There is, however, an additional bias of this type that raises such special difficulties for parapsychological experimentation that it has come to be designated specifically as the *parapsychological experimenter effect*. Essentially the parapsychological experimenter effect in psi research is the partial dependence of the obtained data on the parapsychological abilities of the experimenter (Kennedy & Taddonio, 1976; Schmeidler, 1997; White, 1976). As the parapsychological experimenter effect assumes the existence of psi it is not especially problematic for the issue of the authenticity of ESP, but it does raise the question of whether it is possible for a researcher to investigate the nature of ESP.

Suppose, for example, that a researcher wanted to test the hypothesis that extraverts were better ESP scorers than introverts. It is possible that the experimenter subconsciously might use his or her own precognitive and other extrasensory abilities to locate series of targets which are more susceptible to good scoring and allocate these to the group of extraverted participants. There is indeed some empirical evidence that extrasensory abilities may be utilized nonintentionally (Palmer, 2000; Schechter, 1977). If account is taken of the possibility of psychokinesis (a paranormal influence on physical systems by the mind) it is conceivable that the experimenter subconsciously might influence even the production of target sequences for each subject in a direction favoring the hypothesis. Hence an observed relationship between extraver-

sion and ESP performance might be nothing more than an artifact of the experimenter's subconscious use of his or her own psi to generate results in accordance with this relationship.

To what extent does the parapsychological experimenter effect operate? Anecdotally it has been suggested that some *psi-conducive experimenters* (e.g., Charles Honorton and Marilyn Schlitz in America) seem to obtain a higher rate of significant results than others who only rarely obtain statistically significant ESP findings and have been labeled *psi-inhibitory experimenters* (e.g., British parapsychologists John Beloff and Susan Blackmore). This apparent disparity could be due to the familiar psychological experimenter effects (e.g., upon the subject's motivation), or to the greater psi abilities of the more successful experimenters (the parapsychological experimenter effect), or to other factors such as differences in the professionalism of experimenters and in the conservatism of their hypotheses.

Some study of the issue is being undertaken (e.g., Parker, 1977). Schmeidler and Maher (1981) and Edge and Farkash (1982) report that students rate psi-conducive experimenters' "body language" as communicating greater friendliness and flexibility than does that of psi-inhibitory experimenters, although this correlation has yet to be demonstrated for the experimenters' behavior during the conduct of psi experiments (Palmer, 1993). Again, Smith (2003) found the peer-rated psi-conduciveness of 50 experimenters was correlated with the experimenters' belief in their own PK ability and their belief that it is possible to demonstrate ESP in an experimental study. This might be taken to imply psi-conducive experimenters are more able to use their own psi ability in their studies, but it could also suggest that psi-conducive experimenters are more confident in a positive outcome and thereby can foster a similar outlook in their experimental participants. Interestingly, Smith (2003) found just over half of parapsychologists in his survey had only low to moderate agreement when rating who was psi-conducive or psi-inhibitory. There were very high levels of agreement (over 85 percent) for only 16 of the 50 researchers rated. This suggests that for the majority of researchers, it is not obvious whether they are psi-conducive or psi-inhibitory. The survey did not attempt to discover *actual* (versus perceived) experimenter success rate. Research into parapsychology's experimenter effect could benefit from having a more objective measure of psi-conduciveness, but this sizeable task has not yet been achieved. Finally, in a series of studies the second author (CW) observed that the extent of a psi-experimenter effect was *not* influenced by the experimenter's prior reputation or by the degree to which the experimenter made psi-supportive suggestions during the session, nor by the subjects' confidence, comfort, and perceptions of the experimenters' warmth and professionalism (Watt & Baker, 2002; Watt & Brady, 2002). However, in a study using multiple experimenters who had been selected on the basis of their extreme belief or disbelief in the paranormal, it was found that the strongest psi results were obtained by the believer experimenters (Watt & Ramakers, 2003). Taken together, these studies suggest that the parapsychological experimenter effect does merit more extensive investigation (Palmer, 1997a; Schmeidler, 1997).

Some procedural strategies for minimizing the influence of experimenter psi are suggested by Stanford (1981). One investigative strategy that admittedly has limited application is to analyze data from an old ESP experiment originally performed for other purposes (Beloff, 1986). However, parapsychologists' only general defense against the parapsychological experimenter effect is to conduct replications of one another's experiments. As a given result is confirmed by several independent experimenters perhaps it becomes increasingly unlikely to have been

an artifact of an isolated researcher's subconscious use of his or her own psi. Disinterested parties could be hired to conduct replications (e.g., see Schmidt, Morris & Rudolph, 1986), but we simply do not know the limits of the experimenter effect; even disinterested assistants might learn telepathically of the experimenter's expectations and use their own psi to oblige the experimenter.

With due cognizance of these methodological points we now may review the literature on the experimental investigation of the nature of ESP. Because of the incidence of potential methodological flaws in process-oriented studies (Akers, 1984), the parapsychological experimenter effect, and the inherent unreliability of ESP scores, consideration must be focused on findings that have been replicated or that at least show consistency with related data. Matters to be examined here are patterns of ESP test performance and the role of variables related to the targets, the test environment, and the people engaged in the test. The surveys by Palmer (1978a, 1982) and Schmeidler (1994a) are recommended as an invaluable resource in this regard.

ESP Performance: Patterns and Improvement

What is the character of performance in an experimental ESP task? Apart from the overall hit rate there have been observed certain consistencies in individuals' patterns of performance, particularly in restricted-choiced studies in which participants perform long runs of ESP calls. These patterns will be described briefly.

Psi Missing

Some individuals (and some groups in specific experiments) have been found to score significantly below chance in an ESP task. This is termed psi missing. It is important to note that this does not indicate a lack of ESP (or of psi in general) since the latter would be associated with nonsignificant scores. Rather, psi missing might be viewed as an expression of psi in a way that produces a result opposite to the conscious intent. The participant's guesses are wrong more often than would be expected by chance, that is, the participant shows sensitivity to the targets' identity but tends to make calls at odds with this sensitivity. Consistent missing is a variety of psi missing that entails poor scoring on one symbol due to a consistent tendency to call it another particular symbol (Cadoret & Pratt, 1950; Kelly, Kanthamani, Child & Young, 1975; Kennedy, 1979; Timm, 1969). In more recent years, with the increased use of free-response methods, less attention has been given to psi missing.

As we shall see, psi missing is thought to be in part a consequence of negative elements in mood and attitude or of aspects of personality; these elements may cause psi missers to focus their ESP inaccurately (Crandall, 1985). While observations of psi missing are much less common than psi hitting the former are sufficiently numerous to suggest there is an effect here to be explained (Rao, 1965).

Critics would be inclined to argue that the occurrence of so-called psi missing confirms their view of reported card-guessing data as statistical freaks. These below-chance scores are seen as nothing else than the negative tail of the normal distribution of random guessing scores centered on a mean of 5 hits per run. Two points count against this interpretation. First, under this "normal curve" model the incidence of psi-missing data should be the same as that of psi-hitting results, yet in fact the former is much lower than the latter. Admittedly, this might be due to an as yet unidentified tendency for researchers not to publish data that evidence psi missing. Second, the occurrence of psi missing seems to be correlated with specific psychological variables; this should not be the case if properly controlled ESP tests entail purely random guessing.

Position Effects and Decline Effects

It was noted early in experimental ESP research that performance often declines within defined units or sections of the test (Rhine, 1969; Schmeidler, 1944). Within a run (25 guesses) scoring on the first half frequently is superior to that on the second half. A subject's performance may also gradually fall over time, much to the annoyance of the parapsychologist who waited so long for a consistently good ESP performer. A similar chronological decline in effect size may be found across a set of experiments performed by the same researcher or research group. Such declines may be due to the effects of boredom and the comparative revival of interest at the beginning and the end of each unit of experimentation (Nash, 1989).

Although the occurrence of decline effects received a deal of empirical scrutiny in earlier years, the progression from a card-guessing methodology to computerized procedures has been associated with a lessening of attention to these effects (Palmer, 1978a, p. 171) or indeed, an attempt to prevent them (Schmeidler, 1994a). Nonetheless some decline effects continue to be found (e.g., Dunne, Dobyns, Jahn & Nelson, 1994; Haraldsson & Houtkooper, 1995).

The Differential Effect

The use of two contrasting conditions in an experiment may result in contrasting levels of performance under the two conditions, usually with psi hitting in one and psi missing in the other. This is the *differential effect* (Rao, 1965). Often the differential effect across contrasting conditions appears meaningful (e.g., Carpenter, 1971), but in other instances it seems quite capricious, perhaps signaling the operation of some kind of experimenter effect. Rao and Palmer (1987) cite the differential effect as one of their three examples of a replicable effect in parapsychology. Perhaps it is surprising, then, that more recently parapsychologists have paid little attention to this effect.

Displacement

In some experiments it has been found that while a subject's guesses match the intended targets only at chance level there is a significant tendency for each call to match the target before (or the target after) the intended one. That is, ESP seems to have been displaced either temporally or spatially, an effect known as *displacement*. The effect often is said to have been discovered serendipitously in 1938 by a prominent American experimental physicist and announced by him anonymously ([Abbot], 1938), but earlier references to the concept may be found in the literature (Alvarado, 1989a). Although there have been several studies of displacement (e.g., Crandall, 1985, 1994; Tart, 1978; Soal & Bateman, 1954), Milton (1988a,b) cautions that as so few such experiments are methodologically sound, any generalization on the nature of the phenomenon would be ill-founded. Braud's (1987) review of the empirical literature, however, suggests that displacement effects are linked to negative moods and attitudes, including those induced by unfavorable test situations; impatience, especially when aggravated by the experimental procedure; and distractibility or lack of absorption in the immediate goal or target. Braud suspects too that the ESP subject's curiosity to explore beyond the immediate target may be a significant factor, although this might be interpreted as a motivational element of the distractibility/absorption dimension. There is scope for further experimental study of displacement in relation to the concepts of ESP response inhibition and absorption in experiencing the target. A recent study has begun to explore these issues, working with individuals who have histories of emotional trauma, and observing both backwards and forwards displacement in relation to emotionally-charged targets (de Graaf & Houtkooper, 2004).

Variance Effects

Sometimes a statistical deviation from chance expectation may be manifest not in terms of the average score but in the variance of the data. A variety of variance effects have been reported (for a review see Carpenter, 1977, pp. 243–252), one of which is termed *clustering*. Clustering is the trend toward stringing hits together instead of having each in isolation from the rest (Don, McDonough & Warren, 1995; Kelly, 1982).

Effects in Post Hoc Analyses

The occurrence of many of the above effects cannot yet be anticipated, and in undertaking all manner of post hoc analyses to test for the presence of these various patterns there is a fair probability of turning up a significant result purely by chance; as you will recall, if data are purely random and 20 different statistical analyses are applied to them, then on average one of these analyses nevertheless will yield a "significant" result at the .05 level of probability. Such a blind search for a significant trend through continued re-analysis of performance obviously would leave the experimenter open to the charge of "data bashing" or "hypothesis saving." Indeed, citing Ockam's Razor, Alcock (2003) is critical of such "multiplication of entities." These various effects cannot be regarded as meaningful, therefore, until parapsychologists are better able to specify the conditions under which they would be expected to occur.

Improvement and the Role of Feedback

As indicated previously, often a subject's ESP scores are observed to decline. An American psychologist/parapsychologist Charles Tart (1966, 1977) has argued that chronological declines and poor performance overall are due to inadequate opportunities for learning. If at the end of a run or at the end

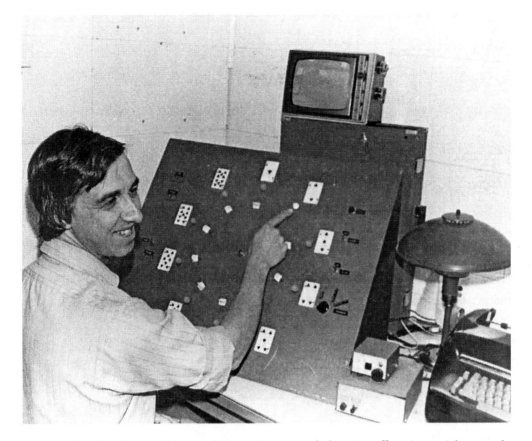

Figure 9. Charles Tart used his ten-choice trainer to study learning effects in ESP (photograph: Charles Tart).

of a session the participant is told the aggregate level of performance (as was usual in the Duke University studies, for example) this would do little to help the individual learn when she or he was "using ESP." Tart recommends that the subject be informed of the correctness of each call as it is made, thereby providing a chance for the subject to determine (even intuitively) what they were doing differently in those trials on which calls were correct. In other words, the ESP task can become one of learning, with appropriate responses being reinforced through provision of immediate feedback. Tart (1976) and others (e.g., Honorton, 1970; Sandford, 1977; Vaughan & Houck, 2000) have reported some improvement in ESP scores under trial-by-trial feedback, but the available data are inconsistent (e.g., Delanoy, Morris & Watt,

in press) and the situation appears rather more complex than a simple learning hypothesis would allow (e.g., Jackson, Franzoi & Schmeidler, 1977). If learning effects do occur they may require much longer training periods than typically studied in experiments to date.

It is still too early to say if ESP performance can be enhanced by application of learning principles but the issue is of such importance as to warrant considerable research effort.

Target Variables in ESP Performance

In tests of ESP the target may be mental as in a telepathic procedure, physical as in clairvoyance, or mental and/or physical as in GESP. Among the targets used by researchers have been the standard ESP symbols, digits, letters, words, colors, line drawings (of animals, for example), paintings, photographs, three-dimensional objects, distant environmental settings, video clips, and music. To ascertain the aspects of target material pertinent to extra-chance performance some studies have focused on various specific physical and psychological dimensions.

Physical Aspects

The size of the targets does not seem to affect performance in restricted-choice ESP tests, particularly if the participants are not informed that target size is to be manipulated. Likewise the distance of the ESP targets from the subject seems to have no clear linear effect upon performance; such effects as do occur are thought to be explicable in terms of the subject's differential perception of the task. (This should not be interpreted as showing conclusively that the extrasensory "signal" is not attenuated by distance; an ESP score is hardly a pure measure of "signal strength.") In recent studies there are indications that dynamic targets (video clips) might be more effective than static ones (e.g., photographs) (Bem & Honorton, 1994; Lantz, Luke & May, 1994). Watt (1988) suggests that the former type of target may be more cognitively salient than the latter, and dynamic targets also bear a much greater similarity to real-life ESP settings than rather sterile geometric symbols or static pictures. When it comes to laboratory testing, parapsychologists, like psychologists, have often sacrificed ecological validity in favor of pragmatic considerations.

Psychological Aspects

Psychological preferences for targets vary across subjects. Some research has found higher ESP scoring with targets that subjects favor for emotional reasons (e.g., using friends' names compared to strangers' names

as targets; Dean & Nash, 1967; see also Carpenter, 1971, and Johnson & Nordbeck, 1972).

In some circumstances, however, negatively toned targets may be more psychologically evocative than emotionally positive material. Thus, many spontaneous extrasensory experiences bear upon traumatic life events (e.g., the death of a loved one). This trend has been pursued in the laboratory context. Using video clips as targets in a dream clairvoyance experiment Sherwood, Dalton, Steinkamp and Watt (2000) observed a greater proportion of hits with emotionally negative targets than with positive or neutral video material. Delanoy's (1989a) survey of the characteristics of successful free-response targets revealed very few consistent findings and suggested that although anecdotally researchers prefer emotionally evocative targets, there is little empirical evidence to support this preference. It may be that, as Warcollier (1948/2001) suggested, individual participants differ so much in their response to different types of target that generalizations are difficult to achieve.

Other Situational Variables in ESP Performance

Facets of the testing situation other than the target material may influence the level of ESP scores. Pertinent variables here include the experimental personnel and the experimental setting and procedure.

Experimental Personnel

The possible influence of the experimenter on the outcome of the study was noted earlier specifically in relation to the parapsychological experimenter effect. There is now a substantial literature documenting the operation of experimenter effects in the broader sense (see White, 1977, for a review). For example, Honorton, Ramsey and Cabibbo

(1975) tested two groups of subjects, one with an experimenter acting in a friendly and supportive way and the other with an experimenter who affected an abrupt, formal and unfriendly manner. The former group achieved significant psi hitting and the latter, psi missing.

Apart from the experimenter (that is, the person who designs and supervises the study) and the subjects themselves, another major person involved in the experimental procedure in a telepathic or GESP study is the sender or agent. Sometimes the agent's role is taken by the experimenter (or a co-experimenter) but in many studies, particularly those concerned with the nature of the agent's contribution to the percipient's performance, other people are recruited to act as agents.

Regrettably little research has been devoted to the contribution of the agent (Carpenter, 1977, pp. 252–257; Kreitler & Kreitler, 1973). A fundamental issue here is whether the agent is essential to significant scoring (Palmer, 1978a, pp. 96–102). One means of assessing this is to compare performance under GESP conditions to that on a clairvoyance task. In some studies of this type the percipients were aware of the difference in procedure and thus the results may have been an artifact of the effect of this knowledge on the subjects' expectations and motivation (for evidence concerning the operation of this artifact see Roe, Sherwood & Holt, 2004). The better studies kept the subjects blind to the fact that some trials were clairvoyant and others permitted GESP. A number of these experiments evidence superior scoring in the GESP condition, suggesting that the agent did make some contribution, but this pattern by no means is universal (e.g., Morris, Dalton, Delanoy & Watt, 1995). One interesting recent study considered whether the sender might be acting as a PK agent in ESP studies. Roe, Holt and Simmonds (2003) compared the ESP scoring based on statements from a receiver in a ganzfeld ESP study (described in more detail in the next section) with that of an electronic random event generator (REG) placed in the vicinity of the receiver. Unbeknownst to the sender, during each session the REG randomly selected descriptive statements from a pool of 768 statements to create a 'pseudo-mentation' that was later judged against the target and decoys. The live receiver obtained a statistically significant 35 percent hit-rate, and the REG hit-rate was comparable at 32.5 percent (chance expectation was 25 percent). These findings suggest that the role of the agent is far from clear and we will return to this issue again in Chapters 6 and 8.

Experimental Setting and Procedure

The success of an ESP experiment might be affected by the procedure and the physical conditions under which the subject completes the test. A variety of procedural variables have been studied, including rate of response (e.g., Milton, 1994), spontaneity of response (Stanford, Frank, Kass & Skoll, 1989a, b), lighting levels (Bevan, 1947), background music (Eilbert & Schmeidler, 1950; Quider, 1984), and reward or punishment (e.g., Casler, 1976; McElroy & Brown, 1950). However, the procedural feature that has perhaps received most empirical attention is the participant's state of mind during the test. More specifically, researchers have examined the conduciveness to ESP of various states of consciousness. The main states employed in such studies have been hypnosis, sensory (perceptual) deprivation or the *ganzfeld*, meditation, progressive relaxation, hypnagogic states, dreaming, and drug intoxication. Except perhaps for the last of these there is substantial evidence suggesting that each of the above states of consciousness is psi conducive (see Honorton, 1977 for a review), although the research is not without its methodological flaws (Schechter, 1984; Sherwood & Roe, 2003; Stanford & Stein, 1994).

In recent years the ganzfeld procedure

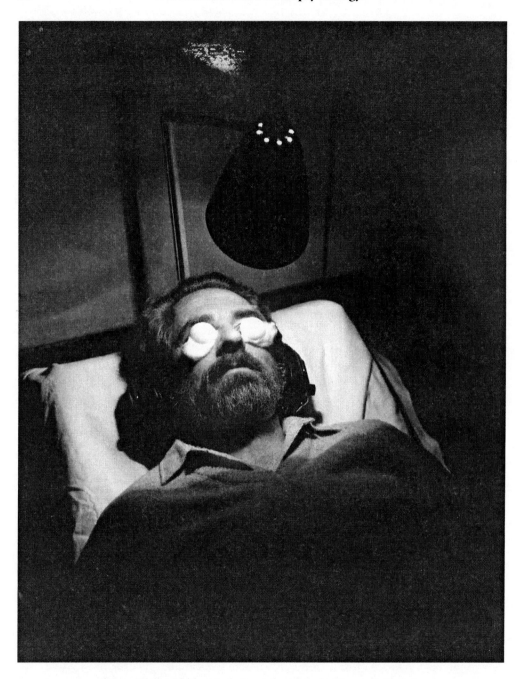

Figure 10. Ganzfeld stimulation (photograph: Harvey J. Irwin).

has been given particular attention. Under this procedure, structured visual stimulation is excluded by placing a half ping-pong ball over each eye of the receiver and directing a red light at them; structured auditory stimulation is excluded by presenting electronic noise (rather like continual soft radio static) through headphones; and the receiver lies on a mattress or in a reclining chair so as to become habituated also to a uniform level of tactile and proprioceptive stimulation. After the first half hour or so the ESP test is commenced, with the receiver simply permitting target-related imagery to come to mind and giving a verbal report of this imagery (the 'mentation'). While the receiver is immersed in the ganzfeld stimulation, in a separate room the sender views the target and attempts to telepathically communicate its contents to the receiver. After the sending period is over, the receiver judges which of four possible targets (the actual target plus three decoys) is most similar to his or her mentation. By chance the hit-rate should be 25 percent, but if the target is correctly identified more often than chance, this may provide evidence of ESP. The ganzfeld methodology has evolved along with technological developments. Original studies used static targets (e.g., postcards of art prints), later ones presented targets such as movie and cartoon excerpts on video tape, and the most recent studies have digitized these clips for computer presentation (e.g., Goulding, Westerlund, Parker & Wackermann, 2004).

In an early assessment of the literature by Honorton (1978), 23 of 42 experiments conducted in ten different laboratories had yielded significant ESP performance under ganzfeld conditions; this success rate of 55 percent was far beyond that expected by chance. Because the ganzfeld effect loomed as a highly replicable phenomenon in parapsychology it became the focus of intense critical debate (Honorton, 1985; Hyman, 1985), the result of which was that it is agreed there is an anomalous effect here to be explained, whether or not the underlying process is authentically extrasensory (Hyman & Honorton, 1986). Additionally, the debate instigated some methodological refinements to the ESP-ganzfeld research (Dalton et al., 1996). Despite these refinements some subsequent research has yielded data similar to the earlier work (Bem & Honorton, 1994; Honorton et al., 1990). Admittedly, a meta-analysis by Milton and Wiseman (1999a) did suggest that the more recent ganzfeld studies had not been successful in eliciting significant

ESP performance. Some researchers have suggested that the greater proportion of chance results in more recent studies may be attributed to these studies being designed to explore ESP process variables rather than being proof-oriented (Bem, Palmer & Broughton, 2001; Storm, 2000; Storm & Ertel, 2001).

Although some commentators (e.g., Wiseman, Smith & Kornbrot, 1996) remain skeptical of the quality of the experimental evidence for the ganzfeld effect, the accumulated data have been cited as scientific testimony not only for the ganzfeld effect but for the existence of psi itself (Bem & Honorton, 1994; Broughton, 1991). Some groups of ganzfeld studies have an effect size (about 0.62; Bem & Honorton, 1994) that is quite impressive by any standards, and further research has been designed to determine more precisely the features of the ganzfeld procedure that make it conducive to psi performance (Bem, 1996; Carpenter, 2005b; da Silva, Pilato & Hiraoka, 2003; Dalton, 1997a; Delanoy, 1989b; Parker, Persson & Haller, 2000; Stanford, 1987a; Stanford, Frank, Kass & Skoll, 1989a,b; Stanford, Kass & Cutler, 1989; Wackermann, Pütz, Büchi, Strauch & Lehmann, 2002; Wezelman & Bierman, 1997). A recent review of the debate over ganzfeld findings (Palmer, 2003) notes that there is considerable variability of results across experimenters, suggesting that work still needs to be done to establish the conditions needed to establish a replicable effect (Milton, 1999).

The reported success of these various psi-conducive states might stem from several sources. Attitudinal factors may be affected, that is, ESP performance may be enhanced by virtue of the fact that while in one of these states of consciousness the individual is more inclined to believe that ESP is possible; the state of consciousness thus may help to break down or suspend the subject's socially conditioned intellectual defenses against the notion of ESP. Other pertinent factors relate more to information-processing characteristics. These psi-conducive states generally encourage greater levels of relaxation and withdrawal of attention from the external world. Thus, ESP appears to be facilitated by minimizing concurrent sensory and proprioceptive stimulation, and by promoting absorption in the internal processes of mentation (Honorton, 1977; Irwin, 1985b; Stanford, 1992). Psi-conducive states of consciousness continue to be of major relevance to contemporary parapsychology, although Alvarado (1998) reports that the recent research focus on the identification of the key cognitive processes underlying psi has unwittingly led to a relative neglect of altered states as such.

Subject Variables in ESP Performance

Parapsychologists have given much attention to the identification of successful ESP subjects. Apart from throwing some light on the nature of ESP such research has the pragmatic justification that if investigators can select a sample of people who are relatively open to extrasensory experiences, then there is a greater chance of achieving statistically significant results in experimental work.

The major personalistic variables that have been investigated are attitudes, mood, and personality, although increasing attention is being given to physiological and cognitive variables. In the following review some reference is made for comparative purposes to the correlates of spontaneous ESP experiences.

Attitudes and Beliefs

The best known work on the contribution of attitudes to ESP performance was conducted by Gertrude Schmeidler (1952; Schmeidler & McConnell, 1958). She began by dividing ESP subjects in two groups, one group designated "sheep" comprising people who believed in the possibility of ESP and a second group of so-called "goats" who rejected that possibility. On pooling scores on ESP tests over a number of such groups Schmeidler established a trend for sheep to score above MCE and for goats to score significantly below chance level.

Separating "the sheep from the goats" in terms of ESP belief therefore also tends to differentiate two types of ESP performer. The result for sheep is interesting although perhaps not surprising: it is consistent with other cognitive research that suggests people attend to information they want to and perceive what they believe can be perceived. The result for goats is most fascinating. Not only does it confirm an effect of attitudes on the occurrence of ESP, it also reminds us of the adage that there are none so blind as those who will not see. But the fact that goats' mean ESP score is significantly below chance suggests these people are not merely directing their attention away from extrasensory information nor blocking its cognitive processing; rather they seem to be identifying ESP targets at an extra-chance level and then unwittingly choosing a different target as their response. By making more incorrect responses than expected by chance, goats seemingly use ESP in a self-defeating endeavor to support their belief that ESP does not exist. It is not that goats are intrinsically insensitive to extrasensory information, but that their attitude affects how they deal with such information.

The *sheep-goat effect* is one of the more successfully replicated relationships in experimental ESP research (Palmer, 1977), even if the overall effect size (0.03) is very small (Lawrence, 1993). Later work, however, indicates that "attitude to ESP" is more complex than one at first might think. "Do I believe in ESP?" may subsume many distinct attitudes and beliefs, including "Would I like ESP to exist?" "Do I think I have ESP?" "Do I think I will exhibit ESP in this particular experiment?" "Can I suspend my natural skepticism toward ESP for the duration of this experiment?" "Do I think this ESP experiment will work (for people in general)?" and "Do I think this experimenter can elicit my ESP?" The measurement, scope and correlates of paranormal belief currently represent a very active area of research (see Chapter 15).

That beliefs are more fundamental in the sheep-goat effect than are specific dimensions of personality and adjustment remains to be established. One experiment by Lovitts (1981), however, suggests the effect does stem from an attitude. When she disguised an ESP test as a procedure for "disproving ESP," the usual scoring pattern was reversed, that is, sheep tended to perform below chance and goats showed psi hitting. This indicates that the sheep-goat effect arises from subjects' use of ESP in conformance with their beliefs about it. Replication of Lovitts's most elegant study is called for. One constructive (i.e., not literal) replication by Wiseman and Smith (2002) was successful and confirmed the sheep-goat effect as a cognitive rather than motivational bias.

Mood

Carpenter (1991) developed a succession of mood scales, each one more refined than its predecessors in its prediction of the total score and variance of restricted-choice ESP performance. This research program indicates that ESP hitting is associated with moods in which the subject feels strong-willed or assertive, detached or dreamy, and agreeable or outgoing; ESP missing is best predicted by a socially anxious mood. These findings are consistent with earlier research suggesting that a psi-conducive state is characterized by relaxation and a belief that success in the ESP task is possible, but Carpenter's view that these features might usefully be regarded as (relatively transient) mood factors is noteworthy. Carpenter also reports that large run-score variance is associated with fearless, dull, and carefree moods, and small variance is related to moods depicted as drifting, annoyed, and task-involved. Carpenter's most recent

research has focused on free-response studies. He analyzed transcripts of over 600 ganzfeld sessions looking at participants' experiences in these sessions. He found that hitting was predicted by neutral or positive physical or emotional experiences whereas missing was associated with anxiety and unhappy adjustment to the situation (Carpenter, 2001, 2005b). Earlier researchers also found that performance on projective tests of mood were associated with ESP performance (Humphrey 1946a,b). Evidently mood does influence ESP scores.

Personality

There has been considerable empirical interest in determining the personality correlates of ESP. The two principal variables investigated in this regard are neuroticism and extraversion.

Neurotic people display either high levels of anxiety or marked reliance upon defense mechanisms directed against anxiety. On the evidence of a substantial number of studies it seems that ESP performance correlates negatively with neuroticism; that is, neurotic subjects tend to score at chance or below MCE whereas stable and well-adjusted people yield above-chance ESP scores (Palmer, 1978a, pp. 130–132). This at least is the dominant trend in studies in which the ESP test is conducted with subjects on an individual basis. When ESP tests are administered to a group of people at one time the relationship with neuroticism does not always emerge, possibly because in this situation neurotic individuals can lose themselves in the crowd and thereby their anxiety is not evoked to the same degree as in the one-to-one setting of an individual assessment of ESP.

Related to neuroticism is defensiveness. A series of studies have found a relatively weak relationship between ESP scores and the strength of general defense mechanisms as indexed by the *Defense Mechanism Test* (DMT): whereas highly defensive subjects tend to score at or below chance expectation in an ESP test, people with low defensiveness show psi hitting (Haraldsson & Houtkooper, 1992, 1995; Haraldsson & Johnson, 1979; Watt, 1994b). The replicability of this relationship has been queried recently by Haraldsson, Houtkooper, Schneider and Bäckström (2002) in terms of its apparent dependence on one specific researcher's scoring of the DMT, although an independent study using a different index of defensiveness (Watt & Morris, 1995) was successful in replicating the relationship.

Extraversion is a personality type in which the individual's interests are directed outward to the world and other people rather than inwards to thoughts and feelings (introversion). A number of studies employing this personality measure have found a positive relationship between extraversion and ESP performance, that is, extraverts typically yield higher ESP scores than introverts (Honorton et al., 1998; Palmer, 1978a, pp. 132–133; Palmer & Carpenter, 1998; Parra & Villanueva, 2003).

While research on the personality correlates of ESP performance is moderately encouraging by its level of consistency and replicability there is some question over its generalization to ESP in everyday situations. The general trend in the research is for the best ESP scorers to have superior social adjustment, that is, to be folk who readily adapt to novel social situations like a psychology experiment. Perhaps then, ESP can occur if the individual is comfortable or relaxed in the given situation, and should this be so, virtually anybody could experience ESP at some time or another, regardless of their personality. This may account for the fact that if experients of *spontaneous* ESP are surveyed there is no definitive trend for them to exhibit the distinctive personality profile thrown up by the experimental research (e.g., Haight, 1979); of course, other explanations of this discrepancy are possible. Other personality correlates of spontaneous ESP (e.g.,

proneness to psychosis, Ross & Joshi, 1992) are addressed in Chapter 15 in the context of paranormal belief.

Physiological Variables

Several studies have documented a relationship between the report of spontaneous extrasensory experiences and the presence of abnormalities in temporal lobe functions (Neppe, 1983; Palmer & Neppe, 2003; Persinger, 1984; Persinger & Makarec, 1987; Persinger & Valliant, 1985), prompting the bald declaration by Persinger (2001, p. 523), "To date there has not been a single type of paranormal experience that is not understandable in terms of known brain functions." But there is meager evidence of relationships between experimental ESP performance and electroencephalographic (EEG) measures. A high amount or density of alpha wave (8 to 13 Hz) activity during the ESP test may be a good predictor of performance, at least if the individual also reports having been in an altered state of consciousness at the time (Palmer, 1978a, pp. 123–128). Alpha waves usually are associated with a relaxed, passive state of mind. In a single-subject design, McDonough, Warren and Don (1989) found an association between hits in an ESP test and increased power in the delta (1 to 3 Hz) and theta (4 to 7 Hz) EEG bands, suggesting a facilitatory effect of low cortical arousal. In a subsequent study with a larger sample however, the same researchers found a differential effect with psi hitting associated with stronger alpha and beta (14 to 30 Hz) activity, and psi missing with delta and theta waves (McDonough, Don & Warren, 1994). More recently, these investigators observed an association between gamma (30 to 70 Hz) activity and the mere presentation of a target symbol (McDonough, Don & Warren, 2000). Evidently the study of the relationship between ESP and EEG needs to take into account distinct stages of information processing.

Some studies have examined the role of cerebral hemispheric specialization under the hypothesis that ESP is a "right hemisphere" task. There are some experimental data to support this view but one study indicates that "left hemisphere" processes also can be a vehicle for psi (Maher & Schmeidler, 1977). In these investigations the distribution of demands upon processing capacity seems to be critical (Irwin, 1979a, pp. 128–137).

More recently, student volunteers at the University of Padova in Italy took part in a clairvoyance study (Sartori, Massacessi, Martinelli & Tressoldi, 2004). While their heart rate was monitored, the students were asked to guess which of four serially-presented pictures a computer had randomly chosen as the target. Heart rate was significantly elevated during presentation of target compared to non-target pictures. Participants' conscious target guesses were at chance level. This may suggest that physiological measures could serve as more sensitive indicators of GESP than conscious guessing. We will return to this issue in Chapters 5 and 6, as there has been a great deal of recent interest in physiological indicators of psi.

Cognitive Variables

A number of studies have correlated ESP performance with scores on standard intelligence tests. Only a few of these experiments have yielded significant data, but interestingly enough the findings generally indicate a positive relationship between ESP scores and IQ (e.g., Nash & Nash, 1958). This is seemingly at odds with the trend for a disproportionately high incidence of spontaneous ESP experiences among people with a poor educational background, at least in some countries (Haraldsson, 1985; Haraldsson & Houtkooper, 1991; Palmer, 1979, p. 245). If the relationship between ESP and IQ is valid it suggests the relatively low level of reporting by people with higher education is a function not of intelligence but of some other

(e.g., social) factor. At the same time the experimental data are not only weak but typically based on very narrow samples of intelligence (e.g., university students). Further, it is notable that there are some reports of highly significant psi hitting in groups of mentally retarded children. Possibly therefore the reported IQ-ESP correlations reflect the operation of some intervening factor such as a capacity to settle into the test situation quickly.

Allied to the popular notion of intelligence is that of creativity. A few studies have sought to compare ESP scores across groups high and low in creativity, but no clear evidence of a relationship between these variables has emerged. Account may have to be taken of the nature of both the measure of creativity and the ESP task (Palmer, 1978a, p. 139); for example, creative people may find restricted-choice tasks very dull (Schmeidler, 1994a). In free-response research, several ganzfeld studies have reported high ESP scoring for participants drawn from "creative" populations (e.g., Dalton, 1997b; Morris, Cunningham, McAlpine & Taylor, 1993) . Perhaps the best-known of these studies (Schlitz & Honorton, 1992) was conducted with an exceptional population — 20 students from the renowned Juilliard School in New York City. These performing arts students obtained a significant hit-rate of 50 percent (double the chance expectation). However, Schlitz and Honorton found no correlation between ganzfeld scores and formal measures of creativity. A more recent ganzfeld study found ESP scores to correlate in the predicted direction with three out of four creativity measures, but not to a statistically significant extent (Roe, McKenzie & Ali, 2001). Nonetheless parapsychological experients reportedly rate artistic creativity as an important purpose of life (Kennedy & Kanthamani, 1995).

The memory skills of the ESP subject have received some measure of attention for theoretical reasons (see Chapter 8). The experimental literature on this topic at first sight shows little consistency but some order may be introduced if account is taken of the type of memory skills entailed. Thus there are indications that ESP scores correlate positively with long-term memory performance, that is, with the ability to retrieve information about past events. Additionally there is some suggestive evidence of a negative correlation between ESP and short-term memory or ability to keep information in mind just for a minute or so; this relationship however is evidentially rather more equivocal than that for long-term memory skills (Irwin, 1979b).

In spontaneous cases of ESP information often is mediated in the form of visual (or other mental) imagery (e.g., White, 1964a). Indeed one of the first author's own surveys (Irwin, 1979c) found that people who in a variety of "normal" psychological tasks adopted the style of a *visualizer* (as opposed to that of a *verbalizer*) tended more often to have their ESP experiences by way of imagery; verbalizers on the other hand more often had intuitive (imageless) extrasensory impressions, although the latter trend did not reach significance. It is appropriate therefore, to explore experimentally the relationship between ESP scores and performance on various measures of mental imagery (for a review see George, 1981; Irwin, 1979a, pp. 98–100; Palmer, 1978a, pp. 139–140).

There are reports of a dependence of ESP scores on spatial abilities (e.g., Freeman, 1970), but the results of research using questionnaire measures of mental imagery are rather inconsistent.

The cognitive style dimension of imagery noted by Irwin (1979c) to be pertinent to spontaneous extrasensory experience has also been investigated tangentially by Mitchell and Drewes (1982). In that experiment subjects with highly verbal interests scored more highly in a verbal ESP task than in a performance ESP task.

Dream recall is another factor of some interest. Several surveys (e.g., Alvarado &

Zingrone, 2003b; Haraldsson, Gudmundsdottir, Ragnarsson, Loftsson & Jonsson, 1977; Palmer, 1979) have obtained a positive relationship between the frequency with which people can recall their dreams and the incidence of spontaneous extrasensory experiences. This could be a reporting bias, because both dream recall and spontaneous ESP experiences are self-reported. However, laboratory ESP tasks are not susceptible to this potential bias, and two of seven experiments have found a positive correlation between dream recall and ESP scores (Honorton, 1972; Palmer, 1978a, p. 140; Palmer, 1982, p. 61). The trend is suggestive but not conclusive. Further, the basis of this correlation is far from clear. It may indicate a psychodynamic factor: people who repress their dreams might not be open to ESP. It may reflect imagery processes: people with certain sorts of skills in mental imagery may recall their dreams more often and achieve high ESP scores.

A dimension that incorporates elements of a cognitive style and other cognitive skills is that of *dissociative tendencies*. In a dissociative state, mental processes are divided or lacking integration in a situation where their integration would normally be expected (Spiegel & Cardeña, 1991). It might reasonably be expected, for example, that a person who has just undergone a major trauma could remember what had happened to them, but many trauma victims are unable to do so, at least initially; the traumatic memories may be said to have been dissociated from normal consciousness. Some people are habitually inclined to dissociate from certain aspects of their experience, that is, they have strong dissociative tendencies. Several recent studies (Pekala, Kumar & Marcano, 1995; Ross & Joshi, 1992; Zingrone & Alvarado, 1994) have found that people who report spontaneous ESP experiences tend to have dissociative tendencies. This cognitive style also has been implicated in laboratory ESP performance (Palmer, 1996). Given that dissociative tendencies can be exacerbated by childhood trauma (Irwin, 1994c) it is not surprising that ESP experients commonly present with a history of abuse during childhood (Ross & Joshi, 1992; Wright, 1999). The latter point will be pursued further in subsequent discussion of the psychological functions of paranormal belief (see Chapter 15).

Psychological dimensions closely related to dissociative processes also are reported to characterize ESP experients and superior performers in ESP experiments. One of these dimensions is hypnotic susceptibility: Pekala et al. (1995) have identified this trait as a correlate of spontaneous ESP experience, and it might also predict experimental ESP scores (Stanford & Stein, 1994). Another variable related to dissociation is *sensation seeking* (Kuley & Jacobs, 1988), that is, a propensity to take risks in the pursuit of novel experiences. Sensation seeking may well be a predictor of both spontaneous ESP experiences and of experimental ESP performance (Curtis & Wilson, 1997; Kumar, Pekala & Cummings, 1993), although further confirmatory studies certainly are called for.

Perhaps more significantly, *psychological absorption*, an empirically identified component of dissociation (Ross, Ellason & Anderson, 1995), appears to play a major role in ESP. Originally educed as the central cognitive feature of the state of hypnosis, absorption is defined formally as "a 'total' attention, involving a full commitment of available perceptual, motoric, imaginative and ideational resources to a unified representation of the attentional object" (Tellegen & Atkinson, 1974, p. 274). As noted earlier in this chapter, situations that are conducive to a state of absorption are recognized as common contexts both for spontaneous extrasensory experience and for high performance in laboratory ESP tests; these situations include hypnosis, sensory deprivation (ganzfeld), meditation, progressive relaxation, and dreaming.

A second factor of the absorption domain, the *capacity* of the individual to achieve an absorbed state, may also be related to ESP. Nadon and Kihlstrom (1987) found the occurrence of spontaneous psi experiences to correlate positively with absorption capacity. The findings of experimental research on this point, however, have been equivocal. A third element of the absorption domain is more concerned with motivation or cognitive style, and it is known as the "need for absorption"; a given person may have adequate absorption capacity and be in a conducive situation yet rarely enter an absorbed state simply because of a disinclination to do so. A recurrent desire to engage in absorbed mentation was found by Irwin (1985b) to be strongly related to the occurrence of spontaneous extrasensory experiences. Indeed, the need for absorbing experiences, dissociative tendencies, fantasy proneness, and the presence of abnormal temporal lobe activity (Neppe, 1983; Persinger, 1984; Persinger & Makarec, 1987; Persinger & Valliant, 1985) might well prove to be essentially indiscriminable as correlates of the occurrence of spontaneous extrasensory experiences. There is nevertheless a need for further research into the role of the dissociation domain in experimental ESP performance.

Several of the foregoing cognitive variables have been encompassed by a hypothesized higher-order dimension termed *transliminality*, that is, the readiness with which subconscious material can cross the threshold of consciousness in a given person (e.g., Thalbourne, 2000). At this stage research on the utility of transliminality for predicting laboratory ESP performance is in the formative stage (e.g., Del Prete & Tressoldi, in press), but the concept certainly holds promise for the conceptual analysis of extrasensory and other parapsychological experiences (see also Myers, 1903).

Demographic Variables

While demographic variables have been incorporated almost as a matter of course in the analyses of data from spontaneous case surveys they have been given rather less attention in the laboratory setting.

Gender differences have been subject to some investigation. Women tend to predominate in ESP case collections but that seems to be a consequence of willingness to contribute to these collections rather than of openness to spontaneous experiences as such. In ESP tests there is no clear trend for differential scoring between the sexes (Palmer, 1978a, pp. 144–146), although in some circumstances gender may interact with other variables to influence performance (Rao, Kanthamani & Norwood, 1983). For example, in GESP and telepathy experiments it is possible that the gender of the subject and that of the agent have some bearing on the ability of the pair to form some sort of rapport which in turn might influence scoring.

Spontaneous ESP experiences are reported more commonly by separated, divorced or widowed individuals than by married people (Haraldsson & Houtkooper, 1991; Palmer, 1979; Zingrone & Alvarado, 1997). This relationship may reflect the role of psychosocial needs rather than that of demographical characteristics as such. An effect of marital status on ESP performance in the laboratory has not been investigated.

In a few experiments age has had an effect on ESP scoring, with children tending to perform better than adolescents and adults. On the other hand, many similar studies have been unsuccessful in demonstrating age-dependent differences in scoring (Palmer, 1978a, pp. 146–148). Again, age (or at least, generation) sometimes is found to be negatively correlated with spontaneous ESP experiences (Levin, 1993; Ross & Joshi, 1992). Like gender, age may be a factor which moderates the influence of more fundamental variables.

Little systematic investigation into the pertinence of race and culture has been undertaken. Certainly the incidence of acknowledged spontaneous telepathic and clairvoyant experiences varies from one country to another, being higher in America than in Europe, for example (Haraldsson, 1985, p. 155; Haraldsson & Houtkooper, 1991), but as the available data are from Western nations the full range of cultural differences in this regard is unknown. Members of so-called primitive societies have been given ESP tests and some have performed well (Rose & Rose, 1951), but there are no data with which adequate cross-cultural comparisons may be made. This has not prevented a few parapsychologists from interpreting the occurrence of ostensibly paranormal experiences in primitive cultures as evidence for the view that ESP is a relic of a form of communication characteristic of a distant epoch of our evolution (see McClenon, 2002; Taylor, 2003) and indeed, that ESP itself may have been a major mechanism of evolution (Hardy, 1950). Freud (1933, p. 76) too regarded ESP as an atavistic phenomenon.

In the preceding sections some factors that affect experimental ESP performance have been discussed. At this point no attempt will be made to draw these findings together, if indeed that is possible. Their relevance to our conception of psi will be considered after we have looked at other aspects of psi.

Nevertheless, it already should be clear that on some points there is a reasonable degree of consistency and coherence in the process-oriented experimental data. A number of relationships have been replicated by independent researchers in disparate contexts, and some observed relationships are compatible with those on allied matters. To the extent that there are consistencies in the data on the nature of ESP it might be argued that there is further support for the authenticity of ESP (Edge et al., 1986, p. 185). Surely if the results of ESP tests were fortuitous or artifactual there would be rather less consistency across experiments linking ESP performance to psychological variables.

While there is some merit in this view it should not be given undue weight. First, the observed level of consistency may be indicative that the extra-chance performance in ESP tests is a real phenomenon, but for reasons outlined earlier this does not demonstrate the authenticity of ESP as opposed to alternative explanations of the anomaly. Second, the determined skeptic may argue that the operation of artifacts in ESP experiments (unintentional sensory cues, subject fraud, etc.) is correlated with various psychological variables and that it is actually these correlations that process-oriented experiments have revealed. For example, ESP scores may be related to extraversion because extraverts are more inclined than introverts to seek means of cheating. This line of argument certainly should not be accepted without subjecting the specific claims to further empirical scrutiny. But the very fact that these arguments can be mounted is sufficient to indicate that the coherence of process-oriented data is, at best, merely supportive of the ESP hypothesis.

Notwithstanding these various grounds for caution, the available data do offer some encouragement to researchers who believe that the concept of ESP is viable, and certainly they provide foundations for theory building.

KEY TERMS AND CONCEPTS

Charles Richet
J. B. Rhine
Duke University
Zener cards/ESP cards
open/closed decks
restricted-choice tests
free-response tests
target
selected/unselected subjects
call
run
hits
misses
critical ratio
mean chance expectation (MCE)
Extra-Sensory Perception
target pool
mentation
judging period
decoy targets
replication
meta-analysis
the definitive experiment
the cumulative record
experimenter effects
the parapsychological experimenter effect
nonintentional psi
psi hitting
psi missing
consistent missing
position effects

differential effect
displacement
ESP focusing
response bias
variance effects
clustering
multiple-aspect targets
psi-conducive states
hypnosis
sensory/perceptual deprivation
ganzfeld
meditation
progressive relaxation
hypnagogic states
dreams
drug intoxication
the sheep-goat effect
Defense Mechanism Test
graphic expansiveness
neuroticism
extraversion
alpha activity
hemispheric specialization
intelligence/scholastic ability
memory skills
imagery skills
visualizer/verbalizer
cognitive style
dissociative tendencies
absorption
demographic factors

STUDY QUESTIONS

1. The work of Charles Richet generally is not as widely acknowledged as it deserves to be. In what respects was it significant?

2. What were J. B. Rhine's principal contributions to parapsychology as a scientific discipline?

3. Why did J. B. Rhine devise the ESP cards?

4. What are the elements of an adequate experimental test of the ESP hypothesis?

5. Discuss the proposition, "ESP is defined ultimately as a statistical anomaly."

6. What criticisms were leveled at the Duke University research into ESP, and how were these taken into account in subsequent research?

7. On what grounds could ESP be shown to be authentic? Has it been authenticated? If so, how? If not, why not?

8. What is the parapsychological experimenter effect in parapsychology, and why is it of major concern?

9. Akers (1984) notes a range of potential flaws in recent process-oriented ESP experiments. Do such studies really have to be as tightly controlled as proof-oriented experiments?

10. Does the notion of a below-chance score in an ESP test make sense? Do the correlates of psi missing help in any way to bring credibility to the notion?

11. Some ESP experiments have incorporated erotic pictures in the target material without informing the participants. Consider the ethical aspects of this procedure.

12. The physical characteristics of targets seem to have scant impact upon ESP scores. Can we therefore discount the idea that ESP is mediated by some unknown form of physical (e.g., electromagnetic) radiation?

13. In light of the findings of process-oriented research, how would you best seek to elicit high scores from subjects in a controlled ESP experiment?

14. As an exercise, set up a simple ganzfeld situation in your own home and experience its (nonparapsychological) effects for about an hour.

15. Under what circumstances have you encountered a spontaneous extrasensory experience? Do these circumstances lend support to the experimental research on psi-conducive states?

16. Drawing on your own experience, what sorts of people do you imagine "sheep" to be? What do you think "goats" are like? How might these differences between sheep and goats actually produce differential performance on ESP tests?

17. Construct a psychological profile of people who perform well in ESP tests. To what extent does this accord with your own impression of people who report spontaneous extrasensory experiences?

18. Is the evidence for the authenticity of ESP strengthened by the coherence of the functional relationships identified in process-oriented ESP research?

5

EXTRASENSORY PERCEPTION AND TIME

Many psychologists reject the notion of ESP on the grounds that if ESP existed it would be at odds with known scientific principles. According to Alcock (1981, p. 191), for example, "if psi exists, science as we know it cannot." As far as contemporaneous ESP is concerned such a view is dubious. Although contemporaneous ESP apparently involves information transfer that cannot be attributed to the operation of the known human senses, by no means is it clear that this is contrary to any scientific principle. That environmental information must come through the senses is a tacit assumption, not a proven principle. Thus contemporaneous ESP, if it exists, could be accommodated by *extending* the present philosophical framework of behavioral science; there is no established principle that would have to be revised or discounted. The conflict between contemporaneous ESP and accepted laws of psychology and physics has been grossly exaggerated by critics for rhetorical purposes, according to Collins and Pinch (1982).

Where ESP seems to relate to events displaced in time the compatibility of ESP and science nevertheless becomes rather strained, and for this reason the issue of ESP and time warrants discussion in its own right. It is to the temporal properties of ESP that we now turn.

Temporal Displacement

In Chapter 4 mention was made of displacement effects. A little more detail on *temporal* displacement is appropriate at this point.

In 1939 an English parapsychologist Whately Carington (1940, 1945) began a series of free-response ESP studies using simple line drawings as targets. The typical procedure of these investigations was as follows. The object drawn as the ESP target for a given night was chosen at random from a dictionary using one of two methods. Carington would randomly insert the blade of a pocketknife into his copy of Webster's dictionary and open it at that page; or he selected a three-digit number from a table of random numbers and interpreted this as a page number in his dictionary. On that particular page Carington located the first word that corresponded to an item which could be drawn, and either he or his wife then drew the item. This became the target picture for the night. The drawing was pinned to Carington's study bookcase from 7 P.M. to 9:30 A.M. the next morning; usually some security measures were observed. This procedure was followed on ten nights, with a different target drawing for each night. About 250 unselected people participated in the investigation. Each night in their own homes they would make a sketch of what they thought to be the target picture for that night, adding a word that named the depicted object.

The number of words counted as hits was determined simply as the frequency of participants who labeled their drawing with the very word Carington had selected from the dictionary. But because some drawable objects (e.g., "cat") are intrinsically more likely to come to a subject's mind than others (e.g., "dolphin") the number of hits on the target night was compared to the incidence of this word on the nights for which it was not the target. That is, Carington operationalized the occurrence of telepathy in terms of a higher incidence of calls of the target word on the night he had selected it than on other nights of the series. A similar procedure was used to rate the presence of hits in the participants' drawings. These were assessed by an independent panel of people who judged each drawing against each target, scoring them 1 point if they unmistakably portrayed the same thing, 0 points if they did not, and ½ point if the correspondence was less clear cut. The panel was not aware of the date on which each target was used and hence the judges were making blind ratings of the correspondence between subjects' drawings and the targets.

The experiment indicated the presence of ESP (or extra-chance guessing). For example, if the target for Night 6 was "pony," the number of people who drew a pony (or horse, etc.) and labeled it "pony" was distinctly higher on Night 6 than that for any other night of the experiment. More interestingly in the present context, the incidence of (say) "pony" drawings on the other nights of the investigation was not uniformly low. Indeed for the nights immediately before and after the night for a given target there were relatively higher frequencies of sketches matching that target than at other stages of the series; these were arranged roughly in a

step-like fashion rising to a maximum on the night of the given target and then falling in a similar (but asymmetrical) manner. The effects of an ESP "stimulus" evidently are not confined to the period in which the target is presented but indeed seem to reach into the future and into the past to some degree. Further experimental work on these bidirectional displacements was undertaken with card guessing tests in the 1930s.

Research into the bases of temporal displacement was reviewed in Chapter 4. In the present context the very occurrence of displacement is the crucial point, for the reason that it suggests a temporal dispersion of the extrasensory "signal" into the future and into the past. Additional investigation of this putative phenomenon has tended to focus either on ESP of past events (*retrocognition*) or on ESP of future events (*precognition*). Each of these facets therefore will be discussed separately.

Retrocognition

Retrocognition literally means "backward knowing" and is defined as direct paranormal access to events that occurred in the past. In this sense retrocognition conceptually is the obverse face of precognition.

An ostensible instance of retrocognition is the so-called Dieppe Raid case (Hastings, 1969; Lambert & Gay, 1952). In August 1951 two English women were holidaying in Puys, France (two miles east of Dieppe). A little after 4 A.M. one night both women were awoken by the sounds of heavy artillery fire, divebombing aircraft, and people's cries. This continued for nearly an hour and occurred twice more during the early hours of morning. The sounds are said to have been similar to those which would have been audible at Puys during an air and sea raid on Dieppe in 1942. Other putative examples of retrocognition are described by Ellwood (1971), MacKenzie (1997), and Dobinson (1998).

The frequency of retrocognitive experiences evidently is very low (Rhine, 1981, p. 53). When Celia Green (1960) analyzed a collection of spontaneous case reports accumulated by the SPR she found 166 were contemporaneous, 108 precognitive, and only 15 retrocognitive. Similarly, in a tally of extrasensory dreams that had been cited in the publications of the ASPR only 4 of 372 were retrocognitive (Stevenson, 1963, p. 182).

The rarity of retrocognitive case reports could be due to several factors (Stevenson, 1963, p. 201). First, if the interval between the retrocognized event and the experience is short the percipient may be inclined to report it as a contemporaneous experience. Second, some experiences which might be construed as retrocognitive may be assigned to other taxonomic categories such as apparitions, reincarnation memories, psychometry, and spirit possession. If the retrocognized event occurred within living memory it is possible too that the experience will be construed as a contemporaneous telepathic impression (Sabine, 1950, p. 43). Third, and probably most important, both experients and researchers may discount experiences occurring after the event because of the possibility of obtaining the information by normal means. For example, the individual may have read of the event or seen a television program on it and have forgotten having done so; information about the event later may be revived from memory as a basis for an imaginal experience with a retrocognitive quality. People alert to the possibility of *cryptomnesia* therefore might not be inclined to make (or in the researcher's case, accept) a report of a retrocognitive experience.

Little effort has been made to subject collections of retrocognitive experiences to content analysis, presumably because the number of such cases in any one collection was too small to justify such analysis. Forman (1978) proposes that retrocognitive experiences begin and end very abruptly, have a dream-like character, focus on some sensory modalities at the exclusion of others, and are specific to a particular place or object. According to MacKenzie (1997) these experiences are associated with specific places (p. 128) and they occur during a trancelike state that is commonly characterized by "feelings of depression, eeriness and a marked sense of silence" (p. 63). Additionally, it is said the thematic content of these experiences often relates to battles of long ago (Ellwood, 1971; Murphy, 1967, p. 4). The evidence for such generalizations nevertheless is limited.

There have been no attempts to investigate retrocognition experimentally, for the simple reason that no suitable research technique has yet been devised and indeed may well be impossible to devise. The problem in this regard is that if performance in a retrocognition task is to be scored there must be a record of the past event against which to check the subject's call, but if such a record exists it would permit the possibility of contemporaneous ESP. That is, the subject may have paranormal access not to the past event but to the existing record of it. While retrocognition is regarded conceptually by some parapsychologists as a feasible form of ESP it does not appear to be one that is open to experimental investigation.

Precognition

Many inspirations of prophets and soothsayers throughout recorded history have a precognitive tone. The previously cited pharaoh's dream of the seven fat kine and the seven lean kine is of this type. Indeed in many cultures omens, oracles, and premonitory visions were accorded great significance (Zohar, 1982, Ch. 1). Precognition therefore is not a peculiarly modern belief.

The Phenomenology of Precognitive Experience

As with other extrasensory experiences spontaneous case collections have been used to ascertain the phenomenological features of precognitive experience.

You will recall the collections by Eleanor Sidgwick (1888–1889) and Saltmarsh (1934) comprised precognitive cases, and other more general case collections such as that compiled by Louisa Rhine have been utilized in comparing precognitive with contemporaneous extrasensory experiences.

Table 1
Form of Precognitive and Contemporaneous ESP Experiences
(*after Rhine, 1954*)

| | *Temporal Category* | |
FORM	*Precognitive*	*Contemporaneous*
Intuitive	19%	35%
Hallucinatory	6%	25%
Realistic dream	60%	19%
Unrealistic dream	15%	21%
TOTAL	100%	100%

Although spontaneous precognitive experiences can take any of the forms shown by contemporaneous extrasensory experiences there is a relatively high incidence of dreams in precognitive case collections (see Table 1). In L. E. Rhine's (1954) American sample 75 percent of precognitive cases were dreams. The corresponding figure in Sannwald's (1963) Western European collection is 60 percent and that in a British study by Orme (1974), 74 percent; similar data are reported by Drewes (2002), Green (1960), Saltmarsh (1934), Sidgwick (1888–1889), and Steinkamp (2000). Most of these are realistic dreams, that is, the precognized event is represented in a fairly literal way. On the other hand, it is possible that unrealistic or symbolic dreams are not recognized for what they are and thus their reported incidence is depressed.

Why might dreams predominate in collections of precognitive cases? Louisa Rhine suggested that the thought of obtaining information about a future event might be so philosophically distasteful to people that such information is permitted to enter conscious-ness only when their intellectual defenses are down, as during a dream. Other explanations, of course, are possible. People's alleged "philosophical distaste" for the concept of precognition might affect their willingness to report such experiences of their own; relatively speaking, dreams might then be more readily acknowledged because if need be, they can hastily be qualified as being mere irrational fantasy and thereby not necessarily indicative of any belief on the part of the experient.

Another major characteristic of precognitive experiences noted by Rhine was that typically the apparent setting of the experience was in the present, not in the future. Thus in the precognitive dream the dreamer perceived the events to be occurring at that time; rarely was there any intrinsic indication that they related to the future. Again, this might reflect the individual's unease with the idea of seeing into the future, although Louisa Rhine suggests that as time is not a concrete thing it can not readily be represented in the form of imagery, that is, the temporal setting generally cannot be conveyed in a dream.

Two British analyses, one by Green (1960) and the other by Orme (1974), have examined the length of time between the precognitive experience and the actual occurrence of the event to which the experience related. In both studies the observed incidence of cases fell as the interval increased. For about half of all cases the precognized event had occurred within two days of the experience, and only about 20 percent of experiences were fulfilled after an interval exceeding one month. A similar trend is reported by Sondow (1988) in her analysis of her own precognitive dreams. These results are consistent with the suggestion of the ESP displacement studies, that the ESP "signal" becomes weaker with time. On the other hand, the data might be due simply to the tendency to forget precognitive experiences that concern events far into the future; admittedly this is a less cogent argument in the case of Sondow's (1988) report, because she recorded her dreams each day and thereby avoided the problem of memory lapses.

Precognitive experiences, like other types of ESP, tend to concern incidents which are emotionally significant to the percipient. In premonitions however, the content often tends to be tragic (e.g., Saltmarsh, 1934; Sannwald, 1963; Schouten, 1982; Steinkamp, 2000), although there may be cultural variations in this trend (Virtanen, 1977/1990) and in addition, it might not be so much the case for the precognitive experiences of children (Drewes, 2002). The death of a close friend or relative is a common theme, as is the occurrence of natural disasters. The sinking of the *Titanic*, the assassination of President Kennedy, and the 1966 Aberfan disaster have been productive areas of research for collectors of precognitive experiences (Barker, 1967; Stevenson, 1960). An intensive phenomenological study by Stowell (1997a,b) identified four types of precognitive dream that were discriminable in terms of the significance of their content for the experient. One type provided information about nontraumatic situations; a second type seemingly brought guidance to the dreamer; another related to negative situations about which it evidently was impossible for the experient to take action; and the final type provided information about situations in which intervention was possible.

Major conceptual problems are raised by the possibility of intervening in precognitive cases (for an analysis of these see Steinkamp, 1997; Struckmeyer, 1970). For example, if someone foresees a particular event and takes effective steps to avoid it the precognized event will not have taken place; how then could the case be regarded as knowledge of a future event?

L. E. Rhine (1955) first examined her case file to see if successful intervention ever was reported. In many cases intervention was not attempted, for a variety of reasons: the

information was too unspecific, was not believed, or was not understood for what it was, or the events were beyond the individual's control or too far developed to be prevented. Some experients evidently did try to intervene in the course of events but were not successful. In other cases the precognized event allegedly was successfully avoided or prevented, but many of these Louisa Rhine felt to be evidentially dubious: that the precognized event would have occurred had the subject not taken the steps she/he did was questionable. In Louisa Rhine's assessment there nevertheless were nine instances in which the event not only was avoided or prevented but seemed bound to have occurred had not the percipient intervened. Similar cases are reported by Drewes (2002) and Steinkamp (2000).

As a possible example of intervention American parapsychologist W. E. Cox (1956) cites data showing that on days on which trains are involved in an accident the level of passenger traffic is relatively low. Cox suggests that people subconsciously precognize the occurrence of train accidents and avoid traveling by train on those days. Again it is possible that railway accidents and low passenger traffic both tend to occur when weather conditions are bad.

If both precognition and intervention are authentic phenomena then on the basis of Rhine's data it would seem that the future is not immutable as some people assume. Louisa Rhine also argues from her analysis that information is not sent from the future back to the percipient but rather (as in other sorts of extrasensory experiences) the percipient is the active element in the situation, paranormally reaching into the future.

Few studies appear to have addressed the personality correlates of reporting precognitive experiences. Rattet and Bursik (2001) found precognitive experients are more extraverted than nonexperients. Hearne (1984) reports experients to be more neurotic than the general population. He did not, however, recruit an appropriate control group of nonexperients. Also Hearne's experients obtained high scores on the personality inventory's "lie scale," suggesting the data are of uncertain reliability.

Spontaneous precognitive cases exhibit much of the same evidential problems as other types of ESP. Nevertheless, because precognized events relate to the future it is possible to investigate their accuracy in prediction. To this end several "premonition bureaus" have been established, including some on the World-Wide Web. People who have a premonition are invited to register it with one of the bureaus before the precognized event takes place. Unfortunately for the proponents of the concept of precognition, the percentage of registered premonitions that prove correct is very low (Shadowitz & Walsh, 1976, p. 117).

Experimental Investigation of Precognition

J. B. Rhine began experimental investigation of precognitive ESP in 1933, although his accumulated results were not published until 1938 (Rhine, 1938). In one of these studies Rhine asked the gifted subject Hubert Pearce to endeavor to predict the order in which ESP targets would appear in a deck that was to be shuffled and cut *after* the calls were recorded. In a series of 212 runs an average of 6.3 hits per run was obtained. A second series of 223 runs yielded an average of 7.1 hits per run. Another experiment utilizing a group of subjects produced a mean of only 5.14, but this was associated with a high level of statistical significance for the total of 113,075 trials completed by the participants. These results are consistent with the idea that experimental subjects can foresee by paranormal means the order of a subsequently generated set of targets.

In J. B. Rhine's early studies it was the experimenter's practice to shuffle the ESP deck without knowledge of the order of the subject's guesses, thereby avoiding the potential criticism of having biased the shuffle. Rhine realized, however, it might be possible for the experimenter unconsciously to use his or her own ESP to get information on the subject's set of calls and to bias the shuffle accordingly. Experiments on the so-called "psychic shuffle" added support to this speculation (Rhine, Smith & Woodruff, 1938). When the Duke laboratory staff constructed mechanical shufflers Rhine (1941) conducted a further investigation of precognition and again obtained supportive data, although on this occasion only at the 0.03 level of significance. With the development of computerized random event generators (REGs) and other instrumented ESP tests significant data in precognition tasks have continued to be reported in the literature (e.g., Schmidt, 1969).

Some process-oriented experimental research has been directed to the nature of precognitive ESP but the quantity of data is very limited in comparison to that for ESP in general. One of the few distinctive trends to emerge is for good precognition performers to be field dependent, that is, to be inclined not to draw too strong a boundary between elements of the perceptual field. There are, however, only a few studies documenting this effect (e.g., Nash & Nash, 1968). Another single investigation suggests that females' precognition scores are on average lower than their clairvoyance scores whereas for males the trend is in the opposite direction (Zenhausern, Stanford & Esposito, 1977). The basis of such an effect, if authentic, is not known (see also Steinkamp et al., 1998). Such other data as are available generally indicate that precognitive test performance has much the same characteristics as contemporaneous ESP, although some studies (e.g., Thalbourne, 1996) do not reveal anything distinctive about the psychological profile of high scorers in precognition experiments.

A few studies have attempted to investigate the tendency in spontaneous case collections for reports of precognition of more distant events to be relatively infrequent. Hutchinson (1940) obtained significantly lower precognition scores on runs for which the targets were selected ten days later than for runs for which target selection took place on the day after the test. This is consistent with the idea that the ESP "signal" becomes weaker in time. On the other hand the participants in this study knew which runs were to be checked after one day and which after ten days, so the data merely may have reflected the subjects' expectations. Also the tests for the ten-day condition usually were conducted last and hence the poorer scores in this condition may be nothing more than a within-session decline effect (Palmer, 1978a, p. 81). Another experiment by Hutchinson with these factors controlled was not successful.

When considered individually, three other card-guessing experiments (Palmer, 1978a, p. 81) and later studies with REGs (Jahn & Dunne, 1987) failed to find any significant negative correlation between precognition scores and the interval between testing and target selection. Honorton and Ferrari's (1989) meta-analysis of precognition experiments published between 1935 and 1987 did reveal a negative correlation, but with the considerable diversity of procedures used in the analyzed pool of studies it is not clear that this finding is anything more than a subtle procedural artifact.

Although further investigation would be justified it does seem likely that people report few spontaneous precognitions of events set far into the future largely because the experience often is forgotten by the time the event takes place. The attentuating temporal displacement effects reported by Carington may therefore have been more a consequence of the nature of experients' information processing mechanisms (particularly in relation to response inhibition or temporal "focusing" on the target) than an indication of the temporal attenuation of an ESP "signal."

Sensing the Future

Some recent research has raised the possibility that precognition may occur even without the person's conscious awareness. At first glance the notion of "precognition without cognition" may strike you as nonsensical, but in Chapter 4 mention was made of the possibility of nonintentional ESP: in this context a person apparently may react to a sensorially inaccessible event without any associated conscious thoughts about that event. Might some instances of precognition also be nonintentional? Research bearing on this question actually arose from an endeavor by some parapsychologists to explore whether unconscious physiological responses might provide more "pure" or sensitive indicators of the operation of psi (both ESP and PK) than conscious indicators such as verbal reports that may be contaminated by cognitive overlay or "noise." The physiological responses that have been investigated in this area include heart rate and electrodermal activity (EDA, previously known as galvanic skin response). EDA is a measure of the electrical conductance of the skin, which increases when our autonomic nervous system becomes aroused or activated and our skin releases sweat, and decreases when we are less aroused and our skin is drier. For instance, the Italian study we described in Chapter 4 (Sartori, Massacessi, Martinelli & Tressoldi, 2004) included a precognition experiment. While their heart rate was measured, participants were shown a series of pictures and were asked to guess which picture would shortly be chosen by the computer as the target. Heart rate was significantly higher for the target compared to the non-target pictures, even though conscious guessing was at chance. This study appears to indicate that the participants' physiology was able to discriminate future targets from non-targets.

The Italian study is unusual in that it only used "calm" pictures as targets. More commonly, research in this area has sought to compare physiological activity in the few seconds prior to the presentation of randomly-selected neutral stimuli with that for strongly arousing stimuli such as photographs depicting violence, bodily mutilation, or scenes of a sexual nature (Radin, 1997b, 2004), audio startle stimuli (Spottiswoode & May, 2003), and even mild electric shocks (Vassy, 2004). Because the dependent measure is physiological rather than cognitive, these have been described as "presentiment" or "prestimulus response" rather than precognition studies. Despite this terminological difference, however, this paradigm is asking whether individuals have some kind of awareness of a future event. Taking an evolutionary perspective, it might be adaptive for an organism to evolve a mechanism for physiological preparedness for an imminent dangerous or threatening event.

So what have these presentiment studies found? Radin (2004) describes a series of four double-blind experiments in which a total of 133 volunteers in the USA and Jamaica participated in over 4,500 trials where their EDA was measured prior to the presentation of randomly selected emotional and calm photos. Two of the studies were independently significant, two showed a positive but non-significant effect, and the four combined studies demonstrated a small but statistically significant effect (p = .0005) in which participants' EDA was higher prior to presentation of emotional photos than of calm photos. Other researchers have replicated this effect using similar methods (e.g., Bierman & Radin, 1997; Spottiswoode & May, 2003; Vassy, 2004). Some researchers have used simulations to suggest that the results in these studies could be methodological artifacts, due the participants having an hypothesised tendency to have gradually increasing EDA in cases where, not having been exposed to an emotional stimulus for some time, they begin to anticipate that the next stimulus will be a distressing one (Dalkvist, Westerlund & Bierman, 2002; Wackermann,

2002). Over the course of a study, all else being equal, this could lead to higher average EDA prior to emotional compared to neutral stimuli. However, both Spottiswoode and May (2003) and Radin (2004) report that in additional analyses they could find no evidence for such an artifact in their data, so although the hypothesised process remains theoretically possible, research to date has failed to find support for the argument that apparent presentiment effects are due to an expectation bias.

This emerging research paradigm seems to provide some early indications that individuals can unconsciously sense imminent future events. As with any developing methodology, researchers must now proceed to further independent replication and exploration of relevant parameters in order to make progress in understanding apparent presentiment effects.

Theoretical Approaches to Precognition

Theories to account for psi phenomena in general will be surveyed in Chapter 8, but precognition warrants brief individual consideration for one fundamental reason: it is not merely that the hypothetical processes underlying precognitive experience are unrecognized in conventional science, but that these processes seem to fly in the face of one of science's central tenets. The apparent paradox in the concept of precognition is that it implies access to information which does not exist. In other words it implies a backward flow of information and this is contrary to the principle of causation, that a cause must precede its effect. Broadly speaking there have been four main approaches to the resolution of this paradox.

Some theorists maintain the paradox springs from the inadequacy of our commonsense view of the world or more precisely, the "naive realism prevalent before the development of modern physics" (Targ &

Puthoff, 1978, p. 169). That the latter is inadequate is demonstrated, they argue, by recent developments in quantum physics which suggest for example, the possibility of a subatomic particle with the property of moving backwards in time. Other parapsychologists reject the notion that the laws of subatomic physics are applicable to aspects of human behavior but nevertheless maintain there is no logical objection to backward causation as would be entailed in the flow of information from the future to the present (e.g., Beloff, 1977a). One of the difficulties with this view concerns the issue of intervention. Suppose that after precognizing a particular event the experient takes steps to prevent that event happening. If these steps are successful the precognized event does not exist and hence there is nothing from which information can flow back to an earlier time. Under the above approach to precognition, therefore, intervention should not be possible. This in turn has implications for the concept of free will (Murphy, 1967).

A few researchers have sought to accommodate the notion of precognition by proposing more complex theories of time (e.g., Dunne, 1927). Our commonsense impression of time is purely linear: at a given moment we are at one point on a dimension linking the past, the present, and the future. It has been proposed that it is possible to move above this linear channel to another temporal plane where points in the past and in the future may be observed. The means of subjecting this and other more sophisticated theories of time (see Stokes, 1987, pp. 102–107) to empirical testing is by no means obvious.

Another possibility is that precognitive experiences merely entail unconscious inferences from extrasensory perception of factors that exist in the *present* (Morris, 1980, p. 22; Mundle, 1964). For example, a premonition of the death of a loved one may be due to extrasensory awareness of such things as that person's present state of health, the unsafe

condition of their car, and so on. This idea readily accommodates the occurrence of intervention. On the other hand, to account for the significant results in laboratory studies of precognition it would be necessary under this approach to argue that subjects are able to obtain extrasensorially some information about the experimenter or the test equipment that helps them to guess (at an extra-chance level) how the targets will be ordered. What such information might comprise is not clear but proponents of this approach argue that assumptions of this nature are far less contentious than those necessitated by a literal awareness of the future. This depiction of precognition is associated with a view of psi known formally as the *intuitive data sorting* hypothesis (recently formulated in a more formal way as the *decision augmentation theory;* May, Utts & Spottiswoode, 1995). Experimental work on this approach has been undertaken (Dobyns, 1996, 2000; May et al., 1995; Radin, 1988; Vassy, 1990), but some recent findings (e.g., Dobyns, 2000) do not favor the hypothesis. Steinkamp, Milton and Morris (1998) also have argued that if precognition arises from real-time ESP followed by an extrapolation to the future, clairvoyance studies should generally show a higher effect size than precognition studies because the latter would entail additional cognitive demands during the stage of extrapolation. The authors' comparative meta-analysis of clairvoyance and precognition experiments failed to substantiate this prediction, prompting them to cast doubt on this model of precognition.

A further option is to reverse the ostensible causal relationship and argue that the precognitive experience in some normal or paranormal way causes the subsequent event. Thus the experience might be communicated extrasensorially to other people who unwittingly act on this information to bring about the incident. Indeed if the possibility of psychokinesis is taken into consideration, perhaps the experient actually brings about the precognized event by psychokinetic means (Braude, 1986; Eisenbud, 1982). In response to this approach it must be said that while there may be something in the notion of a self-fulfilling prophecy there are some precognized incidents that it is hard to envisage being instigated by the experient whether by normal or paranormal means. Is it reasonable to suppose that a person who has a premonition about a natural disaster (earthquake, flood, etc.) or about the commencement of World War III can then actually cause these events? Braude (1986) nevertheless deems such a possibility to be more acceptable conceptually than the notion of backward causation. However, the recent upsurge of presentiment studies have been interpreted as providing evidence of retrocausal effects in humans (e.g., May, Paulinyi & Vassy, 2005) and Radin, Nelson, Dobyns and Houtkooper (2006) urge us to keep an open mind on this possibility.

These are just some of the attempts to resolve the paradox of precognition. Another approach of course, is to deny the existence of precognition and to attribute the reported data to the operation of artifactual factors. For example, extra-chance scores in precognition tests might reflect the experimenter effect: experimenters may use their own psi abilities to produce target series that significantly correspond to the earlier calls of their subjects.

Certainly of all proposed forms of psi,

precognition is the one that parapsychologists themselves feel most uneasy about, according to available survey data (Schmeidler, 1971; R. L. Van de Castle, personal communication, February 2, 1988). In part this lack of conviction stems from the data themselves: among ESP experiments as a whole those on precognition have yielded the results closest to MCE and regardless of the significance level, precognition data thereby are the least convincing of a genuine paranormal means of access to information. Additionally, there is the paradoxical nature of the underlying concept. This is enunciated in an extreme form by McMullen (1978) who asserts the notion of precognition is incoherent because its definition is internally inconsistent: "the self-contradiction is the claim that something which does not exist can be directly known" (p. 19). The resolution of this issue nevertheless will come not through logical analysis but by way of empirical investigation.

Contemporaneous ESP, precognition and retrocognition can be described as the *receptive* aspect of psi in that they seemingly entail paranormal reception of information from the environment. Before examining theories of this process we will look at the other side of psi, namely the *expressive* aspect in which the mind ostensibly influences the structure of a physical system in the environment. The general topic of psychokinesis is the subject of the next chapter.

KEY TERMS AND CONCEPTS

temporal displacement
Carington
retrocognition
Dieppe Raid case
precognition
intervention

premonition bureaus
psychic shuffle
intuitive data sorting
presentiment
receptive psi
expressive psi

STUDY QUESTIONS

1. Compare the phenomenological characteristics of precognitive experiences to those of contemporaneous extrasensory experiences.

2. What generally is regarded as the fundamental paradox in the notion of precognition? Which of the conceptual attempts to resolve this paradox strikes you as the most satisfactory?

3. Consider the implications of precognition for the existence of free will.

4. What is the basic difficulty in casting the concept of retrocognition in an operational form?

5. Consider the following scenario. Euclid the geometer and mathematician of ancient Greece is known to have derived several theorems in plane geometry but the proofs of these particular theorems have not survived. A medium is selected on the basis that his or her own mathematical skills evidenced at school were poor. On being invited to relate psychically to the golden era of ancient Greece the medium produces a proof of a geometrical theorem by way of automatic writing. Contemporary mathematicians confirm both the validity of the proof and the script's identity as the subject of one of Euclid's lost theorems. Would this constitute a definitive demonstration of retrocognition?

6. Compare and contrast temporal displacement in ESP with the phenomena of precognition and retrocognition.

7. Do presentiment studies necessarily imply, paradoxically, that we can have precognition without cognition?

6

PSYCHOKINESIS

To this point our study of parapsychological phenomena has focused on the "receptive" aspects of psi. Thus in ESP the experient acquires some information supposedly by some paranormal means. Chapters 6 and 7 consider the other face of psi, namely its "expressive" character. As well as acquiring information from the environment it may be possible for information to flow from the individual to the environment in a paranormal fashion. The type of expressive psi that has attracted most systematic research is known as *psychokinesis* (PK). The term "psychokinesis" literally means movement by the mind or psyche. That is, PK may entail observable movements of objects paranormally produced by an effort of will. More generally PK is regarded as any direct mental influence upon the structure of a physical system, whether or not observable movement occurs. In short, PK is a phenomenon of mind over matter. Parapsychologists often differentiate between so-called "macro–PK" and "micro–PK." This distinction refers more to the methodology through which PK is studied than to any well-understood theoretical principle. As the name suggests, macro–PK effects are large-scale and detectable with the naked eye (e.g., metal-bending, table-tilting). Micro–PK effects are small-scale, and the use of statistics is needed to detect them (e.g., psychokinetic influence upon the output of an elec-

tronic source of randomness). Psychokinesis and ESP are said to be the two fundamental forms of *psi*.

Spontaneous Cases of PK Experience

Many physical phenomena of spiritualist seances implied the existence of PK. Apports, levitation, spirit raps, materialization, and paranormal movement of objects in the seance room might be categorized as psychokinetic feats (Braude, 1986; Randall, 1982). The 1970s saw the spoon-bending fad inspired by Uri Geller, with many youngsters claiming to have produced distortions in cutlery, keys, and other metal objects by paranormal means. Other people are said to have a similar power to influence the state of a biological system (e.g., psychic healing) or that of photographic film (psychic photography); these two specific expressions of PK will be discussed later in Chapter 7.

For the main part, however, occurrences of the PK experience in everyday life are rather less spectacular, as is evidenced in the following examples.

Maurice Marsh was a colleague of the first author (HJI) for many years and has a long association with parapsychology; indeed he completed his doctoral dissertation on ESP at Rhodes University in South Africa. At one time Maurice was testing a university student for ESP and found she was yielding some promising scores. This trend was appreciated not only by Maurice but by the student herself. One evening the student visited another member of staff (a social anthropologist) and described how well she was performing on the ESP tests. This particular staff member was concerned that his student may be wasting her time participating in such work and after some attempts at gentle discouragement he became sufficiently exasperated to exclaim, "Look, the only thing that could convince me there is anything to this business (i.e., ESP) is if that picture fell down this very instant!" At the moment he pointed to the picture on the wall it fell to the floor. Examination of the picture revealed that the wire on the back of the frame had neither broken nor come adrift, and the hook upon which the picture had been hanging was intact.

A relatively common example of spontaneous PK experience is the stopping of a watch or clock at the time of death of a relative or friend. As Virtanen (1977/1990, p. 71) notes, in folklore the clock symbolizes life; its ticking is evocative of heartbeats, so that when a clock stops it signifies that a life also has ceased. You will recall the old song about the clock that "stopped, short, never to go again when the old man died." Of course, clocks and watches can stop through natural causes, but often in these cases the respondent notes that the timepiece had not wound down, nor was it broken (Rhine, 1981, p. 196). There also are cases in which at the moment an individual experiences a severe crisis a clock starts to tick after years of inaction (Rhine, 1963a, p. 98).

In a case reported to L. E. Rhine (1961, pp. 223–224) a bulb in a floorlamp exploded. According to the woman who witnessed the event the light bulb "had been cold for hours" and there seemed no reason for its explosion. Intuitively she associated the incident with some sort of family trauma. A few days later

she learned that at the time of the PK experience her brother's farmhouse had been destroyed by fire, apparently as the result of an electrical fault.

Another example was reported by the Swiss psychologist Carl Jung (1963, pp. 108–109). His mother heard a loud cracking sound from the sideboard; upon investigation Jung found that the blade of their breadknife had broken into four pieces.

The Phenomenology of PK Experience

Regrettably there are very few large collections of spontaneous PK case reports and even fewer attempts to subject such collections to content analysis. Nevertheless, following along the lines of her work on spontaneous cases of ESP Louisa E. Rhine has analyzed reports of PK submitted to the parapsychology laboratory at Duke University. The principal trends found in that case collection now will be summarized.

The incidence of spontaneous PK cases is relatively low. At the time Rhine conducted her analysis she had on file over 10,000 reports presumptive of ESP and only 178 cases of PK experience (Rhine, 1963a, p. 88). These data may underestimate the occurrence of PK. For example, in Palmer's (1979) survey of psychic experiences about 7 percent of the sample acknowledged having seen an object move without any natural mechanism being evident. But with the incidence of ESP experiences at over 50 percent in Palmer's study PK does seem to be by far the less common of the two fundamental forms of psi experience.

Again it is possible that this comparative trend is exaggerated by various circumstances. Perhaps people do not countenance the possibility of paranormal factors in physical events as readily as they do in mental events. The concept of ESP is sufficiently familiar that it may be used to "explain" certain mental events, but as PK is a less familiar notion it might not occur to the observer that a particular physical effect could have had a paranormal basis and the unaccountable event may soon be forgotten as "just an accident," something of no great interest. The meaningfulness of the event also may be less obvious in PK experiences. While the content of an ESP experience may have very clear links with an actual event it simply may not strike the individual that for example, the stopping of a clock had some connection with the death of a loved one. Further, in comparison with ESP, it typically is difficult in PK experiences to be sure that an undetected but natural cause was not responsible for the observed event. Finally, for some reason a "mind over matter" effect is much less credible than one of ESP. Perhaps this incredulity is motivated by a strong subconscious fear of the existence of such a potentially unlimited destructive force as PK (Grosso, 1989). In any event, the experient may well be comparatively reluctant to acknowledge having had a PK experience.

Nearly all PK cases in Rhine's (1963a) collection involved two people, one who observed the physical effect and another (usually some distance away) who was undergoing a crisis of some sort. In over a half of Rhine's cases the crisis was death (see also Wright, 1998). Typically the two folk in the case were relatives or close friends so that one individual's crisis normally would have elicited an emotional response from the other person.

This might be taken to imply that the individual undergoing the crisis had used a physical effect as a paranormal means of communicating with the observer. This interpretation is challenged by Rhine. Her reason is that there are a few cases in which only one person was involved. For example, a clock may start ticking when the observer is in a state of crisis. Rhine (1963a, p. 106) cites another case in which a man's watch stopped at the moment he himself died. In such cases there would not seem to be any "message"

being sent to an observer. On these grounds Rhine suggests that even when two people feature in a PK case it might be not the distant friend but the observer who is directly responsible for the physical effect. It is hypothesized that the observer extrasensorially perceives the danger faced by the distant friend but rather than admitting this information into consciousness as an intuitive impression or mental image the subconscious mind of the observer uses a physical object as a means of expressing the information.

Certainly the repression of information from consciousness is indicated in many instances. For example, in one case a woman was sitting in her office when suddenly she began to cry. Her employer repeatedly asked her what was the matter but she could not tell him, nor could she stop crying. After some 20 minutes a huge decorative vase fell off its shelf when no one was near it. Subsequently the woman learned that her father had died on the day of the incident (Rhine, 1963a, p. 112). In such cases PK seems to reflect the defense mechanism of *displacement:* extrasensory knowledge for one reason or another cannot be admitted to consciousness and this leads to a state of tension which is released through displacement on to a physical object, a parapsychological version of frustratedly thumping the table with one's fist. (In some cases it is possible that once the tension is released via PK, the extrasensory knowledge may begin to break through into consciousness.)

According to Rhine's analysis it typically is the case that the observer is situated near the affected object and the person in crisis is some distance from it. Some researchers propose that this indicates PK is uninhibited by distance, but their interpretation assumes that the psychokinetic influence stems from the person in crisis rather than from the observer. As noted above such an assumption is questionable. It should be remembered too that there are cases of PK experience in which the presumed referent person was deceased.

Forty-six of Rhine's (1963a, p. 91) 178 cases were of this sort; usually they were construed by the experient as a sign of the referent person's post-mortem survival.

There is some variety in the type of physical effect featured in spontaneous PK experiences. Objects may fall, or they may fracture without falling; mechanical objects may stop functioning or restart after a period of inactivity. Commonly the target object is part of the household decor, an object such as a clock, vase, mirror or framed picture. On the other hand this merely may reflect the frequency with which the respondent is in particular situations or the likelihood of the physical effect being noticed or acknowledged. For example, few reported cases may be set in a shopping center because firstly, observers may spend relatively little time shopping and secondly, if an object falls from a shop shelf its original position is assumed to have been precarious and the involvement of PK simply is not countenanced.

In her main phenomenological analysis of nonrecurrent PK experiences L. E. Rhine (1963a) classified her cases in terms of the physical events reported. The categories she employed and their relative frequencies were as follows: the fall of objects from a wall, mantel, or shelf (36 percent); starting or stopping of clocks (27 percent); breakage or explosion of objects (12 percent); turning on or off of lights (10 percent); opening, shutting, or unlocking of doors (8 percent); and rocking or shaking of objects (7 percent).

This sample of cases nevertheless excludes instances in which the experience was purely auditory (e.g., rapping sounds from a wall). Auditory cases were analyzed separately by Rhine (1963b) on the grounds that they could conceivably have been hallucinatory rather than entailing an objective event. The sample of purely auditory cases included the striking of clocks (12 percent), the ringing of bells (22 percent), and knocks, raps, or less specific noises (66 percent).

On the basis of her analyses Rhine (1963a,b) concluded that the physical phenomena in spontaneous PK experiences are in fact not likely to have been hallucinatory. She cites a number of cases in which the effects were seen or heard by several people. For example, in 57 percent of the purely auditory cases the experient was in the company of at least one other person, and in 92 percent of these instances all persons present were said to have heard the sound.

The condition of the person in crisis (or presumed target person) was found by Rhine (1963a) to interact with the form of the PK experience. The stopping or starting of clocks often was associated with a target person who was dying but rarely with one who was deceased. The fall of objects, on the other hand, was most characteristic of cases with a living target person. Rhine notes, however, that at least a few instances of each form of the PK experience were recorded for each condition of the target person.

Of the above phenomenological trends perhaps the most interesting from the viewpoint of research is that PK might represent a displaced expression of extrasensorially acquired information. Somewhat surprisingly this notion has received little attention in the parapsychological laboratory, although it has been explored to some degree in the context of recurrent spontaneous PK phenomena or poltergeist experiences (as we shall see in Chapter 10).

More recently Heath (2000) undertook detailed phenomenological interviews of individual spontaneous PK experients and identified 17 common themes associated with the experience, some of which accord with trends in the case material reported by Louisa Rhine. It should be said, however, that as Heath's sample comprised only 8 participants the generality of the phenomenological elements identified in her study remains to be determined through further research. Several elements were found by Heath in all PK experiences. These elements include the presence of an altered state of consciousness and an altered sense of time during the experience; a sense of openness to the experience; a sense of connection to the target; a feeling of dissociation from the self; the suspension of the intellect; the presence of playfulness and/or peak levels of emotion; a sense of energy that may have a transcendent quality; the feeling that one's physical state contributes to or reflects the PK energy; the focusing of awareness and a desire for or investment in the psychokinetic event; and a tendency for the PK event to occur at the moment when one stopped concentrating or striving for an effect. In cases where the experient had consciously tried to bring about the PK event, the experient generally described attempts to "guide" the psychokinetic process (e.g., through focusing on the goal and by using visualization) and mentioned the importance of "not trying too hard" to achieve the outcome. The consequences of the PK experience were reported typically to include a positive impact on self-concept or worldview, a sense that one possesses anomalous knowledge, and an appreciation that one has ESP as well as PK experiences. Research like that by Heath is fundamental to achieving an insight into the spontaneous PK experience from the experient's point of view.

Although it could be said the consistencies in spontaneous PK case reports do testify to the authenticity of this parapsychological phenomenon, there are many uncertainties associated with spontaneous case reports as far as their evidential value is concerned. Several of these were discussed in Chapter 3 in the context of ESP. The factor of chance particularly is problematic here. How often do clocks stop and pictures fall at a time when a close friend or relative is *not* in a state of crisis? Unless we have estimates of such occurrences it cannot confidently be asserted that alleged PK incidents of these forms are beyond the realms of pure chance.

Further, it is even more difficult in PK experiences than in those of ESP to rule out the operation of "normal" causes. It is one thing

to be reasonably sure that the content of an ESP experience could not have been acquired by normal means, but rarely can the experient or the researcher demonstrate that a supposed PK effect could not have been due to some normal physical process. Investigation of the authenticity of PK would require properly controlled conditions of observation.

In this light we now turn to a review of experimental PK research.

Experimental Research and the Authenticity of PK

Most spontaneous PK experiences take the form of macro–PK. In order to overcome some of the difficulties in ruling out normal explanations for these experiences, parapsychologists turned to micro–PK methods. These are characterized by large numbers of trials and the use of statistics to detect whether some random physical system is behaving non-randomly when willed by an observer. Experimental PK research began at the Duke University parapsychology laboratory in 1934 when a young professional gambler walked into J. B. Rhine's office and claimed that he could influence the fall of dice purely by his will power. The two men then got down on the floor and began throwing dice. Although Rhine was not particularly convinced by the gambler's demonstration it did occur to him that dice throwing was an appropriate task to use in the laboratory investigation of the authenticity of PK (Rhine, 1970, pp. 2–4).

In J. B. Rhine's initial experiment subjects rolled a pair of dice with the aim of achieving a total in excess of seven on the uppermost faces of the dice. The probability of this event is 5/12. That is, in a run of 12 throws of the two dice it would be expected that purely by chance the sum of the faces would exceed seven on 5 of the throws. A group of 25 participants completed 562 runs (each of 12 rolls) and yielded 5.53 hits per run compared to the MCE of 5, a highly significant result.

The first experimental study therefore was encouraging, but Rhine realized that the dice may have been biased and the data hence were inconclusive. To test whether the results reflected a bias in the dice Rhine repeated the study, first with participants asked to throw a score *less* than seven, and then with the target set at seven itself. Above-chance performance was obtained also under these procedures, suggesting that the initial finding was not an artifact of poorly balanced dice.

Later studies utilized high quality dice as are used in casinos (where slight biases in dice could cause the casino proprietors to lose heavily). Additionally, the face to be thrown in a given run, the so-called *target*, was selected randomly. Methodological improvements also were made in the throwing process. In the early studies subjects held the dice in their hands and threw them against a wall. With throwing by

Figure 11. One of Rhine's dice-rolling machines (photograph: RRC).

hand some degree of "fudging" by the subject may be possible. Subsequent experiments relied on other means of releasing the dice: progressively these included tipping the dice off a ruler and down a slide, pulling a cord to release the dice through a shutter and thence down a slide, spinning the dice in a machine-driven fully enclosed wire-mesh tube, and spinning the dice in a similar perspex device which contained baffles to make the fall of the dice even less open to artifactual manipulation.

L. E. and J. B. Rhine (1943) published a cumulative report on their PK investigations in 1943, by which time the controversy over their ESP work had died down somewhat (L. E. Rhine, 1970, pp. 26–27). The PK task be-

came standardized at 24 throws of a single die; with the probability of throwing the target face on any trial being 1/6, the MCE was 4 hits per run. A number of PK experiments were conducted within this framework, primarily looking at the influence upon performance of various physical factors such as size, weight, and number of dice. Updating the Rhines' report, Radin and Ferrari (1991) conducted a meta-analysis of 148 experimental studies of PK with dice published from 1953 to 1987. When all studies were included, there appeared to be a convincing PK effect. However, many of these studies did not attempt to counteract possible physical bias in the dice by balancing high and low aim throws. When these possibly biased studies were removed, the remaining 69 studies showed a considerably weaker PK effect, though it was still statistically significant.

The 1970s saw a marked resurgence of PK research. Several factors underlying this revival are identified by Stanford (1977, pp. 328–329), but the primary element of the revival was Helmut Schmidt's (1970a) contribution to the development of random event generators (REGs) based on radioactive decay and his use of these devices in PK research.

The operation of an REG can be described (somewhat simplistically) as follows. In essence an REG comprises electronic circuitry connecting three basic components: a radioactive source (or in some cases a source of electronic noise, rather like intermittent radio static), a counter, and a visual display.

The electronic counter has a clock-like face and its indicator can be stopped in any one of a limited number of positions (e.g., four), just as a hand on a clock may point to one of the hours. The indicator on the counter spins around the face at a very high frequency until it is stopped by a signal produced upon the emission of a particle from the radioactive source. The nature of the visual display (the only part of the apparatus open to the observer) is governed by the stopping point of the counter on each trial. Now, the interval between successive emissions of particles from the radioactive source is conceptually random, that is, theoretically it is not possible to predict accurately the position in which the counter next will stop. Hence if an individual can focus on the visual display over a substantial number of trials and in some way

Figure 12. Helmut Schmidt demonstrating one of his REGs (photograph: Helmut Schmidt).

"will" it to change in a specified way to a level beyond chance expectation, a psychokinetic effect is said to be evidenced. The statistical randomness of the REG's output when subjects are *not* attempting to achieve PK effects must regularly be checked.

With REG technology current PK research is methodologically superior to that of the dice-throwing days. The REG can be interfaced with a computer so that the targets and outcomes automatically are recorded and scored without the opportunity for human error. A huge data base also can be obtained in a relatively short period. For example, the Princeton Engineering Anomalies Research Laboratory (PEAR) has reported a 12-year series of experiments in which 91 individuals participated in nearly two and a half million REG-PK trials (Jahn, Dunne, Nelson, Dobyns & Bradish, 1997).

The methodology of the REG-PK research nevertheless has been criticized, principally by Hansel (1980, 1989), Hyman (1981), and Alcock (1990). Some criticisms, such as the possibility of fraud, are ultimately irrefutable but equally as applicable to any topic of research in the behavioral sciences. The insufficient documentation of methodological detail particularly in the earlier publications on REG-PK received some comment; it is notable that more recent papers (e.g., Schmidt, 1991) tend to report the experimental procedure and apparatus very thoroughly. A few other points have been satisfactorily countered by parapsychologists (Rao & Palmer, 1987). One reasonably cogent criticism is that although the experimenters periodically checked their REG apparatus for nonrandomness over extremely long series of trials, this might not have ruled out the presence of nonrandomness in shorter runs of the kind used in the PK experiments. On the other hand, it is difficult to envisage how such biases could yield significant data in the predicted direction in those studies in which experimental (PK-trial) performance was compared directly to control sequences generated by the same REG (e.g., Schmidt, 1976). The problem of short-run biases also would seem to be negated by the significant results of two meta-analyses of the cumulative record of REG-PK studies (Radin & Nelson, 1989, 2003).

Whereas previous REG-PK meta-analyses have been primarily aimed at the question of whether there was any evidence for PK, the most recently-available meta-analysis of REG-PK studies sought not only to update the cumulative database, but also to identify factors, known as moderator variables, that might be associated with success or failure in finding evidence for PK (Bösch, Steinkamp & Boller, 2006a; see also subsequent commentary by Bösch, Steinkamp & Boller, 2006b, Radin, Nelson, Dobyns & Houtkooper, 2006, and Wilson & Shadish, 2006). Consisting of 380 REG-PK studies, this meta-analysis found a significant but very small overall effect size. The effect size was strongly and inversely correlated with the number of trials, so that the smallest studies had the largest effects. The effect size was also highly variable, and this variability was unrelated to the moderator variables studied such as whether participants were selected or unselected, mode of feedback to participants, and type of random source. Bösch and colleagues argue that publication bias, particularly nonreporting of small non-significant studies (known as the "file drawer problem"), is the most parsimonious explanation for the patterns observed in their data. However, in line with our comments on the limits of meta-analysis in Chapter 4, they conclude (Bösch, Steinkamp & Boller, 2006b) that the retrospective nature of this and the previous REG-PK meta-analyses means that the question of authenticity of the PK effect cannot be resolved on the basis of these meta-analyses. They argue, as Kennedy (2004) and others have also done, that trial registers need to be established in order to avoid possible selective reporting of data once study outcome is known. This is becoming common practice in

medical research (where, of course, an artifactual effect could be a matter of life or
death) and some leading journals now have
pre-registration as a *requirement* of consideration for publication (DeAngelis et al., 2004,
2005).

A version of this pre-registration was recently accomplished in an ambitious project
in which an international consortium of research groups planned that each of the three
labs would conduct 250 experimental REG-PK
sessions, each session consisting of 1000 200-
sample trials in each of three different conditions. In the high-aim condition, participants intended to bias the REG output above
its mean. The low-aim condition directed
participants to bias the REG below its mean,
and in the baseline condition participants
willed the REG to perform at baseline level.
The different labs used identical REG equipment and similar methods of testing and
analysis. The overall results, which were included in the Bösch, Steinkamp and Boller
(2006a) meta-analysis, showed a slight tendency for participants to bias the REG in the
specified direction, but not to a statistically
significant extent (Jahn, Mischo, Vaitl,
Dunne, Boller & Houtkooper et al., 2000).
This finding, given that it was based on pre-
registered trials, perhaps offers tangential support for the reporting bias hypothesis put forward by Bösch, Steinkamp and Boller
(2006a,b).

So it seems that despite a great deal of
research, it is still too early to draw a firm
conclusion on the authenticity of psychokinesis based on REG-PK studies. We can at least
safely say that effects in these studies tend to
be very weak. Perhaps, in rightly seeking
greater methodological rigor, parapsychologists have moved too far from the conditions
under which PK would occur in real life. They
might do well to look again to spontaneous
cases of psychokinesis as a source of ideas for
methodological features that might have
greater psychological significance for experimental participants.

That an apparent PK phenomenon necessarily entails a "mind over matter" effect as
implied by the PK hypothesis is another issue.
For example, the REG-PK data might be explained under the *intuitive data sorting* hypothesis: statistically significant performances
may stem not from a psychokinetic process
but from precognitive identification of an appropriate time to commence the experimental series or to make a response in the experimental task (May et al., 1995; Radin & May,
1987; Vassy, 1990). Recent analyses by Dobyns
(1996, 2000) suggest that this explanation
does not fit the data as effectively as the assumption of a direct (PK) influence, but the
simple fact that the intuitive data sorting hypothesis can be proposed is sufficient to indicate that the PK research is not conclusive
for the issue of ontological reality. As is the
case for ESP, unless parapsychologists can
demonstrate the nature of the channel of PK
interaction it cannot be said that a "mind over
matter" effect has been authenticated.

Process-Oriented Experimental Research on PK

By means of the techniques described
above some experimental research into the
nature of PK has been conducted, but the
quantity and scope of available data are far
more restricted than for ESP. Detailed reviews
of the literature are provided by Rush (1977,
1982), Schmeidler (1977, 1982, 1987, 1994b)
and Stanford (1977).

If ESP and PK are to be regarded as expressions of some unitary capacity termed
"psi" the comparison of PK with ESP becomes
crucial and it therefore may be instructive to
outline the trends in experimental PK research
under the same sequence of headings used in
the summary of the ESP literature (see Chapter 4). The following presentation draws in
part upon Irwin (1985e).

PK Performance: Patterns and Improvement

Most of the data on patterns of PK performance are derived from the old research paradigm of dice throwing. In many cases it remains to be shown that the same patterns can be demonstrated under the methodologically superior REG approach.

The bidirectionality of PK: psi missing. In some experimental investigations of PK (e.g., Steilberg, 1975) subjects have scored below MCE to a significant extent, that is, incorrect outcomes were obtained more often than expected by chance. Psi missing therefore occurs in PK. Sometimes this arises in the context of a differential effect (e.g., Gibson & Rhine, 1943). The occurrence of PK missing in association with negative elements in mood or personality is not well documented (Stanford, 1977, p. 330 & pp. 345–348).

There seem to be no reports of consistent missing, that is, a trend towards producing one particular outcome when another is intended.

Position effects. One of the factors prompting the Rhines' publication of their accumulated data in 1943 was the observation of a decline in scoring within each session (Rhine, 1970, p. 29). This suggested to the Rhines that PK has an affinity with ESP. Like ESP tests the majority of dice-throwing studies evidence better performance in the first quarter of the session than in the last quarter; within-run declines also were reported (McConnell, Snowdon & Powell, 1955; Rush, 1977, pp. 34–36). Critics (e.g., Girden, 1962) nevertheless continued to maintain that position effects in these studies were due to chance, bias in the dice, or nonrandom effects in the operation of the dice-rolling apparatus.

Subsequent research with REG methodology has not given much attention to position effects, although some experiments have confirmed the within-session decline (Honorton & May, 1976; Schmeidler, 1987, p. 19)

and position effects across series (Dunne et al., 1994).

The differential effect. As with ESP, PK experiments featuring two contrasting conditions may yield contrasting levels of performance, often with hitting in one condition and missing in the other (e.g., Cox, 1971; McMahan, 1947).

Displacement? It is not clear that spatial or temporal displacement of PK can occur within a run of trials. In the dice research the identity of the target usually was changed for each run rather than for each trial; hence it would not have been meaningful to look for a displacement of PK on to the target for the trial after (or before) the intended one, since both trials had the same target. Nevertheless some researchers (Pratt & Woodruff, 1946; Palmer & Kramer, 1984) have noted positive scoring on the target that was just abandoned, an effect which is suggestive of temporal displacement. Braud (1987, p. 215) also asserts the possibility of spatial displacement, with significant scores being found for dice face outcomes other than the intended one.

Among the more recent REG studies Schmidt (Schmidt, 1976; Schmidt, Morris & Rudolph, 1986; Schmidt & Stapp, 1993) has performed several experiments consistent with the concept of *retro–PK*, that is, the operation of a psychokinetic influence on a past event (or perhaps a future event's influence upon the present). The methodology used by Schmidt can be queried on the grounds that its data also are interpretable in terms of a precognitive parapsychological experimenter effect. That is, the experimenter may unwittingly have used his own psi to select targets that would yield significant results in relation to subjects' subsequent efforts.

Variance effects. There seems to be only one indication that PK "hits" may tend to cluster together rather than being spaced randomly through the run (Schmidt, 2000; *cf.* Stanford, 1977, p. 354). This observation accords with Kelly's (1982) and Don, McDonough and Warren's (1991) suggestions of

ESP clustering. Again, a trend toward clustering might be affected by the frequency with which the targets are changed, whether from trial to trial (as in ESP work) or from run to run (as in most of the PK research).

Improvement and the role of feedback. Providing the subject with trial-by-trial feedback does not seem to lead to an improvement in PK performance: scoring continues to decline within the session (Stanford, 1977, pp. 359–360). In the context of PK Tart's argument for the importance of feedback therefore is not supported. Tart (1983) argues, however, that a prerequisite level of PK ability is necessary for his predicted learning effects to take place. Gissurarson (1997) also suggests that a strong sense of commitment and persistent practice may be important in "learning" PK skills.

Target Variables

Among the target systems that have been used in experimental PK research are rolling dice, tossed coins, falling spheres, falling drops of water, spinning roulette wheels, and various sorts of video displays governed by an REG.

Physical aspects of the target objects have been given some experimental scrutiny.

In the older dice-throwing work the size of the dice had no significant or consistent effect upon PK scores (e.g., Humphrey & Rhine, 1945). Forwald's (1961) methodologically superior study did reveal die size as a factor in level of performance but the nature of the data suggests that size as such was not as fundamental as the extent to which the dice bounced and spun before coming to rest.

The die's density (weight with size held constant) or its component material has not proved to have any linear effect upon scoring. In one study using celluloid dice and lead dice of the same size, the former yielded significant above-chance scoring and the latter scoring below chance to an equal degree (Cox, 1971). This differential effect occurred

without the participants knowing that dice of different densities were being used.

The number of dice thrown on each trial does not seem a pertinent variable at least in the physical sense (Rhine & Humphrey, 1944). At the same time, if only one die is thrown per trial a greater number of trials is required to yield a given quantity of data and as the test progresses the subject working with a single die could become increasingly bored, a situation which might well depress performance. There also are some complex methodological issues in the multiple-dice studies (see Kennedy, 1978, pp. 92–94 for an analysis).

In PK studies with electronically generated targets a very high rate of target generation may impair performance (Schmidt, 1973), but it has been argued that this effect springs from the participant's perception of the tasks rather than from any intrinsic limitations of PK (Stanford, 1977, pp. 353–354). Further evidence bearing on this issue comes from recent REG-PK research designed to randomly intersperse trials consisting of the sum of 200 bits with trials consisting of the sum of 2,000,000 bits. The participants in these studies were unaware whether a trial was "high density" or "low density." Using this protocol, evidence of a PK effect was found in both types of trials, but the direction of effect was reversed for the 2,000,000-bit trials. In other words, for the high density trials the REG output was shifted in the direction *opposite* to the participant's intention (Ibison, 1998), and this unexpected pattern of results was later replicated in a second study (Dobyns, Dunne, Jahn & Nelson, 2004). Given that participants and experimenters were blind as to trial type, psychological factors associated with task perception can be ruled out. The researchers are unable to explain these results, and further research on this question has been hampered due to the subsequent fatal breakdown of the specially-designed REG (Dobyns et al., 2004).

In a study with pictorial stimuli Stanford

(1983) obtained higher PK performance when the target slide had low similarity to other pictures that could be selected by the REG. Although "similarity" here was judged partly in terms of contours and thereby might be deemed a physical dimension, it also entailed some semantic interpretation of the pictures. Whether Stanford's data reflect purely physical or psychological target characteristics therefore is unclear. Certainly the variable of physical similarity or discriminability of REG outcomes warrants further investigation.

In REG research there also is some indication that PK scoring is not influenced by the complexity of the device which generates the target (Schmidt, 1974).

One physical characteristic which may influence PK is the *lability* of the target system, that is, the ease with which the system can change from one state to another, or the amount of "free variability" in the system. In a series of experiments conducted by the American parapsychologist William Braud (1980) labile target systems appeared more open to psychokinetic influence than were systems characterized by high inertia. This is not to say that static targets are impervious to PK (see the section on macro–PK in Chapter 7). Again, it is feasible that Braud's results are due more to psychological than to physical factors: a highly stable system may strike unselected experimental subjects (consciously or subconsciously) as so immutable as to discourage attempts to influence its state. However, a recent study (Holt & Roe, in press) suggests that individual differences may need to be taken into account, as the highest psi scores were obtained when senders with high trait lability interacted with the least labile target system and when low-labile senders interacted with the most labile target system.

Looking globally at the research on physical aspects of PK target systems it would appear that such factors have little effect on PK performance except perhaps by way of their psychological impact on the participant. This accords with similar research into ESP.

Further, these data suggest that it might not be appropriate to think of PK as a paranormally produced physical force. It must be acknowledged, however, that the scope of the PK studies in this regard has been limited. Faith may move mountains, but that PK can do so as readily as it appears to influence dice is a matter yet to be resolved conclusively. Braud's research also serves as a caution that there may be important physical dimensions yet to be explored in this context.

While on the subject of the pertinent characteristics of the target it should be mentioned that PK can occur even when the participant is unaware of the nature or even the existence of the target system. For example, in most REG experiments the subjects are asked to try to influence a video display and as far as they are concerned this display is the "target." On the other hand, it might be presumed that the point at which the REG system is open to PK influence is in the emission of particles from the radioactive source, a part of the system that is unknown to the subjects. Indeed the subjects may even be unaware that they are taking part in a PK experiment. In one study the uninformed participants were given either a boring task or a pleasant task according to the outcome of an REG situated in an adjacent room; the number of people gaining access to the pleasant task exceeded chance (Stanford, Zenhausern, Taylor & Dwyer, 1975). It seems then that PK is directed toward a *goal* rather than necessarily to the underlying physical mechanisms of the target event. This aspect of PK is particularly important in the context of constructing a theoretical account of the phenomenon, and it also offers a viable alternative to the view that PK operates like a physical force. The *teleological* (goal-directed) character of PK is discussed by Stanford (1978); see also Chapter 8.

Related to the question of unconscious psychokinetic influence is a relatively new area of research into the interaction of consciousness with the environment: the "Global

Consciousness Project" (e.g., Nelson, 2001). REGs located in 40 sites around the world run continuously and send data back to the project's headquarters in Princeton, USA. The researchers hypothesize that at moments of coherent or focused human attention (for example, when a large-scale emotional event is witnessed by thousands or even millions of people), the output of the REGs will become less random compared to other times when no such global events are occurring. For instance, it is reported that such non-random REG behavior was observed for the funeral of Princess Diana (Nelson, Bosch, Boller, Dobyns, Houtkooper, Lettieri et al., 1998), around midnight during New Year celebrations worldwide (Nelson, 2001), and during the terrorist attacks in New York on 11th September 2001, whose live broadcast was witnessed aghast by a global audience (Nelson, 2002; Radin, 2002). However, some commentators (Scargle, 2002) have criticized these studies on the grounds of multiple analysis and selective reporting of data and suggest that firmer conclusions may be drawn once this research moves beyond the exploratory phase.

Other Situational Variables

Performance in a PK task may vary with the physical setting of the experiment presumably by way of an effect on the motivation of participants. With psychological factors controlled most physical variables appear irrelevant. For example, PK does not decline with increased distance between the subject and the target system, provided the subject remains unaware of the actual distance (Dickstein & Davis, 1979). There is one study in which PK scoring was significantly higher in light than in darkness (Gibson & Rhine, 1943), but in another study the reverse was observed (McMahan, 1947). Perhaps some subjects find darkness unnerving, while for others it is conducive to relaxation.

As with ESP the experimenter's motiva-

tion, attitudes and handling of subjects can have some bearing on the outcome of a PK study. Some evidence of this is cited in White's (1977) review.

A little work has been conducted on the states of consciousness most conducive to good PK scores (Gissurarson, 1997). There are indications that a relaxed frame of mind is more advantageous than intense striving for an effect (Debes & Morris, 1982; Steilberg, 1975). Thus superior performance may be obtained when the PK task is presented as a kind of game. Similarly, various yoga/meditation techniques seem to be PK conducive (Gissurarson, 1997). Passive visualization of the target also seems more efficacious than thoughts about imagined processes leading to the goal (Levi, 1979; Morris, Nanko & Phillips, 1982). These findings are consistent with the idea that PK performance is facilitated by an unforced state of absorption in the goal of the task (Isaacs, 1986), although the occurrence of spontaneous PK experiences does not seem to be related to a need for absorption (Irwin, 1985b).

The number of subjects tested at one time may be regarded as a situational factor. In one early study employing the dice methodology two subjects trying to achieve the same target face were more effective than when each tried for a different target (Humphrey, 1947). In another experiment the run variance was greater when the pair of subjects aimed for the same target (Feather & Rhine, 1969). Few of these so-called "help or hinder" studies have been undertaken with the more sophisticated REG methodology. An interesting variation of this approach was used by Schmidt (1985), with two subjects making *successive* attempts to influence prerecorded events by means of retro–PK; only the individual who made the first such attempt was associated with a significant effect. There still are too few data upon which to base a decision about additive PK effects across different people.

Subject Variables

Some studies have examined PK performance in relation to the beliefs of the experimental participants. A few sheep-goat experiments have been conducted but unlike ESP a belief in the possibility of PK evidently has little if any effect upon dice-throwing performance (Dale, 1946; Gissurarson, 1991; Gissurarson & Morris, 1991; Stanford, 1977, pp. 330–331). As PK seems even more sensitive than ESP to the subject's level of mental relaxation it is possible that the advantage of a stronger positive attitude to PK is offset to some degree by a concomitant increase in level of arousal. Nevertheless in one study with an REG-PK task Weiner (1982) found a strong positive correlation between performance and belief in the existence of PK; this result was not obtained in her attempted replication of the experiment.

Possibly associated with PK belief is the acknowledgment of personal spontaneous PK experiences. The frequency of prior PK experiences has been found to correlate positively with PK test scores (Gissurarson, 1991; Gissurarson & Morris, 1991).

There is scant evidence that the subject's mood during the test affects scoring level although few studies have addressed this issue directly. Van de Castle (1958) reports that the Expansive/Compressive index of mood may be related to PK performance, although the data are weak and lack independent confirmation. Research on personality correlates of PK has not fared much better. Van de Castle's study indicated also that spontaneous people exhibit higher scores than inhibited subjects. Other studies suggest a negative correlation with anxiety (Broughton & Perlstrom, 1985) and possibly with defensiveness (Watt & Gissurarson, 1995). Few experiments, however, have sought to relate PK performance to major personality variables.

Physiological correlates likewise have been given little attention. Schmidt (1991) failed to establish any relationship between experimental PK performance and heart rate.

Some research on cognitive variables has been undertaken. The capacity for generating mental imagery does not seem to be a correlate of PK scores (Gissurarson & Morris, 1991). Similarly, different imagery strategies in themselves were not observed by Gissurarson and Morris (1990) to affect PK performance differentially, but Stanford (1969) found that people tend to do better in a PK task when they use their preferred mode of cognitive processing; thus habitual visualizers achieve higher PK scores when they visualize the target than when forming free associations to the target. Another investigation by Krieger (1977) revealed a significant relationship between PK and a test of depth of semantic processing; the latter is a factor in establishing information as a secondary (long-term) memory trace, so perhaps PK is linked with long-term memory skills. Although there is some coherence in reported associations between cognitive style and PK performance it must be said there are attempted replications and other studies that have yielded nonsignificant results.

The experimental literature therefore evidences similarity between PK and ESP in some respects. But in other respects the parallelism is less clear. Certainly there are reports of people who are adept in both ESP and PK (Stanford, 1977, pp. 346–347), but this might be due to an attitudinal factor or the like rather than to any fundamental commonality between "two forms of psi." The principal difficulty here is that little research has been directed to the psychological dimensions of PK performance. Much of the current work, despite the welcome improvements in precision and control, still is concerned with the existence of PK and the forms it may take. More of this material is reviewed in the following chapter but at the present point it must be regretted that we are left with comparatively little process-oriented data from which to deduce the modus operandi of PK.

KEY TERMS AND CONCEPTS

psychokinesis (PK)	PK missing
micro–PK	position effects
macro–PK	retro–PK
PK as a displaced reaction	target variables
dice methodology	lability
target face	teleological approach
random event generator (REG)	situational variables
file drawer problem	subject variables
moderator variable	cognitive variables
intuitive data sorting	

STUDY QUESTIONS

1. Define psychokinesis and describe the principal techniques employed in its experimental investigation.

2. Have you had a spontaneous PK experience? If so, did it exhibit any of the phenomenological characteristics reported by Louisa Rhine?

3. What trends have been educed from collections of spontaneous PK case reports? What is the evidential value of such material?

4. To what extent do the patterns in PK test performance parallel those of ESP?

5. Is retro–PK a testable hypothesis? Discuss.

6. Some people are inclined to think of PK as a mentally produced physical force. What experimental findings cast doubt on this simple notion?

7. Suppose you throw a die 100 times and on each throw you attempt to call the outcome. The correspondence between the throws and the calls is statistically significant. How could you determine whether this result was due to ESP or due instead to PK?

8. What is an REG and how do these devices work? What precautions must be observed in using an REG in parapsychological research?

9. The results of an REG-PK experiment might be construed as being due to precognition. Explain the rationale of this view. Might spontaneous cases of PK similarly be attributable to precognition? Conversely, might spontaneous cases of precognition be attributable to PK?

10. Imagine you are designing a new REG-PK user interface. Considering the form of real-life PK experiences, what kind of interface would you use to maximize the psychological motivation and involvement of the participant?

7

SPECIAL TOPICS IN PK RESEARCH

This chapter examines several issues some of which might be said to be on the periphery of PK research but which nevertheless have some affinity with the notion of a "mind over matter" effect. The issues to be discussed are PK and the parapsychological experimenter effect; psychic healing and, related to this, direct mental interaction with living systems; macro–PK; and psychic photography.

PK and the Parapsychological Experimenter Effect

The authenticity of PK would add a whole new dimension to the parapsychological experimenter effect. As you will recall, if we assume the authenticity of ESP, investigations of the nature of psi would be faced with the prospect that before testing commences parapsychologists unwittingly may use their own ESP abilities to identify subjects and target sequences favorable to their hypothesis. If additionally it is assumed that the experimenter may have PK abilities it is conceivable that these too could be used (even subconsciously) to influence the experimental equip-

ment in such a way as to facilitate the production of data consistent with the hypothesis under investigation. Indeed the experimenter's psychokinetic influence might conceivably extend to control over the subjects' responses.

The potential PK component of the parapsychological experimenter effect may be considered in relation to some research into the parapsychological abilities of animals, so-called *anpsi*. A number of laboratory experiments have utilized an REG device to investigate the precognitive or psychokinetic skills of animal subjects (for a review of this work see Nash, 1986, p. 146; Rush, 1982, p. 100). A fairly common procedure here is to apply a moderate electric current to one half of the grid that forms the floor of the test cage. The particular half of the grid to be electrified on each trial is determined randomly by the output of the REG.

The objective of such a procedure is to see if an infra-human animal can use psi to avoid shocks to a statistically significant degree: thus, the animal might employ precognition to ascertain which part of the grid is to be electrified next and then move to the other section of the cage, or PK might be used to ensure that the current tends to be applied to the empty side of the cage. This procedure

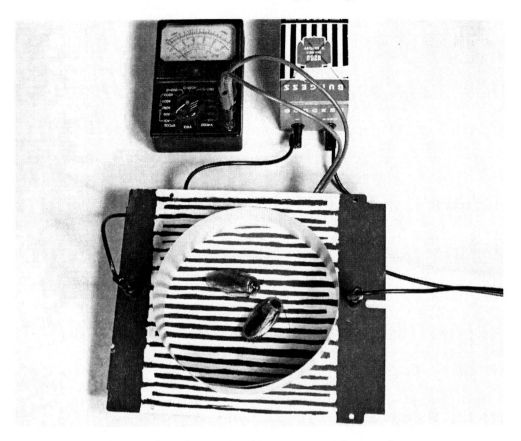

Figure 13. Cockroaches in Schmidt's experiment (photograph: RRC).

has been used with some success to evidence psi in various species including hamsters, guinea pigs, gerbils, cats, laboratory rats, and brine shrimp. Each of these species appeared able to prevent or avoid the electric shocks to a statistically significant degree.

A rather curious result, however, was obtained in an experiment conducted by Schmidt (1970b). The subjects in this investigation were cockroaches! And they too yielded significant data, but in the opposite direction. That is, the cockroaches received *more* shocks than would be expected by chance. There are many possible interpretations of this contrary result.

Perhaps cockroaches are masochistic by nature and actually enjoyed receiving more than their fair share of electric shocks. The sample of cockroaches used by Schmidt may not have been typical of the species: for ex-

ample, a group numerically dominated by neurotic cockroaches (?) may be inclined to psi missing. Again, a plausible explanation may be contrived in terms of the parapsychological experimenter effect. Specifically, Schmidt could dislike cockroaches (which admittedly are rather unlovable in comparison with the other species used in this research); therefore, he could subconsciously have used his own psychokinetic abilities to influence the REG, ensuring that these creatures were punished for being objectionable.

It is not suggested that the data of Schmidt's cockroach study conclusively evidence the parapsychological experimenter effect in operation, but the fact that such an account can be formulated illustrates the problematic character of the "parapsychological experimenter effect" hypothesis. If ESP and PK are authentic the results of *any* process-oriented psi research could be explained away in such terms. Indeed parapsychologists themselves are beginning to resort to this hypothesis in order to "account for" discrepant experimental outcomes. Thus, several skeptical commentators (e.g., Alcock, 1998; Riniolo & Schmidt, 1999) have taken parapsychologists to task for using the concept as an "escape clause" or ad hoc mechanism to explain away any failure to support the psi hypothesis under the laboratory conditions. Perhaps you now can appreciate the extent to which the experimenter effect represents a major conceptual obstacle in contemporary parapsychology. Further discussion of this issue is provided by Palmer (1997a).

Psychic Healing

Some forms of healing might involve an element of PK. Indeed according to some commentators even conventional healing features psychokinetic factors. For example, in the evaluation of medicinal drugs it is usual to include a "placebo" control condition because patients who believe prescribed treatment will alleviate their illness often show an improvement attributable largely to that belief. Mental processes also are known to affect the body's immune system, a matter that is now the subject of a specialist medical field called psychoneuroimmunology (Ader, Felten & Cohen, 1991; Braud, 1986). It has been argued that placebo and other psychosomatic effects instance a "mind over matter" process and thereby can be construed as psychokinetic in nature.

On these grounds the distinction between psychic healing and other sorts of healing may be dubious. But for the sake of definition *psychic healing* is taken here to entail a mode of healing in which there is claimed to be a direct transfer of some form of energy from the healer to the patient or "healee" (Hodges & Scofield, 1995). At a purely conceptual level psychic healing in that sense can be differentiated from orthodox healing, faith healing (in which the effect evidently stems from the authority vested in the healer), and psychic surgery (in which diseased tissue allegedly is removed without the use of surgical instruments). In discussing psychic healing, therefore, the focal question is whether or not it represents a form of PK. That other sorts of healing could also have a PK component is not central to the inquiry.

Throughout recorded history there have been people who claimed the power of healing by "the laying on of hands" and other paranormal techniques. It is only in recent years, however, that the phenomenology of the psychic healing experience has been given scientific attention. In the following review, the experiences of the healer are considered first, followed by those of the patient.

Rituals performed for the purpose of psychic healing are diverse, and variation across cultures is especially marked (Kleinman, 1980; Krippner, 1989; LeShan, 1974). In technologically undeveloped societies, healing rituals are the province of specially designated members of the tribe known as shamans. The shamans' rituals may incorporate trance, incantations, choreography, music, totems, talismans, costumes, herbal preparations, and so on. There is variation too within the rituals of a single culture. In Western countries, for example, healers variously work in a religious or a secular setting, with a mass audience or an individual client, as a benevolent or a business activity. Despite these variations, there do seem to be some phenomenological consistencies in the experiences of psychic healers.

Immediately before the healing process is applied, healers typically enter what seems to be a state of strong psychological absorption, that is, an effortless engrossment in the contents of their experience. Many healers use relaxation, meditation, prayer or some such "centering" technique to induce a low level of arousal in which heart rate, muscle tension, and respiration are decreased (Cooperstein, 1992). Alternatively, healers may perform a vigorous, ritualistic dance or other practice that leads to high arousal (Krippner, 1982). The extremes of arousal are known to be associated with intensely yet passively absorbed mentation (Irwin, 1985b). According to Benor (1986, p. 96) these preparatory exercises are not invariably necessary; some healers are able to enter an absorbed state very rapidly or are habitually in such a state.

The first act of the "treatment" is to "engage with the healee" (Benor, 1986, p. 97). Often this entails the "laying on of hands," that is, healers place their hands in direct contact with the patient's body, perhaps with the patient's clothes still in place. Some healers simply make "passes" or hand movements around the patient's body without actual contact. This process sometimes lasts for several minutes, during which the healer may be aware of various sensations in his or her hands or body. For example, healers may report they experience heat, cold, tingling and prickliness in their hands and rhythmic sensations through the body (Benor, 1986; Cooperstein, 1992). These sensations may vary with the location and the type of physical disorder in the patient. One healer remarked, "I get an ache for a bone injury, a prickle for a nerve problem and for a trapped sciatic nerve, almost an electric shock. For cancer, it's a sensation like worms under the skin and for asthma, it's mites under the skin" (Harvey, 1983, p. 113).

Healers may depict themselves as being in an "altered reality" at this stage. In this state, temporal-spatial, physical, and personal boundaries appear to be permeable (Van Dragt, 1980/1981). The subjective breakdown of the personal barrier between the healer and the healee is particularly salient, creating an impression of intimate "transpersonal merging" or oneness with the healee (Benor, 1986; LeShan, 1974; Van Dragt, 1980/1981). The sense of oneness is marked by an unconditional regard for and empathy with the healee.

Some healers report they feel exhausted at the conclusion of a healing session, but others do not feel at all drained (Harvey, 1983, p. 114). This may be related to the healer's belief in the source of the healing energy, that is, whether the energy is held to be self-generated or to be channeled from an external, cosmic source. Innovative research by Maher, Vartanian, Chernigovskaya and Reinsel (1996) also suggests a reduction in tactile sensitivity in some healers by the end of the session.

Research has yet to determine a detailed personality profile of psychic healers. Many of the highly fantasy-prone participants in the study by Wilson and Barber (1983, p. 363) believed in their ability to heal others, and some were actively involved in the practice of psychic healing. This finding is consistent with the earlier suggestion that healers are able to achieve high absorption in their own mentation. Snel and van der Sijde (1997) also report that healers exhibit an external locus of control, that is, healers see their life more as being under the control of external agencies than as within their own capacity to control. This profile is consistent with the belief of many healers that the healing force emanates from an external source and is merely "channeled" through them as passive mediators.

Let us turn now to the phenomenology of the experience of the psychic healee or patient. The evidence here is much more limited. In technologically undeveloped societies, people may consult a shaman because this is the conventional source of medical assistance. In Western societies, on the other hand, a psychic healer often is approached as a "last resort" when conventional medical treatment has proved unsatisfactory (Harvey, 1983; Schouten, 1997). These healees therefore may be at a low ebb when they first visit the healer's clinic. For this reason much of the initial consultation may be devoted to establishing rapport with the patient and to facilitating a state of relaxation to alleviate the individual's tension and anxiety. The patient typically is placed in a relaxed position for the treatment and may be instructed to relax, to breathe deeply, and to meditate on a deity or other higher power. Other procedures for enhancing relaxation include the ministration of herbal preparations, laying on of hands, and massage of the patient's body.

The healing treatment encourages not only a low level of arousal but also a degree of positive expectation (or at least a suspension of negativism). In the view of many healers, positive expectations in the healee are an important ingredient of psychic healing (Kleinman, 1980; Krippner, 1989; Wirth, 1995).

While the healer performs the healing ritual, the healee may experience various physical sensations (Benor, 1986, p. 97; Harvey, 1983). Among the sensations reported by patients in Harvey's (1983, p. 126) sample were warmth, deep relaxation, calmness, tingling, coldness, spontaneous movement, and discomfort.

Pain is the symptom most frequently reported to be ameliorated through psychic healing. Few healers, however, have had the objective effects of their practices confirmed by scientific investigation. Because cross-cultural evaluations of treatment outcome are problematic (Kleinman, 1980), the focus here will be on research conducted in Western cultures.

One of Britain's most renowned psychic healers Harry Edwards was investigated by a psychiatrist Dr. Louis Rose (1955). The study by Rose focused on 95 patients who claimed to have had their condition alleviated by Edwards. Independent medical records were available for only 37 of the sample, but these data indicated that the efforts of the psychic healer were of no substantial benefit in 34 cases. Only in three patients was there some sustained improvement that might conceivably be attributed to Edwards' powers; again, the observed improvement in these few cases may have been due to spontaneous recovery

or to a placebo effect. In any event there evidently was a marked discrepancy between clients' claims of improvement and the actual medical evidence. Whether the results for Edwards would be comparable to those for other kinds of psychic healers is unknown. One study of a German healer also yielded an essentially null outcome, although there were indications that an improvement in the patient's condition is more likely if the medical disorder is functional rather than organic (Strauch, 1963).

Detailed surveys of clinical investigations of psychic healing in human patients are provided by Schouten (1997) and Abbot (2000); see also Astin, Harkness and Ernst (2000). These authors identify serious methodological flaws in many of these studies, including the lack of appropriate control groups and the absence of double blind procedures. The principal conclusion to be drawn from the available data base seems to be that there may well be an objective effect of psychic healing in human patients but if it does exist, the effect size is very small by comparison with that of the healer's impact on patients' subjective feelings of wellness. That is, evidence of any objective improvement in health status tends to be swamped by patients' reconstruction of and accommodation to the chronic symptoms of their illness (Glik, 1990).

This trend points to a major problem in the scientific investigation of psychic healing. As long as human patients are employed in the study it becomes difficult to rule out alternative explanations of any observed alleviation of illness (e.g., see Beutler, Attevelt, Geijskes, Schouten, Faber & Dorhout Mees, 1987). A "placebo" control condition might be incorporated in the design, but it is very difficult to ensure that the "psychological" treatment given to the placebo group is precisely equivalent to the presumed psychological component of the "psychic healing" condition, and further it could always be argued that the person administering the placebo procedure had unrecognized powers of psychic healing. Considerations such as these have encouraged researchers in this area to make use of animal and other nonhuman target material. It is assumed that animals do not form expectations of a treatment's curative potential in the way that human patients may.

Arguably the best research program conducted along these lines is that by Bernard Grad, an expert in experimental morphology at McGill University in Montreal. In the 1960s Grad worked with a Hungarian psychic Oskar Estebany who was said to have the power of healing by the method of laying on of hands. A review of these studies is provided by Grad (1976). In his first experiment mice were placed on an iodine-deficient diet to produce goiters and then were divided into three groups. The experimental group was treated by Estebany: the healer placed his hands on the outside of the animals' cage for 15 minutes about ten times per week. A control group of mice was kept in a similar cage but was left completely alone. In a second control condition the mice's cage was warmed by electrothermal tapes intended to produce heat equivalent to that from Estebany's hands. Grad found that the rate of goiter development was significantly slower in the experimental group than in the control mice. A second experiment excluded Estebany from the vicinity of the cages. In this study the healer merely held pieces of wool and cotton material that then were put in the cage with the experimental animals. Untreated material was deposited in the control mice's cage. Again the goiters on the control mice grew more quickly than those on the experimental animals, suggesting that the intervention of the healer was beneficial.

Another of Grad's investigations involved the surgical removal of a small piece of skin from the back of each mouse. The wounds on the animals treated by Estebany healed more quickly than those of the control group. A more elaborate replication of this study was conducted with controls on the size of the original wound, temperature and humidity of the animals' housing, amount of handling, and other factors. Mice in the cages held by Estebany showed faster healing than those in other groups; additionally, mice in cages held by skeptical medical students showed *less* improvement than other control animals.

More recent work by Wirth, Johnson, Horvath and MacGregor (1992) has utilized a different research paradigm. Amphibious animals known as salamanders or newts have a remarkable ability to regenerate various parts of their body after an injury. In an experiment designed to capitalize on this ability Wirth et al. surgically removed a section of the forelimb in a sample of anesthetized salamanders, and then invited four psychic healers to try and influence the rate of forelimb regrowth. Regeneration generally was reported to be more rapid in the treated group of animals than in an untreated control group.

While it is difficult to argue that animals can form a psychological expectation of health improvement, it is even more difficult to do so for plants. Some recent research has been conducted looking at the effects of healing on the growth of healthy lettuce seeds. These studies are interesting in several ways. Firstly, they are very well-designed, utilizing a randomized double-blind methodology. Secondly, they are conducted in a real world setting, a farm rather than a test-tube or a laboratory. And thirdly, partly as a result of the first two, they show potential commercial applications of healing in agriculture. In these studies, a healer treated one of four random samples of lettuce seeds, two other samples were unhandled, and one sample was handled by a person who did not claim to have any healing abilities but who attempted to mimic the movements of the healer. The lettuce seeds were then planted out by a person who did not know the sample identities, and were later scored as to various health measures, again blind as to which were the treated and the control samples. In the first study, of three possible health measures, lettuce grown from the treated seeds showed enhanced performance on one, namely, restricted fungal growth (Roney-Dougal & Solfvin, 2002). In the second study, the treated lettuce showed enhanced performance on all three pre-planned outcome variables, having greater weight and less slug and fungal damage than the untreated seeds. Roney-Dougal and Solfvin (2003) conclude that with about a 10 percent larger crop for the treated seeds compared to the control samples, the use of a healer yielded a real practical value for the commercial farmer. One limitation, though, is that only a single healer was used in each study, so that there is some question over the generalizability of the findings.

A more process-oriented line of research in this area is of a biochemical nature. Studies by Sister Justa Smith (1968) and by Rein (1978) report that enzymes kept in a flask show a significantly increased rate of chemical transformation when held by a healer. Further work of this sort might reveal the mechanism underlying the phenomenon of psychic healing. It is feasible, of course, that psychic healing may function in several different ways. For example, as well as affecting the body's enzyme activity a healer may be able to exercise a direct influence upon organic tissue. Thus Braud, Davis and Wood (1979) report PK effects on some biochemical processes in human blood cells. There is, therefore, a measure of experimental support for the notion of a psychokinetic effect upon healing processes, but further investigation is required to broaden and strengthen the field's empirical foundation, particularly in relation to human patients. For further detail, see reviews by Benor (1990) and Solfvin (1984).

The notion of a psychokinetic influence upon healing may more broadly encompass studies on the effects of distant intercessory prayer. While these studies cannot "test God"

(Kennedy, 2002), they may provide some evidence on the question of the effect of human intentionality upon another's health. Positive therapeutic effects of prayer have been reported in controlled studies with patients suffering from coronary illness (e.g., Byrd, 1988; Harris et al., 1999) and distant healing has been shown to be effective in a small study with sufferers of advanced AIDS (Sicher, Targ, Moore & Smith, 1998). However, such studies are plagued by methodological problems (Chibnall, Jeral & Cerullo, 2001) that have led one commentator to suggest that positive results could be experimenter effects (Kennedy, 2002). For instance, how can one control for a seriously ill patient being prayed for by others uninvolved in the study, or for the patient quite understandably praying for herself even if she is in the "no prayer" group? A recent systematic review (Roberts, Ahmed & Hall, 2000) found that the results of studies of distant intercessory prayer are inconclusive but that the topic is a potentially important one that merits further investigation.

Direct Mental Interaction with Living Systems (DMILS)

Due to the methodological challenges that face those trying to ascertain whether some impaired biological system has been healed through human intentionality alone, many researchers have chosen instead to ask a simpler question that is nevertheless consistent with the hypothesis of mental healing: can one person influence a remote biological system through thought alone? This line of research studies the possible occurrence of PK influences upon a wide range of unimpaired biological target systems such as the spatial orientation of swimming fish, the locomotor activity of small mammals, and the rate of hemolysis of in vitro samples of

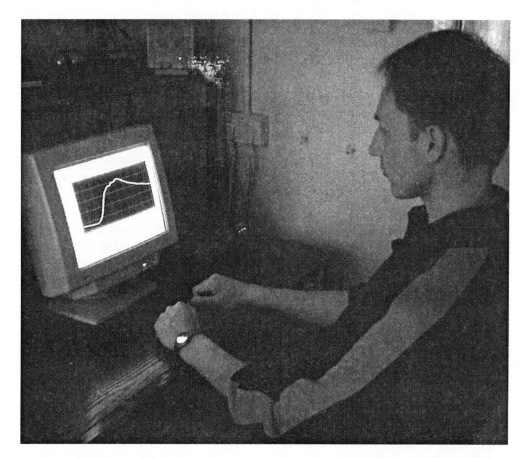

Figure 14. The agent in an EDA-DMILS study (photograph: Koestler Parapsychology Unit).

red blood cells (Braud & Schlitz, 1991). Termed "direct mental interaction with living systems" (DMILS), the most commonly-studied target system is the psychophysiology (e.g., heart rate, blood pressure, electrodermal activity) of a human subject (see surveys by Delanoy, 2001, and Schlitz & Braud, 1997). All DMILS studies use basically the same design. Two individuals are involved, equivalent to the sender/agent and the receiver in an ESP study. The receiver's psychophysiology is constantly measured while, at the same time, the distant agent follows a randomized schedule of experimental and control periods. The receiver is unaware of the schedule; therefore, if direct mental interaction is *not* taking place then on analysis there should be no significant difference in the target person's psychophysiology when experimental periods are compared with control periods. If such a difference is found, and if all other potential artifacts have been ruled out, then a DMILS effect is inferred.

Using this basic method, a great deal of experimental work has been carried out on two main research questions. Firstly, can we detect when we are being stared at from behind, and secondly, can we influence another person at a distance. We shall discuss each in turn.

The feeling of being stared at is commonly reported. For instance, it is often said that while sitting on a bus one can feel unease and, on turning around, find that one is being stared at. However, various sensory cues could operate in this situation. For instance, you might unconsciously have picked up on someone quietly talking about you as they stare, or hear the rustling of their clothing as they gesture towards you. Also, the very action of you turning around could attract the attention of a person who wasn't previously staring at you. For over 100 years, psychologists and parapsychologists have been investigating the feeling of being stared at with gradually increasing methodological sophistication (e.g., Coover, 1913; Schlitz, Wiseman, Watt & Radin, 2006; Sheldrake, 2001). The typical method for eliminating possible sensory cues is to have the receiver (sometimes termed the "staree") in an isolated room that is monitored by a camera, while the staree's EDA (electrodermal activity) is measured. The starer is in a separate room watching a monitor. At random times the live image of the staree is displayed on the starer's monitor, while during control periods the screen is blank or another image is shown. Reviewing the results of 11 remote staring studies, Schlitz and Braud (1997) reported a highly significant difference in EDA in stare periods compared to no-stare periods.

The 1997 review by Schlitz and Braud also summarized the results of 19 remote influence studies. In these, the receiver's EDA is monitored while the remote influencer follows a randomized schedule of influence and control periods. During the influence periods, the influencer thinks about the receiver and mentally attempts to affect the receiver's EDA (see Fig. 14). Different mental strategies might be used in this process. For instance, if the influencer's task is to activate the receiver's EDA, the influencer might visualize the receiver taking part in some arousing activity such as bungee jumping. Sometimes the influencer can see live feedback of the EDA of the receiver and in this case the influencer might focus attention on the visual display and try to cause the shape of the graph to change in the desired direction. During control periods, the influencer turns his or her attention elsewhere. In these remote influence studies, again a highly significant difference was found in EDA activity when influence and control periods were compared.

While Schlitz and Braud (1997) report strong apparent remote staring and remote influence effects, their review included a number of earlier studies that might not have had the methodological sophistication that came to prevail in later years, as is often the case with a developing research paradigm (for some methodological recommendations, see Schmidt & Walach, 2000). Additionally, the completion of a number of remote staring and remote influence studies in recent years meant that an update would be timely. In order to do this and also to investigate whether methodological quality might be associated with study outcome, a meta-analytic review has been recently conducted (Schmidt, Schneider, Utts & Walach, 2004). This meta-analysis went beyond the previous two in that it formally coded each study on 208 different items, 19 of which were associated with different kinds of quality criteria, such as the use of acoustical shielding, having suitable environmental humidity for the EDA measurements, and having pre-planned hypotheses and analyses. In 15 remote staring studies, a small significant effect was obtained. Although study quality was negatively correlated with effect size in the staring studies, the correlation was not statistically significant. So, poor methodology could not account for the significant findings in the remote staring studies. In 36 remote influence studies, a small significant effect was also found, but it appeared that this effect was associated with lesser quality studies, and when the analysis was restricted to the 7 highest-quality studies, results fell to chance levels. Of course, a correlation between study quality and study outcome, though worrying, does not in itself prove that poor quality methodology *caused* the study outcome, and Schmidt and colleagues concluded that both databases showed small effects that were deserving of further independent replication. They also called for theoretical work to explicate possible mechanisms for DMILS phenomena. Perhaps in response to this, Walach

(2005) has drawn from developments in quantum theory to argue that such effects might be understood as a form of "generalized entanglement."

Another recent line of DMILS research that does not use psychophysiological measures as the variable of interest is what might be termed cognitive DMILS, or behavioral DMILS. Consider you have a friend or family member who is going to take an important exam or a driving test. Often you will say to them "I'll be thinking of you," or "fingers crossed." The intuitive feeling behind such sayings is that your positive thoughts may somehow help your friend perform well at their challenge. A number of studies have explored this using the DMILS paradigm, specifically asking whether one person can help another remotely-located person have fewer distractions in a simple attention-focusing task. The receiver's task is to try to focus his or her attention on a candle, and to press a button to provide a count of the times when the attention wanders. At the same time, in a distant room, the sender at random periods mentally attempts to help the receiver have fewer distractions. The majority of studies using this methodology have found evidence of remote helping (Brady & Morris, 1997; Braud, Shafer, McNeill & Guerra, 1995; Edge, Suryani, Tiliopoulos & Morris, 2004; Watt & Ramakers, 2003), though two have failed to replicate this effect (Watt & Baker, 2002; Watt & Brady, 2002). Overall, then, there is some suggestion that DMILS effects may be found using "higher level" cognitive and behavioral measures as well as with the more commonly-used unconscious psychophysiological measures.

Macro–PK

In the classical dice-throwing work the effect of PK upon the rolling die was not directly observable. The die could not be seen to move in a noticeably different way when PK

was being "applied." The evidence for PK here was statistical, not perceptual. The same can be said of the more modern REG research. The PK influence upon the decay of the radioactive source (assuming that to be the physical locus of the effect) is not directly accessible to observation: we have no device which signals that particle n_i is being emitted by virtue of natural causes when particle n_{i+1} is being helped along by PK. As we mentioned in the previous chapter, psychokinetic phenomena which are discernible solely upon statistical analysis are termed *micro–PK*. The magnitude of micro–PK effects (like that of experimental ESP data) typically is small; that is, the deviation from MCE while statistically significant is minor compared with that part of the average performance attributable to chance. Consequently this sort of experimental evidence is scientifically consistent with the notion of PK but is not very convincing at a purely emotional level.

For the latter reason, directly observable PK phenomena would be of considerable interest. Such phenomena collectively are termed *macro–PK*. Thus if it were possible to produce paranormal movement of a stationary object under controlled conditions the testimony of our own senses would be most compelling and the question of the level of statistical significance would virtually be superfluous.

Many of the alleged phenomena of the spiritualistic seance would be categorized as macro–PK. Levitation of objects and people, apportation of objects from distant locations, table tipping, and effects upon weights in a set of scales all involved observable physical effects of an ostensibly paranormal character. Many such incidents, of course, occurred under conditions that cannot be regarded as scientifically controlled. As increasing numbers of physical mediums were detected in fraud, reports of such phenomena became less frequent, although Stevenson (1990a) attributes this decline not to the exposure of mediums but to the inhibitory atmosphere of skepticism promoted by the materialism of contemporary society. A perception of macro–PK phenomena as "anarchic" (Beloff, 1993) nevertheless persists.

A revival of interest in macro–PK with static objects was sparked by a Russian psychic Nina Kulagina in the late 1960s. Films brought out of Russia showed Kulagina apparently moving various nonmagnetic objects by paranormal means. In 1968 parapsychologists attending an international conference in Moscow saw one such film and through contacts made at that conference several Western researchers arranged brief visits to Russia in subsequent years to conduct their own tests with Kulagina. The Soviet authorities evidently did not want to be seen to be encouraging parapsychological research and adequate laboratory facilities unfortunately were not made available. The investigations of Kulagina's macro–PK feats, therefore, were conducted either in her own apartment or in the researchers' hotel rooms, and to this extent controls might not have been of the highest quality. A number of reputable Western parapsychologists nevertheless have reported observing and filming movement of objects without finding the slightest suggestion of any trickery (Keil, Herbert, Ullman & Pratt, 1976). For example, in one instance Kulagina apparently moved a small glass that was inverted inside another inverted glass.

Because of the vagaries of international politics parapsychologists were unable to conduct the kinds of studies necessary to elucidate the nature of Kulagina's performance. Similar phenomena rarely are reported in the West. The ability to psychokinetically displace objects reportedly is possessed by a Frenchman Jean-Pierre Girard, by Felicia Parise in America, and by Suzanne Padfield in Britain, but access to these subjects has been limited and few incisive investigations with them have been published. Further, there were claims that at least Girard had a background as an amateur magician (Shaw, 1996).

The principal macro–PK phenomenon

investigated extensively in the West sprang from the Geller affair. In 1973 the Israeli entertainer Uri Geller appeared on a BBC television program and by apparently paranormal means he bent keys, cutlery and other metal objects, and started allegedly broken watches. The authenticity of Geller's performance is a matter of much debate (as it must be with all folk who derive their living from such performances). Generally Geller has been reluctant to participate in scientific research, preferring the more lucrative television and lecture circuit. He has tended to be uncooperative in projects in which he has agreed to participate and curiously enough the few "scientific" studies with Geller by and large have been methodologically weak (*cf.* Targ & Puthoff, 1974; Marks & Kammann, 1980). There are instances in which Geller has been shown to cheat (Hutchinson, 1988; Jaroff, 2001) and, of course, there are many magicians who claim to be able to replicate Geller's feats under the same conditions in which Geller performs (Fuller, 1975; Randi, 1975). Without adequate testing in properly controlled conditions it is impossible to validate Geller's psychic talents.

More important in the present context is the fact that Geller's performances have encouraged other people to try to achieve macro–PK effects. Many children, the so-called *mini–Gellers*, have reported to parapsychologists with claims of spoon-bending abilities. The majority of these people have been unable to demonstrate their alleged talents in the parapsychological laboratory and when given an opportunity to cheat many (particularly the children) do so (Bender, 1977; Delanoy, 1987; Hanlon, 1975; Pamplin & Collins, 1975). Nevertheless there have been located occasional individuals who are said to bend metal strips by paranormal means under laboratory conditions.

One commonly employed research technique is to enclose a metal strip in a sealed glass tube or other container and to invite the subject to distort the metal psychokinetically (e.g., Wolkowski, 1977). Another method used by the British researcher John Hasted (1981) is to attach piezoelectric sensors or strain gauges to a metal strip and record the deformation of the strip while the subject is under observation; a strain gauge is a filament whose electrical resistance varies as it is stretched or bent.

There are reports from several researchers (Dierkens, 1978; Hasted, 1981; J. Isaacs, 1983; Scutt, 1981) that paranormal metal bending is recorded in these sorts of tests. In other attempts to authenticate this macro–PK phenomenon nitinol wire has been used as the target material. Nitinol has the property of "shape memory": it is machined to a specific shape at a particular temperature and when bent by normal physical means it will revert to its original shape upon reheating to the critical temperature. There are some reports that certain subjects have used PK to destroy the nitinol wire's shape memory (Hasted, 1981, p. 38; Randall & Davis, 1982). However, there has also been a report that a permanent "kink" can be produced in nitinol wire by normal means (Couttie, 1986). The status of this element of PK research therefore remains uncertain.

Some research has been undertaken into the physical characteristics of paranormal metal bending. Metallurgical analysis of some specimens has suggested that macro–PK produces changes in the crystalline structure of the metal in many respects unlike that associated with deformation by normal means. Various effects are cited in this regard, including anomalous hardening, anomalous softening, loop dislocations, a churning-like distortion of the crystals, and chemical transformations (Hasted, 1981). Recordings from strain gauges attached to the metal strip have been taken to imply that the macro–PK effect involves a surface of action that moves along the strip and that may rotate about an axis in its own plane to produce twists in the strip (Hasted & Robertson, 1979).

Little investigation of the psychological correlates of paranormal metal bending has been undertaken. Informal observations point to the importance of mental relaxation and passive attention rather than concentration (Hasted, 1981, p. 160). This characterization of the conducive state of consciousness is consistent with one report of an association between the phenomenon and EEG activity in the alpha band (Dierkens, 1978). Before the psychokinetic event, however, some arousal of the sympathetic nervous system appears necessary.

Paranormal metal bending remains a controversial phenomenon in parapsychology. One source of difficulty is that comparatively few people are actively involved in this area of research and thus the standing of the research relies heavily upon the reputation of a small number of individuals; this is not to denigrate that reputation in any way, but simply to make the point that the acceptability of a phenomenon as authentic is in part a function of the number of researchers who have elicited that phenomenon in their laboratory. This issue is all the more cogent in light of the fact that one team of parapsychologists researching the "Geller effect" was deceived at least to some extent by two conjurors masquerading as psychics (Randi, 1983a,b; Shaw, 1996; Thalbourne, 1995b; Truzzi, 1987).

Despite the controversy metal-bending research is important in two respects. First, by entailing an observable event it could offer more emotionally convincing evidence of the authenticity of PK than have most of the micro–PK experiments. Second, research on the temporal course of the metal-bending action may provide some insight into the physical characteristics of PK, an issue upon which other research paradigms have not been particularly enlightening.

Another putative form of macro–PK has been advanced as having singular evidential value to the psi hypothesis. Beloff (1985) has challenged psychics to produce what he calls a "permanent paranormal object" that would stand as enduring material testimony to the existence of paranormal processes. One such object, he suggests, could comprise two paranormally interlinked seamless rings of differing natural materials (e.g., links made from different types of timber). If such an object could not have been produced by normal means it would represent impressive evidence for the paranormal, according to Beloff.

As yet, no object fulfilling Beloff's criteria has been constructed. Wälti (1990) has reported a Swiss psychic's (unsupervised) creation of a linkage between a square frame of aluminum foil and a square frame of paper. But the materials in these links are manufactured rather than natural. Additionally, there are techniques for producing a linkage between these materials by normal means, as demonstrated by Gardner's (1991) account of duplications of the psychic's feat. It remains to be seen if a permanent paranormal object will be created and, given that it were to be, that the object would lead to a general scientific acceptance of the existence of PK as envisaged by Beloff. The production of a permanent paranormal object nevertheless represents a useful challenge to the abilities of self-proclaimed psychics.

Psychic Photography

If it is possible to influence paranormally the state of a physical system perhaps photographic film might provide a potential target material for such an effect. The psychokinetic production of an image on unexposed film or photographic plates is termed *psychic photography*.

Psychic photography arose historically from spirit photography (Krauss, 1994). From the earliest days of spiritualism some people claimed that when they took a photograph of an individual, faces of deceased folk (often "identified" as the individual's late relatives) also would be found on the processed plate. Others purported to be able to photograph spirits that were summoned to certain mediums' seances. Several psychical researchers investigated these alleged phenomena, but the evidence for spirit photography was not impressive and in many instances clear proof of fraud was established.

Perhaps photographic effects said to depend upon spirit agencies were bound to encounter an antagonistic reception among serious researchers. But in other work there appeared to be evidence that living persons paranormally could affect unexposed photographic materials. Sometimes the individual's mental image seemed to have been projected onto a photographic plate, a phenomenon dubbed "thoughtography" by the Japanese researcher Tomokichi Fukurai (1931). Psychic photography thereby came to be recognized as a field of parapsychological research that could be distinguished from spirit photography.

In more recent times interest in psychic photography has been maintained very largely through the work of the American psychiatrist and parapsychologist Jule Eisenbud with the subject Ted Serios (Eisenbud, 1967, 1977, 1989). Under Eisenbud's supervision Serios reportedly was able to produce anomalous effects on unexposed Polaroid film. The typical procedure here was that Eisenbud would point the camera toward Serios and press the shutter release at the moment signaled by Serios. In some sessions Serios was permitted to hold a small tube in front of the camera lens; this so-called "gismo" became the target of criticism by skeptics (Diaconis, 1978), but even without the device apparently paranormal effects on the film were obtained. These images included completely black or completely white photographs; fuzzy shadows and silhouettes; and pictures of varying clarity, some of which were of specifically identifiable objects. On many occasions Serios was asked to produce a photographic image of a target defined by the experimenter; some of the resulting prints bear an impressive structural resemblance to Serios's mental image of the target. Ian Stevenson and J. G. Pratt also conducted experiments with Serios.

As an area of research psychic photog-raphy remains controversial even among parapsychologists. In part this attitude is due to the small number of experimenters and subjects upon which the literature relies. A greater involvement of independent researchers

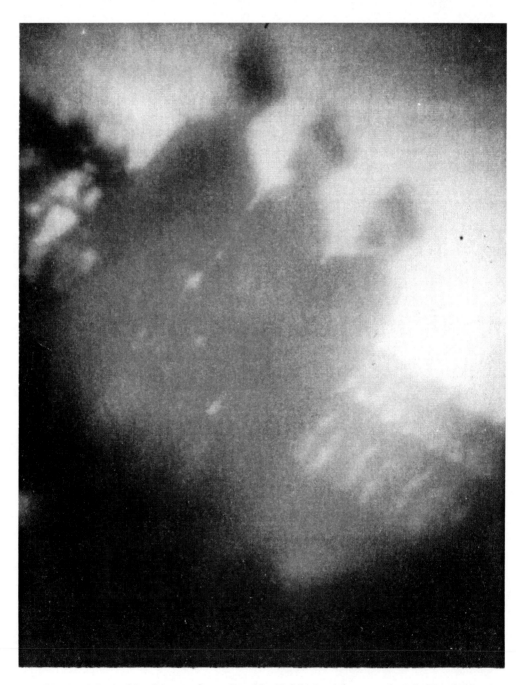

Figure 15. A psychic photograph produced by Ted Serios (photograph: Jule Eisenbud).

would be needed to put psychic photography on a more sound empirical footing. Additionally, parapsychologists' unease over this area of research reflects the fact that fraudulent production of effects upon film is such a simple matter. Photographic technicians have revealed various methods of achieving results similar to the psychics' but by normal means. This has impaired not only the acceptance of the data by other scientists but also the readiness with which parapsychologists are prepared to conduct experiments on psychic photography: charges of being a "pseudoscientist" are hard enough to bear without becoming involved in an activity which is so open to the suspicion of fraud regardless of the care taken in conducting the research.

While some of the alleged forms of PK may be poorly documented it would seem that in many PK experiments there is evidence of a genuine effect. That this effect necessarily entails a "mind over matter" transfer of information is less clear. Discussion of the theoretical aspects of PK and of psi in general is undertaken in the next chapter.

KEY TERMS AND CONCEPTS

PK experimenter effect
anpsi
DMILS
psychic healing
laying on of hands
faith healing
Grad
enzyme activity
Nina Kulagina

Uri Geller
mini–Gellers
paranormal metal bending
Hasted
permanent paranormal object
psychic photography
spirit photography
Eisenbud
Ted Serios

STUDY QUESTIONS

1. How would the existence of PK add to the complexity of the parapsychological experimenter effect?

2. What are the major sources of evidence for macro–PK?

3. Compare the research techniques used to study macro–PK with those for micro–PK. In your view, which of these two areas has generated the more convincing evidence for the authenticity of PK?

4. Discuss the methodological problems of research into psychic healing. To what extent did Grad deal successfully with these problems?

5. What evidence suggests that PK might affect photographic film? Why are many parapsychologists dubious about such effects? If the effects were authentic what light could they throw on the nature of PK?

6. DMILS studies are usually viewed as a form of PK because an agent is being asked to exert an influence over the receiver. Consider how ESP might also produce DMILS effects.

8

THEORIES OF PSI

This chapter considers the major theories designed to account for the two proposed fundamental forms of psi, ESP and PK. It should be noted at the outset that attention is to be focused upon scientific rather than mystical theories.

Theorization has a crucial role to play in scientific endeavor. Empirical research does not achieve scientific advancement merely through the collection of data and the evaluation of isolated hypotheses. Understanding requires that the derived factual information be ordered, integrated, generalized, and interpreted. Further, to permit continuing progress the hypotheses being investigated in isolated projects must be interrelated and coordinated, forming a gradual (albeit not always linear) kind of conceptual progression. These various functions are served by the formulation of a powerful scientific theory or more typically, a few competing theories of this type. Without such theories empirical inquiry achieves no more than a massive collection of piecemeal observations, and genuine progress is inhibited by the lack of any overriding conceptual momentum to steer ongoing hypothesis generation into purposeful channels. Ancillary functions of scientific theories are the prediction of new findings and the clarification of assumptions underlying a particular area of research.

The Australian philosopher Michael Scriven (1962, p. 104) has asserted that whereas psychoanalysis is all theory without any hard facts, parapsychology is just a collection of facts without any theory. At least with regard to the latter part of this comment the position is overdrawn, as there has been a good deal of theorizing about the nature of psi. The point of Scriven's assessment of parapsychology, however, is that the field lacks what could be called an agreed theory. Indeed many scientists ignore the efforts of parapsychologists not simply because the facts themselves are controversial but because the facts are not accommodated by any widely endorsed scientific theory (Beloff, 1972; Churchland, 1987; Flew, 1980). Thus the development of a viable theory of psi is essential both to progress within parapsychology and to the acceptance of the field by other scientists.

Most contemporary theories of psi are designed to accommodate both ESP and PK. This is desirable in part on the ground of the principle of parsimony, but it is also the case that there do not appear to be adequate empirical grounds for supposing ESP and PK to be ontologically independent phenomena (Roe, Davey & Stevens, 2003, 2005; Storm & Thalbourne, 2000; Thalbourne, 2004a).

In essence theories of psi have to address two basic questions: first, how is information mediated between the environment and the individual (in either direction, if ESP and PK are construed as reciprocal processes in this regard); and second, how does psi come to manifest itself in the individual's consciousness and actions in the ways that it does? Most theories have focused on the first issue, that of mediation, as can be seen from earlier commentaries (Chari, 1977; Rao, 1978; Stokes, 1987). This preoccupation is understandable: if there is no clear conceptual appreciation of the mediational phase then the experiential phase might well be dismissed as fantasy or autosuggestion. This survey of theories of psi therefore is organized in three major sections: theories which address the mediational issue, those that are concerned with the experiential phase, and some that in a sense encompass both. Finally there is a discussion of the view that theories of psi are unnecessary because psi does not exist; here some skeptical interpretations of the available data are presented.

Theories of Psi Mediation

Electromagnetic Theories

According to some accounts psi is mediated by some form of electromagnetic radiation. In ESP this radiation is held to affect electrical activity in the brain directly, that is, without going through any recognized sensory organ. In PK electrical activity in the brain is "transmitted" as electromagnetic radiation. Under this approach telepathy for example, would be deemed a sort of "mental radio." Modern proponents of this view include the Russian I. M. Kogan (1966), the Canadian Michael Persinger (1975), and the American Robert Becker (1992). Each of these theorists proposes that psi is mediated by *extremely low frequency* (ELF) waves whose wavelength is so great that they are not impeded by walls or other objects in the manner that light and sound are.

Under Becker's (1992) formulation of the electromagnetic hypothesis, signals conveying the psi information are held to affect not the neurons of the brain but some more primitive system in the brain. This system, possibly involving the glial cells, exists in all living organisms and is posited to operate on the basis of electromagnetic fields. As a rudimentary communication system it may function most effectively during periods of quiet geomagnetic activity (the intensity of the Earth's magnetic field varies as it is subjected to solar particles and cosmic rays) and at times when the individual is engaged in minimal sensory processing.

Persinger (1985, 1989) argues the ELF wave hypothesis is supported by correlations between the incidence of spontaneous ESP experiences and low levels of geomagnetic activity. These correlations have been observed by Persinger and his colleagues for both spontaneous psi experiences and experimental psi performance (Arango & Persinger, 1988; Berger & Persinger, 1991; Lewicki, Schaut & Persinger, 1987; Persinger & Krippner, 1989) and have been confirmed to some degree by independent investigators (Haraldsson & Gissurarson, 1987; Krippner, Vaughan & Spottiswoode, 2000; Wilkinson & Gauld, 1993). Spottiswoode (1997) reports that the relationship seems to be evident only in a two-hour window around 1:30 P.M. local sidereal time, but attempted replications of this trend have yielded mixed findings (e.g., Dalkvist & Westerlund, 2000). Again, because of their correlational nature the data are not conclusive for the ELF-wave hypothesis. For example, the correlation might arise from the facilitation of psi-conducive states of consciousness under conditions of quiet geomagnetic activity rather than from the facilitation of any electromagnetically mediated ESP signal (see Stevens, 1997). Additionally, Hubbard and May (1987) maintain that for statistical reasons current indices of geomagnetic activity are inappropriate to a correlational assessment of the electromagnetic hypothesis (but see Persinger, 1989, pp. 144–147).

Related to the question of geomagnetic activity and psi, five studies have investigated the correlation between restricted-choice ESP task performance and atmospheric electromagnetism. The first study found higher ESP performance was associated with lower atmospheric electromagnetism in the 24 hours prior to the ESP test (Houtkooper, Schienle, Stark & Vaitl, 1999). This relationship failed to reach statistical significance in each of four subsequent studies (Houtkooper, 2003; Houtkooper, Schienle, Stark & Vaitl, 2001) but when all studies are combined they show a small but significant negative correlation between atmospheric electromagnetism and ESP performance (r = -.09). Overall, it may be argued the data show some degree of consistency but evidently the effect is very small and in any event the relationship needs to be independently replicated. Given that atmospheric electromagnetism is often recorded as part of environmental monitoring, there would seem to be the potential to further investigate this question retrospectively, comparing local weather records with the records of ESP studies previously conducted in other laboratories.

There are numerous objections to electromagnetic theories. If psi is mediated by electromagnetic radiation both ESP and PK should obey the inverse square law as do other forms of such radiation; thus if the distance between target and percipient is doubled then the psi "signal" should be attenuated to a quarter of its original strength. That ESP and PK seem independent of distance casts doubt on this suggestion, notwithstanding the fact that performance on ESP/PK tasks is hardly a pure measure of "signal strength." Again, if psi tests were to be conducted in a Faraday cage which is designed to exclude electromagnetic radiation of specific wavelengths, then subjects' scores should be at chance level. In experimental investigations, however, this sort of screening does not appear to eliminate extra-chance ESP or PK effects (Eisenbud, 1977; Tart, 1988; Vasiliev,

1963/1976). The proponents of the ELF wave theory could argue that a Faraday cage would pose no obstacle to ELF waves because the whole cage would resonate at the frequency of these signals; on the other hand it is not clear how the experimental participant could sense and interpret these resonant vibrations.

Apart from the context of Faraday cages it has been calculated that direct cortical detection of ELF waves would require an antenna of considerable proportions, far larger than the human brain. The low information transmission rate of ELF waves and their poor capacity to carry information over a large distance raise further serious doubts about this form of the electromagnetic theory (Stokes, 1987, p. 115). An account of precognition under any of these theories would have to make appeal to the hypothetical existence of so-called "advanced" electromagnetic waves that can travel backward in time, but even this assumption cannot cope with the precognition of an event set even as much as one day into the future (Stokes, 1987, p. 127). It is difficult also to conceive of brain activity instigating sufficiently powerful electromagnetic radiation as is proposed to occur in expressive psi: with current technology the electrical activity of the brain cannot be detected more than a few millimeters from the scalp.

Finally, electromagnetic theories do not explain what variations in the pattern of radiation are the cues to the identity of targets: for example, how does the radiation associated with a square on an ESP card or in a telepathic agent's thoughts differ from that for a circle?

Energy Field Theories

Other theorists attribute psi to some undiscovered or unrecognized form of physical energy (e.g., Wassermann, 1956). This energy is said to radiate from the individual as a *field effect* and mediates extrasensory and psychokinetic phenomena. The quanta of which the energy is comprised are so small that they do not interact with matter, and hence the energy field may pass through solid objects with no difficulty. Interest in these sorts of energy fields (e.g., "bioenergy") is greatest in Europe, particularly in Eastern Europe, and in Japan; research with this orientation often is termed *psychotronics*.

One query to be leveled at this theory is that if the energy passes through matter unimpeded, how is it stopped and detected by the brain in receptive psi? One would have to suppose that the energy is not "stopped" as such but rather has its effect through an interaction with neurological processes as it passes through the brain, just as a magnetic field can induce a flow of electricity.

A more serious criticism is that despite efforts in psychotronic research there is no generally acknowledged demonstration that an energy with the required characteristics actually exists. In terms of theory building it would be legitimate if the energy field was purely hypothetical, but in such circumstances to fulfill the requirements of a scientific theory the postulated energy form still would have to be specified in such a way as to lead to novel implications that can be subjected to empirical testing. Energy field theories of psi unfortunately have not been markedly successful in this regard.

Observational Theories

According to quantum mechanics a physical system such as an atom has an infinite number of potential states, and observation of the system is associated with its "collapse" into one of its component states. An American theoretical physicist Evan Harris Walker (1975) believes the observer's consciousness or intention is responsible for the collapse and he interprets PK phenomena as instances of just this sort of effect. Walker explains ESP in a similar if rather contorted way: here the selection of ESP targets collapses in (partial) accordance with the "percipient's"

consciousness of them. In neither of these paranormal processes is there held to be any transfer of energy; only information is transferred. As quantum state collapse is independent of space and time psi phenomena are not related to these variables. Hence an experimental subject can affect the output of an REG irrespective of the complexity of the device. Even macro-PK and effects on rolling dice are possible because there are quantum processes occurring in individual atoms of the target object, according to Walker.

A broadly similar observational theory by Schmidt (1975) is couched in terms of feedback to a "psi source" or observer by which the probability of a given outcome in a quantum state collapse may be altered, depending on the "strength" of the psi source. In Schmidt's model ESP comprises an influence upon the quantum indeterminacy of neural processes in the brain. The latter notion is developed by Jahn and Dunne (1986) who draw parallels between aspects of mentation and various dimensions of quantum processes.

An advantage of these observational theories is that they are formulated in mathematical terms. Theories of this sort are relatively powerful because they generate precise predictions and thereby are readily accessible to empirical assessment. The level of REG-PK research has risen sharply in the last four decades, in part because of the questions raised by the observational theories. Although Schmidt's theoretical predictions accord with most of those yielded by Walker's theory there are some differences and this too has stimulated experimental investigation. For example, both theories maintain the dependence of a psi effect upon feedback of the outcome to the experimental subject or source of that effect (Millar, 1978); some experimental results (e.g., Braud, 1978; Thorisson, Skulason & Haraldsson, 1991) query this assumption, although it is difficult to be sure who the psi source really is and what manner of feedback is sufficient. On the other hand, PK performance is predicted to be inversely related to the presentation rate of trials under Walker's theory but not under Schmidt's. Experiments to test between the models on this score have yielded somewhat inconsistent results (Stanford, 1977, pp. 351–354), although as we mentioned in Chapter 6, two recent PK-REG studies have found PK performance for high-speed PK trials to reverse direction, that is, contrary to the effect in low-speed trials the apparent PK influence in the fast trials was in the direction opposite to the operator's intention (Dobyns, Dunne, Jahn & Nelson, 2004; Ibison, 1998). These findings seem to pose a problem for observational theories because such theories cannot account for a reversal of effect (Dobyns et al., 2004).

Another strength of observational theories is that they predict the existence of a new phenomenon, namely retro–PK. In Chapter 6 we described some studies apparently demonstrating retro–PK, though the first experiment designed to test this prediction appeared to lend less support for observational theory than for an alternative theory (Bierman & Houtkooper, 1975). This raises the question of what it would take to falsify an observational theory, and it may be that the proponents of observational theories could argue that the theories are as yet insufficiently well-elaborated to take account of hidden variables, so a conclusive test would be premature.

One of the less satisfactory aspects of the observational theories is that they imply a quantum process may be affected by many observers at various times. For example, the results of a completed PK experiment conceivably might have been due in large measure to some particularly powerful psi sources who in the future get feedback about the quantum state collapse by reading the published report of the experimental data. The possibility of contributions by any number of unknown observers at any time is termed the *divergence problem*. That such an effect is

possible has yet to be resolved empirically, although in one study Schmidt (1985) found evidence that a quantum process can become fixed after the first observation and thenceforth be immune to further PK influence. Schmidt (1984) has modified his theory to permit observation to be "complete" at some stage so that the quantum state collapse could not proceed beyond this point. Because additional PK influences by later observers would then not be possible the divergence problem is eliminated by Schmidt's amendment. In ruling out the occurrence of a further PK effect beyond a certain point in time, however, the revised model essentially abandons the assumption of PK's space-time independence.

Another criticism of observational theories is raised by Braude (1979). He points out that they involve a closed causal loop. A psi effect supposedly begins with the observation of its outcome and this retroactively effects the quantum state collapse that underlies the outcome that is observed. That is, in order to bring about an event through psi the occurrence of that event must first be observed. Walker (1984, pp. 282–283) responds to this criticism by arguing that it is misleading to apply everyday temporal logic to a quantum process; rather, under observational theories the observation and the quantum state collapse are aspects of a single event. A more practical limitation of the observational theories is that because the measurement of psi is so unreliable the parameters of the theories' equations are difficult to determine with any precision.

The observational theories have been productive of novel predictions and of research. Their validity nevertheless is yet to be demonstrated conclusively. There is some debate even among quantum physicists that consciousness is a necessary component of state vector collapse (May & Spottiswoode, 1989). As noted earlier, there also are some empirical data that question the necessity of accurate feedback for the successful performance of psi tasks (Braud, 1978; Thorisson et al., 1991), but the difficulty of specifying what constitutes an "observation" leaves such findings open to contention. Indeed, some concern has been expressed that the observational theories' premise of the necessity of feedback may be essentially unfalsifiable (Varvoglis, 1986).

In addition to these empirical issues it appears that some parapsychologists are uneasy about borrowing from theoretical physics some laws that relate to the subatomic world and applying them to human behavior and to macro-physical events. Whether this translation is best regarded as literal or as an analogy (see Amorim, 1994), or indeed is appropriate at all, must be answered by further research. For a skeptical analysis of this issue see 't Hooft (2000); by contrast, for a case that an observational theory admits the possibility of psi see Costa de Beauregard (1998) and Houtkooper (2002).

Some of these difficulties would seem to be avoided in an observational theory recently proposed by von Lucadou, the Model of Pragmatic Information (MPI: von Lucadou, 1995; von Lucadou & Kornwachs, 1980). While retaining many of the relational properties of the earlier theories this model is formulated in the more general terms of systems theory rather than starting at the level of quantum events. That is, von Lucadou agrees that information obtained from a system can interact with the measurement process or "observation," but he does not think it necessary to reduce processes of the mind to features of the quantum theoretical structure of atomic systems. The MPI states that psi effects represent meaningful non-local correlations between a person and a target system. Such non-local correlations cannot be used for information transfer, and thus the MPI predicts difficulty in obtaining replicable evidence for psi under the methods usually used by experimental parapsychologists. The merits of his approach still are under investigation. For instance, it has been suggested that the MPI does not adequately specify how a psi effect would manifest during replication attempts and that therefore the model needs further elaboration before it can be properly tested (Etzold, 2006).

Theories of the Experiential Phase of Psi

Assuming some means of mediating psi information between the (ESP or PK) target and the individual there remains to be explained the experiential facet of the phenomena. In ESP, where is the information admitted to the central nervous system or information processing system, and how does the system deal with it? In PK, what manner of information processing takes place, and at what point of the system is it transmitted or emitted into the environment? As noted above parapsychological theorization on these aspects of psi phenomena has been relatively limited.

Theories of the ESP experience will be considered first. The basic issue here is whether or not ESP operates in a sensory-like fashion, despite the absence of an obvious organ for extrasensory "perception." On this basis a distinction may be drawn between two approaches to the experiential phase of ESP, the *pseudosensory models* and the *memory models*.

Extrasensory perception popularly is spoken of as a "sixth sense," and in essence this is the theoretical orientation of the pseudosensory models. That is, although ESP apparently is not mediated by any of the *known* sensory modalities, perhaps there is some as yet undiscovered organ, a "third eye," responsible for the reception of so-called extrasensory information. Under this pseudosensory approach psi inputs would be processed by the mind in essentially the same manner as sensory inputs.

A pseudosensory model of psi has been proposed by Schmeidler (1991). She proposes that the perceptual processing of psi inputs parallels that of sensory inputs from the most basic level of analysis, namely, the discrimination of a figure from its background. The extent of the pseudosensory processing of the psi input will depend on the strength of the input, according to Schmeidler; it will follow the course of sensory processing to a greater extent if the psi signal is "strong."

A means of assessing pseudosensory models of ESP is to conceptualize the mind as an information processing system, to establish the stages of information processing to which sensory inputs are subject, and then to see if the nature of ESP performance conforms to the characteristics of these respective sensory processing stages. A detailed analysis in these terms is presented by Irwin (1979a; see also Irwin, 1978a,b, 1980a). The conclusion reached there is that the available evidence does not encourage the view that extrasensory information receives the same sorts of processing as a sensory input. For example, unlike a sensory stimulus, the sensory discriminability or "quality" of the ESP target (its contrast, size, form, orientation, etc.) has no systematic effect on ESP performance (apart from effects interpretable in terms of psychological reactions rather than to discriminability as such). On current evidence, depiction of ESP in a pseudosensory framework does not emerge as a promising approach, but as Schmeidler's work demonstrates, some parapsychologists remain open to this option.

Sensory processing is, however, only one mode of human information processing. Another is the ideational mode, in which the information processed by the system (or mind) is obtained not direct from the external environment but from within the system itself. For example, typically a dream or a reminiscence entails the processing of information that already is in the system, specifically in the individual's (long-term) memory. Perhaps the processing of extrasensory information is more akin to processing

in the ideational mode than to that in the sensory mode.

This possibility is encapsulated by the so-called memory models of ESP. According to the memory models, in ESP a trace (or set of traces) in long-term memory becomes activated and the information in these traces represents the foundation of the content of the extrasensory experience. The activated memorial information is mediated from a preconscious to a conscious level by the very same processes that characterize the normal operation of the information processing system in the ideational mode. Just how the memory traces become activated in ESP is unknown and is the subject of speculation: perhaps the process entails the passage of information from the ESP target directly to the relevant memory trace/s, or again memory activation may be a nonmechanistic, teleological process (see the discussion of noncybernetic theories below). At the same time it must be said that this issue pertains to the mediational phase of psi rather than to the experiential phase in itself.

Memory models of ESP have been proposed by Roll (1966, 1987) and Irwin (1979a), and a similar notion is encompassed by Stevens' (2002, p. 239) argument that ESP is "imagination that relates to the target." In Irwin's (1979a) version it is held that the activated memorial information is *structurally* similar to the ESP target. For example, if the target is a star then memories relating to a radial structure (e.g., those for a star, a daisy, a bicycle wheel and so on) will tend to become activated. Among the evidence in support of this notion is the work of Sinclair (1930/ 1962) and Warcollier (1938/1975) in which selected subjects frequently drew remarkably accurate representations of an ESP target but showed little appreciation of its identity or meaning. Again, in a small-scale laboratory study with Zener figures Kreiman (2001) found incorrect guesses for an ESP target tended to correspond to a significant extent to structurally similar targets (i.e, calling "square" for a circle, "star" for a cross).

On the assumption that the systemic source of extrasensory information is in long-term memory a good deal of ESP data begins to become intelligible. For example, the models readily accommodate the known forms of spontaneous ESP experience (including even those rare cases comprising purely emotional reactions or purely semantic associations), as well as such characteristics of experimental ESP performance as position effects and psi missing. The central assumption of the memory models is consistent with reported correlations between ESP scores and long-term memory skills. Further, an experiment by Kanthamani and Rao (1974) employing a task with both memory and ESP components suggests more directly that extrasensory processes are not merely *similar* to those underlying performance in memory tasks but rather they *depend* upon memorial processes for their expression. In addition to this empirical support the memory models are proving of considerable heuristic value in integrating diverse aspects of the experiential phase of ESP (Edge et al., 1986, Ch. 8).

The experiential phase of PK phenomena has received scant attention, primarily because parapsychologists have so few experimental data on the psychological (especially cognitive) correlates of PK. Theorization along these lines nevertheless is pertinent if only to encourage further empirical investigation. The possibility of incorporating PK in a memory framework is pursued by Irwin (1979a, 1980b). Essentially the proposed account is the converse of the memory model of ESP. Thus in PK it is suggested a long-term memory trace (or set of such traces) is active and by some means (whether mechanistic or teleological) a relationship is formed between the nature of the memory trace and the structure of a physical system in the environment. This approach has yet to prove as successful in its application to PK as it has to ESP. One reason for this may spring from the theory's tenet that so-called receptive and expressive

psi are in fact converse facets of a single process. Despite broad implicit endorsement of this idea by parapsychologists and explicit attempts to argue ESP and PK are indivisible (Nash, 1983) the evidence for it is meager (Irwin, 1985e). Indeed a few differences are emerging between the performance characteristics of ESP and those of PK. For example, indications of clustering of ESP hits and the personality and attitudinal correlates of ESP performance are not paralleled in PK. These differences if confirmed and elaborated by further research would suggest the unitarian approach to psi has shaky foundations. There certainly is scope for further theoretical development in the domain of PK's information-processing bases.

Stanford (1974a,b; 1990) has formulated an account of the experiential phase of psi that is closely allied to the approach of the memory models. Stanford's theory is termed the *psi-mediated instrumental response* (PMIR) model. In its most recent form (Stanford, 1990) the PMIR model proposes that psi experiences arise because, under circumstances prevailing in the environment, the individual has some disposition or need for the experience to occur. That is, the psi experience or "psi-mediated response" is fundamentally goal-oriented or adaptive. Stanford further proposes that psi operates below the level of consciousness through the facilitation of responses that are already encoded in memory; in this respect the PMIR model shares some conceptual ground with the memory models. The range of responses thought by Stanford to be facilitated by psi nevertheless is reasonably broad. Under the PMIR model psi may trigger behaviors, feelings, images, associations, desires or memories. These, either singly or in combination, may constitute the psi-mediated response.

One of the features of the PMIR model is that it explicitly accommodates nonintentional psi experiences. In other words, the individual evidently need not be conscious of the circumstances which make the psi-mediated response appropriate. Additionally, Stanford has taken pains to formulate his model as a series of propositions, each designed to be readily accessible to empirical assessment. The PMIR model thereby has served to stimulate research and it should continue to do so for some time. At a more pragmatic level, Stanford's approach has appeal also in the ease of its application to people's spontaneous parapsychological experiences. The notion that psi is fundamentally need-serving has also been subsumed in more recent theories including Taylor's (2003) evolutionary model and Storm and Thalbourne's (2000) psychopraxia model (see also Thalbourne, 2004a).

Recently, Carpenter (2004, 2005a) has proposed a model, termed the *First Sight* model of psi, that is similar in some respects to Stanford's. Carpenter's model assumes an organism has access to events beyond its physical boundaries and that unconsciously the events that are most needed or relevant for the organism are selected for special response. However, Carpenter goes further in suggesting that psi perceptions ubiquitiously form the first stage of *all* perceptions: "Psi processes are posited to function normally as the unconscious leading edge of the development of all consciousness and all intention" (Carpenter, 2004, p. 217). In this bold model, then, psi phenomena are central to our perceptual processes, although we are usually unaware of this.

Stimulated by recent research that shows the central role played by the emotional system in decision making (Bechara, Damasio, & Damasio 2000), Broughton has argued that emotions may be fundamental to the selection of psi-mediated memories (Broughton, 2006). Furthermore, this research may provide a mechanism for the psi-mediated adaptive behavior predicted by Stanford's PMIR model. Thus, Broughton's ideas elegantly combine the memory and PMIR models and integrate these with mainstream developments. Additionally, it is claimed that the First Sight model can help organize findings in memory–ESP research (Carpenter, 2006). All in all this would seem to be a promising area for future research and theorizing.

Other approaches to the experiential phase of psi have not been expounded in adequate detail. There is some exploration within a neurophysiological framework, most notably implicating the temporal lobe as a neuroanatomical locus for psi experiences (e.g., Neppe, 1983; Persinger & Roll, 1986), but this has not yet been refined sufficiently to qualify as a model of the experiential phase.

Noncybernetic Theories

There is one more group of theories which might be said to address both the mediational and the experiential phases of psi, or again be regarded more properly as an alternative to the concepts of ESP and PK. These theories abandon the notion of information flow in psi phenomena and hence they are referred to here as *noncybernetic* models.

The best known theory of this sort is Carl Jung's synchronicity hypothesis. Jung (1955/1985) argued that there exists in nature a tendency for two separate systems to conform to a common structure or to coincide. This tendency however, is held not to involve a cause-effect relationship. That is, it is not a matter of one system being physically linked to the other system and mechanistically causing the latter to conform with it in some degree. Synchronicity is not a causal process, it is *acausal*. When elements of the two systems coincide this "just happens" as a characteristic of the natural world. Hence a series of ESP targets may show extra-chance agreement with a subject's set of calls not because of any transfer of information between targets and the person's mind but because of this acausal tendency of synchronicity. The phenomena of PK are explained similarly. In short, psi experiences are instances of synchronicity or meaningful coincidence.

For people socially conditioned to conceptually structure their world in terms of cause and effect the notion of acausal relationships is difficult to comprehend or at least to appreciate. Not unexpectedly Jung's hypothesis has met with a measure of criticism. The British philosopher Antony Flew (1953) has argued it is nonsensical to speak of a "meaningful coincidence" because this is tautological: a situation is a coincidence only because the association between the two separate events is meaningful and thus the coincidence is defined, not accounted for, by its meaningfulness.

Also meaningfulness is a subjective matter: what is meaningful to one person is not so to another (Falk, 1989). It is difficult to credit the existence of a tendency in the physical world such that a certain situation arises simply because one particular person would find meaning in that situation. The alternative to this interpretation of synchronicity is to suppose that there exists some ultrahuman domain of meaningfulness, where meaning in a coincidence of events is defined in objective terms independent of people's culture and personal history. More crucially perhaps for parapsychological research, if ESP and PK are acausal events then there is no point in conducting experiments on the phenomena: manipulating conditions in such a way as to elicit psi necessarily implies a causal process (Beloff, 1972, 1977b). If a "synchronistic" relationship is shown to be more likely to occur in some situations or with certain sorts of people the relationship may be said to be governed by these situational and personalistic variables and thereby cannot be acausal.

In that synchronicity does not imply any flow of information between mind and target in a psi task it could be argued that it is not an explanation of ESP and PK but an alternative to these concepts. That is, since ESP and PK have been *defined* in terms of information flow they cannot be attributed to synchronicity; rather they would be supplanted by Jung's hypothesis (if the evidence warranted doing so). The extent to which psi processes and synchronicity may be differentiated nevertheless continues to be a matter for vigorous debate (e.g., Mansfield, Rhine-Feather & Hall, 1998; Storm, 1999).

Another theory that abandons the assumption of information flow is Rex Stanford's (1978) conformance theory. Unlike synchronistic accounts the conformance theory proposes that the link between targets and mind is causal but is not physically mediated as often implied in the information-flow or cybernetic approach. Stanford depicts the causal relationship in terms of the *goal* that the relationship achieves; in other words the formation of the relationship is a teleological process. Psi therefore is viewed as organizing loose, disorganized or random processes such that their outcomes accord with the dispositions of someone who (or some organism which) has an interest in those outcomes. A similar model is presented by Ballard (1991).

Noncybernetic models do offer a simple account of psi's evident independence of physical variables such as size, distance, and time. Admittedly scientists are so wedded to explanations in terms of physical or mechanistic causes that the teleological approach is unlikely to appeal to people outside the field of parapsychology (or for that matter to many people within this field). But the viability of a theory must be based on its performance in explanation and prediction, not simply on the conditioned emotions it evokes among conventional scientists. Unlike the synchronicity hypothesis the conformance model is open to empirical testing and thereby is admissible as a scientific theory. Much more research nevertheless is required in order to ascertain if teleological causation provides a satisfactory account of the characteristics of psi.

Skeptical Theories of Psi Phenomena

To this point the analysis has focused on theories that seek to explain the paranormal mediation of information between an individual and the environment and the means by which this information is utilized as the basis of a parapsychological experience. Skeptics on the other hand maintain there is no need to devise any theory of paranormal processes because the available data can be accommodated satisfactorily by appeal to "normal" or conventionally recognized factors. In a sense this view is not so much a theory as an ideological stance. The skeptical position nonetheless is an influential one and thus it deserves our attention.

Under a skeptical approach all spontaneous psi experiences are attributed to such processes as misperception, misinterpretation, inaccurate recall of individual experiences, or chance. The feasibility of this view was surveyed in Chapter 3 and generally is acknowledged by parapsychologists themselves. The central issue for the skeptic therefore is the explanation of the experimental psi data. As noted in Chapters 4 and 7 the common assumption here is that the data are variously an artifact of procedural flaws, a freak outcome of chance, other inappropriate assumptions about sampling, or a product of fraud. Such weaknesses undoubtedly do exist in the database of parapsychology and indeed of behavioral science in general (e.g., Akers, 1984; Bösch, Steinkamp & Boller, 2006; Scargle, 2000), though it cannot be retrospectively proven that these flaws are responsible for data apparently verifying the psi hypothesis. However, in the critics' view their position is further supported by the reportedly low level of replicability of the data and by the fact that there is no definitive psi experiment, none that is immune to claims of actual or potential methodological deficiencies.

At the same time it is possible to maintain that the data of psi experiments attest to a genuine phenomenon (as opposed to an artifact) but that this underlying phenomenon is a normal process rather than psi. Most skeptics have been so intent on dismissing the data that they have given little thought to the development of a theory to account for any valid effect yielded by psi research. One skeptical theory that did take the data seriously was proposed by Goodfellow (1938, 1940).

Goodfellow's argument, originally applied to the data of an ESP experiment conducted during a series of weekly broadcasts by the Zenith Radio Corporation late in 1937, was that the extra-chance correspondence between ESP targets and calls was due purely to nonrandomness in the subjects' selection of calls. When people try to produce any random series (such as in guessing the identities of a random series of ESP symbols) they may in fact show various biases in their responses (Brugger, 1997; Palmer, 1997b; Rapoport & Budescu, 1997; Tune, 1964). Some symbols may be called much more frequently than others; calling the same symbol two or more times in succession may be avoided to the extent that such strings appear more rarely than in a truly random series; and other idiosyncratic sequential interdependencies may arise, such as a tendency to call "circle" immediately after a call of "square." The nonrandomness in the ESP subject's calls is responsible for the deviation of the number of hits from that expected under a random-guessing statistical model, according to Goodfellow. A similar account recently has been advanced by Brugger and his colleagues (Brugger, Landis & Regard, 1990; Brugger, Regard & Landis, 1991).

Can this theory account for the observed correlates of experimental ESP performance? That is, does the tendency to produce a nonrandom series of responses have the same pattern of correlates as ESP scores? Presumably the extent of nonrandomness in a set of calls would be little dependent upon the distance of the targets from the subject, the presence of intervening physical barriers, the size and orientation of the targets, and similar physical variables.

Call randomness may be affected by the subject's mood (Stanford, 1975, p. 156). With regard to attitudinal variables sheep (believers in ESP) have a poorer understanding of statistical probability than do goats or disbelievers (Blackmore & Troscianko, 1985). Additionally, Brugger and his co-workers (Brugger et al., 1990, 1991) found that in comparison to goats, sheep tend to avoid repetition of responses in ESP tests. Although this result was not confirmed in studies by Blackmore and Troscianko (1985), Broughton (1994), Houtkooper and Haraldsson (1997), and Lawrence (1991), the possibility remains that the sheep-goat effect reported in the ESP literature conceivably could reflect nonrandomness of guesses.

Like ESP scores, nonrandomness of response sequences correlates negatively with mathematical education and short-term memory (Tune, 1964) and is subject to experimenter effects (Gault & Goodfellow, 1940).

On the other hand, other correlates of nonrandomness seem to be contrary to those of ESP performance. For example, nonrandomness correlates positively with neuroticism (Wagenaar, 1972) and with age (Tune, 1964). It would be thought too that dissociative tendencies and the identified psiconducive states of consciousness would work to facilitate response spontaneity rather than to encourage nonrandomness (Brugger, 1997). Perhaps some account needs to be taken of the *type* of nonrandomness in response series. That is, a given psychological variable might well be related positively to one style of nonrandomness and negatively to another.

The importance of distinguishing types of nonrandomness becomes evident when the issue of psi missing is countenanced in the context of Goodfellow's approach. Both psi

hitting and psi missing entail deviations from chance but their contrasting direction signals the insufficiency of an undifferentiated concept of nonrandomness as an explanation of ESP scores. Different styles of nonrandomness have indeed been found in association with psi hitting and missing; Morris and Cohen (1971) found subjects who rarely called the same symbol twice in succession in ESP tests achieved psi hitting and those who frequently called doubles showed psi missing. On these grounds, if a psychological variable reportedly correlates in one direction with ESP scores and in the other direction with response nonrandomness this might not be contrary to Goodfellow's theory but instead be a mere consequence of the selected index of nonrandomness. That ESP and nonrandomness show so many of the same correlates (when direction is ignored) might be taken therefore, as encouraging for the spirit of Goodfellow's theory.

Two relatively direct tests of the theory may be considered. First, Houtkooper and Haraldsson (1996) investigated the relationship between nonrandom generation of calls and performance in ESP tests. Consistent with Goodfellow's theory a significant positive correlation (Kendall's tau = .16) was found between repetition avoidance and ESP scores. That is, when ESP calls become increasingly nonrandom there is a greater likelihood that the calls will match the targets, just as Goodfellow predicted. This most intriguing finding warrants urgent replication, preferably with a variety of indices of nonrandomness. Additionally, it remains to be demonstrated that the associated effect size (.24) is sufficient to account both for extra-chance ESP performance and for the pattern of its correlates.

A second source of direct evidence was known even in the earlier card-guessing studies. In Goodfellow's opinion the extra-chance scores yielded by an ESP experiment stem from the comparison of a nonrandom series (the subject's calls) to a random series (the targets). The effect therefore should be evident regardless of the choice of the random series against which the comparison is made; that is, extra-chance scores should be equally likely whether the calls are scored against the actual targets used for that individual or against some other run of ESP symbols not even used as targets in the experiment. But when ESP calls are compared to symbols for which they were not intended the correspondence is found to be at the level of chance (e.g., Greenwood, 1938). (Appeal to the parapsychological experimenter effect to excuse such a finding of course is inappropriate because Goodfellow's theory would not admit any manner of parapsychological influence.) This represents a substantial empirical stumbling-block for the approach advocated by Goodfellow. In the view of some parapsychologists a further cause for unease may be that the theory is applicable only to ESP and not at all to PK; in a PK experiment the subject does not generate the series of targets and thus psychological sources of nonrandomness are not a pertinent issue. Additionally, nonrandomess theories are most relevant for restricted-choice ESP studies, where participants tend to make dozens if not hundreds of calls on only four or five target symbols. As we noted in Chapter 4, most modern ESP research tends not to use restricted-choice methods. For instance, free-response methods such as the ganzfeld typically have only one trial per participant. In this case, randomness of calling is not an issue. Likewise, in the DMILS studies we described in Chapter 7, unconscious psychophysiological measures are used as indicators of possible ESP or PK information, and again randomness of calling is not a relevant factor in these studies. So to some extent nonrandomness theories are undermined by methodological changes over time.

Evidence of some consistencies between the correlates of ESP performance and those of nonrandom response generation, in conjunction with the findings of Houtkooper

and Haraldsson (1997), nevertheless indicate that Goodfellow's theory does warrant further empirical scrutiny.

Other skeptical theories of the psi data have not been developed in detail. Spencer-Brown (1953), Bridgman (1956) and Gilmore (1989) have argued that classical scientific understanding of chance processes may be flawed or simplistic and that the data thought to attest to psi are therefore nothing else than a consequence of inappropriate notions about chance expectation. This argument has yet to be shown to accommodate the observed pattern of correlates of psi performance. Because classical probability theory has been widely applied in scientific fields other than parapsychology, even skeptics are loath to pursue the argument.

Contemporary skeptics generally do not believe the psi data attest to any phenomenon, paranormal or otherwise. Thus the anomalous data are dismissed as unworthy of consideration because of the perceived possibility of fraud (e.g., Hansel, 1966, 1980) or because of claimed procedural errors (e.g., Diaconis, 1978; Hyman, 1985). In that these views deny the existence of any nonartifactual effect they are strictly speaking not theories of psi. Further, they are not open to falsification. In the unlikely event there was a psi experiment for which the skeptic was at a loss to identify openings for fraud or procedural shortcomings it would not prove that an effect could occur in the absence of these artifacts: the latter might exist without being immediately obvious.

There remains a demand for other skeptical theories that address the psi data as indicative of a valid but nonparapsychological effect. The debate over the authenticity of psi is best conducted not by skeptics' seeking to "explain away" the data but by the construction of skeptical theories that generate predictions capable of being pitted against those of the parapsychological models. Such theoretical development would have the fruitful effects of sharpening the assumptions underlying the authenticity issue and encouraging critical empirical investigation of them.

These then are the major types of theory designed to explain psi; some additional approaches, including more mystical accounts, are described by Chari (1977), Rao (1978) and Stokes (1987). Probably a fair if sweeping summary assessment of the position is that older accounts are either not viable or relatively inaccessible to empirical scrutiny, while the more recent models have yet to be given sufficiently exhaustive empirical evaluation for their viability to be assessed. Nevertheless the sophistication of recent theories may signal that the time is near when it will be inappropriate to describe parapsychology as "a set of facts in search of a theory."

KEY TERMS AND CONCEPTS

mediational phase
experiential phase
electromagnetic theories
ELF waves
inverse square law
energy field theories
bioenergy
psychotronics
observational theories

pseudosensory models
memory models
psi-mediated instrumental response
noncybernetic models
synchronicity
acausal phenomena
conformance theory
teleological
skeptical theories

STUDY QUESTIONS

1. What are the functions to be served by a theory in parapsychology?

2. Outline the major types of theory designed to explain the way in which psi is mediated. What objections to each type may be raised?

3. What is the fundamental objective of theories of the experiential phase of psi? Given the range of theories of the mediational phase of psi, are experiential models even necessary?

4. Two noncybernetic models of psi have been formulated by Jung and Stanford respectively. Compare these theories and comment on their capacity to explain what is known about psi.

5. What contributions to parapsychology can be made by skeptical theories of psi phenomena?

9

THE SURVIVAL HYPOTHESIS

The three classical domains of parapsychological research are ESP, PK, and the survival hypothesis. This chapter is concerned with a general introduction to survival research; subsequent chapters will discuss in more depth some topics in parapsychological research which originally were motivated by interest in the survival hypothesis but which now attract research effort in their own right.

The survival hypothesis concerns the notion of postmortem survival, that is, that a disembodied consciousness or some such discarnate element of human personality might survive bodily death at least for a time. The survival hypothesis has obvious religious connotations but these are of no concern in scientific parapsychology. Further, it should be noted that survival does not necessarily imply immortality or eternal existence as promoted in many religious systems (Thouless, 1979). The question of survival is worthy of investigation, not only for what it may tell us about human nature, but also because substantial numbers of the population believe in life after death. For instance, 74 percent of respondents in a 1984 NORC poll indicated a belief in survival (Greeley, 1987). Furthermore, in a 2005 US survey, 20 percent of those polled expressed the belief that it is possible to hear from or communicate mentally with someone who has died (Moore, 2005), a sizeable number even though some-

what less than the 28 percent of Americans who expressed this belief in 2001 (Newport & Strausberg, 2001). Such widely-held beliefs are likely to have an influence over people's behavior. For instance, many of these individuals may be recently bereaved and vulnerable, and may visit and pay for the services of individuals, known as mediums, who claim to be able to communicate with deceased loved ones. So, what evidence is there that mediums can indeed communicate with the dead?

Mediumship and the Survival Hypothesis

You will recall that the early activities of the Society for Psychical Research (SPR) were concerned fundamentally with the issue of discarnate survival. The SPR's investigation of phenomena of the seance room and the collection of cases of spontaneous psychic experiences were designed largely to accumulate empirical data upon which the survival hypothesis might be assessed. Indeed the development of interest in ESP to some degree grew from survival research: ESP was seen to be a possible mode of interaction with the "spirit world" or as an artifact in mediums' acquisition of information that was presented as if gathered from discarnate personalities.

Spiritualistic mediumship thus stands as an historically important component of survival research. Evidentially speaking the most notable seance phenomena bearing on the survival hypothesis have been proxy sittings, "drop in" communicators, xenoglossy, and cross-correspondences.

Proxy Sittings

As mentioned above, one of the problems with so-called spirit communications as evidence for survival is that the medium could be held to have obtained the reported information telepathically from one or more of the sitters at the seance rather than from any discarnate personality. One methodological device to circumvent the possibility of ESP from sitters entails the use of *proxy sitters*. That is, a sitter asks the medium to contact the spirits for information known only to some third party who is not present at the seance. There are some notable cases of successful proxy sittings in which the medium cited specific data not familiar to any of the sitters but which were verified on subsequent consultation with the absent party (e.g., Saltmarsh, 1930–1931; Thomas, 1932–1933).

An objection to proxy sittings as a source of support for the survival hypothesis is that we simply do not know the limits of ESP. For some parapsychologists it is not inconceivable that the medium could use ESP to "reach out" to any sources, including the absent person, from which or from whom the required information may be gleaned. This account of the evidence from proxy sittings assumes that it is not necessary for the medium to know either the identity or the location of pertinent sources in order to achieve extrasensory contact with them; such an interpretation consequently is known as the *super–ESP hypothesis* (Braude, 1986, 1989, 1992; Gauld, 1961). In support of this idea it may be noted that some ostensible spirit communications do appear to have entailed unintentional extrasensory contact with a liv-

ing source (e.g., "Case...," 1923; Dallas, 1924).

"Drop In" Communicators

A "drop in" communicator is an apparently discarnate personality who uninvitedly drops in to a seance yet is not known to either the medium or the sitters. If the "drop in" communicator provides information with which the sitters are unfamiliar and this information subsequently proves veridical, it can be argued that the survival hypothesis is enhanced because the medium here could not have relied upon telepathic contact with the sitters as the basis for the communicated material.

An appeal to the super–ESP hypothesis again might be made as an alternative to the survival interpretation of this phenomenon. That is, the medium conceivably may have used ESP to acquire data from any source about any deceased person; in the dissociated state of the mediumistic trance these data then would form the subconscious informational foundation for a dramatized "spirit" communication. Additionally, while acknowledging there are some impressive reports of "drop in" communicators (Gauld, 1982, Ch. 5) it is difficult if not impossible to demonstrate that the medium could not have had access by normal means to the communicated information at some time prior to the seance; because the experimenter has no *a priori* control over the identity of the "drop in" communicator the operation of fraud or of cryptomnesia remain potential interpretations of these seance communications. The failure to rule out such optional accounts means that the phenomenon of "drop in" communicators can not constitute conclusive evidence for the survival hypothesis.

Xenoglossy

There are some rare instances in which it appears a discarnate personality communicates to a medium some skill the personality demonstrably possessed while alive but which the medium himself/herself does not have. One type of such case is termed xenoglossy: here the medium speaks, writes or understands a language known by the deceased communicator and yet as far as can be ascertained, the medium has never had the opportunity to learn that language. A few cases of mediumistic xenoglossy have been documented in the literature (Gauld, 1982, pp. 101–107; Stevenson, 1974, Ch. 1), although the thoroughness of their investigation generally tends to have been insufficient.

The significance of these cases is that if they are authentic, the super–ESP hypothesis might be held to be hard pressed to accommodate them. Is it really possible for a medium to acquire by the sole means of ESP the vocabulary, pronunciation and grammar of a foreign language? Strictly speaking the answer to this question is that parapsychologists do not know; but if ESP can service such a skill, then the informational bounds of ESP must virtually be limitless. For this reason the survival hypothesis looks increasingly viable to some parapsychologists, despite Braude's (1986, 1989) entreaties that the super–ESP hypothesis should not be dismissed prematurely. Once again, however, there is the substantial problem of excluding fraud by the medium as another explanation of xenoglossy in seance communications.

The Cross-Correspondences

Three early leaders of the SPR Myers, Gurney and Henry Sidgwick died within a short period of one another, and reports soon began to appear that several mediums were receiving communications from these three deceased personalities. The material thus communicated, particularly in the first decade of the twentieth century, became quite voluminous (Saltmarsh, 1938). Of primary interest is that there seem to be certain correspondences between the messages received by different mediums.

Now Myers, Gurney and Sidgwick were classical scholars and the scripts of the seance communications contain many classical references and allusions. Some correspondences between the scripts of independent mediums comprise merely the same obscure word or phrase. But others were much more complex and subtle. For example, two seemingly meaningless messages would be obtained by different mediums and then a third medium would receive some key or clue which enabled the meaningless items to be connected in an allusive yet meaningful way, rather like fitting together pieces of a jigsaw puzzle.

Some psychical researchers (e.g., Piddington, 1908) deemed the cross-correspondences to be evidence that communications received by different mediums in fact came from a common discarnate source and that this source was capable of highly intelligent and creative activity in devising these correspondences. Other parapsychologists (e.g., Podmore, 1910) have suggested one of the mediums, Mrs. Verrall, had a classical education and could therefore have devised the series of cross-correspondences at a subconscious level, then extrasensorially communicated the pieces of the puzzle to the other mediums; the cross-correspondences, however, continued well after Mrs. Verrall's death. At the same time a hypothesis of some form of ESP or super–ESP from living sources might conceivably accommodate the cross-correspondence data. Additionally, the material of the cross-correspondences is very complex and to this extent its evidential value for the survival hypothesis is not readily gauged.

Two Experimental Tests of the Survival Hypothesis

Two tests of survival were proposed subsequently in the context of the performances of mediums. The proposals are Thouless's (1946) "cipher test" and Stevenson's (1968) "combination lock test."

The first of these entails a passage of prose translated into code; the passage can be deciphered only by use of a key word or phrase that is known solely by the person who designs the code. During the lifetime of that person others are invited to use either ESP or cryptographic techniques to discover the key and thereby decipher the passage. If they are unable to do so and an alleged post-mortem communication from the spirit of the test designer conveys the correct key to a medium the notion of survival may be held to be supported.

Researchers had a long wait for the opportunity to enact Thouless's own instances of the cipher test; having published his coded passages in 1946 Thouless died in 1984 at the age of 90. The SPR and another group immediately invited people (presumably with the aid of Thouless's discarnate personality) to nominate the clue that would decode the sequences. For several years no effective solution was forthcoming (Stevenson, Oram & Markwick, 1989), but then in 1996 it was announced that the words "Black Beauty" had been shown to be the cipher for one of Thouless's passages (Berger, 1996; Stevenson, 1996): the decoded passage read, "This is a cipher which will not be read unless I give the key words." Unfortunately the "Black Beauty" solution was computer generated by a cryptographic expert, thereby negating that particular instance of the test of survival devised by Thouless.

More disturbingly, however, Berger (1984) has shown that for Thouless's method of encipherment there may have been no unique key, that is, several different keys might well have decoded such a relatively short sequence. A medium's identification of a key decoding one of Thouless's passages therefore would not have demonstrated that this was the key intended by Thouless and communicated by him posthumously. Berger does present an alternative method of encipherment that appears to possess a unique key, so in this respect perhaps a cipher test of

survival might still be viable. The fact that a solution to one of Thouless's own ciphers eventually was generated by a computer nevertheless raises doubts about the viability of a cipher test, especially when short (e.g., two-word) keys are used. Thouless's remaining unbroken code relies on a key comprising a passage of approximately 100 words from a published book; in this instance the possibility of deciphering the associated passage even with the aid of computer algorithms is presumably remote. But the confidence of many parapsychologists in the cipher test of survival has now been shaken. In any event cipher tests continue to be devised and some have now been set up on the internet (Smith, 2000).

In Stevenson's (1968) test a similar procedure is followed with a combination lock instead of a coded passage; the lock's combination is known only to the person conducting the test and is to be communicated in the form of a code word after that person's death. These techniques have a significant advantage over an older practice in which a message in a sealed envelope was to be identified by a medium after the writer's death (Gay, Salter, Thouless, Firebrace, Phillimore & Sitwell, 1955; Salter, 1958). The latter test becomes useless as soon as the envelope is opened to check mediums' guesses about the contents, whereas if some mediums' initial guesses at the identity of a code key or lock combination are incorrect the test still is operative for any other medium who subsequently should claim to have had a communication from the deceased. A satisfactory result from any of the lock tests has yet to be obtained (Stevenson, 1996; Stevenson, Oram & Markwick, 1989). It might be mentioned that a combination lock set by Thouless was opened after his death, but the combination had deliberately been set to correspond to the "Black Beauty" key Thouless had used for one of his encoded passages (Stevenson, 1996). In other words, computer algorithms successfully identified the key to the encoded passage but the lock combination itself was not directly broken.

Modern-Day Investigations of Mediums

The research reviewed in the above section pertains primarily to historical approaches to the evaluation of mediumship in seances. The study of proxy sittings, drop-in communications, xenoglossy, and cross-correspondences was an attempt to evaluate the evidentiality of the medium's statements with regards to the alleged postmortem survival of an individual. As we have already noted, super-ESP seems as plausible an alternative hypothesis for seance phenomena as the survival hypothesis. However, invoking the principle of parsimony, we should also consider whether, as has sometimes been alleged, the medium is simply skilled at simulating knowledge uniquely relevant to the sitter, for instance by expertly interpreting verbal and non-verbal cues from the sitter, clever guesswork, and making general statements that would apply to most sitters (e.g., Hyman, 1977; Podmore, 1901). Our first section considers controlled tests aimed at eliminating such cues. We then turn to a rare modern-day claim of physical phenomena in the seance.

Mediums in the Laboratory

A number of researchers have grappled with the considerable methodological challenges faced when attempting to evaluate whether mediums are able to make statements that are uniquely relevant to a sitter and that are not contaminated by artifacts (e.g., Pratt & Birge, 1948). As Schouten's (1994) review of this work shows, the resulting studies have obtained mixed results. More recent studies continue to strive to overcome methodological and statistical artifacts, but the methods can be unwieldy (e.g., Robert-son & Roy, 2004) and the results can be the subject of debate (e.g., Hyman, 2003; Schwartz, Russek & Barentsen, 2002).

In one study that claims to overcome previous methodological problems (O'Keeffe & Wiseman, 2005), five professional mediums each gave a reading to five sitters, giving a total of 25 readings. The mediums had no contact with the sitters and had no information about them, and the sitters were all of the same sex, were approximately the same age, and did not know one another. Each sitter then blind-rated their own 5 readings and 20 decoy readings as to their accuracy. The resulting analysis found that there was only one occasion where the sitter gave a higher rating for the reading that was intended for them rather than for the other four sitters; thus the mediums in this study were unable to provide information uniquely relevant to the intended sitters. Whether this result will generalize to other mediums and other sitters remains to be seen but in any case the methodology used appears to eliminate many potential routes for artifactual matches between the sitters and the mediums' readings. This study was published in a mainstream psychology journal, and O'Keeffe and Wiseman note that this methodology may be used for other conceptually similar cases where an expert is claiming to provide information uniquely relevant to an individual, such as a patient in a clinical context, or a potential criminal in a forensic context. As such, this is another case where the methodological challenges facing parapsychologists may give rise to techniques with potential application beyond parapsychology.

Seance Investigations: The Scole Report

In 1999, the Society for Psychical Research (SPR) published an account of a three-year investigation by three senior members of the society into seance phenomena reported in over twenty sittings with four individuals known as the Scole Group (Keen, Ellison & Fontana, 1999), two of whom acted as trance mediums. The investigation also gave rise to a popular book subtitled *Scientific Evidence for Life After Death* (Solomon et al., 1999). Based in Norfolk, England, the Scole group claimed they had obtained messages from spirit communicators and had witnessed various anomalous physical phenomena such as materializations of objects and unusual light effects. While physical seance phenomena were commonplace in Victorian times, modern-day accounts are rare indeed, and it is interesting to see the SPR return to its historical roots with this investigation. The SPR team state that their study is "the first to be made into the activities of a number of persons acting as a team; the first to link alleged oral communications via trance mediums with a variety of photographic, visual, auditory, tactile and tangible phenomena, and the first to investigate a range of tangible physical effects apparently not associated with ectoplasm, and which are susceptible to public inspection outside the seance room" (Keen, Ellison & Fontana, 1999, p. 157). The investigators reported that they were unable to detect signs of fraud or deception, and concluded that their investigation provided evidence of paranormal activity, either from discarnate sources or from living humans. The scale of the study is too great for us to go into any detail. Suffice to say that there is no doubt that the investigators showed great thoroughness in their efforts to study and document the Scole phenomena. However, a number of commentators have pointed out that the seances took place in darkness and that under these conditions it is difficult to rule out potential normal explanations for the phenomena reported. For further details, the reader is referred to the critical comments made by Cornell (1999), Gauld (1999), and West (1999), and replies by Fontana (1999), and Keen and Ellison (1999). We suspect that the conclusion one may draw on the question of whether the Scole Report does indeed

provide scientific evidence of life after death may depend on the reader's a priori beliefs. However, the episode certainly makes an excellent case study of the difficulty of ruling out deception and self-deception in investigations of this kind.

The Survival Hypothesis and the Super–ESP Hypothesis

The prospects look bleak for a critical test between the survival hypothesis and its major alternative, the super–ESP hypothesis. Available evidence can be accommodated by each hypothesis in turn, even if at times they have to be stretched somewhat in order to do so. Moreover, much of the dissatisfaction with each hypothesis seems motivated more by religious beliefs than by objective evaluation of the hypotheses' adequacy. It seems both hypotheses are a little too unspecific for a critical test between them or perhaps even for a crucial test of either one in its own right.

The survival hypothesis has failed to define exactly what it is that is held to survive death and what the fundamental characteristics of this entity would have to be (Grosso, 1979). At the same time the super–ESP hypothesis seeks to explain one unknown (e.g., seance communications) in terms of another unknown, namely ESP. Explanations in terms of a process that has few identifiable constraints or boundary conditions (as ESP and in particular super–ESP have) are extremely awkward to refute empirically. According to Alvarado and Martínez-Taboas (1983) the super–ESP hypothesis simply is untestable because "it postulates an omniscient and omnipotent capacity that cannot be falsified by the scientific method" (p. 58). Even if the survival hypothesis is vague, at least specific forms of it could be open to empirical evaluation (Schmeidler, 1980; Thouless, 1979). On the other hand it is possible this hypothesis itself has an implicit extrasensory component, that is, spirit communications may be mediated extrasensorially and thereby exhibit certain characteristics of ESP. In any event no empirical test has yielded persuasive data in support of either of the rival positions.

There nevertheless are several phenomena that in the view of some researchers strongly testify either to the authenticity or to the feasibility of postmortem survival. Such

phenomena include poltergeists, near-death experiences, out-of-body experiences, apparitions and reincarnation experiences. But these phenomena deserve discussion in a broader context than the survival hypothesis. In subsequent chapters each of these phenomena is considered in turn; some reference to the survival issue is made but coverage is not restricted to this aspect.

KEY TERMS AND CONCEPTS

survival hypothesis
super–ESP hypothesis
proxy sittings
xenoglossy
"drop in" communicators

cross-correspondences
Thouless's cipher test
Stevenson's combination lock test
The Scole Report

STUDY QUESTIONS

1. Why has survival research given so much emphasis to evidence from mediumship? Review and evaluate this evidence.

2. "Human personality and dispositions are encoded wholly in the central nervous system." Explore this proposition in relation to the survival hypothesis, and decide if survival research is compatible with mainstream behavioral science.

3. Examine the status of the survival hypothesis and the super–ESP hypothesis as scientific theories, considering such issues as conceptual parsimony and accessibility for empirical evaluation. Are the two hypotheses necessarily mutually exclusive?

4. What data are required before it will be possible to evaluate adequately the super–ESP hypothesis?

5. Critically discuss the potential of cipher tests and combination lock tests for providing a crucial test between the survival hypothesis and the super–ESP hypothesis.

6. Evaluate the strengths and weaknesses of the method used by O'Keeffe and Wiseman compared to the method used by the Scole group, in evaluating mediumistic abilities.

10

POLTERGEIST EXPERIENCES

The German word *Poltergeist* does not translate precisely into English but roughly speaking it means a noisy, boisterous, troubling spirit or ghost. The term thus reflects the popular folk belief that poltergeist disturbances were the responsibility of the spirit of a deceased person. In this regard the link between poltergeists and the survival hypothesis has a long history. At the same time there was some realization that poltergeist activity may be associated with a particular living person and according to some accounts (e.g., Roll, 1977, p. 382) the word "geist" now is used to designate either a discarnate spirit or the "spirit" of a living individual (for an account of the historical development of this construct see Puhle, 2001).

Poltergeist outbreaks have been reported for centuries (Gauld & Cornell, 1979; Puhle, 1999); indeed there are accounts dating back to the first century A.D. Each year two or three new cases appear in the press. While poltergeists therefore are not common there are sufficient cases for parapsychologists to investigate. By way of illustration a summary of the so-called Sauchie poltergeist is provided below. (Poltergeist cases usually are identified by the name of the town in which the outbreak occurred, although occasionally they are named after the family which was subjected to the disturbances. Sauchie is a town in Scotland and being Scottish the sec-

ond author, CW, can confirm that the correct pronunciation is "sawchee," with the emphasis on the first syllable and a soft guttural "ch" sound as in Loch.) The Sauchie case often is cited in recent literature because it was one of the first modern cases to attract the serious interest of the parapsychological community. The following outline of the case draws upon the detailed report by Owen (1964, Ch. 5).

The Sauchie outbreak began in November 1960 and was documented by A. R. G. Owen, a parapsychologist who at that time was an academic at Trinity College, Cambridge University. Owen did not witness any of the phenomena himself but based his report on interviews with the many witnesses to the disturbances. The Sauchie poltergeist phenomena centered on an 11-year-old girl, Virginia Campbell. Virginia had been raised on a small farm in Ireland where she had led a lonely life, her chief companions being the daughter of the neighbors and a pet dog. In 1960 Virginia's father decided to sell the farm and during the process of winding up the business Virginia was sent to stay with her elder married brother in Sauchie, leaving behind her friend, her dog, and most of her possessions. She appears to have been very upset with this state of affairs.

The first curious incident occurred on the evening of Tuesday, November 22, when a sound like a bouncing ball was heard in Virginia's bedroom, on the stairs, and in the living-room; no cause for this noise was apparent. The following evening Virginia was sitting in the living-room near but not in contact with a heavy sideboard. Her brother and his wife saw the sideboard move outwards about 5 inches (12 cm.) and then return to its original position. Later that evening while Virginia was lying awake in bed loud knocks were heard in her room. A local minister the Rev. Lund was summoned and he concluded that the raps came from the bedhead; he moved Virginia down the bed so that no part of her body was touching the bedhead but found the noises continued. Rev. Lund then saw a large and full linen chest which was standing 18 inches (45 cm.) from the bed rock sideways and move jerkily along parallel to the bed and back again. The chest weighed about 50 pounds (23 kg.). At the suggestion that Virginia's nine-year-old niece sleep with her there was a burst of violent knocking.

On Thursday evening, November 24, Rev. Lund again visited and heard more raps and saw the linen chest rocking. He also saw Virginia's pillow rotate horizontally beneath her head about 60 degrees. Dr. Nisbet, a physician accompanying Rev. Lund, also heard the knockings and saw a curious rippling movement pass across the pillow on which Virginia's head lay.

At school on Friday, November 25, Virginia's teacher saw her trying to hold down her desk lid which several times raised itself to an angle of 45 to 50 degrees. The teacher could see Virginia's hands flat on the lid of the desk and her legs under the desk. Virginia's teacher also saw an empty desk behind Virginia slowly rise about an inch (2 cm.) above the floor and settle down again. That evening Dr. Nisbet again witnessed knocks, movement of the linen chest, rotation of the pillow, and ripples passing across the bedclothes.

On Monday, November 28, a blackboard pointer on the teacher's table began to vibrate and move across the table until it fell off. The table was felt to be vibrating and it swung around anticlockwise. Virginia started to cry and said that she was not responsible. That afternoon Virginia was taken to stay with a relative in a nearby town and there Dr. Nisbet again heard knockings, this time very loud ones.

Virginia returned to Sauchie and on Thursday, December 1, Dr. Nisbet and a colleague succeeded in recording the noises on tape. After this date the phenomena diminished considerably. Minor occurrences persisted for about three months but these are not as well attested as earlier incidents. One of the more reliably documented incidents in this period occurred on Monday, January 23, 1961. Virginia placed a bowl of bulbs on her teacher's table and the bowl moved across the tabletop. Both Virginia and her niece also claimed to have been pinched occasionally by unknown means.

The Phenomenology of Poltergeist Experiences

Various sorts of ostensibly paranormal events are associated with the poltergeist experience. In reviewing these, frequent reference will be made to two major surveys. One involved the tabulation of 116 poltergeist cases by William Roll (1977, 1978a); the other is the monumental compilation of 500 cases by two British parapsychologists Alan Gauld and Tony Cornell (1979).

Movement of objects. One of the most common features of poltergeist activity is the movement of objects. The Sauchie case reportedly involved movement of several articles such as the sideboard, the linen chest, the pillow, the teacher's table, a child's desk, the blackboard pointer, and the bowl of bulbs. In Roll's (1977, p. 387) sample about 90 percent of cases mention recurrent movement of objects; Gauld and Cornell (1979,

p. 226) found 64 percent of cases to feature movement of small objects and 36 percent with movement of large objects such as pieces of furniture.

Sometimes the displaced objects are damaged. In the Miami poltergeist of 1966–1967 (Roll, 1976, Ch. 9) the major incidents were set in the warehouse of a novelty and souvenir firm and many fragile articles were broken.

In some cases the objects move not along the floor but through the air, and when the trajectories of these have been observed they tend to be rather odd. For example, objects may seem to float or fall slowly, as if being carried: the latter impression was noted in 19 percent of Gauld and Cornell's (1979, p. 226) sample. Roll (1977, p. 389) also reports that in 41 percent of cases entailing object movement the trajectories were unusual, being variously described as floating, wavering, zigzagging, hovering, fluttering, and moving in a sinuous fashion. Even movements across the floor or table may be odd: in the Sauchie case the linen chest was said to move in a jerky and rocking manner.

Apportation also may occur, that is, objects may be transported by apparently paranormal means from a remote location. About 20 percent of cases include this effect (Gauld & Cornell, 1979, p. 226).

The "poltergeist" may be selective in regard to the objects moved. Thus some outbreaks are designated *stone-throwing poltergeists* because they predominantly comprise bombardment by rocks and pebbles. These disturbances have occurred in the same basic form in many cultures over the centuries. For example, in A.D. 530 Deacon Helpidius, the physician to Theodoric king of an area now part of Germany, was the target of mysterious showers of stones (Thurston, 1953, pp.

Figure 16. Property damage in the Miami poltergeist case (photograph: William Roll).

187–188). Sometimes the stones in these outbreaks feel hot to the touch. Occasionally the stones have been collected, marked and thrown away, only to reappear in the house plagued by the disturbance (Gauld & Cornell, 1979, p. 228; Roll, 1977, p. 391). In many cases people are hit by the falling stones but it is rare for someone to be hurt: indeed a few witnesses report that stones seemed to "float" down and strike them with less force than expected of a falling object (Roll, 1977, p. 389).

Noises. Another typical manifestation of the poltergeist experience is the outbreak of unaccountable noises, particularly of a percussive type. In Gauld and Cornell's (1979, p. 226) sample about half included mention of rapping, pounding, knocking, and scratching sounds. A similar level of incidence was found in Roll's (1977, p. 387) sample. The poltergeist, therefore, is one of those "things that go bump in the night." There are suggestions that the occurrence of sounds may tend to precede the outbreak of movement of objects (as in the Sauchie case) but data to this effect as yet are weak (Roll, 1977, pp. 387–388).

In most instances the poltergeist noises are heard by several people collectively (Virtanen, 1977/1990). In several modern cases, of which the Sauchie case is one, the noises were recorded on tape, thereby excluding the possibility of mass hallucination. Additionally, there have been some attempts to compare these noises to ones produced in imitation by the investigator. According to one report the poltergeist noises showed a distinctive sound spectrum: the vibrations were damped (died away) more quickly than were the imitative sounds (Whitton, 1975, 1976).

Fires. Incendiary phenomena were mentioned in 11 percent of Gauld and Cornell's (1979, p. 227) cases. Sometimes these represent the major phenomenon of the disturbances: such cases are termed *fire poltergeists* and entail the sudden outbreak of numerous small fires in the household.

In some instances the objects that burst into flame would otherwise be incombustible or would merely smolder if ignited by normal means. A case in Michigan (Solfvin, personal communication, 1979; Solfvin & Roll, 1976) involved the incineration of a wet towel and a roll of toilet paper burned to the core. Forensic analysis of the latter revealed no evidence of chemical impregnation. If ever you have tried to ignite a tightly rolled newspaper you will appreciate the oddity of this event.

Generally these outbreaks are investigated by officials from the fire or police departments. Some of these investigators admit the inexplicability of the phenomena, at least in private; others attribute them to childish pranks and leave the scene before anyone thinks to ask how normally incombustible objects were set alight.

Water inundations. Some poltergeist disturbances exhibit an obsession with water (Bugaj, 1996; Nichols, 2000). Water may begin to seep or spurt from a wall in the house and investigation fails to uncover any natural explanation of this. Other cases focus on the toilet: Brian Nisbet in England once told HJI of his investigations of three poltergeist cases in which the cistern would flush unaccountably and water would be thrown up on the toilet walls.

Comparatively speaking these effects are not common. Gauld and Cornell (1979, p. 227) found such phenomena in only 5 percent of their collection, and Roll (1977, p. 387) cites only two cases.

Bites, scratches, and pinches. Fifteen percent of Gauld and Cornell's (1979, p. 227) collection included various forms of personal assault of an unaccountable nature. People would report being scratched or bitten, the marks on the body being inconsistent with self-infliction. Pinches are relatively more frequent: these occurred in the terminal stages of the Sauchie case, for example.

Demonic persecution. A few cases are of an even more vicious character with sustained persecution of a particular individual or family. Often these persecutions have a religious element: they may center on a clergyman and feature desecration of religious artifacts. In the public's mind demonic poltergeists would be most clearly instanced by the case of the "Amityville Horror"; there is evidence, however, that this case was greatly dramatized by the book's author, if not completely fabricated by the author and the family concerned (Auerbach, 1986, pp. 295–303; Harris, 1986, pp. 9–17; Morris, 1981).

Electronic phenomena. One recent UK case demonstrates how poltergeist-like phenomena might manifest in the computer age. In 1997 two tourists reportedly saw an apparition of the Virgin Mary in a field in Wales, which then became a place of pilgrimage. Subsequently, in their home adjacent to the field, a school headteacher and his family experienced a number of other unusual phenomena, including apparitions, carvings of religious Welsh words, unexplained stains, electrical disturbances, and object displacements. Additionally, during a week-long period in October 1999, allegedly unbeknownst to the family almost 40 email messages containing Welsh religious words were sent to 14 people in the family's email address book. The family is not Welsh or Welsh-speaking. The messages tended not to appear in the Sent mail folder, and several had been sent in the middle of the night. Subsequently, email messages sent by the family occasionally contained Welsh word intrusions, and other computer-related phenomena included the appearance of Welsh religious words or religious images in printouts of documents or as intrusions on screen and, peculiarly, lettering occasionally being printed upside-down or sideways. Unusually, the poltergeist-like outbreak spanned several years. The case was investigated by a member of the SPR (Daniels, 2002), who noted that although the case had some very unusual features, he could not come to a firm conclusion on whether or not the phenomena were hoaxed, paranormal, or a combination of the two.

Other Features of the Poltergeist Experience

Most poltergeist disturbances exhibit recurrent events which tend to diminish rapidly. Usually the outbreaks last between two weeks and two months, although there are cases in the literature said to have persisted for a year or more. In Roll's (1977, p. 388) sample the median duration was two months, but some extraordinarily persistent cases (including one of six years) pulled the mean duration up to five months.

Although some poltergeist cases are said to be centered on a place (Bender, 1982; Osis & McCormick, 1982a; Pierce, 1973), the major part of poltergeist research has been directed to cases in which the outbreak seems to center upon and generally require the presence of a particular individual, the so-called poltergeist *focus* or *agent*. Roll (1977, p. 386) reports that 79 percent of his cases had an alleged focus, and in 42 percent of cases the disturbances "followed" this individual beyond the home. Gauld and Cornell (1979, p. 226) put the incidence of cases with agents at 40 percent. It is possible that many of their older cases were not documented in sufficient detail to permit a judgment of the existence of a focal person. Even if many of the cases do involve a key figure any decision that this person was the poltergeist agent is moot and the judged incidence of person-centered cases thus will depend markedly on the conservatism of the case analysts. In any event now that the concept of a focus is more familiar the considerable majority of contemporary cases investigated by parapsychologists appear to feature a focal person. The Sauchie poltergeist is one such instance.

Another example of a case with a focal individual is the Bremen poltergeist (Bender, 1971, pp. 91–93). In mid–1965 unexplained movements of merchandise occurred in the chinaware department of a Bremen store. Investigations by police and other authorities failed to establish any normal explanation for the events but they evidently were connected in some obscure way with a 15-year-old apprentice employee in the department. The lad was dismissed and the disturbances in the store immediately came to an end. The young man subsequently obtained a job as an apprentice in a Freiburg electrical shop. In March 1966 he was asked to drill holes in a concrete wall and to install wall hooks. The task was done properly but a little later it was found that the hooks came loose in the presence of the young apprentice. He was accused of being to blame. In a test of this a freshly attached hook was observed to come loose within two minutes while the apprentice stood about a yard (meter) from the wall. It is reported that the boy had been "brought up under difficult circumstances" and was living with foster parents at the time of the outbreak.

If a substantial number of poltergeist cases center upon a focal person it is pertinent to inquire into the characteristics of such people. Three biographic factors that have been examined are gender, age and domestic situation.

In both collections of poltergeist cases there is a predominance of female agents. In Roll's (1977, p. 386) sample 61 percent of focal individuals were female; the figure in Gauld and Cornell's (1979, p. 226) collection is 73 percent. Roll suggests that this trend is due to the rarity of male agents in the oldest (1612 to 1899) cases; in the more recent cases the sexes are represented equally. The earlier predominance of females may have been due to the different nature of social pressures across the sexes; again there may have been a reporting bias, with cases either attributed to a "witch" or depicted as place-centered rather than person-centered. In any event the recent data suggest that gender is not a major determinant of poltergeist agency.

In Roll's (1977, pp. 386–387) sample the age of agents ranged from 8 to 78, although the median was 13 years. The tendency for adolescent foci is confirmed in Gauld and Cornell's (1979, p. 226) collection where over 70 percent of agents were under 20 years of age.

An interesting trend is found in regard to the agent's domestic situation. On the assumption that 18 is the age at which a young person might leave home for normal reasons Roll (1977, p. 402) selected from his sample those cases in which the agent was aged 18 or less. Of this group 62 percent were living away from home when the disturbances commenced. In many poltergeist cases, therefore, a young focal individual was not living with his or her natural parents at the time of the outbreak; this was the situation for both the Sauchie and the Bremen poltergeist, for example. Roll (1977, p. 403) also notes that of those cases in which an agent was identified, 41 percent of disturbances occurred when there were changes or other problems in the home or the family which may have affected the agent. In some instances poltergeist agents have been victims of physical abuse by their parents, with no power to defend themselves (Carvalho, 1992). Fifteen percent of focal individuals in Gauld and Cornell's (1979, p. 226) sample were known to be suffering from a mental or emotional problem prior to the outbreak, and in many other cases such a problem was discovered during the period of the poltergeist activities.

The modal picture of the poltergeist agent that emerges is that of a young adolescent, often near the age of pubescence, with cause for personal turmoil and rebellion. This suggests that poltergeist disturbances in some way are associated with emotional conflict in the focal person. The frequency of adolescent cases may indicate further that the agent typically is not in a situation to express the conflict openly. Implications of these trends will be discussed shortly in the context of theories of the poltergeist.

There are some consistencies also in the poltergeist phenomena themselves, despite their ostensibly erratic quality. For example, there may be an obsessive element in the disturbance with activity concentrated on particular objects, particular types of objects, or particular areas such as a certain room or shelf (Roll, 1977, p. 390). In person-centered cases there are suggestions that the number of incidents decreases with distance from the agent; in other words, most activity may tend to occur in the vicinity of the focal person (Roll, 1977, p. 388). Quantitative documentation of this effect, however, is limited.

Theories of the Poltergeist Experience

There are five main theoretical approaches to the poltergeist. The first two emphasize normal causes, the others appeal to either supernatural or paranormal factors.

Fraud. One theory of poltergeist activities is that they simply are childish pranks. Proponents of this view (e.g., Nickell, 2001; Podmore, 1896) point out that it explains why so many cases center around a child and why it reportedly is rare for people to witness the initial stages of movement of a displaced object (Zusne & Jones, 1982, p. 414).

There is a measure of support for this approach. Gauld and Cornell (1979, p. 226) report that in 8 percent of their cases fraud was detected. Roll (1977, p. 392) puts the figure at 16 percent and notes that the identification of fraud is more common in modern cases, presumably because contemporary parapsychologists are more skilled investigators than the people who documented disturbances in earlier times. In the fraudulent cases trickery usually is of a simple, though sometimes skillfully executed, sort. Thus objects would be thrown at judiciously chosen moments and objects overturned or levitated by use of fine horsehair or cotton thread attached to them (Christopher, 1971, pp. 142–163; Owen, 1964, pp. 26–64). Very rarely a mechanical device has been employed to produce various odd effects.

The generality of the "naughty child" account is open to question. The incidence of fraudulent cases is rather low to be taken as evidence in support of the theory, although admittedly it is possible that many other cases identified as fraudulent have not been written up by investigators. The appeal of this theory also may be limited to the more short-lived cases. It is less reasonable to blame a "naughty child" for undetected fraudulent activities in a poltergeist disturbance if the outbreak lasts for years; one Brazilian case, for example, was associated with the same family over a period of 11 years (Amorim, 1990). Again there are some reported poltergeist feats that do not seem possible to achieve by normal means. How did the 11-year-old Virginia Campbell manage to move a heavy sideboard and a large linen chest in the Sauchie case? How do normally incombustible objects burst into flames in some instances of fire poltergeist? Indeed, far from the literature suggesting an underestimation of the incidence of fraud, there are grounds for arguing that many supposedly fraudulent cases in fact are not so. For example, the timing of the identified fraudulent activities bears examination. In many such cases the trickery occurred well after the original outbreak had subsided and thus could be construed as a rather puerile attempt by some of the principals of the case to prolong the attention brought to them by the initial genuine phenomena. Further, in a number of allegedly fraudulent cases a confession was extracted from a youngster under the inducement that the interrogation then would terminate and no further action would be taken. In person-centered cases it hardly is surprising that the focal individual feels some responsibility for the phenomena and hence may confess as much.

It should be noted also that it is not correct that the initial stages of an object's movement are rarely witnessed in poltergeist disturbances. There is a substantial number of cases in which a complete movement or trajectory was observed (e.g., the Sauchie poltergeist). While the occurrence of trickery in some cases is not denied the fraud theory, therefore, is inadequate as a general explanation of the poltergeist.

Misinterpretations. Poltergeist phenomena have been deemed to represent misinterpretations of natural events by nervous or overimaginative folk. For example, the sources of indistinct noises are difficult to locate and hence these might be attributed to paranormal factors. Natural sounds like the activities of rodents behind the skirting boards and waterhammers could be perceived as poltergeist scratching and rapping noises. Minor seismic activity, underground water flows, and shifting house foundations might not be detected yet produce movement of objects that are interpreted as the effects of a poltergeist (Lambert, 1959). Some instances of (apparent) poltergeist experience have indeed been diagnosed as comprising misinterpretations of natural events (Blackmore, 1986a, pp. 195–207). For example, one case of a woman seemingly haunted by the sound of a ticking clock was solved when the source of the sounds was discovered to be a small insect about the size of a pin's head (Eastham, 1988). Lange and Houran (1997) also found a tendency toward heightened perceptual experiences in a group of people visiting a "haunted" theater compared to a group which had been told no more than that the theater was under renovation. These experiences may be evoked by vague or ambiguous somatic and environmental stimuli (Houran, 1997). The findings of Lange and Houran suggest that contextual factors could prime some people to experience poltergeist-like phenomena in particular types of setting (see also Lange & Houran, 1998, 2001).

While "nervous and overimaginative" people might well behave in the above fashion it is unlikely that everyone who witnesses poltergeist phenomena could be categorized thus. At the very least it would seem that the misinterpretation theory would have to be supplemented with such factors as substantial misreporting. Additionally, some of the trends of poltergeist case collections do not sit happily with this approach. In person-centered cases why should the phenomena seem dependent upon the presence of a particular person? And why should these focal individuals tend to be under the age of 20? Also, the trajectories of displaced objects in poltergeist cases are quite unlike those associated with natural shocks to house foundations (Gauld & Cornell, 1979, pp. 334–337). The persistence of poltergeist phenomena does not accord with such natural events as seismic activity. As a broad account of the poltergeist experience this approach leaves much to be desired, although it does fare better if taken in conjunction with the theory of fraudulent activity.

A neuropsychological version of the "misinterpretation" hypothesis has been advanced by Persinger and his colleagues (Gearhart & Persinger, 1986; Persinger & Cameron, 1986; Persinger & Koren, 2001). They cite empirical evidence of a correlation between poltergeist activity and seismic or other geophysical disturbances. These disturbances are viewed not so much as producing any anomalous movements of objects, but rather as generating geomagnetic fields which influence susceptible people's temporal lobe functioning, causing them to feel anxious and thereby disposing them to perceive the environment anomalously. Gauld (1996) also suggests that increased geomagnetic radiation may cause some temporal lobe irritability or behavioral disturbance in the apparent poltergeist agent, possibly inciting some fraudulent activity.

If it proves to be the case that (some) poltergeist phenomena cannot be explained satisfactorily in terms of normal factors there remain two principal theoretical options. The point at issue between these options is encapsulated by the question, "Are poltergeists living or are they dead?" (Stevenson, 1972).

Spirits. In traditional folklore the poltergeist is depicted as the spirit of a deceased person. This account is consistent with many apparently paranormal features of poltergeist phenomena. Thus some poltergeists give the impression of an underlying intelligence. Poltergeist noises have been used as a basis for meaningful communication (in 16 percent of Gauld and Cornell's sample); objects may move as if they are being carried (19 percent of Gauld and Cornell's sample); and some disturbances seem to be directed at specific individuals, particularly the demonic poltergeist cases. These indications of an underlying intelligence are consistent with the spirit theory, although they might also be said to support the fraud theory. Other suggestions of the involvement of spirits are that apparitions are reported in some poltergeist cases (29 percent of Gauld and Cornell's sample, 23 percent of Roll's sample; see also Alvarado

& Zingrone, 1995) and that exorcism may be successful in attenuating the disturbance (60 percent of Gauld and Cornell's cases in which exorcism was attempted).

The spirit theory has its maximum appeal with place-centered cases. On the other hand these cases are not as well attested as person-centered poltergeists and particularly in recent instances the place-centered outbreak is in a distinct minority. As far as the person-centered disturbances are concerned it is not clear under this theory why the poltergeist focus should have a distinctive psychological profile, that is, why only certain sorts of people should attract a poltergeist "spirit." Indeed, why should the "spirit" be attracted only to some people in conflict and not to all of them? Most if not all of the various points of evidence favoring the spirit hypothesis can be accommodated by another theory (see below) that does not rest on an assumption of discarnate entities and to this extent poltergeist experiences in the view of most parapsychologists do not constitute compelling support for the survival hypothesis.

Subconscious PK. A theory of the poltergeist that has gained wide support from parapsychologists in recent years proposes that poltergeist effects are due to the subconscious use of PK as a release from considerable psychological tension. The feasibility of this hypothesis is enhanced by those experimental studies which suggest that a person may be able to employ PK without conscious awareness of either the task to be performed or the situation to which it pertains (e.g., Stanford et al., 1975). Proponents of this approach thus refer to poltergeist activity as *recurrent spontaneous psychokinesis* or RSPK. To the extent that both "poltergeist" and "RSPK" are theory-based terms neither is really satisfactory as purely descriptive nomenclature for a class of phenomena, but each has become entrenched through widespread usage.

Many aspects of the poltergeist experi-

ence are consistent with the subconscious PK interpretation. The theory implies a high level of tension among poltergeist agents and this is confirmed both by survey data and some case study material which includes detailed psychological assessment of the presumed agent (e.g., Palmer, 1974; Roll, 1968). The identification of the source of the trouble as bottled-up aggression may explain the frequency with which children and adolescents are identified as agents, since in comparison with adults children have fewer skills and opportunities for giving socially acceptable expression to their conflicts. The postulated subconscious basis of the phenomena is compatible with their reported susceptibility to post-hypnotic influence (Bender, 1982, p. 131) and with the evident inability of the focal person to bring under conscious control the disturbances that center upon him or her. The childishness of much of the activity accords with the idea that the acts spring from frustration: often our behavior becomes childish when we are intolerably frustrated. Indeed, often it merely needs to be mentioned to the presumed agent that such outbreaks can be a subconscious displacement of tension and the disturbances will dissipate. Similarly, taking a psychoanalytical perspective, it has been suggested that deep-seated psychosexual conflict can create a "poltergeist psychosis," manifesting as poltergeist activity (Carrington & Fodor, 1951; Fodor, 1948). However, as is often the case with the psychoanalytical approach, such an interpretation is difficult to refute.

Apart perhaps from the psychoanalytical versions, the subconscious PK theory appears compatible with available phenomenological data on the poltergeist experience. The incidence of apparitions in poltergeist cases may be a source of some inconvenience, but as apparitions constitute a phenomenon in their own right the point need not be pursued at this juncture. A further advantage of the RSPK theory is that it is more open to empirical testing than is the spirit hypothesis.

This is not to say that the RSPK approach should be accepted uncritically. Let us look more closely at its two main assumptions, first that poltergeist experiences reflect conflict, and second that they employ a psychokinetic mechanism.

Are poltergeist agents really in the grip of psychological conflict? Survey data to this effect actually are inconclusive because control subjects have not been surveyed; thus one might well find similar levels of conflict reported by people (especially adolescents) who are not poltergeist agents. There have been some detailed psychological assessments of focal individuals but often these were methodologically poor: assessments were undertaken by the case researcher or someone who knew the subject was a poltergeist agent and thus had an expectation of finding evidence of conflict. Martínez-Taboas (1984) argues also that these investigators almost exclusively used unreliable projective tests of personality. Those psychological assessments that were performed satisfactorily are too few

in number and too neglectful of comparative data from nonagents to be regarded as conclusive support for the theory's "conflict" postulate.

The assumption of a PK mechanism can be tested by investigating the PK abilities of poltergeist foci. Roll (1977, pp. 391–392) reports only three of six such studies to have yielded significant PK performance, and the German parapsychologist Hans Bender (1974, p. 130) notes that in his experience PK can not be elicited from agents in the laboratory. The direct evidence for the PK postulate therefore is not strong, although it could be argued that conscious PK tests in the laboratory are a poor analogue of subconscious and deeply motivated poltergeist PK. Thus, the poltergeist focus may subconsciously be reluctant to demonstrate laboratory PK because this could imply "ownership" of the poltergeist events; this possibility is consistent with the fact that while PK performance of foci in the parapsychological laboratory is often nonsignificant, their ESP performance usually is above chance (Bender, 1974; Roll, 1977). Again, there are reports of extra-chance patterns in the output of REGs left in the vicinity of poltergeist outbreaks (Gerding, Wezelman & Bierman, 2002; Maher & Hansen, 1997), but there is no evidence here that the source of the apparent PK effects on the REG was the poltergeist focus.

In any event the attribution of poltergeist phenomena to PK is rather like explaining one unknown in terms of another unknown. Parapsychologists know so little about the limitations of PK that they simply are unable to say whether or not it is plausible to accommodate the variety of poltergeist activities under the concept of PK. For example, no laboratory studies have examined the

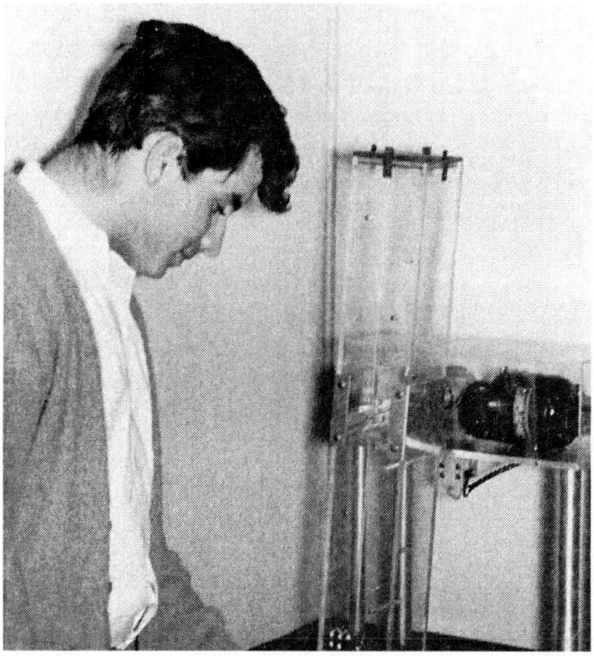

Figure 17. Julio, a poltergeist focus, performing a laboratory PK test (photograph: William Roll).

possibility that PK might produce incendiary phenomena and hence it is precipitate to suppose that PK could explain instances of fire poltergeist activity.

The theory's emphasis upon an individual as the poltergeist agent also might be too simplistic. If one person can use PK activity as a release from psychological conflict then so too could several people. Rogo (1982) drew attention to the need to take account of family dynamics in one poltergeist case. More generally, investigation of the psychodynamics of interpersonal relationships in a given case might well serve to identify multiple poltergeist agents each making significant and interdependent contributions to the RSPK phenomena.

It would appear then that the popularity of the RSPK theory does go somewhat beyond the available evidence. Support for this approach probably stems in some measure from modern parapsychologists' unease with any proposal demanding the assumption of spirit entities. Thus the rejection of the spirit theory while undoubtedly justified on some objective grounds also is intimately bound up with current fashions in parapsychological theorization. Conceptually the poltergeist is subject to the zeitgeist.

Roll's neurological model. Roll has also proposed a neurological version of the RSPK approach (Montago & Roll, 1983; Roll, 1977, pp. 405–410; 1978b). He proposes that RSPK activity is due to eruptions within the central nervous system (CNS), rather like epileptic disturbances. Hence the neurotic conflict said to be characteristic of poltergeist agents is not the direct cause of the poltergeist outbreak but just an incidental consequence of the more fundamental factor of CNS disturbances. In a recent amplification of this approach Roll and Persinger (1998) propose that neuropsychological and psychosocial tensions in the agent can modify the person's electromagnetic energy "profile," and this change modulates and focuses electromagnetic energy in the environment to produce an RSPK event.

In support of this theory Roll has identified a few poltergeist agents whose EEG was symptomatic of epilepsy (e.g., Solfvin & Roll, 1976). He claims further that four percent of his collected cases feature behavioral signs of epileptic disorders and argues that this significantly exceeds the one percent incidence of such signs in the general population. On the other hand, even a rate of four percent cannot be deemed substantial evidence of the potency of this factor in poltergeist cases. Further, among children and adolescents (who form the majority of poltergeist foci) the frequency of EEG abnormalities considerably exceeds one percent and thus Roll's figure might not be particularly deviant (Martínez-Taboas, 1984; Martínez-Taboas & Alvarado, 1981). Some of the "behavioral signs" taken by Roll as indicative of CNS disturbances also are diagnostically dubious (Martínez-Taboas, 1984). Although Roll's interpretation of the RSPK theory is both interesting and more open to empirical scrutiny than the purely psychopathological version its evidential base is not strong.

The general RSPK approach nevertheless does warrant further research effort. In drawing attention to the possible role of psychological conflict in poltergeist cases this theory also merits consideration in the clinical context. Psychologists alert to the theory might be more constructive in their handling of people who come to clinics for guidance in dealing with the poltergeist experience. Counseling in light of an appreciation of the RSPK model at least would be preferable to telling clients that since spooks do not exist, poltergeist disturbances are all in the imagination.

In the final analysis there may be an element of truth in each of the theories of the poltergeist experience. At least some cases do entail fraudulent activity and/or misinterpretation of natural events. If other cases have paranormal origins it is possible too that some are due to an RSPK agent and others to a discarnate entity; this approach is promoted most notably by Stevenson (1972) and Gauld and Cornell (1979, Ch. 18).

Although poltergeist cases cannot justifiably be claimed to provide strong evidential support for the survival hypothesis the fact remains that we are not yet in a position to discount any of the major theoretical approaches to the poltergeist experience.

Key Terms and Concepts

poltergeist
poltergeist focus/agent
recurrent spontaneous psychokinesis (RSPK)

poltergeist psychosis
Roll's neurological model

Study Questions

1. What are the principal forms of poltergeist activity? Is there any independent evidence that these forms can be brought about by psychokinetic means?

2. What are the principal characteristics and correlates of poltergeist experiences?

3. Outline the major theories of the poltergeist, listing the evidential points for and against each theory.

4. To what extent has poltergeist research lent support to the survival hypothesis?

11

NEAR-DEATH EXPERIENCES

Many persons suddenly faced with death have experienced a distinctive state of consciousness in which their existence seemed to be bound neither to a physical body nor to earthly environs. Such a state is termed a *near-death experience* (NDE) and may be defined simply as a transcendental experience precipitated by a confrontation with death. Reports of NDEs come from people who survive the threat to their life. These experients may have been in potentially fatal situations but escaped uninjured, or they may have been seriously ill or hurt and recovered unexpectedly; a few may have been pronounced clinically dead but eventually responded to resuscitative measures. The occurrence of the NDE nevertheless seems to depend not so much on the fact that the experients were dying but rather, that they *perceived* their life to be under serious threat (Gabbard & Twemlow, 1991; Stevenson, Cook & McClean-Rice, 1989).

According to one estimate (Ring, 1980, p. 32) as many as half of all people suffering a serious accident or grave illness have an NDE, although some other surveys suggest its incidence to be much lower, even as little as 6 or 7 percent (Locke & Shontz, 1983; Parnia, Waller, Yeates & Fenwick, 2001). Modal estimates of the NDE's incidence appear to fall in the 10 to 15 percent range (Greyson, 1998b; van Lommel, van Wees, Meyers & Elfferich, 2001). Again,

Schröter-Kunhardt (1993) speculates that the reported incidence of the experience would be much higher but for the dissociative or amnestic consequences of the psychologically traumatic context of the NDE. In other words, a threat to life can be so traumatic that in order to preserve their psychological integrity some people could be unable to recall any NDE they might have had in this context.

The following example of an NDE was obtained by one of HJI's former students Norm McMaster from a man who had cardiac bypass surgery at the age of 55. The experient reports that as he regained consciousness after the operation he was in a great deal of pain. The description of his NDE is extracted from a recorded interview.

> All of a sudden I was standing at the foot of the bed looking at my own body. I knew it was me in bed because there were certain features I could recognize easily. I felt no pain at all. I was a bit puzzled. I wasn't anxious or worried, I just didn't understand what I was doing at the foot of the bed. Then I was travelling. I was at the entrance of a tunnel. There was a light at the end of the tunnel just like sunlight. I had a feeling of comfort and all the pain was gone, and I had a desire to go towards the light. I seemed to float along in a [horizontal] position. When I reached the other end I was in a strange place. Everything was beautiful, yet it was more of a feeling rather than seeing. I could see other people.

They ignored me completely and the next thing I heard a voice saying, "You must go back ... it is not your time." Afterwards I seemed to think it was my father [speaking] but this may have been imagination. Then I was in my bed. There was no sensation of moving back. It was just as though I woke up and all the pain was back and [hospital staff] were working on me.

Although isolated reports on the NDE had been published earlier (see Basford, 1990), interest in NDEs increased greatly in the 1970s. The work of Elisabeth Kübler-Ross drew the attention of researchers and of the general public to the study of death. At the same time, Russell Noyes (1972) began scrutiny of near-death phenomena from a psychiatric perspective, and in 1975 a physician Raymond Moody published a book based on more than a decade of investigation into NDEs during which time he collected about 150 case reports. Moody's (1975) book, *Life After Life*, became an international best seller. In sequels to this book Moody (1977, 1988) explored the implications of the NDE for the survival hypothesis, prompting him to declare that his case collection convinced him of the existence of life after death. Several other books on NDEs now are available, of which the most scientific are those by Ring (1980, 1984), Sabom (1982), Lundahl (1982), Greyson and Flynn (1984), Grey (1985) and Morse (1990). Study of the experience has flourished to the extent that it supports its own specialist journal the *Journal of Near-Death Studies* (formerly *Anabiosis*). With the publication by the American Psychological Association of the book *Varieties of Anomalous Experience* (Cardeña, Lynn & Krippner, 2000), there is some indication that mainstream psychologists increasingly recognize that anomalous experiences such as NDEs and out-of-body experiences (the topic of the following chapter) are worthy of serious study. A comprehensive review of NDE research and theory is provided by Greyson (2000b) in the *Varieties* book.

Study of the NDE necessarily entails retrospective case reports; strict experimental induction of the experience would require us to engineer a perceived threat to a subject's life, a procedure that clearly is unacceptable on ethical grounds. A Canadian researcher Joel Whitton claims to have used a hypnotic technique for inducing experiences with much the same elements as are found in NDEs (Whitton & Fisher, 1986, Ch. 4). This technique could conceivably be represented as an experimental method for NDE induction. Some independent empirical scrutiny of this approach has been undertaken by van Quekelberghe, Goebel and Hertweck (1995). Although the experiences induced under these hypnotic techniques are of interest there must remain some question about the role of expectations of the experience that are generated from familiarity with popular accounts of the NDE. In any event most current data on the NDE comes from case collections and surveys. Admittedly the reliance upon this research strategy is open to the criticism that the fallibility of human memory may make retrospective accounts of the NDE unreliable to some unknown degree, but there is evidence to suggest that the reported features of the NDE do not vary with the length of time since the experience (e.g., Lester, 2003), and thus possible distortion over time does not seem to be a major cause for concern. Furthermore, "prospective" studies can be carried out with populations highly likely to be at risk of death. For instance, hospital cardiac patients frequently suffer cardiac arrest, allowing researchers to interview these patients shortly after resuscitation, hence minimizing changes in recall that may occur over time, and allowing comparisons with patients who have been resuscitated but who did not experience an NDE (e.g., Parnia et al., 2001; van Lommel et al., 2001).

Phenomenological Characteristics of Near-Death Experiences

On the basis of his case collection Moody (1975) identified a common set of elements in NDEs. Broadly speaking these "core" elements are confirmed in the more rigorous studies by Ring (1980), Sabom (1982), Grey (1985), and Lange, Greyson and Houran (2004). Elsaesser Valarino (1997) has offered an even more detailed taxonomy of the NDE's features. Note, however, that a given NDE might not feature all elements and that they need not occur in a fixed order, despite their depiction by Ring (1980) as "stages" and by Lundahl (1993) as a "sequence" of events. The phenomenological elements reported by Moody are

(a) an overwhelming feeling of peace and well-being, including freedom from pain;

(b) the impression of being located outside one's physical body;

(c) floating or drifting through darkness, sometimes described as a tunnel;

(d) becoming aware of a golden light;

(e) encountering and perhaps communicating with a "presence" described by Moody as a "being of light";

(f) having a rapid succession of visual images of one's past; and

(g) experiencing another world of much beauty, perhaps meeting there spirits of deceased relatives and acquaintances with whom one also might communicate.

The characteristics of each of these features will be reviewed in turn.

The Affective Component

Generally this may be described as a sense of emotional detachment, that is, the absence of feelings of fear and pain that otherwise the individual would be experiencing. The state of peace and well-being some-

times is depicted as one of happiness or joyfulness. There may be moments of sadness, loneliness and anxiety during the NDE but these tend to be transient, the overall experience later being described as enjoyable.

The affective component seems to be much the same whether the experient is conscious or behaviorally unconscious (Noyes & Slymen, 1979). In other words, the reported freedom from pain and fear evidently is not a mere consequence of loss of consciousness.

In Ring's (1980, p. 39) survey the feeling of peace was found to be the most common feature of NDEs, being acknowledged by about 60 percent of experients. A survey in the United Kingdom by Fenwick and Fenwick (1995) recorded 88 percent of experients having had this feeling. The participants in the study by the cardiologist Michael Sabom had their NDEs during a heart attack or in heart surgery, and Sabom (1982, p. 206) claims that all experienced calm and peace in the NDE. A similar investigation of cardiac patients by van Lommel et al. (2001), however, yielded an incidence of only 56 percent.

The Out-of-Body Impression

Many experients report the impression of being outside the physical body during the NDE. Estimates of the incidence of this element are rather variable: van Lommel et al. (2001) report the incidence as 24 percent, Ring (1980, p. 45) puts it at 37 percent, a smaller scale study by Greyson and Stevenson (1980, p. 1194) found the incidence to be 75 percent, and in Sabom's (1982, pp. 204–205) sample of NDEs all but one respondent (99 percent) had a sense of bodily separation. Especially if probed, people certainly do tend to describe their NDE as if it had taken place outside their physical body.

The majority of experients have no actual sensations of leaving the physical body, realizing their apparently exteriorized state only when they see their own physical body from the outside. A substantial number of respondents nevertheless do report noises and other sensations accompanying the process of their separation from the body. Many experients also believe that while in the out-of-body state their exteriorized self had a body-like form. These elements will be explored further in Chapter 12 in the context of out-of-body experiences.

It is common for the NDE to consist of an out-of-body impression of nothing more than the experient's immediate environment. The individual can recall apparently looking down upon the physical body and watching the activities of other people trying to lend assistance. Sometimes it is claimed that certain of these out-of-body observations could not have been gathered in any normal fashion (because the individual was unconscious at the time, for example). It is rare, however, for the accuracy of these claims to be checked by NDE investigators. Further, the fact that a person is behaviorally unconscious does not preclude the possibility that some sensory (e.g., auditory) inputs are processed (Lawrence, 1997). There is scant evidence, therefore, that the out-of-body impression of the environment has a paranormal base and is neither pure fantasy nor imagery built upon expectations and partial sensory information. Even if it can be demonstrated that sensorially inaccessible information was incorporated in some NDEs it remains to be shown that this was due to some literal separation of consciousness from the body and not to ESP (assuming this distinction to be legitimate).

The Passage Through Darkness

Sometimes the NDE is not limited to earthly environs and may progress to, or consist entirely of, an experience of some allegedly supernaturalistic realm. Often the transition to this realm is characterized as a rapid passage through darkness. This element is found in about a quarter of NDEs (Ring, 1980, p. 53; Sabom, 1982, p. 206; van Lommel et al., 2001), although the incidence in the survey undertaken by Fenwick and Fenwick (1995) was 51 percent. Moody (1975, pp. 30–34) claims that his experients often

Figure 18. The passage through darkness.

perceived the darkness as a tunnel, but he does not quantify this trend. In the surveys by Ring (1980) and Sabom (1982) it is more common for the darkness to be described as a completely dark and empty space without shape or size; only a small minority of respondents referred to it as a tunnel, funnel, pipe, or the like.

According to Greyson and Stevenson (1980) the tunnel effect is most often cited by executives and professionals as opposed to service workers and laborers. Perhaps there is a class or educational factor operating here but the pertinence of such a factor is unclear and the association thus warrants independent confirmation. No such occupational association was evident in Sabom's (1982, p. 207) analysis. In the study by van Lommel et al. (2001) the more transcendent elements of the NDE were more common among female experients, but replication of this observation is needed.

Seeing a Light

The transition from darkness to the nonphysical realm sometimes is signaled by the appearance of a brilliant light, often described as golden. The light may be so brilliant as to be blinding but at the same time it generally has a magnetic and reassuring quality. In some cases the light may be experienced without the passage through darkness. This element was mentioned by about 30 percent of experients in both Ring's (1980, p. 56) and Sabom's (1982, p. 206) surveys, and 23 percent of experients in the study by van Lommel et al. (2001), although the British survey by Fenwick and Fenwick (1995) put its incidence as high as 72 percent. Owens, Cook and Stevenson (1990) report that the experience of a light was most frequent among those experients whose medical records confirmed that they would have died without medical intervention.

Encountering a "Presence"

Having entered the transcendental environment some kind of cosmic being, angel or religious figure may be encountered (Elsaesser Valarino, 1997; Lundahl, 1992; West, 1998). About 40 percent of Ring's (1980, p. 67) cases include this experience, although Serdahely (1987) reports that occasionally the encounter is set in the dark void or tunnel.

Often the "presence" is not perceived directly but is detected and identified by an intuitive process. Communication between the experient and this being generally concerns the question of whether the individual is to die or to return to the physical body. Many experients had the impression that it was up to themselves to make the choice but sometimes the "presence" commands their return. In some instances the "presence" seems also to have had the role of guide or escort in the transcendental realm (Lundahl, 1992).

Interestingly enough three studies (Greyson & Stevenson, 1980, p. 1195; Ring, 1980, p. 134; Sabom, 1982, p. 207) have revealed no relationship between encounters of a "presence" during an NDE and the experient's prior religious beliefs. On the other hand it is feasible that even the most avowed atheist becomes an instant "believer" when confronted with imminent death, if only for the duration of the threat to life.

Panoramic Life Review

A popular folk belief is that on confrontation with death people will see their life flash before their eyes, and a number of near-death experients do report this. The frequency of the life review generally is put at about 25 percent of NDEs (Ring, 1980, p. 67; Greyson & Stevenson, 1980, p. 1195; Noyes & Kletti, 1977, p. 181), although Stevenson and Cook (1995) and van Lommel et al. (2001) report an incidence of only 13 percent and Sabom's (1982, p. 206) cardiac cases evidenced an atypically low figure of 3 percent. Fenwick and Fenwick (1995) also note that while about 15 percent of their experients mentioned a glimpse of some memories from the past these recollections usually were very fragmentary, and the full life review was much less common. The life review may occur at almost any point in the NDE and indeed, in a few cases it may comprise the entire experience (Stevenson & Cook, 1995).

The panoramic life review consists of unusually vivid, almost instantaneous visual images of either the person's whole life or a few selected highlights of it. In many instances the images may appear in an orderly sequence, from the present to childhood for example, but sometimes the images seem to appear "all at once" (Stevenson & Cook, 1995). The life review occurs without the conscious effort or control of the person; thus experients often remark that they were passive witnesses of the life review.

The following example of a panoramic life review is taken from HJI's file of NDE case reports. At the age of 19 the experient had his chest crushed while working between carriages on a railroad.

> I couldn't breathe while I was stuck in there. The locomotive driver did not realize what was happening. I was unconscious. There was something like a film went through my mind. It went that fast! You get every picture and think you have died. It appears to run for a long time although it is only a few seconds. It was the years of my life — what I had done, wrong or good. I think it was from the beginning of my life — what I have done, where I have been. When I think back I can still see the "film" running; I don't see any pictures anymore but I still have it in my mind.

In some instances experients may rehearse a past event but with greater empathic identification with people they have hurt (Ring, 1992). The panoramic life review occasionally may incorporate fantasies about the future: experients may visualize their death, the reactions of relatives and friends on receiving news of the death, and incidents at the funeral (Fenwick & Fenwick, 1995; Ring, 1982).

The Transcendental Realm

People who undergo an NDE may have a perceptual-like experience of a supernaturalistic environment. This occurred in approximately 20 percent of Ring's (1980, p. 60) cases, 24 percent of experients sampled by Fenwick and Fenwick (1995), 29 percent of experients in the study by van Lommel et al. (2001), and 54 percent of Sabom's (1982, p. 206) cases.

The transcendental realm typically is described as one of preternatural beauty, a pastoral scene with lush green grass, trees, and beautiful flowers. The vividness of the colors is commonly remarked upon. The identification of the setting as nonphysical seems largely to be an intuitive process, although the overwhelming beauty, color, and the soft diffuse lighting may be cues distinguishing the environment from an earthly scene. Occasionally too, lovely music may be heard (Gibson, 1994). The nonphysical realm experienced in NDEs is unlike the biblical stereotype of heaven, although Sabom (1982, p. 209) cites three or four cases in which "St. Peter's Gate" and "streets of gold" are mentioned. It should be noted, however, that the pastoral image is a popular stereotypical notion of the nature of the afterlife (Irwin, 1987b; Kellehear & Irwin, 1990; McDannell & Lang, 1988).

Some experients report meeting deceased relatives and friends in the transcendental realm (Fenwick & Fenwick, 1995; Moody, 1988, p. 10; van Lommel et al., 2001). According to Elsaesser Valarino (1997) the experient is always recognized by the deceased loved one, and typically the experient recognizes the deceased in turn. These beings usually reassure the experient or advise a return to earthly existence. While in the transcendental realm the experient may also encounter some type of boundary, whether a tangible obstacle or an invisible wall (Grey, 1985); it seems to be implicitly understood that if this structure were to be crossed, a return to earthly existence would be impossible.

Contact with a paradisial environment was not correlated with prior religious beliefs in either Ring's (1980, p. 134) or Sabom's (1982, p. 207) sample. Encounters with this realm have been found more commonly among female experients than male experients (Greyson & Stevenson, 1980, p. 1194); possibly this represents nothing more than a response bias, with women being more prepared to admit such an encounter when interviewed by the researcher.

The phenomenological return to the physical body most commonly is instantaneous; that is, the person simply notices that the NDE is over and consciousness is "in" the body (but see Fenwick & Fenwick, 1995). In transcendental cases the termination of the experience ostensibly may be instigated by a command from a discarnate entity. In "earthbound" experiences it may be occasioned by bodily stimulation (e.g., that associated with particular resuscitative measures). Rarely individuals will experience a jolting sensation upon "return." The end of most NDEs, however, is both abrupt and a blank.

The Impact of the Experience

An NDE often has an enduring effect upon the individual's attitudes and values, particularly if death was thought to be imminent and if the NDE included a panoramic life review (Greyson & Stevenson, 1980). These effects might be due to the NDE as such or simply to the close brush with death. According to data obtained by Berman (1974), attitudinal changes are not as marked for people who faced death without undergoing an NDE, suggesting that the NDE itself is crucial to such changes. This result nevertheless is queried by a methodologically superior study conducted by Pope (1991, 1994).

Pope examined attitudes to life, death and suicide among three groups, namely NDErs, a group of people who had been in a life-threatening situation without undergoing a transcendent experience (nonNDErs), and a control group that had neither an NDE nor a close brush with death. Some of the beliefs of NDErs and nonNDErs were found to have changed since their life-threatening incident, but in comparison to the control group it was evident that the NDErs and nonNDErs had changed in precisely the same respects. Pope concluded that, in regard to the attitudes he surveyed, the impact of the NDE was due fundamentally to its occurrence in a life-threatening context rather than to the content of the experience.

Changes reported to occur in experients after an NDE include a renewed sense of the purpose of life; an increased appreciation of life with a determination to live life to the fullest; a greater sense of self-worth; a more tolerant, compassionate attitude to other people; increased religiosity in a universal rather than sectarian sense; decreased materialism and competitiveness; and conviction in life after death, with substantially reduced fear of death but also stronger attitudes against the appropriateness of suicide (Bauer, 1985; Fenwick & Fenwick, 1995; Flynn, 1986; Grey, 1985; Greyson, 1983b, 1992, 1993; Greyson & Stevenson, 1980; Groth-Marnat & Summers, 1998; Musgrave, 1997; Noyes, 1980; Pennachio, 1988; Pope, 1991, 1994; Raft & Andresen, 1986; Ring, 1980, 1984; Sabom, 1982; Sutherland, 1990; van Lommel et al., 2001; Wells, 1993). Experients may also cite an increased incidence of other parapsychological experiences (Fenwick & Fenwick, 1995; Greyson, 1983a; Groth-Marnat & Summers, 1998; Sutherland, 1989). In a comparison of 40 NDErs with 16 individuals who had survived death but had no recall of any concomitant unusual experience one recent study found the former group was relatively more inclined to describe their close call with death as life-changing, but also to depict these after-effects as long-lasting and even increasing over time (Bonenfant, 2004).

These reports of the NDE's impact are based, of course, on the testimony of the experients themselves. According to Atwater (1988) the families of NDErs may draw a somewhat different picture of the changes in the experient. Family members may report difficulty in accommodating to what they see as the experient's indiscriminate expression of love for other people, the perception of social conventions in behavior as "silly," and the sudden fascination with strange mystical and psychic concepts. Indeed, to friends and relatives of some NDErs the latter do not now seem more caring of others but rather, more smug and preoccupied or distant. Family relationships thus may be significantly disrupted (Greyson, 1998a; Insinger, 1991). Some experients themselves encounter difficulties in communicating with other people, finding their experience is to some extent ineffable and not adequately understood by others (Elsaesser Valarino, 1997; West, 1998). Counseling may well be required to assist NDErs adjust to their experience and its emotional and interpersonal sequelae (Clark, 1984; Furn, 1987; Greyson, 1997; Greyson & Harris, 1987; Holden, 1996).

Irrespective of its exact bases, the impact of the NDE upon the experient therefore is notable for its breadth and depth. If only for this reason the NDE would be worthy of serious investigation.

The Negative NDE

Near-death experiences occasionally relate to a transcendental realm that experients may identify as "hell" and is experienced as nightmarish. These cases are relatively rare and their existence is only beginning to be acknowledged (Atwater, 1988, pp. 14–17; Atwater, 1992; Grey, 1985, Ch. 5; Rawlings, 1978, Ch. 7). In his NDE case collection the first author, HJI, has only one example that approaches this "hellish" experience; it was collected by one of his students, Barbara Bramwell, and is examined in greater detail

by Irwin and Bramwell (1988). The NDE is that of a woman in her late forties and arose in the context of a car accident. She describes her presence in a pastoral transcendental realm and her entry into a building that looked rather like a church yet was sensed not to be one.

> I started walking down [the aisle] and I was frightened. There were many pews on each side, and each pew was filled with people wearing black robes with hoods. I couldn't see their faces but if I turned my eyes I could see the inside of the hoods were lined with red. There was no sound at all. I kept walking and walking and then came to three steps which I went up, then walked a little further. I then saw what looked like an altar on which were six silver goblets and a big silver jug. I stood there wondering where I was and what I was doing there, when a door opened to the right of the altar and out came the Devil. He came over to the altar, looked me straight in the eye and told me to pick up a goblet. I picked up a goblet and he picked up the big silver jug and started pouring. I saw that what he was pouring from the jug was fire, and I screamed, dropped the goblet and started to run. I just ran and ran. I didn't know where I was running to. And then I saw a big fence, a stone fence, and the gates opened and I passed through. Then I came to another fence made out of iron bars, and that just opened, and again I ran through. All the time I was getting warmer and warmer and brighter and brighter.

At this point she awoke to find herself in a hospital.

The defining characteristic of so-called *negative* NDEs is their aversive affective tone; these NDEs are not peaceful and calm but instead are nightmarish, marked by fear and anguish. The "hellish" experience illustrated above is one of three apparently distinct types of negative NDE (Ring, 1994). In a second type the experients are seemingly thrust into an existential void, a meaningless environment in which they are taunted by voices claiming that the experients' earthly life never really existed; this experience seems to be a common response to inadequate anesthesia during surgery. A third, much less common form of the negative NDE has essentially the same content as the more typical or "positive" NDE, except that the experients in these cases are extremely frightened by the perception that their life is about to be extinguished. Ring (1994) refers to this type as an *inverted* NDE.

There may be a degree of gross phenomenological parallelism between negative and positive NDEs. For example, the negative NDE can incorporate impressions of being out of the body (Grey, 1985, pp. 63–64), passing through a dark void or tunnel (Grey, 1985, p. 69; Sutherland, 1988, p. 20), contact with a cosmic being (Grey, 1985, p. 66), and entry into a transcendental realm where deceased friends and religious figures may be encountered (Grey, 1985, p. 69; Rawlings, 1978). These parallels prompt Atwater (1988) to declare that positive and negative NDEs have "the same pattern of common elements" (p. 17), even if they differ in detail.

But within this framework of gross similarities, negative NDEs can differ from the positive form (Irwin & Bramwell, 1988). Apart from the defining affective distinction, there is often an element of judgment associated with the negative experience. In positive NDEs experients feel loved unconditionally by the "presence" or cosmic being, and all aspects of their past life, both good and bad, seem acceptable. In negative NDEs, on the other hand, experients report being judged either implicitly or explicitly for past deeds (Grey, 1985, pp. 66–67).

Passage through the dark void or tunnel also may be distinctive. Negative NDErs often describe the movement as in a downward direction (Grey, 1985, p. 70; Lindley, Bryan & Conley, 1981, p. 114; Sutherland, 1988, p. 20), an impression not usually found in other NDEs.

The most marked distinction, however, is in regard to the transcendental environment that the experient may enter. Instead of finding a pastoral scene of preternatural beauty, many negative NDErs report the transcendental setting to be a hellish and barren place: a dark, dank, misty cave or a lake of fire and brimstone, for example (Crookall, 1966; Grey, 1985, pp. 68–72; Rawlings, 1978, Ch. 7). The Devil or other menacing demonic entities may be met in this place. On return to the body, negative experients typically have a sense of having been "spared" from a dreadful fate in order to set their life to a better purpose (Rawlings, 1978, Ch. 7).

The contrasts between positive and negative NDEs might be taken to suggest that the two forms have different origins and hence are distinct phenomena. On the other hand, the occasional occurrence of an NDE that has both positive and negative facets (Abramovitch, 1988; Bonenfant, 2001; Irwin & Bramwell, 1988; Lindley et al., 1981) does point to some commonality of underlying mechanisms.

Greyson and Bush (1992) speculate that the impact of the negative NDE may well be profound and long-lasting, but this issue has yet to be researched. According to Atwater (1992, p. 159), negative experients feel neglected by NDE researchers but at the same time they are a little ashamed to talk about their experience, presumably because the negative NDE carries a stigma in some social circles.

Correlates of the Near-Death Experience

Several surveys of the NDE have included items about the respondent's background with the intention of determining some correlates of the experience (Greyson & Stevenson, 1980; Ring, 1980; Sabom, 1982).

Generally speaking, the incidence of the NDE is not related to such demographic factors as age, gender, socioeconomic level, race (at least within the United States), and marital status.

The NDE's content, on the other hand, may correlate with some of these factors. For example, gender may have a bearing on the reported characteristics of the experience. Sabom (1982, p. 207) found female experients to report encounters with discarnate beings more often than did males. According to Ring (1980, p. 107) and Twemlow and Gabbard (1984, p. 227) there may be an interaction between gender and the circumstances in which the NDE occurs: in the samples of these researchers, women were relatively more likely to have their experience during illness whereas men tended to have their NDE more often in an accident or a suicide attempt. This trend probably reflects a gender difference in lifestyle rather than any inherent difference in susceptibility to the experience.

Positive findings in relation to the variable of occupation have been infrequent and not always consistent. Sabom (1982, p. 207) observed professional people to report fewer encounters with discarnate beings, while in Greyson and Stevenson's (1980, p. 1194) analysis professionals were relatively likely to report the impression of passing through the dark void or tunnel during their NDE.

Religious affiliation and religiosity at the time of the life-threatening incident has no effect upon the likelihood of an NDE nor on the frequency of the various elements of the experience, including the supernaturalistic elements (Ring, 1980; Sabom, 1982). Indeed, there are documented cases of NDE even in skeptics (Lansberry, 1994). High religiosity seems to be more a consequence than a cause of the experience.

The possible effect of age on NDE content has been an issue of special interest. Under any theory that holds the elements of the NDE in some way are a product of social conditioning, it may be predicted that NDEs in childhood would include fewer of the basic phenomenological elements because children have had less extensive social conditioning than have adults. Despite many adults' claims they had an NDE in childhood, it has proved relatively difficult to locate children who have recently had the experience. Among researchers who have been successful in recruiting accounts of NDEs from children are Morse (1990, 1994) and Serdahely (1989, 1990). Making due allowance for children's limited vocabulary and conceptual sophistication, it would seem children's NDEs do exhibit much the same general features as occur in the adult experience (Irwin, 1989b). There might not be a panoramic life review in children's experiences (Serdahely, 1989), and children might be inclined to encounter deceased pets rather than deceased relatives in their experience (Serdahely, 1989), but the sample of children's NDEs still is far too small to establish definitive trends in these respects.

The possible contribution of social conditioning to the NDE can be explored also through cross-cultural research. Despite claims of the NDE's universality (e.g., Holck, 1978) the content of the experience might be affected by the experient's cultural background. In a comparison of NDEs in India with those in America Pasricha and Stevenson (1986) established that Indian experients did not have a panoramic life review nor an out-of-body impression of their physical body, and that they were taken directly by "messengers" to a transcendental realm where a discarnate being consulted some records, decided a mistake had been made and ordered their return to terrestrial life. Counts (1983) found Melanesian cases of NDE to lack the out-of-body impression and the feeling of peace and well-being. Murphy (2001) reports negative elements such as visions of hell and the Lord of the Underworld are common in Thai cases of the NDE, yet these are very rare in Western experiences. Although the samples in the above studies were relatively small, these findings do suggest the elements of the NDE might not be universal. Kellehear's (1993) survey of the cross-cultural literature suggests that the tunnel effect and the panoramic life review are among the most culture-specific features of the NDE, although debate continues on this point (*cf.* Blackmore, 1993b; Kellehear, Stevenson, Pasricha & Cook, 1994). Indeed Rodabough (1985, p. 107) argues more generally that claims for the uniformity of NDEs are overstated.

Social conditioning might influence the NDE rather more directly through the publicity given to this phenomenon in the media (Walker, 1989). Some experients had heard or read about NDEs prior to their own experience: such was the case in 19 percent of Ring's (1980, p. 136) experients. It might be argued, therefore, that this knowledge inspired the occurrence of an NDE when the life-threatening situation arose. Greyson and Stevenson (1980, p. 1195), however, found no relationship between prior knowledge and the incidence of the NDE. More curiously both Ring and Sabom found a *lower* incidence of prior knowledge among experients than among people who had faced death without incurring an NDE. Sabom (1982, p. 57) suggests that this was due to the greater opportunity for nonexperients to have heard of Moody's book before their brush with death: in the surveys by Ring and Sabom nonexperients on average had had their encounter with death more recently than had the experients. Another possibility is that some experients are rather reticent on any items which imply their experience to have been imaginal. In any event experients' seemingly low level of prior knowledge about the NDE makes it unlikely that the claimed degree of uniformity across NDEs is principally an artifact of such knowledge (Alcock, 1978, p. 28), although other sources of social conditioning could still provide the basis for elements of the experience. Two recent studies have investigated whether there is any difference in the characteristics of NDEs experienced prior to the publication of Moody's seminal 1975 book, and those reported after. The first of these was an internet-based questionnaire study completed by 48 pre-1975 NDErs, and 170 individuals who experienced their NDE in 1975 or later. This study found

no difference between the two groups (Long & Long, 2003). However, the retrospective nature of the study means that we cannot rule out the possibility that alterations in recall are more likely to creep in for the pre-1975 group, enhancing the similarity between the two groups. The second study avoided this problem by studying 24 NDE accounts published prior to 1975 to 24 accounts published more recently and matched for relevant demographic and situational variables (Athappilly, Greyson & Stevenson, 2006). This study found that the reports were indistinguishable on fourteen out of fifteen phenomenological features. The exception was an increased frequency of reports of tunnel phenomena in the more recent group. These studies suggest that cultural factors have little influence over the content of NDE reports.

Twemlow and Gabbard (1984) claim that the nature of the NDE may be influenced also by the circumstances of its occurrence. For example, they report that awareness of the golden light was slightly more common when the experient was anesthetized and encounters with discarnate beings were more typical of NDEs that arose when the individual's heart stopped beating. This study unfortunately has two flaws. The technique used for the statistical analysis was inappropriate and did not incorporate a correction for multiple analyses. The sample also comprised people who had had an out-of-body experience in a near-death situation; by excluding cases of NDE that did not incorporate the out-of-body element the generality of the data is uncertain. Further research is warranted on the pertinence of the circumstances of the NDE's occurrence.

Few studies have sought to examine the psychological profile of experients, and even these tend to rely on very small samples. Locke and Shontz (1983) studied a group of students who had had a life-threatening encounter and compared those who experienced an NDE to those who had not. No differences were found between the subgroups in intelligence, extraversion, neuroticism and trait anxiety. Twemlow and Gabbard (1984) similarly report no indications of psychopathology among experients as indexed by measures of psychoticism, hysterical tendencies, danger seeking and general adaptation, although the experients did show a high Absorption capacity on Tellegen and Atkinson's (1974) scale. Using larger samples of near-death experients and nonexperients, Council, Greyson and Huff (1986) found experients to rate highly in psychological absorption and in fantasy-proneness.

Ring and Rosing (1990), on the other hand, report no differential trend toward fantasy proneness among NDErs, although their comparison group comprised nonexperients who had an interest in the NDE. It is feasible that the latter group also would be highly fantasy-prone in comparison to the general population (see also Glicksohn, 1990, pp. 681–682). Because the investigators used a nonstandard index of fantasy proneness the viability of this view can not be assessed through an inspection of their data. Ring and Rosing (1990) and Irwin (1993b) nevertheless note that their NDErs reported the occurrence of considerable abuse and trauma during their childhood, and this factor is known to be predictive of high fantasy proneness. In addition, Ring and Rosing (1990) and Greyson (2000a) report NDErs to score highly on a measure of tendency toward psychological dissociation.

Further research on dissociative processes, and indeed on personality factors more generally, may indicate why some people have an NDE in a life-threatening situation while others do not.

Theories of the Near-Death Experience

The NDE would offer strong support for the survival hypothesis if it could be shown to be what it superficially seems to be, namely a literal separation of the "soul" from the body and its passage to some paradisial realm of postmortem existence. The latter notion of course, is not a description of the NDE but a theory of its basis.

The separationist view of the NDE commonly is embraced by members of the general public, at least in Western countries (cf., Kellehear & Heaven, 1989; Kellehear, Heaven & Gao, 1990). As with so many aspects of the survival issue, however, parapsychologists have yet to devise an adequate test of this theory of the NDE, not really through want of effort but because of the theory's inability to generate unequivocal predictions that a materialistically oriented science can subject to empirical scrutiny. For example, the inclusion of sensorially inaccessible observations in NDEs might be held to discount an imaginal interpretation of the experience in favor of the separationist hypothesis; but such results could equally well be attributed to the operation of ESP in conjunction with a fantasy of separation. Similarly, reports that some NDEs may occur during a state of deep unconsciousness or cortical inactivity (van Lommel et al., 2001) might be taken as persuasive evidence for a separationist account, yet perhaps such experients are recalling a fantasy of separation that in fact was triggered after the period of unconsciousness but which is erroneously attributed to that period (French, 2001). In the absence of a conclusive empirical test the evaluation of the "literal separation" theory has become a matter of disproving other potential theories. Let us, therefore, examine some other options.

For convenience of exposition accounts of the NDE that fall within the scope of conventional science may be dichotomized as either predominantly neurophysiological or predominantly psychological in their orientation.

Neuropsychological Theories

Temporal lobe paroxysm. The temporo-parietal region of the cerebral cortex plays some role in visual imagery and in body image. Thus temporal lobe epilepsy and electrical stimulation of the temporal lobe are characterized by disturbance of these functions. On this basis some commentators (Carr, 1982; Persinger, 1983) have argued that the NDE is an instance of temporal lobe paroxysm, that is, seizure like neural discharges in the temporal lobe or more generally in the limbic system.

This theory is consistent with Britton and Bootzin's (2004) observation of greater paroxysmal activity during sleep in the temporal lobe of near-death experients compared to nonexperients. On the other hand it is difficult to disentangle cause and effect in this correlation, given that the EEG recordings were made after rather than before the NDE. Further, despite some similarities between the NDE and temporal lobe disorders there are several points telling against this approach (Sabom, 1982, pp. 173–174). Perception of the immediate environment typically is distorted in a temporal lobe seizure but seems strikingly realistic in the NDE. A seizure is accompanied by feelings of fear, loneliness, and sadness, whereas the NDE most often is peaceful and calm. Seizures feature auditory imagery more frequently than visual imagery, and sensations of smell and taste are common; the NDE does not conform to this pattern of modalities. In a seizure and in electrical stimulation of the temporal lobe a memory may be revived but invariably it is of no great significance; it is quite unlike the succession of autobiographical highlights that occurs in the panoramic life review associated with the NDE. Finally, seizures and electrocortical stimulation do not evoke images of communicating with deceased relatives in a paradisial setting.

Cerebral anoxia. A shortage of oxygen (or equivalently hypercarbia, an increase in carbon dioxide) in brain metabolism can elicit hallucinatory experiences and thus has been suggested as a physiological basis of the NDE (Blackmore, 1991; Rodin, 1980, pp.

261–262; Schnaper, 1980; Whinnery, 1997). Indeed some subjects with experimentally elevated carbon dioxide levels have experienced an impression of being located outside the body (Sabom, 1982, pp. 176–178). On the other hand in a study of NDEs in cardiac patients Parnia et al. (2001) found experients actually had *higher* oxygen levels at the time of their NDE than did nonexperients. People in a state of cerebral anoxia also tend to have bizarre imagery and thoughts that are quite uncharacteristic of the NDE. Finally, many NDEs do occur in circumstances where cerebral anoxia is extremely unlikely. Perhaps cerebral anoxia is one of many possible physiological cues to a threat to life but at the same time is not the fundamental cause of the experience.

Neuropeptide and neurotransmitter release. Several writers have speculated that the NDE springs from a sudden release of specific neurochemicals in the brain that act on the limbic system and the temporal lobe.

Carr (1982), Jansen (1990) and Jourdan (1994), for example, suggest the involvement of endorphins or endopsychosins. These opiate-like neurochemicals are known to be associated with analgesic effects and a sense of psychological well-being.

Morse, Venecia and Milstein (1989) propose a similar model but based on the neurotransmitter serotonin rather than neuropeptides. Under this account a life-threatening situation is associated with emotional or physiological stress, a neurological effect of which is to alter serotonergic activity. This in turn leads to activation of the temporal lobe, where the NDE is posited to be genetically imprinted.

Saavedra-Aguilar and Gómez-Jeria (1989) have devised a detailed theory of the NDE that incorporates the action of both endorphins and neurotransmitters on the limbic system, the temporal lobe and other connected areas of the brain.

In arguing against this class of theories Sabom (1982, pp. 171–172) maintains that the known analgesic effects of endorphins last much longer than the seconds to minutes typical of the NDE's duration. Endorphins also are not potent hallucinogens, a fact that bears on Blacher's (1989) contention that purely neurochemical accounts can not adequately explain the relatively specific perceptual-like content of NDEs. For example, is it realistic to suppose that images of a paradisial realm are coded genetically in the temporal lobe? Additionally, these theories have yet to be shown to accommodate all the known correlates of the NDE.

Drugs. Some NDEs do occur under the influence of certain medicinal drugs, particularly anesthetics. Perhaps the NDE could be explained as an effect of such drugs. On the other hand, the features of NDEs are rather too specific to be dismissed as drug-induced hallucinations. The latter are notable for their variability across people and they are more bizarre than the NDE. The drug-hallucination theory also is of limited generality since a large number of NDEs, probably the majority, do not occur in the context of drug intoxication.

Massive cortical disinhibition. Siegel (1980) proposed that NDEs are due to massive cortical disinhibition, a view reiterated by Blackmore (1993a) in her depiction of the experience as an artifact of a "dying brain." Thus in certain circumstances (including life-threatening events) control is lost over the random activity of the central nervous system and consciousness reflects the system's efforts to make sense of this endogenous activity. One effect of this, holds Siegel, is to destroy the identification of self with the physical body. Another is for endogenous activity in the optic tract to be interpreted as a perceptual-like experience; specifically, information about the intrinsic structures of the optic tract becomes a basis for the experience of a dark tunnel-shaped structure. In support of his theory Siegel points to elements of experiences induced by drugs that are similar to those of the NDE.

Again there is the problem under this theory of why the particular constellation of elements found in the NDE typically occur only as some isolated components of drug experiences. Further, if Siegel's account of the tunnel effect is correct there should be many other so-called "form constant" experiences in the NDE as there are in drug hallucinations, yet these are notable by their absence from NDEs. Finally, in an NDE why should the "disinhibited brain" activate memories of deceased relatives but evidently not those of living relatives (Serdahely, 1996)? Thus while the approach by Siegel and Blackmore has some novel features it lacks the coherence necessary to accommodate the range of components of NDEs.

Psychological Theories

Depersonalization. Many clinicians, most notably Russell Noyes (1979), are inclined to categorize the NDE as an instance of depersonalization. Depersonalization entails a psychological detachment from one's body; in the case of the NDE the depersonalization would be deemed a defensive psychological reaction to the perceived threat of death. A similar depiction of the NDE is advanced by Roberts and Owen (1988).

On the other hand depersonalization by definition involves not merely a sense of psychological detachment from the body but also much confusion over the identity and reality of one's self. The depersonalized individual feels she or he is not a person. This most certainly is not a characteristic of the NDE: experients typically report that during the NDE their sense of self was strong, clear, and even more real than in normal waking consciousness. The depersonalization theory also assumes that the individual first perceives a threat to life and then has an NDE as a psychological defense. Sabom (1982, pp. 162–163) argues that there are cases in which it would appear that the experient had no appreciation of the life-threatening circumstance until after the onset of the NDE or in some instances after the NDE itself (see also van Lommel et al., 2001).

Motivated fantasy. A milder form of the above theory retains the element of "defensive fantasy" but dispenses with the concept of depersonalization. This approach is associated particularly with the psychoanalytical school and more generally with a psychiatric orientation. The actual motivational basis of the fantasy is variously posited as narcissism (Rank, 1971), the denial of death (Ehrenwald, 1974; Greyson, 1981; Sagan, 1979) or a basic dread of catastrophe (Gabbard & Twemlow, 1991). The content of the fantasy is held to derive from the experient's belief system (Norton & Sahlman, 1995) and from popular social images of an afterlife, including portrayals of heaven in Hollywood movies (Vaisrub, 1977) and media accounts even of the NDE itself (Walker, 1989). In one instance of this theory the observation by van Lommel et al. (2001) that many NDEs may occur during a state of deep unconsciousness has prompted French (2001) to argue that the experience is a fantasy retrospectively generated to "fill in the gap" in cortical activity.

This is a simple theory, and perhaps too much so. Thus the motivational component of the theory is almost tautological: in essence it seems to be proposing that experients have an impression of surviving death because they desire to survive death. Under this theory one also would expect a strong correlation between the occurrence of NDEs and religiosity at the time of the experience, yet as noted above there is no such correlation.

Other consistencies in NDEs do not sit well with the "fantasy" view. Why should so many experients fantasize about passing through a tunnel or darkness, and why should experients' vision of "paradise" be so similar but at the same time so unlike the biblical stereotype? If these images are socially conditioned, how, why, and by whom are they propagated? If the NDE is based in part on accounts of the experience disseminated in the media, why have NDEs not become increasingly homogeneous or stereotyped as the public's familiarity with the experience has grown? In general, theorists of this school give such cursory attention to the details of the NDE that one is tempted to suggest that the motivated fantasy theory is itself motivated fantasy. Perhaps the latter assessment is too harsh but the fact remains that if the NDE is to be depicted as an imaginal event it is necessary to account more precisely for the imaginal origins of each element of the experience. The next psychological theory attempts to do just this.

Archetypes. One way of accounting for the commonality of NDE elements is to assume that these images (the tunnel, the light, the "presence," the paradisial landscape) are "wired" into the brain. That is, people of all cultures and of all eras are born with an inclination to generate certain mental images or *archetypes* that form the mythological elements of our common humanity. These archetypes are held to explain the existence of parallel themes in the folklore of disparate cultures, for example. Originally postulated by Jung (1954/1971), the concept of archetypes has been applied to the NDE by Grosso (1981), Heaney (1983) and Quimby (1989). The near-death archetypal image is envisaged by Grosso as the human race's consensual paradigm of "the best possible way to die," and its teleological function is to structure the passage of consciousness to ultimate completion at the point of death.

On the other hand Jung drew upon a diversity of sources to substantiate his proposed archetypal images, but the evidence for the images of the tunnel, the golden light, and so forth seems to be confined to the experience in question. In other words independent evidence for the existence of the alleged "near-death archetypes" is lacking. How this theory might be put to a more general empirical test also is unclear. In these circumstances it does not seem very constructive to attribute the uniformity of NDEs to the uniformity of people's archetypal images: appeal is being made to one unknown in order to explain another.

It is fair to say that no current neurophysiological or psychological theory of the NDE is satisfactory. It is on these grounds that Sabom (1982) is inclined to the view that the NDE must be a literal experience, one entailing the "soul's" excursion to paradisial environs. Furthermore, none of the rival theories precludes a separationist interpretation, and it is difficult to see how they conclusively could do so: a separation of consciousness from the body could well have the sorts of neurophysiological and psychological correlates upon which the more orthodox theorists focus their attention. Be that as it may, data on NDEs still are too meager to warrant the abandonment of orthodox approaches to the experience. Research into the origins of the individual elements of the experience particularly is required, as it is in this respect that current theories tend to founder. It certainly is premature to assert that the inadequacy of individual orthodox theories enhances the pertinence of the NDE to the survival hypothesis. For further discussion of this issue see Cook, Greyson and Stevenson (1998) and Potts (2002).

Appeal to various conventional psychological factors either singly or in combination may yet provide an adequate account of the experience. In particular, little has been made of Twemlow and Gabbard's (1984) and Council, Greyson and Huff's (1986) finding of high capacity for absorbed mentation among experients. This facet of dissociation has been given considerably closer attention in relation to an allied phenomenon, the out-of-body experience; the latter is the subject of the next chapter.

KEY TERMS AND CONCEPTS

near-death experience (NDE)
Raymond Moody
Kenneth Ring
Michael Sabom
negative NDE

religiosity
prior knowledge
separationist theory
neurophysiological theories
psychological theories

STUDY QUESTIONS

1. Describe the principal phenomenological elements of the NDE.

2. Discuss research on the correlates of the NDE, indicating the potential pertinence of each dimension to our understanding of the experience.

3. List the respects in which the NDE has an impact upon the experient and consider why the experience might have these particular effects.

4. Compare and contrast the major theories of the NDE. In what respects do these theories fail?

5. Discuss the use of the NDE as evidential support for the survival hypothesis.

6. Of what help could a near-death experient be to a terminally ill patient? To what extent should our assessment of this issue depend on the perceived adequacy of the separationist account of the NDE?

7. Early NDE surveys tended to focus on NDE experients alone. What are the values of this approach, and what are its shortcomings?

12

OUT-OF-BODY EXPERIENCES

As noted in the previous chapter, in some NDEs the experient has the impression that consciousness is outside the physical body. This impression, termed an *out-of-body experience*, or OBE, is not confined to near-death circumstances: it may arise in a variety of other situations. The first author, HJI, has reviewed the literature on OBEs (see also Alvarado, 2000), and has collected over 100 OBE accounts. The following report from his collection illustrates a typical case (Irwin, 1985a, p. 1).

> This event occurred some years ago when I was in my twenties. I was in bed and about to fall asleep when I had the distinct impression that "I" was at ceiling level looking down on my body in the bed. I was very startled and frightened; immediately I felt that, I was consciously back in the bed again.

The out-of-body experience may be defined as one in which the center of awareness appears to the experient to occupy temporarily a position which is spatially remote from his or her body. As with the NDE the OBE is defined as an experience, not as a literal event. That the OBE entails a literal separation of consciousness from the body is a theoretical interpretation of the experience rather than a definition of it.

The OBE clearly overlaps the phenomenon of the NDE and many experiences could appropriately be designated by either term.

The two phenomena, however, are not equivalent: there are OBEs that occur in circumstances that are not life-threatening and there are NDEs that do not incorporate the impression of the self being exterior to the body. It may strike you as curious that research on the NDE has to a large degree proceeded independently of that on the OBE, but there are two main factors contributing to this situation. First, NDE research evolved primarily in a medical setting and even now a large proportion of NDE researchers are medical professionals; OBE research, on the other hand, initially received more attention from parapsychologists. At least in the early phase of work on the NDE researchers in fact took care to avoid any reference to the OBE literature for fear of being regarded by colleagues as "occultists." However, perhaps unbeknownst to the medics investigating NDEs, neurologists have been documenting OBEs and other autoscopic (literally, seeing oneself) experiences in their patients since the 1930s (see reviews by Blanke, Landis, Spinelli & Seeck, 2004; Blanke & Mohr, 2005; Brugger, Regard & Landis, 1997), though theorizing on this matter has been described as pre-scientific (Dening & Berrios, 1994). Second, the distinctive theoretical orientation to each phenomenon has been facilitated by different styles of definition: whereas the NDE is defined *contextually* or in relation to its circumstances of occurrence, the OBE is defined *phenomenologically* or in relation to its impression upon experients themselves.

Defining the OBE in experiential or phenomenological terms raises some difficulties. For example, if a psychotic patient reported an OBE, should this experience be categorized as a real OBE or as a psychopathological delusion? Under the above definition it would be admitted as an instance of an OBE because at the time, the experient had the impression of being outside the body. With further research we may be in a position to discriminate the OBEs of psychotics from those of otherwise normal people, but at this stage a distinction between a "real" OBE and a hallucinatory one would be presumptuous. The same applies to OBEs that can be shown to include nonveridical information.

You may recall the story of Hélène Smith's out-of-body excursions to the planet Mars (Chapter 2). That Smith's account of the Martian landscape is at odds with data from space probes does not negate the fact that during the experience Smith believed her "spirit" to be outside her body, and her account thereby qualifies as an OBE report. Veridical and nonveridical OBEs may prove to have different correlates, but this dimension can not properly be used as a criterion for accepting or rejecting OBE reports: veridical experiences might have the same bases as nonveridical ones.

In other cases people report seeing an apparition of a living individual and assert that the latter was having an OBE. Again, unless the individual concerned had an impression of being out of the body at the time, such a case would not qualify as an OBE under the adopted definition.

Data on OBEs rely heavily on retrospective reports. Thus considerable use is made of OBE case collections, surveys of experients (OBErs) and nonexperients (nonOBErs), and self-observations by so-called OBE adepts who reportedly can induce the experience virtually at will. Irwin (1985a, Ch. 2) reviews the ad-

vantages and the limitations of these sources of data; in this regard it is important to note that some of the information on OBEs is available only from the above sources.

Efforts nevertheless have been directed to the development of experimental methods of OBE induction, the objective being to facilitate laboratory investigation of the experience. At the beginning of the twentieth century French researchers pioneered hypnotic suggestion as an OBE induction procedure, but that method now is rarely used because of its strong demand characteristics; that is, because the subject merely may produce verbal responses in compliance with the hypnotist's suggestions the hypnotic performance might not be comparable experientially to a spontaneous OBE (see also Tart, 1998).

More recently Palmer (1978c) has sought to induce experimental OBEs by simulating conditions under which spontaneous experiences occur. His most successful techniques to date involve three fundamental elements. The first is bodily relaxation, usually promoted through a recorded exercise in progressive muscle relaxation. The second involves manipulation of the subject's sensory environment by way of either sensory bombardment or severe sensory restriction and homogeneity; this procedure seems to facilitate the individual's dissociation from exteroceptive processing and to encourage high absorption in mentation. Finally there is an element of expectancy or "mental set" whereby the participant is encouraged to want an OBE and to believe one can occur (Palmer & Lieberman, 1975).

When HJI explored Palmer's techniques, he found the induced experiences to be rather insipid in comparison to spontaneous OBEs, often marked by little more than a vague dissociative feeling. Demand characteristics may be substantial here too. Experimental procedures in OBE research, therefore, are very much in their infancy.

Phenomenological Characteristics of the Out-of-Body Experience

The following review of OBE phenomenology is based upon HJI's earlier collation (Irwin, 1985a, Ch. 3) of data from surveys, case collections, and adepts' self-observation.

Sensations at Onset and Termination

Between 20 and 40 percent of survey respondents report having specific sensations at the onset of the OBE (Irwin, 1985a, pp. 81–82; Poynton, 1975, p. 116). Four main types of experience are cited. There may be percussive noises; that is, the OBEr may hear a buzz, roar, click or crack on "leaving" the body. Vibrations in the physical body may be experienced; these vary from shivering to violent shaking, and from a single jolt to a series of vibrations. Catalepsy sometimes is reported; this state is described as a lack of bodily sensation or a lack of bodily control, with complete rigidity. The start of the experience may be signaled also by a momentary blackout or short period of "mental darkness," after which the experient has the impression of being exteriorized. Some of these onset phenomena are instanced in the following case (Irwin, 1985a, p. 81).

> My first experience was when I was 13 years old. I do not recall anything out of the ordinary at the time nor remember anything that might have led up to it. As I was sleeping I had a strange falling sensation. In my ears and head I had a noise, it went boom boom boom etc. very loudly and quickly. I guess it would be likened to a noise a plane makes but it throbbed more or vibrated. I tried to wake but I felt frozen. I felt my whole body just pinned there.

Onset sensations have been found to correlate with the impression of control during the experience (Irwin, 1985a, p. 84). That is, people who experience these phenomena tend to report that they had greater control

over the way in which the OBE subsequently unfolded.

It must be emphasized, however, that onset sensations are found among a minority of cases. In most OBEs the experient suddenly has the impression of being in an exteriorized state, as in the following experience (Irwin, 1985a, p. 81).

> I was sitting in the bath when I became aware that I was in the ceiling corner of the room looking down at myself in the bath. I watched myself quietly for a while, aware of the light and looking down. Then suddenly I felt frightened and the scene was rapidly lost — I was back once again at ground level, in the bath.

This case also terminated instantaneously, as do the majority of OBEs. Nevertheless up to 40 percent of survey respondents claim to have had definite sensations upon "returning" to the body. These phenomena are much the same as for the onset of the experience: a momentary blackout, noises, vibrations in the physical body, and a sense of immobility or catalepsy. If return to the body is rapid it may be described as a sudden jolt (Alvarado & Zingrone, 1997b).

The OBE may be terminated by an emotional reaction: in two of the cases presented above fear produced an immediate end to the experience. Other cases cite annoyance, mirth, and "consuming love" as having cut short the OBE. The sight of the physical body from the outside may terminate the experience, in many instances apparently because of the emotional response (fear, contempt, revulsion) this sight evokes, but also perhaps because attention is diverted back to the body. Another factor commonly bringing an end to the OBE is the physical body's being touched by someone. Also the experient may "return" to the body by a conscious effort to do so. The OBE therefore may end when attention is drawn to bodily processes or when dissociation from such processes begins to lapse.

Content of the Experience

In the typical OBE experients find themselves instantaneously exteriorized in the immediate vicinity of the physical body, looking down on the environment and perceiving it in an apparently realistic fashion. "Astral flights" to far-off lands and to other planets tend to be the province of the adept, although it is feasible that survey respondents may be less willing to reveal such experiences.

Most OBErs report having seen their own body from the remote location. This is a feature of 50 to 80 percent of survey cases (Gabbard & Twemlow, 1984, p. 19; Irwin, 1985a, p. 88). The appearance of the physical body during an OBE is of interest in the following regard. There is a psychotic condition known as *autoscopy* in which the individual has a hallucination of coming face to face with their own double. A few psychiatrists want to equate the OBE with autoscopy, despite marked phenomenological differences: for example, in autoscopy the individual realizes the vision is hallucinatory and regards consciousness still to be "in" the physical body. Nevertheless one curious aspect of autoscopy is that the hallucinated double usually is a mirror image of the body, that is, it appears laterally reversed (with hair parted on the opposite side, wedding ring on the wrong hand, etc.). Perhaps our mental image of ourselves tends to be laterally reversed because the most common full-length three-dimensional experience of ourselves is in a mirror. If the OBE is a hallucinated image a perceptual-like experience of the physical body from the outside therefore might be expected to be laterally reversed. There seem to be no definitive data on this point, although if OBErs do note the appearance of their physical body from the exteriorized perspective their comments usually are not of the form, "that's just how I look in the mirror," but rather, "so that's how I look to other people."

The out-of-body perception of the environment is described as visually realistic in over 80 percent of cases (Green, 1968a, p. 71). Occasionally some odd effects occur, including wide-angle vision, seeing through objects, and seeing in the dark, but these are uncommon. On the other hand, some OBE accounts do imply a lack of realism in certain respects. For example, an experient may report seeing the physical body as if from a height of 30 feet (9 meters) or more, yet this would have entailed seeing through the roof and the ceiling of the house.

Other less common features are associated particularly with OBEs in life-threatening circumstances (Gabbard, Twemlow & Jones, 1981). Passage through a dark tunnel is reported by up to a quarter of survey respondents (Gabbard & Twemlow, 1984, p. 19; Irwin, 1985a, pp. 93–94); this seems to mark a transitional process, for example, between the body and the exteriorized state or between a naturalistic and a transcendental setting. Experiences of a bright light, discarnate entities, and music also are mentioned in a small minority of OBEs, again most often in a life-threatening context (Alvarado, 2001).

Sensory Modalities

Over 90 percent of OBEs are visual (Green, 1968a, pp. 67–68), often exclusively so. The involvement of other sensory modalities tends to parallel that of normal perceptual experience, or alternatively it could be said to be consistent with imagery generated so as to provide a maximally convincing representation of the normal environment.

Very occasionally an *asensory* OBE is reported, that is, the experient feels exteriorized but has no perceptual-like impression of any environment. In over 300 OBE cases obtained in a British survey Green (1968a, p. 69) found only "a few" asensory experiences. In HJI's collection there is only one in which there was an absence of any perceptual-like awareness of the environment.

Vividness

The vividness or clarity of the perceptual-like experience is striking, according to survey respondents. Again there may be some variation in this respect as vividness usually is low in experimentally induced OBEs.

Control

Some OBErs report having been able to control the content of their experience in some way. In one of HJI's surveys (Irwin, 1985a, p. 100) 46 percent of experients made this claim. There is a general consensus among survey respondents and adepts that such control is purely cognitive: it is a matter of directing attention to a desired state of affairs rather than of exerting "physical" effort. Most often control is exercised in relation to the place the exteriorized self wishes to be; according to some accounts the experience may be directed to a person whose location was unknown at the time. Some OBErs mention that the nature and the very existence of objects can be manipulated in the out-of-body state. Females tend to report more control over OBE content than do males (Irwin, 1985a, p. 101).

Aspects other than content are subject to control. These include the termination of the experience and the activities of the out-of-body or *parasomatic* form. Again it should be noted that many OBEs are so brief and so disconcerting that the idea of control is not even entertained.

Naturalism

About 80 percent of OBEs are purely naturalistic. Possibly this figure partly reflects a response bias: an OBE with a transcendental setting is more easily dismissed by the experient as fantasy and thus not reported.

There is some suggestion that naturalistic cases tend to relate to the world as conceived rather than as perceived. Thus people with sensory deficits often report these not to exist in an OBE (Green, 1968a, pp. 32–33; Irwin, 1987c).

As mentioned earlier, transcendental experiences tend to occur more often under life-threatening circumstances (Gabbard et al., 1981).

Veridicality

Experients typically present their naturalistic OBEs as being completely veridical. The accuracy of out-of-body perception, however, often is assumed rather than proven: if the experience matched the individual's memory of the real-life setting then it is held to have been veridical.

One means of investigating the veridicality of OBEs is to see if a person in an out-of-body state can obtain sensorially inaccessible information. In a survey by Palmer (1979) about 15 percent of OBErs claimed to have acquired information in this fashion. During induced OBEs in experimental tests (e.g., Palmer & Lieberman, 1975) subjects have been able to identify remote targets to a statistically significant degree. This might be attributable to the use of ESP, although in a study conducted by one of HJI's students (Smith & Irwin, 1981) a correlation was found between veridicality and independently judged "OBEness"; that is, the more the induced experience was like a spontaneous OBE the more accurate was the subject's description of a remote target. There is, therefore, some indication that OBEs can be veridical to a degree that mere fantasy could not. Further research on this point is warranted.

In some OBEs nonveridical elements nevertheless do occur. One case (Crookall, 1972, pp. 89–90) included mention of nonexistent bars on the bedroom window; these bars seemed to have some symbolic significance for the experient in preventing him from "leaving" his room.

The Astral Body and the Astral Cord

Some OBErs report their exteriorized self to have had a definite form. In occult literature this is termed the "astral body"; in parapsychological work it is known also as the *parasomatic* form. Estimates of the incidence of parasomatic forms vary widely, from 15 to 84 percent of experiences (Irwin, 1985a, p. 114), but the trend is for the slight majority of OBEs to be parasomatic. Further, even in allegedly *asomatic* experiences the OBEr may imply that the formless exteriorized self had spatial dimensions. For example, the exteriorized self may be said to have had to "squeeze" through a small space or to have been "standing."

The parasomatic form most commonly is a replica of the physical body. A few older experients have depicted their astral body as the image of themselves when they were at their physical peak. Occasionally the parasomatic form is localized as a point or a small sphere, while in other cases its dimensions are more vague, being described as a cloud, a mist, or a band of light.

In about 20 percent of survey cases (Irwin, 1985a, p. 125) the parasomatic form is linked to the physical body by a cord-like structure. This so-called *astral cord* is more common in those case collections in which respondents of a spiritualist persuasion are frequent; here the structure tends to be known as "the silver cord." It is much less common in contemporary cases and is very rare in laboratory induced experiences.

The cord reportedly may join the physical body at either the forehead or in the region of the solar plexis; its connection to the astral body often is on the back. Where experients do report having had an astral cord it usually is on the basis of having seen it, but sometimes it is evidenced merely as a sensation of being tugged toward the physical body. Many experients have the impression that if the cord were broken death would be inevitable.

Psychological Processes During the Experience

Experients tend to characterize their psychological state in an OBE as one of re-laxed alertness, mental clarity, and effortless concentration. In cognitive terms the OBE is marked by a resistance to distraction and total involvement, the state known as psychological absorption. This recalls the earlier suggestion that the experience may be terminated by a loss or disruption of attention. Note, however, that this absorbed state during the OBE typically is achieved and maintained in an effortless manner. Thus, experients depict the OBE's cognitive processes not in terms of internally focused attention (Maitz & Pekala, 1991) but rather as an engrossing, externally oriented or perceptual-like experience.

Emotionally the experient seems to be calm, peaceful, and even emotionally detached during the experience, even in otherwise arousing circumstances. It seems that any emotion with strong bodily concomitants tends to terminate the experience.

Circumstances of Occurrence

Other research on the OBE is more explicitly process-oriented, seeking to illuminate factors underlying the experience. Two major foci for this work have been the OBE's circumstances of occurrence and the sorts of people who are prone to the experience.

Under what circumstances does the OBE take place? For convenience of discussion the experient's mental state and physical state will be considered separately; it is not assumed, however, that these aspects are independent.

Pre-Experience Mental State

In about 60 percent of survey cases the pre–OBE mental state is described as quiescent or calm, rather like the OBE itself. On the other hand the experience also can arise in emotionally arousing circumstances such as confrontation with death; this is found in 25 to 40 percent of cases (Irwin, 1985a, pp. 144–145).

It would seem then that the OBE may occur under a wide range of mental states, but in fact we can be more specific than this. Irwin (1985a, p. 146) asked a group of OBErs to rate their pre–OBE mental state on a ten point scale. Fifteen rated their emotional arousal as having been low (1, 2, or 3); nine rated it as high (8, 9, or 10); and only two respondents chose intermediate ratings. This trend towards extremes of arousal is statistically significant. On these grounds it may be proposed that the OBE occurs when the level of cortical arousal is extreme (either high or low), perhaps unusually extreme for the experient.

At this point it is appropriate to enter a caveat on past OBE research methodology. Much of the phenomenological research into OBEs has relied on cases that have occurred under a variety of states of consciousness. Stanford (1987b) has cautioned that the correlates of OBE phenomenology may well vary with the state of consciousness in which the experience occurs. Additionally, Blackmore (1986b) and Irwin (1986a) signal that deliberately induced and spontaneous experiences may have slightly different phenomenology and correlates. Experimental work by Glicksohn (1991) suggests that the subjective qualities of induced anomalous experiences are codetermined by aspects of the subject's personality and the sensory environment. Future research might usefully give closer attention to the nature of these more complex interaction effects (see also Alvarado, 1997).

Pre-Experience Physical State

Many OBEs occur when sensory input is minimal or under conditions approximating sensory deprivation. Lying on the bed or meditating are common contexts for the experience. At the other extreme the experience also may be precipitated by sensory bombardment or overload, as in the trance states associated with the rhythms of native drums and the dances of the whirling dervishes; in one case in HJI's collection the experient was listening to very loud rock music. Again it is probable that these physical states have their effect by way of cortical arousal.

At the same time the factor of physical inactivity warrants closer scrutiny. Over 90 percent of OBEs (Green, 1968a, p. 50) occur when the individual is physically inactive (lying down, sitting, etc.). This suggests that a lack of somatic (kinesthetic and proprioceptive) stimulation is an important condition for the OBE. Further evidence for this comes from a survey of 11 OBE cases published in the neurological literature over the last 100 years, in which 86 percent of experiences occurred while the experient was lying down, compared to 38 percent of the 8 autoscopic cases (in which people see a double of themselves in extrapersonal space but don't feel outside of their own body) and also 38 percent of the 8 heatoscopic cases (an intermediate form of experience, in which the extrapersonal double is seen but the experient is not sure if they themselves are inside or outside their own body) (Blanke & Mohr, 2005). In other words OBEs seem to be facilitated by a lack of proprioceptive and tactile feedback leading to the person becoming out of touch with bodily processes. This also accords with the indication that attention to bodily processes brings the experience to an end. Of the 5 to 10 percent of cases in which the experient was physically active at the time of the OBE the considerable majority of activities were automatic (e.g., walking) or so highly practiced as to be automatic for the individual concerned (e.g., a professional musician playing an instrument, a minister reading a sermon). In cognitive terms these automatic activities require a negligible amount of attention, that is, the individual may perform them while dissociating from bodily processes.

Induction Processes

Many commentators on mystical experiences have published detailed programs for the deliberate self-induction of the OBE (Rogo, 1983). Although most of these have not been put to rigorous scientific investigation they are worthy of consideration as a source of *hypotheses* about the factors critical to the occurrence of the experience.

At first glance there are as many proposed OBE induction techniques as there are commentators, but once the esoteric rigmarole is stripped away some consistencies can be identified (Irwin, 1985a, pp. 155–170). Physical and mental relaxation are given particular emphasis, reinforcing some of the suggestions made above. The use of mental imagery is a common feature; whether this is important for its own sake or as a focus for one's attention is not clear. Certainly attention or absorption is seen as a fundamental factor: many programs include directions for focusing attention upon a particular thought or object, and some even promote some preparatory training in total absorption. The other characteristic general to all techniques, either implicitly or explicitly, is that of expectation: the individual who follows any proposed induction program is to expect an OBE to happen.

The Experient

Further insight into the nature of the OBE may be gained by determining the sorts of people who have these experiences.

Incidence

There have been few surveys of OBEs among the general population, but estimates of their incidence here range from 8 to 15 percent (Blackmore, 1984a; Palmer, 1979).

Outside of the neurological context, the most frequent target population has been that of university students. In his own studies (Irwin, 1985a, p. 174) HJI has found 20 to 48 percent of Australian undergraduate psychology students to have had the experience.

These figures are comparable to data from other countries. The higher incidence of reported OBEs among university students may reflect various factors such as better memory, higher capacity for self-observation, recency of experience, more willingness to acknowledge "odd" experiences, greater sympathy with academics' surveys, and more frequent experimentation with psychotropic drugs.

Surveys also indicate that the majority of experients have had more than one OBE (e.g., Palmer, 1979). While the experience may not be an everyday one for the individual it nevertheless seems to be a remarkably familiar one on a population basis.

Age

The OBE evidently can occur at any time of life, although current data are not adequate to indicate if the experience is more common at a given phase of life. Although 12-year-old children readily acknowledge OBEs (Glicksohn, 1990), it seems that few reported cases occurred when the experient was less than five years old (Irwin, 1985a, p. 179; Blackmore & Wooffitt, 1990). On the other hand, there are difficulties of recall for this period (how many experiences can you recall from your pre-school years?) and direct questioning of very young children is fraught with such methodological problems as response bias and lack of comprehension.

Gender

In case collections there are more accounts from female experients than from males. Judging from survey data, however, gender does not seem to be a major factor in the incidence of the experience (Irwin, 1985a, p. 181), although it may be linked with the circumstances under which the OBE arises: for example, OBEs under marijuana intoxication are more likely for males presumably because males on average are heavier users of marijuana (Tart, 1971, p. 105).

Other Demographic Variables

The OBE evidently is independent of level of education, marital status, social class and income. Religiosity does not influence either the occurrence of the OBE or the incidence of any specific aspects of OBE content (Irwin, 1985a, pp. 186–189).

There are few data upon which to assess the possible role of race and culture in the OBE. There are differences across cultures in *belief* in the possibility of an OBE, the sorts of people who are thought capable of having an OBE, and the circumstances under which an OBE is held to occur (Sheils, 1978). Some qualitative evidence does suggest that culture may affect OBE content. For example, when shamans of certain primitive tribes have a "magical flight" their parasomatic body often is said to take the form of the tribe's totemic animal.

Prior Knowledge

Certainly the OBE can occur without the experient's prior knowledge of the phenomenon. About 50 to 60 percent of survey cases occurred without such knowledge. Further, prior knowledge does not seem to influence the incidence of the various elements of the experience, including sensations at onset and at termination, the possession of an astral body, and the impression of having control over the experience (Irwin, 1985a, pp. 192–196).

Personality

Several studies have investigated the personality of the OBEr. Gabbard and Twemlow (1984, p. 32) found experients to be comparatively low in "danger seeking," but the control group for their investigation makes this result ambiguous. HJI did not find this tendency among student experients (Irwin, 1980c).

Gackenbach (1978/1979) reports that people who have a high number of OBEs are more unrestrained, imaginative, radical, and bohemian. Similarly, McCreery (1997) found OBErs to be inclined to engage in a type of magical thinking that was not maladjustive. This "unconventional" profile of the OBEr may be misleading. People who are comparatively bohemian may have more OBEs not because they are inherently more susceptible to the experience but because they are more likely to delve into occultism and thus to experiment with OBE induction techniques.

Using the *Jackson Personality Inventory*, Myers, Austrin, Grisso and Nickeson (1983) found OBErs had a greater breadth of interest and taste for complexity than did nonexperients. The population they investigated, however, comprised students of a Jesuit college. It is feasible their data say more about nonOBEing Jesuit college students than they do about the personality of the OBEr. Comparison of the data to college student norms supports this view.

Irwin (1985a, p. 201) did not identify any differences between experients and nonexperients on either the Extraversion or the Neuroticism scales of the *Eysenck Personality Inventory*. Tobacyk and Mitchell (1987a) also report no association between the OBE and measures of avoidant defense styles, narcissism and social desirability.

Cognitive Skills

Imagery skills of OBErs warrant some scrutiny. It might be expected that if the OBE is an imaginal experience it would require some dexterity of imagery skills to conjure up a vivid image of how one's physical body and the immediate environment would appear if observed from a point near the ceiling.

Several parapsychologists have examined the ability to generate vivid visual images and to control or manipulate such images. No differences between experients and nonexperients have been established with questionnaire measures (see Irwin, 1985a, pp. 260–277 for a review). Some performance measures of visual imagery ability, however, have yielded significant results. Cook and Irwin (1983) ascertained that OBErs are comparatively adept in judging how an object would appear from various perspectives (see also the methodologically interesting paper by Amorim, 2003), and Hunt, Gervais, Shearing-Johns and Travis (1992) report a relationship between OBEs and the performance of block designs and embedded figures tests.

In addition to the involvement of general visual imagery skills HJI has found that kinesthetic and somaesthetic imagery is correlated with experients' impression of control over their OBE (Irwin, 1985a, pp. 272–273). This suggests that in order for the exteriorized self to appear to be doing one thing while the physical body is doing another, some skill in somatic imagery is necessary.

Dissociative Processes

Phenomenological analyses of OBEs, as well as the OBE's association with lucid dreams (Alvarado & Zingrone, 1999; Green, 1968a,b; Irwin, 1988a), meditation (Palmer, 1979), and hypnotic susceptibility (Palmer & Lieberman, 1976), raise the possible significance of attentional factors in the OBE. One aspect of this is that during the OBE the individual is out of touch with or dissociating from bodily processes. It therefore may be asked if this is specific to the experience or is a habitual tendency of experients. This issue has not been researched thoroughly but in a questionnaire study HJI did not find experients to have a permanently low level of "body consciousness" (Irwin, 1985a, pp. 279–280).

Another attentional aspect of the OBE is that of absorption. The nature of the experience suggests that OBErs may have a capacity for resisting distraction. That this is not specific to the period of the OBE is suggested by experients' greater inclination toward lucid dreams and meditation and their superior susceptibility to hypnosis. Irwin (1980c,

1981b, 1985a) has established a substantial advantage of experients over nonexperients in capacity for having absorbing experiences. This result has been confirmed by Myers et al. (1983) in America, Glicksohn (1990) in Israel, and Dalton, Zingrone and Alvarado (1999) in Scotland. Further, people who have high Absorption scores are more open to an experimental OBE induction technique (Irwin, 1981b). Thus the dissociative factor of psychological absorption seems to play a major role in the OBE. There are indications too that experients with high absorption capacity are more likely to report a parasomatic form and sensations at termination of their spontaneous OBEs (Irwin, 1985a, pp. 287–288).

Fantasy proneness, a factor strongly related to absorption capacity, reportedly is higher among OBErs than nonOBErs (Hunt et al., 1992; Myers et al., 1983; Wilson & Barber, 1983). Stanford (1987b) reports further that various types of fantasy during childhood may correlate differentially with the circumstances in which the individual's OBE arises, although this finding was not replicated in a subsequent study (Stanford, 1994). Possibly related to this finding is a reported correlation between OBEs and the "aberrant perceptions and beliefs" factor of schizotypy, a disposition to schizophrenic-like behaviors (McCreery & Claridge, 2002).

Psychological absorption and fantasy proneness are dissociative phenomena. The role of dissociative processes in the OBE therefore warrants scrutiny. As yet the empirical literature on this issue is meager, but Alvarado and Zingrone (1997a) and Dalton et al. (1999) reported that the OBE correlates with various pathological (depersonalization) and nonpathological (absorption) components of the dissociative domain. Recently Irwin (2000) found the facet of the dissociation domain most strongly predictive of the occurrence and frequency of OBEs was somatoform dissociation, that is, the tendency to dissociate from bodily sensations. Given that dissociative tendencies may be exacerbated by childhood trauma (Irwin, 1994c) the role of dissociative processes in the OBE would also account for a reported association between the experience and a history of childhood trauma (Bergstrom, 1999; Irwin, 1996). OBErs also have higher self-consciousness, higher social physique anxiety, and score more highly on a measure of somatoform dissociation than non-experients (Murray & Fox, 2005a,b). These findings replicate those of Irwin (2000) and suggest that the OBE is a form of dissociational body experience perhaps arising in part from dissatisfaction with one's body image. This etiology would be particularly pertinent for those experiencing spontaneous OBEs, rather than OBEs arising from alcohol, drugs, or traumatic events. To test this idea, Murray and Fox (2006) examined body image for those who had the out-of-body impression as part of an NDE and in people whose spontaneous OBE was not in a life-threatening context. In line with this hypothesis, spontaneous OBErs scored more highly than the NDErs on measures of somatoform dissociation, body dissatisfaction, and self-consciousness. Murray and Fox (2006) argue that this provides evidence of more than one route to experiencing an OBE, and as we shall see in the following section on OBE theories, there is also evidence that some OBEs may have a neurological cause. However, given that most of the research correlating OBE experiences with measures of dissociation relies on self-report instruments, there is always the possibility that these correlations arise from a form of response bias, such as a readiness to report bodily dissatisfaction and to report OBE experiences. This is a perennial problem with self-report measures.

Needs

The content of many OBEs suggests that the experience may serve some social need, such as the need to be with a particular person. On the other hand there are so many other cases in which social motives are lacking that it is likely such motives affect the content rather than the actual occurrence of the OBE.

One psychoanalytic view of the OBE (e.g., Rank, 1971) is that the experience reflects narcissism, that is, experients have a need to step outside their physical body and admire it as everyone else can. In one of HJI's surveys, however, experients did not exhibit a greater obsession with their body than did nonexperients (Irwin, 1985a, pp. 296–297). Tobacyk and Mitchell (1987a) also observed no difference between OBErs and nonOBErs on the *Narcissistic Personality Inventory*. Thus the need for a narcissistic fantasy does not seem a likely factor in the OBE. Indeed the reverse may be the case: OBErs score more highly on measures of body dissatisfaction, and have lower confidence in their physical self-presentation, than non-experients (Murray & Fox, 2005a).

In a more broadly based investigation of the manifest needs of OBErs Irwin (1981a) found these people to have a higher need for Intraception: this entails a concern with and attention to one's mental processes. This finding accords with the earlier result that experients have a high capacity for absorption. To explore this link further the items of the Absorption questionnaire were reworded to address the respondent's *need* for absorbing experiences rather than the capacity for such experiences. Again OBErs were shown in two studies (Irwin, 1985a, p. 303; Irwin, 1985b) to have a substantially higher need for absorption.

Neurophysiological Correlates

A few studies have recorded neurophysiological data while a subject had an OBE in the laboratory (for a review see Irwin, 1985a, pp. 207–210). For obvious reasons, most of these investigations employed adepts as subjects. In general terms the only correlates of the out-of-body state are for the adept to exhibit the neurophysiological signs of being deeply relaxed and of attending to something. These findings have yet to be replicated with unselected subjects.

The Impact of the Experience

An OBE can affect some of the experient's attitudes. The more complex the OBE experience, the more likely there are to be after-effects (Alvarado & Zingrone, 2003a). The fear of death is reduced in many OBErs (Irwin, 1988b; Osis, 1979). Those OBEs occurring under life-threatening circumstances particularly are associated with a tendency to view death as leading to an afterlife of reward and justification (Irwin, 1988b). The experience will likely be interpreted in spiritual terms if the individual previously was religious or if the OBE occurred in near-death circumstances (Gabbard et al., 1981); however, the OBE generally does not inspire religious conversion in atheists (Irwin, 1985a, pp. 215–216; Palmer, 1979, p. 245). Many experients become interested in psychic phenomena and do some reading in this field (Gabbard & Twemlow, 1984, p. 22; Osis, 1979). Most feel the experience to have been beneficial, providing a better understanding of oneself and increasing awareness of altered states of consciousness and of the possibility of "other realities" (Gabbard & Twemlow, 1984, p. 23; Irwin, 1988b; Osis, 1979). The majority of experients, therefore, would be happy to have another OBE.

Theories of the Out-of-Body Experience

How are OBEs and their correlates to be explained? Broadly speaking, theories of the OBE fall into two categories. First there are the *ecsomatic theories;* they propose that in an OBE a nonphysical element of existence literally separates from the body and subsequently returns to it. Opposed to this approach are the *imaginal theories* that see the OBE as imaginal or hallucinatory (in a nonpejorative sense), a product of purely psychological or physiological factors. Instances of each type of theory will be described and critically reviewed.

Ecsomatic Theories

According to Crookall (1970) we each possess a "superphysical soul body" that in the OBE separates from the physical body and passes through the objectively real worlds of earth, paradise, and hades. Many aspects of Crookall's theory can be criticized but one of the major difficulties for this type of theory springs from the assumption that the soul body exteriorizes into the physical world. If this is the case why do some OBErs report distortions in reality (e.g., bars on the bedroom window), and how are some experients able to manipulate the nature and existence of objects in the out-of-body environment by an effort of will?

Other ecsomatic theorists such as Yram (c.1926/1974) maintain that the out-of-body world is constructed from memory and imagination but is every bit as "real" as the physical world. The out-of-body environment is a world of *thought forms* that can be manipulated by mental processes. But while the out-of-body world is imaginary the OBE is not: the experient's entry into and existence within this world are held to be as real as one's existence in the physical world. You may be uneasy with this interpretation of what is real and what is imaginary. The notion of a world created from memory and imagination nevertheless does accommodate the fact that the OBE may relate to the physical world as the experient conceives it yet also feature some fantasized distortions of the real world.

A source of inconvenience for this approach is that in some OBEs it would seem that experients can acquire information about sensorially inaccessible events of which they previously were ignorant. If the out-of-body world is a product of memory and imagination how is this possible? Some theorists in this camp simply deny that such experiences occur. Others such as Yram resort to introducing another conceptual realm, a "clairvoyant dimension," that during an OBE is accessible in much the same way that the thought world is entered. The latter notion seems little else than an assumption of what is to be explained.

Whiteman (1961) and some other ecsomatic theorists propose that there exists an astral world that has varying degrees of correspondence with the physical world. An OBE consists of the soul's movement into this "astral" world. These theorists would appear to be hedging their bets. If an OBE is veridical, that is because the astral and physical worlds corresponded. If the experience is distorted then the two worlds were not quite in correspondence after all. Unless there is an independent measure of the level of correspondence this notion remains *ad hoc* and contrived.

In general terms the ecsomatic approach is intuitively plausible (especially to people who have had an OBE) and at least at first blush it is conceptually parsimonious. The impression of being outside the body, the perceptual-like awareness of the environment in an out-of-body perspective, and the apparent possession of a parasomatic form linked to the body by a cord, all are explained by one basic and simple notion: that the OBE is literally as it seems to be. But the parsimony of the ecsomatic theory is deceptive. As far as making a minimum of conceptual assumptions is concerned it is just as simple to assert that all out-of-body phenomena are hallucinatory.

On closer inspection the ecsomatic approach is seen not to constitute a very good scientific theory. It tends to provide *post hoc* explanations rather than testable implications. For example, under this theory what

sorts of people are susceptible to OBEs? No specific indications are forthcoming; but if it is mentioned that lucid dreamers are more open to the experience this is "explained" by declaring such people to have inherently "loose" astral entities. Similarly the circumstances of the OBE's occurrence are not explained by the theory but merely cited to be the circumstances under which an OBE might be evoked.

This is not to say that there have been no attempts to test the theory. Some researchers have placed various physical detectors in a target location to see if the subject's exteriorized self can be detected there (for reviews see Alvarado, 1982; Irwin, 1985a, pp. 61–66). Most such studies have yielded null results although in a couple of experiments (e.g., Osis & McCormick, 1980) some unusual recordings from the detectors have been reported. The ecsomatic theory is so pliable, however, that it could accommodate any outcome of a detector study. Null data may be explained on the basis that the exteriorized self is nonphysical and hence would not interact with a physical detector. Positive signals from the instruments may be said to be due to certain "semiphysical" properties of the exteriorized self. On the other hand, critics could attribute such signals to subconscious psychokinetic effects rather than to the presence of any exteriorized entity.

Osis (1974, 1975; Osis & Perskari, 1975) conducted another sort of test of the ecsomatic approach. His experimental task requires a subject to exteriorize to a sensorially inaccessible location and to "look" at a target placed there. Now extra-chance success in such a task potentially could be due either to an OBE or to ESP, so Osis sought to arrange the experimental task in such a way as to provide a test between these rival interpretations. In an attempt to show that exteriorization was possible Osis devised the following method to rule out target identification by ESP.

The target image was generated inside a box and was visible only through a small viewing window on one side of the box. The target had three independent dimensions: shape, background color, and location in one of four segments of the viewing window. Each of these various dimensions was enacted by a different optical mechanism. Thus, argued Osis, the composite image was not in one single place within the box and could not be "scanned" by ESP; it could be apprehended only through the viewing window, either by normal sight or by "exteriorized sight." Using this device Osis claimed that a few subjects gave responses that suggested they could get either the composite image or nothing at all, a finding he construed as supportive of the ecsomatic hypothesis.

That the result could not have been due to clairvoyance, however, is moot. Osis assumed that clairvoyance relates only to physical objects; that is, in this context he held that clairvoyance may be applied to the individual physical components within the box but not to the physical (visual) stimuli emitted through the viewing window. Since parapsychologists do not know the limits of ESP Osis's view of the way in which ESP operates is presumptuous and on these grounds his test of the ecsomatic hypothesis must be deemed inconclusive.

If Osis's work achieved anything at all it was to show how very difficult the ecsomatic theory is to subject to scientific evaluation. Proponents of the approach would respond that this highlights the extent to which a materialistically oriented science is ill-suited to the study of nonphysical phenomena. The problems of ecsomatic theories, however, are more deep-seated than this response would allow. It is not simply a matter of the adequacy of scientific method but whether the ecsomatic hypothesis can predict new relationships and accommodate known relationships without resorting to *ad hoc* assumptions. That ecsomatic theorists in principle can construct a model with these features has yet to be demonstrated.

Imaginal Theories

Probably the majority of psychologists and psychiatrists regard the OBE as hallucinatory (Alvarado, 1992). This may very well prove to be the case but in itself it hardly constitutes a sufficient explanation of the experience. The latter demands some consideration of the origins and bases of the out-of-body hallucination, and it is to theories with this level of specificity that we now turn. As with the NDE, imaginal theories of the OBE may be categorized as either predominantly physiological or predominantly psychological.

Physiological theories. An American parapsychologist, Barbara Honegger (1979), attributes the OBE to a mechanism of biological homeostasis. Homeostasis involves a regulatory response to a sudden shift in physiological state in order to preserve biological integrity. According to Honegger, in certain circumstances such as sensory deprivation, sensory overload, and trauma the human organism loses its biological sense of self and the impression of the existence of self independent of the physical body is created to restore integrity. If the possession of a body is an indispensable part of the individual's sense of self a parasomatic form also will be incorporated in the out-of-body imagery.

Persinger (Persinger, 1993; Munro & Persinger, 1992) has proposed that OBEs may originate as sudden intrusions of right-hemisphere processes into the left hemisphere of the brain. That is, when such intrusions occur, the left hemisphere may become aware of two separate "selves": one of these comprises a disembodied sense of self and the other, awareness of the physical body. Persinger claims support for his theory in observations of an association between a sense of bodily detachment and hemispheric mismatch in temporal-lobe theta activity.

More recently Blanke, Ortigue, Landis and Seeck (2002) reported the elicitation of an OBE in an epileptic woman through focal electrical stimulation of the brain's right angular gyrus during exploratory surgery. The authors conclude that the OBE arises from a failure to integrate complex somatosensory and vestibular information. It should be noted, however, that the angular gyrus is not the only neurological site that has been implicated in OBEs (Neppe, 2002). Blanke and colleagues have recently published data on the phenomenological, neuropsychological, and neuroimaging correlates of OBE and autoscopic phenomena experienced by six neurological patients (Blanke et al., 2004). In five of these patients, brain dysfunction was located in the temporo-parietal junction, which has been implicated in visual body-part illusions and which may have a function in coordinating tactile, proprioceptive and visual information. Further evidence for a neurological model of OBEs comes from a study in which healthy volunteers were asked to imagine themselves having the position and visual perspective of an OBE-experient (Blanke et al., 2005). Evoked potential mapping showed that during this task the temporo-parietal junction was selectively activated, and performance on this task was disrupted when transcranial magnetic stimulation was directed at the temporo-parietal junction. When the volunteers were asked to imagine spatial transformations of external objects, transcranial magnetic stimulation did not disrupt task performance, suggesting that the temporo-parietal junction is particularly implicated in the processing of mental imagery of one's own body. Based on this research, neurologists have argued that further neurological investigations of OBEs may help elucidate the normal neurocognitive mechanisms that mediate awareness of one's body, and self-consciousness (Blanke & Mohr, 2005; Brugger, 2002).

Other physiological theories of the OBE are essentially the same as those listed in Chapter 11 for the NDE. The "temporal lobe paroxysm" hypothesis has some adherents (Eastman, 1962; Persinger, 1983).

The criticisms of the physiological models of the NDE apply equally to the equivalent depictions of the OBE and need not be reiterated. Account also needs to be taken to the fact that OBEs do not occur only under life-threatening circumstances. For example, Siegel's (1980) theory of "massive cortical disinhibition" is based on the assumption of high cortical arousal and as noted previously there appear to be some OBEs that arise under conditions of very low cortical arousal.

Psychological theories. An old theory of the OBE is that it represents a schizophrenic hallucination (Rawcliffe, 1959). Some objections to this view were mentioned in the context of the NDE. Personality test scores of OBErs and nonOBErs offer little support for this approach, and it is hard to imagine a quarter to a third of undergraduate psychology students being subject to schizophrenic hallucinations. Perhaps a less extreme formulation of the theory, namely that the OBE is associated with the more widely distributed schizophrenia-like trait of schizotypy, would have greater viability (McCreery, 1997; McCreery & Claridge, 2002).

The depersonalization model of the NDE has been extrapolated to the OBE by Whitlock (1978). Consistent with this view, Alvarado and Zingrone (1997a) found that the OBE is related to various facets of dissociation, including depersonalization. For the vast majority of experients however, the OBE is a very fleeting instance of depersonalization, one which has been found not to entail the pathological connotations of the severe forms of depersonalization evident in some psychiatric patients (Jacobs & Bovasso, 1996). It is possible therefore that OBEs involve some process that is akin to depersonalization but is nonetheless qualitatively distinct from pathological depersonalization. Further research on this point is called for. Nonetheless, simply labeling the OBE as an instance of depersonalization is insufficient as an explanation of the experience.

Previously mentioned was Rank's (1971)

psychoanalytical theory of the OBE centered on the concept of narcissism. That experients are not preoccupied with their physical appearance (Irwin, 1985a, pp. 296–297) and do not score highly on a measure of narcissistic tendencies (Tobacyk & Mitchell, 1987a) leaves this theory without an empirical base.

A psychiatrist, Jan Ehrenwald (1974), has described the OBE as an imaginal confirmation of the question for immortality, a delusory attempt to assure ourselves that we possess a soul that exists independently of the physical body. Two main lines of evidence speak against Ehrenwald's theory. First, neither the occurrence of the OBE nor the incidence of transcendental elements in it are correlated with religiosity (Irwin, 1985a, pp. 186–189). Second, concern with the existence of an afterlife was not found to affect susceptibility to an experimental OBE induction procedure (Smith & Irwin, 1981).

In some older texts (e.g., Tyrrell, 1942/1963) the OBE is termed traveling clairvoyance or *ESP projection*. Thus it is possible that the perceptual-like content of OBEs is based on ESP, and to provide oneself with a sense of orientation to the remote location a fantasy of mentally traveling to that point is integrated with the extrasensory information. This theory accounts for both veridical and distorted OBEs, although like many other theories it has difficulty in accounting for some phenomenological elements such as onset sensations and the tunnel effect. According to Blackmore (1982, p. 237) the ESP theory also might not be open to being disproved: this would require a test in which an OBE must be elicited when the possibility of ESP is ruled out, and parapsychologists do not know how to engineer the latter conditions. On the other hand it is possible in principle to establish if the properties of the OBE differ from those of ESP and hence the ESP theory could be testable in these terms.

One of the more detailed psychological accounts of the OBE has been formulated by Palmer (1978b). In some respects Palmer's theory is similar to a homeostatic approach. Palmer proposes that in certain situations a lack of proprioceptive feedback threatens the individual's sense of self and the OBE then occurs as an imaginal attempt to re-establish this sense of self and to ensure that the ego has not been destroyed. The perceptual-like aspect of the OBE actually is hypnagogic imagery, according to Palmer; any extrasensory content of the experience in a sense is incidental, reflecting hypnagogic imagery's conduciveness to ESP. The postulated involvement of hypnagogic imagery, however, is open to question. Such imagery tends to be bizarre, disconnected, rapidly changing, not subject to volitional control, most common in childhood, and not about oneself (Schacter, 1976); these features are not typical of the OBE. Nevertheless Palmer's notion of being sensorially out of touch with the body does accord with suggestions made earlier in this review of the OBE.

Blackmore (1984b) has offered a cognitive theory of the OBE. She proposes that at any given time the cognitive system is generating many different models of reality and one is chosen on the basis of its compatibility with current sensory input. In certain circumstances such as stress, sensory information processing is not efficacious and the cognitive system then is more inclined to select a model of reality compiled from information in memory and imagination. Some of these memorial representations of the environment incorporate a bird's-eye view. The OBE entails the experient's acceptance of one of these models as "reality." Blackmore's theory is consistent with the finding by Cook and Irwin (1983) that OBErs are better than nonOBErs in imagining a given scene from a different viewpoint. Blackmore also predicts higher imagery skills among people who deliberately induce OBEs than among spontaneous experients; imagery performance data have yet to confirm this. Research by Irwin (1986a) suggests that Blackmore's theory might have to take cognizance of the distinction between parasomatic and asomatic OBEs; the disposition to construct bird's-eye models of reality could vary across this dimension.

The principal shortcoming in these imaginal theories of the OBE is that they have tended to focus almost exclusively on explaining why the experient feels that the self literally is exteriorized. The diverse phenomenological elements of the OBE all too often have been neglected. An attempt to formulate a more comprehensive theory of the OBE was undertaken by Irwin (2000).

Irwin's dissociational model of the OBE focuses on the role of several facets of dissociation such as somatoform dissociation and psychological absorption (nonpathological dissociation). The model of the OBE is more complex than most, in part a consequence of its comprehensiveness, but in essence the theory seeks to identify the specific dissociative and other processes underlying each phenomenological element of the OBE. The essence of the model is as follows.

The origins of the OBE are hypothesized to lie in a confluence of dissociative factors. Circumstances associated with extreme (either high or low) levels of cortical arousal evoke a state of strong absorption, particularly in the case of a person with a requisite level of absorption capacity and need for absorbing experiences. Alternatively, high absorption may be induced deliberately by the experient. If this state of absorbed mentation is paralleled by a dissociation from somatic (somaesthetic and kinesthetic) stimuli an OBE may occur (see Blanke et al., 2002). People who are prone to this type of somatoform dissociation (Nijenhuis, Spinhoven, van Dyck, van der Hart & Vanderlinden, 1996) may be said to have tendencies toward depersonalization. There may nevertheless be various pathological and nonpathological factors underlying this propensity (Jacobs & Bovasso, 1996) and the OBE therefore should not automatically be diagnosed as a pathological symptom.

In instances where the development of the state of somatic dissociation is gradual the imminent cognitive loss of all somatic contact may be signaled by certain innate biological warning signals, the so-called OBE onset sensations.

The continued orientation of attention away from both exteroceptive and somatic stimuli effectively suspends support for the socially conditioned assumption that the perceiving self is "in" the physical body, fostering the impression that consciousness no longer is tied spatially to the body. This abstract, nonverbal idea of a disembodied consciousness is coded by the cognitive processing system into a passive, generalized somaesthetic image of a static floating self. Consciousness of that image corresponds to the so-called asensory OBE. By means of the dissociative process of synesthesia the somaesthetic image also may be transformed into a visual image, given a basic level of visuospatial skills in the experient.

Strong absorption in this image is a basis for the OBE's perceptual realism. The somaesthetic image also may be transformed into a more dynamic, kinesthetic form and the experient will have the impression of being able to move in the imaginal out-of-body environment. The somatic imagery entailed in this transformation is held to underlie the phenomenon of the parasomatic form. A drawing of attention back to the physical body's state also may be expressed synesthetically by way of the image of the astral cord.

The perceived content of the out-of-body environment is governed by short-term needs. A life-threatening situation for example, may prompt imagery about a paradisial environment; the nature of the latter is held to be a product of social conditioning, although the precise sources of these paradisial stereotypes have yet to be identified fully (see Irwin, 1987b). Because dissociation is psi-conducive it is possible that the out-of-body imagery could incorporate extrasensory information and thereby feature a degree of veridicality not expected of mere fantasy;

evidence of extrasensory elements in sponta-neous OBEs, however, is not yet convincing. Eventual dissipation of somatic dissociation or diversion of attention to somatic or exte-roceptive processes brings the individual's OBE to an end.

It can fairly be said that parapsycholo-gists' recent empirical and theoretical inves-tigations of the OBE have substantially en-hanced scientific understanding of the experience. Although ecsomatic theories have not been conclusively discounted the OBE currently does not look a promising source of support for the survival hypothesis (see also Braude, 2001). Even if the experience were shown to involve a literal separation of a nonphysical element of existence from the physical body there is no certainty that this el-ement could survive the biological death of the body. Notwithstanding that fact, the OBE remains a rewarding topic of scientific study.

KEY TERMS AND CONCEPTS

out-of-body experience (OBE)
out-of-body experients (OBErs)
asensory
asomatic
parasomatic
onset sensations
autoscopy
astral cord
cortical arousal
somatic imagery
somaesthetic
kinesthetic
psychological absorption

ecsomatic theories
Crookall
Osis
imaginal theories
homeostasis
narcissism
ESP projection
Palmer
Blackmore
Irwin
dissociational model
somatoform dissociation

STUDY QUESTIONS

1. Describe a typical OBE and list the principal features of the phenomenon.

2. What are the major methods for researching the OBE? Consider the advantages and dis-advantages of each approach.

3. Some OBEs include elements that do not correspond to physical reality. For example, one experient noted that in her OBE the color and pattern of the bedroom wallpaper had changed. Do these cases demonstrate that the OBE is pure fantasy?

4. Many experients describe their OBEs as completely realistic. If the OBE is not a pro-cess of literal exteriorization of perceptual functions how can this impression be explained?

5. On the basis of the phenomenology of the OBE what factors emerge as of potential significance in the explanation of the experience?

6. Under what circumstances do OBEs occur? What do these circumstances suggest about the nature of the experience?

7. There has been some investigation into the sorts of people who have OBEs. Has this research indicated anything about the underlying processes of the experience?

8. Outline the major theories of the OBE and discuss their viability.

9. Sit in a comfortable chair in a quiet location, close your eyes and perform the following exercise. Imagine that you can transfer your point of observation to a corner of the ceiling and that you can look down into the room and see yourself seated in the chair.

How difficult was this exercise? What does it suggest about the cognitive skills necessary for an OBE if the imaginal hypothesis is valid? Assuming that you did not feel "out of the body" during the exercise, how then can the OBE be claimed to be an imaginal experience of this sort?

13

APPARITIONAL EXPERIENCES

Tales of ghosts, wraiths, and other apparitions have been recorded in virtually all cultures (Rosenblatt, Walsh & Jackson, 1976). In the context of parapsychology these phenomena are so clearly germane to the survival hypothesis that they were accorded special significance from the earliest years of the Society for Psychical Research.

It is difficult to define the term "apparition" without introducing some theoretical assumption about the nature of the phenomena encompassed by that term (Braude, 1986). In essence an apparition is encountered in a perceptual-like experience and relates to a person or animal that is not physically present, with physical means of communication being ruled out. Note that apparitions are not defined in terms of a "spirit form"; such an approach would incorporate a particular theoretical interpretation of an apparitional experience and thus is best avoided in formulating a definition. On the other hand many parapsychologists, while not committing themselves to the authenticity of apparitions, maintain that these phenomena must be defined to be objective or at least semiobjective. We know that people have apparitional experiences but it is held to be pointless to speak of "apparitions" unless we mean this term to refer to the hypothesis of an objective entity. Having defined the term thus, it is up to parapsy-

chologists to ascertain if these hypothesized objective entities actually exist.

A comparable argument may be raised against any definition of the apparition as a hallucination. To the extent that the person represented by the apparition, the so-called *referent person*, is not present in the experient's immediate environment it could be said the apparition is hallucinatory. But this too entails an implicit interpretation of the phenomenon because at least in the view of some researchers the apparition itself could have some manner of objective existence independent of the referent person and thereby be "perceptible" through normal sensory channels. The definition adopted above rightly does not preclude nor presume any theoretical possibility.

The conceptualization of an apparition either as objective or as hallucinatory has been a dominant issue in the past century of parapsychologists' research into these phenomena but as Osis (1986a) points out, this focus has proved hopelessly inconclusive and might even have blinkered investigators to pursue hypotheses along inappropriately narrow paths. In recent years there has been a growing appreciation that we need to study not the apparition per se but rather the *apparitional experience;* that is, it might be best to adopt a phenomenological approach in this field of study. In this context the apparition's seemingly objective features and its seemingly hallucinatory features all are documented simply as aspects of the experience's phenomenology. Thus these featural categories are not deemed *a priori* to be mutually contradictory, nor need they divert research from the determination of other phenomenological dimensions of the apparitional experience. The foregoing definition can readily be reformulated to suit this shift in orientation; thus, the *apparitional experience* is perceptual-like and relates to a person or an animal that is not physically present, with physical means of communication being ruled out.

While an apparitional experience may prove to be hallucinatory it nevertheless should in principle be distinguishable from mirages and perceptual illusions (in which physical means of communication can be ascertained), and rather more problematically, from hallucinations associated with drug states and mental illness (Anderson & Anderson, 1982). Admittedly it may be difficult in practice to decide whether a given report describes an(other) hallucination or is a prima facie case of an apparitional experience, but there are criteria which may help in some instances.

An apparitional experience may convey veridical information of which the experient previously was unaware; this generally is lacking in psychotic and drug-induced hallucinations of another person. An apparitional experience can be related clearly to an identifiable person (or animal); hallucinatory figures typically are anonymous or known to be nonexistent. Finally, an apparition may be experienced by more than one person, whereas a psychotic or drug-related hallucination cannot be shared.

By way of illustration the following collective case of an apparition was researched by the Society for Psychical Research (Gurney et al., 1886, Vol. 2, pp. 617–618). Two brothers sharing a cabin in an old naval ship suddenly were awakened to see the figure of their father standing between their bunks. As one of the brothers sat up, the form vanished. The father had died about the time of the incident. In some collective cases the various accounts of the same experience do show discrepancies; of course, eyewitnesses' reports of objective events also can differ in substantial respects.

A variety of research techniques have been used in the study of apparitional experiences. Needless to say, data on the experience come predominantly from the study of spontaneous cases. Thus case collections and surveys provide information on the phenomenology of the experience and on the types of people who report the experience. Field studies also may be performed for the purpose of naturalistic observation. In these studies some sensing devices may be placed in locations where an apparition is reported to appear and by this means the researcher can seek objective evidence about the ontological reality of the apparitional experience.

In recent years attempts have been made to induce apparitional experiences in the parapsychological laboratory (Moody, 1994; Radin & Rebman, 1996). The procedure involves an experimental participant sitting in a quiet dark room and gazing deeply into a reflective surface such as a mirror. In this setting, known as a *psychomanteum*, the mirror is positioned such that participants see a reflection of the wall above and behind them. Each participant is asked to choose one deceased person who he or she would want to see again. Before the experimental session the participant's relationship with the deceased is discussed in depth, as is any memento of the deceased brought to the laboratory. The participant is then instructed to relax and to gaze into the mirror. According to Moody (1994) 70 percent of participants in the psychomanteum have a visual experience of the deceased. The experimental subjects in Radin and Rebman's (1996) study reported much weaker impressions such as a simple sense of the presence of the deceased, rather than a vivid apparitional experience (see also Hastings et al., 2002). The demand characteristics of this experimental procedure clearly are very high and further research is required in order to demonstrate the utility of the psychomanteum for the study of apparitional experiences.

Phenomenological Characteristics of Apparitional Experiences

Data on the phenomenology of apparitional experience necessarily come from collections of spontaneous cases and anecdotes. Many cases presented to societies for psychical research have been investigated carefully by society members for their evidential reliability, although the usual problems with spontaneous case material apply (Gauld, 1977, p. 604).

Two additional sources of bias spring from the popularity of ghost stories in fiction. First, some supposedly real-life cases initially may have been devised as a good story but then presented as authentic in the hope of enhancing their commercial potential. Second, fictional ghost stories (and folklore too) promote a particular stereotype of an apparitional experience and it is feasible that witnesses' accounts of their experience unwittingly are distorted to conform to these popular expectations. Parapsychologists therefore must be a little wary of accepting consistencies in spontaneous case accounts as indications of the nature of apparitions: in part these consistencies may reveal only the fictional conception of apparitions. One way of minimizing this problem is to give greater credence to consistencies that are not a feature of the popular stereotype, but if taken to an extreme there is a danger here of throwing out the metaphorical baby with the bathwater: some aspects of the fictional stereotype may well be drawn from authentic experiences.

Ignoring fictional anthologies (especially those labeled "true life ghost stories") there are a few case collections testifying to the phenomenology of apparitional experiences. One of the earliest large collections was the SPR's "Census of Hallucinations" (Sidgwick et al., 1894); this was concerned with apparitions of people occurring about the time of their death. Tyrrell's (1942/ 1963) book *Apparitions* was based on a smaller number of cases intensively investigated by the SPR and is a classic in its field. A difficulty with these corroborated cases, however, is that the SPR researchers insisted there be evidence that the experience was more than a mere hallucination. A simple report of an apparitional figure was insufficient; the figure had to communicate information of which the experient could be shown to have been unaware, or the experience had to coincide temporally with an unexpected significant event involving the referent person. These cases' representativeness of all apparitional experiences, therefore, is uncertain. One of the few modern studies is Green and McCreery's (1975) *Apparitions;* this surveys uninvestigated experiences. More recently, Haraldsson (1994) conducted an extensive study of uninvestigated experiences of apparitions of the dead among Icelanders. Apart from these there have been a few surveys of parapsychological experiences that have included items on apparitional experiences (e.g., Haraldsson et al., 1977; Palmer, 1979). The major phenomenological findings of these investigations now will be summarized.

Frequency and Duration

The experience of an apparition is not as uncommon as one might think. In Palmer's (1979) survey of Charlottesville, Virginia, residents and students 17 percent had had an impression of an apparition, and of these about three quarters acknowledged more than one such experience. Twenty percent of a sample of Australian university students reported apparitional experiences (Irwin, 1985b, p. 6). A poll of Icelandic adults by Haraldsson et al. (1977) put the incidence even higher: 31 percent had witnessed an apparition of a deceased person and 11 percent reported an apparition of a living person. In Canada Persinger (1974, p. 69) found 32 percent of survey respondents to acknowledge an apparition of a person or an animal. A large sector of the population therefore has had at least one of these experiences.

The duration of the apparitional experience is variable. In Green and McCreery's (1975, p. 143) survey about half of the respondents considered their experience to have lasted less than one minute, although 20 percent estimated its duration to exceed five minutes.

Sensory Modality

Apparitional experiences tend to be restricted to one or two sensory modalities. Green and McCreery (1975) report that of their cases 61 percent were in one modality only, with a further 25 percent limited to two senses. Most apparitional experiences are visual, 84 percent according to Green and McCreery (see also Haraldsson, 1994; Sidgwick et al., 1894). About a third of cases nevertheless have an auditory component, with 14 percent being a wholly auditory experience. On the other hand the dominance of visual apparitional experiences is not found in every survey (*cf.* Palmer, 1979, p. 228). The reported modality of the apparitional imagery may be in a sensory system that is impaired in the given experient; for example, one "totally deaf" man described hearing the rustle of an apparitional figure's dress (Green & McCreery, 1975, p. 169).

A small number of cases are asensory, comprising the intuitive impression of a "presence" nearby. These instances of a sense of a presence represented only 8 percent of Green and McCreery's (1975, p. 118) cases, although there was a rather higher incidence

in Haraldsson's (1985, p. 152) Icelandic sample and in a sample of Australian university students surveyed by HJI. One of the students reported the experience of strolling along a deserted beach and feeling there was someone walking beside her; although she did not see nor hear anything to indicate there was something there, the sense of a presence was very strong and she felt very comfortable with it.

Taxonomy of Apparitions

The distinction between apparitions of the living and apparitions of the dead can be refined into a more detailed taxonomy. Tyrrell (1942/1963, p. 35ff) proposed four classes of apparitional experiences: experimental cases, crisis cases, postmortem cases, and ghosts or haunting cases. Each of these is described below.

Experimental apparitional experiences. In these cases living people deliberately have endeavored, allegedly with success, to make an apparition of themselves appear before a chosen percipient.

Some of the most famous cases are attributed to S. H. Beard (Gurney et al., 1886, Vol. 1, pp. 93–94). For example, in December 1882 Beard decided to project an apparition of himself to his fiancée Miss L. S. Verity. On the following day Beard visited the Verity family. His fiancée's married sister was visiting her family and without prompting she declared that during the previous night she had seen Beard on two occasions. She told her sister of the experience before Beard's (corporeal) visit. Both women corroborated this account.

These experimental cases are rare. They seem to occur when the agent is asleep or in a trance-like state. They are similar in some respects to OBEs and at least one researcher (Hart, 1956) regarded experimental apparitions and OBEs as the same phenomenon. On the other hand it is not usual for the "projector" to have the conscious impression of being outside the body in an experimental apparition case; conversely, when an individual has an OBE it is very uncommon for that person's apparition (or parasomatic form) to be witnessed at the location to which the person consciously has projected.

The behavior of apparitional figures in experimental cases frequently gives the impression of awareness. Thus in the above case of Beard the apparition is said to have moved to the witness's bedside and taken her hair into his hand.

Crisis apparitional experiences. In crisis cases a recognized apparition is experienced at a time when the person represented by the apparition is undergoing some sort of crisis. By convention an apparitional experience qualifies as a crisis case only if the apparitional figure is experienced no more than 12 hours before or after the crisis. Often the crisis is death; an apparitional experience shortly before or after the referent person's death commonly is known as a wraith. According to Gauld (1977, p. 602) crisis cases are the most frequently reported type of apparitional experience under the SPR criteria for selection. When evidence of veridicality is not required for purposes of corroboration, however, crisis cases are in the minority (Green & McCreery, 1975, p. 179).

The following case of a wraith was investigated by the SPR (Tyrrell, 1942/1963, p. 39). The experient's brother was a pilot and, unbeknown to the woman concerned, had been shot down in France. That same day the experient had a strong feeling that she must turn around; on doing so she was amazed to see her "brother." Assuming that he had been re-posted she turned back to put her baby in a safe place, then went to greet her brother only to find that he was not there. Thinking he was playing a joke she called him and searched the house for him. It was only when no trace of her brother could be found that she felt very frightened, suspecting that he was dead. The loss of her brother in combat on the day of the experience was confirmed two weeks later.

Two points about this case should be appreciated. First, the wraith was mistaken for a real person; and second, at the time of the experience the experient was not thinking of her brother.

In the SPR's investigations an attempt was made to show that wraiths did not appear at the time of the referent person's death purely by coincidence (Gurney et al., 1886, Vol. 2, Ch. 3). On the other hand West's (1948) more recent though less extensive survey for the SPR failed to establish that the timing of crisis apparitions was anything else than a chance process.

Postmortem apparitional experiences. These cases involve an apparition of a person who has been dead for at least 12 hours. About two-thirds of recognized apparitions are of the dead (Green & McCreery, 1975, p. 188; Haraldsson, 1985, 1994; Persinger, 1974, p. 150). One of the most frequently cited instances of this type is the so-called "Chaffin will" case ("Case...," 1927).

In 1905 James Chaffin, a farmer in North Carolina, made a will leaving his estate to his third son Marshall, with his wife and other three sons without support. In 1919 he made a new will under which the whole family was provided for. The second will was not witnessed but was valid under North Carolina law, being in Chaffin's own handwriting. The new will was placed in an old family Bible and a note identifying the will's location was sewn inside his overcoat pocket. In 1921 Chaffin died and as the family did not know of the existence of the new will Marshall inherited the entire estate.

In June 1925 during a vivid dream the second son James experienced an apparition of his father pulling open his overcoat and announcing, "You will find my will in my overcoat pocket." James looked inside the overcoat pocket where he found the message revealing the will's location and after some searching an old Bible was found and the second will located. In December this will was admitted to probate; ten witnesses were prepared to swear that it was in the testator's handwriting.

The Chaffin will case illustrates a common feature of postmortem cases, namely that the apparition seemingly tries to convey specific information that is unknown to the experient. Note also in this case the apparition had both a visual and an auditory component. As with other types of apparition the figure is lifelike and appears suddenly and unexpectedly (Haraldsson, 1994; Tyrrell, 1942/1963, pp. 40–41). A disconcerting feature of the Chaffin will case is that it occurred during a dream. As Gauld (1977, p. 605) comments, on this basis one wonders if almost any extrasensory dream could be regarded also as a veridical apparitional experience. Be that as it may, the case otherwise is representative of postmortem apparitional experiences.

Experiences of ghosts. So-called ghosts are recurrent or haunting apparitions, that is, the same figure is witnessed in the same locality on a number of occasions, often by a number of different experients. The ghosts in these experiences reportedly show less awareness of experients and their surroundings than do other apparitional figures. Additionally, ghosts seem more somnambulistic in their movements. Some ghosts reportedly perform the same actions in the same location on each occasion they are experienced. Recurrent apparitional experiences that are less stereotyped in this regard tend to have a deceased friend or relative as the referent person (Green & McCreery, 1975, p. 65). Recurrent apparitions of animals, particularly cats, also are not uncommon (Green & McCreery, 1975, p. 63).

Tyrrell's taxonomy of apparitions has general acceptance although some parapsychologists (e.g., Gauld, 1982, p. 226) prefer to broaden his "experimental" category to include apparitions of the living that are not crisis cases but which also need not necessarily involve the volitional element implied by experimental cases. Persinger (1974, pp.

151–154) notes that some apparitional experiences relate to past or to future events, and he proposes categories for retrocognitive and precognitive apparitions. Other writers (e.g., Bayless, 1973; Sherwood, 2000) point out that there are occasional reports of other sorts of apparitional experiences, including apparitions of animals and luminous manifestations such as disks of light or figures in a circle of light.

Characteristics of Apparitions

In some cases apparitions are said to have been witnessed by several people at the same time; Green and McCreery (1975, p. 41) report up to eight people simultaneously experiencing an apparition. About a quarter of experients present their case as having been collective (Haraldsson, 1994; Palmer, 1979, p. 228). Not all members of a group necessarily will perceive the apparitional figure. In cases with more than one person present approximately one-third of the apparitions seem to have been collectively experienced (Sidgwick et al., 1894; Tyrrell, 1942/1963).

Most apparitional figures are experienced to be within 10 feet (3 meters) of the subject (Green & McCreery, 1975, p. 123). In the majority of cases, however, the figure is not recognized by the experient (Green & McCreery, 1975, p. 178). About 70 percent of recognized apparitions are of people whom the experient knew to be dead (Green & McCreery, 1975, p. 188; Haraldsson, 1985). This may vary with the age of the individual or more precisely, with the number of deceased persons the individual knew. Thus in Palmer's (1979, p. 228) survey about 60 percent of apparitions witnessed by the older sample of townspeople were of the dead, but for the student sample only 30 percent were of this type.

On the basis of his case collection Tyrrell (1942/1963) determined a number of consistencies in the phenomenological characteristics of apparitional figures. Apparitions appear real and solid. Their appearance changes as the experient moves around it. They occlude objects they move in front of and are occluded by objects they move behind. They may cast a shadow and the experient may perceive their reflection in a mirror. In those respects therefore, apparitional figures are not the transparent misty forms popularized in fiction. Most apparitions evidence awareness of their surroundings (although this is less characteristic of ghosts). For example, if the observer moves around the room the apparitional figure's head reportedly may turn to follow these movements. Also these figures usually are experienced to leave a room by the door rather than to wander aimlessly through a wall (like the fictional stereotype). Noises made by apparitions tend to be appropriate, like the rustle of clothes or the shuffle of feet rather than clanking chains and soulful moans. Some apparitional images are claimed to have spoken, although this is not common; any spoken communication usually is limited to a few words. If the individual is close to the apparition a sensation of coldness may be felt. Most attempts to touch an apparitional figure are unsuccessful but people who did so generally report their hand to have gone through the apparition. The figure may seem to pick up an object or to open a door when physically these have not moved at all. Apparitions usually leave no physical traces such as footprints, nor can they be photographed or tape-recorded, according to Tyrrell.

Green and McCreery's (1975) analysis of apparitional cases yielded several further characteristics. The apparitional figure's background may remain the same or it may be modified as part of the experience. There usually is no discontinuity of experience at the onset and at the termination of apparitional experiences as there sometimes is for example, in the OBE. It is more common for the apparition to enter as a complete figure rather than building up or solidifying before the witness's eyes. At the end of the appari-

tional experience the figure usually vanishes instantly, but in other cases it may fade gradually either as a whole or part by part, or it may be reported to have left as if by its own accord (e.g., by walking out of the room). Many of these phenomenological trends are confirmed in Persinger's (1974, pp. 159–161) Canadian survey.

Finally, Haraldsson (1994) notes that a substantial proportion (30 percent) of recognized apparitional figures in his Icelandic case collection were reported to have died by violent means. In Haraldsson's view this factor accounts for his observation that a majority (67 percent) of apparitional figures are male.

Correlates of the Apparitional Experience

Physical Circumstances

Although the apparitional figure almost inevitably is said to have appeared unexpectedly (Green & McCreery, 1975, p. 135) there are some consistencies in the experience's circumstances of occurrence. It typically arises in familiar everyday surroundings, most often in the experient's home or in its immediate vicinity (Persinger, 1974, p. 157). Only 12 percent of Green and McCreery's (1975, p. 123) cases occurred in a place that the subject had never visited before. In a considerable majority of cases the experient was indoors (Green & McCreery, 1975, p. 123; Persinger, 1974, pp. 157–158) and in daylight or reasonably good artificial light (Haraldsson, 1994).

Demographics

Most demographic variables fail to differentiate apparitional experients from nonexperients. Palmer (1979) found no correlations with gender, race, age and religiosity. Two correlates, however, did show statistical significance. Apparitional experiences were reported more frequently by people with a low educational level and also by widows. Subsequent surveys of bereaved individuals both in the US and the UK found that widows commonly experienced apparitions and sensed the presence of their deceased spouses, that these experiences were usually comforting and helpful, and that in many cases the widows hadn't told others of their experience (Olson, Suddeth, Peterson & Egelhoff, 1985; Rees, 1971; Simon-Buller, Christopherson & Jones, 1988).

Psychological Variables

Psychological conditions of occurrence also have been surveyed. Over 90 percent of respondents in Green and McCreery's (1975, p. 123) study claimed to have been in normal health at the time of the apparitional experience; generally the phenomenon would seem, therefore, not to be a hallucination associated with illness. Most apparitions nevertheless occur when the experient is in a physically inactive state. Concurrent activities reported by Green and McCreery (1975, p. 124) were lying down (38 percent), sitting (23 percent), standing still (19 percent), walking (18 percent) and others (2 percent). Because we spend about a third of our lives lying down (asleep) these data should not be taken to imply that one should adopt a supine position to facilitate an apparitional experience, but the trend toward minimal or "automatic" physical activity is notable. This feature was observed also by Persinger (1974, p. 158) and in a small-scale Australian survey by Campbell (1987). As Thouless (cited by MacKenzie, 1982, p. 28) observed, this suggests that apparitional experiences occur either in circumstances conducive to absorbed mentation or for people with an enduring need for absorption. Traditional tests of personality have rarely been administered to matched groups of apparitional experients and nonexperients. Using the *Eysenck Personality Questionnaire*, McCreery (1986) has noted that experients' scores on psychoticism, neuroticism and extraversion are comparable to normative data for the general population. In a sample of recently bereaved adults, however, Datson and Marwit (1997) found that those who reported an apparitional experience of the deceased were more neurotic and extraverted than were nonexperients. The remaining available psychometric data lie in the domain of cognitive functions. In relation to the above suggestion that experients may have a relatively marked *need* for absorbed mentation, such has been found to be the case by Irwin (1985b, p. 6), although experients and nonexperients evidently do not differ in their *capacity* for psychological absorption (Campbell, 1987). The related factor of fantasy-proneness is a strong discriminator: as a group, apparitional experients are highly inclined to fantasize (Cameron & Roll, 1983; Campbell, 1987; Myers & Austrin, 1985; Osis, 1986b; Wilson & Barber, 1983).

It remains to be shown whether these results imply the apparitional experience to be a pure fantasy or on the other hand, to be an experience that tends to arise when the individual is absorbed in fantasy-like mentation. Under the former interpretation an association between apparitional experiences and skills in mental imagery might be predicted. That is, for the experient to interpret a fantasy as a perceptual experience the person might be expected to be capable of extremely vivid imagery. Such seems to be the case for some (other) hallucinations (Mahoney, 1976/ 1977; Mintz & Alpert, 1972) but in the context of the apparitional experience adequate tests of this elementary hypothesis have yet to be undertaken.

Martin (1915) found three apparitional experients had strong visual imagery and were able to project it on to the environment (so-called eidetic imagery), although she speculated that this capacity is necessary but not sufficient for an apparitional experience. The minuteness of the sample in Martin's study, however, makes generalization inappropriate. In an investigation of 11 experients in a collective apparitional case Osis and McCormick (1982b) found what appears to be a normal distribution of scores on Betts' *Questionnaire upon Mental Imagery* (QMI), but in the absence of corresponding data for non-experients no reliable conclusion can be drawn about the relative vividness of experients' mental imagery. One other apparitional experient tested subsequently by Osis (1986b) checked the highest level of imagery vividness on all items of the QMI scale; again, little can be made of the performance of a single subject.

Using Marks' *Vividness of Visual Imagery Questionnaire* (VVIQ) Campbell (1987) compared the scores of 14 experients with those of 28 gender- and age-matched nonexperients and found the experients to exhibit significantly *lower* vividness of visual imagery. Campbell's finding is not anticipated by any interpretation of the apparitional experience and it is possible her experients deliberately depressed their performance on the VVIQ because of its tacit imputation that their apparitional experience was imaginal. Although further research certainly is warranted there are scant indications here that mental imagery skills make a significant, positive contribution to the apparitional experience.

One recent case study nevertheless raises some interesting possibilities in regard to psychological processes underlying the apparitional experience. The study was conducted by an American psychiatrist living in London, Morton Schatzman (1980). A young married woman called Ruth (a pseudonym) consulted Schatzman when she was seriously troubled by apparitions of her father (the latter was alive and in another country at the time). The apparition had her father's looks, voice and smell. When "he" sat on her bed Ruth allegedly felt and saw the bed sag. The apparition also occluded her view of objects behind it, cast shadows, and was reflected in

a mirror. The figure seemed to appear at times not of Ruth's choosing. The case had marked sexual connotations: the apparition would terrify Ruth with recollections of the time her father had tried to rape her as a child, and subsequently it appeared in her husband's place in bed.

Now, many collectors of case reports would not accept Ruth's story as an instance of an apparition. Some features of the case are uncharacteristic of apparitions: for example, when the apparition appeared in Ruth's bed it was by way of a perceived change in her husband's appearance to that of her father. Some of Ruth's behavior and the sexual tone of the experiences might be construed as symptomatic of psychotic disturbance; indeed Ruth was referred to Schatzman by her physician as a possible schizophrenic, although Schatzman himself dealt with her depression and anxiety as a response to the apparitional experiences rather than as signs of psychosis. Additionally some developments during therapy (to be described shortly) strongly suggest that the experiences were hallucinatory. With past researchers' preoccupation with the objectivity of apparitions Ruth's experiences would be dismissed by many parapsychologists as psychotic hallucinations and not admitted for consideration in relation to apparitions. As far as assessment of the objectivity issue is concerned perhaps this position is a reasonable one. But for the parapsychologist wishing to pursue research on the nature of the apparitional experience Schatzman's treatment of Ruth's case could prove most instructive.

Most psychiatrists in Schatzman's position would work to put an end to Ruth's experiences, but this was not the immediate objective of Schatzman. Rather than encouraging Ruth to dispel the apparition whenever it appeared, he suggested to Ruth that she could and should make the apparition appear at her own wish. Initially she was too frightened to attempt this but with further psychotherapy to relieve the anxiety evoked by the experiences, Ruth achieved some voluntary control over both the occurrences of the experiences and the behavior of the apparitional figure. Later she was able to produce apparitions of other people including her husband, her children, a friend, Schatzman, and even herself (the apparition of herself was *not* her mirror image). By letting her father's apparition "speak" through her, Ruth was able to express his feelings and point of view, thereby lessening her own hatred for her father and her (unjustified) feelings of guilt over her own role in the childhood assault.

One of Schatzman's tests raises some interesting questions about the processes of apparitional experiences. When a person stares at a screen displaying a changing checkerboard pattern the occipital cortex (the visual area of the cerebral cortex) will produce an EEG record (called the evoked response) that changes with the checkerboard stimulus. When Ruth was presented with this stimulus her visual evoked response was normal. Schatzman then asked Ruth to make an apparition appear in front of the screen. The evoked response disappeared, as if something had actually blocked the stimuli, yet the response of the retina and the pupillary reaction to the flashing checkerboard pattern were normal. Evidently low level visual processes are not involved in Ruth's sort of hallucination, but higher level visual processes (say, from the lateral geniculate nucleus) apparently are much the same as in the perception of a real object.

It would be well worth attempting to replicate this result with "normal" subjects in recurrent apparitional cases. Such a study might throw some light on the curious mix of apparently objective and subjective elements of the apparitional experience. In this context it may be noted that later tests of Ruth (Harris & Gregory, 1981) did not reveal evidence of unusual powers of eidetic imagery. If the apparitional experience is hallucinatory the realism of the apparitional figure therefore

might be due not so much to the quality of the imaginal processes responsible for its production but rather to the locus of the imaginal input within the visual information processing system.

Schatzman's idea of controlling apparitional experiences opens up many possibilities for research. For example, it might permit exploration of the underlying personality dynamics of the apparitional experience. Through the experient/s the investigator may administer various psychological tests to the apparitional personality and compare the results of such tests with the manifest needs of the experients and if possible with the psychological profile of the referent person.

The therapeutic technique employed by Schatzman also has implications for current clinical practice. People who attend a psychological clinic for guidance in coming to terms with their apparitional experience are likely to be classified and treated as psychotics or to be told that the experience was a mere perceptual illusion. Schatzman alerts us to other possibilities, but most importantly he shows how the client can be helped to work through the experience to reach their own understanding of it.

Recent studies like that by Schatzman serve to remind us that the objectivity of an apparitional figure is not the only issue of interest or even the most important one. If apparitions should prove to be pure hallucinations the origins and underlying processes of the apparitional experience still would deserve the attention of behavioral scientists.

Theories of Apparitional Experiences

The central issue addressed by the major theories of apparitional experiences is whether apparitional figures are objective or subjective phenomena. As the foregoing review indicates there would seem to be evidence for both views. Apparitions may be deemed objective because sometimes they are perceived by more than one person, and they have been reported to occlude objects, cast shadows, be reflected in a mirror, and change perspective with the experient's movement. On the other hand apparitions seem to be subjective (hallucinatory) phenomena in that some people present might not perceive them, some apparitions are reported to have moved through solid objects, experients may put their hand through the figure, objects may be perceived to have moved when in fact they did not, and apparitions leave no physical traces in circumstances where such traces should be found. An adequate theory of apparitional experiences should be able to accommodate these ostensibly contradictory characteristics.

Spirit

The traditional theory of apparitions is the spirit hypothesis, that is, an apparition is an aspect of the individual's existence that survives bodily death. Hart (1956, 1967) and Crookall (1970) each developed a theory of apparitions along these lines. In essence the approach is equivalent to the ecsomatic models of the OBE and the NDE, with the additional assumption that the ecsomatic element has a continued postmortem existence. Some people are comfortable with such a notion as it relates to apparitions of the dead but are dubious about its applicability to apparitions of living persons. Thus if the spirit leaves the physical body, they argue, the person would die.

There are further, more serious difficulties with this model. To account for both objective and subjective characteristics of apparitions, recourse is made to rather vague concepts such as "semiphysical" and "ultraphysical" states of existence. That is, a spirit can have physical qualities that are the basis of its reportedly objective phenomena, yet still be ethereal and pass through solid objects, for example. This would seem little else

than an *ad hoc* assumption of what is to be explained. A slightly more subtle approach is to argue that the spirit is nonphysical and projects into space, but is perceived only by extrasensory means. This accounts for several features of the experience, although that an extrasensorially perceived nonphysical spirit should be seen to cast shadows is not explained.

A major problem for the spirit hypothesis is the fact that apparitional figures usually are described as being appropriately attired, sometimes with such accessories as a walking stick and a flower in a lapel. Now, our religious heritage leaves us at least potentially tolerant of the notion of the body's "soul," but the implication that our clothes and favored accessories also possess a "soul" seems to some people to be stretching the bounds of credibility. Ecsomatic theorists' attempts to explain apparitional attire in terms of an "etheric double" of the referent person's own clothes (e.g., Crookall, 1966) are conceptually as flimsy as the ghostly garments themselves.

Some relatively direct tests of the spirit hypothesis have been undertaken. Attempts to use various types of sensors and other devices to detect the presence of an apparition (e.g., Maher & Hansen, 1992) nevertheless have yielded fundamentally ambiguous or otherwise inconclusive data. The spirit hypothesis of apparitional experiences now is promoted by a minority of modern parapsychologists (e.g., Osis, 1986a; Stevenson, 1982).

Telepathic Hallucination

Let us turn now to some alternative theories. One early theory was that proposed by Edmund Gurney, a founding member of the SPR. Gurney (Gurney et al., 1886) held that apparitions were hallucinatory and were mediated by telepathy. Thus the experient acquires certain information from the referent individual by extrasensory means and then admits this information to consciousness as a hallucination in the form of that individual's apparition. To accommodate collective cases Gurney had to propose the idea of "contagious telepathy." One person would acquire the extrasensory information and telepathically communicate the nature of the hallucinatory figure to other people present, inducing them to witness the same experience. Again it would seem to be asking a lot of ESP to ensure that different people's images of the apparition exhibit a mutually consistent set of perspectives, as is claimed to have occurred in some collective cases. Also Gurney posed his theory only in relation to apparitions of the living and crisis cases.

An extension of Gurney's theory to postmortem apparitions could require the additional assumptions of the survival hypothesis and of the possibility of telepathic communication by deceased personalities, although some form of super–ESP model might be devised as an alternative. The "telepathic hallucination" theory nevertheless readily accommodates apparitional experiences in which the experient acquires information and those in which the apparitional figure appears appropriately clothed.

Gurney's colleague Frank Podmore (c. 1909) generally reiterated Gurney's theory of veridical apparitions of the living but went further in dismissing out of hand any notion of ghosts as telepathic hallucinations. Experiences of ghosts were a product of an apprehensive subject's imaginative misinterpretation of natural sounds, Podmore (c. 1909, p. 123) asserted.

F. W. H. Myers, another founder of the SPR, devised a theory in many ways similar to that of Gurney. Myers (Gurney et al., 1886, Vol. 2, pp. 277–316; Myers, 1903, Ch. 6 & 7) agreed that apparitions (of the living or of the dead) could be hallucinatory projections of telepathically acquired information, but he proposed further that the referent person sometimes could cause changes in the "metetherial world" which permit the ob-

jective perception of his or her image by people in the vicinity of this change. This would account, for example, for the consistency of different experients' perspectives in certain collective cases. Myers is not very lucid in his specification of this metetherial world but evidently it entails some nonphysical dimension of existence that intertwines with physical space. How one would seek independent evidence of the existence of the metetherial world is unknown. But at least Myers appreciated the problem posed by collective cases and sought to address it in a manner he thought to be justified by the evidence accumulated in the SPR investigations. He also implied that apparitional experiences might not all feature exactly the same underlying process. Gauld (1982, Ch. 16) believes Myers's theory to be less problematic than other current approaches.

Tyrrell (1942/1963), like Gurney and Myers, held apparitions to be engendered telepathically. In Tyrrell's view the referent person and the experients effect a hallucination by a mingling of their subconscious minds, a cooperative production of an apparitional drama. Since all participants contribute to the mental staging of the hallucination the apparition has consistent perspectives for the different experients. People who are unable to perceive the apparition are held not to have taken part in the subconscious dramatic production.

The identification of apparitional experiences with hallucinatory ESP experiences was pursued further by Louisa Rhine (1957). Consistent with her views on the agent's role in other extrasensory experiences Rhine construed the apparitional experient (rather than the referent person) to be the instigator of the experience, reaching out extrasensorially to the referent person and expressing the subconsciously acquired information through the medium of a hallucination of that person. Unlike earlier theorists, therefore, Rhine saw no need to propose the referent person to be an active contributor to the experience.

Green and McCreery (1975) also accept the apparitional experience as hallucinatory, in some cases inspired by extrasensory information about the referent person. In the view of these researchers both the apparitional figure and the environment in which it seemingly appears are hallucinatory in the majority of cases (see also Green & Leslie, 1987), although there may be some experiences in which the figure is hallucinated upon the real environment of the experient.

Imagination and Misattribution

Another approach to apparitional experiences is that the apparition is a pure hallucination. That is, the image has no objective status and its occurrence is not grounded in ESP nor in any other parapsychological process; it is totally a product of the imagination and reflects the experient's suggestibility, expectations, needs, social conditioning and unconscious childhood memories (Houran, 2000; Lange & Houran, 1997, 1998; Rawcliffe, 1959, pp. 372–377; Shapiro, Sherman & Osowsky, 1980). The realism of the experience commonly is ascribed to the properties of hypnagogic imagery (Alcock, 1981, p. 83; Neher, 1980, p. 200; Reed, 1972, p. 39).

This theory is supported by claims of variations in the apparitional experience across historical periods and across cultures in accordance with the social functions served by belief in apparitions (Beyer, 1999; Emmons, 1982, Ch. 8; Finucane, 1984; Thomas, 1971, Ch. 19). On the other hand Gauld (1984) argues the evidence for such claims is unsatisfactory because cases of apparitional experience prior to the seventeenth century are very poorly documented and they cannot be regarded in any way as a random sample of such experiences in their respective historical period. In addition, perhaps social conventions have a greater bearing on how an apparitional case is narrated than on the phenomenology of the associated experience itself (see Herman, 2000). Collective apparitional cases presumably are treated as mass hallucinations under the skeptical theory, although there is some doubt that such an account could accommodate the features of these cases if they have been reported accurately.

There have been some attempts to empirically test the theory that conventional psychological factors may account for apparitional experiences. For instance, it is possible that group hallucinations might be facilitated by an effect of psychological contagion and there is some empirical support for the theory that people's expectations may be a contributory factor in ghost experiences. For example, Houran and Lange (1996) proposed that in any environment, there is a constant supply of events that could be interpreted as paranormal, and that once potential anomalies have been noticed, perceptual contagion will cause increasing numbers of events to be noticed. They tested this theory by asking a married couple to make a 30-day diary of odd events in their home (which had no previous reputation for poltergeist or haunt-type phenomena). The categories of events included visual and auditory phenomena, the unexplained movement of objects, and sensed presences. The couple reported 22 "unusual" events, the frequency of which increased as predicted. Another study analyzed over 900 experiences of haunting to test the theory that contextual variables such as demand characteristics, belief in the paranormal, or situationally-embedded cues, might in part shape the content of such experiences. The researchers' predictions were supported (Lange, Houran, Harte & Havens, 1996). However, a possible weakness to this study is that it is not clear whether the two individuals who rated the experiences were blind to the hypothesis under test.

Two recent studies (Wiseman, Watt, Stevens, Greening & O'Keeffe, 2003) have asked volunteers to record any unusual experiences they had while walking round historical sites, some areas of which had a prior reputation for being haunted, and other areas of which did not. Those participants who reported a prior belief in ghosts reported a significantly greater number of experiences than disbelievers, providing some support for the expectancy hypothesis. However, participants reported significantly more unusual experiences in the "haunted" areas than in the control areas, and this could not be attributed to the participants' prior knowledge of the sites. In most of the studies of this nature, the experiences are often quite subtle and a relatively small proportion are fully-fledged apparitional experiences. So although this work provides some support for the imagination and misattribution model, it is likely that a complete understanding of apparitional experiences will have to take into account other contributory factors, as we will see in the next two sections.

Neuropsychology

Some recent work on the "sense of a presence" may prove a fruitful avenue for future research into apparitional experiences. Persinger and his colleagues (Persinger, 1993; Persinger & Makarec, 1992) have proposed a neuropsychological model of the experience of a sensed presence. Citing previous suggestions that the sense of ("conscious") self is an aggregate property of language processes taking place primarily in the left hemisphere of the brain, Persinger proposes that a homologue of these left hemispheric processes exists in the right hemisphere and is the primary neurological basis of the sense of a presence. This account could be extended to accommodate the experience of an apparition or "ghost" (Persinger, 1993, p. 916). Persinger's theory predicts that the sensed presence or apparitional figure would typically be located to the left of the experient's body, but this does not seem to be the case (Brugger, 1994; Houran, Ashe & Thalbourne, 2003; Ter-

hune, 2004). Some support for Persinger's theory comes from clinical studies that have found females with temporal lobe dysfunction reported subjective ESP experiences including visual and auditory hallucinations, and that these experiences seem associated with left-hemisphere disturbances (Palmer & Neppe, 2003, 2004). Furthermore, sensed presences and visual and auditory hallucinations are not uncommon experiences for high-altitude mountaineers. Neuroscientists have suggested that these experiences arise from the combined effects of disinhibition caused by social isolation, and the effects of oxygen deprivation and high altitude on the functioning of the temporo-parietal junction (Arzy, Idel, Landis & Blanke, 2005).

Physical Environment

An allied approach mentioned earlier in the analysis of poltergeist experiences (Chapter 10) holds that unusual electromagnetic or geomagnetic fields may influence susceptible people's temporal lobe functioning, causing them to have anomalous perceptions such as the experience of an apparition (Persinger & Koren, 2001). There is some case material and correlational evidence in support of this view (e.g., Persinger, Koren & O'Connor, 2001; Terhune, 2003; Wiseman et al., 2003), but at present the research does have methodological limitations. Other aspects of the physical environment may also play a role in apparitional experiences. Inaudible low-frequency sound, known as infrasound, has been associated with sensed presences and visual experiences (Tandy, 2000; Tandy & Lawrence, 1998). The suggestion here is that the unusual physical sensations supposedly caused by infrasound may be interpreted in certain contexts as paranormal, leading to a sense of fear and an attribution that one has sensed or even seen a ghost. Wiseman et al. (2003) also found that reports of unusual experiences in locations with a reputation for being haunted correlated with the physical factors of room area and lighting conditions.

Jawer (2006) has published an interesting paper that brings together many of the above lines of research. He proposes that certain individuals are genuinely neurobiologically "sensitive" and therefore may be responding to subtle environmental characteristics that don't affect others. In a survey comparing 62 self-described sensitives and 50 control participants, the sensitives reported a greater number of apparitional and other psi perceptions, and they tended to be female, first-born or only-children, single, ambidextrous, imaginative, introverted, to recall traumatic events, and to perceive they were sensitive to electrical activity. Intriguingly, 14 percent of sensitives claimed to have suffered a severe electric shock or to have been struck by lighting, whereas none of the controls reported such experiences. The implication of this work is that some individuals who experience apparitions may be genuinely responding to physical characteristics of their environment. This does not dismiss the possibility of a spiritual or psychical cause or correlate to these environmental factors, though the more parsimonious approach would be to regard the environmental factors as the primary cause of the apparitional experiences for certain sensitive individuals. In order to rule out the possibility of response bias since self-report measures were used in Jawer's study, further studies might investigate the ability of sensitives and controls to detect the presence or absence of artificially-generated subtle environmental stimuli, in a double-blind design.

Other recent theories of apparitional experiences are critically surveyed by McCue (2002). Finally, mention may be made of a trend among some contemporary researchers (Evans, 2001; Houran, 2000) to group apparitional experiences with encounters of such other entities as extraterrestrial aliens, the Virgin Mary, phantom hitchhikers, fairies, Men in Black, materializations in the seance room, angels, and bedroom visitors (e.g., the "old hag").

As far as the survival hypothesis is concerned it is assessed by Gauld (1977, pp. 601–607) to have gleaned little substantive empirical support from apparitional experiences, although this conclusion is disputed by Stevenson (1982). It would seem nonetheless that the spirit theory has not proved a productive approach, yet most proponents of the telepathic theories seem compelled to imply some form of discarnate existence in their attempts to account for postmortem apparitional cases. Additionally, a satisfactory account of collective cases and their characteristics has yet to be formulated. It is to be hoped that the recent phenomenological orientation of research into apparitional experiences will generate a new style of theory that is more fruitful and more comprehensive than past approaches have been. Another means of progressing work in this area would be to investigate "control" sites along with "haunt" sites, to take into account the possibility that unusual events may spontaneously occur in any site, and to note potentially informative differences in events experienced in the two different types of location (Houran & Brugger, 2000).

KEY TERMS AND CONCEPTS

apparition
apparitional experience
hallucination
collective case
psychomanteum

"Census of Hallucinations"
Tyrrell
Green & McCreery
incidence
sensory modalities

experimental cases
crisis apparitions
wraiths
postmortem apparitions
ghosts
"objective" characteristics
"subjective" characteristics

Schatzman
spirit hypothesis
ghostly garments
telepathic theories
contagious telepathy
infrasound
environmental sensitivity

STUDY QUESTIONS

1. Critically examine the notion that apparitional experiences signify a psychotic disorder.

2. Outline Tyrrell's taxonomy of apparitional experiences and consider the adequacy of the spirit theory in accounting for each type of experience.

3. List the principal phenomenological consistencies in apparitional case reports. Examine each of these from the perspective of (a) the spirit theory, (b) a telepathic theory, and (c) a skeptical "pure hallucination" approach.

4. Several researchers have given telepathy some emphasis in their accounts of apparitional experiences. What is their purpose in doing this? If one rejects the survival hypothesis is the postulation of a telepathic process viable in all instances of apparitional experience?

5. Of what relevance to apparitional experiences is Schatzman's study of "Ruth"?

6. How can a neuropsychological approach account for the basic features of apparitional experiences, and what features pose a particular challenge for this approach?

14

REINCARNATION EXPERIENCES

Reincarnation is the notion that a non-physical element of human existence not only survives death but subsequently is reborn in another body. In the present context we are concerned specifically with the hypothesis of reincarnation in human form and not with that of metempsychosis or transmigration of souls between different species of animal life. Authors sometimes use the term *past-life experience* (PLE), recognizing that such experiences are necessarily subjectively defined (e.g., Mills & Lynn, 2000), though as we shall see such cases can be investigated in an attempt to find objective verification of the reported experiences.

The concept of reincarnation is widely accepted in many cultures, particularly in the Middle East and in Asia, and it is a significant element in several major religious systems (Head & Cranston, 1977; TenDam, 1990). In the West, however, the concept generally is regarded with much skepticism, although there are indications that Western interest by no means is negligible (Sigelman, 1977); for example, in the early 1980s nearly a quarter of American adults surveyed by the Gallup organization acknowledged a belief in reincarnation (Gallup, 1982, p. 137). This level of incidence has remained relatively stable (Newport & Strausberg, 2001; Moore, 2005). However, even in cultures where belief in reincarnation is widespread, claims of past-life experiences are relatively rare: only one in 500 surveyed in northern India reported a PLE (Barker & Pasricha, 1979).

The so-called Pollock case illustrates a claimed instance of reincarnation. This case, documented by Wilson (1982, Ch. 1; 1984), relies heavily on the testimony of an Englishman named John Pollock. At the age of 19 Pollock converted to Roman Catholicism but posed a problem for parish priests by professing a belief in reincarnation; such a belief is heretical in the view of the Catholic church. Despite the priests' efforts to dissuade him Pollock persisted in his reincarnationist stance and at night would pray that God would provide some proof of reincarnation to resolve the dispute. A few years later Pollock married. His wife Florence did not share his belief in reincarnation.

Two daughters, Joanna and Jacqueline, were born to the Pollocks and the family moved home to Hexham. In May 1957 the girls, aged 11 and 6 years respectively, were hit by a car and killed while walking to an early morning children's mass. Almost immediately John Pollock decided the deaths of his daughters were part of God's response to his prayers for proof of reincarnation and that the girls would be reborn to him. Florence found this attitude most distasteful and for a time their marriage was in serious jeopardy. When Florence fell pregnant early in 1958

208

John declared she would have twin daughters because God was returning Joanna and Jacqueline to their parents. Indeed, twin daughters Jennifer and Gillian were born in October. A faint thin line on the second-born ("younger") Jennifer's forehead and a birthmark on her left hip were said to be identical to marks on Jacqueline, the younger of the dead sisters.

When the twins were four months old the Pollocks moved to another town. Three years later the family revisited Hexham and according to John Pollock the twins immediately behaved as if they knew the town. They were said to have recognized the school and the playground previously frequented by their dead sisters and to have identified their former home, all without any prompting from their parents. Similar incidents allegedly followed. For example, some toys of Joanna and Jacqueline were unpacked and Jennifer is said to have correctly named two dolls and to have assigned a toy of the eldest sister Jacqueline to her first-born twin sister Gillian. Pollock also reports coming upon the twins in the backyard screaming hysterically, "The car! The car! It's coming at us!" Such incidents ceased not long after the twins' fifth birthday. Today Jennifer and Gillian claim to have no memories "belonging" to their late sisters. According to John Pollock he did not discuss with the twins their purported reincarnated status until they were 13.

Although this case is convincing to Pollock himself and to others who subscribe to a belief in reincarnation its evidential bases are not strong. Most of the features of the case rely wholly on the testimony of John Pollock (his wife having died in 1979) and he can not be regarded as an unbiased observer and reporter of the alleged events. Corroborated facts in the case are scant and not convincing of reincarnation. There is no doubt that Joanna and Jacqueline were killed and that the twins were born subsequently. Further, Jennifer does have a birthmark on her left hip, although there now is no sign of the mark on her forehead. But these data are hardly conclusive. Normal genetic principles can account for the similarity of the birthmarks on Jacqueline and Jennifer; birthmarks are known to run in families. On the other hand, as the twins were identical (I. Stevenson, personal communication, 8 November, 2000) it is odd that only Jennifer had the birthmark. The twins' recognition behavior may have been exaggerated by Pollock because of the fervor of his beliefs and the attention his claims received in the British media. Ian Wilson (1984, p. 51) also raises the possibility that the twins overheard their father discussing his beliefs with his wife and then behaved according to their father's expectations.

A further difficulty with the Pollock case is that it does not strictly entail an experient giving a firsthand report of what appeared to be personal memories of a previous existence. That is, while the Pollock case included claims of alleged reincarnation "behavior" it did not exhibit a *reincarnation experience*, one in which the experient spontaneously recalls details of a personal life seemingly led some time before his or her present one. Researchers interested in the reincarnation hypothesis have devoted much of their energy to the pursuit of cases which incorporate such an experience. Note, however, that in conformity with the definitions of other parapsychological experiences there is no assumption that the reincarnation experience necessarily entails recall of a previous existence of the experient; the experience merely *seems* to do so, and it is a task of the researcher to ascertain the bases of these experiences. Matlock (1990) advocates the use of the expression "past life memory cases" for this class of experience, but the terms "reincarnation experience," "past-life experience," or "case of the reincarnation type" seem to have become conventional in the parapsychological literature.

The Phenomenology of Reincarnation Experience

Although the detailed investigation of spontaneous reincarnation experiences is said to have begun in India in the 1920s (Pasricha & Barker, 1981, p. 381), Ian Stevenson of the University of Virginia has been the most prominent, productive, and respected investigator of these cases for over forty years. Stevenson has visited many countries, recording and investigating numerous cases; his detailed observations have been published in a series of books (e.g., Stevenson, 1966, 1975, 1977c, 1987a). Stevenson (1987c) puts great emphasis on the importance of investigating the authenticity of spontaneous cases, and in part for this reason he has worked almost exclusively with the reincarnation experiences of children. It seems also that childhood cases are far richer in detail than experiences in adulthood (Matlock, 1990; TenDam, 1990).

Usually Stevenson locates cases with the aid of fellow parapsychologists and the media. The young experient and witnesses (typically the experient's parents and other family members) are interviewed, usually with the assistance of an interpreter. Where possible, the data in the reincarnation experiences are checked for their veridicality. In some instances, for example, the family of the deceased personality is identified and reported details of the ostensible former life then are checked; a meeting between the experient and the "former" family occasionally can be arranged and the experient's recognition of people and the surroundings is observed. It may be noted that Stevenson trained as a psychiatrist and has written a book on interviewing techniques; one therefore would not expect him to accept human testimony at face value.

Unfortunately the majority of cases documented by Stevenson were no longer "active" at the time of their investigation. That is, the subject of the case had ceased to have recollections of the supposed previous existence and thus the evidence consists mainly of retrospective accounts by other people (e.g., parents) of the experient's statements about that existence. Stevenson nevertheless has been able to interview some experients while they still could access their "past life" memories. One such case is that of Gnanatilleka (Stevenson, 1966, pp. 118–134), a girl born in the village of Hedunawewa, central Sri Lanka in February 1956.

When Gnanatilleka was one year old she mentioned another mother and father, and at the age of 2 she began to make explicit references to a previous life as a boy. She claimed to have parents, two brothers and many sisters living in another town. At first Gnanatilleka did not identify the town but after hearing some visitors speak of Talawakele she nominated that as the location of her (or "his") previous existence. Talawakele is a town about 16 miles (26 kilometers) from Hedunawewa; the climate and vegetation of these two settlements differ considerably and travel between them is difficult and infrequently attempted. Gnanatilleka said she wanted to visit her "other" parents and recalled details of her alleged past life including the names of members of her former family, the father's occupation, descriptions of the parents, the location of family home, and a story she had been taught at school during that previous life.

On the basis of these details a particular family in Talawakele was identified as that of the "previous personality" (as Stevenson terms the subject of an alleged former existence). The previous personality was a lad named Tillekeratne who had died at the age of 12 in November 1954. The cause of Tillekeratne's death remains obscure. He may have had some visceral disease; certainly he is known to have been admitted to hospital following a fall and to have died within a fortnight. Prior to his death he is said to have developed effeminate tendencies. During Stevenson's interview of Gnanatilleka she reported that when she had been a boy she had wanted to be a girl, and now she was happier as a girl. Members of each family denied having any knowledge of the other prior to Gnanatilleka's statements about her previous existence.

In 1960 Gnanatilleka and her family visited Talawakele where she correctly identified several buildings in the town; when she directed her family to the place of her former residence, however, the home was found to be no longer standing. Gnanatilleka later recognized some teachers from Tillekeratne's school. Early in 1961 Gnanatilleka again went to Talawakele where various relatives and acquaintances of Tillekeratne were brought before her and she was asked if she knew each person. In the presence of an independent observer seven members of the previous personality's family and two other people were identified accurately in terms of their relationship with Tillekeratne. A person unknown to Tillekeratne was not recognized by Gnanatilleka. Two people in a crowd outside the house also were recognized spontaneously. Gnanatilleka's behavior towards the people she recognized was said to have been consistent with Tillekeratne's relationship with them.

Figure 19. **Gnanatilleka and her mother in 1966 (photograph: Ian Stevenson).**

During his visit to both Hedunawewa and Talawakele later in 1961 Stevenson was able to confirm the above data of the case by interviewing Gnanatilleka herself, members of the two households concerned, and other witnesses. During the following year, shortly before Gnanatilleka's seventh birthday, Stevenson had word that the young girl's spontaneous recollections of a previous existence had ceased and that she now remembered little about that life.

As Stevenson acknowledges, the Gna-

natilleka case is atypical in some general respects. The majority of reincarnation experiences do not feature such a wealth of information of the sort that is verifiable. Even in many highly detailed experiences the previous personality cannot be identified conclusively with a known person; Stevenson calls these "unsolved cases" and those of the Gnanatilleka type, "solved." And as noted previously, it is not often that a parapsychologist can locate an "active" case in which an experient still has access to memories of a past life;

in most cases the evidence must be compiled from people who witnessed the experient's reminiscences about the previous existence. The Gnanatilleka case nevertheless does serve to illustrate the reincarnation experience, one in which an experient has the spontaneous impression of having lived before and seemingly can recall variously detailed information about that previous existence.

Through the laborious investigations by Stevenson and his assistants an appreciation of the reincarnation experience's phenomenology has emerged.

The incidence of reincarnation experiences is not known precisely. A survey by Barker and Pasricha (1979) in Fatehabad, a district of north India, found the incidence in that population to be about two per thousand, but the generality of this estimate is doubtful. Broadly speaking, cases are more frequent in countries in which the belief in reincarnation is strong (Stevenson, 1977a, p. 646).

A reincarnation experience commonly arises during the waking state in a young child, beginning at the age of 2 to 5 years with the child telling its parents or siblings of a life it led in another time and place. Generally these ostensible recollections arise spontaneously, although especially with the older children in this age range there may be a "stimulus" to the experience through some contact with the setting of the former life (Matlock, 1989). The "intermission" interval between the death of the "previous personality" (as Stevenson calls it) and the birth of the experient is variable, ranging from a few weeks to many years (Wilson, 1982, p. 47) and averaging about 15 months (Pasricha & Stevenson, 1987, p. 244; Stevenson, 1987a, p. 117).

The name of the previous personality often is given, featuring in about one-third of American cases and three-quarters of Indian cases (Stevenson, 1983a, p. 745). The previous personality sometimes is related to the experient, almost invariably is ordinary and undistinguished, and his or her living conditions can be either more or less affluent than those of the experient (Cook, Pasricha, Samararatne, Win Maung & Stevenson, 1983; Stevenson, 1983a, p. 745). Wilson's (1982, p. 50) reanalysis of some of Stevenson's data suggests, however, that a high proportion of cases in India and Sri Lanka relate to a past life of greater wealth or higher caste than that of the experient.

The geographical distance between the settings of the "past" and present lives rarely exceeds 100 miles (160 kilometers) (Wilson, 1982, p. 48); the previous personality and the experient, therefore, in most instances are of the same nationality, speak the same language, and have the same religious background. The previous personality frequently has the same gender as the experient; cross-gender "rebirth" is virtually unknown in Turkish cases but may be as high as 15 percent among American experiences (Stevenson, 1983a, p. 745) and 20 percent in cases from Burma and Thailand (Stevenson, 1977a, p. 655).

Of the various life events of the previous personality recounted by the experient the mode of death often is cited. In a majority of documented cases the mode of death was violent, most particularly in unsolved cases (Cook et al., 1983; Pasricha & Stevenson, 1987; Stevenson, 1983a).

The child's spontaneous memories of the past life gradually cease, typically between the ages of 5 and 8 years (Pasricha & Stevenson, 1987, p. 244; Stevenson, 1983a, p. 745), and soon these apparent recollections have been completely forgotten. Other features of the experience nevertheless may tend to persist somewhat longer. For example, in cross-gender reincarnation experiences the child may show cross-dressing when young and continue to exhibit various signs of cross-gender identification as it grows (Stevenson, 2000). A traumatic incident in the former life, particularly in relation to the instrument and the mode of death, may be the ostensible basis of a phobia in the present life (Stevenson, 1977b, pp. 311–312; 1990b; 2000). Likewise, a birthmark might be construed as the remnant of a wound in a previous existence (Stevenson, 1977b, pp. 318–320; 1993; 2000).

Recent studies have examined statistical associations among the various phenomenological features of reincarnation experiences. Chadha and Stevenson (1988) report that in cases where the previous personality is said to have died by violent means, the interval between that death and the experient's birth is relatively short and the experient begins to speak about the former life at a comparatively early age. On the other hand, there seem to be no interrelationships between the experient's age at the onset of recall, the age at which the previous personality died, and the length of the interval between death and "rebirth" (Stevenson & Chadha, 1990).

Solved and unsolved cases differ somewhat in their phenomenology, according to an analysis of Stevenson's data by Cook et al. (1983). Experiences for which the previous personality has not been positively linked to a known person feature a comparatively high incidence of violent death. The experients of these unsolved cases identify the previous personality by name more frequently and stop talking about the previous life earlier than do subjects of solved cases. Cook et al. are unable to provide an unequivocal explanation of these data but they do speculate that some unsolved cases may incorporate elements of fantasy.

Few distinguishing characteristics of the reincarnation experient have been established. Studies by Haraldsson (1995, 1997) found Sri Lankan children who claimed reincarnation memories had greater verbal skills and better memories than a control group. The two groups did not differ in suggestibility (see also Haraldsson, Fowler & Periyannanpillai, 2000), but those with reincarnation memories are reportedly more dissociative, obsessional, perfectionistic, and inclined to have behavior problems (Haraldsson et al.,

2000). Similar findings are reported for Lebanese children (Haraldsson, 2003). In a survey of Australian adults Robertson and Gow (1999) found those claiming a past-life experience to be more fantasy-prone than other participants and to have a more intuitive and feeling type of personality. For at least some of the experients in this study, however, the past-life experience would have been hypnotically induced.

As noted previously, reincarnation experiences are reported most frequently among cultures that embrace the concept of reincarnation. This fact might be taken to indicate that belief in reincarnation is a fundamental stimulus for the experience. At the same time many cases are known to have occurred among children whose family did not subscribe to such a belief or even was unfamiliar with it (Mills, 1990; Stevenson, 1983a, p. 744). The role of family communication of cultural beliefs about reincarnation is queried further by Pasricha (1990) who reports that Indian stereotypical notions of the characteristics of reincarnation experiences generally do not correspond to the observed characteristics of cases occurring in that country. It is feasible that cultural endorsement of the reincarnation hypothesis influences readiness to report a reincarnation experience rather than the experience's occurrence as such.

The cultural background of experients nevertheless does correlate with some phenomenological features of reincarnation experiences, whether because of the impact of belief systems or for other reasons (Matlock, 1990; Mills & Lynn, 2000). For example, the frequency of cross-gender experiences varies substantially across cultures, with such cases reportedly not occurring at all amongst the Lebanese Druses (Stevenson & Haraldsson, 2003). So too does the incidence of reincarnation experiences featuring a violent death, forming a minority among Sri Lankan cases and a substantial majority in Lebanese Druse cases (Stevenson, 1977a, p. 655) and in American cases (Stevenson, 1983a, p. 745). Cases of "rebirth" of a close relative also have different frequencies across cultures (Stevenson, 1983a, pp. 744–745). Generally these trends are consistent with beliefs about reincarnation in the culture concerned. Stevenson (1977a, p. 634) believes the relationship here to be a circular one, with the incidence of cases serving to sustain the beliefs and the strength of the beliefs encouraging the development and the communication of the experiences.

In compiling an outline of the phenomenology of reincarnation experiences Stevenson frequently has emphasized that his case reports do not "prove" reincarnation; at best, they provide data consistent with the reincarnation hypothesis. For this reason Stevenson continues to refer to them noncommittally as "cases suggestive of reincarnation" or "cases of the reincarnation type." But skeptics have been eager to attack Stevenson's research, presumably because it dares to address a concept that is a scientific heresy. Some of these criticisms may be mentioned briefly; for a more detailed review, see Edwards (1996) and Matlock (1990).

Although Stevenson has explored orthodox accounts of reincarnation experiences he has been accused of being too ready to reject them on insubstantial grounds (Wilson, 1982, p. 50). The quality of his data also has been questioned. Because most of Stevenson's cases rely on retrospective information from witnesses they may have the evidential shortcomings to which such reports usually are vulnerable. But some critics have queried the reliability of Stevenson's observations on the additional ground that so many of them were gathered in communities having a fervent religious commitment to the doctrine of reincarnation. For example, Wilson (1982, p. 50) suggests that Stevenson's frequent reliance on interpreters and assistant investigators, many of whom believe in reincarnation, permits an opportunity for distorting the evidence before it reaches Stevenson. Rogo (1985, p. 85) further asserts that Stevenson has "polished up" some of the weaker cases before their publi-

cation. Although the alleged amendments may be relatively minor, Rogo holds them to be a reflection of Stevenson's systematic bias in favor of the reincarnation hypothesis. Other critics (e.g., Edwards, 1996) charge that Stevenson's interviews of reincarnation claimants and witnesses have been naïve and insufficiently searching.

As with many other types of spontaneous paranormal experiences, it is difficult to assess the statistical likelihood of "solving" a PLE case by chance alone (Haraldsson & Abu-Izzeddin, 2004). Some authors have suggested a way to overcome this difficulty (Mills & Lynn, 2000). One could randomly generate a reincarnation case by selecting from a series of prototypical descriptors. Blind investigators could then attempt to solve the case by trying to find a match. The degree of correspondence found for such fabricated cases could usefully be compared with that found for "real" cases. Mills and Lynn (2000) also point out that in order to make further progress in understanding PLEs, there is a pressing need for a standardized system for coding such experiences and for determining when a case can be considered solved.

Certainly it is to be regretted that such a large part of the data on reincarnation experiences has been accumulated by just one researcher and his associates. Be that as it may, in all the literature on the concept of reincarnation Stevenson's empirical contributions stand as an unparalleled scientific achievement. It is notable also that recent independent investigations of reincarnation experiences (e.g., Haraldsson, 1991; Keil, 1991; Mills, 1989; Mills, Haraldsson & Keil, 1994) are very largely supportive of Stevenson's phenomenological findings.

Theories of the Reincarnation Experience

Skeptical philosophers such as Edwards (1996) have mounted a substantial case that the reincarnation hypothesis is conceptually incoherent. Alternative interpretations of reincarnation experiences therefore warrant careful consideration. In discussing each of his major cases of reincarnation experience Stevenson addresses a range of possible theoretical explanations and assesses their adequacy in accounting for the case under analysis. In addition to the reincarnation hypothesis he considers the hypotheses of fraud, paramnesia, cryptomnesia, ESP with personation, inherited memory, and possession. The nature of each of these theoretical options now will be outlined.

Stevenson (1977a, p. 650) acknowledges that *fraudulent* cases of reincarnation experience have occurred; indeed he has exposed some of them himself (Stevenson, Pasricha & Samararatne, 1988). In several societies a powerful motive for fraud is the status accorded to the family of a person believed to be a reincarnated being. Any case that depends wholly on the unsupported statements of the alleged experient's parents, as does the Pollock case, for example, should therefore be given little evidential weight. With these concessions Stevenson nevertheless feels that reincarnation experiences of young children generally are not likely to be fraudulent because it would be too difficult to coach the child to assume and sustain the unnatural role of being another person. The theatrical skills and the amount of factual information to be learned are thought to be beyond the ability of a young child and any performance thus contrived is expected to be transparent.

Would Gnanatilleka, the experient of Stevenson's Sri Lankan case cited earlier in this chapter, be able and willing at the age of 4 or 5 to simulate her knowledge of and feelings for her "former" family, simply to fulfill some supposed mischievous scheme devised by her parents? Well, some critics would believe so (Zusne & Jones, 1982, pp. 165–166). Wilson (1982, pp. 50–51) discusses possible motives for fraud in several of Stevenson's cases and concludes that Stevenson has been

naïve and precipitate in dismissing this theory. One skeptical version of the fraud hypothesis is that in some cases dishonest parents have heard their child talking about its fantasies (e.g., the imaginary playmate) and have fostered and molded the child's subsequent imaginary experiences to give them a reincarnationist flavor (Chari, 1978, pp. 319–320). The skeptical view of features such as cross-gender identification, phobias and birthmarks is that these are seen more properly as a cause than as a consequence of the reincarnation experience; that is, these features are taken by the child or by its parents as one source of inspiration for a reincarnation fantasy. However, Stevenson counters that statistical comparisons of groups of cases investigated at different times and in different cultures demonstrate a degree of stability and similarity that undermines the suggestion that such experiences should be interpreted as fantasies (Keil & Stevenson, 1999; Pasricha & Stevenson, 1987; Stevenson & Haraldsson, 2003).

Related to the fraud hypothesis is the idea that in cases that are "solved" prior to their being investigated and documented, the families may later quite unintentionally incorporate or confound information about the previous personality gained through their interaction with the family, leading to an artifactual exaggeration of the similarity between the two personalities. However, investigators who have studied and documented cases *prior* to them being solved argue that the evidence for this hypothesis is weak (e.g., Keil & Tucker, 2005).

Another theory of cases of the reincarnation type is that witnesses mistakenly believe the experient is the source of information that actually was obtained elsewhere. For example, in the considerable majority of Stevenson's cases the two families concerned had met before the parapsychologist's investigation and had discussed the life of the previous personality. Some of the details of this discussion could be recalled incorrectly by family members as having been reported by the experient. This process is termed *paramnesia* (Stevenson, 1977a, pp. 650–651). The possible role of paramnesia in reincarnation experiences was suggested long ago by Burnham (1889, p. 432) and still is regarded (Zusne & Jones, 1982, p. 165) as a major flaw in the value of these cases to the reincarnation hypothesis. Stevenson admits that paramnesia may be an element in a few cases but deems it an inadequate explanation of highly detailed experiences reported by careful observers and an inapplicable account of the cases that have been investigated before any meeting between the two families (e.g., Stevenson & Samararatne, 1988). Further, Schouten and Stevenson (1998) found that neither the number nor the percentage of accurate details of a claimed former life is higher if these details are recruited after the two families meet.

Under the hypothesis of *cryptomnesia* it is supposed that the experient has acquired the facts of the previous life by normal means but has forgotten the source of this information and erroneously has ascribed the existence to their own experience. The process of cryptomnesia is well attested in other contexts (Stevenson, 1983b) and may well be due to a neurological dysfunction (Persinger, 1996) but according to Stevenson (1977a, p. 651) as yet no spontaneous reincarnation experience has been demonstrated to have been due to cryptomnesia. He believes further that this hypothesis can not accommodate the many cases in which an experient gave details of a former life before any contact was likely with relatives and acquaintances of the previous personality. Zusne and Jones (1982, p. 154) believe the historical accuracy of "past life" memories is due to cryptomnesia, but in documenting the evidence for this conclusion these authors make no distinction between spontaneous reincarnation experiences and hypnotic regression (the latter is discussed in the next section of this chapter).

Another theory of the reincarnation experience appeals to a parapsychological mechanism, or more specifically, to a combination of ESP *and personation*. Here the child is held to develop a pathological secondary personality that under the influence of the cultural setting is cast into a reincarnationist form. The delusion is buttressed by the use of ESP to obtain information about the deceased person from surviving relations and acquaintances. A form of this hypothesis is explored by Chari (1962). In many instances the hypothesis implies a super–ESP capacity because the experient would have had to recruit information from sources the existence of which was not known by normal means.

Stevenson (1977a, p. 653) argues it is unreasonable to account for the behavioral aspects of reincarnation experiences in terms of ESP. Additionally Chari (1978, p. 316) and Gauld (1982, p. 184) claim that the majority of reincarnation experients do not show signs of any special ESP abilities. Gauld adds that reincarnation experiences do not merely entail diverse pieces of information but these data are integrated and organized in a style appropriate to the previous personality. It should be said that a super–ESP hypothesis, because of its implied omniscience, is untestable by empirical methods, but by the same token our current inability to rule out conclusively the role of ESP in reincarnation experiences effectively renders the reincarnation hypothesis untestable too (Chari, 1978, p. 314).

Another option to the reincarnation hypothesis countenanced by Stevenson is that of *possession*. That is, reincarnation experiences might be due to the experient's being possessed by the spirit of a deceased person. Possession does seem a more apt account of one of Stevenson's (1966, pp. 33–50) cases in which the previous personality did not die until more than three years after the birth of the experient. The possession hypothesis of course, does not appeal to skeptics because both it and the notion of reincarnation subsume the survival hypothesis.

Stevenson also argues against the possession hypothesis on several grounds. First, the experient can recall only a limited amount about the life of the previous personality, whereas a possessing personality would be thought able to provide virtually unlimited data about itself (Stevenson, 1966, p. 346). Second, according to Stevenson (1966, p. 349) the possession hypothesis does not explain the appearance of a birthmark on the experient that is related thematically to the reincarnation experience. Third, there seems no reason for discarnate personalities to be relatively uniform in the period of their possession, "arriving" when the experient is 2 to 4 years and "departing" at 5 to 8 years (Stevenson, 1977a, p. 654). Fourth, although the experient may stop recalling the previous existence the claimed effects on behavior (e.g., by way of a phobia) may persist for some time; under the proposed account why should the possessing personality "vacate" in this piecemeal fashion? Chari (1978, p. 316) maintains additionally that the possession hypothesis does not sit well with the experient's use of the present tense with respect to the current life and the past tense with respect to the previous life.

Stevenson is well aware that arguments against alternative interpretations of the data are in themselves not sufficient to substantially increase the strength of the reincarnation hypothesis. He believes nevertheless that the reincarnation hypothesis is worthy of further serious consideration.

The reincarnation hypothesis itself is not homogeneous. It has a number of varieties, these differing essentially in regard to precisely what it is that is posited to survive death. For example, some versions are couched in terms of the surviving spirit of the deceased person while others focus on the previous personality's "psychic elements" (memories and traits) (Rogo, 1985, Ch. 11). It remains to be seen if these metaphysical distinctions can generate a critical empirical test between them.

As yet it has not been possible to design an effective test between the general reincarnation hypothesis and its conceptual rivals. Further research into the reincarnation experience's phenomenology eventually may enable such a test, but what would really be desirable here is a technique for experimentally evoking reincarnation experiences that permits their investigation under more controlled conditions.

Hypnotic Regression: An Experimental Induction Technique?

It has long been known that suggestions may be made to subjects under hypnosis to return or *regress* to an earlier stage of their life. Participants often respond to these suggestions by behaving as if they were re-experiencing their life at that earlier stage. A logical extension of this technique of hypnotic age regression was to suggest the subject could return to a time before they were born and there encounter a life they had led previously. French spiritualists began to experiment with this procedure in the nineteenth century, and a systematic study of hypnotic regression to past lives was reported by Colonel Albert de Rochas in 1911. Subjects gave variously detailed accounts of a past life, their dramatic performance indicating their experience to be most vivid and personally convincing. During the 1950s the much publicized case of an American woman Virginia Tighe who regressed to an existence as Bridey Murphy in nineteenth-century Belfast (Bernstein, 1956; Ducasse, 1960) confirmed in the popular mind the view of hypnotic regression as an experimental method for liberating our past lives. This belief has been fostered by a plethora of populist paperbacks citing numerous examples of regressed experiences of claimed past lives.

There have been some academically interesting studies of hypnotic regression within phenomenological (Winn, 2002) and therapeutic (Lucas, 1993) frameworks. From the perspective of the professional parapsychologist, however, hypnotic regression has not proved satisfactory as an experimental technique, for the simple reason of its unreliability (Stevenson, 1994). Not that a regressed experience is exceptionally difficult to induce in people preselected for their hypnotic susceptibility (Baker, 1982). But the considerable majority of experiences thus induced are clearly fantasies, marked by historical inaccuracies, malapropisms, anachronisms, and loose narrative (Venn, 1986). The hypnotic state is well documented as a context for imaginative role-playing and for confabulation, a fact that evidently applies also to the majority of performances under the procedure of hypnotic regression (Baker, 1982; Perry, Laurence, Nadon & Labelle, 1986; Spanos, 1988). Expectations of the hypnotically regressed person may also make a contribution, given that most members of the general public believe that hypnosis can recover memories of past lives (Johnson & Hauck, 1999). In addition, there is experimental evidence that hypnotic past-life regressions are shaped by expectations expressed by the hypnotist (Spanos, Menary, Gabora, DuBreuil & Dewhirst, 1991).

The poor efficacy of hypnotic regression as an experimental technique, however, does not necessarily mean that the data it has yielded are of no evidential value to the reincarnation hypothesis. Despite the technique's reputation for generating imaginary past lives there reportedly are occasional cases that appear to show substantial historical and other veridicality, yet the hypnotic subjects declare they have had no opportunity to acquire the information in question by normal means (e.g., Tarazi, 1990). These cases deserve further scrutiny.

In one type of such case an experient to some degree is conversant in the previous personality's language but has not learned that language during the present lifetime.

This phenomenon is known as *xenoglossy*. Sometimes the subject not only makes statements in the "unlearned language" but also can engage in intelligible interactive conversation in that language; this form is termed *responsive xenoglossy*.

Instances of xenoglossy are extremely rare both in the spontaneous reincarnation experience and in the hypnotic state. Of the handful of documented cases one is the so-called Gretchen case (Stevenson, 1984). Here an American woman Dolores Jay was hypnotized by her husband and without any suggestions to regress she presented a trance personality named Gretchen who spoke in German. A few biographical details of the previous personality were established during subsequent hypnotic sessions but most of these data were variously unspecific, unverifiable, or simply incorrect. The Gretchen personality nevertheless was able to speak German responsively. Admittedly the utterances typically were short, simple, repetitive and ungrammatical, but nonetheless they were in reasonably well-pronounced German. In the waking state Dolores Jay declared she had never learned this language and Stevenson's quite extensive investigations seem to confirm that Dolores had had no opportunity to learn German either at school or from people living in her childhood home town. It is impossible, of course, to be absolutely confident on such an issue. Thomason (1987) argues further that a few snippets of ungrammatical German hardly suggest that Dolores Jay had been a fluent speaker of this language in a previous life. These considerations, together with the fact of their exceptional rarity, make cases of responsive xenoglossy more an extraordinary enigma than definitive evidence of reincarnation. Their major fascination lies in the fact that it is difficult to conceive ESP, or even super–ESP, to be the basis of this unlearned knowledge of a foreign language's vocabulary, pronunciation and grammar.

Other cases of hypnotic regression reportedly have incorporated historically veridical information. One notable series was obtained by a British hypnotherapist the late Arnall Bloxham, whose work came to public notice through a BBC television documentary and an associated bestselling book (Iverson, 1976). Bloxham claimed to have tape-recorded hypnotic regressions of over 400 people, although only a few were sufficiently specific to warrant detailed investigation. Two of Bloxham's hypnotic subjects were considered particularly suitable for inclusion in the television documentary. An Englishman Graham Huxtable regressed as a gunner's mate aboard a British frigate some 200 years before. During the regression Huxtable named the ship and its officers and in naval slang he vividly described the conditions and events aboard ship, ending in a dramatic enactment of the sailor's severe wounding in a naval battle.

But Bloxham's most prolific subject was a Welsh woman pseudonymously called Jane Evans who regressed to six quite distinct lives, three of which were depicted in impressive detail. Historically speaking the earliest life was as Livonia in Roman Britain in the year 286 A.D. Livonia's husband was tutor to the youngest son of Constantius, the governor of Britain, and Livonia described the life of a Roman household and gave an account of an unsuccessful coup intended to overthrow Constantius. Another life was as Rebecca, the wife of a Jewish moneylender in the English city of York in the year 1189. In this regression Rebecca recounted anti–Jewish disturbances and at the climax she seemingly relived a mob's massacre of her children and then of herself as they sheltered in the crypt of a York church. A third reported existence was as Alison, the housekeeper of Jacques Coeur who was a merchant prince in medieval France in the middle of the fifteenth century. Alison described Coeur's financial dealings with the king and his mistress, the beautiful Agnes Sorel.

Viewers of the televised documentary on Jane Evans's regressions were struck by two features. First, Evans portrayed each of the roles so convincingly that she seemed to be reliving actual experiences. Second, professional historians examined the content of her regressions and although noting occasional curious fallacies they judged the accounts to be historically accurate to a substantial degree. Now, Evans swore she had never researched any of these historical events. Nevertheless there remains the possibility of cryptomnesia; that is, Evans may have acquired the relevant historical information at some stage but now cannot recall doing so.

Is cryptomnesia a viable explanation of veridical hypnotic regressions? Although as a scientific hypothesis cryptomnesia suffers the defect of not being open to disproof, there certainly are some confirmatory instances. One of the most frequently cited is the Blanche Poynings case (Dickinson, 1911). Under hypnosis the subject, a young woman identified only as "Miss C," regressed as Blanche Poynings, a close friend of Maud the Countess of Salisbury in England under the reign of Richard II. The trance personality gave a wealth of information about the life and times of the Countess and the Earl of Salisbury. Dickinson, an SPR investigator, checked the information and found it to be substantially correct. Miss C on the other hand was unable to imagine how she could have acquired these historically accurate details, as she had never studied the reign of Richard II. To all appearances, therefore, this was a classic case of hypnotic regression to a previous life.

Subsequently, however, Dickinson participated in a seance with Miss C as the medium and contact was made with the "Blanche" personality. Dickinson asked how the information obtained from Blanche during the regression could be verified. After some probing the spirit communicator suggested he read a novel entitled *Countess Maud* and written by Emily Holt. In the normal waking state Miss C could recall a novel by this name and said she had read it, although she was unable to recall the story. Dickinson examined the novel and found it to contain virtually all of the factual material obtained during the regression. In the novel, however, Blanche Poynings herself was a minor character. Miss C's regression evidently was an instance of cryptomnesia, with "forgotten" memories of a historical novel being used unconsciously to construct a narrative from the perspective of one of the novel's minor characters.

Cryptomnesia has been shown to play a role in other "past lives" generated under hypnotic regression. For example, when hypnotized for a second time but without the suggestions for regression, some subjects have been able to identify the source of the information contained in their reported past life, despite being unable to recall the source in the normal waking state (e.g., Zolik, 1958). Indeed the investigation of past life regressions by a Finnish psychiatrist Reima Kampman (e.g., Kampman & Hirvenoja, 1978) suggests that the factual material upon which some regressions are based may be embedded so deeply in unconscious memories that the individual might not have the faintest recollection of it during the waking state.

Given that cryptomnesia *can* be the basis of a past life regression, is there any evidence that the cases collected by Bloxham may be interpreted in this way? This question has been pursued by a researcher in Britain, Melvin Harris (Harris, 1986, pp. 145–163; Wilson, 1982, pp. 233–243). No specific source has been identified for Graham Huxtable's regression as a gunner's mate. Harris located dozens of novels that contain accounts of shipboard life in the era of the regression, but the historically unattested names of the frigate and its officers have not been traced to any specific book.

Harris's investigations of Jane Evans's regressions have proved more fruitful. Her regression as Livonia in Roman Britain evidently is based on the novel *The Living Wood* by Louis de Wohl. Not only does this book contain the historically accurate information that was incorporated in the regression, but both the book and the regression feature at least two fictitious details that de Wohl had invented for dramatic purposes. T. B. Costain's novel *The Moneyman* is nominated as the source of the regression as Alison, the housekeeper of Jacques Coeur. Factual details of Coeur's dealings with the king are common to the novel and the regression. Further, the Alison personality appears to have been unaware that her master was married and had five children, and Costain's book deliberately omitted any reference to Coeur's family life in order to simplify the story. A probable source for another of Jane Evans's six regressions also has been located by Harris. It would seem that cryptomnesia, if not deceit, is at the root of the Evans cases. Evans herself reportedly has declined to be interviewed about the correspondences between her regressions and the novels nominated by Harris (Wilson, 1982, p. 243).

There may remain, of course, some instances of veridical past life regression that to all appearances do not involve a cryptomnesic mechanism. But such cases, and indeed the Evans regressions too, presumably could be accommodated by a super–ESP hypothesis. Hypnotic *progression* to a "future life" might be a potential research technique in this context. If a veridical account of a future life could be obtained it would be explicable in terms of (precognitive) super–ESP but surely not in terms of either cryptomnesia or rekindled memories of another existence. The technique of hypnotic progression unfortunately would be inefficient on two grounds. There would be a substantial delay between the experiment and the evaluation of the data concerning a life in a future time. Additionally, there is nothing to encourage an expectation that the yield of veridical "future life" narratives under this procedure would be high, if they occurred at all; thus attempts at hypnotic progression within the subject's present lifetime to date have generated mere fantasies (Rubenstein & Newman, 1954).

On balance it must be said that hypnotic regression has not proved especially useful to the reincarnation hypothesis either as an experimental induction procedure or as a source of supportive data. In light also of the difficulty of ruling out alternative accounts of spontaneous reincarnation experiences the notion of reincarnation has not proved a fruitful domain for research on the survival hypothesis. In one respect this is surprising: perhaps more than any other phenomenon that has been linked to the survival hypothesis, reincarnation raises the issue of precisely what it is that is alleged to survive bodily death. But while survival has yet to prove an authentic phenomenon, reincarnation experiences remain a thought-provoking topic for phenomenological research.

Key Terms and Concepts

reincarnation
reincarnation experience
past-life experience
Stevenson
solved/unsolved cases
phobias
birthmarks
fraud

paramnesia
cryptomnesia
ESP/super–ESP with personation
inherited memory
possession
hypnotic regression
responsive xenoglossy
Bloxham

Study Questions

1. List the features of a typical case of spontaneous reincarnation experience. Which of these features are instanced in the Gnanatilleka case?

2. How are cases of the reincarnation experience investigated?

3. What potential explanations of reincarnation experiences should be considered by investigators? Is there support for any of these explanations? What are the arguments against them?

4. According to the philosopher of science Karl Popper, a fundamental requirement of a scientific hypothesis is that it be open to disproof. In the context of explanations of reincarnation experiences and past life regressions, why is the hypothesis of cryptomnesia unable to meet the criterion of falsifiability?

5. Do reincarnation experiences vary across different cultures? In light of this, can reincarnation be deemed an objective event?

6. In what respects has the technique of hypnotic regression failed to contribute to an assessment of the reincarnation hypothesis?

7. What features would you require of a case of hypnotic regression before you would accept it as a persuasive example of reincarnation?

15

BELIEF IN THE PARANORMAL

Previous chapters have surveyed research into the nature of various anomalous experiences that seem, at least at first glance, to imply the existence of paranormal processes. It is clear that the authenticity of these hypothesized processes remains a highly contentious issue: some parapsychologists interpret the available evidence to be in support of the existence of the paranormal, but skeptical commentators dismiss the empirical literature as being either inconclusive or methodologically flawed.

Many people nevertheless embrace paranormal beliefs. The Gallup Organization, for example, has carried out a series of polls over the years in which they have asked US citizens to indicate the degree to which they believe in various allegedly paranormal phenomena. In 2005, 41 percent of respondents said they believed in ESP, down from 50 percent in 2001 (Moore, 2005). Similar levels of ESP belief were found by Gallup in 1996 (48 percent) and 1990 (49 percent). In all, about three-quarters of the American population believes in the authenticity of one or more paranormal processes (Moore, 2005). Whether or not psi actually exists, the reality of ESP and PK is widely endorsed by the public. Such belief has attracted a good deal of attention from researchers, and this work is the focus of the present chapter.

It is important to appreciate at the out-set that the scientific investigation of the nature of paranormal belief is legitimate irrespective of the ultimate resolution of the debate on the reality of the paranormal. That is, the nature and the functions of belief in the paranormal can be investigated within an orthodox psychological and sociological framework with scant reference to the actual bases of parapsychological experiences. In this regard, research into paranormal belief may be of interest to parapsychologists and to skeptics alike.

Some of the reasons for this interest may be mentioned briefly. As noted in Chapter 4, belief in ESP is reported to affect performance in laboratory ESP tasks: believers ("sheep") tend to achieve psi-hitting and disbelievers ("goats") show psi-missing. Because of the intrinsic prospect of improved control of experimental ESP performance, this so-called sheep-goat effect has been the principal focus of much of the parapsychological investigation of paranormal belief.

But the study of paranormal belief bears on other issues too. An understanding of the bases of these beliefs might help to account for the experience encountered by many parapsychologists of mental conflict over the evidence they obtain in support of the existence of paranormal processes (Inglis, 1986; McConnell & Clark, 1980; Tart, 1995). Additionally, research on belief, and thence disbelief, in the paranormal may throw some light on the belligerence of many critics' response to parapsychology (Hansen, 1992; Irwin, 1989c). Indeed, McClenon (1982b) reports that among members of the American Association for the Advancement of Science the level of disbelief in ESP is statistically related to the view that parapsychological research is not a legitimate scientific undertaking.

From the skeptical viewpoint, paranormal belief also may be a factor in people's misinterpretation of normal events as paranormal occurrences (Ayeroff & Abelson, 1976; Benassi, Sweeney & Drevno, 1979; Jones & Russell, 1980; Singer & Benassi, 1981, pp. 51–52; Wiseman, Greening & Smith, 2003) and in the selective discounting of information not compatible with a paranormal interpretation (Russell & Jones, 1980; Singer & Benassi, 1981). There has even been a proposal to use the level of paranormal belief in the general population as an index of social dislocation and of the inadequacy of the nation's program of science education (Singer & Benassi, 1981). Thus, advancements in the scientific understanding of paranormal beliefs potentially could have some wide-ranging implications. In any event, the nature of paranormal belief should be of interest in its own right to any professional student of human behavior.

Much of the investigation of paranormal belief has been undertaken by scientists who are not parapsychologists. This has had three major consequences for the literature on paranormal belief.

First, there has been a tendency among skeptical researchers to pursue relationships between paranormal belief and negative psychological characteristics (e.g., gullibility). Although the findings of individual studies conducted under this approach might well be valid, there is a concomitant danger of introducing some bias in the overall depiction of the believer in the paranormal. Certainly it is important to know if paranormal believers tend to be gullible or dogmatic or the like, but collectively this information may be misleading if potential positive psychological characteristics of believers (e.g., empathy) are neglected by researchers.

Second, there is evidence that people's responses to a questionnaire on paranormal belief are open to influence by the demand characteristics of the context of the test. What people reveal about their own beliefs in the paranormal is significantly affected by cues in the test situation that signal the extent to which such beliefs are endorsed by the research team. If the researchers are perceived to be at all skeptical, participants evidently are reluctant to acknowledge fully their paranormal beliefs (Crandall, 1985; Fishbein & Raven, 1967; Layton & Turnbull, 1975). This may be a reason for occasional discrepancies between the findings on paranormal belief reported by parapsychologists and those reported by skeptics (Irwin, 1991c).

Third, the participation of researchers who are not parapsychologists seems to be responsible for substantial variation in what is taken to be the scope of paranormal belief. This variation is most clearly reflected in the currently available measures of paranormal belief. Some measures devised by parapsychologists are purely sheep-goat scales, that is, they index no more than belief in ESP (e.g., Thalbourne & Haraldsson, 1980). Other instruments tap a greater range of parapsychological claims; for example, Sheils and Berg's (1977) questionnaire addresses belief in telepathy, precognition, psychokinesis, astral projection (out-of-body travel), and psychic healing.

At the other extreme, however, are researchers who deem the paranormal to encompass not only parapsychological processes but all manner of magical, superstitious, religious, supernatural, occult and other notions such as UFOs, astrology, déjà vu, the Loch Ness monster, angels, the unluckiness of walking under a ladder, communication with plants, witches, levitation, palmistry, voodoo, and graphology. Many of these notions, of course, fall outside the scope of the paranormal as usually conceived by parapsychologists. On the other hand, the average person might well be inclined to see all these beliefs as falling in the same general category. Inventories marked by this very broad, popularist perspective include the widely used *Paranormal Belief Scale* (PBS: Tobacyk & Milford, 1983), which has seven statistically discriminable subscales that its designers have named traditional religious belief, psi belief, witchcraft, superstition, spiritualism, extraordinary life forms, and precognition (but see also Lange, Irwin & Houran, 2000). The PBS is the scale most commonly used by psychologists who investigate the psychological correlates of paranormal belief, whereas the scales that take a narrower definition of paranormal tend to be used by parapsychologists investigating relationships between belief and performance on laboratory psi tasks (Goulding & Parker, 2001).

Because of this variation in the assessment of paranormal belief, caution should be exercised in accepting at face value any researcher's findings on the nature of such belief; that is, it is as well to ask if "paranormal" is being used by the researcher in a limited parapsychological sense or instead is intended to signify a much broader domain. A research paper that reaches the conclusion "paranormal believers have low intelligence" must be regarded differently if the measure of belief focused on superstitions than if it addressed psi phenomena. The majority of empirical data in fact do relate to paranormal belief in its broadest sense and unless otherwise specified, the generic term "paranormal belief" has the same connotation throughout the remainder of this chapter. It must nevertheless be stressed that the factorial structure of the domain of paranormal belief is an issue of ongoing debate (Lawrence, 1995; Thalbourne, Dunbar & Delin, 1995; Tobacyk, 1995).

Discussion of the topic of paranormal belief also tends to be in terms of "believers"

and "disbelievers." Again, it should be stressed that this convention is largely for convenience of exposition; certainly it should not be taken to imply that people can be simply dichotomized in relation to paranormal belief. Indeed, on the basis of a statistical technique known as cluster analysis Irwin (1997) has identified a four-category typology the respective components of which may be described as traditional religious believers, New Agers, tentative believers, and skeptics. As yet no research has addressed the psychological profiles of the four groups but it as well to remember that empirical generalizations about "paranormal believers" may well be too sweeping.

The *form* of paranormal beliefs held by a given person is strongly influenced by cultural factors such as socialization within the family, peer group processes, dissemination of parapsychological concepts in the media, and formal persuasion by other social institutions such as the church (Irwin, 2006; Schriever, 2000; Sparks, Nelson & Campbell, 1997; Vyse, 1997; Zusne & Jones, 1982). On the other hand the factor of socialization is insufficient to account for the individual's underlying susceptibility to paranormal belief. Irrespective of the specific form of these beliefs why do people endorse them?

Some parapsychologists, having considered the available empirical evidence, conclude that people believe in the paranormal because they have experienced genuinely paranormal phenomena (e.g., Goulding & Parker, 2001). However when we consider the experiences that people report, we cannot disentangle the ontological status of the phenomena giving rise to the experience from the experient's interpretation of these phenomena. Both believers and non-believers in the paranormal have anomalous experiences, but they interpret them in different ways (Irwin, 1985d). Thus, people do not subscribe to paranormal belief because they have witnessed the paranormal in action, but because they have interpreted anomalous experiences in terms of paranormal concepts. Therefore the main theoretical approaches to understanding paranormal belief do not focus on the question of the reality of paranormal phenomena.

These four approaches will be referred to here as the social marginality hypothesis, the worldview hypothesis, the cognitive deficits hypothesis, and the psychodynamic functions hypothesis. It so happens that each of these hypotheses bears on quite distinct groups of the correlates of paranormal belief. This fact anticipates the observation that as yet, no single theoretical approach addresses the full range of data on paranormal belief, but at least it permits the expository convenience of addressing each class of correlates in conjunction with a single associated hypothesis. However, it is regrettable that each of these approaches seems to have progressed largely independently of the others because it is unlikely that a model arising from a single perspective will adequately account for the rich variety of paranormal beliefs that exists (Wiseman & Watt, 2006). The following review considers in turn four major themes, namely, demographic correlates of paranormal belief and the social marginality hypothesis, attitudinal correlates and the worldview hypothesis, cognitive correlates and the cognitive deficits hypothesis, and personality correlates and the psychodynamic functions hypothesis. For a more detailed survey within this framework see Irwin (2006).

Demographic Correlates and the Social Marginality Hypothesis

Interest in demographic correlates of paranormal belief has been prompted primarily by the *social marginality hypothesis*. According to Bainbridge (1978), Lett (1992), and Wuthnow (1976), people most susceptible to paranormal belief are members of so-

cially marginal groups, that is, groups such as the poorly educated or the unemployed that possess characteristics or roles that rank low among dominant social values. The deprivation and alienation associated with marginal status in society is held to encourage such people to appeal to magical and religious beliefs, presumably because these beliefs bring various compensations to the lives of their adherents.

Under the social marginality hypothesis the demographic correlates of paranormal belief should be those that represent indices of social marginality. In the view of sociologists, such indices include (old) age, (female) gender, (low) socioeconomic status, ethnicity, and marital status (being a divorced or separated person). Researchers have sought to relate the endorsement of paranormal belief to each of these factors.

Age. With the major exception of traditional religious beliefs, most paranormal beliefs appear to be stronger in young adults than in elderly people. Indeed, Emmons and Sobal (1981, p. 52) report age to be the strongest of all demographic correlates of paranormal belief.

Age has been found to correlate negatively with global paranormal belief and with specific belief in ESP, witchcraft, spiritualism, superstitions, astrology, New Age tenets, and extraordinary life forms such as the Loch Ness monster (e.g., Boy, 2002; Emmons & Sobal, 1981; Irwin, 2001a; Randall, 1990; Tobacyk, Pritchett & Mitchell, 1988). On the other hand, the relationship appears to be relatively weak (Irwin, 2001a), contrary to the initial claim by Emmons and Sobal (1981). Further, Tobacyk, Pritchett and Mitchell (1988) and Emmons and Sobal (1981) found no significant relationship between age and religious belief, and other studies (e.g., McAllister, 1988) have actually noted an *increase* in religiosity among the elderly.

In seeking to interpret the reported associations between age and paranormal belief it should be noted that all the studies have been cross-sectional rather than longitudinal in design. This makes interpretation somewhat uncertain; although the data might well testify to effects of aging or developmental processes on adherence to paranormal beliefs, they could also reflect generational differences.

In any event, the predominant negative relationship between age and paranormal belief seems at odds with the social marginality hypothesis. Youthfulness is highly valued in Western society, and the aged thereby constitute a socially marginal group. Under the social marginality hypothesis, elderly people should be relatively prone to paranormal belief, yet for most facets of this belief domain the reverse is the case.

Gender. The endorsement of most, but certainly not all, paranormal beliefs is stronger among women than among men.

Women typically show higher scores on measures of global paranormal belief and on scales for specific beliefs in ESP, superstitions, astrology, New Age tenets, black magic, and traditional religious concepts (e.g., Blum, 1976; Boy, 2002; Clarke, 1991; Emmons & Sobal, 1981; Irwin, 1985d, 2001a; Rice, 2003; Thalbourne, 1981; Tobacyk & Milford, 1983). On the other hand, men have a stronger belief in UFOs and extraterrestrials (Clarke, 1991; Rice, 2003) and in extraordinary life forms (Tobacyk & Milford, 1983). Belief in witchcraft generally does not vary with gender (Emmons & Sobal, 1981).

Giving due acknowledgment to the extent that being a woman continues to be socially devalued, these data still offer at best only partial support for the social marginality hypothesis of paranormal belief. Some beliefs in this domain are endorsed more strongly by men than by women. Additionally, it is plausible that the relationship between paranormal belief and gender is mediated not by social marginality but by stereotypical gender roles in a broader sense. The nature of such gender-role effects nevertheless warrants further investigation.

With regard to the related concept of sexual orientation McBeath (1985) speculated that homosexual people are inclined to endorse paranormal beliefs; to the extent that homosexuality continues to be marginalized this speculation is consistent with the social marginality hypothesis. In a comparison of homosexual and heterosexual men Thalbourne (1997) nevertheless found no support for McBeath's view.

Socioeconomic status. The variable of socioeconomic status has been little investigated in relation to paranormal belief, possibly because of the difficulty of its measurement and the perceived intrusiveness of questions that might be used as indices.

In the analysis by Emmons and Sobal (1981) unemployment, an important facet of socioeconomic status, was used explicitly as an indicator of social marginality. The paranormal beliefs they found to correlate with unemployment include those relating to ESP and its individual forms, extraordinary life forms, ghosts, and angels, but in the majority of these instances the relationship was negative. That is, unemployed people generally showed relatively low paranormal belief. This trend is contrary to the social marginality hypothesis. More recently however, MacDonald (1995) reported a positive relationship between financial dissatisfaction and clairvoyant experiences, a finding which might be taken to be consistent with the hypothesis.

Ethnicity. Ethnic background has been included in some investigations of paranormal belief because of the socially marginal status accorded to some ethnic groups within a given society. In the United States this variable usually has been scored in terms of whether or not the participant is black.

Emmons and Sobal (1981) found belief in ESP and in all its individual forms to be *lower* among blacks than among other ethnic groups in the general population, but in a survey of university students Tobacyk, Miller, Murphy and Mitchell (1988) observed blacks to have a higher belief in precognition than did whites. Again, Murphy and Lester (1976) report no dependence of ESP belief upon the ethnic background of college students. Complex interactions may be operating here between ethnicity, geographical region, and educational level. Although these effects warrant further study, when taken in isolation the factor of ethnicity does not look to be particularly promising for the assessment of the social marginality account of ESP belief.

Tobacyk, Miller, Murphy and Mitchell (1988) note further that in their sample of university students, blacks showed stronger belief than whites in spiritualism, superstitions, and witchcraft, whereas white students had the higher level of traditional religious belief. Emmons and Sobal (1981) and Tobacyk, Miller, Murphy and Mitchell (1988) each report belief in extraordinary life forms to be stronger among whites than among blacks. In terms of ethnicity, therefore, the social marginality hypothesis evidently does not apply uniformly across the different dimensions of paranormal belief.

Marital status. Given that divorced and separated people sometimes are seen to have marginal status in society, marital status may be a pertinent demographic variable for study.

Emmons and Sobal (1981) found married people to have relatively strong religious beliefs but also comparatively low levels of belief in ESP and its different forms, astrology, witchcraft, and extraordinary life forms. Wuthnow (1976) similarly found divorced and separated people to have substantially higher belief in astrology than did married, widowed, or "never married" respondents. Although the database still is quite small, marital status is one facet of social marginality that does provide reasonably consistent evidence for the social marginality hypothesis of paranormal belief. But even here, religious belief seems an exception to the trend.

Conclusion. By way of a conclusion to this limited survey of the demographic correlates of paranormal belief, it is appropriate to comment on the standing of the social marginality hypothesis in relation to the empirical evidence. Following the observations of sociologists the variables of age, gender, socioeconomic status, ethnicity, and marital status have each been considered as an index of social marginality. The review of the empirical literature nevertheless has failed to find a single dimension of paranormal belief showing a pattern of correlations with these indices that is uniformly consistent with the social marginality hypothesis. Further, the observed correlations are typically small. Perhaps a complex combination of the indices would provide a basis for future research into the issue (see Rice, 2003), but at present it is fair to say the social marginality hypothesis of paranormal belief (when taken in isolation) does not satisfactorily accommodate the available evidence. The identified demographic correlates nevertheless remain as data to be taken into account in the formulation of an effective theory of paranormal belief.

Attitudinal Correlates and the Worldview Hypothesis

Research on beliefs and activities associated with paranormal belief has a bearing on the *worldview hypothesis*, among other things. According to Zusne and Jones (1982), belief in the paranormal is simply one facet of a broader worldview, a view that is characterized by a highly subjective and esoteric perspective on humanity, life and the world at large. For example, events may be interpreted more in terms of intangible mental and metaphysical processes than in relation to observable or physical factors. Under Zusne and Jones's hypothesis, paranormal belief should tend to be found in conjunction with other beliefs and activities that share the subjective and esoteric orientation. The evidence on this point now will be surveyed.

Religious beliefs. To the extent that some researchers define belief in traditional religious concepts to be a paranormal belief, it may seem redundant to inquire if paranormal beliefs are associated with religious beliefs. On the other hand, the association between religious and nonreligious paranormal beliefs certainly is pertinent to the worldview hypothesis.

Tobacyk and Milford (1983) found traditional religious belief to correlate positively with belief in precognition and witchcraft, but negatively with belief in spiritualism and nonsignificantly with belief in psi, superstition, and extraordinary life forms. According to Clarke (1991), religiosity correlates positively with belief in psychic healing and negatively with UFO belief. Hillstrom and Strachan (2000) reports negative correlations between religiosity and beliefs in telepathy, precognition, psychokinesis, psychic healing, UFOs, reincarnation, and communication with spirits. The worldview hypothesis would predict these relationships to be typically positive. Thus, there is at best only partial support for the view that religiosity should be a concomitant of (nonreligious) paranormal beliefs. Some more recent support comes unexpectedly from a study (Thalbourne, 2003) that tested the popular suggestion that paranormal belief may be a substitute for belief in God. Thalbourne predicted that if this was the case, the two would be negatively correlated. He looked at data from 9 studies, with a total of 1558 participants, in which theism and paranormal belief had been measured. Most of the studies used a measure of paranormal belief that focused on belief in psychic abilities. The median correlation was, contrary to prediction, positive but not large (+0.29), and in no case was the correlation negative. Hergovich, Schott and Arendasy (in press) also found that paranormal belief correlated only weakly with religiosity in those individuals with explicit religious affiliation, and the correlation was higher for those without religious affiliation, leading these researchers to conclude that paranormal belief is not necessarily a substitute for traditional religious belief.

Other beliefs. There are nevertheless some additional indications that paranormal belief is associated with rather subjective notions of the ways in which the world functions.

One respect in which this may be the case is in regard to the human world. The very nature of the dimensions of paranormal belief suggest that paranormal believers see themselves as more than mere physical or biological structures. This impression is borne out by some empirical work. Stanovich (1989) and Svensen, White and Caird (1992) report psi belief to correlate positively with a dualist (mind/body) philosophy of human nature. Paranormal believers' conviction in nonphysical dimensions of human existence is instantiated also in relation to the issue of their postmortem fate; global belief in the paranormal is positively correlated with belief in life after death (Irwin, 1985d; Thalbourne, 1995a). The hypothesis of believers' immersion in subjective aspects of life is supported further by reported associations between the level of belief in ESP or broader parapsychological phenomena and both an inclination to interpret dreams (Haraldsson, 1981; Irwin, 1985d; Thalbourne, 1984) and an inclination to be self-reflective or to devote attention to subjective experience more generally (Davies, 1985; Glicksohn, 1990). Similarly, Irwin (2003a) found New Age beliefs and belief in black magic to correlate positively with the tendency to infer a sense of the world's meaningfulness from life events.

In an endeavor to test directly the worldview hypothesis Zusne and Jones (1982, pp. 192–194) developed the Worldview Scale. This questionnaire comprises items reflecting either a subjective or an objective view of the universe and human behavior. Global belief in the paranormal was observed to be greatest for people scoring high in subjectivism on the Worldview Scale.

There is, therefore, some empirical support for the worldview hypothesis. Now, although most of the available data bear upon global paranormal belief rather than on specific dimensions of belief, this empirical information certainly is informative and should be taken into account by any comprehensive theory of paranormal belief. Nonetheless, the worldview hypothesis does not seem sufficient in itself. Granted the tendency of paranormal believers toward subjectivism, there remains a need for more fundamental determinants of paranormal belief to be ascertained. That is, what styles of cognitive processes and of personality underlie paranormal beliefs and this broader subjectivist belief system alike?

Additionally, there are some types of attitude associated with paranormal belief that it is insufficient to characterize merely as "subjective." The beliefs in question relate to the extent to which life is regarded as subject to the control of the individual.

A cognitive dimension known as *locus of control* refers to people's disposition to believe their fate either to be in their own hands or to be the consequence of external factors beyond their personal control. Those who believe personal outcomes are contingent largely on their own behavior and attributes are said to have internal locus of control. People with external locus of control, on the other hand, believe personal outcomes are governed predominantly by other powerful individuals and institutions, luck, chance, and so on.

There is a general trend for paranormal belief to be associated with an external locus of control. This relationship has been documented in regard to global paranormal belief and to specific beliefs in ESP, precognition, witchcraft, superstitions, spiritualism, and extraordinary life forms (Dag, 1999; Irwin, 1986b; Randall & Desrosiers, 1980; Thalbourne et al., 1995; Tobacyk & Tobacyk, 1992; Tobacyk & Milford, 1983). As a group, paranormal believers therefore are inclined to maintain that they are especially vulnerable to external forces beyond their control. This theme will emerge again in following

sections that address styles of thinking and personality factors in paranormal belief.

The worldview hypothesis has been valuable in drawing attention to the subjective perspective of some beliefs associated with belief in the paranormal. There nevertheless remains a need to take account also of other facets of associated beliefs, particularly as these relate to the issue of control over life events, and to examine the more fundamental matter of the personality dynamics that might be served by these various belief systems.

Cognitive Correlates and the Cognitive Deficits Hypothesis

Many skeptical researchers have had a particular interest in the nature of cognitive processes associated with paranormal belief. The hypothesis underlying this interest usually is not formalized, but for ease of exposition it will here be referred to as the *cognitive deficits hypothesis*. Under this collective view the believer in the paranormal variously is held to be illogical, irrational, credulous, uncritical, and foolish. Alcock (1981, pp. 48–53), for example, depicts paranormal believers as credulous, dogmatic and generally inept in basic intellectual skills. A substantial body of skeptical research therefore has been designed to document hypothesized cognitive deficits associated with paranormal belief. Other researchers have attempted to take a more neutral stance, for example Wiseman and Watt (2006) use the term "misattribution hypothesis" when reviewing this literature.

Educational attainment. As predicted under the cognitive deficits hypothesis, there is a trend for paranormal believers to show relatively poor educational attainment, although findings certainly are mixed (Emmons & Sobal, 1981; Messer & Griggs, 1989;

Musch & Ehrenberg, 2002; Otis & Alcock, 1982; Rice, 2003; Tobacyk, Miller & Jones, 1984). The variability of results in part may be due to different indices of educational attainment used across studies and to confounding effects of such variables as age, socioeconomic status, generational differences, developmental level, social roles associated with particular vocations, and exposure to forms of indoctrination other than education.

Scientific education. A few researchers have sought to relate paranormal belief to the amount of scientific education the individual has had. Students enrolled in the sciences are reported to have a lower belief in the paranormal than do students of the humanities, at least in some surveys (Otis & Alcock, 1982). More recently, a survey of over 350 Spanish university students (Diaz-Vilela & Alvarez-Gonzalez, 2004) found a tendency for higher paranormal belief amongst students of tourism, and lower belief amongst students enrolled on courses in biology, sociology and physics, particularly for religious belief. Students of psychology, education and human resources expressed more neutral beliefs.

It is not clear, however, whether science students' low level of paranormal belief is due to their more scientific style of thinking or to an enculturation process that discourages the acknowledgment of their paranormal beliefs. Educational programs focused more specifically on the paranormal certainly do influence students' acknowledgment of such beliefs, depending on the style of the program (Irwin, 1990b; Morier & Keeports, 1994; Tobacyk, 1983a; Vitulli, 1997).

As indices of cognitive functioning, the variables of scientific education and educational attainment are simply too ambiguous to provide a critical test of the cognitive deficits hypothesis.

Intelligence and reasoning skills. An obvious means of assessing the cognitive deficits hypothesis is the investigation of a relationship between paranormal belief and intelligence (IQ). Surprisingly few such studies have been undertaken.

Killen, Wildman and Wildman (1974) have shown superstitious belief does correlate negatively with IQ, but Jones, Russell and Nickel (1977) report a *positive* correlation between global paranormal belief and intelligence. Although further research clearly is warranted, the finding by Jones et al. would appear to stand as a significant challenge to the cognitive deficits hypothesis.

Greater attention has been given to a link between paranormal belief and reasoning skills. Several skeptical investigators have demonstrated relatively poor critical thinking ability in paranormal believers (Alcock & Otis, 1980; Wierzbicki, 1985). Sappington (1990) also reports that belief in psi seems to be more affected by emotional than rational considerations. But the findings can be conflicting even within individual studies. Hergovich and Arendasy (2005) had their participants complete a measure of critical thinking ability, then an intelligence test to measure reasoning ability, followed by a questionnaire about paranormal experience, and a questionnaire about paranormal belief. The study found no relationship between critical thinking ability and either paranormal belief or experience in a sample of 180 students of psychology, computer science, and arts. However, in the same study those students with lower reasoning ability had higher levels of paranormal belief, but not experience.

Tobacyk and Milford (1983) nevertheless caution that uncritical thinking might not be characteristic of all dimensions of paranormal belief. Only two of the seven dimensions of their *Paranormal Belief Scale* (PBS) correlated with a measure of uncritical inference; thus, traditional religious believers tended to be relatively critical in drawing inferences, and believers in spiritualism were uncritical. A closer look at the Hergovich and Arendasy (2005) study echoes this warning:

the only two PBS sub-scales that were significantly negatively correlated with reasoning ability were concerned with superstitious beliefs and traditional religious beliefs. For the other five sub-scales the correlations, though not positive, were near zero.

Additionally, investigation of the relationship between paranormal belief and reasoning skills may be subject to demand characteristics of the context in which the tests are performed. Although skeptics have found the relationship to be negative, two studies conducted by parapsychologists (Irwin, 1991c; Roe, 1999) failed to confirm this. Recent work by Watt and Wiseman (2002) points to the significance of motivational factors in these studies.

It is feasible that paranormal belief is fundamentally related not so much to reasoning *skill* as to reasoning *style*. Epstein and his co-workers (e.g., Epstein, Pacini, Denes-Raj & Heier, 1996) have shown that people vary in their relative reliance on two styles of reasoning or systems of information processing. The analytical-rational style is a rather slow, deliberative, effortful, conscious and primarily verbal process of conventionally logical or objective analysis of information; the intuitive-experiential style is a rapid, automatic (rather than effortful), subconscious, holistic, and primarily nonverbal ("intuitive") process of subjectively driven analysis of information. Although people will use each of these reasoning styles according to prevailing circumstances, a person may have a habitual preference to rely on one style rather than the other. Wolfradt, Oubaid, Straube, Bischoff and Mischo (1999) found global paranormal belief is associated more strongly with reliance on the intuitive-experiential style than with the analytical-rational style, although both reasoning styles did seem to be implicated, at least in their sample of university students. In a replication with a general community sample Irwin and Young (2002) found all major facets of paranormal belief to correlate positively with the

intuitive-experiential style and negatively with the analytical-rational style. It should be noted, however, that the two reasoning styles serve different cognitive functions, so one can not be regarded as necessarily "inferior" to the other. Thus, the association of paranormal belief with an intuitive-experiential style is a potentially instructive finding, but it is of moot significance for the cognitive deficits hypothesis.

In short, research into paranormal believers' intelligence and reasoning has not yielded unequivocal support for the cognitive deficits hypothesis. Indeed, some contrary findings (Jones et al., 1977) even raise substantial doubts about the general validity of the hypothesis.

Creativity and imagination. Paranormal belief is reported to correlate positively with measures of creativity (Davis, Peterson & Farley, 1974; Thalbourne & Delin, 1994), sensation seeking (Tobacyk & Milford, 1983), and hypnotic susceptibility (Nadon, Laurence & Perry, 1987; Pekala, Kumar & Cummings, 1992). These results suggest that paranormal belief is linked to a cognitive style of fantasizing.

More direct scrutiny of this view is enabled by measures of the personality construct known as fantasy proneness. Fantasy proneness entails a propensity to fantasize a large part of the time and to be deeply absorbed in or fully experiencing what is being fantasized (Lynn & Rhue, 1988). Several studies (e.g., Irwin, 1990a, 1991a; Lawrence, Edwards, Barraclough, Church & Hetherington, 1995) have established that fantasy proneness correlates positively with global paranormal belief and with belief in traditional religious concepts, psi, precognition, witchcraft, spiritualism, and extraordinary life forms. Aspects of the dissociative domain other than fantasy proneness might also be implicated (Irwin, 1994a; Wolfradt, 1997).

The association between paranormal belief and fantasy proneness is of interest not only in its own right but also in relation to the issue of the origins and functions of paranormal belief. Fantasy proneness seems to emerge partly as a result of physical abuse and other trauma during childhood. It is possible therefore, that childhood trauma is an important factor in explaining the individual's fundamental openness to paranormal belief. This issue will be discussed further following a consideration of personality correlates of belief in the paranormal.

Personality Correlates and the Psychodynamic Functions Hypothesis

There undoubtedly are various routes by which an individual may come to believe in specific paranormal concepts. Many people may find such belief is the only satisfactory way they can make intelligible a personal or other anomalous (parapsychological) experience. Socialization to paranormal beliefs also may be a potent mechanism, with the individual gradually absorbing attitudes toward the paranormal conveyed by family members and close friends. Some people may adopt paranormal beliefs in the course of formulating a personal philosophy of life, deriving a sense of self-understanding from ideas promoted by a religious or cultist group or those advanced in popularist New Age literature. A few individuals might even be persuaded of the existence of paranormal processes by the data of parapsychological research. But beyond the specific social context in which paranormal beliefs are molded, there is the matter of the underlying needs met by such beliefs.

It is virtually a psychological axiom that beliefs are held because they serve significant psychodynamic needs of the individual. According to Taylor and Brown (1988), beliefs can achieve this function whether they are grounded in objective reality or are intrinsically illusory, and thus parapsychologists and

skeptics alike are interested in the functions served by paranormal beliefs.

The general view that paranormal beliefs are needs-serving will be termed the *psychodynamic functions hypothesis*. Skeptics usually take this hypothesis to mean that paranormal believers in some respects are psychologically deviant, and although this is not a necessary implication of the psychodynamic functions hypothesis, the personality correlates of paranormal belief clearly are data to be taken into account in this regard.

Social dimensions of personality. Although believers in the paranormal do not seem to be socially withdrawn people (Windholz & Diamant, 1974), Tobacyk (1983b, 1985) has established that global paranormal belief and most of its individual dimensions are related to social alienation and low social interest. That is, paranormal believers as a group are little concerned about the needs or attitudes of other people. This is consistent with previously cited evidence that believers are primarily interested in the world of their own subjective experience (Davies, 1985; Glicksohn, 1990).

Psychological adjustment. Some paranormal believers may have a grandiose sense of their own importance and uniqueness. Tobacyk and Mitchell (1987b) report positive correlations between a measure of narcissism and belief in psi, precognition, witchcraft, and spiritualism. That is, believers might be preoccupied with fantasies of unlimited power and success. The significance of a sense of control once again is indicated.

Dogmatism seems to be a correlate of a few dimensions of paranormal belief, particularly belief in psi, witchcraft, and traditional religious concepts (Alcock & Otis, 1980; Thalbourne et al., 1995; Tobacyk & Milford, 1983). According to Zusne and Jones (1982), such findings are consistent with the notion that paranormal believers have poor psychological adjustment.

Schumaker (1987) claims to have shown global paranormal belief is associated with *superior* psychological adjustment, but he appears to have misconstrued his data by interpreting his index of psychological adjustment as a direct measure when in fact it was inverse (see Irwin, 1991a); that is, Schumaker might be taken instead to have documented an inverse relationship between these beliefs and adjustment. In a replication of Schumaker's procedure Irwin (1991a) found global paranormal belief and belief in witchcraft correlated negatively with psychological adjustment.

Greater scrutiny has been given to the status of paranormal believers and nonbelievers on magical ideation, an index of schizotypy or proneness to psychosis. Measures of magical ideation are found to correlate positively with global paranormal belief and with belief in psi, precognition, witchcraft, superstition, extraordinary life forms, and traditional religious concepts (Irwin & Green, 1998; Peltzer, 2003; Simmonds & Roe, 2000; Thalbourne, 1985, 1994; Thalbourne et al., 1995; Tobacyk & Wilkinson, 1990; Williams, 1989; Williams & Irwin, 1991). There also are reports of an association between psi belief and manic-depressive (bipolar) tendencies (Thalbourne & French, 1995). For a more comprehensive survey of the clinical correlates of paranormal belief see Irwin (2006). In a relatively recent development, paranormal belief has been associated with so-called "healthy schizotypy" (Goulding, 2004, 2005; McCreery & Claridge, 2002), with these authors suggesting that some paranormal beliefs may be adaptive. Similarly, Wiseman and Watt (2004) point out that although the correlates particularly of superstitious beliefs tend to be pathological, most studies have used the PBS to measure superstition. The PBS superstition subscale only contains items referring to "negative" superstitions, that is, items related to the experience of bad luck. When Wiseman and Watt investigated individual differences in scoring on a superstition questionnaire that contained items about bad *and*

good luck, they found different patterns of scoring for the two different types of superstition items. This provides further support for the idea that different paranormal beliefs may serve different psychological functions, as well as adding more voices to the calls for an improved measure of paranormal belief. This line of research might in future be very helpful in developing a detailed understanding of the different causes of such beliefs.

It is possible that many of the foregoing clinical correlates are operating here as indirect indices of reality testing. Reality testing entails "a set of perceptual, cognitive and sensorimotor acts that enables one to determine one's relationship with the external physical and social environments" (Reber, 1995, p. 640). That is, paranormal beliefs may be formed and maintained in part because the person does not subject intuitive interpretations to rigorous critical scrutiny. Some support for this view is reported by Irwin (2003b), though this study used a measure of reality testing that contained items about paranormal belief which may have therefore partially confounded the variables under study. A subsequent replication study by Irwin (2004) with an uncontaminated measure of reality testing also found that deficits in reality testing were associated with relatively high scoring on all seven PBS subscales as well as with the two factors in a more recent version of the PBS (Lange, Irwin & Houran, 2000), namely traditional paranormal beliefs and New Age philosophy.

One facet of psychological adjustment that reportedly does not correlate with paranormal belief is trait anxiety, that is, a disposition toward chronic anxiety. Several studies (e.g., Irwin, 1995; Jones et al., 1977) have failed to identify such a relationship. An acute state of anxiety, on the other hand, is a correlate. Dudley (1999) used an experimental task to manipulate the level of stress or helplessness and found the stressed group of participants tended to increase the strength of their superstitious beliefs. A similar phenomenon was elicited by Keinan (2002). This suggests that the activation of paranormal belief is governed by contextual stress. When a situation appears to be out of control people may therefore be more inclined to appeal to their belief in the paranormal. That is, paranormal belief may serve to enhance feelings of security in the face of a capricious and threatening world. In this respect the activation of paranormal belief functions like a specialized coping mechanism (Callaghan & Irwin, 2003).

Although there certainly is scope for further research, the available literature offers general support for the psychodynamic functions hypothesis. What is required at this point, however, is a specific version of the hypothesis that posits more precisely the nature of the psychodynamics involved. The concluding section of the chapter examines this issue more closely.

Functions and Origins of Paranormal Belief

If paranormal believers do tend to be maladjusted, what might be the origins of such personality disturbance, and what functions might be served by paranormal beliefs in relation to the disturbance? Given that paranormal belief is related to fantasy proneness, a clue to the origins of such belief may be found in one of the antecedent factors in the development of fantasy proneness, namely, a history of abuse in childhood. In an empirical investigation of this idea, Irwin (1992) established a link between paranormal belief and childhood trauma, particularly physical abuse by family members. Less sustained trauma may also have at least a transient effect on children's paranormal beliefs (Terr et al., 1997).

This in turn suggests the nature of some of the psychodynamic functions served by paranormal beliefs. That is, paranormal beliefs may be endorsed because they provide a sense of control over life events (Irwin, 1993a). An assurance of order and meaning in the physical and social world is thought to be essential for emotional security and psychological adjustment. Traumatic events and anomalous experiences, however, pose a potential threat to a state of assurance, in essence because they can be taken to imply the world sometimes is uncertain, chaotic, and beyond the individual's understanding and mastery. By incorporating a system of paranormal beliefs, the individual has a cognitive framework for effectively structuring many events and experiences in life so that they appear comprehensible and thereby able to be mastered, at least intellectually. Under this view, paranormal belief constitutes a cognitive bias through which reality may be filtered without threatening the individual's sense of emotional security. In essence the way in which paranormal beliefs achieve this effect is by creating a transient "illusion of control" (Langer, 1975) over events that are anomalous or are in reality not controllable by the individual.

Empirical research offers support for this view. Blackmore and Troscianko (1985) have shown that a group of paranormal believers had a greater sense of control over a computer task than did a group of nonbelievers, yet the two groups did not differ in their achieved control on the task. Irwin (1992) also found that paranormal believers tend to be perceived by independent judges as being very controlling in their behavior toward other people; that is, paranormal belief is related to a need for interpersonal control. Rudski (2004) found that questionnaire measures of illusion of control were associated with paranormal belief, particularly superstitious and precognition beliefs, again suggesting that such beliefs might give a sense of control over otherwise unpredictable events.

Independent studies also have provided broad support for the psychodynamic approach to paranormal belief. With regard to the key variables in the model French and Kerman (1996) confirmed the interrelationships between childhood trauma, fantasy proneness, and paranormal belief. The noteworthy feature of their study was that they recruited participants with documented histories of childhood abuse, thereby ensuring that the reported abuse history was not an artifact of participants' fantasy proneness. Additionally, Lawrence et al. (1995) conducted an empirical assessment of the model using structural equation modeling techniques. Substantial support for the model was found.

A more recent version of the psychodynamic model (Irwin, 2006) has slightly broadened the nominated developmental origins of paranormal belief from trauma to a childhood in which the person was unable to establish a clear sense of his or her capacity to exert control over life events. Thus, the key developmental antecedent of paranormal belief is proposed to be the child's substantial early experience with diminished control which fosters an enduring need for a sense of mastery over life events. People who lack such a need do not feel so compelled to devise an explanation for the anomalous events they encounter or about which they hear. A strong need for a sense of mastery, on the other hand, drives the formation of parapsychological and other scientifically unaccepted beliefs. The specific beliefs that are created nevertheless are governed or moderated by both the person's information processing style and the person's sociocultural setting. For example, one person may establish an intuitively-experientially grounded belief in ESP, whereas another may develop a more analytically-rationally oriented belief in the power of the devil. Some support for Irwin's revised model comes from a questionnaire study that found the predicted negative correlation between perceived childhood control and paranormal belief (Watt, Watson & Wilson, in press).

The correlation was statistically significant but relatively small (-.18), so childhood control as indexed in this study was not strongly implicated in the development of paranormal belief.

After a paranormal belief is established within the person's system of beliefs, some effort may be made to ensure that this belief is compatible with other cherished beliefs, thereby enabling a reasonably coherent or integrated belief system (e.g., a worldview). This process may entail modification of those beliefs that conflict with the more psychodynamically significant paranormal belief, or even entirely jettisoning a conflicting belief. Generally speaking, however, paranormal beliefs are relatively protected from direct critical scrutiny. Confrontation by a contextual stressor may serve to activate relevant paranormal beliefs of the person, whether at a conscious or subconscious level. The major functional significance of such activation is to attenuate the state of anxiety evoked by the contextual stressor; indeed, the process of anxiety reduction may have a significant role in further reinforcing the intensity of the underlying belief. Other relevant behaviors may be instigated by the activation of the belief. Thus, the person may be inspired to act upon the activated paranormal belief and engage, for example, in belief-associated rituals. In some instances these behaviors may function to maintain the paranormal belief in the longer term, either by ostensibly confirming the belief or by impeding its disconfirmation.

Again, it is stressed that the particular forms of paranormal belief endorsed by the individual will depend very much on the cultural and social environment. In this context special significance is accorded to models provided by parents, peers, teachers, the media, and professional apostles of paranormal beliefs. The functions of these beliefs nevertheless appear to be more fundamentally psychodynamic in nature.

Key Terms and Concepts

social marginality hypothesis

worldview hypothesis

cognitive deficits hypothesis

psychodynamic functions hypothesis

need for control

Study Questions

1. For many parapsychologists the primary issue for research is the authenticity of paranormal processes. Why should people's belief in the paranormal be an issue of any scientific significance?

2. Some researchers have taken the paranormal to subsume all manner of magical, superstitious and occult notions. Consider the advantages and the disadvantages of this approach.

3. Do you think it appropriate to include items on traditional religious concepts in a questionnaire designed to survey paranormal belief? On what grounds should the inclusion or exclusion of such items be decided?

4. In what ways might paranormal beliefs appeal to socially marginal groups? How might the social marginality hypothesis be refined as a guide to future research?

5. Under the worldview hypothesis, in what vocational categories would you expect to find relatively high levels of paranormal belief?

6. How might a need for control over life events constitute a major psychodynamic function of paranormal beliefs?

7. Some empirical findings suggest that paranormal believers as a group are more maladjusted than nonbelievers. Can skeptics justifiably conclude that parapsychologists are psychologically disturbed individuals? What issue does this raise for further research into the personality correlates of paranormal belief?

8. Some parapsychologists maintain that their belief in the authenticity of psi is based purely on the findings of scientific research. Does this contradict the psychodynamic functions hypothesis?

9. How might the psychodynamic functions hypothesis be extended to accommodate the observation that the response of many skeptics to parapsychology is very belligerent?

16

MATTERS OF RELEVANCE

Parapsychology has been held to be relevant in substantial respects to a wide range of academic disciplines (Angoff & Shapin, 1974; Schmeidler, 1976; Watt, in press). This chapter, however, focuses specifically on clinical practice in a parapsychological context and on some suggested practical applications of the findings of parapsychological research. A book could be devoted to each of these topics in their own right, so this chapter aspires to do little else than raise a few major issues.

Parapsychology and Clinical Practice

The parapsychologist, and occasionally the psychologist in the clinic, may be called upon to counsel people about their parapsychological experiences. It is appropriate, therefore, to consider briefly the implications of parapsychology for the clinical context.

One less obvious implication here is the experience of psi in the therapeutic relationship. Thus the client may report telepathic dreams about the therapist, or use psychokinesis in a displaced expression of frustration with the therapeutic relationship, and so on. Some of the most famous examples of psi experiences in the course of therapy were recorded by Freud and Jung. In one case a young woman was describing to Jung (1955/1985, p. 31) a dream in which she was given a golden scarab. At this moment Jung was distracted by the sound of a flying insect knocking against the window. He opened the window, caught the insect and found to his surprise that it strongly resembled a golden scarab. The patient was equally surprised when Jung presented the beetle to her as her "golden scarab." The salutary effect of this experience was to break down the patient's intellectual resistance to therapy. Many other examples of parapsychological experiences during therapy have been documented (e.g., Carvalho, 1996; Devereux, 1953; Eisenbud, 1987; Mintz, 1983; Schwarz, 1980), and the therapeutic context has inspired the administration of psi tests (Carpenter, 1988). Because psi experiences may arise in the therapeutic situation, the therapist should be alert to this possibility and give thought to the experience's likely function(s) in the therapeutic relationship (Calvesi, 1983; Ehrenwald, 1978; Schwarz, 1980).

A circumstance more familiar to parapsychologists, however, is that of being asked to give advice to people who report a parapsychological experience or series of such experiences. These cases may reflect various needs and motives, some of which may be mentioned briefly. It is as well to mention at the outset, however, that the suggestions made below are not intended in any sense as counseling "recipes." Because each person is unique the counseling given in a particular case must be individually tailored. In addition, there may be circumstances in which the parapsychologist with no clinical or counseling training may feel that he or she does not have the appropriate expertise — for instance if an individual appears to be psychotic or delusional. In this case it may be unethical to offer advice or counseling and the case should be referred on to a suitably qualified professional contact, preferably one who does not dismiss outright the possibility that the experiences may reflect the operation of genuine psi. The following points, therefore, are offered merely as issues to be considered in the clinical context.

The Hoaxers

If your interest in parapsychology is known to the public you are bound to encounter people who approach you with tales of preternatural experiences purely out of a sense of mischief. Often such individuals can be identified readily by the exaggerated character of their account, although evidence cited in some previous chapters warns that even genuine parapsychological experients rate highly in fantasy proneness. In any event the very existence of hoaxers serves as a caution that it may be advisable to be noncommittal and nonevaluative in commenting on reported experiences especially in the early phases of the consultation. Of course, even the hoaxer might well benefit from some form of counseling. That the clinician as the intended victim of the hoax would be sufficiently self-controlled to offer counseling is another matter, but it might be borne in mind that the hoax could be a ruse for engaging the counselor's attention, sympathy and support in relation to quite a different problem.

The Seekers of Reassurance

People who genuinely believe they have had a spontaneous parapsychological experi-

ence may approach the parapsychologist or clinician for little else than reassurance, placing the therapist in the role of scientific exorcist (Morris, 1976; Siegel, 1986; Sprinkle, 1988). For those who find their experiences disturbing and frightening, participation in some form of therapy may be beneficial (e.g., Montanelli & Parra, 2004).

A need for reassurance may manifest itself in various degrees. Some people simply may want to talk to someone about their experience rather than seeking counseling as such. Many parapsychological experiences are so uncanny that experients fear friends would only laugh if the incident was confided to them. The opportunity simply to verbalize the experience to a nonevaluative listener permits the experient to reassure themselves that the experience really happened and to make the incident seem more coherent in their own mind.

Other people want confirmation that the experience in fact was paranormal and not delusory. Of course, no definitive judgment can be made on the paranormality of spontaneous parapsychological experiences. If the account seems plausible, reference may be made to other similar experiences to indicate that at least they are common (= normal?), but perhaps it is more fruitful to suggest that the question of authenticity is less important than that of the function served by the experience. The parapsychologist, therefore, might help the individual to work through the experience to establish its personal significance: regardless of the paranormality of the experience, what does the experient take to be its meaning and its place in their life? This is not to suggest that all ostensibly paranormal experiences are crucially meaningful in a psychodynamic sense; the idea of their functional significance certainly should not be pushed dogmatically by the parapsychologist. But the individual's very interest in the status of the experience is often a cue that it is associated with an issue of some psychological significance, and the experient can at least be invited to explore that possibility.

This nonevaluative approach is appropriate also for people who want assurance that parapsychological experiences do not make them abnormal or alien in some sense. Labeling the experience at least may help to normalize it and to reduce the inquirer's level of anxiety and is certainly more constructive than labeling the individual, whether as psychic or as psychotic. It may be useful also to ask about the occurrence of other parapsychological experiences: this may help both experient and clinician to put the focal experience into a broader context. More generally Belz-Merk (2000) recommends attention to the following issues during the course of counseling: dedramatizing and demythologizing the parapsychological experience; assisting the client to explore possible explanations of the experience other than that which the client initially embraced; helping to integrate the experience with the client's self-concept and worldview; and guiding the client towards a restored sense of control over life.

As Weiner (personal communication, June 17, 1988) has noted, the parapsychologist can substantially enhance rapport with a client by feeling comfortable in discussing parapsychological experiences and by demonstrating a readiness not to dismiss the possibility of psi out of hand. Even if the client then is told their particular experience does not appear parapsychological, the advice can be appreciated as more than a statement of mere prejudice and thereby may encourage the individual to face the implications of alternative explanations.

Clients Needful of Therapy

If psi does exist there is little reason for presuming it could not operate in a psychopathological context. Indeed, if we were extrasensorially aware of other people's thoughts about us we probably would be quite paranoid. The roles of psi in at least some psychoses such as schizophrenia have been promoted by Alberti (1974), Ehrenwald (1978), Ullman (1973) and others, and perhaps are at their clearest in (person-centered) poltergeist outbreaks. Therapy in these cases may be more effective if cognizance is taken of the parapsychological elements rather than dismissing their possible paranormality out of hand (Munson, 1985; Rogo, 1974; Snoyman, 1985), although certainly there is scant experimental evidence that psychotic experients do have heightened psi abilities (Greyson, 1977; Rogo, 1975).

People who report parapsychological experiences may well have problems in personality and adjustment of a less extreme type. For example, perhaps OBEs are being used to escape from certain unpleasant aspects of reality that the individual is not prepared to confront. The clinician, therefore, should be alert to possible psychopathological factors underlying parapsychological experiences. By way of illustration, Harary (1982) reports a group therapy case in which a high level of frustration and anxiety was uncovered among workmates who frequently experienced an apparition in their department during the night shift. Again this highlights the importance of exploring the functions played by the parapsychological experience rather than merely labeling the client as psychic or psychotic. It also prompts the point that parapsychologists ethically are obliged to put the needs of an experient ahead of their research interests in the experience.

Even if the therapist believes in the existence of psi, the possibility of psychopathology associated with "pseudo-psi" must be countenanced (Greyson, 1977; McHarg, 1982). For example, some schizophrenics claim that someone is in paranormal control of their mind or that they have extraordinary telepathic powers by which they hear voices talking about them. These cases usually are identifiable by the presence of defective reality testing (Greyson, 1977; Hastings, 1983).

Patients with temporal lobe epilepsy some-times experience bizarre images which they might interpret in parapsychological terms. Belz-Merk (2000) reports that about half of all parapsychological experients who volun-tarily approach a psychological clinic meet diagnostic criteria for a psychological disor-der. Similarly, Weiner (1980, p. 46) com-ments that at least half of the experients who called her laboratory for help had a history of some psychological disturbance. While these parapsychological experiences might not be paranormal, neither are they to be grouped with hoaxers. The individuals con-cerned are very much in need of professional assistance and it would be insensitive of any parapsychologist to have a policy that if a re-ported experience is not likely to be gen-uinely paranormal the inquirer should be shown the door as quickly as possible.

Additionally there arise therapeutic cases which may be regarded as *reactive* in the sense that the individual's anxiety and maladaptive behavior spring from the experience rather than vice versa. Many people are quite disturbed by their parapsychological experience (Hast-ings, 1983; Montanelli & Parra, 2004; Siegel, 1986; Targ, Schlitz & Irwin, 2000; Morris, 1976) and need counseling in order to come to terms with the incident. One of the most common instances of this type is the precog-nitive experience: the experient had a pre-monitory dream of a tragic incident and when the latter actually occurred, felt very guilty for not doing more to prevent the tragedy. Often this sense of responsibility is misguided in that nothing the individual could have done would have prevented or avoided the precognized event. Be this as it may, a useful issue to pur-sue in therapy is the possibility of functions other than intervention that the precognitive experience could be construed to serve. Thus a premonition might be said to have had the purpose of helping the experient to cope with the tragedy when eventually it did occur, or of putting them in a better position to help other affected people to cope.

The NDE is another parapsychological experience that may have disturbing effects on the experient quite apart from the actual threat to life. Although most NDErs are reas-sured by their experience, some are distressed by the command to leave the paradisial realm and to return to their earthly existence (Clark, 1984), and others are frustrated by the experience's ineffability which prevents its profundity being shared with someone else (Greyson & Harris, 1987). Because of the major philosophical and spiritual changes ac-companying an NDE Furn (1987) observes that the NDEr also may feel like a new mem-ber of a cultural minority and may need pro-fessional guidance to adapt emotionally and interpersonally to the "culture shock" of their newly embraced worldview. In other types of cases experients may be upset by a friend's reactions upon hearing about the parapsy-chological experience and some counseling may be required to assist the client's adjust-ment to the secondary effects of the experi-ence upon interpersonal relationships. A more serious variety of reactive case may arise when a person has very frequent parapsy-chological experiences. According to Neppe (1984) such an individual may come to rely upon these experiences as a means of relating to their physical and social environment, with the result that they tend to lose contact with reality to the point of becoming acutely psychotic.

There is a further therapeutic applica-tion of parapsychology that warrants ac-knowledgment and it relates not to people who have had a parapsychological experience but to people who might benefit by having one. For example, you will recall the very profound psychological effects of OBEs and NDEs, particularly with regard to the experi-ent's attitudes to life and death. Whether or not these effects are deemed by others to be delusory they might well be utilized for ther-apeutic purposes. Thus if parapsychologists develop a powerful and reliable technique for the induction of OBEs (or certain types of

OBEs) it could prove of substantial value in counseling programs for terminally ill patients.

A counseling approach to parapsychological experiences clearly raises many considerations of which just a few have been touched on here. As Hastings (1983) observes, there is a great need for both research and training in parapsychological counseling. There are recent indications that interest in this field is growing (Tierney, Coelho & Lamont, in press; Ruttenberg, 2000; White, 1995).

Potential Practical Applications

Parapsychological research may have application in many areas other than the psychological clinic. The *Applied Psi Newsletter* somewhat ambitiously listed potential practical application in the following areas (Mishlove & Kautz, 1982, p. 1):

agriculture and pest control
animal training and interspecies
   communication
contests and gambling
creativity
education and training
entertainment
environmental improvement
executive decision making
finding lost objects
future forecasting
geological exploration
historical investigation
investigative journalism
medicine and dentistry
military intelligence
personnel management
police work
psychotherapy and counseling
safety inspection
scientific discovery
social control
weather prediction and control

To these, other commentators would add dowsing, archeological excavation, and prediction of natural disasters. Furthermore, our previous chapters have reviewed research into direct mental interaction with living systems and psychic healing that clearly has potential application in healthcare. Turning to PK with inanimate systems, Radin (1993) has made the interesting suggestion that neural networks can be used to recognize individuals' PK "signatures" (unique patterns of interaction with random number generators), and provides empirical evidence to support his case. He suggests potential practical applications of such neural networks, for instance a mentally controlled lock, and a psychic switch that might be controlled by a paraplegic (see also Radin, 1997b). We now consider in more detail some areas of potential practical application of psi that have received particular attention from parapsychologists.

Psychic Detection

Can psi be constructively used for the purpose of criminal investigation? There is a long history of criminal cases in which a psychically gifted person is said to have assisted in the apprehension of the perpetrator of the offence (Lyons & Truzzi, 1991). By way of illustration, in 1692 a French wine merchant and his wife were murdered and robbed, and a dowser reportedly used his divining rod to locate and then to identify the three offenders (C. Wilson, 1984). Prior to the twentieth century many alleged cases of psychic detection involved *psychometry:* while holding an object that had been in contact with the victim or the offender, the psychometrist could paranormally obtain information about the crime (Rowe, 1996). Particularly in contemporary cases however, the predominant method of psychic detection involves clairvoyant visions, that is, waking images or dreams about the crime.

There is little in the literature on experimental psi to suggest that psychic abilities would in principle be inapplicable to the investigation of crime. In seeming support of this view are various popular accounts that describe the apparent contribution of a self-professed psychic to the successful solution of a crime (e.g., Friedman, 1982; Lyons & Truzzi, 1991; Tabori, 1974). Such reports have nevertheless been dismissed by skeptical commentators (e.g., Alcock, 1994; Rowe, 1996) as evidentially unsound; that is, it is claimed the reported cases may have well been solved by means that do not involve any paranormal process. Thus, some psychics' "solutions" are said to be imaginative narratives based on rational inferences from what is already known about the crime (as gleaned from reports in the news media and perhaps from police personnel working on the case), on common social trends, and on popular social stereotypes about the characteristics of criminals. In some cases the reported success of a psychic may be attributable to favorable reinterpretation of the predictions after further facts of the case come to light, to confabulatory errors of memory (Alcock, 1994), or indeed, to outright misrepresentation by the psychic (Gordon, 1994; Rowe, 1996) or by the media (Ejvegaard & Johnson, 1981).

Certainly much of the case material popularly proffered for the efficacy of psychic detection comprises relatively informal descriptions of psychic impressions relating to a crime and a superficial, largely subjective assessment of the congruence between these impressions and the subsequently determined facts of the case (Irwin, 2001b). Indeed, the lack of adequate documentation and independent corroboration of the large majority of these cases has made them highly vulnerable to fatal debunking by skeptical commentators (for examples see Hoebens & Truzzi, 1985; Nickell, 1994). It must also be stressed that the anthologies of "psychic detection" cases are highly selective: the relative incidence of valid and invalid psychic solutions of a crime does not seem to have been precisely documented, but the former are

generally conceded to constitute a small minority. Any impression generated by the popularly cited successful cases needs therefore to be set against evidence of the substantial failure of most other psychics' visions to bear unequivocally upon the facts of a given crime (Randi, 1982a).

Of potentially greater evidential value are some attempts to subject psychic detection to critical experimental scrutiny. In some early studies (e.g., Brink, 1960; Tenhaeff, 1955) experimenters invited psychics to use psychometry under laboratory conditions to generate statements about the offender in cases that the police had already solved and for which a conviction had been obtained. The methodology of some of these studies was weak in a few respects; for example, the experimenter sometimes knew the identity of the offender, thereby allowing the possibility that the psychic could capitalize on the experimenter's involuntary facial reactions as a basis for hedging and amending statements about the offender (so-called cold reading techniques; Hyman, 1977). In any event the results obtained by Brink (1960) were null, and although Tenhaeff (1955) reported encouraging observations with a single psychic (Croiset) it is doubtful that these would satisfy the strict criteria required for statistical significance.

More recent studies typically have been more rigorous in methodology and statistical treatment. Two of the principal improvements have been to use a number of self-declared psychic participants rather than one person, and to systematize the measurement of predicted characteristics of the crime and its perpetrator. To date all these studies (O'Keeffe & Alison, 2000; Kocsis, Irwin, Hayes & Nunn, 2000; Reiser & Klyver; 1982; Reiser, Ludwig, Saxe & Wagner, 1979; Wiseman, West & Stemman, 1996) have found that psychics are unable to identify the key characteristics of a crime and the offender beyond the level expected on the basis of chance or on the basis of the application of commonsense and popular social stereotypes about criminals. The current database admittedly rests on a very small sample of criminal cases and thus their generality remains uncertain, but it is fair to say that the efficacy of psychic detection has yet to be soundly demonstrated.

Precognition

A substantial proportion of potential applications concern the phenomenon of precognition. To assess the efficacy of such applications an evaluative program must be designed before the precognized events occur and preferably before the predictions themselves are made. Thus psychics claim to have foreseen events such as the assassination of President Kennedy, but it is very difficult to assess these performances in retrospect: one must ask how many other predictions by these psychics were not fulfilled. Even if predictions in an evaluative program are known in advance they must be sufficiently precise for success and failure to be defined beforehand and there must be some way of estimating the *a priori* likelihood of the precognized events.

Suppose that a sensitive declares, "There will be serious bushfires in the Sydney area next summer." For this prediction to be included in the program, agreement must be reached on the following questions. How serious is "serious"? When does "summer" start and end? What is the extent of "the Sydney area"? Additionally, official records must be consulted to determine the *a priori* probability of this prediction being realized. Thus if Sydney has serious bushfires almost every summer, this prediction would not be worth including in the evaluative program.

Somewhat surprisingly, only a few studies taking the above sorts of precautions have been performed. The subjects of the prediction in these projects have included the time and location of Skylab's return to earth; the time of the release of American hostages in

Iran; the time, location, and magnitude of earthquakes; and the solution of particular crimes. In contrast with the ostensibly spectacular records of psychics' past achievements, the outcomes of these planned and carefully documented investigations have been null in the considerable majority of instances (e.g., Hunter & Derr, 1978; McClenon, 1982a; Reiser, Ludwig, Saxe & Wagner, 1979). Critics would be quick to point out that this confirms their view that psi does not exist, but such a conclusion does not take adequate account of the laboratory research on ESP and PK. Perhaps the conscious control of psi for its use in a specific situation is even more difficult than the data of simplistic laboratory tasks would suggest. Like much of the laboratory research the studies of applied precognition largely seem to lack the elements of personal significance and spontaneity that tend to characterize parapsychological experiences in everyday life.

Financial Gain

Another possible application of psi is in gambling. There are numerous reports of people dreaming which horse would win a major race or having a strong intuitive impression of which outcome to bet on in roulette or dice games. In these circumstances, however, one cannot disentangle the possible operation of psi from that of chance, knowledge, good judgment, and so on (Nash, 1986, p. 67). Research on the application of parapsychology to gambling is meager. A study by Brier and Tyminski (1970) did indicate some extra-chance success in certain "games of chance," but the experimental setup here was highly artificial: participants were not competing but rather cooperating by betting on the option that a majority of the group agreed upon. Another study by Radin and Rebman (1998) studied how lunar cycle, gravitational (tidal) forces and geomagnetic field records predicted daily gaming payout from a Las Vegas casino over a four year period.

These physical variables had been chosen because research elsewhere indicates they might be implicated in psi functioning. Results suggested that payouts were slightly increased on days on or near the full-moon, and reduced on or near the new moon, though not significantly so. Correlations were non-significant for geomagnetic field, and significant for tidal forces, but as the magnitude of the effect is small and the odds are still stacked in favor of the casino, gamblers will nevertheless lose overall.

If psi could be used in real-life gambling it is unlikely to be effective: many players (even unknowingly) may be trying to use psi to their individual advantage with the net effect that nobody's psi is noticeably productive. It must be remembered too that in laboratory psi tasks, the deviation from chance is very small. In gambling a deviation of this magnitude would not be sufficient to compensate for the odds in favor of the casino and in any event would be so small as to hardly bring instant wealth. There is also the daunting prospect that one might prove to be a psi-misser in these situations! Finally, it may be noted that the states of consciousness typically associated with gambling are not those thought to be conducive to psi. In short, the prospects for applying parapsychology to gambling do not look promising.

A similar conclusion may apply to the possibility of using psi in planning investments on the stock market. While there is some experimental evidence suggestive of precognition of stock prices (Targ, Katra, Brown & Wiegand, 1995), in a real-life context this phenomenon presumably would be found both in holders of the stock and in potential buyers, with no net advantage to either group.

Psi Training

To this point we have been considering applied parapsychology in terms of the intentional use of psi to practical ends. The results of parapsychological research also might be said to have been applied in the development of certain programs for "training psi ability." Little research effort has been devoted to the experimental evaluation of these multifaceted programs, but one study that gave volunteers various purportedly psi-conducive exercises to enhance focusing of attention, self-esteem, imagery, and relaxation, found no evidence of improved or above-chance scoring in controlled psi tests (Delanoy, Morris & Watt, in press). To be sure, there are some programs that superficially appear to entail legitimate extrapolations from the data of parapsychological experiments (Mishlove, 1983), but it is doubtful that the programs' customers are fully aware of the degree of replicability of the original experiments or of the fact that the criterion for a successful psi experiment is not perfectly accurate performance but rather performance beyond chance expectation at the .05 level. To this it must be added that many psi development programs appear more commercially than scientifically inspired. Again, it is feasible that the programs have diverse social, educational, and therapeutic benefits of which the preceding comments fail to take due account.

Military

Some national governments are interested in the prospect of utilizing parapsychological research findings for military purposes. In America, for example, the government for over twenty years funded research on the potential application of remote viewing for intelligence-gathering. The work was eventually declassified and expert evaluations of the program were made public (Hyman, 1995; Utts, 1995). Russian attention to military applications has been documented by Ebon (1983). It is said that world superpowers have been investigating the use of ESP and the OBE in espionage and of PK for sabotage (e.g., of radar equipment or missile guidance systems). Some reports of government involvement in these applications may be instances of disinformation, the objective being to incite rival nations to waste some of their defense budget in monitoring parapsychological research. Many parapsychologists nevertheless are disturbed by the idea of their field being subverted towards military ends. Furthermore, if parapsychologists provide evidence of direct mental interaction with living systems, or of psychic healing, there is no logical reason why such abilities might not be directed towards harmful rather than therapeutic ends (Watt, Ravenscroft & McDermott, 1999). On the other hand the inability to control the phenomena and the minuteness of effect typical of psi experiments give little reason to believe that military applications, or indeed many other mooted practical applications, could be successful in the near future. Some commentators (e.g., Jahn, 1984, p. 134) nevertheless believe that a greater emphasis upon practical applications could improve parapsychology's reception among other scientists. The status of parapsychology in the wider scientific community is addressed in the final chapter.

KEY TERMS AND CONCEPTS

psi in therapy
hoaxers
psi in psychopathology
pseudo-psi
psychopathology in psi

reactive cases
practical applications
psychic detection
psi training programs
military applications

STUDY QUESTIONS

1. As a practicing psychologist how would you be inclined to counsel the person in each of the following cases? If possible, try this as a role-playing exercise with you and a fellow student alternately taking the role of therapist and that of client.

(a) A man is uncertain of his sanity after having experienced an apparition of a sister who is living in a distant city.

(b) While meditating a woman had a spontaneous impression of being outside her body and she is curious about her experience.

(c) A man had a precognitive dream of a major accident to a much-loved aunt and now the accident actually has occurred, he feels guilty that he did not warn his aunt beforehand.

(d) A young man living in a homosexual relationship claims that their house is haunted, loud raps being heard in the walls during the night.

(e) A woman had a vision of a friend's accidental death. She thought initially that perhaps she harbored some unrecognized anger toward the friend. When her friend subsequently was killed in an accident, however, the woman began to fear that in some way the vision had caused the death.

(f) A man reports that malfunctions of electrical goods in his home are due to a malicious neighbor's use of PK.

(g) With the objective of securing a publishing contract a woman wants you to attest to her ability to communicate mediumistically with the spirit of John Lennon.

(h) A man reports that he had the impression of smelling his late mother's perfume, upon which he was possessed by her spirit and caused to suffer a fit of convulsions.

(i) A woman who has been a client of yours for some weeks describes a dream in which you were going to marry her but instead you sent your brother to the ceremony; in reality you were thinking you might refer this client to a medical colleague for supplementary treatment.

(j) Following an NDE a hospital patient admits to feeling resentful about being "sent back" to a life of physical pain and even thought fleetingly of suicide as a means of returning to "that beautiful place beyond death."

(k) Under hypnosis during a "quit smoking" program a young man spontaneously "becomes" a Jewish prisoner in a Nazi concentration camp during World War II and he vividly enacts the terrible ordeal of being tortured. After returning him to normal waking consciousness you relate the experience to him and he asks if it arose from a previous life.

2. How might psi be applied in real-life settings? What are the current prospects of such application?

3. In what manner can a psi-development program be evaluated? Is it sufficient that such a program be based entirely on the findings of laboratory experimentation by parapsychologists?

17

EVALUATION OF PARAPSYCHOLOGY AS A SCIENTIFIC ENTERPRISE

In this the final chapter of the text it is appropriate to examine parapsychology from the perspective of the sociology of science. As previous chapters have indicated there has been encouraging progress in the experimental investigation of some parapsychological phenomena and the resulting data seem to show substantial coherence despite numerous lacunae. Although an adequate experimental paradigm is lacking for research into many other parapsychological experiences, even here an impressive body of phenomenological data has been accumulated. In short, future prospects for parapsychological research appear exciting if not guaranteed.

But how is parapsychology currently regarded in the broader context of scientific enterprise? Two general issues arising from this question are considered here. The first of these concerns the efforts of parapsychologists to establish their discipline as a legitimate science; the second issue is the nature of the scientific establishment's responses to these efforts.

Efforts to Establish Parapsychology as a Science

Historically speaking there has been a clear progression in parapsychology from the collection of anecdotal material to the experimental investigation of laboratory analogues of psi phenomena. Thus a major element in parapsychologists' efforts to put their discipline on a scientific footing is the recourse to scientific method. Arguably J. B. Rhine's major contribution to parapsychology was to appreciate the importance of using the investigative mode of the established sciences in order to inquire into the authenticity and nature of ostensibly paranormal events. Certainly people before Rhine had conducted some elementary experiments on ESP, but in the societies for psychical research where much of the research at that time was being undertaken the development of laboratory analogues of psi phenomena was seen as a minor and indeed somewhat peripheral activity. Rhine's pursuit of a sustained and cohesive experimental program of ESP and PK research, with its attention to the identification and control of artifactual variables and its probabilistic evaluation of data, therefore constituted a significant step toward the goal of gaining scientific status for parapsychology. This initiative has been maintained by contemporary parapsychologists through reliance upon the increasingly sophisticated methods of modern conventional science.

Along with scientific procedures the technological hardware of modern science has been incorporated into psi research. Computers and REGs not only permit tighter experimental methods but also to some degree bring the feature of technical precision that is a hallmark of contemporary science. For example, extrasensory targets can be selected under known parameters of randomness and displayed at the moment chosen by the experimenter or by the participant for an exactly defined interval; the participant's response can be recorded and compared to the target without human bias; and all manner of information on response latency and neurophysiological activity can be plotted across the supposed period of psi processing.

But there is much more to the practice of a scientific discipline than methods and hardware. Science is essentially a social activity. It is undertaken by groups of people who impose upon themselves certain codes of conduct or rules for interacting among themselves and for promoting their interests. Thus the contemporary world of professional science is highly institutionalized.

One consequence of this state of affairs is that it does matter where research is carried out. To be truly scientific, experimental research must be performed in a specialized setting called a "laboratory." If the work has (potential or actual) commercial application it may be conducted in a privately owned facility, but in any event a field of research that has any scientific merit must be represented in the laboratories of recognized universities. In the view of the scientific establishment an area of activity that lacks such representation at the university level cannot be regarded as a "proper" science. In this context it can be

said that another important facet of Rhine's contribution was in undertaking his program of research in a university department. The significance of university representation has continued to be recognized with a number of academics pursuing parapsychological research particularly on campuses in America and in Europe. Indeed, over the last two decades some new European sources of funding for parapsychology have seen a substantial increase in European parapsychological research so that the center of gravity for the field has swung from the United States to Europe. Another characteristic of institutionalized science is that of professionalism. Any genuine science is conducted largely by professionals who specialize in their area of expertise. While amateurs did make acknowledged contributions to conventional science in the nineteenth century, this soon changed and today a predominance of amateurs in a field of interest usually would be construed by orthodox scientists as indicative of the field's status as a craft rather than a science. In its early days psychical research too was performed, often on a part-time basis, by amateurs, people who saw such work virtually as a recreational pursuit. Part of the effort to achieve scientific status for modern parapsychology has been directed to the growth of professionalism, the full-time employment of suitably trained personnel in parapsychological research (at least to the extent that available funding and resources permit).

Allied to this feature is the formation of professional societies. In recognized areas of scientific research formal societies are established with the general objectives of promoting the field and facilitating productive interaction among people involved in research. Such societies tend to set high academic qualifications for membership and to accord recognition to major contributors to the discipline by way of higher levels of membership (fellowships) and/or the conferring of special awards each year. A society of this type has been established for parapsychologists: it is called the Parapsychological Association and was founded in 1957. In recent years its membership has remained relatively static at approximately 110 people, with another 100 or so listed as associate members; this membership admittedly is very small in comparison with that of most scientific societies. The Parapsychological Association's qualifications for full membership are that the person (a) hold a doctorate or have a professional affiliation with a recognized academic institution or research organization; (b) have prepared a paper on some aspect of parapsychology that in the opinion of the Association's Council is of high professional caliber and which has been published in a scientific journal or which merits such publication; and (c) be nominated by two members of the Association and elected by a majority vote of the governing Council. (The lower grade of membership, the Associate, may be granted to a person with a bachelor's degree and with no publications.) Interaction among researchers is encouraged through various publications and an annual convention. The Association annually confers a Career Achievement Award and an Exceptional Contribution Award.

In recent times one of the recognized functions of a scientific society has been to devise guidelines concerning the ethics of experimentation in its field. This has been of particular importance in the context of experiments with human or animal participants. The American Psychological Association, for example, has documented in some detail the ethical considerations that apply to psychological research. Similarly, the Parapsychological Association in 1977 established its own Committee on Professional Standards and Ethics with the objective of developing guidelines on these matters for its members. Advice is given on the protection of the rights of participants in parapsychological research with specific reference to the issues of informed consent to participate in a study, confidentiality, deception about the study's pur-

pose, post-test discussion about the study ("debriefing"), professional treatment of human participants, and humane handling of animal subjects.

Other topics addressed are the misuse of research funds; openness in the conduct and reporting of research; acknowledgment of contributors to the study in the text of the research report and in assigning authorship; possible conflicts of interest in acting as a referee on a manuscript submitted for publication; ethics in criticism of other researchers' work; fraud by experimenters or participants; dissemination of information through the public news media; and the maintenance of parapsychology's professional image. Parapsychologists generally have shown themselves to be alert to ethical issues (Gregory, 1982; Stanford, 1988a,b; Thomson, 1986).

In addition to a discipline having its own society it is usual for this society to be affiliated with more general scientific associations to give it a voice in the formulation and promotion of science policy. In the United States this general body is the prestigious American Association for the Advancement of Science (AAAS). The Parapsychological Association was admitted to the AAAS in 1969 (McClenon, 1984). The annual AAAS convention provides parapsychologists with a forum for presenting their research to scientists from other fields and for advancing parapsychology in the context of the AAAS's lobbying on national science policy.

Science is an international activity. Scientific disciplines therefore are not constrained to any one cultural outlook but rather, are represented in numerous countries with a variety of cultural backgrounds. Parapsychological research also is conducted internationally. Parapsychology is represented in some 30 different countries (Angoff & Shapin, 1973; Krippner, 1992). Of all nations the United Kingdom has the largest number of active researchers, but parapsychological research centers or individual parapsychologists are to be found also in such countries as the United States, Sweden, Central and South America (Parra, 1997; Rueda, 1991; Zangari & Machado, 2001), China (Zha & McConnell, 1991), Japan (McClenon, 1989), Australia (Irwin, 1988c; Keil, 1981), India, Iceland (Gissurarson & Haraldsson, 2001), Israel, Spain (Alvarado, 1984; Rueda, 1991), France, Belgium, the Netherlands, Austria, Germany, Switzerland, Italy, Russia, and South Africa. There certainly are some differences of approach that reflect national political and scientific philosophies (e.g., Hess, 1989a), and language barriers may inhibit communication in some respects (Alvarado, 1989c), but parapsychology nonetheless can fairly be said to have wide international representation.

Another characteristic of a scientific discipline is the publication of specialist journals devoted to the subject matter of the field. These journals permit not only the communication of theoretical and empirical research to interested persons but also the enhancement of the status of the area as a legitimate domain for scientific endeavor. Papers submitted to these journals for publication must fulfill certain requirements in their presentation of methodology and data and are subjected to scrutiny by a panel of qualified referees for evaluation as a substantial scientific contribution worthy of publication. In psychology the earliest journals were very broad in scope, containing papers on the whole range of conventional psychological inquiry; today there are numerous highly specialized journals each of which addresses a particular area of psychological research (e.g., imagery, hypnosis, memory, verbal learning, personality, and so on).

Parapsychological research for much of its history had as its only outlet the journals of a few societies for psychical research. In 1937 Rhine established the *Journal of Parapsychology*; today this and the societies' journals constitute the major channels for the dissemination of research in the field. More recently some other major English-language

journals have been established, including the *European Journal of Parapsychology* (from 1975) and the *Journal of Scientific Exploration* (from 1987). Each of these journals observes the rigid code for acceptance of papers that characterizes orthodox scientific journals. Additionally there are a few more specialized publications. For example, *Theta* (since 1963) primarily provides a forum for research pertinent to the survival hypothesis, the *Journal of Near-Death Studies* (formerly *Anabiosis* and published since 1981) features papers on the NDE and related phenomena, and *Exceptional Human Experience* (formerly *Parapsychology Abstracts International* and published since 1983) includes reports of anomalous experiences and commentaries on their phenomenological investigation. Journals in languages other than English include *Cauadernos de Parapsicología, Psi Comunicación, Quaderni di Parapsicologia, Revista Argentina de Psicología Paranormal, Revista Brasileira de Parapsicologia, Revue de Parapsychologie, Revue Francaise de Psychotronique, Tijdschrift voor Parapsychologie,* and *Zeitschrift für Parapsychologie und Grenzgebiete der Psychologie*.

Representation of a discipline in a university setting also is important for training aspiring professionals. The perseverance of academic parapsychologists has seen the establishment of parapsychology courses in many universities and colleges in America, Britain, continental Europe, Australia, India and other countries. One other feature of a genuine science should be mentioned, distasteful though it is. Occasionally professional scientists break the rules of the game and have to be expelled from the field. Such an incident arose in parapsychology with the Levy affair in 1974 (McConnell, 1987, Chapter 11; Rhine, 1974, 1975). Dr. W. J. Levy had worked in Rhine's laboratory for a few years and was interested primarily in psi research with animals (anpsi). In 1974 some students observed Levy tinkering with the automatic recording apparatus being used in one of the laboratory's anpsi experiments. Secret recordings of the data were arranged and on comparison with Levy's reported results, discrepancies were found. When confronted by Rhine, Levy acknowledged his fraudulent activity and was dismissed. Parapsychologists known to be planning to use any of Levy's published work in their papers immediately were advised not to do so. Rhine (1974) published a statement in the *Journal of Parapsychology* giving the details of the affair and advising that *all* of Levy's publications should now be regarded as unacceptable (although Levy claimed he resorted to fraudulent manipulation only when his recent experiments yielded nonsignificant data). In the Levy case parapsychology was shown to be capable of keeping its house in order and not to be inclined to cover up indiscretions for appearance's sake.

In many respects, therefore, parapsychologists have striven to observe the ideals of scientific endeavor and to ensure that their discipline possesses the trappings of an authentic science.

Responses of Critics

How have members of the scientific establishment responded to the efforts of parapsychologists to put their field on a scientific footing? Several anonymous surveys (Evans, 1973; McClenon, 1982b, 1984; Wagner & Monnet, 1979; Warner, 1952; Warner & Clark, 1938) consistently have indicated that while many scientists do not accept unequivocally the existence of psi phenomena they do acknowledge that parapsychological hypotheses should be permitted evaluation in a conventionally scientific manner. The views of the "silent majority," however, are not always reflected in the voices of the scientific establishment, and in science it is the elite groups that wield the greatest political power (Broad & Wade, 1982, Ch. 5).

Some scientists reject parapsychology as a science simply because they can not accept

its empirical findings. On occasion this is tantamount to naked prejudice. For example, the prominent psychologist Donald Hebb wrote in 1951, "why do we not accept ESP as a psychological fact? Rhine has offered us enough evidence to have convinced us on almost any other issue.... I cannot see what other basis my colleagues have for rejecting it.... My own rejection of [Rhine's] views is — in the literal sense — prejudice" (Hebb, 1951, p. 45). And in 1958 the vice president of the AAAS recalled the remarks of the physicist Hermann von Helmholtz: "I cannot believe it. Neither the testimony of all the Fellows of the Royal Society, nor even the evidence of my own senses would lead me to believe in the transmission of thought from one person to another independently of the recognized channels of sensation. It is clearly impossible" (Birge, 1958, cited by Collins & Pinch, 1979, p. 244). More recently the skeptical commentator Ray Hyman (1996) admitted he could not find any methodological flaws in a series of psi experiments, yet he still refused to concede their support for the psi hypothesis in part on the ground that "it is impossible in principle to say that any particular experiment or experimental series is completely free from possible flaws" (p. 40). This *a priori* assumption that the experimental findings of parapsychologists "just can't be true" and hence must be unscientific persists among the scientific elite and among psychologists in particular, scientists in most other fields being rather more receptive (Alcock, 1975; McClenon, 1982b, 1984; McConnell & Clark, 1991; Wagner & Monnet, 1979). The dogmatic presumption that parapsychological data can *never* be persuasive is sometimes referred to as "pseudo-skepticism" (e.g., Meynell, 1996) because, contrary to the spirit of true scientific skepticism, an element of doubt is never entertained. Thus, a pseudo-skeptical worldview has drawn some commentators into making such extravagant assertions as "every claim to persistent, subtle but statistically detectable psychic phenomena has been refuted" (Hacking, 1993, p. 591).

Other commentators reject psi research on grounds derived from the philosophy of science. For example, one such principle is known as Occam's (or Ockham's) Razor and proposes that if two hypotheses account equally well for a given set of data the simplest or most parsimonious should be accepted. Thus, without any regard to the quality of the available data ESP may be ignored under the principle of Occam's Razor because any orthodox alternative hypothesis (fraud, sensory leakage, poor experimental design, etc.) would have the advantage of not positing any new mode of information transfer. By way of illustration of this strategy, Campbell (1971, p. 95) argued, "The problem of fraud is that we know men (sic) can, and do, cheat and dissemble, but we do not know that they have paranormal capacities.... So for any result in psychical research which can be explained either by appeal to paranormal powers or by the hypothesis of fraud, the explanation by fraud is the more rational one." If taken to an extreme, application of this principle would preclude almost any further scientific discovery.

A few scientists have sought to dismiss the experimental literature of parapsychology as utterly fraudulent (e.g, Price, 1955). Their motivation in doing so seems to be little else than the *a priori* conviction that parapsychological phenomena are impossible. There nevertheless has been some evidential support for the argument of fraud. The Levy affair in 1974 is perhaps the most notable instance. Prior to that, in the 1930s the British parapsychologist S. G. Soal had conducted numerous ESP tests in an effort to replicate the work of Rhine and of Jephson but had been so unsuccessful that he became utterly pessimistic about the viability of an experimental approach to psi. On the urging first of Robert Thouless and then of Whately Carington (Mauskopf & McVaugh, 1980, p. 237) however, Soal in 1939 reprocessed his

data in a search for displacement effects. Two of his 160 subjects, Gloria Stewart and Basil Shackleton, were indeed found to exhibit such effects, that is, there was a significant level of psi hitting on the target before or on the target after the intended one (Soal & Bateman, 1954). Further tests with these people reportedly confirmed the pattern of performance. That the displacement was temporal in nature was supported by the fact that when Shackleton was required to increase his rate of response psi hitting was found not on the target for the following trial but on that for two trials ahead. But in 1978 a British researcher, Betty Markwick (1978), reported that in comparing S. G. Soal's set of ESP targets with the table of random numbers purported to be the basis of target selection in his experiments with the subject Shackleton, some serious discrepancies were evident, on nearly all occasions with the effect of enhancing Shackleton's ESP score. Although there is a growing view among scientists that fraud is a relatively likely feature of the operation of a human social institution such as science (John, 1991), the exposure of fraudulent research by Soal and by Levy had a devastating effect on parapsychologists' confidence in each other's findings in the 1980s (Blackmore, 1989).

That some parapsychologists have sometimes cheated is undeniable. What is equivocal is the notion that all parapsychological research is fraudulent, or indeed that there is any justification in Neher's (1980, p. 142) assertion of an unusually high incidence of fraud in this field. Fraud occurs in all branches of science (Broad & Wade, 1982; Kohn, 1987; St. James-Roberts, 1976).

That parapsychology has relatively more frequent cases of experimenter fraud than does psychology is an impression based in part on different modal reactions to such fraud between the two disciplines. When parapsychologists identify an instance of fraud it is given extensive publicity, such is their determination to maintain the integrity of the discipline; indeed the only reason Hansel (1966) was able to cite some attested instances of fraud in ESP experiments was that parapsychologists themselves had published detailed reports of these instances.

On the other hand there is a much stronger tendency among psychologists to turn a blind eye to fraud in their field, the posthumous exposure of Burt's purported deception notwithstanding (Hearnshaw, 1979); their assumption seems to be that the experiment probably would have turned out in the reported manner anyway, so readers are not really being misled (Broad & Wade, 1982, p. 80). In parapsychology there is much effort directed too to the replication of experimental findings and this can assist in the identification of fraudulent practice. Much less interest in experimental replication is shown by psychologists: if the data are theoretically or intuitively plausible academic psychologists today rarely bother with simple replications, if only for the reason that psychology journals generally will not publish a report of such a study. Without routine experimental replications there is no safeguard against experimenter fraud; most exposures of fraud in the orthodox sciences consequently have come through personal disclosure (Broad & Wade, 1982, p. 73). In short, the argument of frequent fraud in parapsychology seems more politically than evidentially founded.

Some attacks on parapsychologists have focused not so much on their integrity as on their professional competence. Hansel's (1966, 1980) scenarios of possible fraud in selected experiments typically portray the experimenter as inept in attempting to establish experimental control. This is not to say that parapsychological experiments have been criticized unjustly; methodological weaknesses can be nominated as readily for these studies (see Akers, 1984) as for the experiments in many areas of orthodox psychology, for example. But skeptics such as Diaconis (1978), Gardner (1981) and Randi (1975, 1982b) maintain that parapsychologists' experimental control is so poor that participants are able to use conjuring tricks to achieve above-chance performance.

A majority of parapsychologists now appreciate the point that in designing some of their experiments the professional advice of a magician could be helpful, and indeed many parapsychologists have sought consultations of this sort (Hansen, 1985, 1990). Nevertheless the skeptics' generalized slur upon parapsychologists' professional competence still rankles. The issue became acute with Randi's (1983a,b) so-called Project Alpha in which Randi, a professional stage magician, arranged for two young conjurers to present themselves as psychics at a parapsychological laboratory (Shaw, 1996). According to Randi the parapsychologists were deceived effectively by the young men during a series of supposedly controlled experiments. The parapsychologists themselves declared that the conjurers had not been successful in tightly controlled experiments; it was acknowledged however, that in some exploratory studies fraudulent performances had been taken by the research team as "encouraging" results and had been reported as such in unrefereed conference research briefs.

Much of the subsequent debate over Randi's hoax has concerned the ethics of the procedure (Thalbourne, 1995b; Truzzi, 1987), although it must be remembered that Randi is a showman and thereby he is not bound by the professional ethics of scientists. Project Alpha has been constructive in reminding parapsychologists that they need to be especially wary in working with people who volunteer themselves as "psychics." On the other hand the hoax certainly did not show parapsychologists as a group to be incompetent in research. From the perspective of the sociology of science Project Alpha is noteworthy in instancing one form of skeptics' attempts to "debunk" parapsychological research.

Some critics (e.g., Hyman, 1980) have argued for the need to respond to parapsychology in a sober and proper manner, but nonetheless a common tactic of skeptics is the use of ridicule. As Meynell (1996, p. 25) observes, some skeptics are not above "subjecting to public contempt and ridicule those who sincerely report evidence which is not to their liking." Parapsychological phenomena are derided as nonsensical and primitive folk beliefs and parapsychological research is belittled as occultism in pseudoscientific garb. This approach is especially characteristic of the Committee for Skeptical Inquiry (CSI, formerly CSICOP). CSI is a group of people originally founded to examine objectively the evidence for paranormal phenomena (Frazier, 1996), but it has maintained an inflexible stance against research into the paranormal (Hansen, 1992), some of its affiliates even resorting to deception in experimental reports (Pinch & Collins, 1984); many of its more evenhanded members consequently have resigned. The most vocal members of CSICOP are journalists, magicians, and philosophers rather than scientists (Hansen, 2001).

Other subversive strategies also are used by skeptical commentators. Articles published in the *Humanist* and in CSI's own periodical the *Skeptical Inquirer* (see Frazier, 1981, 1986, 1991) amalgamate parapsychological research with astrology, vampires, UFOs, pyramid power, numerology, the Bermuda triangle, witchcraft, the Tarot, the Abominable Snowman and the like, encouraging an impression of parapsychology's guilt by association (see also Hines, 2003; Park, 2000). Parapsychology has been depicted by some skeptics as a spiritualist or occultist movement seeking to maintain popular support by adopting a facade of scientific methodology; for example, the discipline is said to be a "pseudoscience" (Alcock, 1981), "voodoo science" (Park, 2000), and "a prime example of magical thinking" (Bunge, 1991, p. 136), its researchers "closet occultists" (Romm, 1977), and its concepts "a reversion to a pre-scientific religio-mystical tradition" (Moss & Butler, 1978, p. 1077). The results

of parapsychological research are dismissed out of hand or are patently misrepresented. Bunge (1991, p. 133), for example, makes the bald declaration, "all of the well-designed parapsychological experiments have produced negative results." Similarly, in a major report commissioned at the request of the US Congress Hyman (1995, p. 325) asserted, "Only parapsychology, among the fields of inquiry claiming scientific status, lacks a cumulative database."

Although parapsychologists deplore these rhetorical devices the fact of the matter is that this is how scientific controversy is waged. As Feyerabend (1975) maintains, it is not so much the logic of the case that determines the outcome of a scientific controversy but rather the rhetorical skills of the advocates for each side.

Other more specific criticisms of parapsychology have been noted in earlier chapters. Some scientists reject the ESP data because while the results may be statistically significant the deviation from chance is so small that it is not convincing of an extrasensory access to information. Others believe that parapsychology cannot be accorded the status of a science as long as it lacks a widely endorsed theory of its phenomena (Churchland, 1987; Flew, 1980). Still other commentators maintain that parapsychology is not a science because its experiments are not guaranteed to be replicable upon demand (Beloff, 1994). Undoubtedly there is a need to build upon existing findings in a more systematic and cumulative way, but this is largely because progress is seriously hampered by a lack of funding and research posts. It is worth remembering that it has been estimated that the total human and financial resources devoted to parapsychology since 1882 is equivalent to the resources available to sustain psychological research in the United States for a mere two months (Schouten, 1993).

Possibly these aspects of parapsychology could be interpreted as characteristic of a young science, one that has yet to achieve the desired level of control over its phenomena. But again, perhaps psi phenomena are inherently weak, capricious, or little open to conscious production or use (Beloff, 1985; Kennedy, 2003; von Lucadou, 1995). Certainly in recent years there are indications that theories of psi are becoming more viable and that experimental findings may be becoming more replicable. Many parapsychologists had hoped that meta-analyses of the findings of psi experiments would silence critics' claims on the issue of replicability (Krippner et al., 1993); when this did not happen, parapsychologists seemingly abandoned much of their effort to assure conventional scientists on this point (Hess, 1993). In the view of Evans (1996, p. 75), "parapsychologists should realize that it is futile to try to convince some of their skeptical opponents." Similarly, Zingrone (2002) has argued that in the past parapsychologists have been too ready to pay attention to skeptical rhetoric. A regrettable consequence of these reactions is that the rival camps are becoming more insular, with each group antagonistic towards the other but simply ignoring the other's criticisms of themselves, thereby dampening the prospects for fruitful interactive dialog which is the essence of constructive scientific debate. As Alcock (2003, p. 30) observed, discussion of the status of parapsychological research may be becoming "a *dialogue aux sourds,* a dialogue of the deaf." Utts makes the same point, saying "There is little benefit in continuing experiments designed to offer proof, since there is little more to be offered to anyone who does not accept the current collection of data" (1995, p. 290).

It is not impertinent to note that the above criticisms of parapsychology might equally be applicable to other accepted areas of scientific research. In psychology, for example, many experimental results comprise small but statistically significant effects, and often the replicability of these effects is either poor or untested. This is not to say that

effect size and repeatability are unimportant, but merely that critics' emphasis upon them in the parapsychology debate is fundamentally for rhetorical purposes (McClenon, 1984, pp. 89–91). One cannot help but feel that many psychologists' antagonism toward parapsychological research is in some measure a projection of anxieties over their own discipline.

The motivations of parapsychology's critics have been the object of considerable speculation (e.g., LeShan, 1966; McConnell, 1977; Wren-Lewis, 1974). Critics undoubtedly believe in the rationality of their case against parapsychology, yet this in itself seems inadequate to account for the belligerence and vehemence of their attacks. Although some parapsychologists regard the implications of psi phenomena to be so far-reaching as to augur a major revolution in materialistic science (Tart, 2003), there is little indication that critics see the fabric of science to be under serious threat and thus this would not appear to be a significant motive.

Tart (1982) proposes that the critics' behavior is fueled by a very strong unconscious emotion, a "fear of psi." Many people are concerned that if psi really were to exist, social interaction would be disrupted, their personal privacy invaded, and their independence open to unfair manipulation by others. In contemplating the possible existence of psi one skeptic was moved to comment, "But what chaos we would have. There would, of course, be no privacy, since by extrasensory perception one could see even into people's minds.... If most people could foresee the future, how would life be with millions of people all attempting to change present circumstances so as to optimize their personal futures?" (Alcock, 1981, p. 191). For such people it is too awful that psi should exist, so its existence simply must not be conceded. In support of Tart's hypothesis that critics are motivated by a fear of psi, Irwin (1985c) reports a significant relationship between a measure of the fear of psi and the respondent's attitude to the appropriateness of parapsychological research. There is considerable scope for further research into the psychodynamics of attitudes to parapsychological research.

Criticism is intrinsic to academic science, of course (Merton, 1973), and this fact is appreciated by parapsychologists themselves (Radin, 1997a). Without dialog, camps can become increasingly polarized, and the potential benefits of constructive mutual criticism are lost (Watt, in press). Criticism plays an important role in the refinement of theories and empirical techniques and thereby serves to stimulate further, more incisive, research. Indeed, some skeptical analyses of parapsychological research have proved very constructive (e.g., Hyman, 1985; Hyman & Honorton, 1986). Furthermore, some topics in parapsychology, such as experimenter effects, can particularly benefit from a collaborative approach between advocates and counter-advocates (e.g., Schlitz, Wiseman, Watt & Radin, 2006). On the other hand, the scientific establishment's reactions to parapsychology tend to go further than this in using criticisms as grounds for maintaining parapsychology's marginal status and denying it the privileges of a scientific discipline. That is, certain activities of skeptical scientists seem designed to create and maintain a cultural boundary between parapsychology and the rest of science (Hess, 1993).

One instance of this is the inhibition of parapsychologists' access to orthodox journals. Publications such as *Science* and *Nature* have been shown to be extremely unwilling to publish articles favoring parapsychological concepts (Collins & Pinch, 1979, pp. 257–258; McClenon, 1984, pp. 114–118; Rockwell, 1979). One fascinating documentation of this is provided by Honorton et al. (1975). Honorton submitted to *Science* a report of a study on experimenter effects in ESP. After it had been revised in the light of earlier comments, the manuscript was scrutinized by four referees, three of whom favored its publication. The dissenting referee clearly was not familiar with parapsychological research,

being unable, for example, to countenance the observation of a mean ESP score that was significantly *below* chance. The editors of *Science* decided not to publish the paper.

Those articles that are accepted for publication in *Science* or in *Nature* frequently are diluted by negative comments made in an accompanying editorial or in a commentary by scientists outside the field (Collins & Pinch, 1979, pp. 258–259); often such commentaries do not appear to have been subjected to the usual editorial processes. Psychology journals also appear to publish a higher proportion of unsuccessful psi experiments than do parapsychological journals (Billig, 1972), while in introductory psychology texts the tendency is either to ignore parapsychological research altogether (Child, 1985; Irwin, 1991b; Lamal, 1989) or to describe only weak and outdated studies (McClenon, Roig, Smith & Ferrier, 2003; Rogo, 1980; Roig, Icochea & Cuzzucoli, 1991).

Recently, however, parapsychological papers reporting evidence for psi (Bem & Honorton, 1994; Storm & Ertel, 2001) were accepted for publication in the prestigious *Psychological Bulletin*, and several other papers have appeared in the *British Journal of Psychology* (e.g., Roe, 1999; Schmidt, Schneider, Utts, & Walach, 2004). Some parapsychologists have interpreted this acceptance as a suggestion of an emerging evenhandedness toward parapsychological research reports among the editors of mainstream psychological journals. On the basis of past experience, other parapsychologists do not share this optimistic outlook, and it must be said that the majority of papers on parapsychological phenomena accepted for publication in the above journals tend to be concerned with the psychology of paranormal belief, or null psi results. It is also discouraging that despite the appearance of parapsychological papers in high profile psychology journals, a recent survey found that 40 percent of introductory psychology textbooks failed to mention parapsychology (McClenon et al., 2003).

Parapsychologists' access to orthodox journals is, of course, a major issue. Parapsychological journals typically have a very small circulation and are rarely read by mainstream scientists. Publication of parapsychological research in orthodox journals therefore would serve to bring such research to the attention of the wider scientific community, and this in turn may have a significant bearing on the acceptance of the discipline by other scientists (Alvarado, 2003). In addition, publication in key orthodox journals could well be prestigious and thereby have consequences for a parapsychologist's promotion within the university system. Parapsychologists' common reliance on lower status outlets for their research (Martin, 1998) may therefore be disadvantageous for their career prospects.

Restrictions also are placed on funds for parapsychological research. Committees that assess research proposals and allocate public funds to them typically have been found to be unsympathetic to parapsychology. The involvement of prominent skeptics in the National Research Council's dismissive assessment of parapsychological research (Druckman & Swets, 1988) may have had serious consequences for future research funding in this field (Palmer, Honorton & Utts, 1989). Even where a university finances much of its own research activity, parapsychological research might not be granted a reasonable level of financial support. Some funds may be available from private sources but limits frequently are imposed on the sorts of investigations that may be conducted under the auspices of these sources; for example, the terms of the grant may constrain the researcher to look into some aspect of the survival hypothesis. In addition, there are several instances in which the administrators of these funding bodies amended the originally designated purpose of the fund so as to exclude support for parapsychological research (Hansen, 2001, pp. 197–198). Thus, a number of parapsychological research programs have been undertaken in privately funded

laboratories that proved to have a frustratingly short life. This may be one factor in the trend for many researchers to withdraw from the field after a relatively brief involvement.

In the university setting there are many other obstacles placed in the way of those who wish to pursue parapsychological research. According to Hansen (2001, p. 185), "Sociologists, psychologists and folklorists are allowed to study *beliefs* about paranormal events, but there is a taboo against attempting to verify their reality." In academia such interests may substantially harm one's chances of promotion, and there continue to be cases of academics being dismissed (Cornwell, 1997) or ostracized (Hastings, 2002) for engaging in parapsychological research. Bem (1996, cited by Trocco, 2002, p. 35) has cautioned, "There are only two kinds of people who should work on this [i.e., parapsychological research]: undergraduates and tenured professors. Everyone else is at risk." Further, there are few openings for academic parapsychologists. Of those Australian academics currently active in parapsychological research or teaching, *none* was appointed originally in this field. There may also be opposition to the teaching of parapsychology in universities and colleges, despite nominal endorsement of the principle of academic freedom in these institutions (Hansen, 1992; Hess, 1993). McCormick (1987) reports a case of the cancellation of parapsychology courses at the University of Hawaii after pressure from a skeptical group affiliated with CSI. Similar events have occurred on other campuses (Lederer & Singer, 1983). The lack of adequate formal acknowledgment of the field on college campuses severely hinders progress in parapsychology and inhibits recruitment of new people to the discipline. On the other hand, a growing number of universities (e.g., in the UK the Universities of Edinburgh, Liverpool Hope, and Northampton) have been open and supportive to parapsychology. At Edinburgh alone over 100 undergraduate student projects and 20 doctoral theses on parapsychological topics were supervised by the late Professor Robert Morris, and the late Dr John Beloff also supervised a number of parapsychology students, a tradition that is now being continued by the second author. Many of these students went on to academic careers at other universities and have continued to pursue parapsychological research. While universities that do not have first-hand experience of parapsychology may be nervous about having such a potentially controversial topic on campus, those that have been exposed to it have found that academic excellence and the study of the paranormal are not mutually exclusive pursuits. Quite the reverse: the methodological challenges facing parapsychologists and the scrutiny to which the field is subjected tend to encourage very high methodological standards. Furthermore, the topic is exciting and attractive to both undergraduate and postgraduate students, and is recognized as an excellent vehicle for learning about scientific methodology.

In view of the reactions of certain influential members of the scientific community it might be asked why anyone would persist in their efforts toward parapsychology's acceptance as a legitimate area for scientific inquiry. Some reasons for doing so are idealistic: parapsychologists genuinely may see their work as scientific and want it acknowledged as such. Other reasons ultimately are more selfish: effective recognition of parapsychology should bring more research funds, greater opportunities for and security of employment, and the chance to specialize in parapsychology instead of pursuing it as an ancillary interest. Additionally the promotion of parapsychology as a science has political functions: it constitutes a response to critics and serves to engender in parapsychologists working in academically isolated positions some sense of professional support and unity (Hess, 1993).

The majority of parapsychologists unfortunately have put themselves at a strategic disadvantage by continuing to present their field as the investigation of the paranormal rather than as the study of parapsychological experiences or experiences that appear to imply the operation of paranormal processes (Blackmore, 1988). Definition in terms of paranormal phenomena inhibits any rapprochement between parapsychologists and their critics because it currently leaves open the question of whether the discipline has any phenomena to investigate: that paranormal phenomena exist is at best uncertain. Further, the very use of the term "paranormal" has the unintended effect of suggesting to conventional scientists that parapsychologists do not think of psi as a natural phenomenon (Honorton, 1993), implying that the subject matter of parapsychology is intrinsically beyond the realms of science. The parapsychologist's adherence to scientific procedures in itself is insufficient; for a field of inquiry to be deemed a science there must additionally be identifiable natural phenomena for investigation by these procedures. The phenomenological context avoids this difficulty. There can be no dispute that people have parapsychological experiences, and the scientific investigation of these experiences by definition then constitutes a science.

This is not to assert that parapsychology should be totally immersed in the world of human consciousness. Under a phenomenological definition of the discipline, the performance of psi experiments still is appropriate because some types of subjective parapsychological events might well prove to have an objective foundation, a basis rooted in the physical world. Until parapsychologists can appreciate that parapsychological experiences can be studied whether or not they are paranormal, parapsychological research will maintain its marginal status in the domain of orthodox science and as Moore (1977) argues, parapsychology will run the risk of its cultural significance progressively fading almost to the point of oblivion, just as happened to nineteenth-century spiritualism.

Perhaps the ultimate survival of parapsychological research will rest on the demise of parapsychology as a discipline. Stevenson (1988) has questioned parapsychologists' continued determination to represent their research activities as a separate field of study. The foundation of a fraternity among scientific parapsychologists seems to have been achieved at a substantial cost of isolation from and ostracism by the mainstream of science. In purely pragmatic terms, parapsychology is in crisis because new researchers and research funds are not being attracted into parapsychology to the degree necessary to sustain it as a discipline. Stevenson suggests that in the future, parapsychological issues might best be pursued within the framework of the orthodox sciences such as psychology and physics.

This option has major implications for the professional training of future researchers. For example, students with an interest in parapsychological topics would be advised to undertake graduate training in an orthodox field rather than by way of a specialist doctoral program in parapsychology. Having become established vocationally as a mainstream research scientist, the individual could then judiciously apply his or her research expertise to parapsychological issues. In this way, the researcher has sufficient expertise to publish in mainstream journals and to bring to the attention of the mainstream community ways in which parapsychology can contribute to problem areas within other disciplines. Parapsychologists cannot assume that, despite the potential implications of psi, other researchers should be interested in reports of relatively small-scale psi effects published in specialist parapsychology journals. Rather than looking inwards and adopting a fortress mentality, they need to look outwards and consider how to make parapsychological research pertinent to other fields (Watt, in press). Another strategy for doing this is to bring to the attention of the mainstream community ways in which parapsychology has already contributed to the development of ideas in mainstream science (e.g., Alvarado, 2002; Hacking, 1988; Kelly & Alvarado 2005).

In some respects this scenario for the future seems like a meek capitulation to the skeptical attacks on parapsychology. Certainly it would entail the abandonment of some hard-won, academically sound graduate programs in parapsychology. But the viability of contemporary parapsychology is under serious threat, and the underlying problems need to be addressed in a realistic manner.

Even if future parapsychological research typically is undertaken within the orthodox scientific disciplines, there may still be opposition to the acceptance of parapsychological issues as germane for scientific scrutiny. Some observers nevertheless see two contemporary movements in the philosophy of science as providing cause for some optimism in this regard.

The first movement is known as *postmodernism* (Griffin, 1988, 1997; Krippner, 1995, 2001). There is a growing disenchantment with the scientistic, deterministic, reductionistic and mechanistic perspectives of contemporary science and their dogmatic domination of our culture. Science seems to have reduced our worldview to factual information, leaving our cultural institutions without a sense of ideals or values. Although science has largely supplanted the traditional cultural mythologies, it has not incorporated the mythic function of providing principles as a guide to living (Krippner, 1988). Modern science's reductionism also seeks causal explanations at the lowest levels, namely in the parts of the object under study; higher causal entities such as consciousness and the individual as a whole are dismissed as unscientific. Postmodernists urge scientists to restore an appreciation of what might loosely be called a "spiritual" dimension in the study of people and their world. This postmodern science would acknowledge the human qualities and the individualism of the person, and it would also seek to understand people holistically rather than in a reductionistic framework. According to Krippner (1988), parapsychological research would fit very neatly into a postmodern view of science.

On the other hand many postmodern writers depict nonscientific approaches as "alternative" worldviews that are equally as legitimate and potentially enlightening as a scientific approach. Under this interpretation, by embracing postmodernism and rejecting scientism parapsychologists might construe their research paradigms not as invalid but as the operationalization of a merely "different" point of view, thereby obviating attacks from skeptical commentators. Admittedly, many parapsychologists must work within a context of institutionalized science if they want research support and a livelihood, so the prospect of depicting their approach as a legitimate alternative to science may have limited appeal. But to the extent that postmodernist perspectives succeed in undermining the cultural assumption that orthodox science is the only valid method of creating knowledge parapsychologists may be more confident in the intellectual value of their professional work.

A related movement in the philosophy of science has its roots in feminism. Feminist scientists such as Bleier (1984), Harding (1986, 1987) and Keller (1983) see modern science as an uncompromising expression of androcentric or "masculine" values. For example, scientists are essentially in pursuit of power; they seek to dominate, subdue, and control nature. Scientists also use methods which emphasize an objective, impersonal, and dispassionate ("logical") approach at the exclusion of subjective, personal, and emotional ("feeling") elements. Even in the social sciences researchers seek to assert control over experimental subjects rather than to engage participants in a collaborative exercise. At the same time as they are adopting a detached methodology scientists tend to be ad-

versarial, highly competitive with their peers and exploitative of their subordinates (Utts, 1994; Zingrone, 1994).

In parapsychological research this dualism is instantiated by the contrast between J. B. Rhine's relentless drive for experimental control over ESP and Louisa E. Rhine's sensitivity to the personal dimensions of spontaneous extrasensory experiences. Stereotypical "feminine" values perhaps may be more evident in parapsychology than in most other disciplines; [for appreciations of women's contributions to parapsychology see Alvarado (1989b), Coly and White (1994), Hess (1989b), and Zingrone (1988)]. Certainly some parapsychologists' preoccupation with the subjective and the "intuitive" aspects of human behavior (Powers, 1991) is extremely irksome to the (almost exclusively male) skeptics.

In any event, a more extensive accommodation of "feminine" values in general science, as advocated by feminists, may provide a context in which a greater variety of parapsychological studies are received as scientifically legitimate. The feminization of science would in part entail the implementation of a pluralistic approach (White, 1992), that is, a recognition of the value of many different research paradigms and a rejection of the view that the laboratory experiment is the epitome of the scientific method. White (1991, 1994) has urged parapsychologists to join in the process of transforming contemporary science to this end. Thus parapsychology could be the first point of implementation of a significant revolution in the philosophy of science.

In the final analysis what fairly can be said of parapsychology? Historically, it has been argued that the research agenda pursued by early psychical researchers contributed to the development of ideas about dissociation and consciousness in mainstream psychology and psychiatry (Alvarado, 2002; Kelly & Alvarado, 2005). Furthermore, while sociological pressures may drive the behavioral sciences towards an increasingly reductionist approach, parapsychologists' study of the interaction between human intentionality and the physical world can help redress the balance. As Emily Kelly put it, "If psychical research does nothing more than continually shake complacent assumptions about fundamental questions concerning mind, consciousness, volition, that alone is a significant contribution to science" (Kelly, 2001, p. 86). Turning to detailed research findings, as far as spontaneous cases are concerned it seems likely that there are numerous instances of self-deception, delusion, and even fraud. Some of the empirical literature likewise might be attributable to shoddy experimental procedures and to fraudulent manipulation of data. Be this as it may, there is sound phenomenological evidence of parapsychological experiences and experimental evidence of anomalous events too, and to this extent behavioral scientists ethically are obliged to encourage the investigation of these phenomena rather than dismissing them out of hand. If all of the phenomena do prove to be explicable within conventional principles of mainstream psychology surely that is something worth knowing, especially in relation to counseling practice; and if just one of the phenomena should be found to demand a revision or an expansion of contemporary psychological principles, how enriched behavioral science would be.

KEY TERMS AND CONCEPTS

scientific method
laboratory analogues
technological hardware
professionalism
scientific societies
Parapsychological Association
American Association for the Advancement
    of Science (AAAS)
specialist journals
Journal of the Society for Psychical Research
*Journal of the American Society for Psychical
    Research*
Journal of Parapsychology
European Journal of Parapsychology
Journal of Scientific Exploration
Theta

Journal of Near-Death Studies
Exceptional Human Experience
university representation
disclosure of fraud
the Levy affair
fraud by Soal
incidence of fraud
Project Alpha
effect size
replicability
critics' motives
access to journals
research funding
parapsychology teaching
postmodernism
feminism in science

STUDY QUESTIONS

1. Why must science generally be conducted in a laboratory? Discuss this issue in relation to the position of contemporary parapsychology.

2. In what ways has the practice of parapsychology developed toward being scientific?

3. Should parapsychology be permitted representation on university campuses? Why, or why not?

4. In what ways has the scientific establishment sought to frustrate the acknowledgment of parapsychology as a science?

5. "The Levy affair demonstrates that experimenter fraud does occur in parapsychology. This field, therefore, cannot be accorded scientific status." Discuss.

6. Consider (a) the significance for parapsychology, and (b) the ethics, of Randi's Project Alpha.

7. Imagine scientists invented a drug that made people aware of the thoughts of every person within a radius of 30 feet (9 meters). What feelings do you have about this situation? Can you appreciate that some people would be very anxious about it?

8. What are the principal options for parapsychology's future development if it is to survive as a scientific discipline?

REFERENCES

[Abbot, C. G.] (1938). A scientist tests his own ESP ability. *Journal of Parapsychology*, **2**, 65–70.

Abbot, N. C. (2000). Healing as a therapy for human disease: A systematic review. *Journal of Alterative and Complementary Medicine*, **6**, 159–169.

Abbott, D. P. (1909). *Behind the scenes with mediums* (3rd ed.). Chicago: Open Court.

Abramovitch, H. (1988). An Israeli account of a near-death experience: A case study of cultural dissonance. *Journal of Near-Death Studies*, **6**, 175–184.

Ader, R., Felten, D. L., & Cohen, N. (Eds.). (1991). *Psychoneuroimmunology* (2nd ed.). San Diego, CA: Academic Press.

Akers, C. (1984). Methodological criticisms of parapsychology. In S. Krippner (Ed.), *Advances in parapsychological research, Vol. 4* (pp. 112–164). Jefferson, NC: McFarland.

Akers, C. (1985). Can meta-analysis resolve the ESP controversy? In P. Kurtz (Ed.), *A Skeptic's Handbook of Parapsychology* (pp. 611–627). Buffalo, NY: Prometheus.

Alberti, G. (1974). Psychopathology and parapsychology: Some possible contacts. In A. Angoff & B. Shapin (Eds.), *Parapsychology and the sciences* (pp. 225–233). New York: Parapsychology Foundation.

Alcock, J. E. (1975). *Some correlates of extraordinary belief.* Paper presented at the 36th Annual Meeting of the Canadian Psychological Association, Quebec.

Alcock, J. E. (1978). Psychology and near-death experiences. *Skeptical Inquirer*, **3**(2), 25–41.

Alcock, J. E. (1981). *Parapsychology: Science or magic? A psychological perspective.* Oxford: Pergamon.

Alcock, J. E. (1990). *Science and supernature: A critical appraisal of parapsychology.* Buffalo, NY: Prometheus Books.

Alcock, J. E. (1994). Afterword: An analysis of psychic sleuths' claims. In J. Nickell (Ed.), *Psychic sleuths: ESP and sensational cases* (pp. 172–190). Buffalo, NY: Prometheus Books.

Alcock, J. E. (1996). Channeling. In G. Stein (Ed.), *The encyclopedia of the paranormal* (pp. 153–160). Amherst, NY: Prometheus Books.

Alcock, J. E. (1998). Science, pseudoscience, and anomaly. *Behavioral and Brain Sciences*, **21**, 303–304.

Alcock, J. (2003). Give the null hypothesis a chance: Reasons to remain doubtful about the existence of psi. *Journal of Consciousness Studies*, **10**, 29–50.

Alcock, J. E., & Otis, L. P. (1980). Critical thinking and belief in the paranormal. *Psychological Reports*, **46**, 479–482.

Alvarado, C. S. (1982). Recent OBE detection studies: A review. *Theta*, **10**(2), 35–37.

Alvarado, C. S. (1984). Psychical research in Spain. *Journal of Parapsychology*, **48**, 219–226.

Alvarado, C. S. (1989a). ESP displacement effects: A review of pre–1940 concepts and qualitative observations. *Journal of the American Society for Psychical Research*, **83**, 227–239.

Alvarado, C. S. (1989b). The history of women in parapsychology: A critique of past work and suggestions for further research. *Journal of Parapsychology*, **53**, 233–249.

Alvarado, C. S. (1989c). The language barrier in parapsychology. *Journal of Parapsychology*, **53**, 125–139.

Alvarado, C. S. (1992). The psychological approach to out-of-body experiences: A review of early and modern developments. *Journal of Psychology*, **126**, 237–250.

Alvarado, C. S. (1996). The place of spontaneous cases in parapsychology. *Journal of the American Society for Psychical Research*, **90**, 1–34.

Alvarado, C. S. (1997). Mapping the characteristics of out-of-body experiences. *Journal of the American Society for Psychical Research*, **91**, 15–32.

Alvarado, C. S. (1998). ESP and altered states of consciousness: An overview of conceptual and research trends. *Journal of Parapsychology*, **62**, 27–63.

Alvarado, C. S. (2000). Out-of-body experiences. In E. Cardeña, S. J. Lynn, & S. Krippner (Eds.), *Varieties of anomalous experience: Examining the scientific evidence* (pp. 183–218). Washington, DC: American Psychological Association.

Alvarado, C. S. (2001). Features of out-of-body experiences in relation to perceived closeness to death. *Journal of Nervous and Mental Disease*, **189**, 331–332.

Alvarado, C. S. (2002). Dissociation in Britain during the late nineteenth century: The Society for Psychical Research, 1882–1900. *Journal of Trauma and Dissociation,* **3**, 9–33.

Alvarado, C. S. (2003). Reflections on being a parapsychologist. *Journal of Parapsychology,* **67**, 211–248.

Avarado, C. S. (2005). On the centenary of Frederic W. H. Myers's *Human Personality and Its Survival of Bodily Death. Journal of Parapsychology,* **68**, 3–43.

Alvarado, C. S., & Martínez-Taboas, A. (1983). The super-psi hypothesis: A review. *Theta,* **11**, 57–62.

Alvarado, C. S., & Zingrone, N. L. (1995). Characteristics of hauntings with and without apparitions: An analysis of published cases. *Journal of the Society for Psychical Research,* **60**, 385–397.

Alvarado, C. S., & Zingrone, N. L. (1997a, August). *Out-of-body experiences and dissociation.* Paper presented at the 40th Annual Convention of the Parapsychological Association, Brighton, England.

Alvarado, C. S., & Zingrone, N. L. (1997b). Out-of-body experiences and sensations of "shocks" to the body. *Journal of the Society for Psychical Research,* **61**, 304–313.

Alvarado, C. S., & Zingrone, N. L. (1999). Out-of-body experiences among readers of a Spanish New Age magazine. *Journal of the Society for Psychical Research,* **63**, 65–85.

Alvarado, C. S., & Zingrone, N. L. (2003a). Exploring the factors related to the after-effects of out-of-body experiences. *Journal of the Society for Psychical Research,* **67**, 161–183.

Alvarado, C. S., & Zingrone, N. L. (2003b, August). *Interrelationships of psychic experiences, dream recall and lucid dreams in a survey with Spanish participants.* Paper presented at the 46th Annual Convention of the Parapsychological Association, Vancouver, Canada.

Amorim, M. (1990). The Guarulhos poltergeist: A reassessment of Andrade's (1984) monograph. *Journal of the Society for Psychical Research,* **56**, 193–207.

Amorim, M. (1994, August). *Do quantum mechanical concepts help to understand psi phenomena?* Paper presented at the 37th Annual Convention of the Parapsychological Association, Amsterdam, The Netherlands.

Amorim, M. (2003). "What is my atavar seeing?": The coordination of "out-of-body" and "embodied" perspectives for scene recognition across views. *Visual Cognition,* **10**, 157–199.

Anderson, R. I. (1987). Spiritualism before the Fox sisters. *Parapsychology Review,* **18**(1), 9–13.

Anderson, R., & Anderson, W. (1982). Veridical and psychopathic hallucinations: A comparison of types. *Parapsychology Review,* **13**(3), 17–23.

Angoff, A., & Shapin, B. (Eds.) (1973). *Parapsychology today: A geographical view.* New York: Parapsychology Foundation.

Angoff, A., & Shapin, B. (Eds.) (1974). *Parapsychology and the sciences.* New York: Parapsychology Foundation.

Arango, M. A., & Persinger, M. A. (1988). Geophysical variables and behavior: LII. Decreased geomagnetic activity and spontaneous telepathic experiences from the Sidgwick collection. *Perceptual and Motor Skills,* **67**, 907–910.

Arzy, S., Idel, M., Landis, T., & Blanke, O. (2005). Why revelations have occurred on mountains? Linking mystical experiences and cognitive neuroscience. *Medical Hypotheses,* **65**, 841–845.

Astin, J. A., Harkness, E., & Ernst, E. (2000). The efficacy of "distant healing": A systematic review of randomized trials. *Annals of Internal Medicine,* **132**, 903–910.

Athappilly, G. E., Greyson, B., & Stevenson, I. (2006). Do prevailing societal models influence reports of near-death experiences? A comparison of accounts reported before and after 1975. *Journal of Nervous and Mental Disease,* **194**, 218–222.

Atwater, P. M. H. (1988). *Coming back to life: The aftereffects of the near-death experience.* New York: Dodd, Mead & Co.

Atwater, P. M. H. (1992). Is there a hell? Surprising observations about the near-death experience. *Journal of Near-Death Studies,* **10**, 149–160.

Auerbach, L. (1986). *ESP, hauntings and poltergeists: A parapsychologist's handbook.* New York: Warner Books.

Ayeroff, F., & Abelson, R. P. (1976). ESP and ESB: Belief in personal success at mental telepathy. *Journal of Personality and Social Psychology,* **34**, 240–247.

Bainbridge, W. S. (1978). Chariots of the gullible. *Skeptical Inquirer,* **3**(2), 33–48.

Baker, R. A. (1982). The effect of suggestion on past-lives regression. *American Journal of Clinical Hypnosis,* **25**, 71–76.

Ballard, J. A. (1991). Rychlakean theory and parapsychology. *Journal of the American Society for Psychical Research,* **85**, 167–181.

Barker, D. R., & Pasricha, S. K. (1979). Reincarnation cases in Fatehabad: A systematic survey in North India. *Journal of Asian and African Studies,* **14**, 231–240.

Barker, J. C. (1967). Premonitions of the Aberfan disaster. *Journal of the Society for Psychical Research,* **44**, 169–181.

Basford, T. K. (1990). *Near-death experiences: An annotated bibliography.* New York: Garland.

Bauer, M. (1985). Near-death experiences and attitude change. *Anabiosis,* **5**, 39–47.

Bayless, R. (1973). *Apparitions and survival of death.* New Hyde Park, NY: University Books.

Bayless, R. (1976). *Voices from beyond.* Secaucus, NJ: University Books.

Bechara, A., Damasio, H., & Damasio, A. R. (2000). Emotion, decision making and the orbitofrontal cortex. *Cerebral Cortex,* **10**, 295–307.

Becker, R. O. (1992). Electromagnetism and psi phenomena. *Journal of the American Society for Psychical Research,* **86**, 1–17.

Bell, M. (1956). A pioneer in parapsychology. *Hibbert Journal,* **54**, 281–285.

Beloff, J. (1972). The place of theory in parapsychology. In R. Van Over (Ed.), *Psychology and extrasensory perception* (pp. 379–395). New York: New American Library.

Beloff, J. (1977a). Backward causation. *Parapsychology Review*, 8(1), 1–5.

Beloff, J. (1977b). Psi phenomena: Causal versus acausal interpretation. *Journal of the Society for Psychical Research*, 49, 573–582.

Beloff, J. (1980). Seven evidential experiments. *Zetetic Scholar*, 6, 91–94.

Beloff, J. (1985). Research strategies for dealing with unstable phenomena. In B. Shapin & L. Coly (Eds.), *The repeatability problem in parapsychology* (pp. 1–21). New York: Parapsychology Foundation.

Beloff, J. (1986). Retrodiction. *Parapsychology Review*, 17(1), 1–5.

Beloff, J. (1993). *Parapsychology: A short history*. London: Athlone Press.

Beloff, J. (1994, August). *The skeptical position: Is it tenable?* Paper presented at the 37th Annual Convention of the Parapsychological Association, Amsterdam, The Netherlands.

Belz-Merk, M. (2000, August). *Counseling and therapy for people who claim exceptional experiences*. Paper presented at the 43rd Annual Convention of the Parapsychological Association, Freiburg, Germany.

Bem, D. J. (1996). Ganzfeld phenomena. In G. Stein (Ed.), *The encyclopedia of the paranormal* (pp. 291–296). Amherst, NY: Prometheus Books.

Bem, D. J., & Honorton, C. (1994). Does psi exist? Replicable evidence for an anomalous process of information transfer. *Psychological Bulletin*, 115, 4–18.

Bem, D. J., Palmer, J., & Broughton, R. S. (2001). Updating the ganzfeld database: A victim of its own success? *Journal of Parapsychology*, 65, 207–218.

Benassi, V. A., Singer, B., & Reynolds, C. B. (1980). Occult belief: Seeing is believing. *Journal for the Scientific Study of Religion*, 19, 337–349.

Benassi, V. A., Sweeney, P. D., & Drevno, G. E. (1979). Mind over matter: Perceived success at psychokinesis. *Journal of Personality and Social Psychology*, 37, 1377–1386.

Bender, H. (1971). New developments in poltergeist research. In W. G. Roll, R. L. Morris, & J. D. Morris (Eds.), *Proceedings of the Parapsychological Association No. 6, 1969* (pp. 81–102). Durham, NC: Parapsychological Association.

Bender, H. (1974). Modern poltergeist research. In J. Beloff (Ed.), *New directions in parapsychology* (pp. 122–143). London: Elek.

Bender, H. (1977). Further investigations of spontaneous and experimental PK by the Freiburg Institute. In J. D. Morris, W. G. Roll, & R. L. Morris (Eds.), *Research in parapsychology 1976* (pp. 202–203). Metuchen, NJ: Scarecrow Press.

Bender, H. (1982). Poltergeists. In I. Grattan-Guinness (Ed.), *Psychical research: A guide to its history, principles and practices* (pp. 123–133). Wellingborough, England: Aquarian Press.

Benor, D. J. (1986). Research in psychic healing. In B. Shapin & L. Coly (Eds.), *Current trends in psi research* (pp. 96–119). New York: Parapsychology Foundation.

Benor, D. J. (1990). Survey of spiritual healing research. *Complementary Medical Research*, 4(3), 9–33.

Berger, A. S. (1984). Experiments with false keys. *Journal of the American Society for Psychical Research*, 78, 41–54.

Berger, A. S. (1996). Thouless test for survival: Failures and claims. *Journal of the American Society for Psychical Research*, 90, 44–53.

Berger, R. E., & Persinger, M. A. (1991). Geophysical variables and behavior: LXVII. Quieter annual geomagnetic activity and larger effect size for experimental psi (ESP) studies over six decades. *Perceptual and Motor Skills*, 73, 1219–1223.

Bergstrom, C. B. (1999). The development of belief in astral travel as an accommodation to childhood sexual abuse: A grounded theory. (Doctoral dissertation, Pepperdine University). *Dissertation Abstracts International*, 59(11-B), 6059.

Berman, A. L. (1974). Belief in afterlife, religion, religiosity and life-threatening experiences. *Omega*, 5, 127–135.

Bernstein, M. (1956). *The search for Bridey Murphy*. Garden City, NY: Doubleday.

Besterman, T. (1932). The psychology of testimony in relation to paraphysical phenomena: Report of an experiment. *Proceedings of the Society for Psychical Research*, 40, 363–387.

Beutler, J. J., Attevelt, J. T. M., Geijskes, G. G., Schouten, S. A., Faber, J. A. J., & Dorhout Mees, E. J. (1987). The effect of paranormal healing on hypertension. *Journal of Hypertension*, 5 (suppl. 5), S551–S552.

Bevan, J. M. (1947). ESP tests in light and darkness. *Journal of Parapsychology*, 11, 76–89.

Beyer, J. (1999). On the transformation of apparition stories in Scandinavia and Germany, c. 1350–1700. *Folklore*, 110, 39–47.

Bierman, D. J., & Houtkooper, J. M. (1975). Exploratory PK tests with a programmable high speed random number generator. *European Journal of Parapsychology*, 1, 3–14.

Bierman, D. J., & Radin, D. I. (1997). Anomalous anticipatory response on randomized future conditions. *Perceptual and Motor Skills*, 84, 689–690.

Billig, M. (1972). Positive and negative experimental psi results in psychology and parapsychology journals. *Journal of the Society for Psychical Research*, 46, 136–142.

Blacher, R. S. (1989). Comments on "A neurobiological model for near-death experiences." *Journal of Near-Death Studies*, 7, 241–242.

Blackmore, S. J. (1982). *Beyond the body: An investigation of out-of-the-body experiences*. London: Heinemann.

Blackmore, S. J. (1984a). A postal survey of OBEs and other experiences. *Journal of the Society for Psychical Research*, 52, 225–244.

Blackmore, S. J. (1984b). A psychological theory of the out-of-body experience. *Journal of Parapsychology*, 48, 201–218.

Blackmore, S. (1986a). *The adventures of a parapsychologist*. Buffalo, NY: Prometheus Books.

Blackmore, S. (1986b). Spontaneous and deliberate OBEs: A questionnaire survey. *Journal of the Society for Psychical Research*, 53, 218–224.

Blackmore, S. (1988). Do we need a new psychical research? *Journal of the Society for Psychical Research*, **55**, 49–59.

Blackmore, S. (1989). What do we really think?: A survey of parapsychologists and sceptics. *Journal of the Society for Psychical Research*, **55**, 251–262.

Blackmore, S. (1991). Near-death experiences: In or out of the body? *Skeptical Inquirer*, **16**(1), 34–45.

Blackmore, S. (1993a). *Dying to live: Near-death experiences*. Buffalo, NY: Prometheus Books.

Blackmore, S. J. (1993b). Near-death experiences in India: They have tunnels too. *Journal of Near-Death Studies*, **11**, 205–217.

Blackmore, S., & Troscianko, T. (1985). Belief in the paranormal: Probability judgments, illusory control, and the "chance baseline shift." *British Journal of Psychology*, **76**, 459–468.

Blackmore, S. J., & Wooffitt, R. C. (1990). Out-of-the-body experiences in young children. *Journal of the Society for Psychical Research*, **56**, 155–158.

Blanke, O., Landis, T., Spinelli, L., & Seeck, M. (2004). Out-of-body experience and autoscopy of neurological origin. *Brain*, **127**, 243–258.

Blanke, O., & Mohr, C. (2005). Out-of-body experience, heatoscopy, and autoscopic hallucination of neurological origin: Implications for neurocognitive mechanisms of corporeal awareness and self consciousness. *Brain Research Reviews*, **50**, 184–199.

Blanke, O., Mohr, C., Michel, C. M., Pascual-Leone, A., Brugger, P., Seeck, M., Landis, T., & Thut, G. (2005). Linking out-of-body experience and self-processing to mental own-body imagery at the temporoparietal junction. *Journal of Neuroscience*, **25**, 550–557.

Blanke, O., Ortigue, S., Landis, T., & Seeck, M. (2002). Stimulating illusory own-body perceptions. *Nature*, **419**, 269–270.

Bleier, R. (1984). *Science and gender: A critique of biology and its theories on women*. New York: Pergamon Press.

Blum, S. H. (1976). Some aspects of belief in prevailing superstitions. *Psychological Reports*, **38**, 579–582.

Bonenfant, R. J. (2001). A child's encounter with the devil: An unusual near-death experience with both blissful and frightening elements. *Journal of Near-Death Studies*, **20**, 87–100.

Bonenfant, R. J. (2004). A comparative study of near-death experience and non-near-death experience outcomes in 56 survivors of clinical death. *Journal of Near-Death Studies*, **22**, 155–178.

Bösch, H. (2004, August). *Reanalyzing a meta-analysis on extra-sensory perception dating from 1940, the first comprehensive meta-analysis in the history of science*. Paper presented at the 47th Annual Convention of the Parapsychological Association, Vienna, Austria.

Bösch, H., Steinkamp, F., & Boller, E. (2006a). Examining psychokinesis: The interaction of human intention with random number generators — A meta-analysis. *Psychological Bulletin*, **132**, 497–523.

Bösch, H., Steinkamp, F., & Boller, E. (2006b). In the eye of the beholder: Reply to Wilson and Shadish (2006) and Radin, Nelson, Dobyns, and Houtkooper (2006). *Psychological Bulletin*, **132**, 533–537.

Boy, D. (2002). Les Français et les para-sciences: Vingt ans de mesures [The French and para-sciences: Twenty years of measures]. *Revue Française de Sociologie*, **43**, 35–45.

Brady, C., & Morris, R. (1997, August). *Attention focusing facilitated through remote mental interaction: A replication and exploration of parameters*. Paper presented at the 40th Annual Convention of the Parapsychological Association, Brighton, UK.

Braud, W. G. (1978). Recent investigations of microdynamic psychokinesis, with special emphasis on the roles of feedback, effort, and awareness. *European Journal of Parapsychology*, **2**, 137–162.

Braud, W. G. (1980). Lability and inertia in conformance behavior. *Journal of the American Society for Psychical Research*, **74**, 297–318.

Braud, W. (1985). The two faces of psi: Psi revealed and psi obscured. In B. Shapin & L. Coly (Eds.), *The repeatability problem in parapsychology* (pp. 150–175). New York: Parapsychology Foundation.

Braud, W. (1986). Psi and PNI: Exploring the interface between parapsychology and psychoneurology. *Parapsychology Review*, **17**(4), 1–5.

Braud, W. (1987). Dealing with displacement. *Journal of the American Society for Psychical Research*, **81**, 209–231.

Braud, W., Davis, G., & Wood, R. (1979). Experiments with Matthew Manning. *Journal of the Society for Psychical Research*, **50**, 199–223.

Braud, W. G., & Schlitz, M. (1991). Consciousness interactions with remote biological systems. *Subtle Energies*, **2**, 1–46.

Braud, W., Shafer, D., McNeill, K., & Guerra, V. (1995). Attention focusing facilitated through remote mental interaction. *Journal of the American Society for Psychical Research*, **89**, 103–115.

Braude, S. E. (1979). The observational theories in parapsychology: A critique. *Journal of the American Society for Psychical Research*, **73**, 349–366.

Braude, S. E. (1986). *The limits of influence: Psychokinesis and the philosophy of science*. New York: Routledge & Kegan Paul.

Braude, S. E. (1989). Evaluating the super–ESP hypothesis. In G. K. Zollschan, J. F. Schumaker & G. F. Walsh (Eds.), *Exploring the paranormal: Perspectives on belief and experience* (pp. 25–38). Bridport, England: Prism Press.

Braude, S. E. (1992). Survival or super-psi? *Journal of Scientific Exploration*, **6**, 127–144.

Braude, S. E. (2001). Out-of-body experiences and survival of death. *International Journal of Parapsychology*, **12**(1), 83–129.

Braude, S. E. (2003). *Immortal remains: The evidence for life after death*. Lanham, MD: Rowman & Littlefield.

Bridgman, P. W. (1956). Probability, logic, and ESP. *Science*, **123**(3184), 15–17.

Brier, R. M., & Tyminski, W. V. (1970). Psi application: Part I. A preliminary attempt. *Journal of Parapsychology*, **34**, 1–25.

Brink, F. (1960). Parapsychology and criminal investigation. *International Criminal Police Review*, **134**, 3–9.

Britton, W. B., & Bootzin, R. R. (2004). Near-death experiences and the temporal lobe. *Psychological Science*, 15, 254–258.

Broad, C. D. (1962). *Lectures on psychical research.* London: Routledge & Kegan Paul.

Broad, W., & Wade, N. (1982). *Betrayers of the truth.* New York: Simon & Schuster.

Broughton, R. S. (1991). *Parapsychology: The controversial science.* New York: Ballantine Books.

Broughton, R. S. (1994). Repetition avoidance in ESP tests: Do sheep and goats really differ? In E. W. Cook & D. L. Delanoy (Eds.), *Research in parapsychology 1991* (pp. 147–150). Metuchen, NJ: Scarecrow Press.

Broughton, R. S. (2006, August). *Memory, emotion and the receptive psi process.* Paper presented at the 49th Annual Convention of the Parapsychological Association, Stockholm, Sweden.

Broughton, R. S., & Perlstrom, J. R. (1985). A competitive computer game in PK research: Some preliminary findings. In R. A. White & J. Solfvin (Eds.), *Research in parapsychology 1984* (pp. 74–77). Metuchen, NJ: Scarecrow Press.

Brugger, P. (1994). Are "presences" preferentially felt along the left side of one's body? *Perceptual and Motor Skills*, 79, 1200–1202.

Brugger, P. (1997). Variables that influence the generation of random sequences: An update. *Perceptual and Motor Skills*, 84, 627–661.

Brugger, P. (2002). Reflective mirrors: Perspective-taking in autoscopic phenomena. *Cognitive Neuropsychiatry*, 7, 179–194.

Brugger, P., Landis, T., & Regard, M. (1990). A "sheep-goat effect" in repetition avoidance: Extra-sensory perception as an effect of subjective probability? *British Journal of Psychology*, 81, 455–468.

Brugger, P., Regard, M., & Landis, T. (1991). Belief in extrasensory perception and illusory control: A replication. *Journal of Psychology*, 125, 501–502.

Brugger, P., Regard, M., & Landis, T. (1997). Illusory reduplication of one's own body: Phenomenology and classification of autoscopic phenomena. *Cognitive Neuropsychiatry*, 2, 19–38.

Bugaj, R. (1996). Two water-poltergeist cases. *Journal of the Society for Psychical Research*, 61, 235–242.

Bunge, M. (1991). A skeptic's beliefs and disbeliefs. *New Ideas in Psychology*, 9, 131–149.

Burdick, D. S., & Kelly, E. F. (1977). Statistical methods in parapsychological research. In B. B. Wolman (Ed.), *Handbook of parapsychology* (pp. 81–130). New York: Van Nostrand Reinhold.

Burnham, W. H. (1889). Memory, historically and experimentally considered. III. Paramnesia. *American Journal of Psychology*, 2, 431–464.

Byrd, R. J. (1988). Positive therapeutic effects of intercessory prayer in a coronary care unit population. *Southern Medical Journal*, 81, 826–829.

Cadoret, R., & Pratt, J. G. (1950). The consistent missing effect in ESP. *Journal of Parapsychology*, 14, 244–256.

Callaghan, A., & Irwin, H. J. (2003). Paranormal belief as a psychological coping mechanism. *Journal of the Society for Psychical Research*, 67, 200–207.

Calvesi, A. (1983). The analytic relationship and its therapeutic factors from a parapsychological viewpoint. *Psychoanalytic Review*, 70, 387–402.

Cameron, T., & Roll, W. G. (1983). An investigation of apparitional experiences. *Theta*, 11, 74–78.

Campbell, J. (1987). *Cognition and the apparitional experience: An exploratory study.* Unpublished master's thesis, University of New England, Armidale, Australia.

Campbell, K. (1971). *Body and mind.* London: Macmillan.

Cardeña, E., Lynn, S. J., & Krippner, S. (Eds.) (2000). *Varieties of anomalous experience: Examining the scientific evidence.* Washington, DC: American Psychological Association.

Carington, W. W. (1940). Experiments on the paranormal cognition of drawings. *Journal of Parapsychology*, 4, 1–129.

Carington, W. W. (1945). *Telepathy: An outline of its facts, theory and implications.* London: Methuen.

Carpenter, J. C. (1971). The differential effect and hidden target differences consisting of erotic and neutral stimuli. *Journal of the American Society for Psychical Research*, 65, 204–214.

Carpenter, J. C. (1977). Intrasubject and subject-agent effects in ESP experiments. In B. B. Wolman (Ed.), *Handbook of parapsychology* (pp. 202–272). New York: Van Nostrand Reinhold.

Carpenter, J. C. (1988). Quasi-therapeutic group process and ESP. *Journal of Parapsychology*, 52, 279–305.

Carpenter, J. C. (1991). Prediction of forced-choice ESP performance. Part III: Three attempts to retrieve coded information using mood reports and a repeated-guessing technique. *Journal of Parapsychology*, 55, 227–280.

Carpenter, J. C. (2001). A psychological analysis of ganzfeld protocols. *Journal of Parapsychology*, 65, 358–359.

Carpenter, J. C. (2004). First sight: Part one. A model of psi and the mind. *Journal of Parapsychology*, 68, 217–254.

Carpenter, J. C. (2005a). First sight: Part two. Elaboration of a model of psi and the mind. *Journal of Parapsychology*, 69, 63–112.

Carpenter, J. C. (2005b, August). *Implicit measures of participants' experiences in the ganzfeld: Confirmation of previous relationships in a new sample.* Paper presented at the 48th Annual Convention of the Parapsychological Association, Petaluma, CA.

Carpenter, J. C. (2006, August). *Relations between ESP and memory in light of the* First Sight *model of psi.* Paper presented at the 49th Annual Convention of the Parapsychological Association, Stockholm, Sweden.

Carr, D. (1982). Pathophysiology of stress-induced limbic lobe dysfunction: A hypothesis for NDEs. *Anabiosis*, 2, 75–89.

Carrington, H., & Fodor, N. (1951). *The study of the poltergeist down the centuries.* New York: Dutton.

Carvalho, A. P. de (1992). A study of thirteen Brazilian poltergeist cases and a model to explain them. *Journal of the Society for Psychical Research*, 58, 302–313.

Carvalho, A. P. de (1996). Transference and possible

spontaneous psi phenomena in psychotherapy. *Journal of the Society for Psychical Research*, **61**, 18–25.

Case of thought-transference, A. (1923). *Journal of the Society for Psychical Research*, **21**, 170–175.

Case of the will of James L. Chaffin. (1927). *Proceedings of the Society for Psychical Research*, **36**, 517–524.

Casler, L. (1976). Hypnotic maximization of ESP motivation. *Journal of Parapsychology*, **40**, 187–193.

Chadha, N. K., & Stevenson, I. (1988). Two correlates of violent death in cases of the reincarnation type. *Journal of the Society for Psychical Research*, **55**, 71–79.

Chari, C. T. K. (1962). Paramnesia and reincarnation. *Proceedings of the Society for Psychical Research*, **53**, 264–286.

Chari, C. T. K. (1977). Some generalized theories and models of psi: A critical evaluation. In B. B. Wolman (Ed.), *Handbook of parapsychology* (pp. 803–822). New York: Van Nostrand Reinhold.

Chari, C. T. K. (1978). Reincarnation research: Method and interpretation. In M. Ebon (Ed.), *The Signet handbook of parapsychology* (pp. 313–324). New York: New American Library.

Chauvin, R. (1985). *Parapsychology: When the irrational rejoins science*. Jefferson, NC: McFarland.

Chibnall, J. T., Jeral, J. M., & Cerullo, M. A. (2001). Experiments on distant intercessory prayer: God, science, and the lesson of Massah. *Archives of Internal Medicine*, **161**, 2529–2536.

Child, I. L. (1985). Psychology and anomalous observations: The question of ESP in dreams. *American Psychologist*, **40**, 1219–1230.

Christopher, M. (1971). *Seers, psychics and ESP*. London: Cassell.

Churchland, P. M. (1987). How parapsychology could become a science. *Inquiry*, **30**, 227–239.

Clark, K. (1984). Clinical interventions with near-death experiencers. In B. Greyson & C. P. Flynn (Eds.), *The near-death experience: Problems, prospects, perspectives* (pp. 242–255). Springfield, IL: Thomas.

Clarke, D. (1991). Belief in the paranormal: A New Zealand survey. *Journal of the Society for Psychical Research*, **57**, 412–425.

Collins, H. M., & Pinch, T. J. (1979). The construction of the paranormal: Nothing unscientific is happening. In R. Wallis (Ed.), On the margins of science: The social construction of rejected knowledge. *Sociological Review Monograph*, No. 27, 237–270.

Collins, H. M., & Pinch, T. J. (1982). *Frames of meaning: The social construction of extraordinary science*. London: Routledge & Kegan Paul.

Coly, L., & White, R. A. (Eds.) (1994). *Women and parapsychology*. New York: Parapsychology Foundation.

Cook, A. M., & Irwin, H. J. (1983). Visuospatial skills and the out-of-body experience. *Journal of Parapsychology*, **47**, 23–35.

Cook, E. W., Greyson, B., & Stevenson, I. (1998). Do any near-death experiences provide evidence for the survival of human personality after death? Relevant features and illustrative case reports. *Journal of Scientific Exploration*, **12**, 377–406.

Cook, E. W., Pasricha, S., Samararatne, G., Win

Maung, U., & Stevenson, I. (1983). A review and analysis of "unsolved" cases of the reincarnation type: II. Comparison of features of solved and unsolved cases. *Journal of the American Society for Psychical Research*, **77**, 115–135.

Cooperstein, M. A. (1992). The myths of healing: A summary of research into transpersonal healing experiences. *Journal of the American Society for Psychical Research*, **86**, 99–133.

Coover, J. E. (1913). The feeling of being stared at. *American Journal of Psychology*, **24**, 570–575.

Coover, J. E. (1975). *Experiments in psychical research at Leland Stanford Junior University*. New York: Arno Press. (Original work published 1917)

Cornell, A. D. (1999). Some comments on the Scole Report. *Proceedings of the Society for Psychical Research*, **58**, 397–403.

Cornwell, T. (1997, October 17). The truth is out there, and so is Dr Radin. *Times Higher Education Supplement*, 23.

Costa de Beauregard, O. (1998). The paranormal is not excluded from physics. *Journal of Scientific Exploration*, **12**, 315–320.

Council, J. R., Greyson, B., & Huff, K. D. (1986, August). *Fantasy-proneness, hypnotizability, and reports of paranormal experiences*. Paper presented at the meeting of the American Psychological Association, Washington, D.C.

Counts, D. A. (1983). Near-death and out-of-body experiences in a Melanesian society. *Anabiosis*, **3**, 115–135.

Couttie, R. D. (1986). Correspondence. *Journal of the Society for Psychical Research*, **53**, 336–337.

Cox, W. E. (1956). Precognition: An analysis. II. Subliminal precognition. *Journal of the American Society for Psychical Research*, **50**, 99–109.

Cox, W. E. (1971). A comparison of different densities of dice in a PK task. *Journal of Parapsychology*, **35**, 108–119.

Crandall, J. E. (1985). Effects of favorable and unfavorable conditions on the psi-missing displacement effect. *Journal of the American Society for Psychical Research*, **79**, 27–38.

Crandall, J. E. (1991). The psi-missing displacement effect: Meta-analyses of favorable and less favorable conditions. *Journal of the American Society for Psychical Research*, **85**, 237–250.

Crandall, J. E. (1994). Which comes first, missing or displacement? In E. W. Cook & D. L. Delanoy (Eds.), *Research in parapsychology 1991* (pp. 75–79). Metuchen, NJ: Scarecrow Press.

Crookall, R. (1966). *The next world—and the next. Ghostly garments*. London: Theosophical Publishing House.

Crookall, R. (1970). *Out-of-body experiences: A fourth analysis*. New York: University Books.

Crookall, R. (1972). *Case-book of astral projection, 545–746*. Secaucus, NJ: University Books.

Curtis, J. T., & Wilson, J. P. (1997). Sensation seeking and ESP test performance: A preliminary investigation. *Journal of the Society for Psychical Research*, **62**, 1–21.

Dag, I. (1999). The relationships among paranormal

beliefs, locus of control and psychopathology in a Turkish college sample. *Personality and Individual Differences*, **26**, 723–737.

Dale, L. A. (1946). The psychokinetic effect: The first ASPR experiment. *Journal of the American Society for Psychical Research*, **40**, 123–151.

Dalkvist, J., & Westerlund, J. (2000, August). *Local sidereal time, global geomagnetic field fluctuations and memory.* Paper presented at the 43rd Annual Convention of the Parapsychological Association, Freiburg, Germany.

Dalkvist, J., Westerlund, J., & Bierman, D. J. (2002, August). *A computational expectation bias as revealed by simulations of presentiment experiments.* Paper presented at the 45th Annual Convention of the Parapsychological Association, Paris, France.

Dallas, H. A. (1924). Communications from the still incarnate at a distance from the body. *Occult Review*, **40**, 26–32.

Dalton, K. (1997a, August). *Exploring the links: Creativity and psi in the ganzfeld.* Paper presented at the 40th Annual Convention of the Parapsychological Association, Brighton, UK.

Dalton, K. (1997b). Is there a formula to success in the ganzfeld? Observations on predictors of psi-ganzfeld performance. *European Journal of Parapsychology*, **13**, 71–82.

Dalton, K. S., Morris, R. L., Delanoy, D. L., Radin, D. I., Taylor, R., & Wiseman, R. (1996). Security measures in an automated ganzfeld system. *Journal of Parapsychology*, **60**, 129–147.

Dalton, K. S., Zingrone, N. L., & Alvarado, C. S. (1999, August). *Exploring out-of-body experiences, dissociation, absorption, and alterations of consciousness with a creative population in the ganzfeld.* Paper presented at the 42nd Annual Convention of the Parapsychological Association, Palo Alto, CA.

Daniels, M. (2002). The "Brother Doli" case: Investigation of apparent poltergeist-type manifestations in North Wales. *Journal of the Society for Psychical Research*, **66**, 193–221.

da Silva, F. E., Pilato, S., & Hiraoka, R. (2003, August). *Ganzfeld vs. no ganzfeld: An exploratory study of the effects of ganzfeld conditions on ESP.* Paper presented at the 46th Annual Convention of the Parapsychological Association, Vancouver, Canada.

Datson, S. L., & Marwit, S. J. (1997). Personality constructs and perceived presence of deceased loved ones. *Death Studies*, **21**, 131–146.

Davey, S. J., & Hodgson, R. (1887). The possibilities of mal-observation and lapse of memory from a practical point of view. *Proceedings of the Society for Psychical Research*, **4**, 381–495.

Davies, M. F. (1985). Self-consciousness and paranormal belief. *Perceptual and Motor Skills*, **60**, 484–486.

Davis, G. A., Peterson, J. M., & Farley, F. H. (1974). Attitudes, motivation, sensation seeking, and belief in ESP as predictors of real creative behavior. *Journal of Creative Behavior*, **8**, 31–39.

Day, R. H. (1969). Extrasensory perception and related phenomena. *Australian Rationalist*, **1**(3), 22–26.

Dean, E. D., & Nash, C. B. (1967). Coincident plethys-mograph results under controlled conditions. *Journal of the Society for Psychical Research*, **44**, 1–14.

De Angelis, C. E., Drazen, J. M., Frizelle, F. A., Gaug, C., Hoey, J., Horton, R., et al. (2004). Clinical trial registration: A statement from the International Committee of Medical Journal Editors. *Journal of the American Medical Association*, **292**, 1363–1364.

De Angelis, C. E., Drazen, J. M., Frizelle, F. A., Gaug, C., Hoey, J., Horton, R., et al. (2005). Is this clinical trial fully registered? A statement from the International Committee of Medical Journal Editors. *Lancet*, **365**, 1827–1829.

Debes, J., & Morris, R. (1982). Comparison of striving and nonstriving instructional sets in a PK study. *Journal of Parapsychology*, **46**, 297–312.

deGraaf, T. K., & Houtkooper, J. (2004). Anticipatory awareness of emotionally charged targets by individuals with histories of emotional trauma. *Journal of Parapsychology*, **68**, 93–128.

Del Prete, G., & Tressoldi, P. E. (in press). Anomalous cognition in hypnagogic state with OBE induction: An experimental study. *Journal of Parapsychology*.

Delanoy, D. L. (1987). Work with a fraudulent PK metal-bending subject. *Journal of the Society for Psychical Research*, **54**, 247–256.

Delanoy, D. L. (1989a). Characteristics of successful free-response targets: Experimental findings and observations. In L. A. Henkel & R. E. Berger (Eds.), *Research in Parapsychology 1988* (pp. 92–95). Metuchen, NJ: Scarecrow Press.

Delanoy, D. L. (1989b). An examination of subject and agent mentation in the ganzfeld. *European Journal of Parapsychology*, **7**, 135–168.

Delanoy, D. L. (2001). Anomalous psychophysiological responses to remote cognition: The DMILS studies. *European Journal of Parapsychology*, **16**, 30–41.

Delanoy, D. L., Morris, R. L., & Watt, C. A. (in press). A study of free-response ESP performance and mental training techniques. *Journal of the American Society for Psychical Research*.

Dening, T. R., & Berrios, G. E. (1994). Autoscopic phenomena. *British Journal of Psychiatry*, **165**, 808–817.

de Rochas, A. (1911). *Les vies successives.* Paris: Charcornac.

Devereux, G. (Ed.) (1953). *Psychoanalysis and the occult.* New York: International Universities Press.

Diaconis, P. (1978). Statistical problems in ESP research. *Science*, **201**, 131–136.

Diaconis, P., & Mosteller, F. (1989). Methods for studying coincidences. *Journal of the American Statistical Association*, **84**, 853–861.

Díaz-Vilela, L., & Alvarez-Gonzalez, C. J. (2004). Differences in paranormal beliefs across fields of study from a Spanish adaptation of Tobacyk's RPBS. *Journal of Parapsychology*, **68**, 405–421.

Dickinson, G. L. (1911). A case of emergence of a latent memory under hypnosis. *Proceedings of the Society for Psychical Research*, **25**, 455–467.

Dickstein, M. L., & Davis, J. W. (1979). A blind PK test over two distances. *Journal of Parapsychology*, **43**, 41–42. (Abstract)

Dierkens, J. C. (1978). Psychophysiological approach to PK states. In B. Shapin & L. Coly (Eds.), *Psi and states of awareness* (pp. 152–166). New York: Parapsychology Foundation.

Dingwall, E. J. (1961). British investigation of spontaneous cases. *International Journal of Parapsychology*, 3(1), 89–97.

Dingwall, E. J. (Ed.) (1967–1968). *Abnormal hypnotic phenomena: A survey of nineteenth-century cases* (4 vols.). London: Churchill.

Dobinson, G. (1998). The case for retrocognition. *Journal of the Society for Psychical Research*, 62, 337–346.

Dobyns, Y. H. (1996). Selection versus influence revisited: New method and conclusions. *Journal of Scientific Exploration*, 10, 253–267.

Dobyns, Y. H. (2000). Overview of several theoretical models on PEAR data. *Journal of Scientific Exploration*, 14, 163–194.

Dobyns, Y. H., Dunne, B. J., Jahn, R. G., & Nelson, R. D. (1992). Response to Hansen, Utts, and Markwick: Statistical and methodological problems of the PEAR remote viewing *(sic)* experiments. *Journal of Parapsychology*, 56, 115–146.

Dobyns, Y. H., Dunne, B. J., Jahn, R. G., & Nelson, R. D. (2004). The MegaREG Experiment: Replication and interpretation. *Journal of Scientific Exploration*, 18, 369–397.

Dommeyer, F. C. (1975). Psychical research at Stanford University. *Journal of Parapsychology*, 39, 173–205.

Don, N. S., McDonough, B. E., & Warren, C. A. (1995). Signal processing analysis of forced-choice ESP data: Evidence for psi as a wave of correlation. *Journal of Parapsychology*, 59, 357–380.

Donovan, J. M. (1998). Reinterpreting telepathy as unusual experiences of empathy and charisma. *Perceptual and Motor Skills*, 87, 131–146.

Drewes, A. A. (2002). Dr. Louisa Rhine's letters revisited: The children. *Journal of Parapsychology*, 66, 343–370.

Druckman, D., & Swets, J. A. (Eds.) (1988). *Enhancing human performance: Issues, theories, and techniques*. Washington, DC: National Academy Press.

Ducasse, C. J. (1960). How the case of "The Search for Bridey Murphy" stands today. *Journal of the American Society for Psychical Research*, 54, 3–22.

Dudley, R. T. (1999). The effect of superstitious belief on performance following an unsolvable problem. *Personality and Individual Differences*, 26, 1057–1064.

Dunne, B. J., Dobyns, Y. H., Jahn, R. G., & Nelson, R. D. (1994). Series position effects in random event generator experiments. *Journal of Scientific Exploration*, 8, 197–211.

Dunne, B. J., Jahn, R. G., & Nelson, R. D. (1983). *Precognitive remote perception, (Technical Note PEAR 83003)*. Princeton, NJ: Engineering Anomalies Research Laboratory, Princeton University.

Dunne, J. W. (1927). *An experiment with time*. London: Macmillan.

Eastham, P. (1988). Ticking off a poltergeist. *Journal of the Society for Psychical Research*, 55, 80–83.

Eastman, M. (1962). Out-of-the-body experiences. *Proceedings of the Society for Psychical Research*, 53, 287–309.

Ebon, M. (1983). *Psychic warfare: Threat or illusion?* New York: McGraw-Hill.

Edge, H., & Farkash, M. (1982). Further support for the psi-distributed hypothesis. In W. G. Roll, R. L. Morris, & R. A. White (Eds.), *Research in parapsychology 1981* (pp. 171–172). Metuchen, NJ: Scarecrow Press.

Edge, H. L., Morris, R. L., Palmer, J., & Rush, J. H. (1986). *Foundations of parapsychology: Exploring the boundaries of human capability*. Boston: Routledge & Kegan Paul.

Edge, H. L., Suryani, L. K., Tiliopoulos, N., & Morris, R. L. (2004). Two cognitive DMILS studies in Bali. *Journal of Parapsychology*, 68, 289–321.

Edwards, P. (1996). *Reincarnation: A critical examination*. Amherst, NY: Prometheus Books.

Ehrenwald, J. (1974). Out-of-the-body experiences and the denial of death. *Journal of Nervous and Mental Disease*, 159, 227–233.

Ehrenwald, J. (1978). *The ESP experience: A psychiatric validation*. New York: Basic.

Eilbert, L., & Schmeidler, G. R. (1950). A study of certain psychological factors in relation to ESP performance. *Journal of Parapsychology*, 14, 53–74.

Eisenbud, J. (1967). *The world of Ted Serios*. New York: Morrow.

Eisenbud, J. (1977). Paranormal photography. In B. B. Wolman (Ed.), *Handbook of parapsychology* (pp. 414–432). New York: Van Nostrand Reinhold; reprinted by McFarland, Jefferson NC.

Eisenbud, J. (1982). *Paranormal foreknowledge: Problems and complexities*. New York: Human Sciences Press.

Eisenbud, J. (1987). Psi in psychotherapy. *ASPR Newsletter*, 13, 29–30.

Eisenbud, J. (1989). *The world of Ted Serios: "Thoughtographic" studies of an extraordinary mind* (2nd ed.). Jefferson, NC: McFarland.

Ejvegaard, R., & Johnson, M. (1981). Murderous ESP: A case of story fabrication. *European Journal of Parapsychology*, 4, 81–98.

Ellwood, G. F. (1971). *Psychic visits to the past: An exploration of retrocognition*. New York: New American Library.

Elsaesser, Valarino, E. (1997). *On the other side of life: Exploring the phenomenon of the near-death experience*. New York: Plenum Press.

Emmons, C. F. (1982). *Chinese ghosts and ESP: A study of paranormal beliefs and experiences*. Metuchen, NJ: Scarecrow Press.

Emmons, C. F., & Sobal, J. (1981). Paranormal beliefs: Testing the marginality hypothesis. *Sociological Focus*, 14, 49–56.

Epstein, S., Pacini, R., Denes-Raj, V., & Heier, H. (1996). Individual differences in intuitive-experiential and analytical-rational thinking styles. *Journal of Personality and Social Psychology*, 71, 390–405.

Estabrooks, G. H. (1961). A contribution to experimental telepathy. *Journal of Parapsychology*, 25, 190–213. (Original work published 1927)

Etzold, E. (2006). Does psi exist and can we prove it? Belief and disbelief in parapsychological research. *European Journal of Parapsychology*, 21, 38–57.

Evans, C. (1973). Parapsychology: What the questionnaire revealed. *New Scientist*, 57, 209.

Evans, D. (1996). Parapsychology: Merits and limits. In M. Stoeber & H. Meynell (Eds.), *Critical reflections on the paranormal* (pp. 47–86). Albany, NY: State University of New York Press.

Evans, H. (2001). The ghost experience in a wider context. In J. Houran & R. Lange (Eds.), *Hauntings and poltergeists: Multidisciplinary perspectives* (pp. 41–61). Jefferson, NC: McFarland.

Falk, R. (1989). Judgment of coincidences: Mine versus yours. *American Journal of Psychology*, 102, 477–493.

Faraday, M. (1853). Experimental investigation of table-moving. *The Athenaeum*, No. 1340, 801–803.

Feather, S. R., & Rhine, L. E. (1969). PK experiments with same and different targets. *Journal of Parapsychology*, 33, 213–227.

Fenwick, P., & Fenwick, E. (1995). *The truth in the light: An investigation of over 300 near-death experiences.* London: Headline.

Feyerabend, P. (1975). *Against method.* London: Verso.

Finucane, R. C. (1984). *Appearances of the dead: A cultural history of ghosts.* Buffalo, NY: Prometheus Books.

Fishbein, M., & Raven, B. H. (1967). The AB scales: An operational definition of belief and attitude. In M. Fishbein (Ed.), *Readings in attitude theory and measurement* (pp. 183–189). New York: Wiley.

Fisk, G. W., & Mitchell, A. M. J. (1953). ESP experiments with clock cards: A new technique with differential scoring. *Journal of the Society for Psychical Research*, 37, 1–14.

Flew, A. (1953). Coincidence and synchronicity. *Journal of the Society for Psychical Research*, 37, 198–201.

Flew, A. (1980). Parapsychology: Science or pseudo-science? *Pacific Philosophical Quarterly*, 61, 100–114.

Flournoy, T. (1900). *From India to the planet Mars: A study of a case of somnambulism with glossolalia.* New York: Harper.

Flynn, C. P. (1986). *After the beyond: Human transformation and the near-death experience.* Englewood Cliffs, NJ: Prentice-Hall.

Fodor, N. (1948). The poltergeist — psychoanalyzed. *Psychiatric Quarterly*, 22, 195–203.

Fontana, D. (1999). Scole: Additional responses. *Proceedings of the Society for Psychical Research*, 58, 440–447.

Forman, J. (1978). *The mask of time: The mystery factor in timeslips, precognition and hindsight.* London: MacDonald & Jane.

Forwald, H. (1961). A PK experiment with die faces as targets. *Journal of Parapsychology*, 25, 1–12.

Frazier, K. (Ed.) (1981). *Paranormal borderlands of science.* Buffalo, NY: Prometheus Books.

Frazier, K. (Ed.) (1986). *Science confronts the paranormal.* Buffalo, NY: Prometheus Books.

Frazier, K. (Ed.) (1991). *The hundredth monkey and other paradigms of the paranormal.* Buffalo, NY: Prometheus Books.

Frazier, K. (1996). Committee for the Scientific Investigation of Claims of the Paranormal (CSICOP). In G. Stein (Ed.), *The encyclopedia of the paranormal* (pp. 168–181). Amherst, NY: Prometheus Books.

Freeman, J. A. (1970). Sex differences in ESP response as shown by the Freeman picture-figure test. *Journal of Parapsychology*, 34, 37–46.

French, C. C. (2001). Dying to know the truth: Visions of a dying brain, or false memories? *The Lancet*, 358, 2010–2011.

French, C. C. (2003). Fantastic memories: The relevance of research into eyewitness testimony and false memories for reports of anomalous experiences. *Journal of Consciousness Studies*, 10, 153–174.

French, C. C., & Kerman, M. K. (1996, December). *Childhood trauma, fantasy proneness and belief in the paranormal.* Paper presented at the Annual Conference of the British Psychological Society, London.

Freud, S. (1933). *New introductory lectures on psychoanalysis.* London: Hogarth Press.

Friedman, R. (Ed.). (1982). *Murder most eerie: Homicide and the paranormal.* Virginia Beach, VA: Donning.

Fukurai, T. (1931). *Clairvoyance and thoughtography.* London: Rider.

Fuller, U. (1975). *Confessions of a psychic.* Teaneck, NJ: Fulves.

Furn, B. G. (1987). Adjustment and the near-death experience: A conceptual and therapeutic model. *Journal of Near-Death Studies*, 6, 4–19.

Gabbard, G. O., & Twemlow, S. W. (1984). *With the eyes of the mind.* New York: Praeger.

Gabbard, G. O., & Twemlow, S. W. (1991). Do "near-death experiences" occur only near death? — Revisited. *Journal of Near-Death Studies*, 10, 41–47.

Gabbard, G. O., Twemlow, S. W., & Jones, F. C. (1981). Do "near death experiences" occur only near death? *Journal of Nervous and Mental Disease*, 169, 374–377.

Gackenbach, J. I. (1979). A personality and cognitive style analysis of lucid dreaming. (Doctoral dissertation, Virginia Commonwealth University, 1978). *Dissertation Abstracts International*, 39-B, 3487.

Gallup, G. H., & Newport, F. (1991). Belief in paranormal phenomena among adult Americans. *Skeptical Inquirer*, 15, 137–146.

Gallup, G., with Proctor, W. (1982). *Adventures in immortality: A look beyond the threshold of death.* New York: McGraw-Hill.

Gardner, M. (1981). *Science — Good, bad and bogus.* Buffalo, NY: Prometheus Books.

Gardner, M. (1991). How to fabricate a PPO. *Journal of the Society for Psychical Research*, 58, 43–44.

Gardner, M. (1992). *On the wild side.* Buffalo, NY: Prometheus Books.

Gauld, A. (1961). The "super-ESP" hypothesis. *Proceedings of the Society for Psychical Research*, 53, 226–246.

Gauld, A. (1977). Discarnate survival. In B. B. Wolman (Ed.), *Handbook of parapsychology* (pp. 577–630). New York: Van Nostrand Reinhold.

Gauld, A. (1982). *Mediumship and survival: A century of investigations.* London: Heinemann.

Gauld, A. (1984). Review of "Appearances of the Dead: A Cultural History of Ghosts" by R. C. Finucane. *Journal of the Society for Psychical Research*, 52, 330–333.

Gauld, A. (1996). Poltergeists. In G. Stein (Ed.), *The encyclopedia of the paranormal* (pp. 540–544). Amherst, NY: Prometheus Books.

Gauld, A. (1999). Comments on the Scole Report. *Proceedings of the Society for Psychical Research*, **58**, 404–424.

Gauld, A., & Cornell, A. D. (1979). *Poltergeists*. London: Routledge & Kegan Paul.

Gault, R. H, & Goodfellow, L. D. (1940). Sources of error in psycho-physical measurements. *Journal of General Psychology*, **23**, 197–200.

Gay, K., Salter, W. H., Thouless, R. H., Firebrace, R. H., Phillimore, M., & Sitwell, C. (1955). Report on the Oliver Lodge posthumous test. *Journal of the Society for Psychical Research*, **38**, 121–134.

Gearhart, L., & Persinger, M. A. (1986). Geophysical variables and behavior: XXXIII. Onsets of historical and contemporary poltergeist episodes occurred with sudden increases in geomagnetic activity. *Perceptual and Motor Skills*, **62**, 463–466.

Gendin, S. (1998). Guessing. *Philosophia: Philosophical Quarterly of Israel*, **26**, 435–440.

George, L. (1981). A survey of research into the relationships between imagery and psi. *Journal of Parapsychology*, **45**, 121–146.

Gerding, J. L. F., Wezelman, R., & Bierman, D. J. (2002). The Druten disturbances: Exploratory RSPK research. *European Journal of Parapsychology*, **17**, 3–15.

Gibson, A. S. (1994). Near-death experience patterns from research in the Salt Lake City region. *Journal of Near-Death Studies*, **13**, 115–127.

Gibson, E. P., & Rhine, J. B. (1943). The PK effect: III. Some introductory series. *Journal of Parapsychology*, 7, 118–134.

Gilmore, J. B. (1989). Randomness and the search for psi. *Journal of Parapsychology*, **53**, 309–340.

Giorgi, A. (1997). The theory, practice, and evaluation of the phenomenological method as a qualitative research procedure. *Journal of Phenomenological Psychology*, **28**, 235–260.

Girden, E. (1962). A review of psychokinesis (PK). *Psychological Bulletin*, **59**, 353–388.

Gissurarson, L. R. (1991). Some PK attitudes as determinants of PK performance. *European Journal of Parapsychology*, **8**, 112–122.

Gissurarson, L. R. (1997). Methods of enhancing PK task performance. In S. Krippner (Ed.), *Advances in parapsychological research, Vol. 8* (pp. 88–125). Jefferson, NC: McFarland.

Gissurarson, L. R., & Haraldsson, E. (2001). History of parapsychology in Iceland. *International Journal of Parapsychology*, **12**(1), 29–50.

Gissurarson, L. R., & Morris, R. L. (1990). Volition and psychokinesis: Attempts to enhance PK performance through the practice of imagery strategies. *Journal of Parapsychology*, **54**, 331–370.

Gissurarson, L. R., & Morris, R. L. (1991). Examination of six questionnaires as predictors of psychokinesis performance. *Journal of Parapsychology*, **55**, 119–145.

Glicksohn, J. (1990). Belief in the paranormal and subjective paranormal experience. *Personality and Individual Differences*, **11**, 675–683.

Glicksohn, J. (1991). The induction of an altered state of consciousness as a function of sensory environment and experience seeking. *Personality and Individual Differences*, **12**, 1057–1066.

Glik, D. C. (1990). The redefinition of the situation: The social construction of spiritual healing experiences. *Sociology of Health & Illness*, **12**, 151–168.

Goodfellow, L. D. (1938). A psychological interpretation of the results of the Zenith radio experiment in telepathy. *Journal of Experimental Psychology*, **23**, 601–632.

Goodfellow, L. D. (1940). The human element in probability. *Journal of General Psychology*, **23**, 201–205.

Gordon, H. (1994). "The man with the radar brain": Peter Hurkos. In J. Nickell (Ed.), *Psychic sleuths: ESP and sensational cases* (pp. 21–29). Buffalo, NY: Prometheus Books.

Goulding, A. (2004). Schizotypy models in relation to subjective health and paranormal beliefs and experiences. *Personality and Individual Differences*, **37**, 157–167.

Goulding, A. (2005). Healthy schizotypy in a population of paranormal believers and experients. *Personality and Individual Differences*, **38**, 1069–1083.

Goulding, A., & Parker, A. (2001). Finding psi in the paranormal: Psychometric measures used in research on paranormal beliefs/experiences and in research on psi-ability. *European Journal of Parapsychology*, **16**, 73–101.

Goulding, A., Westerlund, J., Parker, A., & Wackermann, J. (2004). The first digital autoganzfeld study using a real-time judging procedure. *European Journal of Parapsychology*, **19**, 66–97.

Grad, B. R. (1976). The biological effects of the "laying on of hands" on animals and plants: Implications for biology. In G. R. Schmeidler (Ed.), *Parapsychology: Its relation to physics, biology, psychology, and psychiatry* (pp. 76–89). Metuchen, NJ: Scarecrow Press.

Greeley, A. (1987). The "impossible": It's happening. *Noetic Sciences Review*, **2**, 7–9.

Green, B. F., & Hall, J. A. (1984). Quantitative methods for literature reviews. *Annual Review of Psychology*, **35**, 37–53.

Green, C. (1960). Analysis of spontaneous cases. *Proceedings of the Society for Psychical Research*, **53**, 97–161.

Green, C. (1968a). *Out-of-the-body experiences*. London: Hamish Hamilton.

Green, C. E. (1968b). *Lucid dreams*. London: Hamish Hamilton.

Green, C., & Leslie, W. (1987). The imagery of totally hallucinatory or "metachoric" experiences. *Journal of Mental Imagery*, **11**, 75–82.

Green, C., & McCreery, C. (1975). *Apparitions*. London: Hamish Hamilton.

Greenwood, J. A. (1938). Analysis of a large chance control series of ESP data. *Journal of Parapsychology*, **2**, 138–146.

Gregory, A. (1982). Ethics and psychical research. In I. Grattan-Guinness (Ed.), *Psychical research: A guide to its history, principles and practices* (pp. 284–291). Wellingborough, England: Aquarian Press.

Grey, M. (1985). *Return from death: An exploration of the near-death experience*. London: Arkana.

Greyson, B. (1977). Telepathy in mental illness: Deluge or delusion? *Journal of Nervous and Mental Disease*, 165, 184–200.

Greyson, B. (1981). Toward a psychological explanation of near-death experiences: A response to Dr. Grosso's paper. *Anabiosis*, 1, 88–103.

Greyson, B. (1983a). Increase in psychic phenomena following near-death experiences. *Theta*, 11, 26–29.

Greyson, B. (1983b). Near-death experiences and personal values. *American Journal of Psychiatry*, 140, 618–620.

Greyson, B. (1992). Reduced death threat in near-death experiencers. *Death Studies*, 16, 523–536.

Greyson, B. (1993). Near-death experiences and antisuicidal attitudes. *Omega*, 26, 81–89.

Greyson, B. (1997). The near-death experience as a focus of clinical attention. *Journal of Nervous and Mental Disease*, 185, 327–334.

Greyson, B. (1998a). Biological aspects of near-death experiences. *Perspective in Biology and Medicine*, 42, 14–32.

Greyson, B. (1998b). The incidence of near-death experiences. *Medicine & Psychiatry*, 1, 92–99.

Greyson, B. (2000a). Near-death experiences. In E. Cardeña, S. J. Lynn, & S. Krippner (Eds.), *Varieties of anomalous experience: Examining the scientific evidence* (pp. 315–352). Washington, DC: American Psychological Association.

Greyson, B. (2000b). Dissociation in people who have near-death experiences: Out of their bodies or out of their minds? *The Lancet*, 355, 460–463.

Greyson, B., & Bush, N. E. (1992). Distressing near-death experiences. *Psychiatry*, 55, 95–110.

Greyson, B., & Flynn, C. P. (Eds.) (1984). *The near-death experience: Problems, prospects, perspectives*. Springfield, IL: Thomas.

Greyson, B., & Harris, B. (1987). Clinical approaches to the near-death experiencer. *Journal of Near-Death Studies*, 6, 41–52.

Greyson, B., & Stevenson, I. (1980). The phenomenology of near-death experiences. *American Journal of Psychiatry*, 137, 1193–1196.

Griffin, D. R. (1988). Introduction: The reenchantment of science. In D. R. Griffin (Ed.), *The reenchantment of science: Postmodern proposals* (pp. 1–46). Albany, NY: State University of New York Press.

Griffin, D. R. (1997). *Parapsychology, philosophy, and spirituality: A postmodern exploration*. Albany, NY: State University of New York Press.

Grosso, M. (1979). The survival of personality in a mind-dependent world. *Journal of the American Society for Psychical Research*, 73, 367–380.

Grosso, M. (1981). Toward an explanation of near-death phenomena. *Journal of the American Society for Psychical Research*, 75, 37–60.

Grosso, M. (1989). The psi-ring of Gyges. *Journal of the American Society for Psychical Research*, 83, 1–6.

Groth-Marnat, G., & Summers, R. (1998). Altered beliefs, attitudes, and behaviors following near-death experiences. *Journal of Humanistic Psychology*, 38, 110–125.

Gurney, E., Myers, F. W. H., & Podmore, F. (1886). *Phantasms of the living* (2 vols.). London: Trübner.

Guthrie, M., & Birchall, J. (1883). Record of experimentation in thought-transference at Liverpool. *Proceedings of the Society for Psychical Research*, 1, 263–283.

Hacking, I. (1988). Telepathy: Origins of randomization in experimental design. *Isis*, 70, 427–251.

Hacking, I. (1993). Some reasons for not taking parapsychology very seriously. *Dialogue: Canadian Philosophical Review*, 32, 587–594.

Hagio, S. (1994). A survey-interview approach to spontaneous psi experiences in a group of Japanese students. In E. W. Cook & D. L. Delanoy (Eds.), *Research in parapsychology 1991* (pp. 157–158). Metuchen, NJ: Scarecrow Press.

Haight, J. (1979). Spontaneous psi cases: A survey and preliminary study of ESP, attitude, and personality relationships. *Journal of Parapsychology*, 43, 179–204.

Hall, T. H. (1962). *The spiritualists: The story of Florence Cook and William Crookes*. London: Duckworth.

Hall, T. H. (1984). *The enigma of Daniel Home: Medium or fraud?* Buffalo, NY: Prometheus Books.

Hanlon, J. (1975). But what about the children? *New Scientist*, 66, 567.

Hansel, C. E. M. (1966). *ESP: A scientific evaluation*. New York: Scribners.

Hansel, C. E. M. (1980). *ESP and parapsychology: A critical re-evaluation*. Buffalo, NY: Prometheus Books.

Hansel, C. E. M. (1989). *The search for psychic power: ESP & parapsychology revisited*. Buffalo, NY: Prometheus Books.

Hansen, G. P. (1985). A brief overview of magic for parapsychologists. *Parapsychology Review*, 16(2), 5–8.

Hansen, G. P. (1990). Deception by subjects in psi research. *Journal of the American Society for Psychical Research*, 84, 25–80.

Hansen, G. P. (1992). CSICOP and the skeptics: An overview. *Journal of the American Society for Psychical Research*, 86, 19–63.

Hansen, G. P. (2001). *The trickster and the paranormal*. Philadelphia, PA: Xlibris.

Hansen, G. P., Utts, J., & Markwick, B. (1992). Critique of the PEAR remote-viewing experiments. *Journal of Parapsychology*, 56, 97–113.

Haraldsson, E. (1981). Some determinants of belief in psychical phenomena. *Journal of the American Society for Psychical Research*, 75, 297–309.

Haraldsson, E. (1985). Representative national surveys of psychic phenomena: Iceland, Great Britain, Sweden, USA and Gallup's multinational survey. *Journal of the Society for Psychical Research*, 53, 145–158.

Haraldsson, E. (1991). Children claiming past-life memories: Four cases in Sri Lanka. *Journal of Scientific Exploration*, 5, 233–261.

Haraldsson, E. (1994). Apparitions of the dead: Analysis of a new collection of 350 reports. In E. W. Cook & D. L. Delanoy (Eds.), *Research in parapsychology 1991* (pp. 1–6). Metuchen, NJ: Scarecrow Press.

Haraldsson, E. (1995). Personality and abilities of children claiming previous-life memories. *Journal of Nervous and Mental Disease*, 183, 445–451.

Haraldsson, E. (1997). A psychological comparison between ordinary children and those who claim previous-life memories. *Journal of Scientific Exploration*, 11, 323–335.

Haraldsson, E. (2003). Children who speak of past-life experiences: Is there a psychological explanation? *Psychology and Psychotherapy: Theory, Research and Practice*, 76, 55–67.

Haraldsson, E., & Abu-Izzeddin, M. A. (2004). Three randomly selected Lebanese cases of children who claim memories of a previous life. *Journal of the Society for Psychical Research*, 68, 65–85.

Haraldsson, E., Fowler, P. C., & Periyannanpillai, V. (2000). Psychological characteristics of children who speak of a previous life: A further field study in Sri Lanka. *Transcultural Psychiatry*, 37, 525–544.

Haraldsson, E., & Gissurarson, L. R. (1987). Does geomagnetic activity effect extrasensory perception? *Personality and Individual Differences*, 8, 745–747.

Haraldsson, E., Gudmundsdottir, A. Ragnarsson, A., Loftsson, J., & Jonsson, S. (1977). National survey of psychical experiences and attitudes toward the paranormal in Iceland. In J. D. Morris, W. G. Roll, & R. L. Morris (Eds.), *Research in parapsychology 1976* (pp. 182–186). Metuchen, NJ: Scarecrow Press.

Haraldsson, E., & Houtkooper, J. M. (1991). Psychic experiences in the Multinational Human Values Study: Who reports them? *Journal of the American Society for Psychical Research*, 85, 145–165.

Haraldsson, E., & Houtkooper, J. M. (1992). Effects of perceptual defensiveness, personality and belief on extrasensory perception tasks. *Personality and Individual Differences*, 13, 1085–1096.

Haraldsson, E., & Houtkooper, J. M. (1995). Meta-analyses of 10 experiments on perceptual defensiveness and ESP: ESP scoring patterns and experimenter and decline effects. *Journal of Parapsychology*, 59, 251–271.

Haraldsson, E., Houtkooper, J. M., & Hoeltje, C. (1987). The Defense Mechanism Test as a predictor of ESP performance: Icelandic study VII and meta-analysis of 13 experiments. *Journal of Parapsychology*, 51, 75–90.

Haraldsson, E., Houtkooper, J. M., Schneider, R., & Bäckström, M. (2002). Perceptual defensiveness and ESP performance: Reconstructed DMT ratings and psychological correlates in the first German DMT-ESP experiment. *Journal of Parapsychology*, 66, 249–270.

Haraldsson, E., & Johnson, M. (1979). ESP and the Defense Mechanism Test (DMT). Icelandic study No. III. A case of experimenter effect? *European Journal of Parapsychology*, 3, 11–20.

Harary, S. B. (1982). The marshmallow ghost: A group-counseling approach to a case of reported apparitions. In W. G. Roll, R. L. Morris, & R. A. White (Eds.), *Research in parapsychology 1981* (pp. 187–189). Metuchen, NJ: Scarecrow Press.

Harding, S. (1986). *The science question in feminism*. Ithaca, NY: Cornell University Press.

Harding, S. (Ed.) (1987). *Feminism and methodology: Social science issues*. Bloomington, IN: Indiana University Press.

Hardy, A. C. (1950). Telepathy and evolutionary theory. *Journal of the Society for Psychical Research*, 35, 225–238.

Harris, J., & Gregory, R. L. (1981). Tests of the hallucinations of "Ruth." *Perception*, 10, 351–354.

Harris, M. (1986). *Investigating the unexplained*. Buffalo, NY: Prometheus Books.

Harris, W. S., Gowda, M., Kolb, J. W., Strychacz, C. P., Vacek, J. L., Jones, P. G., et al. (1999). A randomized, controlled trial of the effects of remote, intercessory prayer on outcomes in patients admitted to a coronary care unit. *Archives of Internal Medicine*, 159, 2273–2278.

Hart, H. (1956). Six theories about apparitions. *Proceedings of the Society for Psychical Research*, 50, 153–239.

Hart, H. (1967). Scientific survival research. *International Journal of Parapsychology*, 9, 43–52.

Harvey, D. (1983). *The power to heal: An investigation of healing and the healing experience*. Wellingborough, England: Aquarian Press.

Hasted, J. (1981). *The metal-benders*. London: Routledge & Kegan Paul.

Hasted, J. B., & Robertson, D. (1979). The detail of paranormal metal-bending. *Journal of the Society for Psychical Research*, 50, 9–20.

Hastings, A. (1983). A counseling approach to parapsychological experience. *Journal of Transpersonal Psychology*, 15, 143–167.

Hastings, A. (1987). The study of channeling. In D. H. Weiner & R. D. Nelson (Eds.), *Research in parapsychology 1986* (pp. 152–153). Metuchen, NJ: Scarecrow Press.

Hastings, A. (2002). The resistance to belief. *Journal of Near-Death Studies*, 21, 77–98.

Hastings, A., Hutton, M., Braud, W., Bennett, C., Berk, I., Boynton, T., Dawn, C., Ferguson, E., Goldman, A., Greene, E., Hewett, M., Lind, V., McLellan, K., & Steinbach-Humphrey, S. (2002). Psychomanteum research: Experiences and effects on bereavement. *Omega*, 45, 211–228.

Hastings, R. J. (1969). An examination of the Dieppe Raid case. *Journal of the Society for Psychical Research*, 45, 55–63.

Head, J., & Cranston, S. L. (Eds.) (1977). *Reincarnation: The phoenix fire mystery*. New York: Crown.

Heaney, J. J. (1983). Recent studies of near-death experiences. *Journal of Religion and Health*, 22, 116–130.

Hearne, K. M. T. (1984). A survey of reported premonitions and of those who have them. *Journal of the Society for Psychical Research*, 52, 261–270.

Hearnshaw, L. S. (1979). *Cyril Burt, psychologist*. London: Hodder & Stoughton.

Heath, P. R. (2000). The PK zone: A phenomenological study. *Journal of Parapsychology*, 64, 53–72.

Hebb, D. O. (1951). The role of neurological ideas in psychology. *Journal of Personality*, 20, 35–55.

Hergovich, A., & Arendasy, M. (2005). Critical thinking ability and belief in the paranormal. *Personality and Individual Differences*, 38, 1805–1812.

Hergovich, A., Schott, R., & Arendasy, M. (in press). Paranormal belief and religiosity. *Journal of Parapsychology*.

Herman, D. (2000). Pragmatic constraints on narrative processing: Actants and anaphora resolution in a corpus of North Carolina ghost stories. *Journal of Pragmatics*, **32**, 959–1001.

Hess, D. J. (1989a). The poltergeist and cultural values: A comparative interpretation of a Brazilian and an American case. In L. A. Henkel & R. E. Berger (Eds.), *Research in parapsychology 1988* (pp. 64–66). Metuchen, NJ: Scarecrow Press.

Hess, D. J. (1989b). Gender, hierarchy, and the psychic: An interpretation of the culture of parapsychology. In L. A. Henkel & R. E. Berger (Eds.), *Research in parapsychology 1988* (pp. 104–106). Metuchen, NJ: Scarecrow Press.

Hess, D. J. (1993). *Science in the New Age: The paranormal, its defenders and debunkers, and American culture*. Madison, WI: University of Wisconsin Press.

Hillstrom, E. L., & Strachan, M. (2000). Strong commitment to traditional Protestant religious beliefs is negatively related to beliefs in paranormal phenomena. *Psychological Reports*, **86**, 183–189.

Hines, T. (2003). *Pseudoscience and the paranormal* (2nd ed.). Amherst, NY: Prometheus Books.

Hodges, R. D., & Scofield, A. M. (1995). Is spiritual healing a valid and effective therapy? *Journal of the Royal Society of Medicine*, **88**, 203–207.

Hodgson, R. (1892). A record of certain phenomena of trance. *Proceedings of the Society for Psychical Research*, **8**, 1–167.

Hodgson, R. (1898). A further record of observations of certain phenomena of trance. *Proceedings of the Society for Psychical Research*, **13**, 284–582.

Hoebens, P. H., & Truzzi, M. (1985). Reflections on psychic sleuths. In P. Kurtz (Ed.), *A skeptic's handbook of parapsychology* (pp. 631–643). Buffalo, NY: Prometheus Books.

Holck, F. H. (1978). Life revisited (parallels in death experiences). *Omega*, **9**, 1–11.

Holden, J. M. (1996). Effect on emotional well-being of hypnotic recall of the near-death experience. *Journal of Near-Death Studies*, **14**, 273–280.

Holt, N. J., & Roe, C. A. (in press). The sender as a PK agent in ESP studies: The effects of agent and target system lability upon performance at a novel PK task. *Journal of Parapsychology*.

Home, D. D. (c. 1973). *Incidents in my life* (2nd ed.). Secaucus, NJ: University Books. (Original work published 1864)

Honegger, B. (1979). Correspondence. *Parapsychology Review*, **10**(2), 24–26.

Honorton, C. (1970). Effects of feedback on discrimination between correct and incorrect ESP responses. *Journal of the American Society for Psychical Research*, **64**, 404–410.

Honorton, C. (1972). Reported frequency of dream recall and ESP. *Journal of the American Society for Psychical Research*, **66**, 369–374.

Honorton, C. (1975). Objective determination of information rate in psi tasks with pictorial stimuli. *Journal of the American Society for Psychical Research*, **69**, 353–359.

Honorton, C. (1977). Psi and internal attention states. In B. B. Wolman (Ed.), *Handbook of parapsychology* (pp. 435–472). New York: Van Nostrand Reinhold.

Honorton, C. (1978). Psi and internal attention states: Information retrieval in the ganzfeld. In B. Shapin & L. Coly (Eds.), *Psi and states of awareness* (pp. 79–90). New York: Parapsychology Foundation.

Honorton, C. (1985). Meta-analysis of psi ganzfeld research: A response to Hyman. *Journal of Parapsychology*, **49**, 51–91.

Honorton, C. (1993). Rhetoric over substance: The impoverished state of skepticism. *Journal of Parapsychology*, **57**, 191–214.

Honorton, C., Berger, R. E., Varvoglis, M. P., Quant, M., Derr, P., Hansen, G. P., Schechter, E., & Ferrari, D. C. (1990). Psi ganzfeld experiments using an automated testing system: An update and comparison with a meta-analysis of earlier studies. In L. A. Henkel & J. Palmer (Eds.), *Research in parapsychology 1989* (pp. 25–32). Metuchen, NJ: Scarecrow Press.

Honorton, C., & Ferrari, D. C. (1989). "Future telling": A meta-analysis of forced-choice precognition experiments, 1935–1987. *Journal of Parapsychology*, **53**, 281–308.

Honorton, C., Ferrari, D. C., & Bem, D. J. (1998). Extraversion and ESP performance: A meta-analysis and a new confirmation. *Journal of Parapsychology*, **62**, 255–276.

Honorton, C., & May, E. C. (1976). Volitional control in a psychokinetic task with auditory and visual feedback. In J. D. Morris, W. G. Roll, & R. L. Morris (Eds.), *Research in parapsychology 1975* (pp. 90–91). Metuchen, NJ: Scarecrow Press.

Honorton, C., Ramsey, M., & Cabibbo, C. (1975). Experimenter effects in extrasensory perception. *Journal of the American Society for Psychical Research*, **69**, 135–149.

Houran, J. (1997). Ambiguous origins and indications of "poltergeists." *Perceptual and Motor Skills*, **84**, 339–344.

Houran, J. (2000). Toward a psychology of "entity encounter experiences." *Journal of the Society for Psychical Research*, **64**, 141–158.

Houran, J., Ashe, D. D., & Thalbourne, M. A. (2003). Encounter experiences in the context of mental boundaries and bilaterality. *Journal of the Society for Psychical Research*, **67**, 260–280.

Houran, J., & Brugger, P. (2000). The need for independent control sites: A methodological suggestion with special reference to haunting and poltergeist field research. *European Journal of Parapsychology*, **15**, 30–45.

Houran, J., & Lange, R. (1996). Diary of events in a thoroughly unhaunted house. *Perceptual and Motor Skills*, **83**, 499–502.

Houtkooper, J. M. (2002). Arguing for an observational theory of paranormal phenomena. *Journal of Scientific Exploration*, **16**, 171–185.

Houtkooper, J. M., & Haraldsson, E. (1996, August). *Reliabilities and psychological correlates of guessing and scoring behavior in a forced choice ESP task*. Paper presented at the 39th Annual Convention of the Parapsychological Association, San Diego, CA.

Houtkooper, J. M. (2003). An ESP experiment with natural and simulated sferics: Displacement scores and psychological variables. *European Journal of Parapsychology*, **18**, 49–64.

Houtkooper, J. M., & Haraldsson, E. (1997). Reliabilities and psychological correlates of guessing and scoring behavior in a forced-choice ESP task. *Journal of Parapsychology*, **61**, 119–134.

Houtkooper, J. M., Schienle, A., Stark, R., & Vaitl, D. (1999). Atmospheric electromagnetism: The possible disturbing influence of natural sferics on ESP. *Perceptual and Motor Skills*, **89**, 1179–1192.

Houtkooper, J. M., Schienle, A., Stark, R., & Vaitl, D. (2001). Atmospheric electromagnetism: Attempted replication of the correlation between natural sferics and ESP. *Perceptual and Motor Skills*, **93**, 754–756.

Hövelmann, G. H., & Krippner, S. (1986). Charting the future of parapsychology. *Parapsychology Review*, **17**(6), 1–5.

Hubbard, G. S., & May, E. C. (1987). Aspects of measurement and application of geomagnetic indices and extremely low frequency electromagnetic radiation for use in parapsychology. In D. H. Weiner & R. D. Nelson (Eds.), *Research in parapsychology 1986* (pp. 79–82). Metuchen, NJ: Scarecrow Press.

Humphrey, B. M. (1946a). Success in ESP as related to form of response drawings: I. Clairvoyance experiments. *Journal of Parapsychology*, **10**, 78–106.

Humphrey, B. M. (1946b). Success in ESP as related to form of response drawings: II. GESP experiments. *Journal of Parapsychology*, **10**, 181–196.

Humphrey, B. M. (1947). Help-hinder comparison in PK tests. *Journal of Parapsychology*, **11**, 4–13.

Humphrey, B. M., & Rhine, J. B. (1945). PK tests with two sizes of dice mechanically thrown. *Journal of Parapsychology*, **9**, 124–132.

Hunt, H. T., Gervais, A., Shearing-Johns, S., & Travis, F. (1992). Transpersonal experiences in childhood: An exploratory empirical study of selected adult groups. *Perceptual and Motor Skills*, **75**, 1135–1153.

Hunter, R., & Derr, J. (1978). Prediction monitoring and evaluation program. *Earthquake Information Bulletin*, **10**, 93–96.

Hutchinson, L. (1940). Variations of time intervals in pre-shuffle card-calling tests. *Journal of Parapsychology*, **4**, 249–270.

Hutchinson, M. (1988). A thorn in Geller's side. *British and Irish Skeptic*, **2**(4), 9–11.

Hyman, R. (1977). "Cold reading": How to convince strangers that you know all about them. *The Zetetic*, **1**(2), 18–37.

Hyman, R. (1980). Pathological science: Towards a proper diagnosis and remedy. *Zetetic Scholar*, **6**, 31–39.

Hyman, R. (1981). Further comments on Schmidt's PK experiments. *Skeptical Inquirer*, **5**, 34–40.

Hyman, R. (1985). The ganzfeld psi experiment: A critical appraisal. *Journal of Parapsychology*, **49**, 3–49.

Hyman, R. (1995). Evaluation of the program on anomalous mental phenomena. *Journal of Parapsychology*, **59**, 321–351.

Hyman, R. (1996). Evaluation of a program on anomalous mental phenomena. *Journal of Scientific Exploration*, **10**, 31–58.

Hyman, R. (2003). How *not* to test mediums: Critiquing the afterlife experiments. *Skeptical Inquirer*, **27**(1), 20–30.

Hyman, R., & Honorton, C. (1986). A joint communiqué: The psi ganzfeld controversy. *Journal of Parapsychology*, **50**, 351–364.

Ibison, M. (1998). Evidence that anomalous statistical influence depends on the details of the random process. *Journal of Scientific Exploration*, **12**, 407–423.

Inglis, B. (1977). *Natural and supernatural: A history of the paranormal from earliest times to 1914*. London: Hodder & Stoughton.

Inglis, B. (1986). Retrocognitive dissonance. *Theta*, **13/14**(1), 4–9.

Insinger, M. (1991). The impact of a near-death experience on family relationships. *Journal of Near-Death Studies*, **9**, 141–181.

Irwin, H. J. (1978a). ESP and the human information processing system. *Journal of the American Society for Psychical Research*, **72**, 111–126.

Irwin, H. J. (1978b). Psi, attention, and processing capacity. *Journal of the American Society for Psychical Research*, **72**, 301–313.

Irwin, H. J. (1979a). *Psi and the mind: An information processing approach*. Metuchen, NJ: Scarecrow Press.

Irwin, H. J. (1979b). On directional inconsistency in the correlation between ESP and memory. *Journal of Parapsychology*, **43**, 31–39.

Irwin, H. J. (1979c). Coding preferences and the form of spontaneous extrasensory experiences. *Journal of Parapsychology*, **43**, 205–220.

Irwin, H. J. (1980a). Information processing theory and psi phenomena. In B. Shapin & L. Coly (Eds.), *Communication and parapsychology* (pp. 25–43). New York: Parapsychology Foundation.

Irwin, H. J. (1980b). PK and memory: An information-processing model of psychokinetic effects. *Journal of the American Society for Psychical Research*, **74**, 381–394.

Irwin, H. J. (1980c). Out of the body Down Under: Some cognitive characteristics of Australian students reporting OOBEs. *Journal of the Society for Psychical Research*, **50**, 448–459.

Irwin, H. J. (1981a). The psychological function of out-of-body experiences: So who needs the out-of-body experience? *Journal of Nervous and Mental Disease*, **169**, 244–248.

Irwin, H. J. (1981b). Some psychological dimensions of the out-of-body experience. *Parapsychology Review*, **12**(4), 1–6.

Irwin, H. J. (1985a). *Flight of mind: A psychological study of the out-of-body experience*. Metuchen, NJ: Scarecrow Press.

Irwin, H. J. (1985b). Parapsychological phenomena and the absorption domain. *Journal of the American Society for Psychical Research*, **79**, 1–11.

Irwin, H. J. (1985c). Fear of psi and attitude to parapsychological research. *Parapsychology Review*, **16**(6), 1–4.

Irwin, H. J. (1985d). A study of the measurement and the correlates of paranormal belief. *Journal of the American Society for Psychical Research*, **79**, 301–326.

Irwin, H. J. (1985e). Is psi a unitary domain? Analysis in terms of performance patterns. *Parapsychological Journal of South Africa*, 6, 34–46.

Irwin, H. J. (1986a). Perceptual perspective of visual imagery in OBEs, dreams and reminiscence. *Journal of the Society for Psychical Research*, 53, 210–217.

Irwin, H. J. (1986b). The relationship between locus of control and belief in the paranormal. *Parapsychological Journal of South Africa*, 7, 1–23.

Irwin, H. J. (1987a). Charles Bailey: A biographical study of the Australian apport medium. *Journal of the Society for Psychical Research*, 54, 97–118.

Irwin, H. J. (1987b). Images of heaven. *Parapsychology Review*, 18(1), 1–4.

Irwin, H. J. (1987c). Out-of-body experiences in the blind. *Journal of Near-Death Studies*, 6, 53–60.

Irwin, H. J. (1988a). Out-of-body experiences and dream lucidity: Empirical perspectives. In J. Gackenbach & S. LaBerge (Eds.), *Conscious mind, sleeping brain: New perspectives in lucid dreaming* (pp. 353–371). New York: Plenum Press.

Irwin, H. J. (1988b). Out-of-body experiences and attitudes to life and death. *Journal of the American Society for Psychical Research*, 82, 237–251.

Irwin, H. J. (1988c). Parapsychology in Australia. *Journal of the American Society for Psychical Research*, 82, 319–338.

Irwin, H. J. (1989a). Extrasensory experiences and the need for absorption. *Parapsychology Review*, 20(6), 9–10.

Irwin, H. J. (1989b). The near-death experience in childhood. *Australian Parapsychological Review*, 14, 7–11.

Irwin, H. J. (1989c). On paranormal belief: The psychology of the sceptic. In G. K. Zollschan, J. F. Schumaker & G. F. Walsh (Eds.), *Exploring the paranormal: Perspectives on belief and experience* (pp. 305–312). Bridport, UK: Prism Press.

Irwin, H. J. (1990a). Fantasy proneness and paranormal beliefs. *Psychological Reports*, 66, 655–658.

Irwin, H. J. (1990b). Parapsychology courses and students' belief in the paranormal. *Journal of the Society for Psychical Research*, 56, 266–272.

Irwin, H. J. (1991a). A study of paranormal belief, psychological adjustment and fantasy proneness. *Journal of the American Society for Psychical Research*, 85, 317–331.

Irwin, H. J. (1991b). The presentation of parapsychology in psychology texts. *Australian Parapsychological Review*, 18, 21–23.

Irwin, H. J. (1991c). The reasoning skills of paranormal believers. *Journal of Parapsychology*, 55, 281–300.

Irwin, H. J. (1992). Origins and functions of paranormal belief: The role of childhood trauma and interpersonal control. *Journal of the American Society for Psychical Research*, 86, 199–208.

Irwin, H. J. (1993a). Belief in the paranormal: A review of the empirical literature. *Journal of the American Society for Psychical Research*, 87, 1–39.

Irwin, H. J. (1993b). The near-death experience as a dissociative phenomenon: An empirical assessment. *Journal of Near-Death Studies*, 12, 95–103.

Irwin, H. J. (1994a). Paranormal belief and proneness to dissociation. *Psychological Reports*, 75, 1344–1346.

Irwin, H. J. (1994b). The phenomenology of parapsychological experiences. In S. Krippner (Ed.), *Advances in parapsychological research, Vol. 7* (pp. 10–76). Jefferson, NC: McFarland.

Irwin, H. J. (1994c). Proneness to dissociation and traumatic childhood events. *Journal of Nervous and Mental Disease*, 182, 456–460.

Irwin, H. J. (1995). Las creencias paranormales y las funciones emocionales [Paranormal belief and emotional functioning]. *Revista Argentina de Psicologia Paranormal*, 6, 69–76.

Irwin, H. J. (1996). Childhood antecedents of out-of-body and déjà vu experiences. *Journal of the American Society for Psychical Research*, 90, 157–173.

Irwin, H. J. (1997). An empirically derived typology of paranormal believers. *European Journal of Parapsychology*, 13, 1–14.

Irwin, H. J. (2000). The disembodied self: An empirical study of dissociation and the out-of-body experience. *Journal of Parapsychology*, 64, 261–277.

Irwin, H. J. (2001a). Age and sex differences in paranormal beliefs after controlling for differential item functioning. *European Journal of Parapsychology*, 16, 102–106.

Irwin, H. J. (2001b). Psychic detection: The use of psi in criminal investigation. *Australian Journal of Parapsychology*, 1, 61–71.

Irwin, H. J. (2003a). Paranormal beliefs and the maintenance of assumptive world views. *Journal of the Society for Psychical Research*, 67, 18–25.

Irwin, H. J. (2003b). Reality testing and the formation of paranormal beliefs. *European Journal of Parapsychology*, 18, 15–28.

Irwin, H. J. (2004). Reality testing and the formation of paranormal beliefs: A constructive replication. *Journal of the Society for Psychical Research*, 68, 143–152.

Irwin, H. J. (2006). *The psychology of paranormal belief*. New York: Parapsychology Foundation.

Irwin, H. J., & Bramwell, B. A. (1988). The devil in heaven: A near-death experience with both positive and negative facets. *Journal of Near-Death Studies*, 7, 38–43.

Irwin, H. J., & Green, M. J. (1998). Schizotypal processes and belief in the paranormal: A multidimensional study. *European Journal of Parapsychology*, 14, 1–15.

Irwin, H. J., & Young, J. M. (2002). Intuitive versus reflective processes in the formation of paranormal beliefs. *European Journal of Parapsychology*, 17, 45–53.

Isaacs, E. (1983). The Fox sisters and American spiritualism. In H. Kerr & C. L. Crow (Eds.), *The occult in America: New historical perspectives* (pp. 79–110). Urbana, IL: University of Chicago Press.

Isaacs, J. (1983). A twelve-session study of micro-PKMB training. In W. G. Roll, J. Beloff & R. A. White (Eds.), *Research in parapsychology 1982* (pp. 31–35). Metuchen, NJ: Scarecrow Press.

Isaacs, J. D. (1986). PK and conscious awareness. In D. H. Weiner & D. I. Radin (Eds.), *Research in para-*

psychology 1985 (pp. 162–163). Metuchen, NJ: Scarecrow Press.

Iverson, J. (1976). *More lives than one?* London: Souvenir Press.

Jackson, M., Franzoi, S., & Schmeidler, G. R. (1977). Effects of feedback on ESP: A curious partial replication. *Journal of the American Society for Psychical Research*, 71, 147–155.

Jacobs, J. R., & Bovasso, G. (1996). A profile analysis of psychopathology in clusters of depersonalization types. *Dissociation*, 9, 169–175.

Jahn, R. G. (1984). On the representation of psychic research to the community of established science. In R. A. White & R. S. Broughton (Eds.), *Research in parapsychology 1983* (pp. 127–138). Metuchen, NJ: Scarecrow Press.

Jahn, R. G., & Dunne, B. J. (1986). On the quantum mechanics of consciousness, with application to anomalous phenomena. *Foundations of Physics*, 16, 721–772.

Jahn, R. G., & Dunne, B. J. (1987). *Margins of reality: The role of consciousness in the physical world.* San Diego, CA: Harcourt Brace Jovanovich.

Jahn, R. G., Dunne, B. J., Nelson, R. D., Dobyns, Y. H., & Bradish, G. J. (1997). Correlations of random binary sequences with pre-stated operator intention: A review of a 12-year program. *Journal of Scientific Exploration*, 11, 345–367.

Jahn, R. G., Mischo, S., Vaitl, D., Dunne, B., Boller, E., Houtkooper, J., et al. (2000). Mind/machine interaction consortium: PortREG replication experiments. *Journal of Scientific Exploration*, 14, 499–555.

James, W. (1886). Report of the committee on mediumistic phenomena. *Proceedings of the American Society for Psychical Research* [Original Series], 1, 102–106.

Jansen, K. L. R. (1990). Neuroscience and the near death experience: Roles for the NMDA-PCP receptor, the sigma receptor and the endopsychosins. *Medical Hypotheses*, 31, 25–29.

Jaroff, L. (2001). The magician and the think tank. In P. Kurtz (Ed.), *Skeptical odysseys: Personal accounts by the world's leading paranormal inquirers* (pp. 95–100). Amherst, NY: Prometheus Books.

Jawer, M. (2006). Environmental sensitivity: Inquiry into a possible link with apparitional experience. *Journal of the Society for Psychical Research*, 70, 25–47.

Jenkins, E. (1982). *The shadow and the light: A defense of Daniel Dunglas Home, the medium.* London: Hamish Hamilton.

Jephson, I. (1928). Evidence for clairvoyance in card-guessing. *Proceedings of the Society for Psychical Research*, 38, 223–268.

John, I. D. (1991). Differences in scientists' discourse about scientific fraud and impropriety. *Australian Psychologist*, 26, 120–122.

Johnson, M., & Nordbeck, B. (1972). Variation in the scoring behavior of a "psychic" subject. *Journal of Parapsychology*, 36, 122–132.

Johnson, M. E., & Hauck, C. (1999). Beliefs and opinions about hypnosis held by the general public: A systematic evaluation. *American Journal of Clinical Hypnosis*, 42, 10–20.

Jones, W. H., & Russell, D. (1980). The selective processing of belief disconfirming information. *European Journal of Social Psychology*, 10, 309–312.

Jones, W. H., Russell, D. W., & Nickel, T. W. (1977). Belief in the Paranormal Scale: An objective instrument to measure belief in magical phenomena and causes. *Journal Supplement Abstract Service, Catalog of Selected Documents in Psychology*, 7, 100 (MS 1577).

Jourdan, J. (1994). Near-death and transcendental experiences: Neurophysiological correlates of mystical traditions. *Journal of Near-Death Studies*, 12, 177–200.

Jung, C. G. (1963). *Memories, dreams, reflections.* London: Collins.

Jung, C. G. (1971). *The archetypes of the collective unconscious.* Princeton, NJ: Princeton University Press. (Original work published 1954)

Jung, C. G. (1985). *Synchronicity: An acausal connecting principle.* London: Routledge & Kegan Paul. (Original work published 1955)

Kampman, R., & Hirvenoja, R. (1978). Dynamic relation of the secondary personality induced by hypnosis to the present personality. In F. H. Frankel & H. S. Zamansky (Eds.), *Hypnosis at its bicentennial* (pp. 183–188). New York: Plenum Press.

Kanthamani, H., & Rao, H. H. (1974). A study of memory-ESP relationships using linguistic forms. *Journal of Parapsychology*, 38, 286–300.

Kaptchuk, T. J. (1998). Intentional ignorance: A history of blind assessment and placebo controls in medicine. *Bulletin of the History of Medicine*, 72, 389–433.

Keen, M., & Ellison, A. (1999). Scole: A response to critics. *Proceedings of the Society for Psychical Research*, 58, 425–439.

Keen, M., Ellison, A., & Fontana, D. (1999). The Scole Report. *Proceedings of the Society for Psychical Research*, 58, 149–392.

Keene, M. L. (1976). *The psychic Mafia.* New York: Dell.

Keil, H. H. J., Herbert, B., Ullman, M., & Pratt, J. G. (1976). Directly observable voluntary PK effects: A survey and tentative interpretation of available findings from Nina Kulagina and other known related cases of recent date. *Proceedings of the Society for Psychical Research*, 56, 197–235.

Keil, J. (1981). Recent developments in Australia. *Parapsychology Review*, 12(2),16–18.

Keil, J. (1991). New cases in Burma, Thailand, and Turkey: A limited field study replication of some aspects of Ian Stevenson's research. *Journal of Scientific Exploration*, 5, 27–59.

Keil, J., & Stevenson, I., (1999). Do cases of the reincarnation type show similar features over many years? A study of Turkish cases a generation apart. *Journal of Scientific Exploration*, 13, 189–198.

Keil, J., & Tucker, J. (2005). Children who claim to remember previous lives: Cases with written records made before the previous personality was identified. *Journal of Scientific Exploration*, 19, 91–101.

Keinan, G. (2002). The effects of stress and desire for control on superstitious behavior. *Personality and Social Psychology Bulletin*, 28, 102–108.

Kellehear, A. (1993). Culture, biology, and the near-death experience. *Journal of Nervous and Mental Disease*, **181**, 148–156.

Kellehear, A., & Heaven, P. (1989). Community attitudes toward near-death experiences: An Australian study. *Journal of Near-Death Studies*, 7, 165–172.

Kellehear, A., Heaven, P., & Gao, J. (1990). Community attitudes toward near-death experiences: A Chinese study. *Journal of Near-Death Studies*, **8**, 163–173.

Kellehear, A., & Irwin, H. J. (1990). Five minutes after death: A study of beliefs and expectations. *Journal of Near-Death Studies*, **9**, 77–90.

Kellehear, A., Stevenson, I., Pasricha, S., & Cook, E. (1994). The absence of tunnel sensations in near-death experiences from India. *Journal of Near-Death Studies*, **13**, 109–113.

Keller, E. F. (1983). Gender and science. In S. Harding & M. B. Hintikka (Eds.), *Discovering reality: Feminist perspectives on epistemology, metaphysics, methodology, and philosophy of science* (pp. 187–205). Dordrecht, Holland: Reidel.

Kelly, E. F. (1982). On grouping of hits in some exceptional psi performers. *Journal of the American Society for Psychical Research*, 76, 101–142.

Kelly, E. F., Kanthamani, H., Child, I. L., & Young, F. W. (1975). On the relation between visual and ESP confusion structures in an exceptional ESP subject. *Journal of the American Society for Psychical Research*, 69, 1–31.

Kelly, E. W. (2001). The contributions of F. W. H. Myers to Psychology. *Journal of the Society for Psychical Research*, **65**, 65–90.

Kelly, E. W., & Alvarado, C. S. (2005). Frederic William Henry Myers, 1843–1901. *American Journal of Psychiatry*, *162*, 34.

Kennedy, J. E. (1978). The role of task complexity in PK: A review. *Journal of Parapsychology*, **42**, 89–122.

Kennedy, J. E. (1979). Consistent missing: A type of information-processing error in ESP. *Journal of Parapsychology*, **43**, 113–128.

Kennedy, J. E. (2002). Commentary on "Experiments on distant intercessory prayer" in *Archives of Internal Medicine*. *Journal of Parapsychology*, **66**, 177–182.

Kennedy, J. E. (2003). The capricious, actively evasive, unsustainable nature of psi: A summary and hypotheses. *Journal of Parapsychology*, **67**, 53–74.

Kennedy, J. E. (2004). A proposal and challenge for proponents and skeptics of psi. *Journal of Parapsychology*, **68**, 157–167.

Kennedy, J. E., & Kanthamani, H. (1995). Association between anomalous experiences and artistic creativity and spirituality. *Journal of the American Society for Psychical Research*, **89**, 333–343.

Kennedy, J. E., & Taddonio, J. L. (1976). Experimenter effects in parapsychological research. *Journal of Parapsychology*, **40**, 1–33.

Kennedy, J. L. (1939). A methodological review of extrasensory perception. *Psychological Bulletin*, **36**, 59–103.

Kenny, M. G. (1986). *The passion of Ansel Bourne: Multiple personality in American culture*. Washington, DC: Smithsonian Institution Press.

Killen, P., Wildman, R. W., & Wildman, R. W. (1974). Superstitiousness and intelligence. *Psychological Reports*, **34**, 1158.

Kleinman, A. (1980). *Patients and healers in the context of culture: An exploration of the borderland between anthropology, medicine, and psychiatry*. Berkeley, CA: University of California Press.

Kocsis, R. N., Irwin, H. J., Hayes, A. F., & Nunn, R. (2000). Expertise in psychological profiling: A comparative assessment. *Journal of Interpersonal Violence*, 15, 311–331.

Kogan, I. M. (1966). Is telepathy possible? *Telecommunication and Radio Engineering*, **21** (No. 1, Part 2), 75–81.

Kohn, A. (1987). *False prophets: Fraud and error in science and medicine*. New York: Blackwell.

Krauss, R. H. (1994). *Beyond light and shadow* [T. Brill & J. Gledhill, Trans.]. Munich: Nazraeli Press.

Kreiman, N. (2001). Posible identidad topologica entre figuras Zener, en los experimentos de eleccion forzosa. *Cuadernos de Parapsicología*, **34**(1), 1–5.

Kreitler, H., & Kreitler, S. (1973). Subliminal perception and extrasensory perception. *Journal of Parapsychology*, 37, 163–188.

Krieger, J. (1977). Hemispheric specialization in intentional versus nonintentional psi performance. *Journal of Parapsychology*, **41**, 40–42. (Abstract)

Krippner, S. (1982). Psychic healing. In I. Grattan-Guinness (Ed.), *Psychical research: A guide to its history, principles and practices* (pp. 134–143). Wellingborough, England: Aquarian Press.

Krippner, S. (1988). Parapsychology and postmodern science. In D. R. Griffin (Ed.), *The reenchantment of science: Postmodern proposals* (pp. 129–140). Albany, NY: State University of New York Press.

Krippner, S. (1989). The healing process: How native healers contribute to knowledge. *Australian Parapsychological Review*, 14, 3–6.

Krippner, S. (1992). Parapsicologia: Una perspective internacional [Parapsychology: An international perspective]. *Revista Argentina de Psicologia Paranormal*, **3**, 44–52.

Krippner, S. (1995). Psychical research in the postmodern world. *Journal of the Society for Psychical research*, **89**, 1–18.

Krippner, S. (2001). Psi and postmodernity in the twenty-first century. *International Journal of Parapsychology*, **12**(1), 128.

Krippner, S., Braud, W., Child, I. L., Palmer, J., Rao, K. R., Schlitz, M., White, R. A., & Utts, J. (1993). Demonstration research and meta-analysis in parapsychology. *Journal of Parapsychology*, **57**, 275–286.

Krippner, S., Vaughan, A., & Spottiswoode, J. (2000). Geomagnetic factors in subjective precognitive dream experiences. *Journal of the Society for Psychical Research*, 64, 109–118.

Kuley, N. B., & Jacobs, D. F. (1988). The relationship between dissociative-like experiences and sensation seeking among social and problem gamblers. *Journal of Gambling Behavior*, 4, 197–207.

Kumar, V. K., Pekala, R. J., & Cummings, J. (1993). Sensation seeking, drug use and reported paranormal beliefs and experiences. *Personality and Individual Differences*, **14**, 685–691.

Lamal, P. A. (1989). Attending to parapsychology. *Teaching of Psychology*, 16, 28–30.

Lambert, G. W. (1959). Scottish haunts and poltergeists: A regional study. *Journal of the Society for Psychical Research*, 40, 108–120.

Lambert, G. W. (1976). D. D. Home and the physical world. *Journal of the Society for Psychical Research*, 48, 298–314.

Lambert, G. W., & Gay, K. (1952). The Dieppe Raid case: A collective auditory hallucination. *Journal of the Society for Psychical Research*, 36, 607–618.

Lamont, P. (1999, August). *How convincing is the evidence for D. D. Home?* Paper presented at the 42nd Annual Convention of the Parapsychological Association, Palo Alto, CA.

Lamont, P. (2005). *The first psychic: The peculiar mystery of a notorious Victorian wizard.* London: Little, Brown.

Lange, R., Greyson, B., & Houran, J. (2004). A Rasch scaling validation of a "core" near-death experience. *British Journal of Psychology*, 95, 161–177.

Lange, R., & Houran, J. (1997). Context-induced paranormal experiences: Support for Houran and Lange's model of haunting phenomena. *Perceptual and Motor Skills*, 85, 95–98.

Lange, R., & Houran, J. (1998). Delusions of the paranormal: A haunting question of perception. *Journal of Nervous and Mental Disease*, 186, 637–645.

Lange, R., Houran, J., Harte, T. M., & Havens, R. A. (1996). Contextual mediation of perceptions in hauntings and poltergeist-like experiences. *Perceptual and Motor Skills*, 82, 755–762.

Lange, R., & Houran, J. (2001). Ambiguous stimuli brought to life: The psychological dynamics of hauntings and poltergeists. In J. Houran & R. Lange (Eds.), *Hauntings and poltergeists: Multidisciplinary perspectives* (pp. 280–306). Jefferson, NC: McFarland.

Lange, R., Irwin, H. J., & Houran, J. (2000). Top-down purification of Tobacyk's Revised Paranormal Belief Scale. *Personality and Individual Differences*, 29, 131–156.

Langer, E. J. (1975). The illusion of control. *Journal of Personality and Social Psychology*, 32, 311–328.

Lansberry, L. D. (1994). First-person report: A skeptic's near-death experience. *Skeptical Inquirer*, 18, 431–432.

Lantz, N. D., Luke, W. L. W., & May, E. C. (1994). Target and sender dependencies in anomalous cognition experiments. *Journal of Parapsychology*, 58, 285–302.

Lawrence, M. (1997). *In a world of their own: Experiencing unconsciousness.* New York: Praeger.

Lawrence, T. R. (1991). Subjective random generations and the reversed sheep-goat effect: A failure to replicate. *European Journal of Parapsychology*, 8, 131–144.

Lawrence, T. R. (1993, August). *Gathering in the sheep and the goats…: A meta-analysis of forced-choice sheep-goat ESP studies, 1947–1993.* Paper presented at the 36th Annual Convention of the Parapsychological Association, Toronto, Canada.

Lawrence, T. R. (1995). How many factors of paranormal belief are there? A critique of the Paranormal Belief Scale. *Journal of Parapsychology*, 59, 3–25.

Lawrence, T. [R.], Edwards, C., Barraclough, N., Church, S., & Hetherington, F. (1995). Modeling childhood causes of paranormal belief and experience: Childhood trauma and childhood fantasy. *Personality and Individual Differences*, 19, 209–215.

Layton, B. D., & Turnbull, B. (1975). Belief, evaluation, and performance on an ESP task. *Journal of Experimental Social Psychology*, 11, 166–179.

Leahey, T. H., & Leahey, G. E. (1983). *Psychology's occult doubles: Psychology and the problem of pseudoscience.* Chicago: Nelson-Hall.

Lederer, R. J., & Singer, B. (1983). Pseudoscience in the name of the university. *Skeptical Inquirer*, 7(3), 57–62.

LeShan, L. (1966). Some psychological hypotheses on the non-acceptance of parapsychology as a science. *International Journal of Parapsychology*, 8, 367–385.

LeShan, L. (1974). *The medium, the mystic, and the physicist.* New York: Viking Press.

Lester, D. (2003). Depth of near-death experiences and confounding factors. *Perceptual and Motor Skills*, 96, 18.

Lett, J. (1992). The persistent popularity of the paranormal. *Skeptical Inquirer*, 16, 381–388.

Levi, A. (1979). The influence of imagery and feedback on PK effects. *Journal of Parapsychology*, 43, 275–289.

Levin, J. S. (1993). Age differences in mystical experience. *The Gerontologist*, 33, 507–513.

Lewicki, D. R., Schaut, G. H., & Persinger, M. A. (1987). Geophysical variables and behavior: XLIV. Days of subjective precognitive experiences and the days before the actual events display correlated geomagnetic activity. *Perceptual and Motor Skills*, 65, 173–174.

Lindley, J. H., Bryan, S., & Conley, B. (1981). Near-death experiences in a Pacific Northwest American population: The Evergreen study. *Anabiosis*, 1, 104–124.

Locke, T. P., & Shontz, F. C. (1983). Personality correlates of the near-death experience: A preliminary study. *Journal of the American Society for Psychical Research*, 77, 311–318.

Long, J. P., & Long, J. A. (2003). A comparison of near-death experiences occurring before and after 1975: Results from an internet survey. *Journal of Near-Death Studies*, 22, 21–32.

Lovitts, B. E. (1981). The sheep-goat effect turned upside down. *Journal of Parapsychology*, 45, 293–309.

Lucas, W. (1993). *Regression therapy: A handbook for professionals. Vol. 1: Past-life therapy.* Crest Park, CA: Deep Forest Press.

Lundahl, C. R. (Ed.) (1982). *A collection of near-death research readings.* Chicago: Nelson-Hall.

Lundahl, C. R. (1992). Angels in near-death experiences. *Journal of Near-Death Studies*, 11, 49–56.

Lundahl, C. R. (1993). The near-death experience: A theoretical summarization. *Journal of Near-Death Studies*, 12, 105–118.

Lynn, S. J., & Rhue, J. W. (1988). Fantasy proneness: Hypnosis, developmental antecedents, and psychopathology. *American Psychologist*, 43, 35–44.

Lyons, A., & Truzzi, M. (1991). *The blue sense: Psychic detectives and crime.* New York: Mysterious Press.

McAllister, I. (1988). Religious change and secularization: The transmission of religious values in Australia. *Sociological Analysis*, 49, 249–263.

McBeath, M. K. (1985). Psi and sexuality. *Journal of the Society for Psychical Research*, 53, 65–77.

McClenon, B., Roig, M., Smith, M. D., & Ferrier, G. (2003). The coverage of parapsychology in introductory psychology textbooks: 1990–2002. *Journal of Parapsychology*, 67, 167–179.

McClenon, J. (1982a). Two experiments in the practical application of psi. *Journal of Parapsychology*, 46, 59. (Abstract)

McClenon, J. (1982b). A survey of elite scientists: Their attitudes toward ESP and parapsychology. *Journal of Parapsychology*, 46, 127–152.

McClenon, J. (1984). *Deviant science: The case of parapsychology*. Philadelphia, PA: University of Pennsylvania Press.

McClenon, J. (1989). Parapsychology in Japan. *Parapsychology Review*, 20(4), 13–15.

McClenon, J. (2002). Content analysis of an anomalous experience collection: Evaluating evolutionary perspectives. *Journal of Parapsychology*, 66, 291–316.

McConnell, R. A. (1977). The resolution of conflicting beliefs about the ESP evidence. *Journal of Parapsychology*, 41, 198–214.

McConnell, R. A. (1987). *Parapsychology in retrospect: My search for the unicorn*. Pittsburgh, PA: Author.

McConnell, R. A., & Clark, T. K. (1980). Training, belief, and mental conflict within the Parapsychological Association. *Journal of Parapsychology*, 44, 245–268.

McConnell, R. A., & Clark, T. K. (1991). National Academy of Sciences' opinion on parapsychology. *Journal on the American Society for Psychical Research*, 85, 333–365.

McConnell, R. A., Snowdon, R. J., & Powell, K. F. (1955). Wishing with dice. *Journal of Experimental Psychology*, 50, 269–275.

McCormick, D. L. (1987). A lawsuit in Hawaii. *ASPR Newsletter*, 13, 14.

McCreery, C. (1986, September). *Spontaneous experiences and the Eysenck Personality Questionnaire*. Paper presented at the 10th International Conference of the Society for Psychical Research, Trinity College, Cambridge, England.

McCreery, C. (1997). Hallucinations and arousability: Pointers to a theory of psychosis. In G. Claridge (Ed.), *Schizotypy: Implications for illness and health* (pp. 251–273). Oxford: Oxford University Press.

McCreery, C., & Claridge, G. (2002). Healthy schizotypy: The case of out-of-the-body experiences. *Personality and Individual Differences*, 32, 141–154.

McCue, P. A. (2002). Theories of haunting: A critical overview. *Journal of the Society for Psychical Research*, 66, 1–21.

McDannell, C., & Lang, B. (1988). *Heaven: A history*. New Haven, CT: Yale University Press.

MacDonald, W. L. (1995). The effects of religiosity and structural strain on reported paranormal experiences. *Journal for the Scientific Study of Religion*, 34, 366–376.

McDonough, B. E., Don, N. S., & Warren, C. A. (1994, August). *EEG in a ganzfeld psi task*. Paper presented at the 37th Annual Convention of the Parapsychological Association, Amsterdam, The Netherlands.

McDonough, B. E., Don, N. S., & Warren, C. A. (2000, August). *Gamma band ("40 Hz") EEG and unconscious target detection in a psi task*. Paper presented at the 43rd Annual Convention of the Parapsychological Association, Freiburg, Germany.

McDonough, B. E., Warren, C. A., & Don, N. S. (1989). EEG analysis of a fortuitous event observed during the psi testing of a selected subject. *Journal of Parapsychology*, 53, 181–201.

McElroy, W. A., & Brown, W. R. K. (1950). Electric shocks for errors in ESP card tests. *Journal of Parapsychology*, 14, 257–266.

McHarg, J. F. (1982). The paranormal and the recognition of personal distress. *Journal of the Society for Psychical Research*, 51, 201–209.

MacKenzie, A. (1982). *Hauntings and apparitions*. London: Heinemann.

MacKenzie, A. (1997). *Adventures in time: Encounters with the past*. London: Athlone Press.

McMahan, E. A. (1947). A PK experiment under light and dark conditions. *Journal of Parapsychology*, 11, 46–54.

McMullen, T. (1978). A basic confusion in the concept of "psi phenomena." In J. P. Sutcliffe (Ed.), *Conceptual analysis and methods in psychology: Essays in honour of W. M. O'Neil* (pp. 15–20). Sydney: Sydney University Press.

Maher, M. C., & Hansen, G. P. (1992). Quantitative investigation of a reported haunting using several detection techniques. *Journal of the American Society for Psychical Research*, 86, 347–374.

Maher, M. C., & Hansen, G. P. (1997, August). *Quantitative investigation of a legally disputed "haunted house."* Paper presented at the 40th Annual Convention of the Parapsychological Association, Brighton, England.

Maher, M. [C.], & Schmeidler, G. R. (1977). Cerebral lateralization effects in ESP processing. *Journal of the American Society for Psychical Research*, 71, 261–271.

Maher, M. C., Vartanian, I. A., Chernigovskaya, T., & Reinsel, R. (1996). Physiological concomitants of the laying-on of hands: Changes in healers' and patients' tactile sensitivity. *Journal of the American Society for Psychical Research*, 90, 77–96.

Mahoney, P. J. (1977). Some observations on the imagery of a group of hallucinating psychiatric patients. (Doctoral dissertation, University of Tennessee, 1976). *Dissertation Abstracts International*, 37(8-B), 4152–4153.

Maitz, E. A., & Pekala, R. J. (1991). Phenomenological quantification of an out-of-the-body experience associated with a near-death event. *Omega*, 22, 199–214.

Mansfield, V., Rhine-Feather, S., & Hall, J. (1998). The Rhine-Jung letters: Distinguishing parapsychological from synchronistic events. *Journal of Parapsychology*, 62, 3–25.

Marks, D. F. (1986). Investigating the paranormal. *Nature, 320*, 119–124.

Marks, D., & Kammann, R. (1980). *The psychology of the psychic*. Buffalo, NY: Prometheus Books.

Markwick, B. (1978). The Soal-Goldney experiments with Basil Shackleton: New evidence of data manipulation. *Proceedings of the Society for Psychical Research, 56*, 250–277.

Martin, B. (1998). Strategies for dissenting scientists. *Journal for Scientific Exploration, 12*, 605–616.

Martin, L. J. (1915). Ghosts and the projection of visual images. *American Journal of Psychology, 26*, 251–257.

Martínez-Taboas, A. (1984). An appraisal of the role of aggression and the central nervous system in RSPK agents. *Journal of the American Society for Psychical Research, 78*, 55–69.

Martínez-Taboas, A., & Alvarado, C. S. (1981). Poltergeist agents: A review of recent research trends and conceptualizations. *European Journal of Parapsychology, 4*, 99–110.

Matlock, J. G. (1989). Age and stimulus in past life memory cases: A study of published cases. *Journal of the American Society for Psychical Research, 83*, 303–316.

Matlock, J. G. (1990). Past life memory case studies. In S. Krippner (Ed.), *Advances in parapsychological research, Vol. 6* (pp. 184–267). Jefferson, NC: McFarland.

Mauskopf, S. H., & McVaugh, M. R. (1980). *The elusive science: Origins of experimental psychical research*. Baltimore: Johns Hopkins University Press.

May, E. C., Paulinyi, T., & Vassy, Z. (2005). Anomalous anticipatory skin conductance response to acoustic stimuli: Experimental results and speculation about a mechanism. *Journal of Alternative and Complementary Medicine, 11*, 587–588.

May, E. C., & Spottiswoode, S. J. P. (1989). A Michelson-interferometer Schrödinger cat: The death of the observation theories. In L. A. Henkel & R. E. Berger (Eds.), *Research in parapsychology 1988* (p. 63). Metuchen, NJ: Scarecrow Press.

May, E. C., Utts, J. M., & Spottiswoode, S. J. P. (1995). Decision augmentation theory: Toward a model of anomalous mental phenomena. *Journal of Parapsychology, 59*, 195–220.

Medhurst, R. G., & Goldney, K. M. (1964). William Crookes and the physical phenomena of mediumship. *Proceedings of the Society for Psychical Research, 54*, 25–157.

Merikle, P. M., Smilek, D., & Eastwood, J. D. (2001). Perception without awareness: Perspectives from cognitive psychology. *Cognition, 79*, 115–134.

Merton, R. K. (1973). *The sociology of science: Theoretical and empirical investigations*. Chicago: University of Chicago Press.

Messer, W. S., & Griggs, R. A. (1989). Student belief and involvement in the paranormal and performance in introductory psychology. *Teaching of Psychology, 16*, 187–191.

Meynell, H. (1996). On investigation of the so-called paranormal. In M. Stoeber & H. Meynell (Eds.), *Critical reflections on the paranormal* (pp. 23–45). Albany, NY: State University of New York Press.

Millar, B. (1978). The observational theories: A primer. *European Journal of Parapsychology, 2*, 304–332.

Mills, A. (1989). A replication study: Three cases of children in Northern India who are said to remember a previous life. *Journal of Scientific Exploration, 3*, 133–184.

Mills, A. (1990). Moslem cases of the reincarnation type in Northern India: A test of the hypothesis of imposed identification. Part I: Analysis of 26 cases. *Journal of Scientific Exploration, 4*, 171–188.

Mills, A., Haraldsson, E., & Keil, H. H. J. (1994). Replication studies of cases suggestive of reincarnation by three independent investigators. *Journal of the American Society for Psychical Research, 88*, 207–219.

Mills, A., & Lynn, S. J. (2000). Past-life experiences. In E. Cardeña, S. J. Lynn, & S. Krippner (Eds.), *Varieties of anomalous experience: Examining the scientific evidence* (pp. 283–313). Washington, DC: American Psychological Association.

Milton, J. (1988a). Critical review of the displacement effect: I. The relationship between displacement and scoring on the intended target. *Journal of Parapsychology, 52*, 29–55.

Milton, J. (1988b). Critical review of the displacement effect: II. The relationship between displacement and psychological and situational variables. *Journal of Parapsychology, 52*, 127–156.

Milton, J. (1992). Effects of "paranormal" experiences on people's lives: An unusual survey of spontaneous cases. *Journal of the Society for Psychical Research, 58*, 314–323.

Milton, J. (1994). Guessing strategies and confidence-call criteria of uninstructed participants in a forced-choice ESP experiment. *Journal of the Society for Psychical Research, 60*, 65–77.

Milton, J. (1996). Establishing methodological guidelines for ESP studies: A questionnaire survey of experimenters' and critics' consensus. *Journal of Parapsychology, 60*, 289–334.

Milton, J. (1997). Meta-analysis of free-response ESP studies without altered states of consciousness. *Journal of Parapsychology, 61*, 279–320.

Milton, J. (1999). Should ganzfeld research continue to be crucial in the search for a replicable psi effect? Part I. Discussion paper and introduction to an electronic-mail discussion. *Journal of Parapsychology, 63*, 309–333.

Milton, J., & Wiseman, R. (1997). *Guidelines for extrasensory perception research*. Hatfield, England: University of Hertfordshire Press.

Milton, J., & Wiseman, R. (1999a). Does psi exist? Lack of replication of an anomalous process of information transfer. *Psychological Bulletin, 125*, 387–391.

Milton, J., & Wiseman, R. (1999b). A meta-analysis of mass-media tests of extrasensory perception. *British Journal of Psychology, 90*, 235–240.

Milton, J., & Wiseman, R. (2001). Does psi exist? Reply to Storm and Ertel (2001). *Psychological Bulletin, 127*, 434–438.

Mintz, E. E. (1983). *The psychic thread: Paranormal and transpersonal aspects of psychotherapy*. New York: Human Sciences Press.

Mintz, S., & Alpert, M. (1972). Imagery vividness, reality testing, and schizophrenic hallucinations. *Journal of Abnormal Psychology*, 79, 310–316.

Mishlove, J. (1983). *Psi development systems*. Jefferson, NC: McFarland.

Mishlove, J., & Kautz, W. H. (1982). An emerging new discipline! *Applied Psi Newsletter*, 1(1), 1.

Mitchell, J. L., & Drewes, A. A. (1982). The rainbow experiment. *Journal of the American Society for Psychical Research*, 76, 197–215.

Montago, E. de A., & Roll, W. G. (1983). A neurological model for psychokinesis. In W. G. Roll, J. Beloff, & R. A. White (Eds.), *Research in parapsychology 1982* (pp. 272–273). Metuchen, NJ: Scarecrow Press.

Montanelli, D. G., & Parra, A. (2004). A clinical approach to the emotional processing of anomalous/paranormal experiences in group therapy. *Journal of the Society for Psychical Research*, 68, 129–142.

Moody, R. A. (1975). *Life after life*. Covington, GA: Mockingbird.

Moody, R. A. (1977). *Reflections on life after life*. Covington, GA: Mockingbird.

Moody, R. A. (1994, August). *A latter-day psychomanteum*. Paper presented at the 37th Annual Convention of the Parapsychological Association, Amsterdam, The Netherlands.

Moody, R. A., with Perry, P. (1988). *The light beyond*. New York: Bantam.

Moore, D. W. (2005). *Three in four Americans believe in paranormal*. Washington, DC: Gallup Poll News Service, June 16.

Moore, R. L. (1977). *In search of white crows: Spiritualism, parapsychology, and American culture*. New York: Oxford University Press.

Morier, D., & Keeports, D. (1994). Normal science and the paranormal: The effect of a scientific method course on students' beliefs. *Research in Higher Education*, 35, 443–453.

Morris, F. (1976). Emotional reactions to psychic experiences. In M. Ebon (Ed.), *The satan trap: Dangers of the occult* (pp. 205–216). Garden City, NY: Doubleday.

Morris, R. L. (1980). Psi functioning within a simple communication model. In B. Shapin & L. Coly (Eds.), *Communication and parapsychology* (pp. 1–24). New York: Parapsychology Foundation.

Morris, R. L. (1981). The case of the Amityville Horror. In K. Frazier (Ed.), *Paranormal borderlines of science* (pp. 170–178). Buffalo, NY: Prometheus Books.

Morris, R. L., & Cohen, D. (1971). A preliminary experiment on the relationships among ESP, alpha rhythm and calling patterns. In W. G. Roll, R. L. Morris, & J. D. Morris (Eds.), *Proceedings of the Parapsychological Association No. 6, 1969* (pp. 22–23). Durham, NC: Parapsychological Association.

Morris, R. L., Cunningham, S., McAlpine, S., & Taylor, R. (1993, August). *Toward replication and extension of autoganzfeld results*. Paper presented at the 36th Annual Convention of the Parapsychological Association, Toronto, Canada.

Morris, R. L., Dalton, K., Delanoy, D. L., & Watt, C. A. (1995, August). *Comparison of the sender/no sender condition in the ganzfeld*. Paper presented at the 38th Annual Convention of the Parapsychological Association, Durham, North Carolina.

Morris, R. L., Nanko, M., & Phillips, D. (1982). A comparison of two popularly advocated visual imagery strategies in a psychokinesis task. *Journal of Parapsychology*, 46, 1–16.

Morse, M., with Perry, P. (1990). *Closer to the light: Learning from children's near-death experiences*. New York: Villard Books.

Morse, M. L. (1994). Near death experiences and death-related visions in children: Implications for the clinician. *Current Problems in Pediatrics*, 24, 55–83.

Morse, M. L., Venecia, D., & Milstein, J. (1989). Near-death experiences: A neurophysiologic explanatory model. *Journal of Near-Death Experiences*, 8, 45–53.

Moss, S., & Butler, D. C. (1978). The scientific credibility of ESP. *Perceptual and Motor Skills*, 46, 1063–1079.

Mulholland, J. (1979). *Beware familiar spirits*. New York: Scribner. (Original work published 1938)

Mundle, C. W. K. (1964). Does the concept of precognition make sense? *International Journal of Parapsychology*, 6, 179–198.

Munro, C., & Persinger, M. A. (1992). Relative right temporal-lobe theta activity correlates with Vingiano's Hemisphere Quotient and the "sensed presence." *Perceptual and Motor Skills*, 75, 899–903.

Munson, R. J. (1985). *Clinical applications of psi: Three cases*. Paper presented at the 12th annual conference of the Southeastern Regional Parapsychological Association, Duke University, Durham, NC.

Munves, J. (1997). Richard Hodgson, Mrs. Piper and "George Pelham": A centennial reassessment. *Journal of the Society for Psychical Research*, 62, 138–154.

Murphy, G. (1967). Direct contacts with past and future: Retrocognition and precognition. *Journal of the American Society for Psychical Research*, 61, 3–23.

Murphy, K., & Lester, D. (1976). A search for correlates of belief in ESP. *Psychological Reports*, 38, 82.

Murphy, T. (2001). Near-death experiences in Thailand. *Journal of Near-Death Studies*, 19, 161–178.

Murray, C. D., & Fox, J. (2005a). Body image in persons with and without prior out-of-body experiences. *British Journal of Psychology*, 96, 441–456.

Murray, C. D., & Fox, J. (2005b). The out-of-body experience and body image: Differences between experients and non-experients. *Journal of Nervous and Mental Disease*, 193, 70–72.

Murray, C. D., & Fox, J. (2006). Differences in body image between people reporting near-death and spontaneous out-of-body experiences. *Journal of the Society for Psychical Research*, 70, 98–109.

Musch, J., & Ehrenberg, K. (2002). Probability misjudgment, cognitive ability, and belief in the paranormal. *British Journal of Psychology*, 93, 169–177.

Musgrave, C. (1997). The near-death experience: A study of spiritual transformation. *Journal of Near-Death Studies*, 15, 187–201.

Myers, F. W. H. (1903). *Human personality and its survival of bodily death*. London: Longmans, Green.

Myers, F. W. H., Lodge, O. J., Leaf, W., & James, W.

(1890). A record of observations of certain phenomena of trance. *Proceedings of the Society for Psychical Research*, **6**, 436–659.

Myers, S. A., & Austrin, H. R. (1985). Distal eidetic technology: Further characteristics of the fantasy-prone personality. *Journal of Mental Imagery*, **9**, 57–66.

Myers, S. A., Austrin, H. R., Grisso, J. T., & Nickeson, R. C. (1983). Personality characteristics as related to the out-of-body experience. *Journal of Parapsychology*, **47**, 131–144.

Nadon, R., & Kihlstrom, J. F. (1987). Hypnosis, psi, and the psychology of anomalous experience. *Behavioral and Brain Sciences*, **10**, 597–599.

Nadon, R., Laurence, J., & Perry, C. (1987). Multiple predictors of hypnotic susceptibility. *Journal of Personality and Social Psychology*, **53**, 948–960.

Nash, C. B. (1978). Effect of response bias on psi mediation. *Journal of the American Society for Psychical Research*, **72**, 333–338.

Nash, C. B. (1983). An extrasensory observational theory. *Journal of the American Society for Psychical Research*, **52**, 113–116.

Nash, C. B. (1986). *Parapsychology: The science of psiology*. Springfield, IL: Thomas.

Nash, C. B. (1989). Intra-experiment and intra-subject scoring declines in "Extra-Sensory Perception after Sixty Years." *Journal of the Society for Psychical Research*, **55**, 412–416.

Nash, C. B., & Nash, C. S. (1958). Checking success and the relationship of personality traits to ESP. *Journal of the American Society for Psychical Research*, **52**, 98–107.

Nash, C. S., & Nash, C. B. (1968). Effect of target selection, field dependence, and body concept on ESP performance. *Journal of Parapsychology*, **32**, 248–257.

Negro, P. J., Palladino-Negro, P., & Louza, M. R. (2002). Do religious mediumship dissociative experiences conform to the sociocognitive theory of dissociation? *Journal of Trauma and Dissociation*, **3**, 51–73.

Neher, A. (1980). *The psychology of transcendence*. Englewood Cliffs, NJ: Prentice-Hall.

Nelson, R. D. (2001). Correlation of global events with REG data: An internet-based, nonlocal anomalies experiment. *Journal of Parapsychology*, **65**, 247–272.

Nelson, R. D. (2002). Coherent consciousness and reduced randomness: Correlations on September 11, 2001. *Journal of Scientific Exploration*, **16**, 549–570.

Nelson, R., Bösch, H., Boller, E., Dobyns, Y., Houtkooper, J., Lettieri, A., et al. (1998). Global resonance of consciousness: Princess Diana and Mother Teresa. *Electronic Journal for Anomalous Phenomena*, *eJAP*. http://www.psy.uva.nl/eJAP.

Neppe, V. M. (1983). Temporal lobe symptomatology in subjective paranormal experients. *Journal of the American Society for Psychical Research*, **77**, 1–29.

Neppe, V. M. (1984). Subjective paranormal experience psychosis. *Parapsychology Review*, **15**(2), 7–9.

Neppe, V. M. (2002). "Out-of-body experiences" (OBES) and brain localisation: A perspective. *Australian Journal of Parapsychology*, **2**, 85–96.

Newport, F., & Strausberg, M. (2001, June). *Gallup poll release: Americans' belief in psychic and paranormal phenomena is up over last decade*. Retrieved June 12, 2001, from the World Wide Web: *http://www.gallup.com/poll/releases/pr010608.asp*

Nichols, A. A water poltergeist in Florida. *International Journal of Parapsychology*, **11**(2), 143–159.

Nickell, J. (Ed.). (1994). *Psychic sleuths: ESP and sensational cases* (pp. 172–190). Buffalo, NY: Prometheus Books.

Nickell, J. (2001). Phantoms, frauds, or fantasies? In J. Houran & R. Lange (Eds.), *Hauntings and poltergeists: Multidisciplinary perspectives* (pp. 214–223). Jefferson, NC: McFarland.

Nijenhuis, E. R. S., Spinhoven, Ph., van Dyck, R., van der Hart, O., & Vanderlinden, J. (1996). The development and psychometric characteristics of the Somatoform Dissociation Questionnaire (SDQ-20). *Journal of Nervous and Mental Disease*, **184**, 688–694.

Norton, M. C., & Sahlman, J. M. (1995). Describing the light: Attribution theory as an explanation of the near-death experience. *Journal of Near-Death Studies*, **13**, 167–184.

Noyes, R. (1972). The experience of dying. *Psychiatry*, **35**, 174–184.

Noyes, R. (1979). Near-death experiences: Their interpretation and significance. In R. Kastenbaum (ed.), *Between life and death* (pp. 73–88). New York: Springer.

Noyes, R. (1980). Attitude change following near-death experiences. *Psychiatry*, **43**, 234–242.

Noyes, R., & Kletti, R. (1977). Panoramic memory: A response to the threat of death. *Omega*, **8**, 181–194.

Noyes, R., & Slymen, D. J. (1979). The subjective response to life-threatening danger. *Omega*, **9**, 313–321.

O'Keeffe, C., & Alison, L. (2000). Rhetoric in "psychic detection." *Journal of the Society for Psychical Research*, **64**, 26–38.

O'Keeffe, C., & Wiseman, R. (2005). Testing alleged mediumship: Methods and results. *British Journal of Psychology*, **96**, 165–179.

Olson, P. R. Suddeth, J. A., Peterson, P. L., & Egelhoff, C. (1985). Hallucinations of widowhood. *Journal of the American Geriatrics Society*, **33**, 543–547.

Oppenheim, J. (1985). *The other world: Spiritualism and psychical research in England, 1850–1914*. Cambridge: Cambridge University Press.

Orme, J. E. (1974). Precognition and time. *Journal of the Society for Psychical Research*, **47**, 351–365.

Osis, K. (1974). Out-of-body research at the ASPR. *ASPR Newsletter*, No. 22, 1–3.

Osis, K. (1975). Perceptual experiments on out-of-body experiences. In J. D. Morris, W. G. Roll, & R. L. Morris (Eds.), *Research in parapsychology 1974* (pp. 53–55). Metuchen, NJ: Scarecrow Press.

Osis, K. (1979). Insiders' views of the OBE: A questionnaire survey. In W. G. Roll (Ed.), *Research in parapsychology 1978* (pp. 50–52). Metuchen, NJ: Scarecrow Press.

Osis, K. (1986a). Apparitions old and new. In K. R. Rao (Ed.), *Case studies in parapsychology* (pp. 74–86). Jefferson, NC: McFarland.

Osis, K. (1986b). Characteristics of purposeful action in an apparition case. *Journal of the American Society for Psychical Research, 80*, 175–193.

Osis, K., & McCormick, D. (1980). Kinetic effects at the ostensible location of an out-of-body projection during perceptual testing. *Journal of the American Society for Psychical Research, 74*, 319–329.

Osis, K., & McCormick, D. (1982a). A poltergeist case without an identifiable living agent. *Journal of the American Society for Psychical Research, 76*, 23–51.

Osis, K., & McCormick, D. (1982b). A case of collectively observed apparitions and related phenomena. In W. G. Roll, R. L. Morris, & R. A. White (Eds.), *Research in parapsychology 1981* (pp. 120–123). Metuchen, NJ: Scarecrow Press.

Osis, K., & Perskari, B. (1975). *Perceptual tests of the out-of-body hypothesis.* Unpublished manuscript, American Society for Psychical Research, New York.

Otis, L. P., & Alcock, J. E. (1982). Factors affecting extraordinary belief. *Journal of Social Psychology, 118*, 77–85.

Owen, A. (1990). *The darkened room: Women, power and spiritualism in late Victorian England.* Philadelphia, PA: University of Pennsylvania Press.

Owen, A. R. G. (1964). *Can we explain the poltergeist?* New York: Garrett.

Owens, J. E., Cook, E. W., & Stevenson, I. (1990). Features of "near-death experience" in relation to whether or not patients were near death. *The Lancet, 336*, 1175–1177.

Palmer, J. (1974). A case of RSPK involving a ten-year-old boy: The Powhatan poltergeist. *Journal of the American Society for Psychical Research, 68*, 1–33.

Palmer, J. (1977). Attitudes and personality traits in experimental ESP research. In B. B. Wolman (Ed.), *Handbook of parapsychology* (pp. 175–201). New York: Van Nostrand Reinhold.

Palmer, J. (1978a). Extrasensory perception: Research findings. In S. Krippner (Ed.), *Advances in parapsychological research, Vol. 2: Extrasensory perception* (pp. 59–243). New York: Plenum Press.

Palmer, J. (1978b). The out-of-body experience: A psychological theory. *Parapsychology Review, 9*(5), 19–22.

Palmer, J. (1978c). ESP and out-of-body experiences: An experimental approach. In D. S. Rogo (Ed.), *Mind beyond the body* (pp. 193–217). New York: Penguin.

Palmer, J. (1979). A community mail survey of psychic experiences. *Journal of the American Society for Psychical Research, 73*, 221–251.

Palmer, J. (1982). ESP research findings: 1976–1978. In S. Krippner (Ed.), *Advances in parapsychological research, Vol. 3* (pp. 41–82). New York: Plenum Press.

Palmer, J. (1993). Confronting the experimenter effect. In L. Coly & J. D. S. McMahon (Eds.), *Psi research methodology: A re-examination* (pp. 44–64). New York: Parapsychology Foundation.

Palmer, J. (1996, August). *Further studies with the Perceptual esp Test: Feast and famine.* Paper presented at the 39th Annual Convention of the Parapsychological Association, San Diego, CA.

Palmer, J. (1997a). The challenge of experimenter psi. *European Journal of Parapsychology, 13*, 110–125.

Palmer, J. (1997b). Hit-contingent response bias in Helmut Schmidt's automated precognition experiments. *Journal of Parapsychology, 61*, 135–141.

Palmer, J. (2000). Covert psi in computer solitaire. *Journal of Parapsychology, 64*, 195–211.

Palmer, J. (2003). ESP in the ganzfeld: Analysis of a debate. *Journal of Consciousness Studies, 10*, 51–68.

Palmer, J., & Carpenter, J. C. (1998). Comments on the extraversion-ESP meta-analysis by Honorton, Ferrari, and Bem. *Journal of Parapsychology, 62*, 277–282.

Palmer, J. A., Honorton, C., & Utts, J. (1989). Reply to the National Research Council study on parapsychology. *Journal of the American Society for Psychical Research, 83*, 31–49.

Palmer, J., & Kramer, W. (1984). Internal state and temporal factors in psychokinesis. *Journal of Parapsychology, 48*, 1–25.

Palmer, J., & Lieberman, R. (1975). The influence of psychological set on ESP and out-of-body experiences. *Journal of the American Society for Psychical Research, 69*, 193–213.

Palmer, J., & Lieberman, R. (1976). ESP and out-of-body experiences: A further study. In J. D. Morris, W. G. Roll, & R. L. Morris (Eds.), *Research in parapsychology 1975* (pp. 102–106). Metuchen, NJ: Scarecrow Press.

Palmer, J., & Neppe, V. M. (2003). A controlled analysis of subjective paranormal experiences in temporal lobe dysfunction in a neuropsychiatric population. *Journal of Parapsychology, 67*, 75–98.

Palmer, J., & Neppe, V. M. (2004). Exploratory analyses of refined predictors of subjective ESP experiences and temporal lobe dysfunction in a neuropsychiatric population. *European Journal of Parapsychology, 19*, 44–65.

Pamplin, B. R., & Collins, H. (1975). Spoon bending: An experimental approach. *Nature, 257*, 8.

Parapsychological Association (1989). Terms and methods in parapsychological research. *Journal of Humanistic Psychology, 29*, 394–399.

Park, R. L. (2000). *Voodoo science: The road from foolishness to fraud.* New York: Oxford University Press.

Parker, A. (1977). Parapsychologists' personality and psi in relation to the experimenter effect. In J. D. Morris, W. G. Roll, & R. L. Morris (Eds.), *Research in parapsychology 1976* (pp. 107–109). Metuchen, NJ: Scarecrow Press.

Parker, A., Persson, A., & Haller, A. (2000). Using qualitative ganzfeld research for theory development: Top-down processes in psi-mediation. *Journal of the Society for Psychical Research, 64*, 65–81.

Parnia, S., Waller, D. G., Yeates, R., & Fenwick, P. (2001). A qualitative and quantitative study of the incidence, features and aetiology of near death experiences in cardiac arrest survivors. *Resuscitation, 48*, 149–156.

Parra, A. (1997). Parapsychological developments in Argentina (1900–1995). *Journal of the American Society for Psychical Research, 91*, 103–109.

Parra, A., & Villanueva, J. (2003). Personality factors and ESP during ganzfeld sessions. *Journal of the Society for Psychical Research, 67*, 26–36.

Pasricha, S. (1990). Three conjectured features of reincarnation-type cases in North India: Response of persons unfamiliar with actual cases. *Journal of the American Society for Psychical Research*, **84**, 227–233.

Pasricha, S. K., & Barker, D. R. (1981). A case of the reincarnation type in India: The case of Rakesh Gaur. *European Journal of Parapsychology*, **3**, 381–408.

Pasricha, S., & Stevenson, I. (1986). Near-death experiences in India. *Journal of Nervous and Mental Disease*, **174**, 165–170.

Pasricha, S., & Stevenson, I. (1987). Indian cases of the reincarnation type two generations apart. *Journal of the Society for Psychical Research*, **54**, 239–246.

Pekala, R. J., Kumar, V. K., & Cummings, J. (1992). Types of high hypnotically-susceptible individuals and reported attitudes and experiences of the paranormal and the anomalous. *Journal of the American Society for Psychical Research*, **86**, 135–150.

Pekala, R. J., Kumar, V. K., & Marcano, G. (1995). Anomalous/paranormal experiences, hypnotic susceptibility, and dissociation. *Journal of the American Society for Psychical Research*, **89**, 313–332.

Peltzer, K. (2003). Magical thinking and paranormal beliefs among secondary and university students in South Africa. *Personality and Individual Differences*, **35**, 1419–1426.

Pennachio, J. (1988). Near-death experiences and self-transformation. *Journal of Near-Death Studies*, **6**, 162–168.

Perry, C., Laurence, J., Nadon, R., & Labelle, L. (1986). Past lives regression. In B. Zilbergeld, M. G. Edelstien, & D. L. Araoz (Eds.), *Hypnosis: Questions and answers* (pp. 50–61). New York: Norton.

Persinger, M. A. (1974). *The paranormal. Part I. Patterns.* New York: mss Information Corporation.

Persinger, M. A. (1975). ELF waves and ESP. *New Horizons*, **1**(5), 232–235.

Persinger, M. A. (1983). Religious and mystical experiences as artifacts of temporal lobe function: A general hypothesis. *Perceptual and Motor Skills*, **57**, 1255–1262.

Persinger, M. A. (1984). Propensity to report paranormal experiences is correlated with temporal lobe signs. *Perceptual and Motor Skills*, **59**, 583–586.

Persinger, M. A. (1985). Subjective telepathic experiences, geomagnetic activity and the ELF hypothesis: Part II. Stimulus features and neural detection. *Psi Research*, **4**(2), 4–23.

Persinger, M. A. (1989). Psi phenomena and temporal lobe activity: The geomagnetic factor. In L. A. Henkel & R. E. Berger (Eds.), *Research in parapsychology 1988* (pp. 121–156). Metuchen, NJ: Scarecrow Press.

Persinger, M. A. (1993). Vectorial cerebral hemisphericity as differential sources for the sensed presence, mystical experiences and religious conversions. *Perceptual and Motor Skills*, **76**, 915–930.

Persinger, M. A. (1996). Feelings of past lives as expected perturbations within the neurocognitive processes that generate the sense of self: Contributions from limbic liability and vectorial hemisphericity. *Perceptual and Motor Skills*, **83**, 1107–1121.

Persinger, M. A. (2001). The neuropsychiatry of paranormal experiences. *Journal of Neuropsychiatry and Clinical Neuroscience*, **13**, 515–524.

Persinger, M. A., & Cameron, R. A. (1986). Are earth faults at fault in some poltergeist-like episodes? *Journal of the American Society for Psychical Research*, **80**, 49–73.

Persinger, M. A., & Koren, S. A. (2001). Predicting the characteristics of haunt phenomena from geomagnetic factors and brain sensitivity: Evidence from field and experimental studies. In J. Houran & R. Lange (Eds.), *Hauntings and poltergeists: Multidisciplinary perspectives* (pp. 179–194). Jefferson, NC: McFarland.

Persinger, M. A., Koren, S. A., & O'Connor, R. P. (2001).Geophysical variables and behavior: CIV. Power-frequency magnetic field transients (5 microTesla) and reports of haunt experiences within an electronically dense house. *Perceptual and Motor Skills*, **92**, 673–674.

Persinger, M. A., & Krippner, S. (1989). Dream ESP experiments and geomagnetic activity. *Journal of the American Society for Psychical Research*, **83**, 101–116.

Persinger, M. A., & Makarec, K. (1987). Temporal lobe epileptic signs and correlative behaviors displayed by normal populations. *Journal of General Psychology*, **114**, 179–195.

Persinger, M. A., & Makarec, K. (1992). The feeling of a presence and verbal meaningfulness in context of temporal lobe function: Factor analytic verification of the Muses? *Brain and Cognition*, **20**, 217–226.

Persinger, M. A., & Roll, W. G. (1986). The temporal lobe factor in psi phenomena. In D. H. Weiner & D. I. Radin (Eds.), *Research in parapsychology 1985* (p. 119). Metuchen, NJ: Scarecrow Press.

Persinger, M. A., & Valliant, P. M. (1985). Temporal lobe signs and reports of subjective paranormal experiences in a normal population: A replication. *Perceptual and Motor Skills*, **60**, 903–909.

Piddington, J. G. (1908). A series of concordant automatisms. *Proceedings of the Society for Psychical Research*, **22**, 19–416.

Pierce, H. W. (1973). RSPK phenomena observed independently by two families. *Journal of the American Society for Psychical Research*, **67**, 86–101.

Pinch, T. J., & Collins, H. M. (1984). Private science and public knowledge: The Committee for the Scientific Investigation of the Claims of the Paranormal and its use of the literature. *Social Studies of Science*, **14**, 521–546.

Piper, A. L. (1929). *The life and work of Mrs. Piper.* London: Kegan Paul, Trench, Trübner.

Podmore, F. (1896). Poltergeists. *Proceedings of the Society for Psychical Research*, **12**, 45–115.

Podmore, F. (1901). On Professor Hyslop's report on his sittings with Mrs. Piper. *Proceedings of the Society for Psychical Research*, **17**, 374–388.

Podmore, F. (1902). *Modern spiritualism: A history and a criticism. Vol. II.* London: Methuen.

Podmore, F. (c. 1909). *Telepathic hallucinations: The new view of ghosts.* London: Milner.

Podmore, F. (1910). *The newer spiritualism.* London: Fisher Unwin.

Polidoro, M. (2003). *Secrets of the psychics: Investigating paranormal claims.* Amherst, NY: Prometheus Books.

Pope, J. E. (1991). *Near-death experiences and attitudes towards life, death and suicide.* Unpublished master's thesis, University of New England, Armidale, Australia.

Pope, J. [E.] (1994). Near-death experiences and attitudes towards life, death and suicide. *Australian Parapsychological Review,* 19, 23–26.

Potts, M. (2002). The evidential value of near-death experiences for belief in life after death. *Journal of Near-Death Studies,* 20, 233–258.

Powers, R. (1991). Women's knowing, women's spirit. *Theta,* 17, 44–47.

Poynton, J. C. (1975). Results of an out-of-body survey. In J. C. Poynton (Ed.), *Parapsychology in South Africa* (pp. 109–123). Johannesburg: South African Society for Psychical Research.

Prasad, J., & Stevenson, I. (1968). A survey of spontaneous psychical experiences in school children of Uttar Pradesh, India. *International Journal of Parapsychology,* 10, 241–261.

Pratt, J. G., & Birge, W. R. (1948). Appraising verbal test material in parapsychology. *Journal of Parapsychology,* 12, 236–256.

Pratt, J. G., Rhine, J. B., Smith, B. M., Stuart, C. E., & Greenwood, J. A. (1940). *Extrasensory perception after sixty years: A critical appraisal of the research in extrasensory perception.* New York: Holt.

Pratt, J. G., & Woodruff, J. L. (1946). An exploratory investigation of PK position effects. *Journal of Parapsychology,* 10, 197–207.

Price, G. R. (1955). Science and the supernatural. *Science,* 122, 359–367.

Price, G. R. (1956). Where is the definitive experiment? *Science,* 123, 17–18.

Prince, W. F. (1928). *Noted witnesses for psychic occurrences.* Boston: Boston Society for Psychic Research.

Prince, W. F. (1930). *The enchanted boundary.* Boston: Boston Society for Psychic Research.

Puhle, A. (1999). Ghosts, apparitions and poltergeist incidents in Germany between 1700 and 1900. *Journal of the Society for Psychical Research,* 63, 292–305.

Puhle, A. (2001). Learning from historical cases: Six selected poltergeist cases from the 1700s in Germany. *European Journal of Parapsychology,* 16, 61–72.

Quider, R. F. (1984). The effect of relaxation/suggestion and music on forced-choice ESP scoring. *Journal of the American Society for Psychical Research,* 78, 241–262.

Quimby, S. L. (1989). The near-death experience as an event in consciousness. *Journal of Humanistic Psychology,* 29, 87–108.

Radin, D. I. (1988). Effects of a priori probability on psi perception: Does precognition predict actual or probable futures? *Journal of Parapsychology,* 52, 187–212.

Radin, D. I. (1993). Neural network analyses of consciousness-related patterns in random sequences. *Journal of Scientific Exploration,* 7, 355–373.

Radin, D. I. (1997a). *The conscious universe: The sci-*entific truth of psychic phenomena. San Francisco: HarperEdge.

Radin, D. I. (1997b). Unconscious perception of future emotions: An experiment in presentiment. *Journal of Scientific Exploration,* 11, 163–180.

Radin, D. I. (2002). Exploring relationships between random physical events and mass human attention: Asking for whom the bell tolls. *Journal of Scientific Exploration,* 16, 533–547.

Radin, D. I. (2004). Electrodermal presentiments of future emotions. *Journal of Scientific Exploration,* 18, 253–273.

Radin, D. I., & Ferrari, D. C. (1991). Effects of consciousness on the fall of dice: A meta-analysis. *Journal of Scientific Exploration,* 6, 61–83.

Radin, D. I., & May, E. C. (1987). Testing the intuitive data sorting model with pseudorandom number generators: A proposed method. In D. H. Weiner & R. D. Nelson (Eds.), *Research in parapsychology 1986* (pp. 109–111). Metuchen, NJ: Scarecrow Press.

Radin, D. I., & Nelson, R. D. (1989). Evidence for consciousness-related anomalies in random physical systems. *Foundations of Physics,* 19, 1499–1514.

Radin, D. I., & Nelson, R. D. (2003). Research on mind-matter interacitons (MMI): Individual intention. In W. B. Jonas & C. C. Crawford (Eds.), *Healing, intention and energy medicine: Research and clinical implications* (pp. 39–48). Edinburgh: Churchill Livingstone.

Radin, D. I., Nelson, R. D., Dobyns, Y., & Houtkooper, J. (2006). Reexamining psychokinesis: Comment on the Bösch, Steinkamp, and Boller (2006) meta-analysis. *Psychological Bulletin,* 132, 529–532.

Radin, D. I., & Rebman, J. M. (1996). Are phantasms fact or fantasy? A preliminary investigation of apparitions evoked in the laboratory. *Journal of the Society for Psychical Research,* 61, 65–87.

Radin, D. I., & Rebman, J. M. (1998). Seeking psi in the casino. *Journal of the Society for Psychical Research,* 62, 193–219.

Raft, D., & Andresen, J. J. (1986). Transformations in self-understanding after near-death experiences. *Contemporary Psychoanalysis,* 22, 319–346.

Rand Corporation (1955). *A million random digits and 100,000 normal deviates.* New York: Free Press.

Randall, J. L. (1982). *Psychokinesis: A study of paranormal forces through the ages.* London: Souvenir Press.

Randall, J. L., & Davis, C. P. (1982). Paranormal deformation of nitinol wire: A confirmatory experiment. *Journal of the Society for Psychical Research,* 51, 368–373.

Randall, T. M. (1990). Belief in the paranormal declines: 1977–1987. *Psychological Reports,* 66, 1347–1351.

Randall, T. M., & Desrosiers, M. (1980). Measurement of supernatural belief: Sex differences and locus of control. *Journal of Personality Assessment,* 44, 493–498.

Randi, J. (1975). *The magic of Uri Geller.* New York: Ballantine.

Randi, J. (1982a). Atlanta child murderer: Psychics' failed visions. *Skeptical Inquirer, 7*(1), 12–13.

Randi, J. (1982b). *Flim-flam! Psychics, ESP, unicorns and other delusions.* Buffalo, NY: Prometheus Books.

Randi, J. (1983a). The Project Alpha experiment: Part 1. The first two years. *Skeptical Inquirer, 7*(4), 24–33.

Randi, J. (1983b). The Project Alpha experiment: Part 2. Beyond the laboratory. *Skeptical Inquirer, 8*(1), 36–45.

Rank, O. (1971). *The double: A psychoanalytical study.* Chapel Hill, NC: University of North Carolina Press.

Rao, K. R. (1965). The bidirectionality of psi. *Journal of Parapsychology, 29*, 230–250.

Rao, K. R. (1978). Theories of psi. In S. Krippner (Ed.), *Advances of parapsychological research, Vol. 2: Extrasensory perception* (pp. 245–295). New York: Plenum Press.

Rao, K. R. (Ed.) (1984). *The basic experiments in parapsychology.* Jefferson, NC: McFarland.

Rao, K. R., Kanthamani, H., & Norwood, B. (1983). Sex-related differential scoring in two volitional studies. *Journal of Parapsychology, 47*, 7–21.

Rao, K. R., & Palmer, J. (1987). The anomaly called psi: Recent research and criticism. *Behavioral and Brain Sciences, 10*, 539–551.

Rapoport, A., & Budescu, D. V. (1997). Randomization in individual choice behavior. *Psychological Review, 104*, 603–617.

Rattet, S. L., & Bursik, K. (2001). Investigating the personality correlates of paranormal belief and precognitive experience. *Personality and Individual Differences, 31*, 433–444.

Rawcliffe, D. H. (1959). *Illusions and delusions of the supernatural and the occult.* New York: Dover.

Rawlings, M. (1978). *Beyond death's door.* Nashville, TN: Nelson.

Reber, A. S. (1995). *The Penguin dictionary of psychology* (2nd ed.). London: Penguin Books.

Reed, G. (1972). *The psychology of anomalous experience.* London: Hutchinson.

Reed, G. (1989). The psychology of channeling. *Skeptical Inquirer, 13*, 385–390.

Rees, D. W. (1971). The hallucinations of widowhood. *British Medical Journal, 778*(4), 37–41.

Rein, G. (1978). *Healing energy and neurochemistry.* Paper presented at the 2nd International Conference of the Society for Psychical Research, Cambridge, England.

Reiser, M., & Klyver, N. (1982). A comparison of psychics, detectives, and students in the investigation of major crimes. In M. Reiser (Ed.), *Police psychology: Collected papers* (pp. 260–267). Los Angeles, CA: LEHI.

Reiser, M., Ludwig, L., Saxe, S., & Wagner, C. (1979). An evaluation of the use of psychics in the investigation of major crimes. *Journal of Police Science and Administration, 7*, 18–25.

Rhine, J. B. (1934). *Extra-sensory perception.* Boston: Boston Society for Psychic Research.

Rhine, J. B. (1936). Some selected experiments in extrasensory perception. *Journal of Abnormal and Social Psychology, 31*, 216–228.

Rhine, J. B. (1938). Experiments bearing on the precognition hypothesis. *Journal of Parapsychology, 2*, 38–54.

Rhine, J. B. (1941). Experiments bearing upon the precognition hypothesis: III. Mechanically selected cards. *Journal of Parapsychology, 5*, 1–58.

Rhine, J. B. (1948). *The reach of the mind.* London: Faber & Faber.

Rhine, J. B. (1969). Position effects in psi test results. *Journal of Parapsychology, 33*, 136–157.

Rhine, J. B. (1974). Comments: A new case of experimenter unreliability. *Journal of Parapsychology, 38*, 215–225.

Rhine, J. B. (1975). Comments: Second report on a case of experimenter fraud. *Journal of Parapsychology, 39*, 306–325.

Rhine, J. B., & Humphrey, B. M. (1944). PK tests with six, twelve, and twenty-four dice per throw. *Journal of Parapsychology, 8*, 139–157.

Rhine, J. B., & Pratt, J. G. (1954). A review of the Pearce-Pratt distance series of ESP tests. *Journal of Parapsychology, 18*, 165–177.

Rhine, J. B., Smith, B. M., & Woodruff, J. L. (1938). Experiments bearing on the precognition hypothesis: II. The role of ESP in the shuffling of cards. *Journal of Parapsychology, 2*, 119–131.

Rhine, L. E. (1951). Conviction and associated conditions in spontaneous cases. *Journal of Parapsychology, 15*, 164–191.

Rhine, L. E. (1953a). Subjective forms of spontaneous psi experiences. *Journal of Parapsychology, 17*, 77–114.

Rhine, L. E. (1953b). The relation of experience to associated event in spontaneous ESP. *Journal of Parapsychology, 17*, 187–209.

Rhine, L. E. (1954). Frequency of types of experience in spontaneous precognition. *Journal of Parapsychology, 18*, 93–123.

Rhine, L. E. (1955). Precognition and intervention. *Journal of Parapsychology, 19*, 1–34.

Rhine, L. E. (1956). The relationship of agent and percipient in spontaneous telepathy. *Journal of Parapsychology, 20*, 1–32.

Rhine, L. E. (1957). Hallucinatory psi experiences: II. The initiative of the percipient in hallucinations of the living, the dying, and the dead. *Journal of Parapsychology, 21*, 13–46.

Rhine, L. E. (1961). *Hidden channels of the mind.* New York: Morrow.

Rhine, L. E. (1962a). Psychological processes in ESP experiences. Part I. Waking experiences. *Journal of Parapsychology, 26*, 88–111.

Rhine, L. E. (1962b). Psychological processes in ESP experiences. Part II. Dreams. *Journal of Parapsychology, 26*, 172–199.

Rhine, L. E. (1963a). Spontaneous physical effects and the psi process. *Journal of Parapsychology, 27*, 84–122.

Rhine, L. E. (1963b). Auditory psi experience: Hallucinatory or physical? *Journal of Parapsychology, 27*, 182–198.

Rhine, L. E. (1970). *Mind over matter: Psychokinesis.* New York: Macmillan.

Rhine, L. E. (1981). *The invisible picture: A study of psychic experiences.* Jefferson, NC: McFarland.

Rhine, L. E., & Rhine, J. B. (1943). The psychokinetic effect. I. The first experiment. *Journal of Parapsychology,* 7, 20–43.

Rice, T. W. (2003). Believe it or not: Religious and other paranormal beliefs in the United States. *Journal for the Scientific Study of Religion,* 42, 95–106.

Richardson, A. (1999). Subjective experience: Its conceptual status, method of investigation, and psychological significance. *Journal of Psychology,* 133, 469–485.

Richeport, M. M. (1992). The interface between multiple personality, spirit mediumship, and hypnosis. *American Journal of Clinical Hypnosis,* 34, 168–177.

Richet, C. (1888). Further experiments in hypnotic lucidity or clairvoyance. *Proceedings of the Society for Psychical Research,* 6, 66–83.

Richet, C. (1923). *Thirty years of psychical research: Being a treatise on metapsychics.* London: Collins.

Ring, K. (1980). *Life at death: A scientific investigation of the near-death experience.* New York: Coward, McCann & Geoghegan.

Ring, K. (1982). Precognitive and prophetic visions in near-death experiences. *Anabiosis,* 2, 47–74.

Ring, K. (1984). *Heading toward omega: In search of the meaning of the near-death experience.* New York: Morrow.

Ring, K. (1992). Review of David Lorimer's "Whole in One." *Journal of Near-Death Studies,* 10, 241–245.

Ring, K. (1994). Solving the riddle of frightening near-death experiences: Some testable hypotheses and a perspective based on "A Course in Miracles." *Journal of Near-Death Studies,* 13, 5–23.

Ring, K., & Rosing, C. J. (1990). The Omega Project: An empirical study of the NDE-prone personality. *Journal of Near-Death Studies,* 8, 211–239.

Riniolo, T. C., & Schmidt, L. A. (1999). Testing psi and psi-missing: Do skeptics negatively influence ESP experiments? *Skeptic,* 7(4), 74–76.

Roberts, G., & Owen, J. (1988). The near-death experience. *British Journal of Psychiatry,* 153, 607–617.

Roberts, L., Ahmed, I., & Hall, S. (2000). Intercessory prayer for the alleviation of ill health (Cochrane Review). *The Cochrane Database of Systematic Reviews,* Issue 2. Art. No.: CD000368.

Robertson, S., & Gow, K. M. (1999). Do fantasy proneness and personality affect the vividness and certainty of past-life experience reports? *Australian Journal of Clinical and Experimental Hypnosis,* 27, 136–149.

Robertson, T. J., & Roy, A. E. (2004). Results of the application of the Robertson-Roy protocol to a series of experiments with mediums and participants. *Journal of the Society for Psychical Research,* 68, 18–34.

Rockwell, T. (1979). Pseudoscience? Or pseudocriticism? *Journal of Parapsychology,* 43, 221–231.

Rodabough, T. (1985). Near-death experiences: An examination of the supporting data and alternative explanations. *Death Studies,* 9, 95–113.

Rodin, E. A. (1980). The reality of death experiences: A personal perspective. *Journal of Nervous and Mental Disease,* 168, 259–263.

Roe, C. A. (1999). Critical thinking and belief in the paranormal: A re-evaluation. *British Journal of Psychology,* 90, 85–98.

Roe, C. A., Davey, R., & Stevens, P. (2003). Are ESP and PK aspects of a unitary phenomenon? A preliminary test of the relationship between ESP and PK. *Journal of Parapsychology,* 67, 343–366.

Roe, C. A., Davey, R., & Stevens, P. (2005). Are ESP and PK aspects of a unitary phenomenon? The effects of deception when testing the relationship between ESP and PK. *Journal of the Society for Psychical Research,* 69, 18–32.

Roe, C. A., Holt, N. J., & Simmonds, C. A. (2003). Considering the sender as a PK agent in ganzfeld ESP studies. *Journal of Parapsychology,* 67, 129–146.

Roe, C. A., McKenzie, E. A., & Ali, A. N. (2001). Sender and receiver creativity scores as predictors of performance at a Ganzfeld ESP task. *Journal of the Society for Psychical Research,* 65, 107–121.

Roe, C. A., Sherwood, S. J., & Holt, N. J. (2004). Interpersonal psi: Exploring the role of the sender in ganzfeld GESP tasks. *Journal of Parapsychology,* 68, 361–380.

Rogo, D. S. (1974). Psychotherapy and the poltergeist. *Journal of the Society for Psychical Research,* 47, 433–446.

Rogo, D. S. (1975). Psi and psychosis: A review of the experimental evidence. *Journal of Parapsychology,* 39, 120–128.

Rogo, D. S. (1980). Parapsychology and psychology textbooks. *Research Letter of the University of Utrecht Parapsychology Laboratory,* No. 10, 9–17.

Rogo, D. S. (1982). The poltergeist and family dynamics: A report on a recent investigation. *Journal of the Society for Psychical Research,* 51, 233–237.

Rogo, D. S. (1983). *Leaving the body: A practical guide to astral projection.* Englewood Cliffs, NJ: Prentice-Hall.

Rogo, D. S. (1985). *The search for yesterday: A critical examination of the evidence for reincarnation.* Englewood Cliffs, NJ: Prentice-Hall.

Roig, M., Icochea, H., & Cuzzucoli, A. (1991). Coverage of parapsychology in introductory psychology textbooks. *Teaching of Psychology,* 18, 157–160.

Roll, W. G. (1966). ESP and memory. *International Journal of Neuropsychiatry,* 2, 505–521.

Roll, W. G. (1968). Some physical and psychological aspects of a series of poltergeist phenomena. *Journal of the American Society for Psychical Research,* 62, 263–308.

Roll, W. G. (1976). *The poltergeist.* Metuchen, NJ: Scarecrow Press.

Roll, W. G. (1977). Poltergeists. In B. B. Wolman (Ed.), *Handbook of parapsychology* (pp. 382–413). New York: Van Nostrand Reinhold.

Roll, W. G. (1978a). Understanding the poltergeist. In W. G. Roll (Ed.), *Research in parapsychology 1977* (pp. 183–195). Metuchen, NJ: Scarecrow Press.

Roll, W. G. (1978b). Towards a theory for the poltergeist. *European Journal of Parapsychology,* 2, 167–200.

Roll, W. G. (1987). Memory and the long body. *Theta,* 15, 10–29.

Roll, W. G., & Persinger, M. A. (1998, August). *Poltergeist and nonlocality: Energetic aspects of RSPK.* Paper presented at the 41st Annual Convention of the Parapsychological Association, Palo Alto, CA.

Romm, E. G. (1977). When you give a closet occultist a Ph.D., what kind of research can you expect? *Humanist, 37*(3), 12–15.

Roney-Dougal, S. M., & Solfvin, J. (2002). Field study of enhancement effect on lettuce seeds: Their germination rate, growth and health. *Journal of the Society for Psychical Research, 66,* 129–143.

Roney-Dougal, S. M., & Solfvin, J. (2003). Field study of an enhancement effect on lettuce seeds: A replication study. *Journal of Parapsychology, 67,* 279–298.

Rose, L. (1955). Some aspects of paranormal healing. *Journal of the Society for Psychical Research, 38,* 105–121.

Rose, L., & Rose, R. (1951). Psi experiments with Australian aborigines. *Journal of Parapsychology, 15,* 122–131.

Rosenblatt, P. C., Walsh, R. P., & Jackson, D. A. (1976). *Grief and mourning in cross-cultural perspective.* New Haven, CT: hraf Press.

Ross, C. A. (1989). *Multiple personality disorder: Diagnosis, clinical features, and treatment.* New York: Wiley.

Ross, C. A., Ellason, J. W., & Anderson, G. (1995). A factor analysis of the Dissociative Experiences Scale (DES) in dissociative identity disorder. *Dissociation, 8,* 229–235.

Ross, C. A., & Joshi, S. (1992). Paranormal experiences in the general population. *Journal of Nervous and Mental Disease, 180,* 357–361.

Rowe, W. (1996). Psychic detectives. In G. Stein (Ed.), *The encyclopedia of the paranormal* (pp. 584–597). Amherst, NY: Prometheus Books.

Rubenstein, R., & Newman, R. (1954). The living out of "future" experiences under hypnosis. *Science, 119,* 472–473.

Rudski, J. (2004). The illusion of control, superstitious belief, and optimism. *Current Psychology: Developmental, Learning, Personality, Social, 22,* 306–315.

Rueda, S. A. (1991). Parapsychology in the Ibero-American world: Past and present developments. *Journal of Parapsychology, 55,* 175–207.

Rush, J. H. (1977). Problems and methods in psychokinesis research. In S. Krippner (Ed.), *Advances in parapsychological research, Vol. 1: Psychokinesis* (pp. 15–78). New York: Plenum Press.

Rush, J. H. (1982). Problems and methods in psychokinesis research. In S. Krippner (Ed.), *Advances in parapsychological research, Vol. 3* (pp. 83–114). New York: Plenum Press.

Russell, D., & Jones, W. H. (1980). When superstition fails: Reactions to disconfirmation of paranormal beliefs. *Personality and Social Psychology Bulletin, 6,* 83–88.

Ruttenberg, B. H. (2000). The role of paranormal experiences in healing, growth, and transformation: A study in clinical parapsychology. (Doctoral dissertation, Institute of Transpersonal Psychology). *Dissertation Abstracts International, 61,* 1095B.

Saavedra-Aguilar, J. C., & Gómez-Jeria, J. S. (1989). A neurobiological model for near-death experiences. *Journal of Near-Death Studies, 7,* 205–222.

Sabine, W. H. W. (1950). Is there a case for retrocognition? *Journal of the American Society for Psychical Research, 44,* 43–64.

Sabom, M. B. (1982). *Recollections of death: A medical investigation.* New York: Harper & Row.

Sagan, C. (1979). *Broca's brain: Reflections on the romance of science.* New York: Random House.

St. James-Roberts, I. (1976). Cheating in science. *New Scientist, 72,* 466–469.

Salter, W. H. (1958). F. W. H. Myers' posthumous message. *Proceedings of the Society for Psychical Research, 52,* 1–32.

Saltmarsh, H. F. (1930–1931). A report on the investigation of some sittings with Mrs. Warren Elliot. *Proceedings of the Society for Psychical Research, 39,* 47–184.

Saltmarsh, H. F. (1934). Report on cases of apparent precognition. *Proceedings of the Society for Psychical Research, 42,* 49–103.

Saltmarsh, H. F. (1938). *Evidence of personal survival from cross-correspondences.* London: Bell.

Sandford, J. (1977). Report of three experiments examining the effect of feedback on the direct cognition of an electronic timer. *Journal of Parapsychology, 41,* 36–37. (Abstract)

Sannwald, G. (1963). On the psychology of spontaneous paranormal phenomena. *International Journal of Parapsychology, 5,* 274–292.

Sappington, A. A. (1990). The independent manipulation of intellectually and emotionally based beliefs. *Journal of Research in Personality, 24,* 487–509.

Sartori, L., Massacessi, S., Martinelli, M., & Tressoldi, P. E. (2004). Physiological correlates of ESP: Heart rate differences between targets and nontargets. *Journal of Parapsychology, 68,* 351–360.

Scargle, J. (2000). Publication bias: The "file-drawer" problem in scientific inference. *Journal of Scientific Exploration, 14,* 91–106.

Scargle, J. (2002). Commentary: Was there evidence of global consciousness on September 11, 2001? *Journal of Scientific Exploration, 16,* 571–577.

Schacter, D. L. (1976). The hypnagogic state: A critical review of the literature. *Psychological Bulletin, 83,* 452–481.

Schatzman, M. (1980). *The story of Ruth.* New York: Putnam's.

Schechter, E. I. (1977). Nonintentional ESP: A review and replication. *Journal of the American Society for Psychical Research, 71,* 337–374.

Schechter, E. I. (1984). Hypnotic induction vs. control conditions: Illustrating an approach to the evaluation of replicability in parapsychological data. *Journal of the American Society for Psychical Research, 78,* 1–27.

Schlitz, M., & Braud, W. (1997). Distant intentionality and healing: Assessing the evidence. *Alternative Therapies, 3,* 62–73.

Schlitz, M. J., & Honorton, C. (1992). Ganzfeld psi performance within an artistically gifted population.

Journal of the American Society for Psychical Research, **86**, 83–98.

Schlitz, M., Wiseman, R., Watt, C., & Radin, D. (2006). Of two minds: Sceptic-proponent collaboration within parapsychology. *British Journal of Psychology*, **97**, 313–322.

Schmeidler, G. R. (1944). Position effects as psychological phenomena. *Journal of Parapsychology*, **8**, 110–123.

Schmeidler, G. R. (1952). Personal values and ESP scores. *Journal of Abnormal and Social Psychology*, **47**, 757–761.

Schmeidler, G. R. (1971). Parapsychologists' opinions about parapsychology, 1971. *Journal of Parapsychology*, **35**, 208–218.

Schmeidler, G. R. (Ed.) (1976). *Parapsychology: Its relation to physics, biology, psychology, and psychiatry.* Metuchen, NJ: Scarecrow Press.

Schmeidler, G. R. (1977). Research findings in psychokinesis. In S. Krippner (Ed.), *Advances in parapsychological research, Vol. 1: Psychokinesis* (pp. 79–132). New York: Plenum Press.

Schmeidler, G. R. (1980). Looking ahead: A method for research on survival. *Journal of the Academy of Religion and Psychical Research*, **3**, 16–22.

Schmeidler, G. R. (1982). PK research: Findings and theories. In S. Krippner (Ed.), *Advances in parapsychological research, Vol. 3* (pp. 115–146). New York: Plenum Press.

Schmeidler, G. R. (1987). Psychokinesis: Recent studies and a possible paradigm shift. In S. Krippner (Ed.), *Advances in parapsychological research, Vol. 5* (pp. 9–38). Jefferson, NC: McFarland.

Schmeidler, G. R. (1991). Perceptual processing of psi: A model. *Journal of the American Society for Psychical Research*, **85**, 217–236.

Schmeidler, G. R. (1994a). ESP experiments 1978–1992: The glass is half full. In S. Krippner (Ed.), *Advances in parapsychological research, Vol. 7* (pp. 104–197). Jefferson, NC: McFarland.

Schmeidler, G. R. (1994b). PK: Recent research reports and a comparison with ESP. In S. Krippner (Ed.), *Advances in parapsychological research, Vol. 7* (pp. 198–237). Jefferson, NC: McFarland.

Schmeidler, G. R. (1997). Psi-conducive experimenters and psi-permissive ones. *European Journal of Parapsychology*, **13**, 83–94.

Schmeidler, G. R., & Lewis, L. (1968). A search for feedback in ESP: Part II. High ESP scores after two successes on triple-aspect targets. *Journal of the American Society for Psychical Research*, **62**, 255–262.

Schmeidler, G. R., & Maher, M. (1981). The nonverbal communications of psi-conducive and psi-inhibitory experimenters. In W. G. Roll & J. Beloff (Eds.), *Research in parapsychology 1980* (pp. 121–124). Metuchen, NJ: Scarecrow Press.

Schmeidler, G. R., & McConnell, R. A. (1958). *ESP and personality patterns.* New Haven, CT: Yale University Press.

Schmidt, H. (1969). Precognition of a quantum process. *Journal of Parapsychology*, **33**, 99–108.

Schmidt, H. (1970a). A quantum mechanical random number generator for psi tests. *Journal of Parapsychology*, **34**, 219–224.

Schmidt, H. (1970b). PK experiments with animals as subjects. *Journal of Parapsychology*, **34**, 255–261.

Schmidt, H. (1973). PK tests with a high-speed random number generator. *Journal of Parapsychology*, **37**, 105–118.

Schmidt, H. (1974). Comparison of PK action on two different random number generators. *Journal of Parapsychology*, **38**, 47–55.

Schmidt, H. (1975). Toward a mathematical theory of psi. *Journal of the American Society for Psychical Research*, **69**, 301–319.

Schmidt, H. (1976). PK effect on pre-recorded targets. *Journal of the American Society for Psychical Research*, **70**, 267–291.

Schmidt, H. (1984). Comparison of a teleological model with a quantum collapse model of psi. *Journal of Parapsychology*, **48**, 261–276.

Schmidt, H. (1985). Addition effect for PK on prerecorded targets. *Journal of Parapsychology*, **49**, 229–244.

Schmidt, H. (1991). Search for a correlation between PK performance and heart rate. *Journal of the American Society for Psychical Research*, **85**, 101–117.

Schmidt, H. (2000). PK tests in a pre-sleep state. *Journal of Parapsychology*, **64**, 317–331.

Schmidt, H., Morris, R., & Rudolph, L. (1986). Channeling evidence for a PK effect to independent observers. *Journal of Parapsychology*, **50**, 1–15.

Schmidt, H., & Stapp, H. (1993). PK with prerecorded random events and the effects of preobservation. *Journal of Parapsychology*, **57**, 331–349.

Schmidt, S., Schneider, R., Utts, J., & Walach, H. (2004). Distant intentionality and the feeling of being stared at: Two meta-analyses. *British Journal of Psychology*, **95**, 235–247.

Schmidt, S., & Walach, H. (2000). Electrodermal activity (EDA) — state of the art measurement and techniques for parapsychological purposes. *Journal of Parapsychology*, **64**, 139–163.

Schnaper, N. (1980). Comments germane to the paper entitled "The reality of death experiences" by Ernst Rodin. *Journal of Nervous and Mental Disease*, **168**, 268–270.

Schouten, S. A. (1981). Analysing spontaneous cases: A replication based on the Sannwald collection. *European Journal of Parapsychology*, **4**, 9–48.

Schouten, S. A. (1982). Analysing spontaneous cases: A replication based on the Rhine collection. *European Journal of Parapsychology*, **4**, 113–158.

Schouten, S. A. (1983). A different approach for analyzing spontaneous cases, with particular reference to the study of Louisa E. Rhine's case collection. *Journal of Parapsychology*, **47**, 323–340.

Schouten, S. A. (1993). Are we making progress? In L. Coly and J. McMahon (Eds.), *Psi research methodology, a re-examination: Proceedings of an international conference.* NY: Parapsychology Foundation.

Schouten, S. A. (1994). An overview of quantitatively evaluated studies with mediums and psychics. *Journal of the American Society for Psychical Research*, **88**, 221–254.

Schouten, S. A. (1997). Psychic healing and complementary medicine. In S. Krippner (Ed.), *Advances in parapsychological research, Vol. 8* (pp. 126–210). Jefferson, NC: McFarland.

Schouten, S. A., & Stevenson, I. (1998). Does the sociopsychological hypothesis explain cases of the reincarnation type? *Journal of Nervous and Mental Disease*, 186, 504–506.

Schriever, F. (2000). Are there different cognitive structures behind paranormal beliefs? *European Journal of Parapsychology*, 15, 46–67.

Schröter-Kunhardt, M. (1993). A review of near death experiences. *Journal of Scientific Exploration*, 7, 219–239.

Schumaker, J. F. (1987). Mental health, belief deficit compensation, and paranormal beliefs. *Journal of Psychology*, 121, 451–457.

Schwartz, G. E., Russek, L. G., & Barentsen, C. (2002). Accuracy and replicability of anomalous information retrieval: Replication and extension. *Journal of the Society for Psychical Research*, 66, 144–156.

Schwarz, B. E. (1980). *Psychic-nexus: Psychic phenomena in psychiatry and everyday life*. New York: Van Nostrand Reinhold.

Scriven, M. (1962). The frontiers of psychology: Psychoanalysis and parapsychology. In R. G. Colodny (Ed.), *Frontiers of science and philosophy* (pp. 79–129). Pittsburgh, PA: University of Pittsburgh Press.

Scutt, D. C. (1981). An investigation into metal bending "Geller effect" with Ori Svoray. *Journal of the Society for Psychical Research*, 51, 1–6.

Serdahely, W. J. (1987). The near-death experience: Is the presence always the higher self? *Omega*, 18, 129–134.

Serdahely, W. J. (1989). A pediatric near-death experience: Tunnel variants. *Omega*, 20, 55–62.

Serdahely, W. J. (1990). Pediatric near-death experiences. *Journal of Near-Death Studies*, 9, 33–39.

Serdahely, W. J. (1996). Questions for the "dying brain hypothesis." *Journal of Near-Death Studies*, 15, 41–53.

Shadowitz, A., & Walsh, P. (1976). *The dark side of knowledge*. Reading, MA: Addison-Wesley.

Shapiro, T., Sherman, M., & Osowsky, I. (1980). Preschool children's conception of ghosts. *Journal of the American Academy of Child Psychiatry*, 19, 41–55.

Shaw, S. (1996). Psychokinetic metal bending. In G. Stein (Ed.), *The encyclopedia of the paranormal* (pp. 613–619). Amherst, NY: Prometheus Books.

Sheils, D. (1978). A cross-cultural study of beliefs in out-of-the-body experiences. *Journal of the Society for Psychical Research*, 49, 697–741.

Sheils, D., & Berg, P. (1977). A research note on sociological variables related to belief in psychic phenomena. *Wisconsin Sociologist*, 14, 24–31.

Sheldrake, R. (2001). Experiments on the sense of being stared at: The elimination of possible artefacts. *Journal of the Society for Psychical Research*, 65, 122–137.

Sherwood, S. J. (2000). Black Dog apparitions. *Journal of the American Society for Psychical Research*, 94, 151–164.

Sherwood, S. J., Dalton, K., Steinkamp, F., & Watt, C. (2000). Dream clairvoyance Study II using dynamic video-clips: Investigation of consensus voting judging procedures and target emotionality. *Dreaming*, 10, 221–236.

Sherwood, S. J., & Roe, C. A. (2003). A review of dream ESP studies conducted since the Maimonides dream ESP programme. *Journal of Consciousness Studies*, 10, 85–109.

Sicher, F., Targ, E., Moore, D., & Smith, H. S. (1998). A randomized double-blind study of the effect of distant healing in a population with advanced AIDS: Report of a small-scale study. *Western Journal of Medicine*, 169, 356–363.

Sidgwick, Mrs. H. [E. M.] (1888–1889). On the evidence for premonitions. *Proceedings of the Society for Psychical Research*, 5, 288–354.

Sidgwick, Mrs. H. [E. M.] (1891). On the evidence for clairvoyance. *Proceedings of the Society for Psychical Research*, 7, 30–99.

Sidgwick, H., Johnson, A., Myers, F. W. H., Podmore, F., & Sidgwick, E. M. (1894). Report on the Census of Hallucinations. *Proceedings of the Society for Psychical Research*, 10, 25–422.

Siegel, C. (1986). Parapsychological counseling: Six patterns of response to spontaneous psychic experiences. In D. H. Weiner & D. I. Radin (Eds.), *Research in parapsychology 1985* (pp. 172–174). Metuchen, NJ: Scarecrow Press.

Siegel, R. K. (1980). The psychology of life after death. *American Psychologist*, 35, 911–931.

Sigelman, L. (1977). Multi-nation surveys of religious beliefs. *Journal for the Scientific Study of Religion*, 16, 289–294.

Simmonds, C. A., & Roe, C. A. (2000, August). *Personality correlates of anomalous experiences, perceived ability and beliefs: Schizotypy, temporal lobe signs and gender*. Paper presented at the 43rd Annual Convention of the Parapsychological Association, Freiburg, Germany.

Simon-Buller, S., Christopherson, V. A., & Jones, R. A. (1988). Correlates of sensing the presence of a deceased spouse. *Omega*, 19, 21–30.

Sinclair, U. (1962). *Mental radio* (2nd ed.). Springfield, IL: Thomas. (Original work published 1930)

Singer, B., & Benassi, V. A. (1981). Occult beliefs. *American Scientist*, 69, 49–55.

Smith, E. L. (1972). The Raudive voices — objective or subjective? A discussion. *Journal of the Society for Psychical Research*, 46, 192–200.

Smith, M. D. (2003). The psychology of the "psi-conducive" experimenter: Personality, attitudes towards psi, and personal psi experience. *Journal of Parapsychology*, 67, 117–128.

Smith, [M.] J. (1968). Paranormal effects on enzyme activity. *Journal of Parapsychology*, 32, 281. (Abstract)

Smith, P., & Irwin, H. J. (1981). Out-of-body experiences, needs, and the experimental approach: A laboratory study. *Parapsychology Review*, 12 (3), 1–4.

Smith, S. (2000). *The afterlife codes: Searching for evidence of the survival of the soul*. Charlottesville, VA: Hampton Roads.

Snel, F. W. J. J., and van der Sijde, P. C. (1997). Perceived control by "powerful others" in paranormal healers. *Psychological Reports*, 81, 543–546.

Snoyman, P. (1985). Family therapy in a case of alleged RSPK. *Parapsychological Journal of South Africa*, 6, 75–90.

Soal, S. G., & Bateman, F. (1954). *Modern experiments in telepathy*. London: Faber & Faber.

Solfvin, G. F., & Roll, W. G. (1976). A case of RSPK with an epileptic agent. In J. D. Morris, W. G. Roll, & R. L. Morris (Eds.), *Research in parapsychology 1975* (pp. 115–120). Metuchen, NJ: Scarecrow Press.

Solfvin, J. (1984). Mental healing. In S. Krippner (Ed.), *Advances in parapsychological research, Vol. 4* (pp. 31–63). Jefferson, NC: McFarland.

Solomon, G., Solomon, J., & Scole Experimental Group (1999). *The Scole experiment: Scientific evidence for life after death*. London: Piatkus Books.

Sondow, N. (1988). The decline of precognized events with the passage of time: Evidence from spontaneous dreams. *Journal of the American Society for Psychical Research*, 82, 33–51.

Spanos, N. P. (1988). Past-life hypnotic regression: A critical review. *Skeptical Inquirer*, 12, 174–180.

Spanos, N. P., Menary, E., Gabora, N. J., DuBreuil, S. C., & Dewhirst, B. (1991). Secondary identity enactments during hypnotic past-life regressions: A sociocognitive perspective. *Journal of Personality and Social Psychology*, 61, 308–320.

Sparks, G. G., Nelson, C. L., & Campbell, R. G. (1997). The relationship between exposure to televised messages about paranormal phenomena and paranormal beliefs. *Journal of Broadcasting & Electronic Media*, 41, 345–359.

Spencer-Brown, G. (1953). *Probability and scientific interference*. New York: Longmans, Green.

Spiegel, D., & Cardeña, E. (1991). Disintegrated experience: The dissociative disorders revisited. *Journal of Abnormal Psychology*, 100, 366–378.

Spiritualism exposed: Margaret Fox Kane confesses to fraud. (1985). In P. Kurtz (Ed.), *A skeptic's handbook of parapsychology* (pp. 225–233). Buffalo, NY: Prometheus Books. (Original work published 1888)

Spottiswoode, J. (1997). Geomagnetic fluctuations and free-response anomalous cognition: A new understanding. *Journal of Parapsychology*, 61, 3–12.

Spottiswoode, J., & May, E. C. (2003). Skin conductance prestimulus response: Analyses, artifacts and a pilot study. *Journal of Scientific Exploration*, 17, 617–641.

Sprinkle, R. L. (1988). Psychotherapeutic services for persons who claim UFO experiences. *Psychotherapy in Private Practice*, 6, 151–157.

Stanford, R. G. (1969). "Associative activation of the unconscious" and "visualization" as methods for influencing the PK target. *Journal of the American Society for Psychical Research*, 63, 338–351.

Stanford, R. G. (1974a). An experimentally testable model for spontaneous psi events. I. Extrasensory events. *Journal of the American Society for Psychical Research*, 68, 34–57.

Stanford, R. G. (1974b). An experimentally testable model for spontaneous psi events. II. Psychokinetic events. *Journal of the American Society for Psychical Research*, 68, 321–356.

Stanford, R. G. (1975). Response factors in extrasensory performance. *Journal of Communication*, 25(1), 153–161.

Stanford, R. G. (1977). Experimental psychokinesis: A review from diverse perspectives. In B. B. Wolman (Ed.), *Handbook of parapsychology* (pp. 324–381). New York: Van Nostrand Reinhold.

Stanford, R. G. (1978). Toward reinterpreting psi events. *Journal of the American Society for Psychical Research*, 72, 197–214.

Stanford, R. G. (1981). Are we shamans or scientists? *Journal of the American Society for Psychical Research*, 75, 61–70.

Stanford, R. G. (1983). Possible psi-mediated perceptual effects of similarity of REG alternatives to the PK target: A double-blind study. In W. G. Roll, J. Beloff, & R. A. White (Eds.), *Research in parapsychology 1982* (pp. 178–181). Metuchen, NJ: Scarecrow Press.

Stanford, R. G. (1987a). Ganzfeld and hypnotic-induction procedures in ESP research: Toward understanding their success. In S. Krippner (Ed.), *Advances in parapsychological research, Vol. 5* (pp. 39–76). Jefferson, NC: McFarland.

Stanford, R. G. (1987b). The out-of-body experience as an imaginal journey: The developmental perspective. *Journal of Parapsychology*, 51, 137–155.

Stanford, R. (1988a). Ethics and professional social responsibility in parapsychological research and publication: Part I. *Parapsychology Review*, 19(3), 1–5.

Stanford, R. (1988b). Ethics and professional social responsibility in parapsychological research and publication: Part II. *Parapsychology Review*, 19(4), 1–7.

Stanford, R. G. (1990). An experimentally testable model for spontaneous psi events: A review of related evidence and concepts from parapsychology and other sciences. In S. Krippner (Ed.), *Advances in parapsychological research, Vol. 6* (pp. 54–167). Jefferson, NC: McFarland.

Stanford, R. G. (1992). The experimental hypnosis-ESP literature: A review from the hypothesis-testing perspective. *Journal of Parapsychology*, 56, 39–56.

Stanford, R. G. (1994). Developmental correlates of out-of-body experiences (OBEs) in specific states of consciousness: A replication failure. *Journal of Parapsychology*, 58, 197–199.

Stanford, R. G., Frank, S., Kass, G., & Skoll, S. (1989a). Ganzfeld as an ESP-favorable setting. Part I. Assessment of spontaneity, arousal, and internal attention state through verbal transcript analysis. *Journal of Parapsychology*, 53, 1–42.

Stanford, R. G., Frank, S., Kass, G., & Skoll, S. (1989b). Ganzfeld as an ESP-favorable setting. Part II. Prediction of ESP-task performance through verbal-transcript measures of spontaneity, suboptimal arousal, and internal attention state. *Journal of Parapsychology*, 53, 95–124.

Stanford, R. G., Kass, G., & Cutler, S. (1989). Session-based verbal predictors of free-response ESP-task performance in Ganzfeld. In L. A. Henkel & R. E. Berger (Eds.), *Research in parapsychology 1988* (pp. 79–84). Metuchen, NJ: Scarecrow Press.

Stanford, R. G., & Stein, A. G. (1994). A meta-analysis

of ESP studies contrasting hypnosis and a comparison condition. *Journal of Parapsychology*, **58**, 235–269.

Stanford, R. G., Zenhausern, R., Taylor, A., & Dwyer, M. A. (1975). Psychokinesis as psi-mediated instrumental response. *Journal of the American Society for Psychical Research*, **69**, 127–133.

Stanford, T. W. (1903). *Psychic phenomena: A narrative of facts.* Melbourne: Bruce & Davies.

Stanovich, K. E. (1989). Implicit philosophies of mind: The Dualism Scale and its relation to religiosity and belief in extrasensory perception. *Journal of Psychology*, **123**, 5–23.

Steilberg, B. J. (1975). "Conscious concentration" versus "visualization" in PK tests. *Journal of Parapsychology*, **39**, 12–20.

Steinkamp, F. (1997, August). *Backwards causation, precognition and the intervention paradox.* Paper presented at the 40th Annual Convention of the Parapsychological Association, Brighton, England.

Steinkamp, F. (1998, August). *A guide to independent coding in meta-analysis.* Paper presented at the 41st Annual Convention of the Parapsychological Association, Palo Alto, CA.

Steinkamp, F. (2000). Acting on the future: A survey of precognitive experiences. *Journal of the American Society for Psychical Research*, **94**, 37–59.

Steinkamp, F., Milton, J., & Morris, R. L. (1998). A meta-analysis of forced-choice experiments comparing clairvoyance and precognition. *Journal of Parapsychology*, **62**, 193–218.

Stevens, P. (1997, August). *Human sensing of weak electromagnetic fields: A possible relationship to psi?* Paper presented at the 40th Annual Convention of the Parapsychological Association, Brighton, England.

Stevens, P. (2002). Can we differentiate between ESP and imagination? *Journal of the Society for Psychical Research*, **66**, 239–246.

Stevenson, I. (1960). A review and analysis of paranormal experiences connected with the sinking of the *Titanic. Journal of the American Society for Psychical Research*, **54**, 153–171.

Stevenson, I. (1963). A postcognitive dream illustrating some aspects of the pictographic process. *Journal of the American Society for Psychical Research*, **57**, 182–202.

Stevenson, I. (1966). Twenty cases suggestive of reincarnation. *Proceedings of the American Society for Psychical Research*, **26**, 1–362.

Stevenson, I. (1968). The combination lock test for survival. *Journal of the American Society for Psychical Research*, **62**, 246–254.

Stevenson, I. (1970). *Telepathic impressions: A review and report of thirty-five new cases.* Charlottesville, VA: University Press of Virginia.

Stevenson, I. (1971). The substantiality of spontaneous cases. In W. G. Roll, R. L. Morris, & J. D. Morris (Eds.), *Proceedings of the Parapsychological Association No. 5, 1968* (pp. 91–128). Durham, NC: Parapsychological Association.

Stevenson, I. (1972). Are poltergeists living or are they dead? *Journal of the American Society for Psychical Research*, **66**, 233–252.

Stevenson, I. (1974). *Xenoglossy: A review and report of a case.* Charlottesville, VA: University Press of Virginia.

Stevenson, I. (1975). *Cases of the reincarnation type. Vol. I: Ten cases in India.* Charlottesville, VA: University Press of Virginia.

Stevenson, I. (1977a). Reincarnation: Field studies and theoretical issues. In B. B. Wolman (Ed.), *Handbook of parapsychology* (pp. 631–663). New York: Van Nostrand Reinhold.

Stevenson, I. (1977b). The explanatory value of the idea of reincarnation. *Journal of Nervous and Mental Disease*, **164**, 305–326.

Stevenson, I. (1977c). *Cases of the reincarnation type. Vol. II: Ten cases in Sri Lanka.* Charlottesville, VA: University Press of Virginia.

Stevenson, I. (1980). Gaither Pratt: An appreciation. *Journal of the American Society for Psychical Research*, **74**, 277–295.

Stevenson, I. (1982). The contribution of apparitions to the evidence for survival. *Journal of the American Society for Psychical Research*, **76**, 341–358.

Stevenson, I. (1983a). American children who claim to remember previous lives. *Journal of Nervous and Mental Disease*, **171**, 742–748.

Stevenson, I. (1983b). Cryptomnesia and parapsychology. *Journal of the Society for Psychical Research*, **52**, 1–30.

Stevenson, I. (1984). *Unlearned language: New studies in xenoglossy.* Charlottesville, VA: University Press of Virginia.

Stevenson, I. (1987a). *Children who remember previous lives: A question of reincarnation.* Charlottesville, VA: University Press of Virginia.

Stevenson, I. (1987b). Changing fashions in the study of spontaneous cases. *Journal of the American Society for Psychical Research*, **81**, 1–10.

Stevenson, I. (1987c). Why *investigate* spontaneous cases? *Journal of the American Society for Psychical Research*, **81**, 101–109.

Stevenson, I. (1988). Was the attempt to identify parapsychology as a separate field of science misguided? *Journal of the American Society for Psychical Research*, **82**, 309–317.

Stevenson, I. (1990a). Thoughts on the decline of major paranormal phenomena. *Proceedings of the Society for Psychical Research*, **57**, 149–162.

Stevenson, I. (1990b). Phobias in children who claim to remember previous lives. *Journal of Scientific Exploration*, **4**, 243–254.

Stevenson, I. (1993). Birthmarks and birth defects corresponding to wounds on deceased persons. *Journal of Scientific Exploration*, **7**, 403–410.

Stevenson, I. (1994). The case of the psychotherapist's fallacy: Hypnotic regression to "previous lives." *American Journal of Clinical Hypnosis*, **36**, 188–193.

Stevenson, I. (1996). The opening of Robert Thouless's combination lock. *Journal of the Society for Psychical Research*, **61**, 114–115.

Stevenson, I. (2000). The phenomenon of claimed memories of previous lives: Possible interpretations and importance. *Medical Hypotheses*, **54**, 652–659.

Stevenson, I., & Chadha, N. K. (1990). Can children be stopped from speaking about previous lives? Some further analyses of features in cases of the reincarnation type. *Journal of the Society for Psychical Research*, **56**, 82–90.

Stevenson, I., & Cook, E. W. (1995). Involuntary memories during severe physical illness or injury. *Journal of Nervous and Mental Disease*, **183**, 452.

Stevenson, I., Cook, E. W., & McClean-Rice, N. (1989). Are persons reporting "near-death experiences" really near death? A study of medical records. *Omega*, **20**, 45–54.

Stevenson, I., & Haraldsson, E. (2003). The similarity of features of reincarnation type cases over many years: A third study. *Journal of Scientific Exploration*, **17**, 283–289.

Stevenson, I., Oram, A. T., & Markwick, B. (1989). Two tests of survival after death: Report on negative results. *Journal of the Society for Psychical Research*, **55**, 329–336.

Stevenson, I., Pasricha, S., & Samararatne, G. (1988). Deception and self-deception in cases of the reincarnation type: Seven illustrative cases in Asia. *Journal of the American Society for Psychical Research*, **82**, 1–31.

Stevenson, I., & Samararatne, G. (1988). Three new cases of the reincarnation type in Sri Lanka with written records made before verifications. *Journal of Scientific Exploration*, **2**, 217–238.

Stokes, D. M. (1987). Theoretical parapsychology. In S. Krippner (Ed.), *Advances in parapsychological research, Vol. 5* (pp. 77–189). Jefferson, NC: McFarland.

Storm, L. (1999). Synchronicity, causality, and acausality. *Journal of Parapsychology*, **63**, 247–269.

Storm, L. (2000). Research note. Replicable evidence of psi: A revision of Milton's (1999) meta-analysis of the ganzfeld databases. *Journal of Parapsychology*, **64**, 411–416.

Storm, L. (2003). Remote viewing by committee: RV using a multiple agent/multiple percipient design. *Journal of Parapsychology*, **67**, 325–342.

Storm, L., & Ertel, S. (2001). Does psi exist? Comments on Milton and Wiseman's (1999) meta-analysis of ganzfeld research. *Psychological Bulletin*, **127**, 424–433.

Storm, L., & Ertel, S. (2002). The ganzfeld debate continued: A response to Milton and Wiseman (2001). *Journal of Parapsychology*, **66**, 73–82.

Storm, L., & Thalbourne, M. A. (2000). A paradigm shift away from the ESP-PK dichotomy: The theory of psychopraxia. *Journal of Parapsychology*, **64**, 279–300.

Stowell, M. S. (1997a). Precognitive dreams: A phenomenological study. Part I: Methodology and sample cases. *Journal of the American Society for Psychical Research*, **91**, 163–220.

Stowell, M. S. (1997b). Precognitive dreams: A phenomenological study. Part II: Discussion. *Journal of the American Society for Psychical Research*, **91**, 255–304.

Strauch, I. (1963). Medical aspects of "mental" healing. *International Journal of Parapsychology*, **5**, 135–165.

Struckmeyer, F. R. (1970). Precognition and the "intervention paradox." *Journal of the American Society for Psychical Research*, **64**, 320–326.

Sutherland, C. (1988). The near-death experience: "Claiming life for the first time." *Pallicom*, **8**(2), 18–23.

Sutherland, C. (1989). Psychic phenomena following near-death experiences: An Australian study. *Journal of Near-Death Studies*, **8**, 93–102.

Sutherland, C. (1990). Changes in religious beliefs, attitudes, and practices following near-death experiences: An Australian study. *Journal of Near-Death Studies*, **9**, 21–31.

Svenson, S. G., White, K. D., & Caird, D. (1992). Replications and resolutions: Dualistic belief, personality, religiosity, and paranormal belief in Australian students. *Journal of Psychology*, **126**, 445–447.

Tabori, P. (1974). *Crime and the occult: How ESP and parapsychology help detection*. New York: Taplinger.

Tandy, V. (2000). Something in the cellar. *Journal of the Society for Psychical Research*, **64**, 129–140.

Tandy, V., & Lawrence, T. R. (1998). The ghost in the machine. *Journal of the Society for Psychical Research*, **62**, 360–364.

Tanner, A. E. (1910). *Studies in spiritism*. New York: Appleton.

Tarazi, L. (1990). An unusual case of hypnotic regression with some unexplained contents. *Journal of the American Society for Psychical Research*, **84**, 309–344.

Targ, E., Schlitz, M., & Irwin, H. J. (2000). Psi-related experiences. In E. Cardeña, S. J. Lynn, & S. Krippner (Eds.), *Varieties of anomalous experience: Examining the scientific evidence* (pp. 219–252). Washington, DC: American Psychological Association.

Targ, R. (1994). Remote-viewing replication: Evaluated by concept analysis. *Journal of Parapsychology*, **58**, 271–284.

Targ, R., Katra, J., Brown, D., & Wiegand, W. (1995). Viewing the future: A pilot study with an error-detecting protocol. *Journal of Scientific Exploration*, **9**, 367–380.

Targ, R., & Puthoff, H. (1974). Information transmission under conditions of sensory shielding. *Nature*, **252**, 602–607.

Targ, R., & Puthoff, H. (1978). *Mind-reach*. London: Granada.

Tart, C. T. (1966). Card guessing tests: Learning paradigm or extinction paradigm? *Journal of the American Society for Psychical Research*, **60**, 46–55.

Tart, C. T. (1971). *On being stoned: A psychological study of marijuana intoxication*. Palo Alto, CA: Science & Behavior Books.

Tart, C. T. (1976). *Learning to use extrasensory perception*. Chicago, IL: University of Chicago Press.

Tart, C. T. (1977). Toward conscious control of psi through immediate feedback training: Some considerations of internal processes. *Journal of the American Society for Psychical Research*, **71**, 375–407.

Tart, C. T. (1978). Space, time, and mind. In W. G. Roll (Ed.), *Research in parapsychology 1977* (pp. 197–249). Metuchen, NJ: Scarecrow Press.

Tart, C. T. (1982). The controversy about psi: Two psychological theories. *Journal of Parapsychology*, 46, 313–320.

Tart, C. T. (1983). Learning to use psychokinesis: Theoretical and methodological notes. In W. G. Roll, J. Beloff, & R. A. White (Eds.), *Research in parapsychology 1982* (pp. 97–99). Metuchen, NJ: Scarecrow Press.

Tart, C. T. (1988). Effects of electrical shielding on GESP performance. *Journal of the American Society for Psychical Research*, 82, 129–146.

Tart, C. T. (1995). Fears of the paranormal in ourselves and our colleagues: Recognizing them, dealing with them. *Subtle Energies*, 5, 35–67.

Tart, C. T. (1998). Six studies of out-of-body experiences. *Journal of Near-Death Studies*, 17, 73–99.

Tart, C. T. (2003). Spiritual motivations of parapsychologists? Empirical data. *Journal of Parapsychology*, 67, 181–184.

Tart, C. T., Puthoff, H. E., & Targ, R. (1980). Information transmission in remote viewing experiments. *Nature*, 284, 191.

Taylor, R. (2003). Evolutionary theory and psi: Reviewing and revising some need-serving models in psychic functioning. *Journal of the Society for Psychical Research*, 67, 1–17.

Taylor, S. E., & Brown, J. D. (1988). Illusion and well-being: A social psychological perspective on mental health. *Psychological Bulletin*, 103, 193–210.

Tellegen, A., & Atkinson, G. (1974). Openness to absorbing and self-altering experiences ("Absorption"), a trait related to hypnotic susceptibility. *Journal of Abnormal Psychology*, 83, 268–277.

TenDam, H. (1990). *Exploring reincarnation* (A. E. J. Wils, Trans.). London: Arkana.

Tenhaeff, W. H. C. (1955). Psychoscopic experiments on behalf of the police. *Proceedings of the First International Conference of Parapsychological Studies* (pp. 107–109). New York: Parapsychology Foundation.

Terhune, D. (2003). Temporal lobe lability and self-reported haunting type experiences: A questionnaire study with an undergraduate sample. *Australian Journal of Parapsychology*, 3, 20–35.

Terhune, D. (2004). Investigation of reports of a recurrent sensed presence: Assessing recent conventional hypotheses. *Journal of the Society for Psychical Research*, 68, 153–167.

Terr, L. C., Bloch, D. A., Michel, B. A., Shi, H., Reinhardt, J. A., & Metayer, S. (1997). Children's thinking in the wake of Challenger. *American Journal of Psychiatry*, 154, 744–751.

Thalbourne, M. A. (1981). Extraversion and the sheep-goat variable: A conceptual replication. *Journal of the American Society for Psychical Research*, 75, 105–119.

Thalbourne, M. A. (1984). Some correlates of belief in psychical phenomena: A partial replication of the Haraldsson findings. *Parapsychology Review*, 15(2), 13–15.

Thalbourne, M. A. (1985). Are believers in psi more prone to schizophrenia? In R. A. White & J. Solfvin (Eds.), *Research in Parapsychology 1984* (pp. 85–88). Metuchen, NJ: Scarecrow Press.

Thalbourne, M. A. (1994). Belief in the paranormal and its relationship to schizophrenia-relevant measures: A confirmatory study. *British Journal of Clinical Psychology*, 33, 78–80.

Thalbourne, M. A. (1995a). Further studies of the measurement and correlates of belief in the paranormal. *Journal of the American Society for Psychical Research*, 89, 233–247.

Thalbourne, M. A. (1995b). Science versus showmanship: A history of the Randi hoax. *Journal of the American Society for Psychical Research*, 89, 344–366.

Thalbourne, M. A. (1996). An attempt to predict precognition scores using transliminality-relevant variables. *Journal of the Society for Psychical Research*, 61, 129–140.

Thalbourne, M. A. (1997). Testing the McBeath hypothesis: Relation of sexual orientation and belief in the paranormal. *Psychological Reports*, 81, 890.

Thalbourne, M. A. (2000). Transliminality: A review. *International Journal of Parapsychology*, 11, 1–34.

Thalbourne, M. A. (2003). Theism and belief in the paranormal. *Journal of the Society for Psychical Research*, 67, 208–210.

Thalbourne, M. A. (2004a). *The common thread between ESP and PK*. New York: Parapsychology Foundation.

Thalbourne, M. A. (2004b). A note on paranormal belief and paranormal experience: Their levels, absolute and relative. *Journal of the Society for Psychical Research*, 68, 115–121.

Thalbourne, M. A., & Delin, P. S. (1994). A common thread underlying belief in the paranormal, creative personality, mystical experience and psychopathology. *Journal of Parapsychology*, 58, 3–38.

Thalbourne, M. A., Dunbar, K. A., & Delin, P. S. (1995). An investigation into correlates of belief in the paranormal. *Journal of the American Society for Psychical Research*, 89, 215–231.

Thalbourne, M. A., & French, C. C. (1995). Paranormal belief, manic-depressiveness, and magical ideation: A replication. *Personality and Individual Differences*, 18, 291–292.

Thalbourne, M. A., & Haraldsson, E. (1980). Personality characteristics of sheep and goats. *Personality and Individual Differences*, 1, 180–185.

Thomas, C. D. (1932–1933). A consideration of a series of proxy sittings. *Proceedings of the Society for Psychical Research*, 41, 139–185.

Thomas, K. (1971). *Religion and the decline of magic*. London: Weidenfeld & Nicolson.

Thomason, S. G. (1987). Past tongues remembered? *Skeptical Inquirer*, 11, 367–375.

Thomson, S. (1986). Ethical dimensions of psi capability. *Applied Psi*, 5(1), 8–14.

't Hooft, G. (2000). Physics and the paranormal: A theoretical physicist's view. *Skeptical Inquirer*, 24(1), 27–30.

Thorisson, K. R., Skulason, F., & Haraldsson, E. (1991). Effects of belief in ESP and distorted feedback on a computerized clairvoyance task. *Journal of Parapsychology*, 55, 45–58.

Thouless, R. H. (1942). The present position of experimental research into telepathy and related phenomena. *Proceedings of the Society for Psychical Research, 47,* 1–19.

Thouless, R. H. (1946). A test of survival. *Proceedings of the Society for Psychical Research, 48,* 253–263.

Thouless, R. H. (1979). Theories about survival. *Journal of the Society for Psychical Research, 50,* 1–8.

Thouless, R. H., & Wiesner, B. P. (1948). The psi processes in normal and "paranormal" psychology. *Proceedings of the Society for Psychical Research, 48,* 177–196.

Thurston, H. (1953). *Ghosts and poltergeists.* London: Burns Oats & Washbourne.

Tierney, I., Coelho, C., & Lamont, P. (in press). Distressed by anomalous experience: Early identification of psychosis. *Clinical Psychology Forum.*

Tietze, T. R. (1985). The "Margery" affair. *Journal of the American Society for Psychical Research, 79,* 339–379.

Timm, U. (1969). Mixing-up of symbols in ESP card experiments (so-called consistent missing) as a possible cause for psi-missing. *Journal of Parapsychology, 33,* 109–124.

Tobacyk, J. J. (1983a). Reduction in paranormal belief among participants in a college course. *Skeptical Inquirer, 8,* 57–61.

Tobacyk, J. (1983b). Paranormal beliefs, interpersonal trust, and social interest. *Psychological Reports, 53,* 229–230.

Tobacyk, J. J. (1985). Paranormal beliefs, alienation and anomie in college students. *Psychological Reports, 57,* 844–846.

Tobacyk, J. J. (1995). What is the correct dimensionality of paranormal beliefs? A reply to Lawrence's critique of the Paranormal Belief Scale. *Journal of Parapsychology, 59,* 27–46.

Tobacyk, J., & Milford, G. (1983). Belief in paranormal phenomena: Assessment instrument development and implications for personality functioning. *Journal of Personality and Social Psychology, 44,* 1029–1037.

Tobacyk, J., Miller, M. J., & Jones, G. (1984). Paranormal beliefs of high school students. *Psychological Reports, 55,* 255–261.

Tobacyk, J., Miller, M., Murphy, P., & Mitchell, T. (1988). Comparisons of paranormal beliefs of black and white university students from the Southern United States. *Psychological Reports, 63,* 492–494.

Tobacyk, J. J, & Mitchell, T. (1987a). The out-of-body experience and personality adjustment. *Journal of Nervous and Mental Disease, 175,* 367–370.

Tobacyk, J. J., & Mitchell, T. (1987b). Out-of-body experience status as a moderator of effects of narcissism on paranormal beliefs. *Psychological Reports, 60,* 440–442.

Tobacyk, J., Pritchett, G., & Mitchell, T. (1988). Paranormal beliefs in late-adulthood. *Psychological Reports, 62,* 965–966.

Tobacyk, J. J., & Tobacyk, Z. S. (1992). Comparisons of belief-based personality constructs in Polish and American university students: Paranormal beliefs, locus of control, irrational beliefs, and social interest. *Journal of Cross-Cultural Psychology, 23,* 311–325.

Tobacyk, J. J., & Wilkison, L. V. (1990). Magical thinking and paranormal beliefs. *Journal of Social Behavior and Personality, 5*(4), Special Issue, 255–264.

Trocco, F. (2002). On the fringes of credibility: The boundary question between science and non-science. *Skeptic, 9*(2), 32–39.

Troland, L. T. (1976). A technique for the experimental study of telepathy and other alleged clairvoyant processes. *Journal of Parapsychology, 40,* 194–216. (Original work published 1917)

Truzzi, M. (1987). Reflections on "Project Alpha": Scientific experiment or conjuror's illusion? *Zetetic Scholar, 12/13,* 73–98.

Truzzi, M. (1997). Reflections on the sociology and social psychology of conjurors and their relations with psychical research. In S. Krippner (Ed.), *Advances in parapsychological research, Vol. 8* (pp. 221–271). Jefferson, NC: McFarland.

Tune, G. S. (1964). A brief survey of variables that influence random-generation. *Perceptual and Motor Skills, 18,* 705–710.

Twemlow, S. W., & Gabbard, G. O. (1984). The influence of demographic/psychological factors and preexisting conditions on the near-death experience. *Omega, 15,* 223–235.

Tyrrell, G. N. M. (1963). *Apparitions.* New York: Collier. (Original work published 1942)

Ullman, M. (1973). Psi and psychiatry: The need for restructuring basic concepts. In W. G. Roll, R. L. Morris, & J. D. Morris (Eds.), *Research in parapsychology 1972* (pp. 110–113). Metuchen, NJ: Scarecrow Press.

Ullman, M., & Krippner, S. (1970). Dream studies and telepathy. *Parapsychological Monographs, No. 12.* New York: Parapsychology Foundation.

Ullman, M., & Krippner, S., with Vaughan, A. (1989). *Dream telepathy: Experiments in nocturnal ESP* (2nd ed.). Jefferson, NC: McFarland.

Utts, J. (1988). Successful replication versus statistical significance. *Journal of Parapsychology, 52,* 305–320.

Utts, J. (1991). Replication and meta-analysis in parapsychology. *Statistical Science, 6,* 363–403.

Utts, J. (1994). Social, institutional, and cultural influences of gender on science. In L. Coly & R. A. White (Eds.), *Women and parapsychology* (pp. 28–44). New York: Parapsychology Foundation.

Utts, J. (1995). An assessment of the evidence for psychic functioning. *Journal of Parapsychology, 59,* 289–320.

Vaisrub, S. (1977). Afterthoughts of afterlife. *Archives of Internal Medicine, 137,* 150.

Van de Castle, R. L. (1958). An exploratory study of some personality correlates associated with PK performance. *Journal of the American Society for Psychical Research, 52,* 134–150.

Van Dragt, B. (1981). Paranormal healing: A phenomenology of the healer's experience. (Doctoral dissertation, Fuller Theological Seminary, 1980). *Dissertation Abstracts International, 41,* 3905B.

van Lommel, P., van Wees, R., Meyers, V., & Elfferich, I. (2001). Near-death experience in survivors of cardiac arrest: A prospective study in the Netherlands. *The Lancet, 358,* 2039–2045.

van Quekelberghe, R., Goebel, P., & Hertweck, E. (1995). Simulation of near-death and out-of-body experiences under hypnosis. *Imagination, Cognition and Personality*, **14**, 151–164.

Varvoglis, M. P. (1986). Goal-directed and observer-dependent PK: An evaluation of the conformance-behavior model and observational theories. *Journal of the American Society for Psychical Research*, **80**, 137–162.

Vasiliev, L. L. (1976). *Experiments in distant influence*. New York: Dutton. (Original work published 1963)

Vassy, Z. (1990). Experimental study of precognitive timing: Indications of a radically noncausal operation. *Journal of Parapsychology*, **54**, 299–320.

Vassy, Z. (2004). A study of telepathy by classical conditioning. *Journal of Parapsychology*, **68**, 323–350.

Vaughan, A., & Houck, J. (2000). Intuition-training software: A second pilot study. *Journal of the Society for Psychical Research*, **64**, 177–184.

Venn, J. (1986). Hypnosis and the reincarnation hypothesis: A critical review and intensive case study. *Journal of the American Society for Psychical Research*, **80**, 409–425.

Virtanen, L. (1990). *"That must have been ESP!" An examination of psychic experiences* (J. Atkinson & T. Dubois, Trans.). Bloomington, IN: Indiana University Press. (Original work published 1977)

Vitulli, W. F. (1997). Beliefs in parapsychological events or experiences among college students in a course in experimental parapsychology. *Perceptual and Motor Skills*, **85**, 273–274.

von Lucadou, W. (1995). The model of pragmatic information (MPI). *European Journal of Parapsychology*, **11**, 58–75.

von Lucadou, W., & Kornwachs, K. (1980). Development of the system theoretic approach to psychokinesis. *European Journal of Parapsychology*, **3**, 297–314.

Vyse, S. A. (1997). *Believing in magic: The psychology of superstition*. New York: Oxford University Press.

Wackermann, J. (2002, August). *On cumulative effects and averaging artefacts in randomised S-R experimental designs*. Paper presented at the 45th Annual Convention of the Parapsychological Association, Paris, France.

Wackermann, J., Pütz, P., Büchi, S., Strauch, I., & Lehmann, D. (2002). Brain electrical activity and subjective experience during altered states of consciousness: Ganzfeld and hypnagogic states. *International Journal of Psychophysiology*, **46**, 123–146.

Wagenaar, W. A. (1972). Generation of random sequences by human subjects: A critical survey of literature. *Psychological Bulletin*, **77**, 65–72.

Wagner, W. M., & Monnet, M. (1979). Attitudes of college professors toward extrasensory perception. *Zetetic Scholar*, **5**, 7–16.

Walach, H. (2005). Generalized entanglement: A new theoretical model for understanding the effects of complementary and alternative medicine. *Journal of Alternative and Complementary Medicine*, **11**, 549–559.

Walker, E. H. (1975). Foundations of paraphysical and parapsychological phenomena. In L. Oteri (Ed.), *Quantum physics and parapsychology* (pp. 1–53). New York: Parapsychology Foundation.

Walker, E. H. (1984). A review of criticisms of the quantum mechanical theory of psi phenomena. *Journal of Parapsychology*, **48**, 277–332.

Walker, F. O. (1989). A nowhere near-death experience: Heavenly choirs interrupt myelography. *Journal of the American Medical Association*, **261**, 3245–3246.

Wälti, B. (1990). A permanent paranormal object? Preliminary report on an unusual experiment with Silvio. *Journal of the Society for Psychical Research*, **56**, 65–70.

Warcollier, R. (1975). *Experimental telepathy*. New York: Arno Press. (Original work published 1938)

Warcollier, R. (2001). *Mind to mind*. Charlottesville, VA: Hampton Roads. (Original work published 1948)

Warner, L. (1952). A second survey of psychological opinion on ESP. *Journal of Parapsychology*, **16**, 284–295.

Warner, L., & Clark, C. C. (1938). A survey of psychological opinion on ESP. *Journal of Parapsychology*, **2**, 296–301.

Wassermann, G. D. (1956). An outline of a field theory of organismic form and behavior. In G. E. Wolstenholme & E. C. P. Millar (Eds.), *Ciba Foundation symposium on extrasensory perception* (pp. 53–72). Boston: Little, Brown.

Watt, C. A. (1988). Characteristics of successful free-response targets: Theoretical considerations. In L. A. Henkel & R. E. Berger (Eds.), *Research in parapsychology 1988* (pp. 95–99). Metuchen, NJ: Scarecrow Press.

Watt, C. A. (1990–1991). Psychology and coincidences. *European Journal of Parapsychology*, **8**, 66–84.

Watt, C. A. (1994a). Making the most of spontaneous cases. In S. Krippner (Ed.), *Advances in parapsychological research, Vol. 7* (pp. 77–103). Jefferson, NC: McFarland.

Watt, C. A. (1994b). Meta-analysis of DMT-ESP studies and an experimental investigation of perceptual defense/vigilance and extrasensory perception. In E. W. Cook & D. L. Delanoy (Eds.), *Research in parapsychology 1991* (pp. 64–68). Metuchen, NJ: Scarecrow Press.

Watt, C. A. (1996). Knowing the unknown: Participants' insight in three forced-choice ESP studies. *Journal of the American Society for Psychical Research*, **90**, 97–114.

Watt, C. A. (in press). Parapsychology's contribution to psychology: A view from the front line (Parapsychological Association Presidential Address). *Journal of Parapsychology*.

Watt, C. A., & Baker, I. S. (2002). Remote facilitation of attention focusing with psi-supportive versus psi-unsupportive experimenter suggestions. *Journal of Parapsychology*, **66**, 151–168.

Watt, C. A., & Brady, C. (2002). Experimenter effects and the remote facilitation of attention focusing: Two studies and the discovery of an artifact. *Journal of Parapsychology*, **66**, 49–72.

Watt, C. A., & Gissurarson, L. R. (1995). Exploring defensiveness and psychokinesis performance. *European Journal of Parapsychology, 11,* 92–101.

Watt, C. A., & Morris, R. L. (1995). The relationships among performance on a prototype indicator of perceptual defense/vigilance, personality, and extrasensory perception. *Personality and Individual Differences, 19,* 635–648.

Watt, C. A., & Nagtegaal, M. (2004). Reporting of blind methods: An interdisciplinary survey. *Journal of the Society for Psychical Research, 68,* 105–114.

Watt, C. A., & Ramakers, P. (2003). Experimenter effects with a remote facilitation of attention focusing task: A study with multiple believer and disbeliever experimenters. *Journal of Parapsychology, 67,* 99–116.

Watt, C. A., Ravenscroft, J., & McDermott, Z. (1999). Exploring the limits of direct mental influence: Two studies comparing "blocking" and "cooperating" strategies. *Journal of Scientific Exploration, 13,* 515–535.

Watt, C. A., Watson, S., & Wilson, L. (in press). Cognitive and psychological mediators of anxiety: Evidence from a study of paranormal belief and perceived childhood control. *Personality and Individual Differences.*

Watt, C. [A.], & Wiseman, R. (2002). Experimenter differences in cognitive correlates of paranormal belief and in psi. *Journal of Parapsychology, 66,* 371–385.

Weiner, D. H. (1980). Psi counseling: The situation at research laboratories. In W. G. Roll (Ed.), *Research in parapsychology 1979* (pp. 45–46). Metuchen, NJ: Scarecrow Press.

Weiner, D. H. (1982). The effects of preferred cognitive mode and goal conceptualization in an intentional PK task. *Journal of Parapsychology, 46,* 56–57. (Abstract)

Weiner, D. H., & Haight, J. (1986). Charting hidden channels: Louisa E. Rhine's case collection project. In K. R. Rao (Ed.), *Case studies in parapsychology* (pp. 14–30). Jefferson, NC: McFarland.

Weisberg, B. M. (2004). *Talking to the dead: Kate and Maggie Fox and the rise of Spiritualism.* New York: HarperSanFrancisco.

Wells, A. D. (1993). Reincarnation beliefs among near-death experiencers. *Journal of Near-Death Studies, 12,* 17–34.

West, D. J. (1948). A mass-observation questionnaire on hallucinations. *Journal of the Society for Psychical Research, 34,* 187–196.

West, D. J. (1982). Thoughts on testimony to the paranormal. *Parapsychology Review, 13*(5), 1–8.

West, D. J. (1999). The Scole investigation: Commentary on strategy and outcome. *Proceedings of the Society for Psychical Research, 58,* 393–396.

West, T. (1998). On the encounter with a divine presence during a near-death experience. In R. Valle (Ed.), *Phenomenological inquiry in psychology: Existential and transpersonal dimensions* (pp. 387–405). New York: Plenum Press.

Wezelman, R., & Bierman, D. J. (1997, August). *Process oriented ganzfeld research in Amsterdam.* Paper presented at the 40th Annual Convention of the Parapsychological Association, Brighton, England.

Whinnery, J. E. (1997). Psychophysiologic correlates of unconsciousness and near-death experiences. *Journal of Near-Death Studies, 15,* 231–258.

White, R. A. (1964a). A comparison of old and new methods of response to targets in ESP experiments. *Journal of the American Society for Psychical Research, 58,* 21–56.

White, R. A. (1964b). Approaches to the study of spontaneous cases. *International Journal of Parapsychology, 6,* 227–240.

White, R. A. (1976). The limits of experimenter influence on psi test results: Can any be set? *Journal of the American Society for Psychical Research, 70,* 333–369.

White, R. A. (1977). The influence of experimenter motivation, attitudes, and methods of handling subjects in psi test results. In B. B. Wolman (Ed.), *Handbook of parapsychology* (pp. 273–301). New York: Van Nostrand Reinhold.

White, R. A. (1990). An experience-centered approach to parapsychology. *Exceptional Human Experience, 8,* 7–36.

White, R. A. (1991). Feminist science, postmodern views, and exceptional human experience. *Exceptional Human Experience, 9,* 2–11.

White, R. A. (1992). Review of approaches to the study of spontaneous psi experiences. *Journal of Scientific Exploration, 6,* 93–126.

White, R. A. (1994). The relevance to parapsychology of a feminist approach to science. In L. Coly & R. A. White (Eds.), *Women and parapsychology* (pp. 1–20). New York: Parapsychology Foundation.

White, R. A. (1995). EHE counseling: An ongoing annotated bibliography. *EHE News, 2,* 26–30.

Whiteman, J. H. M. (1961). *The mystical life.* London: Faber & Faber.

Whitlock, F. A. (1978). The psychiatry and psychopathology of paranormal phenomena. *Australian and New Zealand Journal of Psychiatry, 12,* 11–19.

Whitton, J. L. (1975). Qualitative time-domain analysis of acoustic envelope of psychokinetic table rappings. *New Horizons, 2*(1), 21–24.

Whitton, J. L. (1976). Paramorphic table rappings: Acoustic analysis. *New Horizons, 2*(2), 7–11.

Whitton, J. L., & Fisher, J. (1986). *Life between life.* Garden City, NY: Doubleday.

Wierzbicki, M. (1985). Reasoning errors and belief in the paranormal. *Journal of Social Psychology, 125,* 489–494.

Wilkinson, H. P., & Gauld, A. (1993). Geomagnetism and anomalous experiences, 1868–1980. *Proceedings of the Society for Psychical Research, 57,* 275–310.

Williams, L. (1989). *An exploratory study of the relationship between paranormal belief, magical ideation and schizotypy.* Unpublished honors thesis, University of New England, Armidale, Australia.

Williams, L. M., & Irwin, H. J. (1991). A study of paranormal belief, magical ideation as an index of schizotypy and cognitive style. *Personality and Individual Differences, 12,* 1339–1348.

Wilson, C. (1984). *The psychic detectives: The story of psychometry and paranormal crime detection.* London: Pan Books.

Wilson, I. (1982). *Reincarnation? The claims investigated.* Harmondsworth, England: Penguin.

Wilson, I. (1984). A tragic double act. In P. Brooke-smith (Ed.), *Life after death* (pp. 49–51). London: Orbis.

Wilson, D. B., & Shadish, W. R. (2006). On blowing trumpets to the tulips: To prove or not to prove the null hypothesis: Comment on Bösch, Steinkamp, and Boller (2006). *Psychological Bulletin,* **132,** 524–528.

Wilson, S. C., & Barber, T. X. (1983). The fantasy-prone personality: Implications for understanding imagery, hypnosis, and parapsychological phenomena. In A. A. Sheikh (Ed.), *Imagery: Current theory, research, and application* (pp. 340–387). New York: Wiley.

Windholz, G., & Diamant, L. (1974). Some personality traits of believers in extraordinary phenomena. *Bulletin of the Psychonomic Society,* **3,** 125–126.

Winkelman, M. (1981). The effect of formal education on extrasensory abilities: The Ozolco study. *Journal of Parapsychology,* **45,** 321–336.

Winn, D. S. (2002). *The phenomenology of past-life experiences.* Lewiston, NY: Mellon Press.

Wirth, D. P. (1995). The significance of belief and expectancy within the spiritual healing encounter. *Social Science & Medicine,* **41,** 249–260.

Wirth, D. P., Johnson, C. A., Horvath, J. S., & Mac-Gregor, J. D. (1992). The effect of alternative healing therapy on the regeneration rate of salamander forelimbs. *Journal of Scientific Exploration,* **6,** 375–390.

Wiseman, R. (1996). Witnesses to the paranormal (how reliable?). In G. Stein (Ed.), *The encyclopedia of the paranormal* (pp. 829–834). Amherst, NY: Prometheus Books.

Wiseman, R. (2001). The psychology of psychic fraud. In R. Roberts & D. Groome (Ed.), *Parapsychology: The science of unusual experience* (pp. 51–59). London: Arnold.

Wiseman, R., Greening, E., & Smith, M. (2003). Belief in the paranormal and suggestion in the séance room. *British Journal of Psychology,* **94,** 285–297.

Wiseman, R., & Morris, R. L. (1994). Modeling the stratagems of psychic fraud. *European Journal of Parapsychology,* **10,** 31–44.

Wiseman, R., & Morris, R. L. (1995). *Guidelines for testing psychic claimants.* Hatfield, England: University of Hertfordshire Press.

Wiseman, R., & Smith, M. D. (2002). Assessing the role of cognitive and motivational biases on belief in the paranormal. *Journal of the Society for Psychical Research,* **66,** 178–186.

Wiseman, R., Smith, M., & Kornbrot, D. (1996). Exploring possible sender-to-experimenter acoustic leakage in the PRL autoganzfeld experiments. *Journal of Parapsychology,* **60,** 97–128.

Wiseman, R., & Watt, C. (2004). Measuring superstitious belief: Why lucky charms matter. *Personality and Individual Differences,* **37,** 1533–1541.

Wiseman, R., & Watt, C. (2006). Belief in psychic ability and the misattribution hypothesis: A qualitative review. *British Journal of Psychology,* **97,** 323–338.

Wiseman, R., Watt, C., Stevens, P., Greening, E., & O'Keeffe, C. (2003). An investigation into alleged "hauntings." *British Journal of Psychology,* **94,** 195–211.

Wiseman, R., West, D., & Stemman, R. (1996). An experimental test of psychic detection. *Journal of the Society for Psychical Research,* **61,** 34–45.

Wolfradt, U. (1997). Dissociative experiences, trait anxiety and paranormal beliefs. *Personality and Individual Differences,* **23,** 15–19.

Wolfradt, U., Oubaid, V., Straube, E. R., Bischoff, N., & Mischo, J. (1999). Thinking styles, schizotypal traits and anomalous experiences. *Personality and Individual Differences,* **27,** 821–830.

Wolkowski, Z. W. (1977). Reflections on psychokinetic phenomena. In J. D. Morris, W. G. Roll, & R. L. Morris (Eds.), *Research in parapsychology 1976* (pp. 207–209). Metuchen, NJ: Scarecrow Press.

Wooffitt, R. (2000). Some properties of the interactional organization of displays of paranormal cognition in psychic-sitter interaction. *Sociology,* **34,** 457–479.

Wooffitt, R. (2003, August). *The organization of demonstrations of paranormal cognition in psychic-sitter interaction.* Paper presented at the 46th Annual Convention of the Parapsychological Association, Vancouver, Canada.

Wren-Lewis, J. (1974). Resistance to the study of the paranormal. *Journal of Humanistic Psychology,* **14**(2), 41–48.

Wright, S. H. (1998). Experiences of spontaneous psychokinesis after bereavement. *Journal of the Society for Psychical Research,* **62,** 385–395.

Wright, S. H. (1999). Paranormal contact with the dying: 14 contemporary death coincidences. *Journal of the Society for Psychical Research,* **63,** 258–267.

Wuthnow, R. (1976). Astrology and marginality. *Journal for the Scientific Study of Religion,* **15,** 157–168.

Wyndham, H. (1937). *Mr. Sludge, the medium: Being the life and adventures of Daniel Dunglas Home.* London: Bles.

Yram. (1974). *Practical astral projection.* New York: Weiser. (Original work published c.1926)

Zangari, W., & Machado, F. R. (2001). Parapsychology in Brazil: A science entering young adulthood. *Journal of Parapsychology,* **65,** 351–356.

Zenhausern, R., Stanford, R. G., & Esposito, C. (1977). The application of signal detection theory to clairvoyance and precognition tasks. In J. D. Morris, W. G. Roll, & R. L. Morris (Eds.), *Research in parapsychology 1976* (pp. 170–173). Metuchen, NJ: Scarecrow Press.

Zha, L., & McConnell, T. (1991). Parapsychology in the People's Republic of China: 1979–1989. *Journal of the American Society for Psychical Research,* **85,** 119–143.

Zingrone, N. L. (1988). Authorship and gender in American parapsychology journals. *Journal of Parapsychology,* **52,** 321–343.

Zingrone, N. L. (1994). Women and parapsychology. In

L. Coly & R. A. White (Eds.), *Women and parapsychology* (pp. 218–225). New York: Parapsychology Foundation.

Zingrone, N. L. (2002). Controversy and the problems of parapsychology. *Journal of Parapsychology*, **66**, 3–30.

Zingrone, N. L., & Alvarado, C. S. (1994, August). *Psychic and dissociative experiences: A preliminary report.* Paper presented at the 37th Annual Convention of the Parapsychological Association, Amsterdam, The Netherlands.

Zingrone, N. L., & Alvarado, C. S. (1997, August). *"Broken" marital relations and claims of parapsychological experiences.* Paper presented at the 40th Annual Convention of the Parapsychological Association, Brighton, England.

Zohar, D. (1982). *Through the time barrier: A study in precognition and modern physics.* London: Heinemann.

Zolik, E. S. (1958). An experimental investigation of the psycho-dynamic implications of the hypnotic "previous existence" fantasy. *Journal of Clinical Psychology*, **14**, 179–183.

Zorab, G. (1970). Test sittings with D. D. Home at Amsterdam (1858). *Journal of Parapsychology*, **34**, 47–63.

Zusne, L., & Jones, W. H. (1982). *Anomalistic psychology: A study of extraordinary phenomena of behavior and experience.* Hillsdale, NJ: Lawrence Erlbaum Associates.

Name Index

SUBJECT INDEX

AAAS 223, 249, 251
Aberfan disaster 87
Absorption, psychological 79; and apparitional experience 199; and ESP 38, 74, 79; and NDE 168; and OBE 178, 180, 189–190; and PK 106; and psychic healing 111, 112
Agent, PK 94, 149–150; telepathic 37, 49, 71
Alpha waves: and ESP 76; and metal bending 120
American Society for Psychical Research (ASPR) 20, 21, 51, 85; *Journal* 250
Animal magnetism 12
Animal psi (Anpsi) 2, 109–111, 250
Anxiety 168, 233–234
Apparitional experiences 1, 7, 30, 144, 152, 153, 192–206; case of Ruth 200–201; circumstances of occurrence 198–199; collective cases 193, 203; correlates 198–201; crisis cases 196; experimental cases 195, 196; haunting cases 197; incidence 194–195; phenomenology 194–195; postmortem cases 196, 197; theories 201–206
Applications 237–245; *see also* Clinical practice
Apports 18, 22, 24–26, 94, 118
Archetypes 171–172
ASPR *see* American Society for Psychical Research
Astral cord 178, 185
Authenticity 7–8, 9, 11, 27; of ESP 30, 31, 40–45, 46, 48–64; of PK 98–102; and spontaneous cases 29, 30, 40–45, 210
Automatic writing 18, 22–23
Autoscopy 173, 176

Backward causation 90, 91
Belief in the paranormal 2, 31, 32, 41–42, 74–75, 138, 204, 222–235; correlates 225–234;

incidence 222; theories 225–235
Billet reading 44
British Journal of Psychology 256

Call 52
Case collection 29–31, 39–46, 138, 174, 194
Catalepsy 175
Cerebral anoxia 169
Chance 44–45, 49, 50, 51–53, 61, 98, 136; *see also* Coincidence
Channeling 15
Chronological declines 67, 68
Cipher test 140–141
Clairaudience 5
Clairvoyance 5, 12, 30, 51, 53, 71
Clinical practice 40, 155, 164, 201, 237–241
Clock cards 54
Clustering: in ESP 68; in PK 103–104
Coincidence 45, 132
Cold reading techniques 20, 21, 22, 43–44, 242
Combination lock test 141–142
Conformance theory 133
Conjuring 4, 17, 253
Consistent missing: in ESP 67; in PK 103
Control *see* Spirit guide
Corroboration 29
Cortical disinhibition 170, 187
Counseling *see* Clinical practice
Creativity 77, 231
Critical ratio 53
Criticisms: of ESP research 54, 57, 68; of parapsychology 222, 251–257; of PK research 101, 123; of psychic healing research 113–114; of reincarnation research 214
Cross-correspondences 21, 140
Cryptomnesia 23, 85, 145, 216
CSICOP 254, 257
Cultural relativity 3–4, 166

Cumulative record of research 59–60; *see also* Meta-analysis

Darkness 14, 17, 71, 106
Decline effects 67, 68, 89, 103
Defense Mechanism Test 75–76
Definitive ESP experiment 58–59
Density 104
Depersonalization 170, 182, 187
Dieppe Raid case 84
Differential effect: in ESP 67; in PK 103
Direct voice communication 15
Displacement: in ESP 68; in PK 96, 103; temporal 83–84, 103
Dissociation 22, 27, 78–79, 98, 174, 179, 182–183, 189–190, 212
Distance: and ESP 70, 126; and PK 96, 106, 126, 150
Divergence problem 128
"Down through" technique 52
Dreams 31, 33–34; ESP in 33–37, 55, 70, 71, 79; Maimonides research 55; and precognition 86; realistic 33, 34; unrealistic 34
"Drop in" communicators 139
Drug intoxication 71, 170, 180
Duke University 30, 51, 98

Ectoplasm 16
EEG measures 76, 120, 155, 169
ELF waves 125–126
Endorphins 169
Epilepsy 155, 186
ESP cards 51, 52
ESP performance: and absorption 68, 74, 79; and age 80; and attitudes 74–75; and beliefs 74–75; and creativity 77; and cognitive style 78, 88; and cognitive variables 85–88, 98; and demographic variables 79–80; and dissociation 78–79; and distance 70; and dream recall 78; and experimenter variables 70–71; and feed-